VIOLENCE
A CONTEMPORARY
READER

STEPHEN T. HOLMES, PH.D.
University of Central Florida

RONALD M. HOLMES, ED.D.
University of Louisville

PEARSON

Prentice
Hall

Upper Saddle River, New Jersey 07458

Library of Congress Cataloging-in-Publication Data

Violence: a contemporary reader / [edited by] Stephen T. Holmes,
   Ronald M. Holmes.
      p. cm.
   ISBN 0-13-112097-2
   1. Violence.   I. Holmes, Stephen T.   II. Holmes, Ronald M.

   HM886.V55 2004
   303.6—dc22

                                        2003026421

> *This book is dedicated
> to Isabella Grace.
> Welcome to the family.*

Publisher: Stephen Helba
Executive Editor: Frank Mortimer, Jr.
Assistant Editor: Korrine Dorsey
Production Editor: Marianne Hutchinson, Pine Tree Composition, Inc.
Production Liaison: Barbara Marttine Cappuccio
Director of Manufacturing and Production: Bruce Johnson
Managing Editor: Mary Carnis
Creative Director: Cheryl Asherman
Cover Design Coordinator: Miguel Ortiz
Cover Designer: Ruta Fiorino
Marketing Manager: Tim Peyton
Editorial Assistant: Barbara Rosenberg
Formatting and Interior Design: Pine Tree Composition, Inc.
Printing and Binding: R.R. Donnelley & Sons

Copyright © 2004 by Pearson Education, Inc., Upper Saddle River, New Jersey 07458.
Pearson Prentice Hall. All rights reserved. Printed in the United States of America. This publication
is protected by Copyright and permission should be obtained from the publisher prior to any prohibited reproduction, storage in a retrieval system, or transmission in any form or by any means, electronic, mechanical, photocopying, recording, or likewise. For information regarding permission(s),
write to: Rights and Permissions Department.

Pearson Prentice Hall™ is a trademark of Pearson Education, Inc.
Pearson® is a registered trademark of Pearson plc
Prentice Hall® is a registered trademark of Pearson Education, Inc.

Pearson Education LTD
Pearson Education Singapore, Pte. Ltd.
Pearson Education, Canada, Ltd
Pearson Education—Japan
Pearson Education Australia PTY, Limited
Pearson Educaçion de Mexico, S.A. de C.V.
Pearson Education Malaysia, Pte. Ltd.

10 9 8 7 6 5 4 3 2 1
ISBN 0-13-112097-2

CONTENTS

PREFACE

In American society, violence has become a part of the culture. We witness violent acts daily and are the predominant news on the nightly newscasts. Murders, assaults, rapes, and other acts of personal violence occur on a routine basis. We as citizens have become sensitized to the perpetration of violence. We accept that personal violence as inevitable and usually only become sensitive to that violence when we are touched by it. Why is that so? Is it because of the overwhelming number of incidents? Are we "overexposed" to the point where we accept a sense of complacency, where we see violence as inevitable?

In this book, we deal with various forms of personal violence. Some of the cases of violence are common, some emerging, and perhaps some in a reclining numbers. We are interested in the various forms of personal violence while paying attention to the forms that you, as a reader, are interested in as well.

The book is divided into sections that deal with different types of violence. The Introduction deals with the various definitions of violence, the frequency of violent crimes in this country, and the various forms of criminal violence. Basically, this is an introduction to crimes of violence and the various forms it takes. The first section deals with domestic violence in its many forms: spouse abuse, partner homicide, the abuse of children within the family including homicide, and so on. The second section contains information concerning various forms of interpersonal violence when sex is a motivating factor.

The third section deals with an emerging form of violence, school violence. Of course, violence in the school has been a common occurrence, but the character of that violence has changed. The school shootings in Arkansas, Kentucky, Colorado, and other states have become such a concern that many people no longer believe our schools are safe houses set apart from larger society. When we were growing up, school violence took the form of boys fighting in the alleys after school; however, that day may well be over. This is no longer the sole manifestation of school violence; it is now more insidious and life threatening.

The fourth section examines serial violence or incidences of mass murder. In this section we present a series of chapters that not only discuss the types of perpetrators but also give you a glimpse into their minds. The fifth section includes three chapters that discuss the ramifications of this violence on children. One chapter examines the importance of breaking this cycle of violence. The second discusses the challenges that children who have befell victims to this violence face as they enter adulthood. And the third examines the causes and consequences of violence on our nation's youth.

The sixth section examines a wide variety of issues where institutions have incorporated violence into their cultural ethos. The first chapter in this section looks at police organizations and officers and dispels the myth that police officers believe that force should be applied more fervently in minority populations. The others examine institutions where hate and violence have become part of their member's culture.

The seventh section makes some observations about violence in contemporary society and discusses what the future holds in regard to violence for not only our children but grandchildren.

ACKNOWLEDGMENTS

There are people in our discipline who we wish to thank for their interest and support of our work. There is always a danger when one lists people to thank; there is always the chance that a name or two is omitted. We wish to apologize in advance for this. Nonetheless, we move on: Sgt. David Rivers, Metro-Dade (Florida) Sheriff's Office; Drs. David Fabianic and Bernie McCarthy, University of Central Florida; Parole Officer James Massie, Louisville, Kentucky; Dr. Eric Hickey, California State University at Fresno; Dr. Larry Gaines, California State University at San Bernandino; Steven Egger, at the University of Houston at Clearlake; and Dr. Jack Levin, Northeastern University. There are those we talked with and gave us some inside information: Lt. George Barret (retired) of the Louisville Police Department; Sheriff Charles Cox, Miami County, Ohio; Major Henry Ott, Louisville Fire Department; Rick Sanders, Drug Enforcement Administration; Thomas Harris, author; and others.

We would also like to thank our reviewers for their time and effort in making this book even better. The reviewers include: Lucien X. Lombardo, Old Dominion University, Norfolk, Virgina; David McElreath, Washburn University, Topeka, Kansas; Thomas Petee, Auburn University, Auburn, Alabama; Leonore Simon, East Tennessee State University, Johnson City, Tennessee; and Patrick D. Walsh, Loyola University–New Orleans, New Orleans, Louisiana.

Our families deserve special attention. Even at the time we are writing this section, our wives are shopping at Bed, Bath, and Beyond. They deserve special attention and praise, we think.

Stephen T. Holmes
University of Central Florida

Ronald M. Holmes
University of Louisville

Introduction
Violence in the United States

Violence as a human social problem has been a topic of research in criminal justice for years. Never was it more visible than in the attack on the United States on September 11, 2001. The terrorist attacks in New York, Washington, D.C., and Pennsylvania almost paralyzed our country. Perhaps not since the attack on Pearl Harbor that launched our involvement in World War II was violence so visible and painful. Such acts of large-scale violence have scarred our consciousness and countryside. But there are many smaller acts of violence that occur with such frequency and predictability that they affect many, even if they are not aware of it.

The attention that acts of personal violence receive has done little to lower the rates of personal predation. Plans for the reduction of such crimes of violence have met with little success, although official government statistics still claim that there has been a reduction in violence. In fact, if we put faith in our official government statistics, it is clear that the rate of violent crime is on the decline. Examining trends from the National Victimization Survey, violent crime is at its lowest rate since 1972 (Rennison, 2002). Further data from combing the National Crime Victimization Survey (NCVS) and the Uniform Crimes Report (UCR) indicate that crime is at its lowest level in decades. As shown in Figure I.1, the violent crime rate, composed of indicators representing the rates for rape, robbery, assault, and homicide, shows significant reductions. The Bureau of Justice Statistics claims that these data indicate that overall the violent crime rate has been reduced by approximately 50 percent since 1973, primarily because the number of reported rapes, robberies, and assaults has decreased significantly. Interestingly enough, the homicide rate has remained static during the included reporting periods (Rennison, 2002).

Other official data attest to our current low rate of violent crime. For instance, not only has violent crime recorded by the NCVS and UCR shown consistent reductions, but so have other indicators, including the number of crimes reported to the police and the number of arrests of violent criminals. As shown in Figure I.2, the combination of these indicators purports to say the same thing: Violent crime in the United States appears to be on the decline and may be at its lowest level in years.

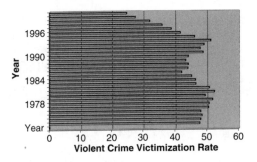

Figure I.1   Adjusted violent victimization rates: number of victim-izations per 1000 population, age 12 and over.

These findings, while important, do not preclude or in any way lessen the problem of crimes of violence in our society. Violent crime is still a major problem and one that needs to be addressed. There may be no better time than the present (a period of decline) to look at trends and try to understand why the rate of violent crime has dropped significantly in recent years.

If the causes of violent crime are related to the actions of the system actors, then these best practices need to be documented and recorded to keep the rate of crime at the current level and lower it further. However, if the causes of violent crime lie in the environment, then the causes and consequences need to be explored further.

While this book does not purport or even attempt to examine or discuss the causes of violent behavior in contemporary Western society, it does examine many of the new and less obvious new forms of violence that are appearing with alarming frequency. These emerging forms of violence not only threaten to raise our awareness of the cost of violent crime, but they may be considered part of the violent crime rate and thereby account for a new and unexpected increase in the overall amount of violent crime in this country.

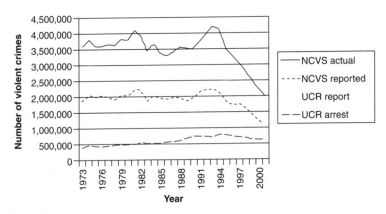

Figure I.2   Comparison of violent crime indicators using both UCR and NCVS (1973–2001).

The unique nature of the crimes discussed in this book is not only timely but is also of great interest to the general public and students of crime and criminology. Just what is it about crimes of violence that galvanizes the attention of our citizens? Is there something indigenous and unique to the United States that makes us a violent population? Is there something psychologically rewarding about the daily exposure to the stories of violent crimes that appear in the media? In other words, what is it about violence that makes it both attractive and at the same time repugnant? Is there something mystical about the crimes and the criminals who commit these random and sometimes non-random crimes of violence?

These are some of the questions that we will address in this book. These, and other questions, will be directed in avenues of intellectual examination, such as violent crimes committed by serial killers, mass killers, killers in the workplace, and school violence.

There is something attractive about personal violence in many people's views. The media often depicts violence in a positive way: One may obtain what is desired by being an aggressor. This act of aggression is directed often toward those who are most vulnerable: women, the elderly, and children. Movies such as *Copycat, Hannibal, Braveheart, The Patriot,* and many others too numerous to mention contain a message that violence, gratuitous or not, works. Indeed, some movies use violence even in a comedy. If enough violence is used, then one gets a desired reward. We witness the violence but not the pain and suffering of those who are being violated, fatally or not. We only see the connection between the use of physical force and what one can realize if the physical force is used deliberately and forcefully. One serial killer stated,

> I know what violence means. I know that it can bring me intrinsic benefits plus the realization that it is for me a manner in which I can become important. I become an omnipotent being, next to God, only slightly below Him in being and presence. After all, the women I killed, I did with a full realization that I was in control. I held their fates in my hands. I could permit them another minute of life if I only chose to do so. Did I want them to live another day? If so, I permitted that. Did I want them to die within the hour? That too was within my ability. Suffice it to say, I was in full command of my faculties. I knew I was a god. In one of my more brutal assaults, I become a fourth personality. So instead of the three persons of one God, I became more important that the Father, the Son, and the Holy Spirit because now I "forced" an addition to the Trinity. It now had to be a Magnificent Quartet: the Father, the Son, the Holy Spirit, and me. What made that all possible? Violence. It made me powerful. Without it I was nothing. With it, I became as God. Truly a very heady feeling.

VIOLENCE IN THE UNITED STATES

So what is it about our attraction and repulsion to violence? Certainly crime and criminals and the acts of violence they commit attract us. Since the release of *Red Dragon* over ten years ago, audiences and readers have been mesmerized by the words and deeds of Hannibal Lecter. His actions in

Silence of the Lambs and *Hannibal* were closely monitored as he moved from one act of violence to the next. We have been almost convinced that he is an actual person. Other movies of the same ilk show a similar trend in interest. Violence holds our attention. The media arranges telecasts that feature shootings, killings, and other sorts of violent acts. The shooting at Columbine held our interest and attention for weeks; there was even a nationally televised program in memory of the shooting a year later. Shootings and other forms of violence are reported almost instantly. When a disgruntled employee or a student opens fire in a workplace or a school, national attention is focused on that site immediately. One gets a message that all employees carry weapons to their workplace or every student has a gun in a locker.

What is the story of violence in America? How prevalent is it? The 2001 National Crime Victimization Survey reported that of all 28.8 million crimes reported,

- 74 percent (18.3 million) were property crimes.
- 24 percent (5.7 million) were crimes of violence.
- 2 percent were personal thefts (Rennison, 2002).

There is a gross difference between the numbers of crime and the personal toll that these same crimes have on the human psyche of the victim. The violation of the private space and humanness of a victim is something that can never be replaced. It is a violation that renders the victim different from what that person had been. One rape victim, for example, stated in a personal interview that the rapist did not kill her but he did kill the person she was. In other words, the woman would never be the same after that sexual attack. She would forever be a different person.

This argument, or the transformation of a person after being the victim of a violent crime, while acknowledged in academic circles, is rarely discussed. Anyone who has had his or her house or car broken into experiences similar feelings. It is a violation of the most personal order. Victims feel that their homes are not safe and that their cars and personal property can be taken at anytime. And there is little if anything that the police or anyone else can do about it. In situations like these, people respond in one of two ways: They either engage in proactive methods and arm themselves with a weapon (gun) or may even install an alarm. Or second, they retreat. That is, they slowly pull themselves away from society and choose not to engage in it anymore for fear of repeat victimization.

CHARACTER OF VIOLENCE

Violence has changed over the years. We have witnessed violent acts of terrorism. Who would have thought that an American could have committed such an atrocious act as the bombing of a federal courthouse in Oklahoma City, resulting in the death of scores of men, women, and children? Initially, many people in this country (including the authors) believed that some foreign terrorist or group had to have committed this crime. Certainly a person born and raised in this country could not be capable of such an atrocity. No American would have such a mind-set of hate. Yet an American committed that act. Timothy McVeigh became a household name connected with a heinous act of mass murder under the guise of some sense of perverted patriotism. That act of violence has forever changed the manner in which we go about living our lives and the way we think of our own safety.

Who would have thought of the remote possibility of more than 3000 deaths taken on one day in the country's largest city? Who will forget where they were in the morning of September 11, 2001? Who can forget the pictures of one Trade Center tower on fire and the astonishing picture of the second airplane ramming into the second tower? There were endless hours of media coverage and newscasts of the victims, their families, and the heroes we have made of the firefighters and the police officers who gave their lives in the struggle to rescue others at ground zero. The aftermath of this act of terrorist violence has affected the mind of every American. We have in this instance placed a face on the responsible agent. We have gone to war to punish those responsible for the murder of the victims. There are suspicions that the acts of international terrorism will not stop. The threat of more acts of terrorism seems a real possibility despite the varied strategies mounted by the United States to predict and thwart such acts of violence. Will there be more acts of skyjacking or using an airplane as a fatal projectile? Only time will tell, but it is likely. It may take the form of a person strapped to a bomb in a crowded restaurant or another form of terrorism, but there is no doubt that there will be an act of violence directed toward innocent people.

Other acts of violence have become more of a steady diet in the course of our daily news reports. Domestic violence, child abuse, sexual abuse, and other forms of personal violence remind us each day of how we human beings treat each other. Only within a week of this writing a young husband and father dropped his days-old child and killed it. He has been arrested and charged with murder. He is presently awaiting his trial in court.

There seems no end to the manner in which we predate on others. We believe that despite all of the best intentions of those in the government, social services, law enforcement, and mental health professionals, there will be no end to the violence, and the best we can hope for is a gradual reduction in the rate and violent content of those acts. Sadly, this is a miserable forecast. But it may be the best we can ask for.

Is our dedication to violence an aberrant interest? Perhaps. But regardless of the negative or positive endorsement of this statement, it is nonetheless an interest that many people share. Knowing that violence takes many forms and its perpetration ebbs and flows with societal growth, we intend to examine the many and varied forms of personal violence extant in American society. Be it serial murder, mass murder, domestic violence, murder in the workplace, school shootings, and other manifestations of violence, we will examine some of the components of violence through the writings of many of the academics and theorists who deal with violence as part of their academic studies.

This book contains many original chapters written especially for this endeavor. We consider this to be a strong point of the book. We have also chosen carefully other previously written articles that we consider "classics" in the treatment of violence.

Let us begin.

REFERENCES

Rennison, C. M. (2002). *Criminal Victimization, 2001: Changes 2000–2001 with Trends 1993–2001* (No. NCJ 194610). Washington, D.C.: U.S. Department of Justice, Bureau of Justice Statistics.

SECTION 1

DOMESTIC AND OTHER FORMS OF PERSONAL VIOLENCE

V iolence is not new to American society. Some have even said that since our nation was formed out of revolution, it was founded on an act of violence. While it is not our desire to discuss or even debate whether the Revolutionary War was an act of violence, it is important to note that violence has a rich tradition in this country.

The chapters in this section focus not on overt acts of violence that are commonly known or seen by people every day, but rather those covert acts of violence that often are hidden from public view. These domestic acts usually occur between family members or others that we live with, work by, or see with some frequency. In this section, we have chosen three chapters that focus on different aspects of this type of violence. These include the effects of alcohol on interpersonal violence and stalking behavior.

The first chapter, "Alcohol and Violence," looks at the use of alcohol as a contributing factor in most incidents of violence. According to the authors, alcohol or some other type of mood-altering drug plays a role in the majority of homicides or assaults and was a factor in 25% of all arrests in 1998. They present further evidence of the link between alcohol and violence by claiming that the frequent consumption of alcohol is by itself one of the most stable and reliable predictors of being involved (either as an offender or victim) in a violent crime. The strength of this chapter lies not with presented empirical or anecdotal evidence suggesting the linkage between alcohol and violence, but rather the theoretical framework that Mustaine and Tewksbury present. They attempt to frame the relationship between alcohol and violence into current criminological theories. While some theories are better at describing this relationship than others, they cover some of the new and evolving theories that have been generated to describe this specific relationship.

The second chapter in this section deals with the extent of stalking in contemporary American society. The authors begin by discussing the definition of stalking behavior and the legal and cultural context in which this type of crime occurs. They then discuss the evolution of typologies of stalkers in contemporary society and describe the different types. The authors conclude by noting that it is important to define and differentiate between the varieties of different stalkers because each type denotes varying degrees of risk between the offender and the object of their affection. Thus, the authors state, if these categories are easily defined and the types of offenders can be seen in a different context, it is much easier to understand their offending behavior than by lumping all stalkers into one or a few varied types.

The third chapter also examines the crime of stalking in contemporary society. However, unlike the modal type of stalking behavior, where an individual is obsessed with another, there is a variant of this behavior that is not discussed often. This type of stalking behavior deals with clients who, after the termination of services with their treatment providers, continue to contact their counselors. This type of stalking consists of victim threats, unwanted harassment, or the relentless pursuit of the clinicians by their patients. The chapter cites various sources that claim that about 25 to 50 percent of clinicians have been tracked, followed, or otherwise harassed by individuals that they once treated. Of these cases, very few reported physical violence, but 26 percent reported being harassed, and approximately 14 percent suffered some type of property damage at their home or place of employment.

To study this phenomenon more closely, the authors identified and tracked 16 cases where the patient had communicated threats of violence to the treatment staff. They found that females are more likely than males to communicate such threats, and when there is some type of violence involved, the clinical stalkers are usually less violent than the general stalking population.

Most important, this study finds that there are very few differences other than the ones noted between clinical stalkers and those in the general population. This being the case, the authors argue that the general typology of stalkers can be applied even to this very small subclass of offenders.

CHAPTER 1

ALCOHOL AND VIOLENCE

Elizabeth Ehrhardt Mustaine and Richard Tewksbury

Abstract: Violence is not a random event in our society. There are some very distinct, well-known patterns to violence, including types of persons involved, and when, where, and under what conditions violence is most likely to occur. Among the strongest predictors of violence is the presence of alcohol in a social setting. However, it is not the mere presence of alcohol that is important to violence. Rather, it is the amount of alcohol consumed, where and when it is consumed, and the types of persons who are involved in drinking events. People who drink are more likely than nondrinkers to be both victims and perpetrators of violence. Similarly, persons who drink more frequently and who drink greater quantities of alcohol are also known to be more likely to be involved in violence. This chapter discusses the relationship between alcohol and violence (as well as other negative consequences of drinking) and examines the conditions under which the presence of alcohol is more and less likely to be associated with violence.

INTRODUCTION

Among the many aspects of American society that people, regardless of their age, race, sex, or location, have to contend with on a regular basis are the effects of violence and the presence of alcohol. Almost without exception both violence and alcohol can be found in communities of all sizes, political persuasions, and compositions. And in almost all instances both violence and the effects of alcohol bring some form of suffering to people in these communities. This is not to say that all instances of violent behavior or all instances of alcohol consumption are bad and should be eliminated from society. What this is saying, however, is that there is a very well-established relationship between alcohol consumption and the presence of violence.

Research has consistently shown the linkages that persist between alcohol consumption and violent behavior or victimization. Using many different methodologies, including national statistics, surveys, observation, and field work, and many different samples, including college students, urban adults, youth, bar patrons, city blocks, and communities, researchers have regularly illustrated the connection between alcohol and violence. However, what is less clear or consistent is why this association is so strong. We will discuss the research supporting the linkage between alcohol and violence and then explore some theoretical explanations for why this relationship persists.

RATES OF VIOLENT CRIME IN AMERICA

National statistics have been collected for decades and can provide myriad information about the incidence of violence in the United States. In 1998 more than 2.5 million completed violent crimes occurred in the United States, according to reports from victims (U.S. Department of Justice, 2000). An additional 5.5 million attempts or threats of violence were also recorded. The official numbers on crime, however, are much lower. According to the FBI's Uniform Crime Reports, in 1999 there were "only" 1,430,693 violent crimes reported to law enforcement agencies in the United States, a reduction of 6.7 percent from the year before (Federal Bureau of Investigation, 2000).

More specifically, among the major forms of violent crime (homicide, rape, robbery, and assault), assault is by far the most common, with 916,383 reported in 1999. However, it should be noted that most assaults do not involve serious injuries to victims (U.S. Department of Justice, 2000). In contrast to assault, homicide is the least common of all violent offenses; "only" 15,533 homicides were reported in 1999 (Federal Bureau of Investigation, 2000).

Persons known to the victims commit the majority of violent crimes that are completed; nearly 6 out of every 10 violent crime events occur between persons who are acquainted (U.S. Department of Justice, 2000). Although most people fear being attacked by strangers, the reality is that the persons most likely to be violent are those whom we know, including our family members.

Violence is not a random event. Rates of violent victimization differ radically across various groups of people, places, circumstances, and settings. For example, young adolescents and young adults are most likely to be victimized by crimes of violence. The rate of violent victimization for persons between the ages of 12 and 24 is more than double the violent victimization rate of persons between ages 35 and 49 and four to six times the rate for persons over the age of 50 (U.S. Department of Justice, 2000).

However, age is not the only important demographic characteristic for understanding the distribution of violence in our society. So too is gender an important consideration. Men are about one-third more likely than women to be victims of violent crime (U.S. Department of Justice, 2000). Further, when age and sex are considered together, the differences become even more clear. Men between the ages of 12 and 24 are nearly 50 percent more likely than women in this age category to be a victim of a violent crime (U.S. Department of Justice, 2000). Again, this is in contrast to the levels of concerns, fears, and assumptions that are common in our country. The only violent offense for which men are not the most likely victims is rape/sexual assault, where women are more than ten times as likely as men to be victimized.

Another characteristic that influences variations in violent crime victimization is race/ethnicity. African Americans are more likely to be victims of violent crimes than whites and persons of all other races. The rate of violent crime victimization for African Americans is approximately 15 percent higher than is the rate of violent crime victimization for whites. African Americans are also more than 50 percent as likely as persons of other races (other than whites) to be violent crime victims (U.S. Department of Justice, 2000). When we consider race and sex together, we find that for both men and women, African Americans have higher rates of violent crime victimization than do whites for almost all forms of violence (U.S. Department of Justice, 2000).

Another element important in the consideration of violent crime variation is place. Rates of violent crime do vary somewhat across different sized communities. Urban communities have higher rates of violent crime than suburban and rural communities. The rate of violent crime in urban communities (especially communities of more than one million residents) is approximately 50 percent higher than in rural communities. Suburban areas have only slightly higher rates than do rural communities (U.S. Department of Justice, 2000). These national surveys make clear the conclusion that violent victimization is not a random event but illustrates clear patterns across groups and spaces in society.

Rates of violent offending also exhibit similar patterns. Similar to violent victimization, one such group variation is age. For example, of all arrests for violent offenses, 30 percent are of persons under the age of 21. Approximately 27 percent of all arrests are of persons 25–34 years old (U.S. Department of Justice, 2000). What this suggests, rather clearly, is that violence is largely an activity of the young. Especially for persons over the age of 30, violence is a somewhat rare experience.

Also similar to violent victimization variations, gender is influential in the commission of violent crime. Specifically, of all persons arrested for the four violent index crimes (homicide, rape, robbery and assault), 83 percent are males (U.S. Department of Justice, 2000). Violence is not only an activity of the young, it is primarily an activity of young men.

Race/ethnicity is also related to violent crime offending variation. Proportionately, African Americans are more likely to be arrested for violent crime commission (40.2 percent of all violent crime arrests) than persons of all other races/ethnicities. Further, the intersection of age and race is more pronounced, with 42.3 percent of all arrests for violent crime by youth under 18 being African American (U.S. Department of Justice, 2000). Additionally, age and gender also interact. Of the under 18 arrests for violent crime, 83.3 percent are males.

Finally, more arrests for violent crimes take place in urban areas. Again, research draws the conclusion that violence is not random but is associated with socially contextual variables such as group membership and location.

RATES OF ALCOHOL USE/MISUSE IN AMERICA

Research can also tell us a lot about who drinks alcohol, how much people drink, and the contexts in which drinking is most common. National statistics show that two out of every three Americans over the age of 18 reports at least occasionally consuming alcohol (Pastore & Maguire, 2000, p. 259). Although rates of heavy and binge drinking may generally be holding steady, the frequency with which individuals drink at such levels (consuming more than

5 drinks at one time) may be decreasing. Further, data from the U.S. Department of Health and Human Services (2000) show that since 1985 the proportion of Americans that report heavy or binge drinking recently (during the past month) has declined from 20.2 percent of all persons to 15.6 percent. While a decline, this remains a significant portion of the population. This also means that binge drinking continues to be a serious problem in society and a significant public policy consideration.

Similar characteristics influence variations in alcohol consumption as those that influence variations in violence victimizations. To elaborate, men (70 percent) are more likely than women (58 percent) to report drinking. This is especially true among the youngest drinkers (those under the age of 21). White Americans (66 percent) are more likely than persons of other races (49 percent) to drink. Interestingly, the likelihood of drinking increases as both education and income increase (Crawford, 1995; U.S. Department of Health and Human Services, 2000). This may be contrary to the assumptions of many persons, who believe that "lower class" persons (i.e., those with less education and fewer financial resources) are more likely to drink alcoholic beverages.

Similar to drinking alcohol, the amount of alcohol consumed varies by demographic characteristics; heavy and binge drinking are most common among more highly educated persons, as well as men, whites, and persons with full-time jobs (U.S. Department of Health and Human Services, 2000). Nonetheless, it is important to recognize that heavy/binge drinking is most common among young adults. Nearly one-third (31.7 percent) of 18–25-year-olds report binge drinking, a rate 44 percent higher than persons aged 26 to 34 and 166 percent percent higher than for persons over the age of 35. Rather clearly, heavy alcohol use, just like violence, is primarily a young person's activity and an activity of men.

The fact that some persons are not legally able to drink (due to age) does not appear to have a significant influence on actual drinking patterns. Even though illegal, persons younger than the legal drinking age also are frequently identified as consumers of alcohol. As reported by the Centers for Disease Control and Prevention (2003), in 1999 81 percent of high school students had drunk at least once in their lives, and nearly three out of every four (73.8 percent) reported drinking in the previous year. The proportion of high school seniors who report consuming alcohol has, however, been decreasing; in the mid-1980s more than 85 percent of high school seniors reporting consuming alcohol (Johnston et al., forthcoming). Additionally, drinking frequently begins at a very early age; fully one-third of high school students report that they first began drinking before the age of 13.

Even more pronounced than the rate and frequency of alcohol consumption among high school students are the data concerning drinking by college students. More than 83 percent of college students drink alcohol (Johnston et al., forthcoming), and when college students drink they often drink heavily. College students largely report that when they drink they both drink heavily and drink with the intent to get drunk. Approximately one in 20 college students report that they drink every single day (Johnston et al., forthcoming).

Given the strong relationship between alcohol consumption and violence, perhaps it should not be surprising that the experience of each seems to vary along similar demographic characteristics. A comparison between the factors that influence variation in alcohol consumption and those that are associated with violent victimization and offending shows that while not all characteristics are held in common, each is higher among males, youth, and students.

NEGATIVE EXPERIENCES ASSOCIATED WITH ALCOHOL USE

Many have recognized that drinking alcohol, especially heavy drinking, can have serious negative consequences, both for society in general and for individuals personally. In terms of society in general, there are some rather serious social problems associated with alcohol. These problems include legal and health problems associated with drinking and driving, medical problems, social problems, sexual assault and, of course, criminal violence.

Drinking and Driving

In 1998 more than 995,000 drivers were arrested for driving under the influence of alcohol (U.S. Department of Justice, 1997). Included in this statistic are approximately 11,000 drivers under the age of 18. Additionally, national data on automobile accidents suggest that nearly one in three drivers had some measurable blood alcohol content (Hedlund, 1994). The prevalence of alcohol in fatal motor vehicle accidents is much higher; in 1996, 41 percent of all fatalities due to automobile accidents involved alcohol and 18.7 percent of all drivers in fatal traffic accidents had blood alcohol concentrations of .1 of higher (U.S. Department of Transportation, 1997). Alcohol is especially prevalent in single-vehicle traffic fatalities, as 61 percent of single vehicle accident deaths involved alcohol (Logan & Schwilke, 1995). This relationship is even stronger in the case of traffic accidents occurring between midnight and 3 A.M. (U.S. Department of Transportation, 1997). For these accidents, 79 percent involved alcohol. In raw numbers, more than 17,000 individuals are killed in automobile accidents involving alcohol annually (U.S. Department of Transportation, 1996). Also, 35.5 percent of all pedestrians killed had blood alcohol concentrations of .10 or above (U.S. Department of Transportation, 1997). What these statistics show us is that drinking and driving does have very significant consequences.

Health Problems

More generally, alcohol is responsible for more than 110,000 deaths each year in the United States (National Institute on Alcohol Abuse and Alcoholism [NIAAA], 1999). According to statistics from the NIAAA (NIAAA, 1999), the economic cost to U.S. society for alcohol use/abuse/addiction in 1995 was estimated at $167 billion. This represents costs associated with medical consequences, lost earnings due to premature death or illness, automobile accidents, fire, and costs incurred by the criminal justice system. Medical consequences alone stemming from alcohol use are estimated at close to 16 billion dollars annually (NIAAA, 1999).

Individual Consequences

In addition, alcohol may pose significant personal problems for individuals. For example, among self-identified heavy drinkers, one in seven persons reports their work/school activities suffering, one in every six reports some type of emotional or psychological problem arising from drinking, and one in nine reports a physical health problem (U.S. Department of Health and Human Services, 2000).

As we might expect, persons who drink more often and drink larger quantities of alcohol are more likely to suffer a variety of problems resulting from their drinking. Wechsler and colleagues (1994, 1995) reported that among the consequences reported more often by binge drinkers are arguments with friends, getting hurt or injured, damaging property, and engaging in unprotected sex. Additionally, psychological research clearly shows that the consumption of alcohol is related to aggression (Abbey & Ross, 1992) and a lowering of inhibitions.

Unwanted Sex and Rape

Another problematic issue experienced by alcohol drinkers involves predatory sexual offenses. Research has found that persons who drink heavily and who binge drink are less likely to practice safer sex (Parker et al., 1994; Prince & Bernard, 1998; Sigmon & Gainey, 1995) and therefore more likely to experience negative consequences (unwanted pregnancies, sexually transmitted diseases, HIV) of sexual activity. Some researchers have even documented the fact that young adults who drink only moderately (not heavily or binging) have a lower likelihood of practicing unprotected sex (Keller et al., 1991). Additionally, students who drink report a lower likelihood of using condoms for sexual intercourse (Desiderato & Crawford, 1995). This is especially true for male college students (Noell et al., 1993). What we see here are the disinhibiting effects of alcohol; when one drinks his or her decision-making abilities are impaired and he or she is more likely to take risks. These risks may very well result in serious problems.

In addition to being more likely to engage in unprotected sex, persons (especially women) who drink are also more likely to engage in unwanted sex or sex against their will. Eighty-two percent of college students who report having been coerced or forced into sexual intercourse against their will report being intoxicated at the time (Presley et al., 1998). Relatedly, young women are more susceptible to unwanted sexual come-ons, fondling, and groping when they are intoxicated, especially when they are in the presence of intoxicated males (Fox & Sobol, 2000).

In fact, more often than not it is both the perpetrators and victims of sexual assault that have been drinking prior to an assault taking place. Most frequently the perpetrator and victim have been drinking together (Abbey & Ross, 1992; Koss & Oras, 1982; Miller & Marshall, 1987; Ullman & Knight, 1993). To elaborate, according to sexual assault victims, nearly two-thirds of them perceived that their attackers were intoxicated (Dobrin et al., 1996). Further, studies of college students involved in sexual assault incidents consistently show that a large proportion of those involved (both men and women) were under the influence of alcohol at the time of the sexual assault incident.

Muelenhard and Linton (1987) report 55 percent of the men and 53 percent of the women involved in sexual assaults on college campuses are under the influence of alcohol. Frintner and Rubinson (1993) report that 71 percent of female victims and 81 percent of male perpetrators of campus sexual assaults were drinking at the time of the incident. Several other researchers report similar findings: The majority of victims and perpetrators were drinking at the time of the sexual assault (Koss, 1998; Ward et al., 1991). Warshaw (1988) reports a similar finding for acquaintance rape: Seventy-five percent of men and 55 percent of women involved have been drinking or using illegal drugs.

Sexual assault is not the only sexually predatory crime associated with alcohol. Research has also shown that stalking victimization is also influenced by drinking patterns. Specifically, among the significant predictors of stalking victimization risks are women who get drunk in public frequently and women who drink at home often (Mustaine & Tewksbury, 1999). Obviously, then, there are negative consequences related to sexual activity that are directly related to alcohol consumption.

THE INTERSECTION OF ALCOHOL AND CRIME/VIOLENCE

In very simple terms, alcohol is closely linked with crime, especially violent crime. "About 3 million violent crimes occur each year in which victims perceive the offender to have been drinking at the time of the offense" (Greenfield, 1998, p. v). Or, as succinctly summarized by Miethe and McCorkle (1998, p. 239), alcohol is a "major precipitating factor [sic] in the onset of many crime incidents. The use of drugs and alcohol are common correlates of public order disturbances, violent offenses, and property crimes. As substances that impair judgement and reduce inhibitions, the majority of homicides and assaults involved alcohol and drug use by either victims, offenders, or both." Specifically, 23.6 percent of all arrests in 1998 (or more than 2.6 million) were alcohol related (U.S. Department of Justice, 2000). Very directly, alcohol is implicated in a greater proportion of criminal offenses than any other drug (Pernanen, 1991).

Research has also found that alcohol is related to heavy or serious involvement in crime. For example, one significant predictor of deep involvement in crime (being both an offender and victim of physical assault) is frequent consumption of alcohol (Mustaine & Tewksbury, 2000). Likewise, individuals who drink more frequently are not only at increased risk of one violent victimization, but also repeated or multiple victimizations (Lasley & Rosenbaum, 1988). Additionally, those who get drunk frequently during the week are at significantly greater risk of being victims of assault (Mustaine & Tewksbury, 2000). Similarly, robbery offenders are less likely than other violent offenders to be under the influence of alcohol when they commit their offenses (Zawitz et al., 1993).

When individuals drink, and especially when they chronically abuse alcohol, their risks for violent death are significantly increased (Rivara et al., 1997). This fact, or rather the relationship between alcohol consumption and homicide (as both offender and victim), is one of the most basic criminological understandings of the twentieth century (Wolfgang, 1958). However, it is not only individuals who drink that are at increased risk of violence and death, but the mere fact that one lives in a home with a drinker also significantly raises the chances of being a homicide victim. "Alcohol use and abuse by victims and offenders is present in the majority of murders and physical assaults" (Miethe & McCorkle, 1998, p. 215).

One population where the relationship between drinking and involvement in violence is easiest to see is among college students. When college students are involved in crime—as either victims or offenders—alcohol is very likely to be present (Abbey, 1991; Koss et al., 1987; Pezza & Bellotti, 1995). For example, 69 percent of students who have been physically assaulted report being intoxicated at the time of the event (Presley et al., 1998). Further, research has found that alcohol consumption by youth is frequently in a group context; this fact, combined with the disinhibiting effects of alcohol, may be related to youth crime (Miethe & McCorkle, 1998).

The link between alcohol use and crime is seen very clearly when we look at the nature of the offenses that result in individuals going to prison. More than one-third of all state prison inmates reports drinking during or immediately prior to the crime for which they are incarcerated. Individuals incarcerated for violent offenses (41 percent) are more likely than those incarcerated for property crimes (34.5 percent) to report being "under the influence of alcohol" when they committed their crimes. For violent offenses this is a rate 43 percent higher than the number of inmates under the influence of illegal drugs at the time of their offense (U.S. Department of Justice, 1999). These patterns do not only apply to offenders in prison, however. Even among offenders on probation—presumably those whose offenses are less serious—fully 40 percent report having been "under the influence" of alcohol at the time of their offenses (U.S. Department of Justice, 1998).

Contrary to popular assumptions, alcohol is the only psychoactive substance that has been shown to commonly increase aggression levels in users (Pernanen, 1991; Roth, 1994). Common assumptions in our society hold that "drugs" in general are associated with aggression and violence; however, this has not been supported in the clinical or social research. The question then becomes, why? Why is alcohol so strongly related to crimes of violence? Beginning to answer this question, we turn to an examination of research findings regarding the social context of alcohol and violence. Certainly an important aspect of each are social attitudes and expectations regarding the use and effects of alcohol and violence.

THE SOCIAL CONTEXT OF ALCOHOL AND VIOLENCE

Location

When we talk about the role of contexts, we are focusing our attention on issues of settings and patterns of activities. Contextual factors are very important in understanding how alcohol and violence are related. There are some settings in which alcohol's relationship to violence is stronger than for other settings, and there are patterns of behaviors involving alcohol that have been shown to be associated with increased likelihood of violence occurring.

The locations where people drink are important for creating opportunities and barriers to the release of aggression and violent tendencies. This leads to the suggestion that the alcohol and violence relationship may be best explained by looking not only at the individuals involved and their characteristics but rather the settings where both alcohol and violence are found. For instance, Lasley (1989) and Mustaine and Tewksbury (1998) have both shown that drinking—and getting drunk—in public places is significantly associated with increased risk of being robbed or assaulted. Somewhat relatedly, Lasley and Rosenbaum (1988) have shown how time spent in bars increases violent crime risks. Presumably this increased risk is attributable to being exposed to potential offenders being present who may perceive drinkers as less able to protect themselves and therefore more easily accessible/vulnerable.

A different approach to assessing the effects of context is looking at specific drinking locations. As reported by Roncek and Maier (1991), when a tavern/bar is in a neighborhood there is an increased level of crime in the neighborhood. Specifically, for every additional tavern on a city block, the probability of violent crime increases by 17.6 percent. Clearly, being in or near locations where alcohol is consumed increases one's likelihood of being a crime victim, even if one is not drinking. Bars are settings that are associated with a large range of types of behaviors, including both property and violent offenses. As such, by their very nature, bars enhance target suitability, by either attracting offenders or making people prone to victimization (Cohen & Felson, 1979). When we look specifically at women, we know that those women who drink in bars (or other public places) have increased risks of being victims of both physical and sexual assault (Fillmore, 1985; Fox & Sobol, 2000; Mustaine & Tewksbury, 1998b, 1999; Parks & Miller, 1997; Schwartz & Pitts, 1995; Tanioka, 1986). This increased risk is not a small risk; nearly one-half of women in one study report some form of sexual victimization after drinking in a bar, with more than one one-quarter (28.8 percent) experiencing unwanted sexual contact while actually in a bar (Parks & Miller, 1997).

Another way of thinking about the interrelationship among bars, alcohol, and violence is to examine the bar as a structural place where drinking and violence occur. As conditions or structural elements of the bar are changed, the amount of drinking or violence can change as well. Using place theory as a guiding principle, Fox and Sobol (2000) suggested that bars typically promote a drinking context that is susceptible to drinking-related problems. Given this, they analyzed how management controls and practices—as well as patrons' lifestyles—at urban bars affected the amount of predatory sexual offending and disorder within the bar. Specifically, they found that when the bouncers scrutinized patrons' behavior more closely, there were fewer outbreaks of violence at the bar. Relatedly, when patrons came and left the bar in groups, they were less likely to be victims of predatory assault than those who arrived and departed by themselves.

Another location where the linkages among alcohol, crime, and violence are underscored is the college campus. Crimes on college campuses are overwhelmingly associated with alcohol (Abbey, 1991; Engs & Hanson, 1994; Sloan, 1994). The relationship among these factors is even stronger on college campuses than in the rest of society. However, it is important to keep in mind that most crimes on college campuses are not violent crimes (Sloan, 1994).

Patterns of Behavior

Not only the setting where drinking occurs, but also when people drink and other activities accompanying drinking are well known to influence the (largely negative) consequences stemming from alcohol consumption. Several researchers, and a variety of theoretical approaches, have focused on assessing and explaining this phenomenon. Lasley (1989) focused his explanation of alcohol's contributing role to violent crime on the lifestyles of individuals. This research approach focuses on the role of frequent out-of-home nighttime social activities and frequent consumption of alcohol on the risks of violent victimization. As Lasley's findings suggest, when young men drink frequently, especially at nighttime social activities away from their homes, the likelihood of them being assaulted or robbed increases. This line of thinking was extended by Mustaine and Tewksbury (1998a) when they added to Lasley's model by looking at situational factors about alcohol consumption, specifically, how men and women may be at differential degrees of risk for assault and robbery.

This more refined approach shows that it is not only drinking frequently that puts individuals at heightened risk of violent victimization, but it is the frequency of drinking, whether or not one gets drunk when drinking, and where one drinks that have significant influences on risks of violent victimization. Specifically, individuals who frequently drink, get drunk in public places, and do a greater amount of their drinking in their own homes are at increased risks of being assaulted and/or robbed. This is the general pattern when considering all persons. When looking specifically at men, being drunk in a public place and doing a smaller proportion of one's drinking at the home of a friend is related to increased risks of assault and robbery. For women the only measure of alcohol consumption that is a significant predictor of assault and robbery victimization is the frequency of drinking. As a woman drinks more days of the week, her chances of being robbed or assaulted increase (Mustaine & Tewksbury, 1998a). This line of research suggests that persons who drink and are out and about in public are more likely to be violently victimized. The usual explanation for this is that by being seen in public in an intoxicated state they are perceived by others as "easy" targets.

Theoretical Explanations for the Linkage
Between Alcohol and Violence

There are a number of theories available for explaining the well-established link between alcohol and violence. Understanding these explanations is obviously important for understanding violence in general. However, while we have a number of available theories, none is necessarily the "right" or only way to explain this relationship. Knowing that alcohol and violence are related is crucial, but that is only half of the story. For example, what is it about the effects of alcohol that cause an increase in the violent behavior of the user? What are the linkages between the use of alcohol and violent incidents? What is it about the social aspects of drinking alcohol and violence that causes these two behaviors to frequently occur together in similar locations and among similar people? Why is alcohol the only psychoactive substance that appears to be related to violent behavior? These are some of the questions that theorists have attempted to answer. Some theoretical explanations for the relationship between alcohol and violence are focused and concern only that connection. Others happen within the context of broader criminological theories. What follows is a review of these theoretical explanations.

THREE FOCUSED THEORIES

Focused theories are those that have a smaller scope: They attempt to explain only the linkage between alcohol use and involvement in violent and aggressive behavior (Parker & Auerhahn, 1998).

Selective Disinhibition

Stemming from earlier weaknesses in the conceptualization of alcohol (namely, that alcohol had universal effects on behavior), Parker (1993) and Parker and Rebhun (1995) suggested that the effects of alcohol were related to the social context in which it was consumed. The theory suggests that alcohol causes a reduction in the inhibitions of individuals, selectively, depending on the circumstances, the norms of the individuals using alcohol, and other factors specific to the situation. In other words, the use of alcohol may lower the inhibitions of an individual in a particular setting, and as a result the individual is more likely to act violently. In a different setting, however, this same individual may consume alcohol and not act violently. Further, a different individual drinking alcohol in the first setting may not be tempted to act violently. These distinctions are all related to the setting and the norms of the individual and the circumstance. To elaborate, Parker and Rebhun establish some principles: Some individuals, because of their norms and culture, may be more likely to act violently than others. Additionally, some settings are more conducive to the use of violence than other settings. Further, alcohol may act as an inhibition reducer, but it does not cause people to do things they would normally be opposed to doing.

In bringing these principles together, these theorists focus on the concepts of active and passive constraint. Active constraint refers to the instances where an individual must consciously and deliberately restrain themselves from acting in a certain fashion in order to not engage in that behavior. Passive constraint suggests that there are times when persons need not be so diligent in restraining themselves from acting in certain ways, because they are really not interested in behaving that way anyway.

Alcohol only influences violent behavior when active constraint is present. When individuals who must earnestly work to stop themselves from behaving violently in a certain setting are drinking alcohol, it is likely that the disinhibiting effects of alcohol will lessen their abilities to constrain themselves. However, when individuals who are drinking are in settings where they are not really thinking of acting violently anyway, it is unlikely that alcohol will change that orientation. In this way, then, alcohol only selectively disinhibits individuals who are drinking alcohol. As such, violence and alcohol are only related when the setting, other individuals in the setting, and/or personal and cultural norms facilitate of the use of violence.

Violence and Intoxication

A similar yet distinct theory for explaining how alcohol and violence are related is proposed by Fagan (1990, 1993). In this theory he suggests that there are only a few areas of similarity among all of the work in various disciplines (biological, cultural, physiological, psychiatric, psychological, psychopharmacological, and social) regarding the effects of alcohol. Among these similarities is the idea that intoxication has a significant impact on behavior and cognitive functioning, and this impact is dependent on the social context and the contextual meanings for how people act when they are intoxicated. As such, when a person who has been drinking becomes involved in violence, it may be because he or she is suffering an impairment in judgment, is misreading social cues, or has fewer resources on which to draw when navigating social situations. Fagan suggests that these effects will be even greater in settings where there is lessened or no formal or informal social control mechanisms at play to guide behavior.

Alcohol Availability and Violence

Another theory exploring the linkages between alcohol and violence focuses not on how alcohol does or does not effect particular people in particular settings but rather centers on the effects of differential availability of alcohol. This theory, which usually looks at youth violence, suggests that areas with higher numbers of alcohol distribution outlets have higher rates of youth violence (Alaniz et al., 1998). This relationship can be explained in one of two ways. First, by drawing on selective disinhibition theory, we can say that areas with higher alcohol availability are likely to be areas where "anything goes" and likely will have norms that encourage the use of violence as well. Thus, active constraint is likely to be disinhibited. Second, when youths drink alcohol, they typically do so in relatively private, out-of-the-way places (like in a deserted park, in a car parked on a seldom used road). These locations have little, if any, effective forms of social control. In the absence of social control mechanisms, violence is more likely to erupt.

THREE GENERAL CRIMINOLOGICAL THEORIES

The following general criminological theories specifically incorporate a discussion of alcohol and its effect on violent crime. These theories' primary purposes includes an explanation for the occurrence of criminal behavior in general. Certainly each can apply an informed discussion for the incidence of violent behavior specifically as well. Many general criminological theories do not specifically mention the link between alcohol and violence, but some do.

Self-Control Theory

In their book *A General Theory of Crime,* Gottfredson and Hirschi (1990) suggest that poor parenting, which gives rise to poor self-control, is the primary cause of all forms of criminal and deviant behavior. Characteristics of people who lack self-control are that they tend to have a present time orientation, they are self-centered, they are less able to defer gratification, they lack diligence and persistence, and they are adventuresome, active, and physical.

Focusing on alcohol, these theorists suggest that persons who consume alcohol lack self-control, as alcohol consumption is something that interferes with the delaying of gratification and the attainment of longer-term goals and plans. The addition of violence into the equation here is simple: Persons who drink alcohol already have low self-control, so they are already prone to other forms of criminal or deviant behavior, and, as such, are more likely to act violently, and alcohol simply adds to that propensity.

Inequality, Strain, and Anomie Theories

These theories suggest that there is a link between relative inequality and violence and that alcohol simply adds to this linkage. Relative deprivation, poverty, and violence are related through the frustration and pressure that build up when persons are unable to attain societally defined goals, like financial comfort. In this manner, violence may be one of the few options left to persons who do not have the economic resources to handle the problems and crises of everyday life. Alcohol simply adds to this effect because of the well-known relationship between the use of alcohol and the use of violence. If relative deprivation causes frustration and stress, which in turn causes violent behavior, than this should happen more often in areas where alcohol consumption is highest. Further, frustration and stress may increase one's use of alcohol (as a coping mechanism), which in turn would increase one's use of violence.

Routine Activity Theory

Routine activity theory emphasizes the settings and contexts of criminal behavior. This theory proposes that three elements are necessary for a crime to occur: potential offenders, suitable targets, and incapable or absent guardians. To elaborate, crimes will not occur if potential offenders are unable to find targets they deem worthy, or, in the face of a desirable target, offenders feel they there are others (or things) around who may interfere with the successful commission of the crime. Finally, even in places where an unguarded, suitable target exists, it will not be attacked if there is no potential offender around. In this way, then, persons are at higher risk for violence when their daily lifestyles bring them into close proximity, or otherwise make them vulnerable, to potential offenders, without the aid of guardianship.

This theory is furthered by the introduction of the concept "hotspot." Hotspots are places where the convergence in space and time of the three necessary crime elements happens frequently and regularly. Routine activity researchers suggest that examples of hotspots are public places, especially public places where alcohol (given the strong relationship between alcohol and violence) is regularly present (Roncek & Maier, 1991). Hotspots may also be places where groups are drinking in settings where violence is expected and socially acceptable. As such, if persons' lifestyles incorporate frequent visits to hotspots, or reduce their ability to protect themselves while at a hotspot, their risks for violent victimization are increased, especially at night.

The key to understanding how alcohol is related to violence and routine activities is severalfold. First, persons who drink alcohol frequently, especially in public places, are more likely to experience violence, because they are less able to protect themselves. Second, persons who frequent hotspots where alcohol is present are more likely to experience violence because of the increased amount of violence happening at these places. Third, persons who are drinking are likely to be with others who are drinking. These others are more likely to act as potential offenders, thus increasing the odds that that person will be violently victimized.

SUMMARY

As seen, alcohol and violence are closely and consistently related. This relationship has persisted regardless of the source of research, type of methodology used, sample or population under investigation, or nature of the theoretical explanation. Research finds that persons arrested for violent offenses are likely to have been drinking during them; victims of violent offenses are likely to have been drinking and to perceive their attackers were intoxicated. Prisoners report they had been drinking prior to or during the offenses for which they have been incarcerated.

We have also noted that other sources of information detail the association between alcohol consumption and violent behavior. While the characteristics of individuals who are involved in violence and those who consume alcohol are not identical, they are similar. Younger persons, males, ethnic minorities, urban dwellers, and students are more likely to be involved in violence. At the same time, younger persons, males, students, and well-educated persons are more likely to consume alcohol. Further, persons who are in the vicinity of men who are drinking are more likely to be targets for violent aggression. Clearly, the similarities in group characteristics indicate an important connection in the relationship between alcohol and violence.

Finally, several researchers have proposed theoretical explanations for the connection between violence and alcohol. Several criminological theories incorporate specific discussions that detail this highly important relationship: inequality/strain/anomie theories, self-control theory, and routine activity theory. Some theorists have focused exclusively on the linkage between alcohol and violence and have written theories that explain just that: selective disinhibition, violence and intoxication, and alcohol availability and violence.

Given the myriad ways that researchers have focused on, written about, and researched the relationship between alcohol and violence, this is an important link to understand. By having a clear appreciation of this association, we may be better able to guide policy in ways to reduce violence, to treat violent offenders, and to assist those persons who are mired in alcohol abuse.

REFERENCES

Abbey, A. (1991). "Acquaintance rape and alcohol consumption on college campuses: how are they linked?" *Journal of the American College Health Association,* 39:165–169.

Abbey, A. & L. Ross. 1992."The role of alcohol in understanding mis-perceptions and sexual assault." Paper presented at the meeting of the American Psychological Society, Washington, DC.

Alaniz, M. L., R. N. Parker, A. Gallegos, & R. S. Cartmill. (1998). "Immigrants and violence: The importance of context." *Hispanic Journal of Behavioral Sciences,* 20(2).

Centers for Disease Control. (1999). *YRBSS: Youth Risk Behavior Surveillance System.* Retrieved November 10, 2003, from *http://apps.nccd.cdc.gov/YRBSS/ GraphV.asp?Site=XX&Cat=3&Qnum=Q40&Year=1999&ByVar=Q2*

Cohen, Robyn L. (1992). *1989 Survey of Local Jails: Drunk Driving.* Washington, DC: Bureau of Justice Statistics.

Cohen, Lawrence, and Marcus Felson. (1979). "Social change and crime rate trends: A routine activities approach." *American Sociological Review,* 44: 588–608.

Crawford, Catherine M. (1995). "Alcohol consumption patterns among undergraduates: The impact of family income." *Journal of Alcohol and Drug Education,* 40: 1–9.

Desiderato, L. L., & H. J. Crawford. (1995). "Risky sexual behavior in college students: Relationships between number of sexual partners, disclosure of previous risky behavior, and alcohol use." *Journal of Youth and Adolescence,* 24(1): 55–68.

Dobrin, Adam, Brian Wiersema, Colin Loftin, & David McDowall. (1996). *Statistical Handbook on Violence in America.* Phoenix: The Oryx Press.

Engs, Ruth C., & David J. Hanson. (1994). "Boozing and brawling on campus: A national study of violent problems associated with drinking over the past decade." *Journal of Criminal Justice,* 22: 171–180.

Fagan, Jeffrey. (1990). "Intoxication and aggression in drugs and crime." In *Crime and Justice: A Review of Research* (eds. Michael Tonry & James Q. Wilson), vol. 13: 241–320. Chicago: University of Chicago Press.

Fagan, Jeffrey. (1993). "Interactions among drugs, alcohol, violence." *Health Affairs,* 12 (4): 65–79.

Federal Bureau of Investigation. (2000). *Crime in the United States–1999.* Washington, DC: U.S. Department of Justice.

Fillmore, K. M. (1985). "The social victims of drinking." *British Journal of Addictions,* 80: 307–314.

Fox, James G., & James J. Sobol. (2000). "Drinking patterns, social interaction and barroom behavior: A routine activities approach." *Deviant Behavior,* 21: 429–450.

Frintner, Mary Pat, & Laurna Rubinson. (1993). "Acquaintance rape: The influence of alcohol, fraternity membership, and sports team membership." *Journal of Sex Education and Therapy,* 19, (4): 272–284.

Gottfredson, Michael, & Travis Hirschi. (1990). *A General Theory of Crime.* Palo Alto, CA: Stanford University Press.

Greenfield, Lawrence A. (1998). *Alcohol and Crime: An Analysis of National Data on the Prevalence of Alcohol Involvement in Crime.* Washington, DC: Bureau of Justice Statistics.

Hedlund, James H. (1994). "If they didn't drink, would they crash anyway? The role of alcohol in traffic crashes." *Alcohol, Drugs, and Driving,* 10 (2): 115–125.

Johnston, Lloyd D., Patrick M. O'Malley, & Jerald G. Bachman. (Forthcoming). *National Survey Results on Drug Use from the Monitoring the Future Study, 1975–1999.* Vol. 1. Washington, DC: U.S. Department of Health and Human Services, National Institute on Drug Abuse.

Keller, S. E., J. A. Bartlett, S. J. Schleifer, R. L. Johnson, E. Pinner, & B. Delaney. (1991). "HIV-relevant sexual behavior among a healthy inner-city heterosexual adolescent population in an endemic area of HIV." *Journal of Adolescent Health Care,* 12 (1): 44–48.

Koss, M., C. Gidycz, & N. Wisniewski. (1987). "The scope of rape: Incidence and prevalence of sexual aggression and victimization in a national sample of higher education students." *Journal of Consulting and Clinical Psychology,* 55(22): 162–170.

Koss, M., & C. Oras. (1982). "Sexual experience survey: A research instrument investigating sexual aggression and victimization." *Journal of Consulting and Clinical Psychology,* 50: 455–457.

Koss, Mary. (1988). "Hidden rape: Sexual aggression and victimization in a national sample of students in higher education." A. Burgess (ed.), *Rape and Sexual Assault* (Volume 2, pp. 3–25). New York: Garland.

Lasley, James. (1989). "Drinking routines/lifestyles and predatory victimization: A causal analysis." *Justice Quarterly,* 6(4): 529–542.

Lasley, James, & Jill Rosenbaum. (1988). "Routine activities and multiple personal victimization." *Sociology and Social Research,* 73: 47–50.

Logan, B. K. & E. W. Schwilke. (1996). "Drug and alcohol use in fatally injured drivers in Washington state." *Journal of Forensic Sciences,* 41 (3): 505–510.

Miller, B., & J. Marshall. (1987). "Coercive sex on the university campus." *Journal of College Student Personnel,* 28: 38–47.

Miethe, Terance D., & Richard McCorkle. (1998). *Crime Profiles: The Anatomy of Dangerous Persons, Places, and Situations.* Los Angeles: Roxbury.

Muelenhard, Charlene L., & Melanie A. Linton. (1987). "Date rape & sexual aggression in dating situations: Incidence and risk factors." *Journal of Counseling Psychology,* 34, (2): 186–196.

Mustaine, Elizabeth Ehrhardt, & Richard Tewksbury. (1998a). "Specifying the role of alcohol in predatory victimization." *Deviant Behavior,* 19, (2): 173–199.

Mustaine, Elizabeth Ehrhardt, & Richard Tewksbury. (1998b). "Victimization risks at leisure: A gender-specific analysis." *Violence and Victims,* 13(3): 231–249.

Mustaine, Elizabeth Ehrhardt, & Richard Tewksbury. (1999). "A routine activity theory explanation for women's stalking victimizations." *Violence Against Women,* 5(1): 43–62.

Mustaine, Elizabeth Ehrhardt, & Richard Tewksbury. (2000). "Comparing the lifestyles of victims, offenders, and victim-offenders: A routine activity theory assessment of similarities and differences for criminal incident participants." *Sociological Focus,* 33 (3): 339–362.

National Institute on Alcohol Abuse and Alcoholism. (1999). *The Economic Costs of Alcohol and Drug Abuse in the United States* (publication no. 98-4327). Bethesda, MD: Lewin Group.

Noell, J., A. Biglan, J. Berendt, L. Ochs, C.W. Metzler, D. Ary, & K. Smolkowski. (1993). "Problematic sexual situations for adolescents: Alcohol and unsafe sex." *Health Values,* 17(6): 40–49.

Parker, D. A., T. C. Harford, & I. M. Rosenstock. (1994). "Alcohol, other drugs, and sexual risk-taking among young adults." *Journal of Substance Abuse,* 6(1):87–93.

Parker, Robert Nash. (1993). "Alcohol and theories of homicide." In *Advances in Criminological Theory* (eds. Freda Adler & W. Laufer) vol. 4: 113–142. New Brunswick, NJ: Transaction.

Parker, Robert Nash, and Kathleen Auerhahn. (1998). "Alcohol, drugs and violence." *Annual Review of Sociology,* 24: 291–311.

Parker, Robert Nash, and L. A. Rebhun. (1995). *Alcohol and Homicide: The Deadly Combination of Two American Traditions.* Albany: State University of New York Press.

Parks, Kathleen A., & Brenda A. Miller. (1997). "Bar victimization of women." *Psychology of Women Quarterly,* 21: 509–526.

Pastore, Ann L., & Kathleen Maguire (eds.). (2000). *Sourcebook of Criminal Justice Statistics* [Online]. Available: *http://www.albany.edu/sourcebook/.*

Pernanen, Kai. (1991). *Alcohol and Human Violence.* New York: Guilford Press.

Pezza, P., & A. Bellotti. (1995). "College campus violence: Origins, impacts, and responses." *Educational Psychology Review,* 7(1): 105–123.

Presley, Cheryl A., Jami S. Leichliter, & Philip W. Meilman. (1998). *Alcohol and Drugs on American College Campuses: A Report to College Presidents.* Carbondale, IL: Core Institute, Southern Illinois University.

Prince, A., and A. L. Bernard. (1998). "Alcohol use and safer sex behaviors of students at a commuter university." *Journal of Alcohol and Drug Education,* 43(2): 1–19.

Rivara, F. P., B. A. Mueller, G. Somes, C. T. Mendoza, N. B. Rushforth, & A. L. Kellermann. (1997). "Alcohol and illicit drug abuse and the risk of violent death in the home."*Journal of the American Medical Association,* 278(7): 569–575.

Roncek, Dennis, and Pamela Maier. (1991). "Bars, blocks, and crimes revisited: Linking the theory of routine activities to the empiricism of 'hot spots'." *Criminology,* 29(4): 725–753.

Schwartz, Martin D., and Victoria L. Pitts. (1995). "Exploring a feminist routine activities approach to explaining sexual assault." *Justice Quarterly,* 12(1): 9–31.

Sigmon, S. B., & R. Gainey. (1995). "High-risk sexual activity and alcohol consumption among college students." *College Student Journal,* 29: 128.

Sloan, John. (1994). "The correlates of campus crime: An analysis of reported crimes on college and university campuses." *Journal of Criminal Justice,* 22: 51–61.

Tanioka, Ichiro. (1986). "Evidence links smoking to violent crime victimization." *Sociology and Social Research,* 71(1): 58.

Ullman, S., & R. Knight. (1993). "The efficacy of women's resistance strategies in rape situations." *Psychology of Women Quarterly,* 17(1): 23–41.

U.S. Department of Health and Human Services. (2000). *National Household Survey on Drug Abuse: Main Findings 1998.* Rockville, MD: Substance Abuse and Mental Health Services Administration.

U.S. Department of Justice. (1997). *Crime in the United States, 1996.* Washington, DC: Federal Bureau of Investigation.

U.S. Department of Justice. (1998). *Substance Abuse and Treatment of Adults on Probation, 1995.* Washington, DC: Bureau of Justice Statistics.

U.S. Department of Justice. (1999). *Substance Abuse and Treatment, State and Federal Prisoners, 1997.* Washington, DC: Bureau of Justice Statistics.

U.S. Department of Justice. (2000). *Criminal Victimization in the United States, 1998.* Washington, DC: Bureau of Justice Statistics.

U.S. Department of Transportation. (1996). *Traffic Safety Facts 1995.* Washington, DC: National Highway Traffic Safety Administration.

Ward, Sally K., Kathy Chapman, Ellen Cohn, Susan White, & Kirk Williams. (1991). "Acquaintance rape and the college social scene." *Family Relations,* 40: 65–71.

Warshaw, Robin. (1988). *I Never Called It Rape.* New York: Harper & Row.

Wechsler, H., A. Davenport, G. Dowdall, B. Moeykens, & S. Castillo. (1994). "Health and behavioral consequences of binge drinking in college." *Journal of the American Medical Association,* 272: 672–1677.

Wechsler, H., G. Dowdall, A. Davenport, & E. Rimm. (1995). "A gender-specific measure of binge drinking among college students." *American Journal of Public Health,* 85: 982–985.

Wolfgang, Marvin. (1958). *Patterns of Criminal Homicide.* Philadelphia: University of Pennsylvania Press.

Zawitz, Marianne W., Patsy A. Klaus, Ronet Bachman, Lisa D. Bastian, Marshall M. DeBerry, Jr., Michael R. Rand, & Bruce M. Taylor. (1993). *Highlights from 20 Years of Surveying Crime Victims: The National Crime Victimization Survey, 1973–92.* Washington, DC: Bureau of Justice Statistics.

CHAPTER 2

STALKING IN AMERICA: TYPES AND METHODS OF CRIMINAL STALKERS[1]

Ronald M. Holmes and Stephen T. Holmes

INTRODUCTION

When Robert Bardo went to the door of Rebecca Schaeffer, of the TV series *My Sister Sam,* and fatally shot her, the level of consciousness was raised concerning the dangers of stalkers. Several years earlier, Arthur Jackson stalked and stabbed actress Theresa Saldana. John Hinckley, Jr., shot at Ronald Reagan in an attempt to impress actress Jodie Foster. A farmer in Canada has written scores of letters to singer Anne Murray.

Not only those in the entertainment field or politics are stalked. Husbands *and* wives seek out their former mates to terrorize. Unbalanced persons send letters and make phone calls to athletes and targeted strangers for purposes of terrorizing and even sexually assaulting and murder. There may be no one truly safe from a predatory stalker.

Little is known about the mind and mentality of one who stalks. Meager research has been done to empirically study this phenomenon. What has been done is often lacking in research rigor and theory testing. Therefore, we are truly only in a beginning stage in our analyses and scientific study of this most serious personal concern.

Also lacking is an analysis of different types of stalkers, differences influenced by behavioral patterns and expected rewards, material or psychological. This is the purpose of this chapter.

WHAT IS STALKING?

More than two dozen states have initiated laws to combat this social problem of stalking. Kentucky, for example, has passed House Bill 445, which defines stalking as "an intentional course of conduct which is 1. directed at a specific

---

[1]This chapter was first printed in 1993 in the *Journal of Contemporary Criminal Justice,* 9(4), 317–327.

person or persons; 2. which seriously alarms, annoys, intimidates or harasses the person or persons; and 3. which serves no legitimate purpose."

Of course there are other definitions of stalking. Other states too have passed laws with similar language. But as varied as the laws or definitions, just as divergent are the persons and the behaviors involved in these predatory *acts*.

Stalking takes many forms: phone calls, letters, personal confrontations. etc. For example, in Oregon, a 24-year-old man sent letters and presents to an 11-year-old girl. Professing his lasting love for the child, the man wrote letters to her which said, "When I seen [sic] her, when I look into her eyes, my mind goes blank. . . . I will wait for ten years. I will and about sex I don't want none until our honeymoon." The man is now serving a sentence at the Oregon State Correctional Institute (Hallman, 1992).

Methods within the stalking process become an important and integral part of the act. Norris (1988) discusses the process of the stalk as it concerns the sex offender. It appears as a starting point in the selection process of the serial predator. Holmes (1989,) has also examined the stalking of the sexual predator. He lists "the stalk" as one of the five steps in the selection and the execution of serial murder. Hazelwood (1989) extends a similar discussion with the serial rapist.

LITERATURE REVIEW

Criminal stalking has only recently been an area of examination by those interested in the criminal mind. Dietz and colleagues (1991) analyzed threatening letters sent to members of the U.S. Congress. This study attempted to gauge the seriousness of the threats. Realizing the numbers of such letters range in the hundreds each year and rising, there was a need to develop an index of personal safety to these public servants.

Other people are targets of a different type of stalker, the erotomaniac. This person suffers a delusional belief that one is passionately loved by another. In *The New Statesman and Society* (1990, p. 32), five basic characteristics of this form of stalker were listed:

1. A difficult and psychologically troubled domestic environment
2. A domineering parent
3. A transference of love and devotional interest to a person who is unobtainable
4. A history of dramatic demonstrations of love, including threats of suicide, dangerous and very public statements and sometimes physical attacks
5. Irrational and inappropriate attempts to dissuade the love object and turn the rejection into a gesture of love

Historically diagnosed as paranoids, Arieti (1959) suggests that erotomaniacs suffer from a "monodelusional disorder" with a "good prognosis" for successful rehabilitation. This is hardly encouraging remarks from those who suffer at the hands of these stalkers.

The academic literature has centered its discussion of stalkers in terms of a medical model. Only recently have other articles appeared which examine this behavioral phenomenon from a different perspective. Vernon Geberth (1992), a retired New York homicide detective, for example, lists two different types of stalkers. One is the psychopathic personality stalker. Invariably a male, and representing the largest population of stalkers, he comes from a dysfunctional family; violence is the norm. He stalks because he has lost control over a subject (e.g., a former girlfriend or a wife) and exercises too frequently fatal violence.

Table 2.1
Selected Stalkers and Their Victims

Stalkers	Victims
Joni Penn	Sharon Gless, actress
Mark David Chapman	John Lennon, musician
Arthur Jackson	Theresa Saldana, actress; John F. Kennedy, President of the United States; Teresa Berganza, singer
John Hinckey, Jr.	Jodie Foster, actress
Tina Ledbetter	Michael J. Fox, actor
Stephen Stillabower	Madonna, musician; Sean Penn, actor
Ken Gause	Johnny Carson, TV host
Nathan Trupp	Michael Landon, actor; Sandra Day O'Connor, Supreme Court Justice
Ralph Nau	Olivia Newton John, singer; Marie Osmond, singer; Cher, singer; Farrah Fawcett, actress/model
John Smetek	Justine Bateman, actress
Robert Bardo	Rebecca Schaeffer, actress
Billie Jackson	Michael Jackson, singer
Margaret Ray	David Letterman, TV host
Roger Davis	Vanna White, TV star
Brook Hull	Teri Garr, actress
Ruth Steinhagen	Eddie Waitkus, baseball player
Daniel Vega	Donna Mills, actress
Robert Keiling	Anne Murray, singer

Information for the stalkers and the victims in this table was obtained from sources including Gebertli (1992); *U.S. News and World Report,* 1992. In the mind of a stalker. Vol. 1112. February 17:28-30; *People Weekly,* 1990. When fans turn into fanatics, nervous celebs call for help from security expert Gavin DeBecker. Vol. 33. February 12:103-106; *People Weekly,* 1989. Vicious crime, double jeopardy. Vol. 31. June 5:44-49; *People Weekly,* 1990. Vanna White and Teri Garr ask the courts to protect them from fans who have gone too far. Vol. 34. July 16:41; *People Weekly,* 1989. Justine Bateman becomes the latest celebrity to be menaced by an obsessive fan. Vol 32. September 25:112-113; *People Weekly,* 1989. An innocent life, a heartbreaking death. Vol. 32. July 31:60-66; Lurie, R. 1990. Guns n' roses. *Los Angeles Magazine.* Vol. 35, February. 88-94; *Time,* 1989. A fatal obsession with the stars. Vol. 134. July 31:43-44; *New Statesman and Society,* 1990. Erotomania. Vol. 3. July 27:31-32.

The psychotic personality stalker is the second type. This stalker, either male or female, becomes obsessed with an unobtainable love object. Geberth places the erotomaniac in this category.

Geberth lists three types of stalking: erotomania, almost 10 percent of all stalkers; love obsession, which includes 43 percent of all stalkers where the victim is a stranger to the stalker but is obsessed and mounts a campaign of harassment to make the victim aware of the stalker's existence; and finally the simple obsession stalker, who accounts for 47 percent of the stalkers who know the victim, perhaps a neighbor or former boss, and begin then a campaign of harassment. Geberth remarks that this typology was gathered from research done in Los Angeles.

Regardless of the number of articles that appear in both the professional literature as well as trade magazines (e.g., *Time, The Los Angeles Magazine, People Weekly,* and *U.S. News & World Report*), stalking is a formidable problem. Moreover, stalking had been viewed from little more than a cursory position. It is only now that serious efforts are made to examine stalking as a major social enigma.

TYPOLOGY OF STALKERS

As evident in any specific type of human behavior, people behave differently from disparate motivational factors and anticipated gains. These variations in behavior stem from many constitutional and/or experiential factors. It may indeed be biology or environment, or personal chemistry or more likely a unique combination of these factors that we do not at this time understand. Social and behavioral scientists, neurologists and physicians, psychologists, and psychics all have their theories that explain human behavior. We do not understand the human condition, criminal or not.

One initial effort is to develop a typology of stalkers. This has been done in the case of serial murder (Holmes & DeBurger, 1985, 1988). Developing such a typology based on motivation and gain, four types of serial killers were developed. From this exercise, a better understanding was gained to investigate crimes of sequential killers.

A typology of stalkers will be described. Within each type of stalker the motives and anticipated gains will be examined. Within each type these two elements function for the predator a personal justification. In addition to the motivational and gain factors, we have offered other discriminating elements that are unique to each type of stalker: celebrity, lust. hit, love-scorned, domestic, and political.

By analyzing more than six score of stalking cases, trained raters were given the task to place each individual case into one of six types. The raters were trained using test cases, and the variables (victims, method of selection, motivation, anticipated gain, fatal violence used, personal affinity, and sexual motivation) were coded by a university professor, a doctoral student in criminal justice, and a masters-level student in the administration of justice.

Celebrity Stalker

The celebrity stalker is one who stalks someone famous. Typically, the victim is in the entertainment profession: recording artist, actor or actress, or athlete (football, baseball, etc.).

Table 2.2
Typology of Stalkers

	Celebrity	Lust	Hit	Scorned	Domestic	Political
VICTIMS						
Nonstranger				X	X	
Stranger	X	X	X			X
SELECTION						
Random		X				
Planned	X		X	X	X	X
MOTIVATION						
Intrinsic	X	X		X	X	X
Extrinsic			X			
ANTICIPATED GAIN						
Psychological	X	X		X	X	X
Material			X			
INTENDED FATAL VIOLENCE						
Yes	X	X	X		X	X
No				X		
SEXUALLY MOTIVATED						
Yes		X				
No	X		X	X	X	X

This type of stalker will pursue a personal stranger. Although this victim is well known on an impersonal level (a famous TV star, for example), the target is personally unknown. Robert Bardo sent Rebecca Schaeffer love letters two years before he killed her. At one time he traveled by bus from Arizona to Hollywood to personally deliver flowers and a giant Teddy bear. Refused admittance, he later obtained her address from a private detective. He rang the bell at her front door, and when she opened it, he fatally wounded her. Bardo had written to his sister months before and confessed an imaginary love affair with Schaeffer but wanted to eliminate something he could not obtain.

The victim is carefully selected by the celebrity stalker. The motivation is inward and the anticipated gain is psychological. As with the case of Bardo-Schaeffer, violence is often fatal. Sometimes when not, it is only because the stalker was unsuccessful. This is illustrated by the case of Arthur Jackson's knife-wielding assault on Theresa Saldana. A delivery man just happened to come upon the attack and wrestled the knife away from Jackson only after he had stabbed her eleven times. His intent was to kill.

With the celebrity stalker, there is no personal affinity, no lines of bloodship by family or marriage. And, of course, the act itself is not sexually motivated.

The Lust Stalker

The lust stalker is motivated by a perverse sense of sexual predation. This type of sexual offender is typically a serialist and if a serial murderer is of the hedonistic or power/control type (Holmes & DeBurger, 1985, p. 1988). Despite many claims that this type of stalker will select ideal victim types (e.g., those with specific physical, personal or occupational traits), the victims themselves are typically strangers. The hunt itself may be quite involved or a spur-of-the-moment occasion. What is the anticipated gain is a sexual experience, a psychological gain. Too often the lust stalker will undergo an escalation into violence that includes the murder of the victim. Again, there is no personal relationship, through blood or marriage, with the selected victim.

Jerry Brudos, a serialist from Oregon, would be an excellent example of the lust stalker. Using a ruse to "arrest" his victims, taking them to his home, he killed at least four women. To one woman, he cut off an ankle; another he cut off a left breast; to a third, both breasts; and finally, with the fourth victim, he sent electrical shocks through her body while she hung from a rafter in his garage. Brudos was arrested while stalking his fifth victim, a young college woman (Stack, 1983).

The Hit Stalker

The example of stalker is the professional killer. Such a stalker would be the murderer for hire. The victims are strangers. They have been carefully selected already by the employee of the professional murderer. The anticipated gain is material, the money or other monetary goods which will be realized from successful predation. Fatal violence is the norm; no sexual acts are demanded. Again, there is no personal relationship.

An example of the hit stalker is Richard Kuklinski. An admitted professional killer (*The Ice Man,* HBO Special, 1991), Kuklinski coldly and dispassionately described his selection of victims and the manner in which he disposed of his victims. He even relates leaving his home on Christmas Eve while assembling toys for his children to go into town to kill a man.

The Love-Scorned Stalker

Unlike most stalkers, the love-scorned stalker intends violence, usually not fatal violence, against someone known. The victim, then, is known to the stalker. There is psychological gain. The predator believes the victim, once realizing how much the stalker really cares, will return that affection. A personal relationship exists between the stalker and the victim, though not by blood or marriage. There has been at one time or another a personal relationship in which too many times the stalker has misunderstood the depth of that relationship. There is no sexual component to the stalking, although the act of the assault may take on a sexual element.

An 18-year-old college coed, Melissa (not her correct name), went to the police for protection. She said that a young man, also a freshman at the same university that she attended, had been writing her letters and following her to her part-time job as well as walking behind her, darting behind bushes and buildings on the campus. She had known the stalker since their freshman year in high school. Upon further investigation, it was found that the young man had broken into her house, went through her bedroom, and stolen panties and bras. Upon developing an analysis of the situation, the man was encouraged to seek hospitalization for his mistaken belief that Melissa was in love with him and wanted to have his babies.

The Domestic Stalker

The domestic stalker at one time shared an intimate part of the victim's everyday life. This is a factor that differentiates the domestic stalker from the love-scorned stalker. The former at one time shared a relationship and life experiences. This relationship was inclusive of, but not limited to, love.

All too frequently a case is reported when an estranged husband hunts his former wife. Often the stalking is a long-term affair, and the confrontation between the two results with tragic consequences. The motivation is psychological, "to get even" with that individual who once shared an important part of the stalker's life.

Recently an estranged husband was stalking his wife for days. He finally approached her outside a daycare center where she had left their only child. Getting into her car to travel to work, he ran up to her car, shot her in the face, and then shot himself. He died at the scene. The anticipated gain is perversely psychological; fatal violence is too often the goal. The target was one with whom he shared an intimate connection. Again, there is no sexual motivating factor involved in the selection of the victim or the perpetration of violence in the finalization of the stalking episode.

The Political Stalker

The intended victim of the political stalker is a personal stranger. It may be the president of the United States, the mayor of a large city, a minor city leader, or someone else. The history of this country has more than its share of those who have stalked public officials, including our presidents. In many cases, the public officials have been only wounded. Unfortunately, in too many other cases, the victims have been murdered.

The victims of the political stalker are carefully selected and the process of stalking is planned. There is usually a political ideology that precipitates the stalking and the intended fatal violence that ensues. As noted, sexual motivations are missing in this form of predation. When Lee Harvey Oswald shot President Kennedy, the president was not personally known to the assassin. They were strangers. There was no money exchanged, as far as we know, from a terrorist organization to Oswald for killing the president. Apparently it was a political ideology that accounted for the motivation to murder. John Wilkes Booth killed Lincoln because of political ideologies that were different from those espoused by the president. Lynette Fromme shot President Ford almost certainly motivated by the influence of the relationship with Charlie Manson and the family's political leanings.

The political stalker is fundamentally different from the other stalkers we have mentioned. The lust stalker is motivated by a predatory sense of sex as conquest. The hit stalker anticipates a material gain. The celebrity stalker hopes to bask in the reflected glory or the celebrity or believes the target shares the affectionate relationship that is in his mind only.

Within each type we have discussed a type of stalker and the behavioral and psychological dynamics involved with each. This is the first step in the understanding of the stalker and perhaps, then, a step toward prevention.

Table 2.3
Presidential Stalkers

Year	President	Stalker	Age	Location	Weapon	Injury
1835	Andrew Jackson	Richard Law	35	U.S. Capitol	Handgun	None
1865	Abraham Lincoln	John Wilkes Booth	26	Ford Theater	Handgun	Death
1881	John Garfield	Charles Guiteau	38	Train Station	Handgun	Death
1901	William McKinley	Leon Czolgosz	28	U.S. Exposition	Handgun	Death
1912	Theodore Roosevelt	John Shrank	36	Hotel	Handgun	Injury
1933	Franklin Roosevelt	Guiseppe Zangara	32	Public Park	Handgun	None
1950	Harry S. Truman	Griselio Torresola & Oscar Collazo	25	Blair House	Handgun	None
1960	John Kennedy	Richard Pavlick	69	Motorcade	Explosives	None
1963	John Kennedy	John Harvey Oswald	24	Motorcade	Rifle	Death
1974	Richard Nixon	Samuel Byck	44	Airport	Handgun	None
1975	Gerald Ford	Lynette Fromme	26	Public Park	Handgun	None
1975	Gerald Ford	Sarah Moore	45	Hotel	Handgun	None
1981	Ronald Reagan	John Hinckley, Jr.	25	Hotel Sidewalk	Handgun	Wound to Body

Adapted from Sifakis, C. (1991) *Encyclopedia of Assassinations*. New York: Facts on File.

CONCLUSION

Stalking is a social condition that is attracting more attention not only from those in the criminal justice system but also those in the social and behavioral sciences. As criminal justice practitioners we are concerned with the early identification of those who stalk their victims. By gaining some insight into the mentality and the mind-set of the stalker, this may be the first step in the detection of those who will start this form of violence.

There must be an effort at early identification of the stalkers. One initial step is to make differential judgments concerning various types of stalkers. This has been the focus of this chapter. By the development of such a typology, this is the first step into an analysis of stalking as well as the personal risk of the potential victim.

REFERENCES

"A fatal obsession with the stars." *Time,* (1989). Vol 134, July 31: 43–44.
"An innocent life, a heartbreaking death." *People Weekly,* (1989). Vol. 32, July 31: 60–66.
Arieti, S. (1959). *American Handbook of Psychiatry,* 1st ed., Vol 1. New York: Basic Books, pp. 525–551.
Dietz, P., D. Matthews, D. Martell, T. Stewart, D. Hrounda, & J. Warren, (1991). Threatening and Otherwise Inappropriate Letters to Members of the United States Congress. *Journal of Forensic Sciences, 36*(5), 1445–1468.
"Erotomania." *New Statesman and Society.* (1990). Vol. 3, July 27: 31–32.
Geberth, V. (1992). "Stalkers." *Law and Order,* 40(10): 138–143.
Hallman, T. (1992). "Stalker robs girl of innocence." *The Oregonian,* Monday, March 9, A1–A8.
Hazelwood, R., & Warren, J. (1989). The Serial Rapist: His Characteristics and Victims. *FBI Law Enforcement Bulletin, 58*(2), 18–25.
"Justine Bateman becomes the latest celebrity to be menaced by an obsessive fan." *People Weekly,* (1989). Vol 32, September 25:112–113.
Holmes. R., & J. DeBurger. (1985). "Profiles in terror the serial murderer." *FBI Law Enforcement Bulletin,* XLIX (September): 29–34.
Holmes. R., & J. DeBurger. (1988). *Serial Murder.* Newbury Park, CA: Sage Publications.
Lurie, R. (1990). "Guns n' roses." *Los Angeles Magazine,* Vol. 35, February, 88–94.
Norris, J. (1988). *Serial Killers: The Growing Menace.* New York. Dolphin Books.
Rudden, M., J. Sweeney, & A. Frances. (1990). "Diagnosis and clinical course of erotomanic and other delusional patients." *American Journal of Psychiatry,* 147: 625–628.
Sifakis, C. (1991). *Encyclopedia of Assassinations.* New York: Facts on File.
Stack, A. (1983). *The Lust Killer.* New York: Signet Books.
"Vanna White and Teri Garr ask the courts to protect them from fans who have gone too far." *People Weekly,* (1990). Vol 34, July 16: 41.
"Vicious crime, double jeopardy." *People Weekly,* (1989). Vol. 31, June 5: 44–49.
"When fans turn into fanatics, nervous celebs call for help from security expert Gavin DeBecker." *People Weekly,* (1990). Vol. 33, February 12.

CHAPTER 3

STALKING AS A VARIANT OF A TERMINATED THERAPEUTIC RELATIONSHIP: PATIENTS WHO THREATEN THEIR TREATMENT PROVIDERS—A META-ANALYSIS

Joseph A. Davis and Angela M. Gonsalez[1]

Abstract: Much of what is known about threats brought about in the form of stalking conduct has been depicted in the popular press and national media. Threats against mental health clinicians are often commonplace in today's society. However, reports of threats against clinicians, either implicit or explicit, and their outcome were examined closer by looking at the reported existing case study(s) or research literature on the subject of threatening behavior, particularly, threatening behavior found in the form of stalking pursuit behavior, and the research was quite limited and lacks depth in terms of descriptive information and empirical data. The potential for threats involving stalking cases always exists. However, it is rare to find threats that involve stalking pursuit behavior that focus on mental health clinicians. When this is the case, such behavior constitutes a form and type of workplace violence. The relationship between patient and clinician is a therapeutic one, established with specific guidelines (i.e., limitations, boundaries, etc.) for the purposes of communication, disclosure, consent, confidentiality, and treatment. Unfortunately, deeply seated dysfunction or pathological illness comes up in counseling, psychotherapy, and early intervention that is not amended, mitigated, or resolvable even when using the best and most reliable proven practices and techniques in the field. These unresolved pathological issues could transfer to the clinician. The researcher(s), over the course of this preliminary study, noted a disturbing recent trend in the number of reported cases that have targeted mental health clinicians as victims of threats, unwanted harassment, and relentless pursuit from their patients in the form of stalking behavior. Despite the earnest attempts on behalf of the clinician or health agency to therapeutically establish rapport, set boundaries, diagnose, and develop an effective treatment plan for their patients, trends in the form of threatening behavior or stalking are increasing. Presently, this review and study of threats, particularly threats in the form of stalking pursuit behavior against clinicians, is ongoing and currently a work in progress.

---

[1]The researchers would like to thank Ms. Veronica Bejar, Director of the McNair Scholars' Program at San Diego State University, for all her research support.

INTRODUCTION

Although a number of professionals have studied threats and stalking behavior, the prevalence and frequency rate of threatening behavior, stalking, and related crimes against targeted medical professionals and mental health clinicians is still relatively unknown (Lion & Herschler, 1998). Furthermore, few studies have been reported in the literature that focus on stalking, threats of violence, and crimes against current or former mental health treatment providers (Davis, 2001b).

Stalking is viewed as an age-old phenomenon. As a topic of psychiatric focus, it was discussed in the ancient writings of Hippocrates and researched extensively in the early twentieth century by French psychiatrist Dr. G.G. de Clerambault. Furthermore, stalking was given national attention and infamous notoriety with the tragic death of former rock star John Lennon in 1980, and viewed as a "fatal attraction" starring actor Michael Douglas and actress Sharon Stone in theaters or on video across the nation (Davis, 2001b; Davis & Chipman, 1997; Orion, 2001).

Stalking is unique as the repetitive, harassing, long-term course of conduct and behavior that reflects the internal dynamics of the stalker's motivating mental state and possible dysfunctional disorder (Davis, 2001a–c; Holmes, 1993; Johnson, 1993; Wells, 1996). Furthermore, the investigation of a stalking case is quite difficult. The numerous and progressive acts of a stalker that comprises an intentional pattern of behavior and course of conduct require a continuity of purpose: harassment designed to control the victim and place him or her in fear (Davis, 2001b; Holmes, 1993; Ugolini & Kelly, 2001; Wells, 1996).

In 1990, the first antistalking legislation was passed in the state of California. In just six years, all 50 states followed California with their own antistalking legislation. Public awareness has encouraged federal legislation to stop criminal stalking behavior as a course of conduct and crime and to give victims a measure of protection (National Institutes of Justice [NIJ], 1993). The U.S. government now has in place a federal statute prohibiting the act of stalking (Johnson, 1993; Jordan, 1995; Walsh, 1996).

History and Development

Stalking behavior, historically characterized as romantic, obsessive advances, has recently been identified as psychopathological by the mental health, law enforcement, and legal communities (Meloy, 1996, 1998; Williams, 1996). Stalking behavior is broad in scope and can be evaluated as to potential threat as well as charted on a continuum with gradient variations of mental disorder and resultant injury to the victim (Davis, 2001a, b; Dietz et al., 1991; Meloy, 1998; Wells, 1996; Zona et al., 1993).

Erotomania, the delusional belief that the stalker is passionately loved by an unattainable victim, often a celebrity, is classified diagnostically as a delusional disorder known as de Clerambault's syndrome (Goldstein, 1987; Zona, et al., 1993) (see also the *Diagnostic and Statistical Manual of Mental Disorders, Fourth Edition*, DSM-IV, Axis-I, Clinical Disorders: Delusional Disorder, Erotomanic Type) (American Psychiatric Association [APA], 1994). The subject goes to extreme lengths to contact or make his or her presence known to the victim. However, the incidence of physical injury is anecdotal (Davis, 1997; Dietz et al., 1991; Meloy, 1992; Menzies et al., 1995; Williams et al., 1996; Zona et al., 1993).

Media coverage of these occurrences of injury has dramatically increased the public awareness of stalking pursuit behavior. Media attention directed toward a high-profile target, such as Rebecca Schaeffer (killed by convicted stalker Robert Bardo) or David Letterman, has publicly exposed the devastating fears, injury, and pain of the celebrity, opening the floodgates for numerous victims recoiling in fear behind bolted doors, drawn curtains, and unanswered telephones (Davis, 2001b, c; Davis et al., 1997). Press coverage of celebrity victims and their families has given a reverberating voice to the thousands of unrecognized victims who were forced into hiding, terrorized into silence, and ignored or disbelieved when they finally summoned the courage to seek help (Collins & Wilkas, 2001; Davis, 1997; Dietz et al., 1991; Williams et al., 1996; Zona et al., 1993).

Stalker Typology

The simple obsessional stalker is the most common. This type of stalking generally begins when the relationship between the two people has gone bad or there is a perception of mistreatment (Wells, 1996). It is usually preceded by domestic violence or other assaultive behavior (Kurt, 1995; Williams et al., 1996). Often rationalized, excused, or denied until the victim has suffered irreparable harm, this behavior is not limited to the poor, the uneducated, or the incompetent. The simple obsessional stalker may reveal indices of personality disorder; however, the stalking is more often the result of the power struggle of the insecure stalker following his or her perceived rejection by the helpless victim. In fact, schizophrenia, hallucinations, or bizarre behavior, if more than incidental, remove the behavior from classification within the stalking continuum (Williams et al., 1996; Zona et al., 1993). The stalker's life from all outward appearances is seemingly normal (Edwards, 1992).

The middle ground of the stalking spectrum is that held by the love obsessional type. This stalking behavior type orchestrates a calculated and relentless harassment campaign intended to make the victim aware of the stalker's existence. Victims are frequently known to their stalkers (Albrecht, 2001; Kurt, 1995; Holmes, 1993; Orion, 2001; Tjaden & Thoennes, 1997). Frequently they are coworkers, a friend of a friend, a bank teller, a grocery store clerk, a former domestic partner, or a mechanic (Davis, 2001a, b; Davis et al., 1997; Holmes, 1993, 2001). The communication efforts of the stalker are creative yet unintelligible from the perception of the victim: a cellophane wrapped rat for Valentine's Day, severed fingernails of a stranger, or assorted issues of *Texas Monthly Magazine* (Boles, 2001; Dietz et al., 1991).

The recognition and identification of stalking behavior as criminal is difficult, because from all outward appearances, most of the stalker's acts are considered normal behavior (Edwards, 1992; Morin, 1994). Some of the conduct may involve criminal activity such as trespass, vandalism, threatening phone calls, petty theft offenses, or domestic violence (Clarke, 1990; Davis, 2001b; Fein et al., 1995; Holmes, 1993, 2001; Wells, 1996). However, these offenses, if charged at all, are generally not dealt with severely. The nominal punishments—credit for time served or brief probationary periods—are minimal deterrents to obsessional behavior.

Until the media blitz following the murder of television actress Rebecca Schaeffer by Robert Bardo in 1990 and resultant public awareness as to the seriousness and degree of stalking in our society, the law enforcement and legal communities failed to look far beyond isolated misdemeanor convictions. The heightened awareness and increased understanding of stalking behavior has presented the criminal history of the stalker in a focused perspective to demonstrate empirically the escalation of the violence (Johnson, 1993; Morin, 1994). The stalker does not stop until he or she is stopped. Stalking involves certain elements of control, manipulation, fear, and psychological power over the victim (Clarke, 1990; Davis, 2001a, b; Davis et al., 1997; Dietz et al., 1991; Hammell, 1996; Holmes, 1993, 2001; Meloy, 1989, 1996, 1998, 1999; Zona et al., 1993).

RESEARCH METHOD

Procedure

It is hypothesized that those patients who harass, stalk, or assault their mental health treatment providers as reported in the scientific literature are no different than those stalkers found in the general population who stalk ordinary citizens. A small sample of stalkers who stalk their treatment providers (mental health clinicians) will be identified and compared to the existing literature on general stalker types. Furthermore, from the sample identified, female threateners (females who stalk and harass their clinicians) will be compared to male threateners (males who stalk their clinicians). Differences within the sample, if any, will be reported from the comparison and subsequent analysis.

The data obtained for this preliminary study were taken from the number of carefully selected and anecdotally reported cases found in the scientific literature. The researcher took to task an in-depth but broad review of the current and past scientific and medical-psychiatric-psychological-sociological literature stemming over a period involving the last 20 years.

The in-depth review and investigation examined the current and existing literature over this period of time from only peer-reviewed scientific journals, the published journal entries, and a few select books on the subject at hand that involved reported instances of violence or threats of violence by patients involving targeted clinicians. Particularly, threats (implied or explicit), actual violence, unwanted harassment, relentless pursuit, and stalking behavior toward mental health clinicians and counseling treatment providers were gleaned and identified from multiple cases reported in the literature.

For the purposes of this literature review and study, threats in either written or oral communication form that implicitly or explicitly suggest a wish or intent to harm, injure, damage or even kill the target victim will be identified. Furthermore, threats that involve the wish or intent to do damage or harm indirectly to the targeted victim (i.e., property damage or destruction, etc.) will also be included. Threats can be instrumental (intent is to control the victim) or expressive (mood, affect, behavioral, etc.). Both are examined in this review. Finally, harassment will also be examined. Harassment is defined as the persistent and unwelcome communication of demands or feelings. Harassment can occur within many different contexts. However, when taken in context with stalking, harassment can be viewed as a persistent pattern of behavior and course of conduct involving unwelcome communication leading to the victim experiencing a degree of physical or psychological fear.

Case Analysis

Clinical-forensic cases meeting the researcher's selected criterion for this study (i.e., reported unwanted pursuit, harassment, implied or explicit threats and stalking, etc.) were identified from the scientific literature and coded based on the type of threatening behavior toward the clinician.

Where possible, additional coding for background information, such as the treatment setting (inpatient or outpatient), gender, and age and type of clinician (e.g., social worker, psychologist, psychiatrist, nurse, marriage counselor) was noted. Additionally, again where possible, coding for background information such as patient gender and psychiatric diagnosis was identified and noted.

RESULTS

Empirical Studies

Only a few empirical studies regarding threats made toward or the actual stalking of clinicians were identified in the scientific literature. However, a total of sixteen actual clinical cases were examined for further in-depth analysis and comparison. Each clinical study was gleaned, identified, and coded from the review of the literature by the researcher as meeting the criterion for this study. The identified empirical studies and additional clinical cases examined that are noteworthy from this literature review are briefly summarized here.

Two particular studies of interest, conducted by Miller (1985) and more recently by researchers Buckley and Resnick (1994), examined the phenomenon of threats made toward mental health clinicians and behaviors carried out in the form of stalking by patients. Miller (1985), as reported in Meloy (1998), surveyed a select sample and group of forensic psychiatrists and found that 55 percent of the 480 participating clinicians reporting had been threatened (physically). Furthermore, according to Miller (1985) in survey, as reported in Meloy (1998), 14 percent of the reporting clinicians sampled has actually been physically assaulted.

In the Resnick and Buckley survey and clinical study conducted in 1994 at an annual meeting of the Oregon Psychiatric Association and Society, 90 clinicians were sampled regarding stalking. As reported in Meloy (1998), 26 of the 90 clinicians had experienced some type of stalking behavior. Additionally, 24 clinicians have experienced a person waiting for them either at their place of employment (i.e., private practice, clinic, hospital, etc.) or at their private residence. Finally, 13 of the respondents stated that each had experienced some type of property damage at their residence, or place of employment.

Studies by Lion (1995), Lion and Herschler (1998), Miller (1985), and Resnick and Buckley (1994) suggest a high incidence for stalking among clinicians and have identified a possible trend toward some clinicians being more prone to stalking than others. The incidence of stalking among clinicians as found by these researchers is under investigation to test the idea of multiple incidences of stalking and stalking proneness suggested to be found in some clinicians.

As determined from the review of the literature, the results of the findings suggest that women patients stalk clinicians more than male patients. Furthermore, it is known that women more frequently seek counseling and psychotherapy than men in American society (Davis, 2001b). Therefore, in relation to stalking and those in counseling or those receiving mental health treatment, this is in direct contrast to the general population. More men than women typically engage in stalking behavior. Roughly, it is reported in the literature that about 80 percent of those who perpetrate this crime and engage in stalking behavior are men, and 20 percent are women. Conversely, 80 percent of the victims are women and 20 percent are men (Davis, 2001b, c; National Institutes of Justice, 1993; Tjaden et al., 1998).

Case Studies

Sixteen cases were examined as found in the current and existing literature regarding communicated threats of violence and stalking. A brief summary of these cases is provided. Nine cases involving females who harassed and stalked their mental health treatment providers were identified. In comparison, seven male cases were identified from the literature.

In review of the clinical cases, it was found that written or oral communications occur in most stalking cases regardless of the gender. These findings are consistent with the research of Meloy (1989, 1998, 1999), as he reported that this type of communication occurs in about 50 to 75 percent of all stalking cases. Moreover, most stalkers are typically not violent. However, when they are, the physical injury that they cause is not considered severe or lethal (Meloy, 1996, 1998, 1999).

Stalkers (either male or female, as found in this review) who threaten or harass clinicians were found to be consistent with the current literature in terms of comparison to general stalkers. It has been identified by many researchers (Brown et al., 1996; Davis, 2001a, b; Davis & Chipman, 1997; Harmon et al., 1995; Meloy, 1996, 1998, 1999) that most stalkers, including those who stalk clinicians, are diagnosed as having a both an Axis I and Axis II disorder (e.g., alcoholism or a mood disorder with a personality disorder, typically Cluster B—narcissistic, histrionic, or borderline disorder with features of Cluster A [paranoid personality, paranoia] and Cluster C [compulsive personality and compulsivity]). Hare (1991) and Meloy (1996) found that the antisocial personality disorder is less likely to be found among stalker types, which makes up about 10 percent of stalkers diagnostically.

Several researchers (Harmon et al., 1995; Kienlen et al., 1997; Meloy, 1996, 1998; Zona et al., 1993; 1998) have found that psychotic stalkers are infrequent as an Axis-I disorder among all stalkers and make up approximately only one in five stalkers. Furthermore, as reported by Kienlen and others, psychotic stalkers are more likely to stalk strangers (Holmes, 1993; Kienlen et al., 1997).

Consistent with this review, in descriptive comparison to those patients who stalk their clinicians, of the 16 cases analyzed, the stalker patient profile was as shown in Tables 3.1 and 3.2.

Table 3.1
Female Patients Who Stalk their Treatment Providers

Sample (N = 9)	Axis II Diagnosis	Axis I Diagnosis	Other indicators	Contact or threat
Case 1:	Borderline personality	Alcoholism	Self-mutilation	Verbal threats
Case 2:	Borderline personality	None	Suicidal, sex abuse	Arson, kills pet
Case 3:	Borderline, w/paranoia	None	Psychosocial stressors	Verbal threats
Case 4:	None	Dissociative disorder	Sex or physical abuse	Vandal, kills pet
Case 5:	Borderline personality	None	Psychosocial stressors	Assault, att. bomb.
Case 6:	None	Depression	Psychosocial stressors	Assaultive behavior
Case 7:	None	Schizophrenia	Psychosocial stressors	Verbal threats
Case 8:	Borderline personality	Substance use	Psychosocial stressors	Crime of homicide
Case 9:	None	Delusional disorder	Erotomania	Property crime

Table 3.2
Male Patients Who Stalk their Treatment Providers

Sample (N = 7)	Axis II Diagnosis	Axis I Diagnosis	Other Indicators	Type of Contact
Case 1:	Antisocial personality	Intermittent explosive	Psychosocial stressors	Verbal threats
Case 2:	None	Schizophrenia	Psychotic break	Verbal threats
Case 3:	None	Impulsive disorder	Psychosocial stressors	Verbal threats
Case 4:	Borderline personality	None	Psychosocial stressors	Verbal threats
Case 5:	None	Alcoholism	Psychosocial stressors	Property crime
Case 6:	None	Schizophrenia	Psychosocial stressors	Verbal threats
Case 7:	Borderline personality	Substance use	Psychosocial stressors	Verbal threats

DISCUSSION

From the few number of empirically based studies as well as from various clinical-forensic cases reviewed and found in literature, individuals who stalk clinicians when compared to stalkers in general make up a very small subset of threateners in terms of the overall stalker-threatener population. The differences between general stalkers and those who stalk their clinicians were found to be minimal.

The findings of this review suggest that stalkers who threaten their clinicians with physical violence or property damage reflect in their behavior similar patterns of conduct as nonclinician threateners. Additionally, the study and review provides some additional reinforcement and confirmation that stalkers, regardless of whether they are clinician stalkers or not, typically use similar types of tactics for communication purposes (e.g., verbal threats) and clinically present with similar *DSM* diagnostic features found in both Axis I and Axis II disorders (e.g., substance use disorders or mood disorders as well as Cluster B personality disorders).

The review found minimal differences when comparing females who stalk their clinicians versus males who stalk their clinicians. However, one interesting aspect to the review and study when comparing the two groups found that the females threateners engaged not only in an abundance of verbal threatening behaviors and communication styles (similar and consistent with the male stalker sample) but also engaged in more diverse crimes as well as more violent conduct that involved instances such as property destruction (arson) and homicide (human as well as animals or personal pets).

There were several limitations identified within the study. The weaknesses were a limited number of empirically based studies and cases represented in the literature from which to draw, extrapolate, and infer scientific conclusions. The small number of studies and cases are believed to limit valid generalizations to the stalker population from which the cases came until more in-depth research can be accomplished on this subject using specific hypotheses and sampling methods. Furthermore, cases studies are frequently vulnerable to researcher subjective biases. Cases may be selected for a variety of reasons because of their inherent dramatic versus typical attributes or because each case may fit neatly into the researchers' schema.

Despite all of the limitations identified in this review and study, a few strengths were identified and found. Case studies in general provide a useful model for background information for developing, designing, and planning additional investigations in the field of psychology and social-behavioral sciences. Furthermore, because of the intensity of the review process, often important variables, processes, trends, and interactions surface that bring with them more precise empirical attention. Finally, this process breaks new ground on the topic and often provides an additional source of direction to develop and refine hypotheses for further empirical study.

CONCLUSION

In general, threats against mental health clinicians are commonplace. Where there is a vocalized threat by a patient, the potential for violence does exist. Further investigation on stalking and, particularly, those who stalk their treatment providers has no conclusive results as additional research is needed. This preliminary study and review of the literature suggests and confirms that instances of threats of violence do exist with this clinical sample.

Research over the past decade suggests that public perception and awareness regarding the conduct of stalking has increased and the reporting of stalking and stalking-related crossover crimes has also increased. Not only has stalking increased within the general population, but within the last decade, a trend toward the stalking of treatment providers has increased as well with multiple instances being reported in the scientific literature.

More empirical research on the stalking of mental health treatment providers and clinicians is needed. This is a work in progress. Efforts are underway to investigate this growing trend and phenomena further beyond this review.

REFERENCES

Albrecht, S. F. (2001). Stalking, stalkers, and domestic violence: Relentless fear and obsessive fantasy. In J. A. Davis (Ed.), *Stalking Crimes and Victim Protection: Prevention, Intervention, Assessment and Case Management* (pp. 81–95). Boca Raton, FL: CRC Press.

American Psychiatric Association. (1994). *Diagnostic and Statistical Manual for the DSM-IV*. Washington, DC: American Psychiatric Association.

Boles, G. S. (2001). Developing a model approach to confronting the problem of stalking: Establishing a threat management unit. In J. A. Davis (Ed.), *Stalking Crimes and Victim Protection: Prevention, Intervention, Assessment and Case Management* (pp. 337–349). Boca Raton, FL: CRC Press.

Brown, G. P., W. R., Dubin, J. R. Lion, & J. Garry, (1996). Threats against clinicians: a preliminary classification. *Bulletin of the American Academy of Psychiatry and the Law*, 24(3): 367–376.

Buckley, R., & M. Resnick, (1994). Stalking survey: Oregon psychiatric society, Portland, Oregon. March 4–5, 1994. Unpublished manuscript. In J. R. Meloy (1998), *The Psychology of Stalking*. San Diego: Academic Press.

Clarke, J. W. (1990). *On Being Mad or Merely Angry: John W. Hinckley, Jr. and Other Dangerous People*. Princeton NJ: Princeton University Press.

Collins, M. J., & M. B. Wilkas, (2001). Stalking trauma syndrome. In J. A. Davis (Ed.). *Stalking Crimes and Victim Protection: Prevention, Intervention, Assessment and Case Management* (pp. 317–334). Boca Raton, FL: CRC Press.

Davis, J. A. (2001a). Assessment of potential threat and future prediction of violence: A second look. *Journal of Police and Criminal Psychology*. Fall Edition, 2001. Society of Police and Criminal Psychology, San Marcos, Texas. Submitted January 2001. Revised March 2001. Accepted for publication, April 2001.

Davis, J. A. (2001b). *Stalking Crimes and Victim Protection: Prevention, Intervention, Assessment and Case Management*. Boca Raton, FL: CRC Press.

Davis, J. A. (November, 2001c). *Stalking, harassment and threats against clinicians: A meta-analysis*. Workshop presentation to the Los Angeles County Psychological Association, Fall 2001. Annual convention, Los Angeles, California.

Davis, J. A. & M. A. Chipman. (1997). A forensic psychological typology of stalking and stalkers. *Journal of Clinical Forensic Medicine* 4: 166–172.

Davis, J., & M. Chipman. (1997). Stalkers and other obsessional types: A review and forensic psychology typology of those who stalk. *Journal of Clinical Forensic Medicine*, 4, 166–172.

Davis, J., R. L. Siota, & L. M. Stewart. (1999). Future prediction of dangerousness and violent behavior: psychological indicators and considerations for conducting an assessment of potential threat. *Canadian Journal of Clinical Medicine*, 6(3): 44–59.

Dietz, P. E. (1984). A remedial approach to harassment. *Virginia Law Review*, 70: 475, 506–544.

Dietz, P. E., D. Matthews, C. Van Duyane, D. Martell, C. Parry, T. Stewart, J. Warren & J. Crowder. (1991). Threatening and otherwise inappropriate letters to Hollywood celebrities. *Journal of Forensic Sciences*, 36(1): 185–209.

Edwards, L. (December, 1992). Trespassers of the heart. *Eyewitness*, 34–40.

Fein, R. A., B. Vosskuil & G. A. Holden. (1995). Threat assessment: An approach to prevent targeted violence. *National Institute of Justice—Research in Action*. September 1–7.

Goldstein, R. L. (1987). More forensic romances: De Clerambault's syndrome in men. *Bulletin of the American Academy of Psychiatry and Law*, 15: 267–274.

Hammell, B. F. (1996). *Stalking: The Torment of Obsession: The STOP Program (Stalking Treatment Options Program)*. San Diego District Attorney Antistalking Case Conference, San Diego.

Harmon, R., R. Rosner & H. Owens. (1995). Obsessional harassment and erotomania in a criminal court population. *Journal of Forensic Sciences*, 40(2): 188–196.

Harmon, R. M. (1998). *Anti-Stalking Legislation: A New Answer for an Age-Old Problem*. Conference presentation, American Academy of Forensic Sciences, 50th Anniversary meeting, San Franscisco.

Holmes, R. M. (1993). Stalking in America: Types and methods of criminal stalkers. *Journal of Contemporary Criminal Justice*, 9: 317–327.

Holmes, R. M. (2001): Criminal stalkers: A typology of those who stalk. *In Stalking Crimes and Victim Protection: Prevention, Intervention, Assessment and Case Management* (pp. 19–29). CRC Press. Boca Raton, FL: CRC Press.

Jordan, T. J. (1995). The efficacy of the California stalking law: Surveying its evolution, extracting insights from domestic violence cases. *Hastings Women's Law Journal*, 6: 363–383.

Johnson, P. (1993). When creeps come calling. *Law Enforcement Quarterly,* February–April, 9–10, 32.

Kienlen, K. K., D. L. Birmingham, K. B. Solberg, J. T. O'Regan & J. R. Meloy. (1997). A comparative study of psychotic and nonpsychotic stalkers. *Journal of the American Academy of Psychiatry and Law,* 25(3): 317–334.

Kurt, J. (1995). Stalking as a variant of domestic violence. *Bulletin of the American Academy of Psychiatry and Law,* 23(2): 219–230.

Lion, J. R., & L. A. Herschler. (1998). The stalking of clinicians by their patients. In J. R. Meloy (Ed.), *The Psychology of Stalking* (pp. 163–174). San Diego: Academic Press.

Lion, J. R. (1995). Verbal threats against clinicians. In B.S. Eichelman and A. C. Hartwig (Eds.), *Patient Violence and the Clinician* (pp. 43–52). Washington, DC: American Psychiatric Press.

Menzies, R. P. D., J. P. Fedeoroff, C. M. Green & K. Isaakson. (1995). Prediction of dangerous behavior in male erotomania. *British Journal of Psychiatry,* 166: 529–536.

Meloy, J. R. (1989). Unrequited love and the wish to kill: Diagnosis and treatment of borderline erotomania. Editorial on Love and Violence. Menninger Foundation, 477–491.

Meloy, J. R. (1998.) *The Psychology of Stalking: A Clinical-Forensic Comparison.* San Diego: Academic Press.

Meloy, J. R. (1999). Stalking: An old behavior, a new crime. *The Psychiatric Clinics of North America,* 22 (1): 85–99.

Meloy, J. (1996). Stalking (Obsessional Following): A Review of Some Preliminary Studies. *Aggression and Violence Behavior, 1,* 147–162.

Miller, R. (1985). The harassment of forensic psychiatrists outside of court. *Bulletin of the American Academy of Psychiatry and the Law,* 13(4): 337–343.

Morin, K. (1994). The phenomenon of stalking: Do existing state statutes provide adequate protection? *San Diego Justice Journal,* 1: 123.

Orion, D. (2001). Erotomania, stalking and stalkers: A personal experience with a professional perspective. In J. A. Davis (Ed.), *Stalking Crimes and Victim Protection: Prevention, Intervention, Assessment and Case Management* (pp. 69–79). Boca Raton, FL: CRC Press.

The National Institutes of Justice. (1993). A project to develop a model anti-stalking code for states. *Final Summary Report Presented to the National Institute of Justice,* 92, October.

Tjaden, P., & N. Thoennes. (1998). *Prevalence, Incidence, and Consequences of Violence Against Women: Findings From the National Violence Against Women Survey.* Washington, D.C.: National Institute of Justice, U.S. Department of Justice.

Tjaden, P., & N. Thoennes, (1997). *Stalking in America: Finding from the National Violence Against Women Survey.* Denver: Center for Policy Research.

Ugolini, J. A., & K. Kelly. (2001). Case management strategies regarding stalkers and their victims: A practical approach from a private industry perspective. In J. A. Davis (Ed.), *Stalking Crimes and Victim Protection: Prevention, Intervention, Assessment and Case Management* (pp. 301–315). Boca Raton, FL: CRC Press.

Walsh, K. L. (1996). Safe and sound at last? Federalized anti-stalking legislation in the United States and Canada. *Dickinson Journal of International Law* 14: 373–402.

Wells, K. (1996). California's anti-stalking law—a first. *Law Enforcement Quarterly,* August–October, 9–12.

Williams, W. L., J. C. Lane, & M. A. Zona. (February, 1996). Stalking: Successful intervention strategies. *The Police Chief Magazine,* Alexandria, Virginia, 3–6.

Zona, M. A., K. S. Kaushal, & J. C. Lane. (1993). A comparative study of erotomanic and obsessional subjects in a forensic sample. *Journal of Forensic Sciences,* 38(4): 894–903.

Zona, M., Palarea, R., & J. Lane. (1998). Psychiatric Diagnosis and the Offender-Victim Typology of Stalking. In J. Meloy (Ed.), *The Psychology of Stalking* (pp. 113–137). San Diego: Academic Press.

SECTION 2

SEXUAL CRIMES AND VIOLENCE

T he chapters in this section deal with a variety of topics ranging from work in the sex industry, to sexual victimization of college women, to the misuse of the Internet by pedophiles. In this day, when we witness an Amber alert almost daily, it is important to study and understand how sex and sexual expression is intimately involved in our daily lives and how these connecting links can often turn violent. This section examines a wide range of issues and is sure to generate a great deal of discussion.

The first chapter, *The Transformative Power of Sex Work,* examines a controversial position. For example, some believe that women are objectified by the sex work industry. They are used as pawns for the sexual gratification of men. However, Perrucci offers a different point of view. She offers the possibility that the sex industry actually empowers women. Considering the strip club as a microcosm of society, both men and women experience power and objectification, and the experience reflects the contradictions of life in this society. In this chapter, women are not seen as pawns in the hands of men, but rather as controllers of their own destiny.

The second chapter examines the sexual victimization of college women. Fisher, Cullen, and Turner examine the serious and often hidden problem of sexual victimization of women on college campuses across the United States. They claim that women in colleges and four-year universities are at a greater risk of victimization than women in the general population in comparable age groups. This chapter was taken from a larger study funded by the National Institute of Justice and the Bureau of Justice Statistics to examine this phenomenon and correct the biases found in previous research. These biases include the use of a national representative sample of college women, assessing the full range of sexual victimization, and using a two-stage screen questionnaire with detailed questions about their victimizations using plain and explicit language. The authors found that over the course of a female's typical college career, she runs about a 20 to 25 percent chance of being a victim of a completed or attempted rape. These percentages are somewhat higher than most would suspect and not the type of data that many colleges and universities would want published. Not only do these statistics seem to be larger than previous official statistics indicate, but when these authors compared their study's findings with the similar questions taken from the National Crime Victimization Survey, the results were consistently higher than previous estimates.

The third chapter in this section deals with the use of the Internet by pedophiles to troll for and locate child victims or to ascertain/distribute child pornography. There is perhaps no greater concern for any parent today than the concern about whom their child interacts with on the Internet. Today, over 50 percent of all homes are equipped with a PC and subscribe to some form of Internet service. This chapter delves specifically into just how pedophiles and others with a sexual interest in children are now using the Internet and e-mail to locate potential victims, distribute child pornography, and join virtual communities where they can share their fantasies and collaborate in any one of many forbidden activities. While this chapter is somewhat now dated (it was first published in 1997), the issues are true today as they were then. Since its publication, law enforcement agencies have made great strides in their efforts to police and patrol these chatrooms; however, there still remains much to be done. The problems with victims and offenders in multiple jurisdictions still hound many efforts to bring these offenders to justice. While not mentioned specifically in the chapter, one contemporary perspective of the musings of pedophiles on the Internet is that their active engagement in these forums may indeed serve as a safety valve where those with a proclivity toward children may be able to live their fantasies through the net and not actually physically violate our nation's youth. This does not mean that the police should relax their enforcement efforts, however; it just means that more research needs to be done looking at and comparing the trends of child sexual victimization by adults and the proliferation of the Internet.

The fourth chapter examines the right of the state to restrict the use of computers by pedophiles on probation to either contact unsuspecting children or download illicit images of youth in various states of undress. While this chapter was originally written in 1995, many jurisdictions have yet to address this critically important topic. While state probation and parole agencies adequately monitor those entrusted to their supervision, the use of the Internet by these offenders to collect or distribute child pornography often occurs under the radar of the supervision plan. The founding principles of the terms of probation in many jurisdictions is to see that these offenders keep away from the environmental and societal triggers that brought them under supervision in the first place. For instance, random drug testing programs are designed to ensure that the client remains drug free. However, pedophiles represent a special case. Since many preferential pedophiles often retain a collection of pornography close at hand, they may use a personal computer with Internet access maintain their "addiction." The authors claim that the courts have addressed this issue and seem to infer that prohibiting the use of the Internet is too restrictive. Thus, the only way to adequately monitor these offenders is to make it a condition of their probation that officers may search their homes, computer hard disks, or other electronic storage mediums to ensure that they are not in possession of child pornography. Further, the authors state that it is often prudent to make pedophiles under the supervision of the state provide all available records relating to their screen names and computer accounts to make sure that they are not participating in chat-room discussions with unsuspecting children or other pedophiles.

CHAPTER 4

THE TRANSFORMATIVE POWER OF SEX WORK[1]

Alissa C. Perrucci

REFLEXIVE STATEMENT

Abstract: Women's subjectivity—their feelings and expressions of themselves as persons—is complicated by the ways in which women's sexuality is deemed transgressive. Women become sexual beings in a world of conflicted messages and double binds. They are taught that they must contain their sexuality at the same time that they are rewarded for augmenting their sexual desirability. For both workers and customers, the world of sex work is typically seen as a deviant expression of sexual desire. However, the gendered dynamics within this world are often not so different from those in everyday sexual relationships. The context of sex work highlights the dynamics of power (for men) and objectification (of women), but a closer look reveals that sex workers arc indeed expressing a sense of empowerment. It is tempting for academic feminism to declare that any feelings of empowerment are evidence of a false consciousness or rationalizations for their choice of work. Our task becomes to not only acknowledge that human experience is conflicted, but also search for the catalysts for such conflicts within the social discourse on feminine sexuality. A serious and genuine consideration of the voices of persons that are marginalized within a culture is key to changing that discourse. Subversion of any repressive understanding of sexuality must begin with an understanding of the social construction of sexuality and desire, and that objectification and empowerment coexist for both genders.

INTRODUCTION

Sex work is a context that can transform the power dynamics of gendered interactions. This transformation is accomplished through aspects of the sex worker's subjectivity: her sense of privacy and her sexuality. The way a woman chooses to embody her sexuality in the context of her work transforms the discourse of masculine and feminine desire and sexuality. A woman's

---

[1]This article first appeared in *Humanity and Society,* Vol. 24(4), November 2000.

feelings about doing sex work, and the revelation or concealment of those feelings in the context of that work, are aspects of her agency and ultimately, her subjectivity. This chapter is based on interviews with five exotic dancers in the Pittsburgh area. Interviews focused on the dancers' experience of privacy, how they protected their privacy, and the significance of violated privacy. A qualitative analysis of the data revealed that dancers consider body parts and processes, feelings and desires, personal information, and role identities to be private. A sense of privacy is possible when a dancer can control the revelation and concealment of these aspects of body and self. A sense of control is significant because it is tied to one's sense of autonomy and agency; a woman's personhood is acknowledged and legitimates her ability to make choices regarding her sexuality. Specifically, the choice to reveal or conceal aspects of self and body is empowering. In the seductive play of the strip club, both participants—customer and dancer—engage in differing degrees of self-disclosure and self-concealment. If this play is kept within the boundaries of the club's rules, privacy remains intact. Dancer and customer then have the freedom to inhabit a mutually satisfying space of sexual expression. In contrast, the customer's concealment of his motivations and desires is problematic for the dancer's sense of control and, ultimately, her privacy.

For some dancers, it is important to conceal certain body parts and keep aspects of their personal lives separate from their jobs. For others, the context of sex work is a site of liberation and freedom from repressive notions of feminine sexuality. Sex work becomes the possibility for the public expression of sexuality precisely because it exists within the realm of fantasy. The play of exotic dancing depends in part on the mystery that surrounds both participants and their willingness to engage with one another within the boundaries and rules of the club. The transformative power of sex work originates in the dancer's control over what she reveals and/or conceals during the customer-dancer encounter. The sense of control gives way to a sense of privacy and agency and is ultimately the grounds by which she can feel empowered.

The structure of the strip club is founded on a set of rules that both limit and facilitate the customer's fantasy. The interactions between dancers and customers are constructed in part by discourses that govern heterosexual interactions. In order to keep the structure of fantasy intact, the dancer must, at times, conceal personal feelings and desires. If she enjoys dancing, she may find that her desire shows itself when she is at work. If she dislikes her job, she will most likely conceal her true feelings. The revelation and concealment of these feelings is her choice, just as it was her choice to be a dancer. Women become sex workers for many reasons. Some enjoy the work, some want a flexible schedule and a high hourly wage, while others have few alternatives. Those who state that sex work is not part of feminist discourse believe that women are degraded no matter what they experience. However, whether or not a woman enjoys dancing, she can decide what stance she will take toward the dynamics within that system.

Kappeler (1986) maintains that sex workers do not have power. The structure of representation in society, specifically pornographic representation, is such that it confines women to positions of subordination and elevates men to positions of power. These gender-specific positions are infused in the language and images of both pornography and the everyday world. Of central importance to the antipornography debate is that pornography, through the objectification of women, radically distorts attitudes about and behaviors toward women. Objectification—the limitation of women's actions, freedoms, and possibilities—perpetuates socially constructed gender inequality by narrowing the conceptualization of the feminine. The images and fantasies of pornography seduce the viewer into subscribing to a new reality of feminine sexuality. More than a mere representation of actual sexual practices, pornography constructs and perpetuates a skewed picture of feminine sexuality and desire. What is represented in pornography comes to reside in the world along with other objects and things; it is not simply fantasy. For Kappeler, there is no freedom for the subject to create her own sexual reality within pornography.

Many feminists who support pornography propose that the variation of its images and scripts provide for the possibility that men can be objects for women, and that men can be dominated and objectified. Kappeler argues that there cannot be "equal exploitation" (1986, p. 50), because the model for objectification is based on women and is ultimately created by, and for, men. A man need not be the actual viewer or maker of pornography, but the man-as-subject stands, for Kappeler, as the third term in every pornographic relation. No matter how creative pornography becomes, nor how many images portray women in positions of supposed dominance and power, it is impossible to place objectification on equal terms between the genders. Men depend on the representation of women to demonstrate their power as well as their very existence. The fantasies and images of pornography are reality, and not just in the sexual arena; the residue of representation is everywhere. The viewing and self-expression that is involved in watching pornography is an action that exists in the world and shapes reality.

Feminists have long struggled with the possibility of a positive side to pornography and sex work, and many are caught between the belief that pornography is detrimental while at the same time experiencing pleasure and power through it (Williams, 1989). It offers an arena of sexual freedom where a woman is encouraged to explore her sexuality without shame or stigma (McElroy, 1995). It liberates a space for sexuality and fantasy much in the same manner as did the feminist movement. Paglia scolds the "middle class feminist" mentality of arrogance, conceit, and prudery" (1994, p. 57) that portrays the sex worker as a victim. Instead of serving to imprison women in roles of submission and objectification, pornography profoundly demonstrates "men's excruciating obsession with and subordination to women" (1994, p. 58). The prostitute becomes "the ultimate liberated woman, who lives on the edge and whose sexuality belongs to no one" (1994, p. 58). She rejects the interpretation that pornography only serves to denigrate and shame women and limit their sexual and individual freedom: "Sexual objectification is characteristically human and indistinguishable from the art impulse. There is nothing degrading in the display of any part of the human body" (1990, p. 62). To characterize pornography as deviant or immoral upholds misogynist, repressive views of women's sexuality. The dancer personifies the mystery of feminine sexuality because in the act of stripping the reproductive organs can never be fully seen (Paglia, 1994). While Kappeler sees power as an impossibility for women in pornography, Paglia views women as clearly dominant in this realm of sexual expression.

On stage, dancers command the attention of customers who follow their every move. Men come to the strip bar night after night to drink and watch dancers. They stand at the edge of the stage with dollar bills extended, waiting patiently for the dancers to attend to them. Some men sit at the bar and watch because they are too shy to tip. Others spend their entire paychecks and overdraw their credit cards. However, a customer can violate a dancer's privacy. At times, she may feel "like a piece of meat or a piece of shit" from the way that he looks at her or tries to touch her. Objectification is a possibility for the dancer just as are feelings of power. Most important, a shared feeling of respect and mutual understanding that coexists between dancer and customer is essential to a balance of power and the existence of a shared space of sexual expression.

THE MYSTERY OF THE DANCER'S DESIRE

The persona of the exotic dancer involves the creation and projection of a particular embodied sexuality; this is part of her performance. To be successful, a dancer must entice customers to pay for individual attention. Her dance routine, makeup, and costumes are chosen to reflect customers' preferences, as well as her own. A dancer must pay attention to tipping customers, even if she finds them disagreeable. At times, it is the mystery of the dancer's desire that fascinates the customer. He may pursue the truth of her thoughts, feelings, and personal life. He might ask her personal questions or try to touch her. Most customers, however, follow the rules and take responsibility for constructing their fantasies within these parameters. In the tension between her own and her customers' desires, a dancer must, at times, "swallow [her] pride" and go out on stage. At times, dancers strive to create the appearance of feeling seductive or attracted to a customer, even if their true feelings are contrary. According to Erica,

> A lot of times if you're not in the mood, you've got cramps or whatever or if you're sick, the way I get into my dancing I think of my boyfriend. You know, making love to him or how he turns me on and that actually helps me dance better.

Despite what her customers might be imagining, Erica was, at times, thinking of her boyfriend in order to dance more seductively. Other times, she felt sick or uncomfortable in her body. Nevertheless, she projected an aura of coolness and control. Erica professed a love for dancing. It was better than "killing [her]self working two jobs" for less pay; it enabled the lifestyle that she enjoyed and helped her plan financially for her future once she stopped dancing. She was angered by customers who conflated her performance on stage with her nondancer identity. She considered herself to be a performer and relished this aspect of her job. She created the illusion of sexual desire for customers, and this gave her a feeling of power. Erica enjoyed the game that occurred within the boundaries of the club's rules and having license to "jack off" customers. This expression is slang for teasing or playing around with another's expectations. Erica enjoyed the flirtations that occurred with her customers, but she also had regular customers with whom she sat and conversed.

People tell me I enjoy my job too much. I love teasing guys! I mean think about it. I'm getting paid just to jack 'em off, you know! And if I want to, I can drink and party a little bit. As long as you can control yourself, you're fine.

In slight contrast, Shelley preferred to feel comfortable and "relaxed" while on stage dancing; she considered herself to be an entertainer. It was less important to her to try to be "sexy," because that did not feel natural to her. Regardless of her customers' interpretations of her performance, Shelley stated that she did not always *intend* to appear seductive or overtly sexual.

I feel like I'm here to entertain. I like to have a good time. I like to dance and most of the time I'm more relaxed than I am sexy because I try to be sexy and then I'll just burst out laughing because I can't handle it.

Shelley was not ashamed of her costume because it was similar to a bathing suit and athletic gear. Although she would never show her genitals, she was not as worried about her breasts because they were small, and her nipples were covered by pasties. She felt that her small breasts made her body less sexual. Having less flesh to conceal, she was less of a sexual object, and even less like an exotic dancer. By comparing her costume to a bathing suit, dancing became more like a public behavior and less like a revelation of private body parts.

As long as I have my G-string on I feel cool. I feel like I'm in basically nothing more than a bathing suit. Some of my bathing suits probably show more. And when I'm working out at the gym I'm in about the same attire, you know? And I don't have big breasts so I don't feel like I'm really showing anything there.

Brooke differed from the other participants in that she enjoyed dancing nude, and she did not stress the importance of separating a private self from her exotic dancer persona. Brooke was outspoken, assertive, and took on somewhat of a supervisory role with her coworkers. She had strong ethics of self-control and responsibility. Her certainty that customers took pleasure in her nudity gave her the confidence to present herself in a way that she considered to be authentic. This confidence was not equaled when she danced in pasties and a G-string.

I enjoy being naked. When I dance totally nude I enjoy being naked. It lets me express myself the way I wanted to express myself. Because what you see is what you get! There ain't no hiding nothing.

Brooke was true to herself, from her full disclosure of her body to her feelings about being naked. Although there were times when she felt self-conscious about her body, she believed that there were remedies to help conceal flaws and accentuate stronger features. In contrast, Shelley believed that showing her genitals to strangers was too intimate. Erica had "no problem dancing nude." She emphasized that she did not do so by choice. Both Erica and Shelley enjoyed the performance aspect of their jobs. They considered themselves to be skilled entertainers and relished the seductive play of dancing. They also expressed more of a need for privacy in terms of a separation between private self and dancer persona. It was important to Erica that her job remained a secret from her family, and she had a hard time "staying in character" when persons that she knew from her everyday life came into the club. Although Shelley did not describe a conflict between her worlds, she did state that she had begun to drink more heavily at work in order to tolerate customers' insensitive remarks. All three women stressed the importance of a mutual respect between dancer and customer that was necessary for each to be comfortable in her or his role. When this was not possible, each stressed that there were times when true feelings were covered over in order to protect themselves from the customers' violating behaviors.

Just as dancers expected customers to leave their fantasies at the door when the night was over, they assumed that intimate others would not subject them to the demands of work once they arrived at home. It was difficult for Nicole's boyfriend to understand that the character she created at work was not who she wanted to be at home, nor was it representative of her sexuality within their relationship. He expected the same favors and attention that Nicole granted her customers.

> [My boyfriend] expects me to come home and dance for him. I keep telling him, "look, it's my, job. I don't like it and I sure as hell don't want to do it when I'm done with five or six hours of work". [He says,] "If I was a mechanic, you'd want me to fix your car." I said that's different. I said that ain't a mind game. Being a mechanic you get your fingers dirty. I said I can go be a mechanic and I'll work on your car.

The reality, or truth, of Nicole's desire was a mystery to her partner. He was jealous of the type of attention that Nicole granted her customers, believing that she withheld her true sexuality from him. He treated her like a dancer when she was at home, pursuing the truth of her desire. Nicole was unable to fully separate her dancer life from her everyday life. She felt that the two worlds had contaminated one another. Being an exotic dancer was something that she wanted to hide from her kids, and she wanted customers to stay out of her everyday life. Six months prior to our interview a customer had been stalking her, and he was recently allowed back into the club. She felt that her hold on personal safety was tenuous and adamantly declared that she had "no privacy." The mystery of Nicole's desire was sought by both customers and intimate others. She had little recourse to protecting her privacy, but she continued to dance. However, she had positive relationships with many of her regular customers because they respected her boundaries.

THE MYSTERY OF THE CUSTOMER'S DESIRE

A dancer's ability to maintain an aura of ambiguity surrounding her own desires facilitates her sense of privacy. The ambiguity of the customer's desires, on the other hand, is detrimental to a sense of control and privacy, because dancers depend on the customer's predictability in order to plan their self-presentation. Nicole was often disturbed by the mystery of a customer's thoughts. Usually, she was conscious of the fact that he was staring at her body. The *unknown* aspects of his thoughts and feelings detracted from her sense of control.

> It's having to deal with the fact that people are standing there looking at you to-tally naked with whatever's going through their mind and they don't even have the decency to tip you for it.

It was especially unnerving to consider that a customer might be focusing on a flaw or a particular characteristic of her body. In these moments, she be-came self-conscious. However, she quickly resigned herself to the task at hand by focusing on making money. She could "block out" an undesirable interac-tion with a customer if she concentrated on the desirable financial outcome.

Dancers expected customers to follow the club's rules so that the intimate nature of the relationship would remain on the level of fantasy. Any uncer-tainty regarding the customer's expectations inhibited a dancer's ability to prepare herself for an interaction. New customers presented the possibility of unusual demands or expectations. Regular customers required little assess-ment on the part of the dancers because their behaviors were predictable. It was less likely that a regular customer would try to break the rules by touch-ing or asking personal, intrusive questions. Regular customers made the job pleasant because they were friendly, happy to see the dancers, always tipped, and sometimes even brought them gifts. An unfamiliar face meant that a dancer had to assess the new person's motivations and anticipate his reactions. Brooke always remained attentive and alert when she approached a new cus-tomer, particularly during a lap dance, where she would be more vulnerable to intrusions of privacy.

> You read the guy. If you're doing stage work you really don't worry about it. But in a private dance, you read the guy and you never let your guard down because even the nicest person can turn into a Mr. Hyde. They might be really nice and sweet and give you a five-dollar tip up front and then turn around and expect you to do something to them instead of just for them.

Participants agreed that it was easier to dance for female customers than male customers, because women did not usually have the same impulse to ask personal questions, make rude remarks, or demand favors. According to Nicole, the motivations of heterosexual female customers were usually simple and clear.

> The girls that'll come in as girls and tip you—there's nothing to it. It don't bother me at all. . . . It's actually more comfortable because I know the girls ain't trying to score. They ain't in here to get a piece of ass. They're just in here because they know you're working and they're here to have a beer or they're in here to see their friends. They know you're in here for the money so they'll give you a dollar or two.

Erica, Nicole, and Brooke felt that female customers had a better under-standing of a woman's motivations for being an exotic dancer. They believed that female customers were sympathetic to the fact that the dancers' seductive behavior was part of their job and was a performance. Female customers were generally more supportive and did not make their work more difficult by pursuing a fantasy relationship with them. In addition, participants said that it was easy to dance for me because my intentions were clear and they understood my expectations. Of my presence in the club, Erica stated, "Girls like you, you're just—you're cool. You're there to have a good time, to party."

Erica and Brooke felt uncomfortable the first time that they danced for a female customer, especially if it was a private dance, but with time it became less awkward. After Brooke ascertained the customer's preferences, the situation became immediately less ambiguous, and she regained a sense of control.

> There's an awkwardness. . . . You also got to remember it's awkward for her. Especially if she's not . . . both ways, you know, it's awkward for her. She's looking around this way and this way. If you do something she's interested in by not showing all and just being seductive and dancing for both of them they enjoy that a lot better and then you feel more comfortable.

A female customer, who was not bisexual and was at the club with her boyfriend or friends, was uncomfortable when Brooke approached her aggressively. Such a woman might find it difficult to make eye contact with the dancer. A woman in this situation might be more comfortable if Brooke kept a greater distance from her. When dancers knew what female customers expected from them, they were able to stay comfortably in character because they could prepare how to approach them. Thus, it was important to assess a female customer's motivations. Brooke used this information to adjust her own behavior, make the woman feel more comfortable, and give the woman the type of attention that she preferred.

> When a woman comes in and she's not with a man . . . you need to find out why she's there. You need to talk to her. . . . Now the ones that come in with their boyfriends to get excited, you just dance sexy for them. You don't necessarily do it to them and then they appreciate that a lot better than if you were doing it to them because they don't really want you to do it to them.

Knowing that there were many different reasons why a woman might come to a strip club, Brooke watched her customers carefully to gauge their reactions. A female customer could be there unwillingly and feel awkward or embarrassed if the dancer gave her too much attention, or she might be dissatisfied unless she was "treated like a man," received a lap dance, and was touched by the dancer.

When the gender or sexual orientation of a customer was unclear or unknown, dancers had less information with which to prepare themselves. Nicole was initially uncomfortable when a customer's gender identity was ambiguous. In such instances, she had less information to ascertain the motivations of that particular customer. Sometimes Nicole did not realize that there were lesbians in the club, because they appeared to be very masculine. She did not like being surprised by the gender or sexual orientation of a customer, because "when someone comes in and they're not who they're supposed to be . . . it just catches you off guard." She needed information about gender to gauge the interaction. The ambiguity or mystery of their gender identity made their desire a mystery as well. It became more difficult for her to embody her character in way that promoted a sense of power and privacy.

> The one thing I didn't like is when I was working at a club and there were girls dressed up as guys. They were straight up wanna-be dudes. And I actually, honest-to-God thought they were guys. And they're sitting at the stage and they're tipping me like crazy. I'm like, cool! And I'm trying to talk to one and it was a female voice. [1 became] totally uncomfortable. I didn't expect it. And you're just sitting there like, "Now, how do I actually talk to this person?"

It did not matter to Nicole which preference a customer had, as long as she knew it in advance. She stated that she felt comfortable dancing and changing in front of a transgendered person who used to work at her club, because she knew what gender that person *wanted to be.* Nicole's comfort with a transgendered coworker was cemented once she understood that person's sexual orientation. Brooke and Erica, while acknowledging the initial awkwardness of dancing for lesbian and bisexual women, adjusted their stance toward these customers in such a way that they met the needs of both parties.

Dancers relied on cultural norms of male heterosexual desire in order to predict how a male customer would behave toward them. Unfamiliar male customers were a source of anxiety, because dancers were familiar with the ways that men tended to violate their privacy. But regular male customers were a pleasure, because their behavior was predictable and respectful of dancers' privacy. Even though women tended to be hassle-free customers, they still warranted close inspection until the dancer was sure of their motivations and expectations. Persons become intelligible subjects through their conformity or nonconformity to gender roles (Butler, 1990). Even in the context of dancing for women, the customer's desires and motivations can be a mystery to the dancer. Although from experience they knew that women were less likely to violate their privacy, every situation merited caution on the part of the dancer. Dancers simply wanted to know what kind of desire their customers were approaching them with, no matter what their gender or sexual orientation. In sex work, as in the everyday world, a person's gender identity is the primary source of information in determining their desire (Schwartz & Rutter, 1998). Dancers know and predict differences in customers' behaviors based on their experiences, as well as cultural understandings and sexual behaviors.

PRIVACY, DESIRE, AND POWER

Deciphering the dynamic of power between men and women in the world of sex work must begin by acknowledging that desire, libido, and sexual drives have historically been characterized as essentially masculine (Chodorow, 1989; Fink, 1995; Freud, 1989; Irigaray, 1985). Feminine sexuality is the "natural" recipient of that desire. If the strip club is envisioned as a system that operates solely on male desire and men's fantasies, then there is no possibility for the freedom of women's desire to exist as authentic or self-creating. Being a sex worker means that at times one must indeed focus on the customer's desire, while at other times one can explore one's own sexual possibilities. The means by which sexual freedoms are limited in sex work occur when both participants—dancer and customer—inhabit roles that define particular styles of sexual interaction. For example, the body types of dancers reflect the dominant trends in what is considered to be sexually appealing for men, and the fetishistic quality of clothes and shoes worn by the dancers may appear, to some, to be limitations of sexual expression. However, if one visits enough clubs one begins to see variation even in these areas.

The club's rules, and the breaking of those rules, are also ways of participating in a game that re-creates and perpetuates norms of gendered desire. Women are coy, seductive, and inherently desirable. The customer's desire must be controlled by the imposition of limits on physical contact. The dancer's sexuality is created within this context in the same way that the customers' behaviors are modeled after society's expectations of masculinity. A reality of masculine and feminine desires and behaviors is generated accordingly. This reality may correspond with, or deviate from, the dancer's own felt sense of her sexuality. In this way, the dancer's acquiescence to these dominant trends reinforces stereotypes, especially if her own true feelings are incongruent with the way that she expresses herself. However, it is too simplistic to view sex workers as being the "perpetrators" of this style of (hetero)sexual interaction.

If we listen to the narratives of women who enjoy sex work, we see evidence of transformation through the freedom of self-expression. If we cannot even entertain the possibility of an authentic transformation of power in gendered interaction, we continue to limit women's (as well as men's) possibilities in the expression of desire. Ironically, this view denies the sex worker her subjectivity and her freedom, which is the very act that many accuse the male customer of committing on a nightly basis. To subscribe to a theory that excludes the possibility of power for sex workers divides women into mutually exclusive groups by virtue of their degree of sexual promiscuity. Modesty, virginity, and chastity become the measure of a woman's worth as a person and whether or not she is a feminist (Pendleton, 1997). This logic assumes that the female body has an essential value that is preserved only when its sexual expression is concealed and guarded and limits the contexts in which said sexual desire is deemed authentic and appropriate. It also characterizes men as sexual predators against whom women must fight to preserve their chastity.

In the everyday world, women suppress their desire in congruence with the dominant sexual morality (Queen, 1997). In the context of sex work, the possibility arises that the expression of desire becomes the locus of power. On the other hand, when the dancer's privacy is violated, her creation of the appearance of intimacy and eroticism is her power. Her power then resides in the mystery of her body, her hidden sexuality, and her skill of seduction. The dancer's ability *to manipulate* the appearances of intimacy, desire, and eroticism becomes a dynamic of power. This ability to manipulate appearances is akin to Enck and Preston's (1988) description of creating the "illusion of intimacy" (1988, p. 370) as well as Boles and Garbin's term "counterfeit intimacy" (1974, p. 136). However, deeming the customer-dancer interaction as inauthentic or manipulative on the part of either of its participants obscures the possibility that much of the time dancer and customer desire and acknowledge this very "illusion" as a form of being in relationship to one another. The very essence of the roles of dancer and customer can be mutually satisfying to both participants, particularly when both preserve the limits of the relationship by following rules and respecting one another. Of course, there are many customers who are frustrated by the rules of the club (Erickson & Tewksbury, 2000) and dancers for whom sex work exposes the performative nature of heterosexual courting, masculinity, and femininity (Delacoste & Alexander, 1987; Nagle, 1997; Ronai, 1992). Thus, both the withholding as well as the expression of sexuality are ways that men and women are together in relationship both in sex work as well as socially legitimated sexual unions. Each style of relating has gains and losses. Because masculinity and femininity do not occur in a vacuum, but instead in the culturally infused space of being with others, persons may call on a sense of privacy in order to preserve integrity of body and self. While negotiating an uncertain space with another person, control over self-exposure balances feelings of objectification and power.

The cultural discourse of feminine sexuality is infused with the rhetoric of shame and repression in an effort to limit women's sexual freedom. Historically, women's worth as persons has been measured in terms of an adherence to sexual practices created for the sole purpose of reducing their value to their (re)productive capabilities (Rubin, 1975). By limiting women's sexual freedom, the culture maintains a system of personal liberty and economic freedom for men. Motivated by punitive shame, the culture continues to marginalize sex workers. As a result, all women internalize society's shame regarding expressions of feminine sexuality (Queen, 1997). A radical sex work movement might prefer that sex workers disclose their choice of occupation for political reasons. Keeping one's identity hidden is seen as complicit with society's wish to silence sex workers. However, one must consider a woman's reasons for concealing aspects of her identity. Sex workers who do not have the support of partners and family and suffer a hostile work environment have fewer motivations to self-disclose, nor do they enjoy the privilege of understanding their work as political or transformative. For these women, the realm of privacy becomes the locus of subversion and part of the process of integrating feminism, feminine sexuality, and sex work. Butler (1990) states that the subversion of a system of power relations is only possible within that system; there is no subject that transcends the situation.

> There is no self that is prior to the convergence or who maintains an "integrity" prior to its entrance into this conflictual cultural field. There is only a taking up of the tools where they lie, where the very "taking up" is enabled by the tool lying there (Butler, 1990, p. 145).

A "taking up of the tools," I believe, includes both the dancer's tactics to protect her privacy and the customer's attempts to violate it. The dancer's privacy—what she conceals, keeps hidden, or keeps for herself—may include her desire. Her sense of privacy is what makes her a subject; it also makes her a person. The mystery within which a dancer shrouds a private sexuality can be empowering. Or she may choose to reveal herself, as Brooke did, in order to feel truly liberated. Her privacy, as part of her subjectivity, is her way of making something her own within the context of her work. If she employs a sense of privacy to protect aspects of body and self, she can inhabit multiple social roles and conceal the discrepancies of desires and behaviors between roles. When a woman has a persona, she is part of the public realm; she is a person (Brown, 1966). If a woman is figured to have no persona or no public face, she can be controlled. With no recourse to the persona and no distinction between public and private, she cannot move freely in either context. When one has privacy, one can occupy several roles as a *sexual being* and as a whole person. To deny a dancer's experience of privacy is to deny her personhood. It is to objectify her just as she is objectified in her work situation and to negate the value of her existence.

The context of the strip club is the scene of a potential gender-power transformation. On the surface, we find familiar themes of feminist discourse: the naked body, the gaze, active subject and passive object, commodification, subjugation, perversion, and desire. These terms generally allocate power to one gender and powerlessness to the other. This dichotomy limits forms of gendered interaction. Sex work subverts this dichotomy. It grants a space for a different sexuality for women: one that is not exclusively procreative, one where women are in control of how they show themselves to others. It becomes the foundation of subjectivity and freedom.

The strip club is a cultural artifact where gender and sexual relations are created, re-created, and perpetuated. I do not believe that it is so different from other contexts, just that the dynamics are more transparent. The strip club is not simply a place for sexual release, nor is it a subculture that fosters crime and deviancy. On the surface, the world of sex work represents the enactment and perpetuation of stereotypes of gender and sexual behavior, the "eternal mystery" of feminine sexuality that men hope to solve a dollar at a time. But both customers and dancers return to the club, night after night. Each participant experiences power and objectification. The phenomenology of the strip club and the exotic dancers' experience deepens our understanding of the sometimes conflicted and ambiguous way that we live out the construction of gendered behaviors while at the same time subverting and transcending them. An awareness of the true complexities and inherent contradictions within gendered interaction is a first step for greater tolerance in the movement toward gender and sexual freedom.

REFERENCES

Boles, Jacqueline, & Albeno Garbin. (1974). The strip club and stripper-customer patterns of interaction. *Sociology and Social Research,* 58: 136–144.

Brown, Norman. (1966). *Love's Body.* New York: Random House.

Butler, Judith. (1990). *Gender Trouble.* New York: Routledge.

Chodorow, Nancy. (1989). *Feminism and Psychoanalytic Theory.* New Haven, CT: Yale University Press.

Delacoste, Frederique, and Priscilla Alexander. (1987). *Sex Work: Writings by Women in the Sex Industry.* Pittsburgh: Cleis Press.

Enck, Graves E., & James Preston. (1988). Counterfeit intimacy: A dramaturgical analysis of an erotic performance. *Deviant Behavior,* 9: 369–381.

Erickson, David John, and Richard Tewksbury. (2000). The 'gentlemen' in the club: A typology of strip club patrons. *Deviant Behavior,* 21: 271–293.

Fink, Bruce. (1995). *The Lacanian Subject.* Princeton: Princeton University Press.

Freud, Sigmund. (1989). Three essays on the theory of sexuality. In P. Gay (Ed.), *The Freud Reader* (pp. 239–292). New York: W.W. Norton & Co.

Irigaray, Luce. (1985). *This Sex Which Is Not One.* C. Porter (Trans.). New York: Cornell University Press.

Kappeler, Suzanne. (1986). *The Pornography of Representation.* Minneapolis: University of Minnesota Press.

McElroy, Wendy. (1995). *A Woman's Right to Pornography.* New York: St. Martin's Press.

Nagle, Jill. (1997). *Whores and Other Feminists.* New York: Routledge.

Paglia, Camille. (1990). *Sexual Persona.* New York: Vintage Books.

Paglia, Camille. (1994). *Vamps and Tramps.* New York: Vintage Books.

Pendleton, Eva. (1997). Love for sale: Queering heterosexuality. In J. Nagle (Ed.), *Whores and Other Feminists* (pp. 73–82). New York: Routledge.

Queen, Carol. (1997). Sex radical politics, sex-positive feminist thought, and whore stigma. In J. Nagle (Ed.), *Whores and Other Feminists* (pp. 125–135). New York: Routledge.

Ronai, Carol Rambo. (1992). The reflexive self through narrative: A night in the life of an erotic dancer/researcher. In C. Ellis & M. Flaherty (Eds.), *Investigating Subjectivity: Research on Lived Experience* (pp. 102–124). London: Sage Publications, Inc.

Rubin, Gayle. (1975). The traffic in women: Notes on the 'political economy' of sex. In R. Reiter (Ed.), *Toward an Anthropology of Women* (pp. 157–210). New York: Monthly Review Press.

Schwartz, Pepper, & Virginia Rutter. (1998). *The Gender of Sexuality.* Thousand Oaks, CA: Pine Forge Press.

Williams, Linda. (1989). *Hard Core. Power, Pleasure, and the Frenzy of the Visible.* Berkeley: University of California Press.

CHAPTER 5

THE SEXUAL VICTIMIZATION OF COLLEGE WOMEN*

Bonnie S. Fisher, Francis T. Cullen, and Michael G. Turner

INTRODUCTION

During the past decade, concern over the sexual victimization of female college students has escalated. In part, the interest in this problem has been spurred by increasing attention to the victimization of women in general; until the relatively recent past, female victims received very little attention. However, this is no longer true. Terms such as *date rape* and *domestic violence* have entered the public lexicon and signify the unprecedented, if still insufficient, notice given to women who have been victimized.

Attention to the sexual victimization of college women, however, also has been prompted by the rising fear that college campuses are not ivory towers but, instead, have become hot spots for criminal activity. Researchers have shown that college campuses and their students are not free from the risk of criminal victimization.[1] It is noteworthy that large concentrations of young women come into contact with young men in a variety of public and private settings at various times on college campuses.

Previous research suggests that these women are at greater risk for rape and other forms of sexual assault than women in the general population or in a comparable age group.[2] College women might, therefore, be a group whose victimization warrants special attention.

Recognizing these risks, the U.S. Congress passed the Student Right-to-Know and Campus Security Act of 1990 (hereafter referred to as the act). This legislation mandates that colleges and universities participating in federal student aid programs "prepare, publish, and distribute, through appropriate publications or mailings, to all current students and employees, and to any applicant for enrollment or employment upon request, an annual security

---

*Source: Fisher, B., Cullen, F., & Turner, M. (2000). *The Sexual Victimization of College Women (Research Report).* Washington, DC: National Institute of Justice and Bureau of Justice Statistics, U.S. Department of Justice.

report" containing campus security policies and campus crime statistics for that institution (see 20 U.S.C. 1092(f)(1)).[3]

Congress has maintained an interest in campus crime issues, passing legislation that requires higher educational institutions to address the rights of victims of sexual victimization and to collect and publish additional crime statistics (e.g., murder and nonnegligent manslaughter, arson). For example, Congress amended the act in 1992 to include the Campus Sexual Assault Victims' Bill of Rights, which requires colleges and universities (1) to develop and publish as part of their annual security report their policies regarding the awareness and prevention of sexual assaults and (2) to afford basic rights to sexual assault victims.[4] The act was amended again in 1998 to include additional reporting obligations, extensive campus security-related provisions, and the requirement to keep a daily public crime log; some states already required a public log (Public Law 105-244).[5] The 1998 amendments also officially changed the name of the act to the Jeanne Clery Disclosure of Campus Security Policy and Campus Crime Statistics Act. In 1999, the U.S. Department of Justice awarded $8.1 million to 21 colleges and universities to combat sexual assault, domestic violence, and stalking.[6] In 2000, 20 additional schools were awarded $6.8 million. Two national-level studies are currently in the field. The first study examines how institutions of higher education respond to the report of a sexual assault. The second one is a multisite evaluation of the programs and policies implemented in the aforementioned 41 schools.

WHAT WE KNOW ABOUT SEXUAL VICTIMIZATION OF COLLEGE WOMEN

Like government officials, researchers also have given attention to the sexual victimization of college women and have conducted a number of studies.[7] Although illuminating, much of the research is generally characterized by one or more of the following limitations:

- The failure to use a randomly selected, national sample of college women. (Many studies have sampled students at only one college or at a limited number of institutions.)
- The failure to assess the various ways in which women can be victimized. (Most studies have focused on a limited number of types of sexual victimization.)
- The failure to use question wording or sufficiently detailed measures that prevent biases that might cause researchers to underestimate or overestimate the extent of sexual victimization.
- The failure to collect detailed information on what occurred during the victimization incident.
- The failure to explore systematically the factors that place female students at risk for sexual victimization.
- The failure to study whether women have been stalked—a victimization that, until recently, had not received systematic research.

The National College Women Sexual Victimization (NCWSV) study, described in this report and funded by the National Institute of Justice (NIJ), attempted to build on, and surmount the limitations of, existing research on the sexual victimization of college students by

- Employing a nationally representative sample of college women.
- Assessing a range of sexual victimizations, including stalking.
- Measuring sexual victimization using a two-stage process starting with "behaviorally specific" screen questions that attempted to cue respondents to recall and report to the interviewer different types of sexual victimization experiences they may have had. Those who reported a victimization were then asked a series of questions, called an incident report, to verify what type of sexual victimization, if any, had occurred.
- Acquiring detailed information on each victimization incident, including the type of penetration(s) or unwanted sexual contact experienced and the means of coercion, if any, used by the offender.
- Examining how the risk of being sexually victimized was affected by a variety of variables, including demographic characteristics, lifestyles, prior victimization, and the characteristics of the college or university attended.

In addition, the research project contained a comparison component designed to assess how rape estimates that use the two-stage process (behaviorally specific questions and incident reports) compared with rape estimates drawn from a sample of college women who completed a survey based on the National Crime Victimization Survey (NCVS). The comparison component was funded by the Bureau of Justice Statistics (BJS).[8]

The resulting data furnish perhaps the most systematic analysis of the extent and nature of the sexual victimization of college women in the past decade.

WHO WAS SURVEYED?

NCWSV study results are based on a telephone survey of a randomly selected, national sample of 4446 women who were attending a two- or four-year college or university during fall 1996. The questions were asked between February and May 1997. The sample was limited to schools with at least 1000 students and was stratified by the size of the total student enrollment (1000–2499; 2500–4999; 5000–19,999; 20,000 or more) and the school's location (urban, suburban, and rural). Schools were randomly chosen using a probability proportional with the size of the total female enrollment. Students were then randomly selected using a sampling frame provided by the American Student List Company. This company provided the school address and telephone number for each student in the sample.

Each sample member was sent a letter describing the study and research protocol approximately 2 weeks prior to when a trained female interviewer called using a computer-aided telephone interviewing system.[9] The response rate was 85.6 percent.[10]

The comparison component used the same two-stage methodology as the main study except victimization was measured by using the screen questions and the incident report employed by NCVS. One purpose of the comparison component was to conduct a methodological experiment that would provide insight into the extent to which rape estimates are influenced by survey methods.

HOW WAS SEXUAL VICTIMIZATION MEASURED?

Measurement of sexual victimization was based on responses to "screen questions" and on a reference period for the victimization. In addition to the victimization measures, survey questions and secondary data sources were used to investigate the factors that potentially placed women at risk of being sexually victimized.

Two-Stage Measurement Design: The Screen Question-Incident Report Methodology

With important exceptions noted later, sexual victimization was measured largely by following the two-stage measurement format of NCVS. NCVS first asks a series of screen questions that seek to determine if a respondent has experienced an act that may possibly be a victimization. If the respondent answers "yes," then for each of the times that the act was experienced, the respondent is asked by the interviewer to complete an incident report. This report contains detailed questions about the nature of the events that occurred in the incident. The report is used to classify the type of victimization that took place; that is, responses to questions in the incident report—not the screen questions—are used to categorize whether a victimization occurred and, if so, what type.

Some researchers have contended that the screen questions as worded in NCVS are not detailed enough to identify all women who have experienced a rape or another type of sexual assault. A respondent may not answer "yes" to a screen question unless it is worded in a way that reflects the experience the respondent has had. To rectify this limitation, researchers have argued that sexual victimization should be measured with screen questions that are both numerous and detailed enough that respondents will not misunderstand what is being asked.[11]

NCWSV, therefore, used a series of behaviorally specific screen questions that sought to assess whether respondents had experienced a range of sexual victimizations. A behaviorally specific question, for example, is one that does not ask simply if a respondent "had been raped"; rather, it describes an incident in graphic language that covers the elements of a criminal offense (e.g., someone "made you have sexual intercourse by using force or threatening to harm you . . . by intercourse I mean putting a penis in your vagina"). The same logic can be used to ask about other forms of sexual victimization, such as sexual coercion or unwanted sexual contact.

Examples of the screen questions used in the NCWSV study are listed in Exhibit 5.1. Each completed rape screen question asks the respondent about a different form of penetration in which force or the threat of harm was used. A statement then follows each question that defines the type of penetration. For example, anal sex is defined as "putting a penis in your anus or rectum." The

Exhibit 5.1
Survey Screen Questions

Women may experience a wide range of unwanted sexual experiences in college. Women do not always report unwanted sexual experiences to the police or discuss them with family and friends. The person making the advances is not always a stranger, but can be a friend, boyfriend, fellow student, professor, teaching assistant, supervisor, coworker, somebody you meet off campus, or even a family member. The experience could occur anywhere: on or off campus, in your residence, in your place of employment, or in a public place. You could be awake, or you could be asleep, unconscious, drunk, or otherwise incapacitated. Please keep this in mind as you answer the questions.

Now, I'm going to ask you about different types of unwanted sexual experiences you may have experienced since school began in fall 1996. Because of the nature of unwanted sexual experiences, the language may seem graphic to you. However, this is the only way to assess accurately whether or not the women in this study have had such experiences. You only have to answer "yes" or "no."

- Since school began in fall 1996, has anyone made you have sexual intercourse by using force or threatening to harm you or someone close to you? Just so there is no mistake, by intercourse I mean putting a penis in your vagina.
- Since school began in fall 1996, has anyone made you have oral sex by force or threat of harm? By oral sex, I mean someone's mouth or tongue making contact with your vagina or anus or your mouth or tongue making contact with someone else's genitals or anus.
- Since school began in fall 1996, has anyone made you have anal sex by force or threat of harm? By anal sex, I mean putting a penis in your anus or rectum.
- Since school began in fall 1996, has anyone ever used force or threat of harm to sexually penetrate you with a foreign object? By this, I mean, for example, placing a bottle or finger in your vagina or anus.
- Since school began in fall 1996, has anyone attempted but not succeeded in making you take part in any of the unwanted sexual experiences that I have just asked you about? For example, did anyone threaten or try but not succeed to have vaginal, oral, or anal sex with you or try unsuccessfully to penetrate your vagina or anus with a foreign object or finger?
- Not counting the types of sexual contact already mentioned, have you experienced any unwanted or uninvited touching of a sexual nature since school began in fall 1996? This includes forced kissing, touching of private parts, grabbing, fondling, and rubbing up against you in a sexual way, even if it is over your clothes.
- Since school began in fall 1996, has anyone attempted but not succeeded in unwanted or uninvited touching of a sexual nature?
- Since school began in fall 1996, has anyone made or tried to make you have sexual intercourse or sexual contact when you did not want to by making threats of nonphysical punishment, such as lowering a grade, being demoted or fired from a job, damaging your reputation, or being excluded from a group for failure to comply with requests for any type of sexual activity?

(continued)

Exhibit 5.1

Survey Screen Questions (*Continued*)

- Since school began in fall 1996, has anyone made or tried to make you have sexual intercourse or sexual contact when you did not want to by making promises of rewards, such as raising a grade, being hired or promoted, being given a ride or class notes, or getting help with coursework from a fellow student if you complied sexually?
- Since school began in fall 1996, has anyone made or tried to make you have sexual intercourse or sexual contact when you did not want to by simply being overwhelmed by someone's continual pestering and verbal pressure?

other screen questions provide examples of the behaviors that respondents were asked about.

The NCWSV rape screen questions are similar, if not identical, to those used by Kilpatrick and his associates[12] and by Tjaden and Thoennes.[13] The use of behaviorally specific screen questions is an important difference between the current survey and NCVS. The NCVS screen questions begin with a reference to a type of criminal victimization that may have been experienced (e.g., "were you attacked or threatened"), which is then followed by a list of short cue responses about the potential victimization. This list includes cues regarding specific places or situations in which the victimization could have occurred (e.g., "at work or at school"); objects that could have been used (e.g., "with any weapon, for instance, a gun or knife"); actions that could have been associated with the victimization (e.g., "face-to-face threats"); actions that constitute a criminal victimization (e.g., "rape, attempted rape, or other types of sexual attack"); and people who might have perpetrated the criminal act (e.g., "a relative or family member"). There is also a screen question that asks about "incidents involving forced or unwanted sexual acts."[14]

Drawing on the NCVS screen question and incident report methodology, the NCWSV screen questions were followed by a detailed incident report that (1) clarified what type of victimization, if any, had occurred and (2) collected information about various aspects of the incident (e.g., victim-offender relationship, whether the victimization took place on or off the college campus, whether the incident was reported to the police). Responses to the screen questions were not used to classify the type of victimization reported by the respondent. Instead, classification was based on the responses in the incident report to questions about (1) the type of penetration experienced (e.g., penile-vaginal, anal, oral); (2) the type of unwanted sexual contact experienced (e.g., touching, grabbing, or fondling); and (3) the means of coercion used by the perpetrators (e.g., force, threat of force). Like Koss and colleagues and NCVS, the incidents were classified using a hierarchical algorithm; that is, incidents were classified by the most severe type of sexual victimization that occurred within an incident.[15] For example, if within an incident report the victim answered questions indicating she had experienced a completed rape and attempted sexual coercion, the incident was classified as a completed rape.

Reference Period

To limit potential response bias due to recall or memory decay, the NCWSV survey questions used a reference period that had a clear starting date for students. Thus, respondents were asked if they had experienced a sexual victimization "since school began in fall 1996." The survey was conducted in 1997 between late February and early May. On average, the reference period for the victimization covered almost 7 months (6.91 months).[16] To participate in the study, respondents had to be enrolled in a college or university at the start of the 1996 fall semester.

Risk Factors

In addition to the victimization measures, the NCWSV survey contained questions about respondents' demographic characteristics, lifestyles or routine activities, living arrangements, prior sexual victimizations, and so forth. Secondary data sources were used to measure the characteristics of the schools the respondents attended (e.g., size of enrollment, location, crime rate). These individual- and institution-level variables were used in multivariate analyses that investigated which factors potentially placed women at risk of being sexually victimized.

WHAT TYPES OF SEXUAL VICTIMIZATION WERE MEASURED IN THE NCWSV STUDY?

Measures of 12 types of sexual victimization were constructed; they are defined in Exhibit 5.2. Most important, the NCWSV study included measures of both completed and attempted rape as well as threats of rape. The study also measured completed, attempted, and threatened sexual coercion (penetration with the use of nonphysical forms of coercion) and unwanted sexual contact (sexual contact, but not penetration, with force or threat of force). In addition, the study measured stalking and visual and verbal forms of sexual victimization.

Exhibit 5.2
Descriptions of Types of Victimizations

Type of victimization	Definition
Completed rape	Unwanted completed penetration by force or the threat of force. Penetration includes penile-vaginal, mouth on your genitals, mouth on someone else's genitals, penile-anal, digital-vaginal, digital-anal, object-vaginal, and object-anal.
Attempted rape	Unwanted attempted penetration by force or the threat of force. Penetration includes penile-vaginal, mouth on your genitals, mouth on someone else's genitals, penile-anal, digital-vaginal, digital-anal, object-vaginal, and object-anal.

(continued)

Exhibit 5.2

Descriptions of Types of Victimizations (*Continued*)

Type of victimization	Definition
Completed sexual coercion	Unwanted completed penetration with the threat of physical punishment, promise of reward, or pestering/verbal pressure. Penetration includes penile-vaginal, mouth on your genitals, mouth on someone else's genitals, penile-anal, digital-vaginal, digital-anal, object-vaginal, and object-anal.
Attempted sexual coercion	Unwanted attempted penetration with the threat of nonphysical punishment, promise of reward, or pestering/verbal pressure. Penetration includes penile-vaginal, mouth on your genitals, mouth on someone else's genitals, penile-anal, digital-vaginal, digital-anal, object-vaginal, and object-anal.
Completed sexual contact with force or threat of force	Unwanted completed sexual contact (not penetration) with or the threat of force. Sexual contact includes touching; grabbing or fondling of breasts, buttocks, or genitals, either under or over your clothes; kissing; licking or sucking; or some other form of unwanted sexual contact.
Completed sexual contact without force	Any type of unwanted completed sexual contact (not penetration) with the threat of nonphysical punishment, promise of reward, or pestering/verbal pressure. Sexual contact includes touching; grabbing or fondling of breasts, buttocks, or genitals, either under or over your clothes; kissing; licking or sucking; or some other form of unwanted sexual contact.
Attempted sexual contact with force or threat of force	Unwanted attempted sexual contact (not penetration) with force or the threat of force. Sexual contact includes touching; grabbing or fondling of breasts, buttocks, or genitals, either under or over your clothes; kissing; licking or sucking; or some other form of unwanted sexual contact.
Attempted sexual contact without force	Unwanted attempted sexual contact (not penetration) with the threat of nonphysical punishment, promise of reward, or pestering/verbal pressure. Sexual contact includes touching; grabbing or fondling of breasts, buttocks, or genitals, either under or over your clothes; kissing; licking or sucking; or some other form of unwanted sexual contact.
Threat of rape	Threat of unwanted penetration with force and threat of force. Penetration includes penile-vaginal, mouth on your genitals, mouth on someone else's genitals, penile-anal, digital-vaginal, digital-anal, object-vaginal, and object-anal.

(continued)

Exhibit 5.2
Descriptions of Types of Victimizations (*Continued*)

Type of victimization	Definition
Threat of contact with force of or threat of force	Threat of unwanted sexual contact with force and threat force. Sexual contact includes touching; grabbing or fondling of breasts, buttocks, or genitals, either under or over your clothes; kissing; licking or sucking; or some other form of unwanted sexual contact.
Threat of penetration without force	Threat of unwanted penetration with the threat of non-physical punishment, promise of reward, or pestering/verbal pressure. Penetration includes penile-vaginal, mouth on your genitals, mouth on someone else's genitals, penile-anal, digital-vaginal, digital-anal, object-vaginal, and object-anal.
Threat of contact without force	Threat of unwanted sexual contact with the threat of nonphysical punishment, promise of reward, or pestering/verbal pressure. Sexual contact includes touching; grabbing or fondling of breasts, buttocks, or genitals, either under or over your clothes; kissing; licking or sucking; or some other form of unwanted sexual contact.

HOW EXTENSIVE IS RAPE AMONG COLLEGE WOMEN?

Exhibit 5.3 reports the extent of rape found in the NCWSV study. As shown, 2.8 percent of the sample had experienced either a completed rape (1.7 percent) or an attempted rape incident (1.1 percent). The victimization rate was 27.7 rapes per 1000 female students.

Exhibit 5.3
Extent of Rape, by Number of Victims, and Number of Incidents, by Type of Victimization Incident

Type of victimization	Victims			Incidents	
	Number of victims in sample	Percentage of sample	Rate per 1000 female students	Number of incidents	Rate per 1000 female students
Completed rape	74	1.7	16.6	86	19.3
Attempted rape	49	1.1	11.0	71	16.0
Total	123	2.8	27.7[a]	157	35.3

[a] Total has been rounded (from 27.665 to 27.7).

We recognize that a hierarchical scoring procedure is not the only way to count victims and incidents, especially because we have multiple victims. Another estimation procedure is to count the total number of completed rape victims and the total number of attempted rape victims separately. For example, suppose there were two incident records for respondent 00: One incident was classified as a completed rape, and the other was classified as an attempted rape (recall that using a hierarchical scoring procedure, respondent 00 would be counted as a completed rape victim). Respondent 00 would now count as a completed rape victim and as an attempted rape victim. Using this "separate" counting procedure, there were 57 attempted rape victims, or 1.3 percent of the sample.

Because some women were victimized more than once, the rate of incidents was higher than the rate of victims (35.3 per 1000 students). Of the 123 victims, 22.8 percent (n = 28) were multiple-rape victims.

A separate analysis, again using the same hierarchical scoring procedure, found that when rates were computed for only undergraduate students, the percentage of students victimized was 1.8 percent for rape and 1.3 percent for attempted rape. The comparable figures for nonundergraduate students were, respectively, 0.8 percent and 0 percent.[17]

At first glance, one might conclude that the risk of rape victimization for college women is not high; "only" about 1 in 36 college women (2.8 percent) experience a completed rape or attempted rape in an academic year. Such a conclusion, however, misses critical, and potentially disquieting, implications. The figures measure victimization for slightly more than half a year (6.91 months). Projecting results beyond this reference period is problematic for a number of reasons, such as assuming that the risk of victimization is the same during summer months and remains stable over a person's time in college. However, if the 2.8 percent victimization figure is calculated for a 1-year period, the data suggest that nearly 5 percent (4.9 percent) of college women are victimized in any given calendar year. Over the course of a college career— which now lasts an average of 5 years—the percentage of completed or attempted rape victimization among women in higher educational institutions might climb to between one-fifth and one-quarter.[18]

Furthermore, from a policy perspective, college administrators might be disturbed to learn that for every 1000 women attending their institutions, there may well be 35 incidents of rape in a given academic year (based on a victimization rate of 35.3 per 1000 college women). For a campus with 10,000 women, this would mean the number of rapes could exceed 350.

Even more broadly, when projected over the nation's female student population of several million, these figures suggest that rape victimization is a potential problem of large proportion and of public policy interest.

HOW DO THE NCWSV RAPE ESTIMATES COMPARE WITH THE RAPE ESTIMATES BASED ON THE NATIONAL CRIME VICTIMIZATION SURVEY?

The sexual victimization literature contains a great deal of discussion about how rape estimates from the nation's federally sponsored victimization survey, NCVS, compare with estimates from other national surveys. This issue was examined through a comparison component.[19] Like the main NCWSV study, the comparison study was conducted in the 1996–1997 academic year, from late March to mid-May. The sample size was 4432 college women; the response rate was 91.6 percent.[20]

Every effort was made to ensure that, aside from using different screen and incident report questions, the methodology used in both the main and comparison components was the same. Thus, both components (1) contacted sample members with a letter that explained the purpose of the survey, (2) employed the same sampling design and sampling frame, (3) used the same reference period for victimization ("Since school began in fall 1996 . . ."), and (4) measured victimization using the screen question-incident report methodology. Both components also were conducted by the same survey research firm (see endnote 10) and were administered by trained female interviewers using a computer-aided telephone interviewing system.

However, in assessing the influence of different methodologies for measuring sexual victimization, the two studies differed on one methodological issue: the wording of the screen questions and the wording of the incident-level questions used to determine the type of incident. As previously described, the main study substantially modified the NCVS format to include a range of behaviorally specific screen questions. In contrast, the comparison component used a format that was closely aligned with the survey format of NCVS. All of the screen questions used in the comparison component came directly from NCVS, as did the incident-level questions used to determine what type of violent victimization the respondent had experienced.[21] Both components used a hierarchical algorithm to classify the type(s) of victimization that the respondent described in the incident report.

We should note, however, that the methodology used in the comparison component differs from that used in NCVS in one respect. In addition to structured responses to the survey questions, NCVS interviewers record a brief "verbatim description" of the victimization incident from those respondents who report experiencing rape or sexual assault. These verbatim responses are used to clarify what occurred in an incident and to code whether an incident should count as a sexual victimization. Thus, according to BJS staff,

> In the NCVS, all questionnaires for which any rape or sexual assault code is entered in any of the pertinent items are reviewed to determine whether the codes reflect the written entries in the summaries. Where there are clear indications that the coded entries are not correct, they are edited, using guidelines developed by BJS and Bureau of Census staffs. This procedure has proven beneficial towards improving the NCVS estimates of rape and sexual assault by removing, to the extent possible, the discrepancies existing between the coded and written entries.[22]

In our comparison component study, the estimates were not adjusted using verbatim responses.[23] We do not know how much this consideration affects the findings reported for the comparison component that is, again, based on NCVS methodology. None of the *Criminal Victimization in the United States* annual publications report how much the NCVS estimates are adjusted using verbatim responses or whether such adjustments cause estimates to increase or decrease compared with estimates coded solely on respondents' answers to the structured screen and incident-report questions.

NCVS defines rape as

> Forced sexual intercourse including both psychological coercion as well as physical force. Forced sexual intercourse means vaginal, anal, or oral penetration by the offender(s). This category also includes incidents where the penetration is from a foreign object such as a bottle. Includes attempted rapes, male as well as female victims, and both heterosexual and homosexual rape. Attempted rape includes verbal threats of rape.

This definition guided the classification of incidents in the comparison study as a completed rape, an attempted rape, or a threat of rape. In the Criminal Victimization in the United States series published by BJS, estimates for attempted rape and threats of rape are reported separately. The same is true in this report so as to compare rape estimates from the two components of the study.

How do the rape estimates from these two studies compare? It should be noted that studies that use behaviorally specific screen questions generally find higher levels of sexual victimization than those reported by NCVS.[24] Most important, this finding has occurred in recent research using a national-level sample and behaviorally specific questions.[25]

Looking at Figure 5.1, it is clear that estimates from the comparison study for completed rape, attempted rape, and threats of rape are considerably lower than the respective estimates from the main study. The percentage of the sample that reported experiencing a completed rape in the comparison study was 11 times smaller than the percentage of victims in the main component (0.16 percent compared with 1.7 percent). The attempted rape estimate from the comparison component was six times smaller than the attempted rape estimate (0.18 percent compared with 1.1 percent) from NCWSV. A similar pattern was evident for threats of rape; the estimate based on the comparison component was four times smaller than the NCWSV estimate (0.07 percent compared with 0.3 percent).

What accounts for these differences? Given the similarities between the two studies, it would appear that the differences most likely stem from the wide range of behaviorally specific screen questions used in the NCWSV

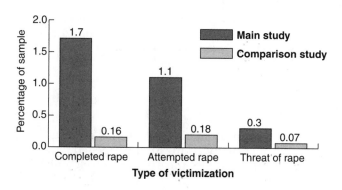

Figure 5.1 Comparison of rape estimates between the NCWSV main study and comparison component study.

study. Compared with the NCVS screen questions employed in the comparison component, the use of graphically worded screen questions in NCWSV likely prompted more women who had experienced a sexual victimization to report this fact to the interviewer. Their responses in the incident report determined whether those answering "yes" to a rape screen question were subsequently classified as rape victims.[26] Even so, it appears that behaviorally specific screen questions are more successful in prompting women who have in fact been sexually victimized to answer in such a way that they are then "skipped into" the incident report by interviewers.

What is unknown, however, is whether behaviorally specific screen questions produce higher estimates of victimization in general or only higher estimates of sexual victimization. It is possible that, due to the sensitive nature of sexual victimization, graphically descriptive screen questions are needed to prompt reluctant victims to report their victimization to interviewers. The other possibility, however, is that a large set of behaviorally specific questions would result in more victim reports for any type of victimization, including property crimes and other forms of violent crime (e.g., aggravated assault, robbery). Future research on NCVS methodology might profit from exploring this issue.

DO WOMEN DEFINE THEIR VICTIMIZATION AS A RAPE?

In each incident report, respondents were asked, "Do you consider this incident to be a rape?" For the 86 incidents categorized as a completed rape, 46.5 percent ($n = 40$) of the women answered "yes," 48.8 percent ($n = 42$) answered "no," and 4.7 percent ($n = 4$) answered "don't know." Among women who experienced other forms of sexual victimization ($n = 1318$), it is noteworthy that 3.4 percent ($n = 42$) defined their sexual victimization as a rape and 1.1 percent ($n = 14$) answered "don't know."

Some scholars believe that the failure of women to define a victimization as a rape calls into question whether researchers have truly measured the crime of rape.[27] Others suggest, however, that the true prevalence of rape is best measured by carefully worded questions on victimization surveys, such as NCWSV.[28] Women may not define a victimization as a rape for many reasons (such as embarrassment, not clearly understanding the legal definition of the term, or not wanting to define someone they know who victimized them as a rapist) or because others blame them for their sexual assault.[29] Which of these reasons is more or less correct cannot be definitively substantiated here because little systematic research has examined why women do or do not define as a rape an incident that has met the researcher's criteria for a rape.

HOW EXTENSIVE ARE OTHER FORMS OF SEXUAL VICTIMIZATION?

Exhibit 5.4 presents the extent of victimization across 10 forms of sexual victimization other than rape. Threats of sexual victimization happened less often than other forms of sexual victimization. Across the 10 types of victimization

Exhibit 5.4

Extent of Sexual Victimization

Type of victimization	Victims			Incidents	
	Number of victims in sample	Percentage of sample	Rate per 1000 female students	Number of incidents	Rate per 1000 female students
Completed or attempted					
Completed sexual coercion	74	1.7	16.6	107	24.1
Attempted sexual coercion	60	1.3	13.5	114	25.6
Completed sexual contact with force or threat of force	85	1.9	19.1	130	29.2
Completed sexual contact without force	80	1.8	18.0	132	29.7
Attempted sexual contact with force or threat of force	89	2.0	20.0	166	37.6
Attempted sexual contact without force	133	3.0	29.9	295	66.4
Threats					
Threat of rape	14	0.31	3.2	42	9.5
Threat of contact with force or threat of force	8	0.18	1.8	50	11.3
Threat of penetration without force	10	0.22	2.3	50	11.3
Threat of contact without force	15	0.34	3.4	75	16.9
Total	568			1,161	

in Exhibit 5.4, the incident rate per 1000 female students ranged from a low of 9.5 to a high of 66.4.

Figure 5.2 presents the data in a slightly different form and contains rape incidents. This exhibit illustrates the percentages of women in the sample who had experienced at least one victimization in three separate categories: (1) physical force, (2) nonphysical force, and (3) either physical or nonphysical force or both. Because the third category includes respondents who have experienced both types of victimization, its percentage is not computed by summing the percentages in the physical and nonphysical categories. As is shown, 15.5 percent of the college women were sexually victimized during the current academic year. In the sample, 7.7 percent experienced an incident involving the use or threat of physical force, and 11.0 percent experienced a victimization that did not involve force.

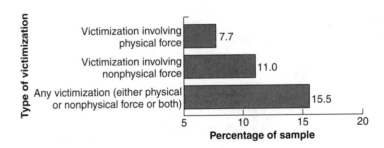

Figure 5.2 Percentage of sample having at least one victimization incident.

HOW EXTENSIVE IS PRIOR SEXUAL VICTIMIZATION?

Respondents were also asked if they had experienced sexual victimization incidents before starting school in fall 1996. These incidents were measured only with single questions, not incident reports (that is, the two-stage process of screen questions followed by an incident report was not used). To limit bias, we attempted to use the detailed questions shown in Exhibit 5.5. Still, the findings must be assessed in light of this methodological limitation.

As Exhibit 5.5 shows, about 1 in 10 college women said they had experienced a rape, while the same proportion stated that they were victims of an attempted rape. Almost the same proportion also had sexual intercourse or contact in which they were subject to threats of nonphysical punishment or promises of reward. Unwanted or uninvited sexual contacts were widespread, with more than one-third of the sample reporting these incidents.

DO VICTIMS KNOW THEIR OFFENDERS?

Most victims knew the person who sexually victimized them. For both completed and attempted rapes, about 9 in 10 offenders were known to the victim. Most often, a boyfriend, ex-boyfriend, classmate, friend, acquaintance, or coworker sexually victimized the women. College professors were not identified as committing any rapes or sexual coercions, but they were cited as the offender in a low percentage of cases involving unwanted sexual contact. The victim-offender relationship for rape incidents is displayed in Figure 5.3.

Variation in the type of sexual victimization that occurred on a date was evident. With regard to date rape, 12.8 percent of completed rapes, 35.0 percent of attempted rapes, and 22.9 percent of threatened rapes took place on a date.

WHEN DOES SEXUAL VICTIMIZATION OCCUR?

The vast majority of sexual victimizations occurred in the evening (after 6 P.M.). For example, 51.8 percent of completed rapes took place after midnight, 36.5 percent occurred between 6 P.M. and midnight, and only 11.8 percent took place between 6 A.M. and 6 P.M.

Exhibit 5.5

Percent of Sample Who Were Sexually Victimized Before the Start of the 1996 School Year

Type of victimization	Yes (percentage)	No (percentage)
Rape[a]	10.1	89.9
Attempted rape[b]	10.9	89.1
Threatened, attempted, or completed unwanted/uninvited sexual contact[c]	35.5	64.5
Sexual intercourse or contact with nonphysical threats/rewards[d]	8.6	91.4
Any other unwanted or uninvited sexual intercourse/contact[e]	5.9	94.1

[a]Prior to school starting in fall 1996, did anyone ever make you have vaginal, oral, or anal intercourse including penetrating you with a penis, a finger, or a foreign object by using force or threatening to harm you?

[b]Prior to school starting in fall 1996, did anyone ever attempt but not succeed in making you have vaginal, oral, or anal intercourse—including penetrating you with a penis, a finger, or a foreign object by using force or threatening to harm you?

[c]Prior to school starting in fall 1996, have you ever experienced any unwanted or uninvited touching of a sexual nature, or threats or attempts of such touching, including forced kissing, touching of private parts, grabbing, fondling, and rubbing up against you in a sexual way?

[d]Prior to school starting in fall 1996, has anyone ever tried to make you have sexual intercourse or sexual contact when you did not want to by making either threats of nonphysical punishment or promises of reward if you complied sexually?

[e]Prior to school starting in fall 1996, is there any type of unwanted or uninvited sexual intercourse or physical sexual contact that you ever experienced that was not covered in the questions thus far?

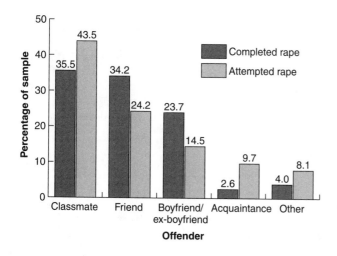

Figure 5.3 Victim-offender relationship for rape victimizations committed by single offenders.

WHERE DOES SEXUAL VICTIMIZATION OCCUR?

The majority of sexual victimizations, especially rapes and physically coerced sexual contact, occurred in living quarters. Almost 60 percent of the completed rapes that occurred on campus took place in the victim's residence, 31 percent occurred in other living quarters on campus, and 10.3 percent took place in a fraternity. Off-campus sexual victimizations, especially rapes, also occurred in residences. However, particularly for sexual contacts and threatened victimizations, incidents also took place in settings such as bars, dance clubs or nightclubs, and work settings.

ARE WOMEN VICTIMIZED ON OR OFF CAMPUS?

College women are victimized both on campus and off campus. For nearly all types of sexual victimization, however, off-campus victimization is more common (Exhibit 5.6). This conclusion must be qualified because off-campus sexual victimizations may take place in bars and nightclubs or in student residences close

Exhibit 5.6
The Location of Victimization by On-Campus and Off-Campus Location, by Type of Victimization

	Location of victimization[a]	
	On campus percentage (*n*)	Off campus percentage (*n*)
Type of victimization		
Completed or attempted		
Completed rape	33.7 (29)	66.3 (57)
Attempted rape	45.1 (32)	54.9 (39)
Completed sexual coercion	29.0 (31)	71.0 (76)
Attempted sexual coercion	46.5 (53)	53.5 (61)
Completed sexual contact with force or threat of force	34.6 (45)	65.4 (85)
Completed sexual contact without force	38.6 (51)	61.4 (81)
Attempted sexual contact with force or threat of force	33.9 (56)	66.1 (109)
Attempted sexual contact without force	35.9 (106)	64.1 (189)

(continued)

Exhibit 5.6

The Location of Victimization by On-Campus and Off-Campus Location, by Type of Victimization (*Continued*)

	Location of victimization[a]	
Type of victimization	On campus percentage (*n*)	Off campus percentage (*n*)
Threats		
Threat of rape	45.2 (19)	54.8 (23)
Threat of contact with force or threat of force	44.0 (22)	56.0 (28)
Threat of penetration without force	48.0 (24)	52.0 (26)
Threat of contact without force	54.1 (40)	45.9 (34)

[a] Don't know (*n* = 2) not included.

to campus. Thus, even if a student is victimized off campus, she may be engaged in an activity that is connected to her life as a student at the college she attends.

DO SEXUAL VICTIMS TAKE PROTECTIVE ACTIONS DURING THE INCIDENT?

As Exhibit 5.7 shows, for nearly all forms of sexual victimization, the majority of female students reported attempting to take protective actions during the incident. For both completed rape and sexual coercion, victims of completed acts were less likely to take protective action than those who experienced attempted

Exhibit 5.7

Percentage of Victims Taking Protective Action, by Type of Victimization

Type of victimization	Victim attempted to protect herself (n)
Completed or attempted	
Completed rape	65.1 (56)
Attempted rape	91.5 (65)
Completed sexual coercion	46.7 (50)
	(*continued*)

Exhibit 5.7
Percentage of Victims Taking Protective Action, by Type of Victimization (*Continued*)

Type of victimization	Victim attempted to protect herself (n)
Completed or attempted	
Attempted sexual coercion	74.3
	(84)
Completed sexual contact with force or threat of force	87.6
	(113)
Completed sexual contact without force	81.8
	(108)
Attempted sexual contact with force or threat of force	89.8
	(149)
Attempted sexual contact without force	76.6
	(226)
Threats	
Threat of rape	81.0
	(34)
Threat of contact with force or threat of force	86.0
	(43)
Threat of penetration without force	60.0
	(30)
Threat of contact without force	66.7
	(50)

victimization. This finding suggests that the intended victim's willingness or ability to use protection might be one reason attempts to rape or coerce sex failed.

Figure 5.4 reports the most common forms of protective action taken by victims during rape incidents. Note that the most common protective action was using physical force against the assailant. Nearly 70 percent of victims of attempted rape used this response—again, a plausible reason many of these acts were not completed. Other common physical responses included removing the offender's hand, running away, and trying to avoid the offender. Verbal responses also were common, including pleading with the offender to stop, screaming, and trying to negotiate with the offender.

ARE VICTIMS HURT IN THE VICTIMIZATION INCIDENTS?

Victims in the sample generally did not state that their victimization resulted in physical or emotional injuries. In about one in five rape and attempted rape incidents, victims reported being injured, most often citing the response "bruises, black-eye, cuts, scratches, swelling, or chipped teeth." The percentage injured by other types of victimization was lower, ranging from 0 percent (completed sexual contact without force) to 16.7 percent (threatened rape).

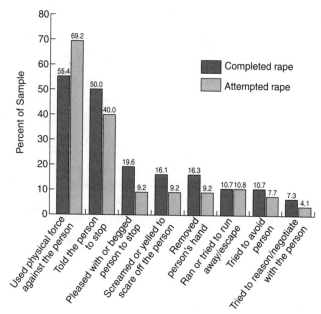

Percentages may be greater than 100 because a respondent could give more than one response

Figure 5.4   Most common forms of protective actions used in rape incidents.

ARE SOME WOMEN MORE AT RISK OF BEING SEXUALLY VICTIMIZED?

Multivariate logit models for each type of sexual victimization measured were estimated to predict the likelihood of having been victimized. Consistent across the models, it was found that four main factors consistently increased the risk of sexual victimization: (1) frequently drinking enough to get drunk, (2) being unmarried, (3) having been a victim of a sexual assault before the start of the current school year, and (4) living on campus (for on-campus victimization only).

DO WOMEN REPORT VICTIMIZATION INCIDENTS TO THE POLICE?

Few incidents of sexual victimization were reported to law enforcement officials. Thus, fewer than 5 percent of completed and attempted rapes were reported to law enforcement officials. In about two-thirds of the rape incidents, however, the victim did tell another person about the incidents. Most often this person was a friend, not a family member or college official.

Victims gave a number of reasons for not reporting their victimizations to law enforcement officials (Exhibit 5.8). Some reasons indicated that they did

Exhibit 5.8
Reasons for Not Reporting Incident to the Police, by Type of Victimization

Type of Incident	Incident was not reported % (n)	Did not want family to know about % (n)	Did not want other people to know about % (n)	Lack of proof that incident happened % (n)	Fear of being treated hostilely by police % (n)
Completed or attempted					
Completed rape	95.2 (82)	44.4 (36)	46.9 (38)	42.0 (34)	24.7 (20)
Attempted rape	95.8 (68)	32.4 (22)	32.4 (22)	30.9 (21)	8.8 (6)
Completed sexual coercion	100.0 (107)	41.9 (44)	43.8 (46)	33.3 (35)	8.6 (9)
Attempted sexual coercion	100.0 (114)	21.2 (24)	19.5 (22)	15.9 (18)	2.7 (3)
Completed sexual contact with force or threat of force	99.2 (128)	19.5 (25)	16.4 (21)	21.9 (28)	9.4 (12)
Completed sexual contact without force	98.5 (129)	4.7 (6)	11.7 (15)	18.0 (23)	4.7 (6)
Attempted sexual contact with force or threat of force	97.0 (160)	13.8 (22)	21.9 (35)	23.1 (37)	8.8 (14)
Attempted sexual contact without force	99.3 (293)	7.2 (21)	10.2 (30)	18.1 (53)	4.4 (13)
Threats					
Threat of rape	90.5 (38)	26.3 (10)	34.2 (13)	31.6 (12)	13.2 (5)
Threat of contact with force or threat of force	90.0 (45)	22.2 (10)	20.0 (9)	20.0 (9)	8.9 (4)
Threat of penetration without force	100.0 (50)	20.0 (10)	22.0 (11)	24.0 (12)	4.0 (2)
Threat of contact without force	98.7 (74)	6.8 (5)	8.1 (6)	21.6 (16)	8.1 (6)

Percentages may be greater than 100 because respondents could give more than one response.

Fear of being treated hostilely by other parts of the justice system % (n)	Not clear it was a crime or that harm was intended % (n)	Did not know how to report % (n)	Police wouldn't think it was serious enough % (n)	Police wouldn't want to be bothered % (n)	Afraid of reprisal by assailant or others % (n)	Did not think it was serious enough to report % (n)	Other % (n)
6.2 (5)	44.4 (36)	13.6 (11)	27.2 (22)	25.9 (21)	39.5 (32)	65.4 (53)	7.4 (6)
1.5 (1)	39.7 (27)	7.4 (5)	33.8 (23)	13.2 (9)	25.0 (17)	76.5 (52)	1.5 (1)
1.9 (2)	58.1 (61)	14.3 (15)	24.8 (26)	21.9 (23)	31.4 (33)	71.4 (75)	1.9 (2)
2.7 (3)	46.9 (53)	6.2 (7)	28.3 (32)	18.6 (21)	11.5 (13)	86.7 (98)	0 (0)
0 (0)	37.5 (48)	7.0 (9)	37.5 (48)	30.5 (39)	22.7 (29)	81.3 (104)	3.1 (4)
1.6 (2)	43.0 (55)	5.5 (7)	29.7 (38)	18.8 (24)	12.5 (16)	91.4 (117)	0.8 (1)
6.3 (10)	37.5 (60)	10.0 (16)	31.3 (50)	22.5 (36)	23.8 (38)	80.0 (128)	2.5 (4)
1.4 (4)	39.6 (116)	6.1 (18)	22.9 (67)	18.4 (54)	10.9 (32)	88.4 (259)	2.7 (8)
7.9 (3)	39.5 (15)	13.2 (5)	34.2 (13)	31.6 (12)	26.3 (10)	65.8 (25)	2.6 (1)
4.4 (2)	51.1 (23)	13.3 (6)	37.8 (17)	26.7 (12)	17.8 (8)	68.9 (31)	4.4 (2)
4.0 (2)	46.0 (23)	6.0 (3)	30.0 (15)	30.0 (15)	12.0 (6)	88.0 (44)	2.0 (1)
6.8 (5)	31.1 (23)	2.7 (2)	21.6 (16)	9.5 (7)	13.5 (10)	83.8 (62)	0 (0)

not see the incidents as harmful or important enough to bring in the authorities. Thus, the common answers included that the incident was not serious enough to report and that it was not clear that a crime was committed. Other reasons, however, suggested that there were barriers to reporting. Such answers included not wanting family or other people to know about the incident, lack of proof the incident happened, fear of reprisal by the assailant, fear of being treated with hostility by the police, and anticipation that the police would not believe the incident was serious enough and/or would not want to be bothered with the incident.

HOW EXTENSIVE IS STALKING?

In addition to the 12 types of sexual victimization (Exhibit 2), this research assessed a form of victimization that has been infrequently studied: stalking. In general, for behavior to qualify as stalking, the attention given to someone must be repeated and it must create fear in a reasonable person. Accordingly, stalking was measured with this screen question:

> "Since school began in fall 1996, has anyone—from a stranger to an ex-boyfriend—repeatedly followed you, watched you, phoned, written, e-mailed, or communicated with you in other ways that seemed obsessive and made you afraid or concerned for your safety?" If a respondent answered "yes," she was then given an incident report that asked detailed questions about the stalking that occurred.

The survey indicated an incidence rate of 156.5 per 1000 female students. Indeed, fully 13.1 percent of the female students in the sample (n = 581) had been stalked since the school year began. This figure approximates what was found in a pretest of the survey conducted on students attending one university. It also is similar to the 6-month prevalence figure reported by Mustaine and Tewksbury,[30] which, in a survey of 861 women attending 9 postsecondary institutions, found that 10.5 percent of the female students reported that they had been stalked.[31]

In contrast, Tjaden and Thoennes's national study of women reports much lower annual rates of stalking: 1 percent to 6 percent, depending on the definition of stalking used.[32] Compared with the current study, the lower extent of stalking in Tjaden and Thoennes's research may be because (1) their study used a more restrictive definition of stalking; (2) their study focused on females across the life course (age 18 to 80 years or older), rather than on younger women among whom stalking is more prevalent; and (3) their study did not focus specifically on college students. It may be that the social domain of college places women in situations and in contact with a range of men that increase the chances of being stalked.

It should be noted, however, that like the study by Tjaden and Thoennes, the estimates in this study of the extent of stalking vary depending on the criteria used to define what counts as stalking victimization.[33] Again, more than 13 percent of the women in the sample were stalked if this victimization is defined as a woman experiencing repeated, obsessive, and frightening behavior that made the victim afraid or concerned for her safety. Even so, if we were to decide that such behavior counts as a stalking victimization only if the person were actually threatened with harm—a requirement for criminal stalking in many states—the extent of stalking victims in the sample falls to 1.96 percent. These results suggest that, in the future, researchers should examine how estimates of the extent of stalking may vary widely depending on the criteria used to define what "counts" as a stalking victimization.

WHAT IS THE NATURE OF STALKING INCIDENTS?

As with other sexual victimizations, four in five victims knew their stalkers. Of the stalkers who were known, they were most often a boyfriend or ex-boyfriend (42.5 percent), classmate (24.5 percent), acquaintance (10.3 percent), friend (5.6 percent), or coworker (5.6 percent). Female students were infrequently stalked by college professors or graduate assistants.

Stalking incidents lasted an average of 60 days. About 30 percent of the female students were stalked only off campus; the remaining victims were stalked either only on campus or both on and off campus. The most common forms of stalking behaviors reported by victims were being telephoned (77.7 percent), having an offender waiting outside or inside places (47.9 percent), being watched from afar (44.0 percent), being followed (42.0 percent), being sent letters (30.7 percent), and being e-mailed (24.7 percent).[34] Almost two-thirds of the sample indicated that they were stalked at least two to six times a week.

Although some victims reported being physically injured, the most common consequence was psychological: Almost 3 in 10 women said they were "injured emotionally or psychologically" from being stalked. In 15.3 percent of incidents, victims reported that the stalker either threatened or attempted to harm them. In 10.3 percent of incidents, the victim reported that the stalker "forced or attempted sexual contact."

In nearly three-fourths of incidents, victims reported that they had taken "actions as a result of their stalking." Exhibit 5.9 shows actions victims took following stalking incidents. Two of the most common responses were "to avoid the stalker" (43.2 percent) or, conversely, "to confront the stalker" (16.3 percent). Beyond the data in Exhibit 5.9, in about 17 percent of incidents, victims reported the stalker to the police. In contrast, in more than 9 in 10 incidents, victims confided in someone—such as a friend, family member, or roommate—that they were being stalked.

ARE SOME WOMEN MORE AT RISK OF BEING STALKED?

A multivariate logit model was estimated to predict the likelihood of being stalked. The risk of being a stalking victim was increased by a number of factors: the propensity to be in places with alcohol; living alone; being in a dating relationship, especially early in the relationship, as opposed to being married or living with an intimate partner; being an undergraduate; being from an affluent family; and having experienced sexual victimization before the beginning of the current academic year. Also, among racial/ethnic groups, Asian/Pacific Islander women were significantly less likely to be stalked while American Indian/Alaska Native women were significantly more likely

Exhibit 5.9
Actions Taken by Victim as a Result of Stalking Incidents

Actions	Percentage[a]	n
Avoidance		
Avoided or tried to avoid the stalker	43.2	210
Did not acknowledge messages or e-mails	8.8	43
Moved residence	3.3	16
Dropped a class the stalker was in or taught	1.4	7
Quit job	0.8	4
Changed colleges or university	0.4	2
Changed majors	0.2	1
Legal/Judicial		
Sought a restraining order	3.9	19
Filed a grievance or initiated disciplinary action with university officials	3.3	16
Went forward with criminal charges	1.9	9
Filed civil charges	1.2	6
Self-Protection		
Got caller ID	4.9	24
Improved security system of residence	4.1	20
Began traveling with companion	3.9	19
Bought a weapon	1.9	9
Took a self-defense class	0.4	2
Psychological		
Became less trustful or more cynical of others	5.6	27
Sought psychological counseling	2.9	14
Confrontation		
Confronted the stalker	16.3	79
Other Actions taken but not specified	21.8	106

[a] Percentages may be greater than 100 because respondents could give more than one response.

to be stalked compared with women in other racial/ethnic groups. Notably, American Indian/Alaska Native women had the highest likelihood of any racial/ethnic group to experience a stalking. This is consistent with Tjaden and Thoennes's research, which reported that American Indians/Alaska Natives are at greatest risk of being stalked.[35]

WHAT IS THE EXTENT OF VISUAL AND VERBAL SEXUAL VICTIMIZATION?

Finally, this research measured the extent to which women were involuntarily exposed to visual images and verbal comments that would generally be considered sexually victimizing. Since these relatively "minor" types of victimization were plentiful, it was not possible to obtain a detailed report on each incident. Instead, results showed only whether a type of victimization was experienced and, if so, how many times it happened both on and off campus.

As Exhibit 5.10 reveals, most respondents did not experience visual victimization. Still, about 6 percent of female students had been shown pornographic pictures, almost 5 percent had someone expose their sexual organs to them, and 2.4 percent were observed naked without their consent. Verbal victimizations, moreover, were commonplace. About half the respondents were subjected to sexist remarks and to catcalls and whistles with sexual overtones. One in five female students received an obscene telephone call and was asked intrusive questions about her sex or romantic life. One in ten students had false rumors spread about her sex life.

CONCLUSIONS

The sexual victimization of college students has emerged as a controversial issue, pitting feminist scholars who claim that the sexual victimization of women is a serious problem against conservative commentators who claim that such victimization is rare and mostly a fictitious creation of ideologically tainted research.[36] The research reported here undoubtedly will not settle this debate; battle lines are solidly entrenched and how the data are interpreted will, to a degree, lie in the "eye of the beholder." However, the current study attempts to add a judicious voice to this conversation by attempting to furnish a methodologically sound assessment of the extent and nature of the sexual victimization of female students.

To summarize, the national-level survey of 4446 college women suggests that many students will encounter sexist and harassing comments, will likely receive an obscene phone call, and will have a good chance of being stalked or of enduring some form of coerced sexual contact. During any given academic year, 2.8 percent of women will experience a completed and/or attempted rape. This figure is not based only on broadly worded, behaviorally specific screen questions because all victimization incidents reported in the screen questions were verified through subsequent questions in the incident report. Furthermore, the level of rape and other types of victimization found in the survey becomes an increasing concern when the victimization figures are projected over a full year, a full college career, and the full population of women at one college or at colleges across the nation.

The results also hold important methodological implications. The comparison component study sponsored by the Bureau of Justice Statistics allowed the rare opportunity to conduct a quasiexperiment in how the methods used to measure sexual victimization might potentially affect estimates of victimization. Thus, two randomly selected samples of college women were surveyed using very similar methodology, with one noteworthy exception: A different way of measuring sexual victimization was used with each sample. Results showed that a methodology that uses behaviorally specific screen questions in combination with an incident report yields considerably higher estimates of completed, attempted, and threatened rape than are found using NCVS methodology.

Exhibit 5.10
The Extent of Verbal and Visual Victimization

	Percentage and number of victims for sample	Total number of victimizations[a]	Rate per 1000 female students	Number of victimizations per victim	Percentage and number of victimizations on campus	Percentage and number of victimizations off campus
Type of verbal victimization						
General sexist remark in front of you	54.3 (2,398)	31,434	7,070.2	13.0	50.6 (15,894)	49.4 (15,540)
Cat calls, whistles about your looks, or noises with sexual overtones	48.2 (2,129)	29,609	6,660.0	13.9	38.6 (11,423)	61.4 (18,186)
Obscene telephone calls or messages	21.9 (973)	4,885	1,099.0	5.0	59.8 (2,922)	40.2 (1,963)
Asked questions about sex or romantic life when clearly none of their business	19.0 (844)	4,694	1,055.8	5.6	41.2 (1,933)	58.8 (2,761)
False rumors about sex life with them or other people	9.7 (431)	1,166	262.3	2.7	59.7 (696)	40.3 (470)
Type of visual victimization						
Someone exposed you to pornographic pictures or materials when you did not agree to see them	6.1 (272)	865	194.6	3.2	59.9 (518)	40.1 (347)

Item						
Someone exposed their sexual organs to you when you did not agree to see them	4.8 (214)	568	127.8	2.7	34.0 (193)	66.0 (375)
Anyone, without your consent, observed or tried to observe you while you were undressing, nude, or in a sexual act	2.4 (105)	302	67.9	2.9	44.0 (133)	56.0 (169)
Anyone, without your consent, showed other people or played for other people photographs, videotapes, or audiotapes having sex or in a nude or seminude state	0.3 (15)	18	4.0	1.2	44.4 (8)	55.6 (10)
Anyone, without your consent, photographed, videotaped, or audio taped you having sex or in a nude or seminude state or in a nude or seminude state	0.2 (8)	9	2.0	1.1	77.8 (7)	22.2 (2)

[a] The distributions for the number of victimization variables are right censored because they include the value "97 or more."

89

Future research should explore the implications of this finding for NCVS. As noted, it was not determined whether using a number of behaviorally specific screen questions tends to increase estimates of only rape or whether the technique would also increase estimates of other types of victimization (i.e., the more widely in scope and the more closely in detail that possible victimizations are probed, the more victims are prompted to report their victimization to interviewers). However, assuming that the methodology used in this study is defensible, it seems likely that NCVS underestimates the true incidence of rape victimization in the United States.

We should note, however, one other possible factor that might have contributed to the differences in victimization between the main and comparison components: the "context" of two surveys. In the main component of NCWSV, the respondents were instructed in an initial contact letter and in instructions during the interview that the survey was focusing on "unwanted sexual experiences." In contrast, the comparison component was patterned after NCVS, which is a crime survey. In this part of the study, respondents were sent an initial letter that mentioned the "increasing concern about criminal victimizations that women may experience during college," and the interview itself contained questions measuring victimization by other types of criminal offenses. It is conceivable, therefore, that respondents on the main component study were sensitized to report a broad range of sexual victimization incidents they experienced, while those on the NCVS-based comparison component limited their reports to the incidents they defined as criminal. If so, this contextual difference would mean that the comparison component was measuring a much narrower domain of sexual victimization. One caution in this line of reasoning is that, as discussed previously, nearly half of the completed rape victims defined their victimization as a "rape," a clear criminal offense. Even when the count of rape victims is limited to this group, the prevalence of rape victims is several times greater in the main component than in the comparison components. Still, the impact of survey context on respondents' responses to sexual victimization questions remains an area that warrants further research.

Of course, many other methodological issues in addition to the use of behaviorally specific screen questions and survey context will have to be addressed in the quest to design surveys capable of achieving more accurate estimates of rape and other forms of sexual victimization. These would include, but not be limited to, issues such as the differential meaning that words used in questions might have to respondents, the impact of the sequencing of questions on answers, the use of more verbatim descriptions of victimization incidents in coding "what happened" in a sexual assault, and perhaps the use of computer-aided personal interviewing as a means of encouraging respondents to disclose traumatic events. In short, systematic, rigorous experimental research into the factors that affect victim responses and, in turn, victimization estimates—especially in the sensitive area of rape and sexual assault—remains in its beginning stages.

Although exceptions exist, most sexual victimizations occur when college women are alone with a man they know, at night, and in the privacy of a residence. Most women attempt to take protective actions against their assailants but are then reluctant to report their victimization to the police. Although based on fewer cases, these same patterns were found as well in the comparison component survey, which used NCVS methodology.[37] The analysis also revealed that some college women were more at risk of being victimized than others. Several factors appeared to increase various types of victimization: living on campus, being unmarried, getting drunk frequently, and experiencing prior sexual victimization.

Finally, in the aftermath of this study, an important challenge remains: taking the information found and developing programs and policies that may reduce female students' risk of victimization. Minor forms of sexual victimization—sexist statements, harassing catcalls, sexually tainted whistles—appear to be commonplace. How can a more civil environment be achieved without compromising free speech? Much is known about the circumstances under which sexual victimization, including rape, most often occurs. How can this information be used in crime prevention programs, including rape awareness seminars designed for women or rape prevention seminars designed for men? Furthermore, the relatively high prevalence of stalking—a form of victimization often ignored by college officials—is cause for concern. What strategies can women use to prevent or end stalking? What programs might colleges implement to control or counsel men who stalk? More generally, how can the lives of college women—whether on, close to, or off campus—be made safer and thus free from the costs imposed by the experience of sexual victimization?

NOTES

1. Bonnie S. Fisher et al., "Crime in the ivory tower: The level and sources of student victimization," *Criminology* 36 (1998): 671–710.
2. Walter DeKeseredy and Katharine Kelly, "The Incidence and Prevalence of Women Abuse in Canadian University and College Dating Relationships," *Canadian Journal of Sociology* 18 (1993): 137–159; Fisher et al., "Crime in the Ivory Tower"; Mary P. Koss, Christine A. Gidycz, and Nadine Wisniewski, "The Scope of Rape: Incidence and Prevalence of Sexual Aggression and Victimization in a National Sample of Higher Education Students," *Journal of Counseling and Clinical Psychology* 55 (1987): 162–170.
3. John J. Sloan, Bonnie S. Fisher, and Francis T. Cullen, "Assessing the Student Right-to-Know and Campus Security Act of 1990: An Analysis of the Victim Reporting Practices of College and University Students," *Crime and Delinquency* 43 (1997): 248–268.
4. "The Jeanne Clery Act Information Page," at *www.campussafety.org* (Security On Campus: College and University Campus Safety Information On-Line, maintained by Security on Campus, Inc., King of Prussia, Pennsylvania, 2000).
5. Bonnie S. Fisher, "Campus Crime and Fear of Victimization: Judicial, Legislative, and Administrative Responses," *The Annals of the American Academy of Political and Social Science* 539 (1995): 85–101; Michael C. Griffaton, "State-Level Initiatives and Campus Crime," in *Campus Crime: Legal, Social, and Policy Perspectives,* edited by Bonnie S. Fisher and John J. Sloan III (Springfield, IL: Charles C. Thomas, 1995).
6. "Justice Department Awards $8.1 Million to Colleges and Universities to Combat Violence Against Women," edited by Daniel S. Carter, at *www.campussafety.org* (Security on Campus: College and University Campus Safety Information On-Line, maintained by Security on Campus, Inc., King of Prussia, Pennsylvania, 2000).
7. DeKeseredy and Kelly, "The Incidence and Prevalence of Women Abuse"; Fisher et al., "Crime in the Ivory Tower"; Koss et al., "The Scope of Rape."
8. In the comparison component, the screen questions and incident questions were virtually identical to those used in NCVS. In designing the comparison component, two minor changes were made to NCVS. First, slight word changes or additional

responses to the response sets of questions in the incident report were made to capture plausible response from a college student sample. For example, to determine to which authority the victim reported the victimization, "campus police" was included in the response set. Second, a few questions were added to the NCVS incident report. For example, questions about offender characteristics included a question about fraternity membership.

9. Most of the sample (*n* = 4,446) were full-time students (90.1 percent) and undergraduates (86.1 percent). Freshmen at 4-year schools/first-year students at 2-year schools made up 24.2 percent of the sample; sophomores at 4-year schools/second-year students at 2-year schools, 22.0 percent; juniors, 17.5 percent; seniors, 22.4 percent; graduate students, 12.1 percent; and others (postdoctorate, continuing education, certification programs), 1.7 percent. As expected, the sample was youthful: Slightly more than 76 percent of the sample was between the ages of 17 and 22 years (mean = 21.54, standard deviation = 4.25). Most of the sample were white, non-Hispanic (80.6 percent), followed by African American, non-Hispanic (7.0 percent), Hispanic (6.2 percent), Asian/Pacific Islander, non-Hispanic (3.4 percent), American Indian/Alaska Native, non-Hispanic (0.8 percent), and mixed or other (1.5 percent). Less than 1 percent (0.5) of respondents refused or did not know their race or ethnicity.

10. The interview was conducted by the firm of Shulman, Ronca, and Bucuvalas, Inc., and lasted an average of 25.9 minutes. This is the same firm that Tjaden and Thoennes (1998) employed for the National Violence Against Women Study.

11. Bonnie S. Fisher and Francis T. Cullen, *The Extent and Nature of Sexual Victimization among College Women: Results from a National-Level Study* (unpublished report, Washington, DC: U.S. Department of Justice, National Institute of Justice, 1999); Bonnie S. Fisher and Francis T. Cullen, "Measuring the Sexual Victimization of Women: Evolution, Current Controversies and Future Research," in *Criminal Justice 2000, Volume 4: Measurement and Analysis of Crime,* edited by David Duffee (Washington, DC: U.S. Department of Justice, National Institute of Justice, 2000).

12. Dean G. Kilpatrick, Christine N. Edmunds, and Anne Seymour, *Rape in America: A Report to the Nation* (Arlington, VA: National Victim Center, 1992).

13. Patricia Tjaden and Nancy Thoennes, *Stalking in America: Findings from the National Violence against Women Survey, Research in Brief* (Washington, DC: U.S. Department of Justice, National Institute of Justice, 1998, NCJ 169592).

14. Questionnaires are available in portable document format (pdf) files from the BJS Web site, at *www.ojp.usdoj.gov/bjs/quest.htm* (July 24, 2000).

15. Koss et al., "The Scope of Rape."

16. The minimum reference period was 6 months, and the maximum was 8 months (standard deviation = 20.3 days).

17. Nonundergraduates made up 13.8 percent of the sample. They included graduate students, postdoctorate fellows, continuing education students, certification students, and others.

18. These projections are suggestive. To assess accurately the victimization risk for women throughout a college career, longitudinal research following a cohort of female students across time is needed.

19. Bonnie S. Fisher and Frances T. Cullen, *Violent Victimization against College Women: Results from a National-Level Study* (unpublished report, Washington, DC: U.S. Department of Justice, Bureau of Justice Statistics, 1999).

20. The interviews lasted, on average, 12.7 minutes. Most of the sample (*N* = 4,432) were full-time students (89.3 percent) and undergraduates (82.1 percent). Freshmen at 4-year schools/first-year students at 2-year schools made up 19.9 percent of the sample; sophomores at 4-year schools/second-year students at 2-year schools, 19.5 percent; juniors, 17.3 percent; seniors, 25.4 percent; graduate students, 16.6 percent; and others (postdoctorate, continuing education, certification programs), 1.6 percent.

As expected, the sample was youthful; 61 percent of the sample was between the ages of 17 and 22 years (mean = 23.18, standard deviation = 4.79). Most of the sample was white, non-Hispanic (81.6 percent), followed by African American, non-Hispanic (6.9 percent), Hispanic (5.1 percent), Asian/Pacific Islander, non-Hispanic (3.5 percent), American Indian/Alaska Native, non-Hispanic (0.7 percent), and mixed or other (1.8 percent). Less than 1 percent (0.5) of respondents refused or did not know their race or ethnicity.

21. Some of the incident-level questions had to be modified to reflect the characteristics of a college sample. For example, locations where an incident occurred included on-campus locations, such as a residence hall room or the library.

22. Personal communication with Jan Chaiken and Michael Rand, April 14, 2000.

23. In the comparison component study, we collected verbatim responses for all incidents. We subsequently explored how the use of verbatim responses can potentially affect estimates of completed rape, attempted rape, and threat of rape. See Fisher and Cullen, *Criminal Justice 2000.*

24. DeKeseredy and Kelly, "The Incidence and Prevalence of Women Violence"; Koss et al., "The Scope of Rape"; Nancy A. Crowell and Ann W. Burgess, editors, *Understanding Violence against Women,* by the Panel on Violence Against Women, National Research Council (Washington, DC: National Academy Press, 1996).

25. Tjaden and Thoennes, *Stalking in America.*

26. Rape victims also have screened into an incident report based on a "yes" to other sexual victimization screen questions (Fisher and Cullen, *Criminal Justice 2000*).

27. Neil Gilbert, "Advocacy Research and Social Policy," in *Crime and Justice: A Review of Research,* edited by Michael Tonry (Chicago: University of Chicago Press, 1997).

28. Mary P. Koss, "The Underdetection of Rape: Methodological Choices Influence Incidence Estimates," *Journal of Social Issues* 48 (1992): 61–75; Mary P. Koss, "The Measurement of Rape Victimization in Crime Surveys," *Criminal Justice and Behavior* 23 (1996): 55–69.

29. Victoria L. Pitts and Martin D. Schwartz, "Promoting Self-Blame in Hidden Rape Cases," *Humanity and Society* 17(4) (1993): 383–398.

30. Elizabeth Ehrhardt Mustaine and Richard Tewksbury, "A Routine Activity Theory Explanation of Women's Stalking Victimizations," *Violence Against Women* 5(1) (1999): 43–62.

31. Mustaine and Tewksbury provide no definition of stalking. Instead, to operationalize stalking, surveyed respondents were asked whether, during the prior 6 months, they had been a victim of behavior that they defined as stalking.

32. Tjaden and Thoennes, *Stalking in America.*

33. Ibid.

34. Of the 696 incidents, in 11 incidents the respondents refused to discuss the incident, and in 13 incidents the respondents did not tell us the form(s) of the stalking behavior. Reported percentages are based on 672 incidents.

35. Ibid.

36. Gilbert, "Advocacy Research and Social Policy."

37. Fisher and Cullen, *Violent Victimization among College Women.*

MISUSE OF THE INTERNET BY PEDOPHILES: IMPLICATIONS FOR LAW ENFORCEMENT AND PROBATION PRACTICE*

Keith F. Durkin

INTRODUCTION

Child sexual abuse is widely recognized as an especially serious problem in the United States. A voluminous body of scientific literature indicates that children who are sexually molested suffer a variety of physical, psychological, and social damage because of their victimization (see Browne & Finkelhor, 1986; Burgess & Lottes, 1988; Conte & Berliner, 1988; Lurigio et al., 1995). Adults who sexually abuse children are considered to be among the most serious deviants in our society. Consequently, they often come to the attention of criminal justice agencies. Because of prison overcrowding, probation is a common punishment for child sex abusers. However, the supervision of individuals who have been convicted of sexually abusing children poses serious challenges to probation departments since these individuals are difficult to manage and frequently recidivate (Lurigio et al., 1995). Recent developments involving the misuse of the Internet by pedophiles—adult males whose sexual preference is for children[1]—further complicate this already problematic situation.

Advances in telecommunication technology have made possible the existence of vast computer networks collectively referred to as the Internet or the "information superhighway." An estimated 30 to 40 million people in more than 160 nations have access to the Internet (Elmer-Dewitt, 1995). This global network consists of tens of thousands of interconnected computer networks, including those at academic, government, and business facilities, as well as commercial online services (e.g., America Online, Prodigy, and Compuserve) and private bulletin board systems. There appear to be four ways in which pedophiles are misusing the Internet: to traffic child pornography, to locate children to molest, to engage in inappropriate sexual communication with children, and to communicate with other pedophiles.

---

*This article first appeared in *Federal Probation*, 61 (Sept. 1997), pp. 14–18.

The abuse of the Internet by pedophiles has received a modest amount of attention lately. Recent criminal investigations have led to the arrest of numerous pedophiles for trafficking child pornography and soliciting sex from children online. For example, in September 1995, as part of a law enforcement operation dubbed "Innocent Images," FBI agents arrested more than a dozen people for transmitting child pornography and soliciting children for sexual purposes via America Online, the nation's largest commercial service provider. The impetus for this investigation was the case of a missing 10-year-old Maryland boy who was lured from his home by online pedophiles (Marshall, 1995). In a statement about this investigation, Attorney General Janet Reno said, "We are not going to let exciting new technology be misused to exploit and injure children" (Swisher, 1995, p. A1).

The purpose of this chapter is to document the ways in which the Internet is being misused by pedophiles. Special consideration is afforded to the implications that these deviant activities have for law enforcement and probation practice. In a recent article, Davis et al. (1995) called attention to the need to control the computer access of child sexual abusers who are on probation. Although these authors briefly mentioned a few of the ways in which pedophiles are misusing computer technology, their primary focus was on the development of valid conditions of probation to limit or prohibit computer access for these offenders. The information presented here reinforces the need to restrict the computer access of convicted child sexual abusers who are on probation. An adequate understanding of the ways in which pedophiles can misuse the Internet certainly will be useful to probation officers in supervising pedophiles and to law enforcement personnel in developing investigative strategies to combat the problem.

PEDOPHILES ON THE INTERNET

One of the primary ways in which pedophiles are misusing the Internet is to exchange child pornography. Traditionally, pedophiles would traffic this material via clandestine newsletters or other tightly controlled exchange networks (Carter, 1995). Now pornographic pictures can be transmitted through computer networks. For instance, in a 1993 law enforcement effort called "Operation Long Arm," federal agents served over 30 warrants against individuals who were using computer networks to import illegal child pornography from Denmark (Durkin & Bryant, 1995). Pedophiles also can obtain text stories with pedophiliac themes from the Internet. Although such textual descriptions of children participating in various types of sexual activities are not illegal, pedophiles collect these narratives for prurient purposes (Lanning, 1992). These stories are fairly common on the Internet. One study estimated that they comprised approximately 10 percent of the content of one of the major Internet newsgroups dedicated to "erotica" (Williams & McShane, 1995).

A trend of particular concern is pedophiles' use of the Internet to locate children to molest. One prosecuting attorney remarked that "instead of hanging around the playground looking for the loneliest kid, potential child molesters simply have to log on" (Kantrowitz et al., 1994, p. 40). Through the chat rooms available on many commercial Internet services, some pedophiles seek to contact youngsters to arrange meetings for sexual purposes.[2]

Consequently, the number of reports of children being molested by pedophiles they met via the Internet is growing. Recently, "a number of people have been arrested for traveling across state lines to meet undercover agents posing as minors they had met on-line" (Swisher, 1995, p. A13).

Another way in which pedophiles are misusing the Internet is to engage in inappropriate sexual communication with children. The anonymity of the Internet affords a pedophile the ability to misrepresent his identity. He can assume the identity of a young person and attempt to engage in sexually explicit online discussions with youngsters that he meets in computer chat rooms. Moreover, there also have been reports of children who use the Internet receiving unsolicited computer files containing pornographic pictures that were sent to them by adult users (Rubenstein, 1996).

Pedophiles also can use the Internet to correspond with each other. Regarding this communicative potential of computer networks, Lanning (1992) wrote,

> There is a modern invention that is of invaluable assistance to the pedophile: the computer. . . . Now instead of putting a stamp on a letter or package, they can use their computers to exchange information (p. 30).

This communication can transpire via chat rooms or Internet newsgroups dedicated to discussions for pedophiles, as well as directly through e-mail. One particularly noteworthy example of this phenomenon is the Usenet newsgroup alt.support.boy-lovers.[3] According to this newsgroup's frequently asked questions list (FAQ), which is regularly posted to acquaint new users with the purpose of this particular computer forum.

Alt.support.boy-lovers is a forum for males to discuss their feelings toward boys. It is intended to provide a sense of peer support for those having difficulties with their feelings, for boy-lovers who feel isolated with their orientation, and for those who have no other avenue of discussion than via a group such as this. This Internet newsgroup receives between 150 and 200 message postings each month.

Durkin (1996) examined a sample of this newsgroup's postings. He determined that this computer forum serves two major functions for pedophiles. First, it appears to serve a validation function for its users. Pedophiles have a need for such validation (Lanning, 1992). Individuals who posted to this newsgroup frequently provided advice and encouragement to other users. Some pedophiles posted messages in which they sought personal support from other users. For instance, one indicated that he felt so isolated that he was experiencing suicidal ideations. Another wrote of how his car was burned by neighbors who had discovered his deviant sexual orientation. Other pedophiles offered support and encouragement to these individuals in subsequent postings. Other users may conceivably receive vicarious validation from reading these postings. These pedophiles probably are not the only users who have experienced suicidal ideations or had their property vandalized because of their pedophiliac orientation. The support that these two particular pedophiles received may have provided affirmation to other pedophiles.

The overall tone and demeanor of this newsgroup also may serve a validation function. In the context of this computer forum, pedophiles are referred to as "boy-lovers." In fact, this newsgroup is called alt.support.boy-lovers. However, in the context of the larger society, pedophiles typically are referred to with such pejorative appellations as "perverts" and "child molesters." The use of the term *boy-lover* may help pedophiles maintain a positive self-concept despite such strong societal condemnation.

Durkin (1996) also found that this newsgroup appears to serve an information function for its users. A wide assortment of information of interest to pedophiles was regularly posted to this forum. There were frequent postings that provided users with instructions on how to obtain novels, poetry, and comic books for pedophiles via mail order or computer. Postings that contained information about the North American Man/Boy Love Association (NAMBLA) also were quite common. NAMBLA is a pedophile organization that advocates the abolition of laws regarding the age of consent, as well as the release of all men incarcerated for "non-coercive" sexual contacts with minors (de Young, 1984). This group, with an estimated membership of 1000, has its organizational headquarters in New York City and local chapters in Boston, Los Angeles, San Francisco, and Toronto (Vito & Holmes, 1994). These postings contained excerpts from NAMBLA publications, as well as information on how to become a member of this organization.

SIGNIFICANCE OF INTERNET MISUSE BY PEDOPHILES

The misuse of the Internet by pedophiles constitutes a significant development in the area of sexual deviance that has several problematic aspects. First, pedophiles are using the Internet as an outlet for deviant sexual gratification. Because of the existence of the Internet, a motivated pedophile now can obtain child pornography through his computer rather than via mail order. Most pedophiles derive sexual gratification from this material (Vito & Holmes, 1994). Additionally, pictorial child pornography, such as that available on the Internet, can be used as a tool in child molestation by desensitizing the victim to nudity and sexual activity (Lanning, 1992). One especially troubling way in which pedophiles are using the Internet as an outlet for deviant sexual gratification is to locate children to molest. The Internet affords a pedophile the opportunity to contact children from the privacy of his home and arrange meetings with them for sexual purposes. The apparent purpose of using the Internet to engage in inappropriate sexual discussions with minors is also of a sexual nature.

An additional aspect of this phenomenon that is significant is the fact that the Internet is serving as a social consolidation mechanism for these sexual deviants. Durkin and Bryant (1995) observed that the Internet can provide an enormous, and extremely rapid, contact network for people of related interests, including those related to sexual deviancy. Individuals can seek, identify, and communicate with fellow deviants of a similar carnal persuasion across the country, and even around the world. Information from deviant subcultures can be broadly disseminated, and interested new persons can be recruited (p. 187).

It normally has been assumed that most pedophiles are isolated individuals with little or no social contact with agemates (Prendergast, 1991). Computer forums such as alt.support.boy-lovers constitute a supportive social context in which pedophiles can provide validation to each other. This appears to be an unprecedented development in the area of pedophiliac behavior. Moreover, members of pedophile organizations such as NAMBLA can use the Internet to proselytize and thus expose hundreds of other pedophiles to their group's deviant ideology.

Another significant aspect of this phenomenon is the distinct possibility that the supportive social context afforded by the Internet may encourage some pedophiles to molest children. The Internet provides an unprecedented source of support and information for these individuals. There is the distinct possibility that some pedophiles may refine or act on their deviant proclivities because of their exposure to the Internet. Pedophiles who participate in these computer groups also may conspire with each other to victimize children. For example, two Virginia men used a computer bulletin board in an attempt to locate a young boy to use in a "snuff film" (Durkin & Bryant, 1995). Fortunately, a law enforcement agent was monitoring this computer service and discovered their despicable plot. When these men were arrested, police found that one of the two pedophiles had a supply of muriatic acid to apply to the youngster's corpse.

DISCUSSION

There are tremendous difficulties associated with investigating criminal activities regarding misuse of the Internet by pedophiles. As with most forms of criminal and deviant behavior that are related to computer technology, the actions of pedophiles have far outpaced the ability of the law enforcement community to respond effectively (Carter, 1995). Most agencies are simply ill equipped to deal with high-tech crimes (Coutorie, 1995). Since the misuse of the Internet by pedophiles is a relatively new phenomenon, most law enforcement agencies, particularly at the state and local levels, lack the experience and expertise to confront this problem. Although it is relatively easy for pedophiles to traffic child pornography on the Internet, it is difficult for law enforcement personnel to track this material (Reske, 1994). Moreover, whenever a pedophile uses a computer in an effort to find children to molest, he is typically doing so anonymously from the privacy of his residence. Additionally, because the Internet transcends geographical boundaries, criminal cases related to pedophiles' misuse of the Internet typically involve the jurisdiction of more than one law enforcement agency.

Davis et al. (1995) suggested that a key element in locating pedophiles "who misuse computers is adequate training and awareness by criminal justice agencies" (p. 47). A strong commitment to cooperation among members of the law enforcement community is imperative. Those officers and agencies with expertise in this area must be willing to share their knowledge with others. Such cooperation not only will be useful in disseminating information between various agencies but will help prevent any conflicts between agencies from different jurisdictions that may occur during the course of an investigation.

Although misuse of the Internet by pedophiles poses serious challenges to law enforcement agencies, it presents important opportunities as well. Investigators should be aware that any pedophile with computer access may engage in the type of activities described in this article. As Kosid-Uthe (1992) recommended, the search warrant for the residence of a pedophile who is suspected of involvement in illegal activities should specify computer equipment and files. This should be done whether or not the impetus for the investigation was illegal activities associated with the suspect's Internet use. This type of search can yield evidence of criminal activity such as computer files that contain child pornography. Computer files also may contain copies of correspondence in which the pedophile was trying to arrange meetings with children for sexual purposes. In a study of messages posted to an Internet newsgroup frequented by pedophiles, Durkin (1996) found that some of these postings appeared to be tantamount to admissions of child molestation. If a pedophile posted such a message, a copy of it may be in his computer files.

An important way in which the law enforcement community can combat the problem of Internet misuse by pedophiles is through educating parents about practical steps they can take to prevent their children from being victimized by online pedophiles. Parents should be encouraged to monitor closely the computer activities of their children. Also, they should forbid their children from giving out any personal information, such as the child's last name, address, and phone number, to anyone online. Moreover, parents should instruct their children never to agree to an in-person meeting with someone from the Internet. Parents also should be urged to report any suspicious activity (e.g., adults attempting to solicit sex from or sending obscene materials to their children) to police immediately.

Misuse of the Internet by pedophiles also presents problems for probation agencies. Probation is a particularly common punishment for individuals who sexually abuse children. However, these individuals are difficult to manage and frequently recidivate (Lurigio et al., 1995). Recent trends in Internet misuse present additional problems for the management of pedophiles who are on probation. The Internet may serve as a conduit for illegal or otherwise deviant activities that constitute a violation of the general terms of a pedophile's probation. He can obtain illegal child pornography or arrange meetings with children for sexual purposes through the Internet. A pedophile also can obtain text stories that describe children engaging in sexual activity via the Internet. Although this child "erotica" is not technically illegal, the possession of such material may constitute a probation violation. Additionally, a pedophile typically is forbidden from associating with minors as a term of his probation. However, a pedophile can readily interact with youngsters on the Internet. As previously mentioned, this computer interaction may include inappropriate sexual communications. For instance, a pedophile can assume the online identity of a 13-year-old boy and enter the computer chat rooms frequented by youngsters and attempt to engage in sexual discussions with them. However, these probation violations involving Internet misuse are difficult to detect due to the privacy and anonymity associated with computer technology.

A common disposition for convicted sex offenders is probation with mandated treatment (Furby et al., 1989). However, compared to other sex offenders, pedophiles are the most difficult to treat (Prendergast, 1991; Vito & Holmes, 1994). There is the distinct possibility that use of the Internet by pedophiles may undermine the treatment efforts that are a condition of probation. For instance, cognitive therapy is currently a very popular type of treatment for pedophiles. The target of this therapy is cognitions "that promote their deviant activities and allow them to deny, minimize, and rationalize their behavior" (Lurigio et al., 1995, p. 73). Cognitive therapies operate on the assumption that cognitions cause behavior (Jenkins-Hall, 1989). However, an offender on probation can participate in the Internet discussion groups that provide a supportive social environment for pedophiles. In a study of one of these groups, Durkin (1996) found that many of these postings contained statements that attempted to rationalize child molestation and pedophilia. Exposure to these forums would certainly be detrimental to cognitive treatment efforts.

It is imperative that probation officers are familiar with the various ways in which pedophiles are misusing the Internet. A pedophile can participate in illegal or otherwise deviant activities via the Internet that constitute a violation of the general terms of his probation. Moreover, there is a strong likelihood that the use of the Internet by a convicted pedophile may subvert treatment efforts. Consequently, it is important that the Internet access of a pedophile who is on probation be restricted. In order to construct specific terms of probation concerning computer use, the reader is directed to the insightful discussion of Davis et al. (1995) on this crucial matter.

CONCLUSION

Recent developments in computer technology have made possible the existence of the Internet or "information superhighway." While millions of people use the Internet, the misuse of this medium by pedophiles is clearly reason for concern. Pedophiles are misusing the Internet in several ways: to traffic child pornography, to locate children to molest, to engage in inappropriate sexual communication with children, and to communicate with other pedophiles. The use of the Internet by pedophiles constitutes a significant development in pedophiliac behavior. Pedophiles are using the Internet as an outlet for deviant sexual gratification and as a social consolidation mechanism. Moreover, the supportive social context afforded by the Internet may encourage some pedophiles to victimize children.

These developments present serious challenges to law enforcement. Most agencies are not prepared to deal with this problem. Furthermore, the activities of pedophiles on the Internet are difficult to detect. Adequate training programs and cooperation between agencies are needed to deal with the problem. Investigators need to be aware that any pedophile with Internet access may be involved in the activities described in this article. A careful search of a pedophile's computer equipment and files may yield important evidence of criminal activity. Also, law enforcement agencies need to undertake a campaign to educate parents about steps they can take to prevent their children from being victimized by pedophiles who use the Internet.

The misuse of the Internet by pedophiles also presents difficulties for probation agencies. A pedophile can use the Internet to engage in activities that constitute a violation of the general terms of his probation. The use of the Internet by a pedophile also may undermine the treatment efforts that are a mandated condition of his probation. It is important that probation officers are aware of the possible problems associated with the Internet use of pedophiles under their supervision. It is strongly recommended that the Internet access of any pedophile who is on probation be restricted or prohibited.

NOTES

1. The terms *pedophile* and *child molester* are frequently confused. The term "pedophilia" typically refers to a sexual orientation or preference (Faller, 1990), whereas the term "child molestation" normally refers to actual behavior. A pedophile is an adult "whose sexual fantasies and erotic imagery focuses on children as sexual partners" (Lanning, 1992, p. 2). On the other hand, a child molester is an adult "who engages in any type of sexual activity with individuals legally defined as children" (Burgess & Lottes, 1988, p. 6). Not all pedophiles commit acts of child molestation. However, even if a pedophile does not molest children, he may participate in related activities that are unlawful such as the possession of child pornography (Lanning, 1992; Prendergast, 1991). Although there have been a few cases of women committing acts of child molestation, virtually all pedophiles are male. For instance, Faller (1990) noted that she had never encounter a female offender who fit the definition of pedophilia. Therefore, masculine pronouns will be used to refer to pedophiles in this article.
2. Computer chat rooms are interactive discussion groups. These groups are "actually a window in which comments from many users scroll by" (Markoff, 1992, p. A5). Many of the commercial services, such as America Online and CompuServe, have these chat rooms. These chat rooms cater to individuals with similar characteristics or interests such as teenagers, senior citizens, or various hobbyists.
3. Usenet is a collection of thousands of discussion groups, known as newsgroups, distributed over the Internet. They are devoted to nearly every possible topic ranging from astronomy to yoga. Some of these groups are dedicated to discussions of sexual deviance. There are groups dedicated to nearly every conceivable sexual proclivity, including bestiality, transvestism, sadomasochism, and pedophilia. The user of one of these groups can read and post messages. These postings are organized in an archival format and can be read in a fashion similar to the daily newspaper.

REFERENCES

Browne, A., & D. Finkelhor. (1986). "Impact of child sexual abuse: A review of the literature." *Psychological Bulletin,* 99(1): 66–77.

Burgess, A. W., & I. Lottes. (1988). "Overview of child sexual abuse." In A. W. Burgess & C. W. Grant (Eds.), *Children Traumatized in Sex Rings* (pp. 1–6). Arlington, VA: National Center for Missing and Exploited Children.

Carter, D. L. (1995, July). "Computer crime categories: How technocriminals operate." *FBI Law Enforcement Bulletin,* pp. 21–26.

Conte, J. R., & R. Berliner. (1988). "The impact of sexual abuse on children: Empirical findings." In L. Walker (Ed.), *Handbook of Sexual Abuse on Children* (pp. 72–93). New York: Springer Publishing Company.

Coutorie, L. E. (1995). "The future of high technology crime: A parallel Delphi study." *Journal of Criminal Justice,* 23(1): 13–27.

Davis, L., M. McShane, & F. P. Williams. (1995). "Controlling computer access to pornography: Special conditions for sex offenders." *Federal Probation,* 59(2): 43–48.

De Young, M. (1984). "Ethics and the lunatic fringe: The case of pedophile organizations." *Human Organizations,* 43(1): 72–74.

Durkin, K. F. (1996). *Accounts and Sexual Deviance in Cyberspace: The Case of Pedophilia.* Unpublished doctoral dissertation, Virginia Polytechnic Institute and State University, Blacksburg, VA.

Durkin, K. F., & C. D. Bryant. (1995). "Log on to sex: Some notes on the carnal computer and erotic cyberspace as an emerging research frontier." *Deviant Behavior,* 16(3): 179–200.

Elmer-Dewitt, P. (1995, Spring). "Welcome to cyberspace." *Time* (Special Issue), pp. 4–11.

Faller, K. (1990). *Understanding Child Sexual Maltreatment.* Newbury Park, CA: Sage.

Furby, L., M. R. Weinrott, & L. Blackshaw. (1989). "Sex offender recidivism: A review." *Psychological Bulletin,* 105(1): 3–30.

Jenkins-Hall, K. D. (1989). "Cognitive restructuring." In D. R. Laws (Ed.), *Relapse Prevention with Sex Offenders* (pp. 207–215). New York: The Guilford Press.

Kantrowitz, B., P. King, & D. Rosenberg. (1994, April 14). "Child abuse in cyberspace." *Newsweek,* p. 40.

Kosid-Uthe, J. (1992). "Considerations in obtaining and using expertise search warrants in cases of preferential child molesters." In K. V. Lanning (Ed.), *Child Molesters: A Behavioral Analysis* (3rd ed.) (pp. 45–59). Arlington, VA: National Center for Missing and Exploited Children.

Lanning, K. V. (1992). *Child Molesters: A Behavioral Analysis.* (3rd ed.). Arlington, VA: National Center for Missing and Exploited Children.

Lurigio, A. J., M. Jones, & B. E. Smith. (1995). "Child sexual abuse: Its causes, consequences, and implications for probation practice." *Federal Probation,* 59(3): 69–76.

Markoff, J. (1992, March 22). "Sex by computer: The latest technology fuels the oldest drives." *New York Times,* p. A5.

Marshall, S. (1995, September 14). "On-line child pornography busted." *USA Today,* p. A1.

Prendergast, W. E. (1991). *Treating Sex Offenders in Correctional Institutions and Outpatient Clinics: A Guide to Clinical Practice.* New York: The Haworth Press.

Reske, H. J. (1994, December). "Computer porn a prosecutorial challenge: Cybersmut easy to distribute, difficult to track, open to legal questions." *ABA Journal,* p. 40.

Rubenstein, C. M. (1996, March). "Internet dangers." *Parents,* pp. 145–149.

Swisher, K. (1995, September 14). "On-line child pornography charged as 12 are arrested." *Washington Post,* pp. A1, A13.

Vito, G. F., & R. M. Holmes. (1994). *Criminology: Theory, Research, and Policy.* Belmont, CA: Wadsworth.

Williams, F. P., & M. McShane. (1995). *Erotica and the Internet.* Paper presented at the annual meeting of the Academy of Criminal Justice Sciences, Boston, MA.

CHAPTER 7

CONTROLLING COMPUTER ACCESS TO PORNOGRAPHY: SPECIAL CONDITIONS FOR SEX OFFENDERS*

Laura Davis, Marilyn D. McShane, and Frank P. Williams

INTRODUCTION

Sex offenders are one of the most controlled populations in the criminal justice system. Public demand often results in laws and agency mandates that require a higher level of supervision for this population. Starting in 1995, 12 new laws specifically targeting sex offenders go into effect in California. Included in these new laws are increases in penalties for first offender perpetrators of aggravated rape or child molestation, a state-maintained 900 toll number that alerts people to registered sex offenders living in their area, and restrictions against ex-sex offenders gaining custody of their children, including those conceived in the criminal act. The legislation also bars sex offenders from unsupervised visits with their children (Gillam, 1995).

A distinction must be made regarding pedophiles and child molesters. A pedophile is an individual who fantasizes about sexual contact with children while a child molester actually commits that act in some form. Therefore, although it is possible to be labeled a pedophile, unless one acts on an urge, he or she is not a child molester. According to McCary and McCary (1984, p. 225), approximately 30 percent of sex offenders are classified as pedophiles and most pedophiles are men. Additionally, most pedophile sex offenders are less aggressive than rapists.

Child molesters are most commonly divided into two groups. A fixated child molester is an individual who exhibits a persistent pattern of primary interest in children. A regressive child molester's sexual interest in children is a departure from a primary sexual orientation toward adults. Another categorization developed by Dietz (1983) divides child molesters into either situational or preferential offenders. Situational child molesters are defined as individuals who do not have a preference for children but engage in molestation due to low self-esteem or poor coping skills. They may be sexually

---

*This article first appeared in *Federal Probation*, 59(2), pp. 43–48 (1995).

indiscriminate and may exhibit a life pattern of using and abusing others including children or those suffering from psychological disorders, including mental retardation or senility. Preferential child molesters are pedophiles who manifest fantasies and active sexual behavior targeted solely toward children. The four major characteristics of the preferential child molester are (1) long-term and persistent pattern of behavior, (2) children as the preferred sex objects, (3) sexual fantasies focusing on children, and (4) well-developed techniques in obtaining victims (Lanning, 1992, p. 15).

PREFERENTIAL CHILD MOLESTERS

Preferential child molesters have a much higher probability of molesting a large number of victims per offender than do situational offenders. Hanson and colleagues (1993) noted that the risk factor for reoffending is much higher for molesters who select extrafamiliar victims. These molesters exhibit high levels of predictable sexual behavior known as sexual rituals and may have specific victim age and gender preferences (Lanning, 1992). Recidivism rates for same sex versus opposite sex offenders are mixed, with the best risk predictor appearing to be history of prior convictions (Hanson et al., 1993). Other research indicates that pedophiles who join organizations looking for victims are usually exclusively male and target male victims (Abel et al., 1994). According to McCary and McCary (1984), the rate of recidivism for homosexual pedophiles is approximately 13 to 28 percent. Additionally, the rate of recidivism among heterosexual child molesters is approximately one-half that of homosexual child molesters.

Several specific patterns of behavior and offender characteristics are present in most preferential child molesters. Extroverted offenders will use seduction to entice victims while introverted offenders, lacking the interpersonal skills necessary to attract victims, will employ covert methods such as obscene phone calls, exhibitionism, or the molesting of very young children. In much smaller numbers, the sadistic child molester must inflict pain or suffering on the child (Lanning, 1992). Characteristics of preferential child molesters include frequent changes in employment or residence, prior arrests, and multiple victims. The profile of a pedophile is an individual who is for the most part male, over 25 years of age, single and never married who lives alone or with parents, has an excessive interest in and associates mainly with children, and has increased access to children (Hanson et al., 1993; Lanning, 1992). Becket and Kaplan (1989) found that 58 percent of adult offenders admitted to sex crimes committed as adolescents. A study by Abel et al. (1994) determined that offenders' awareness of their pedophilia occurred at an early age.

Most preferential child molesters "collect" some form of child pornography or erotica as well as nonsexual materials such as children's games, photo albums, and art work (Abel et al., 1994). According to Lanning (1992), the size of the collection is based on the offender's socioeconomic status, living arrangements, and age. The older the child molester, the larger the collection is likely to be. The material is kept in a highly organized, ritualistic fashion. Child molesters may also produce homemade pornographic, erotic, or nonpornographic matter that relates to children such as diaries, fantasy writings, personal letters, and telephone and address books. This material can be obtained in a number of ways including newsletters through pedophile support groups, detective magazines, and, most recently, computers and CD-ROM disks (Lanning, 1992).

COMPUTER CHILD PORNOGRAPHY

With the advent of the Internet and advanced computer technology, the potential for computer abuse has increased. Recently, an e-mail tip from a Switzerland source led police officers to an Internet site in Birmingham, England. A 3-month investigation led to the eventual arrest of the distributor after downloading revealed 60 pages of file names and images relating to child pornography (Sussman, 1995).

Most people, including children, have access to almost any form of electronic information. Contel has made cash assistance and advice on Internet use available to every public school and library in its service area (Van Curen, 1995). This may include a plethora of pornographic material, including photographs, pictures, bulletin boards, referrals, and "talk" networks. While erotic photographs of juveniles are relatively rare on the Internet, pedophilic stories are relatively common and have been estimated to constitute about 10 percent of the content of one of the major erotica usegroups (Williams & McShane, 1995).

Detective Bill Dworin (personal communication, January, 19, 1995) of the Los Angeles Police Department's Sexually Exploited Child Unit states that a primary concern in the department is the monitoring of Teen Talk, e-mail, Prodigy, and bulletin boards that are used by minors. He explains that many child sex molesters keep their "collections" in the computer. This includes the use of diaries, the viewing and downloading of child pornography, contact with other pedophiles through bulletin boards, and a potential for contact with children by accessing such programs as Teen Talk and e-mail. Detective Dworin notes that offenders skilled with computers may even establish passwords that are very difficult to access. Investigations by police and probation officers preparing pre-sentence investigation reports help assess the techniques pedophiles may use in perpetrating sex crimes.

INVESTIGATION

Lanning (1992, p. 31) states that an affidavit for a search warrant must "set forth the probable cause to believe that the suspect is a preferential child molester and set forth expert opinions concerning traits and characteristics of such offenders." If there is probable cause to believe that an offender is a preferential child molester, then it is also likely that the offender has some form of child pornography or erotica.

Detective Dworin notes that his involvement in an investigation may occur after a police officer has taken the original report or initially by his unit. The detective is alerted to possible misuse of a computer by an offender through either a search of the offender's home or from information obtained from the victim. For example, in a recent case a suspect had been visiting homes under the guise of a Department of Children's Services worker. The suspect would molest his victims and take pictures of them. An investigation of the suspect's background revealed that he was employed as a systems operator. Therefore, specific wording in the search warrant included confiscation of computers and computer paraphernalia. The offender's computer contained stories about his molestations, phony IDs, and pictures of his victims. Detective Dworin further notes that he has observed an increase in the use of computers by these offenders. Each case is handled in a "situation to situation" basis, however.

The pre-sentence report is also important in developing terms and conditions for supervision. The probation officer completing the report should review all information available including police reports, psychological reports, victim statements, and prior criminal history. Psychological reports will most likely include indication that the offender is a preferential child molester. Police reports may reveal a potential for computer misuse by the offender. Additionally, when conducting an interview with the offender, the probation officer should explore the necessity of the offender owning or using a computer, the offender's computer knowledge, and, if indicated in the police report or other information, what types of information the offender accesses, passwords or codes that allow access to the Internet, CD-ROM storage, and other relevant information regarding the possible use of the computer for storing pornography or for accessing victims. Only after a thorough investigation has been conducted can offenders be properly classified.

CLASSIFICATION

Hanson and colleagues (1993) note that accurate information about potential for reoffending is important to effective management of this population. The researchers found that rates of recidivism were highest for offenders who selected boys and lowest for incest offenders. Kalichman (1991) studied levels of psychological disturbance in 144 sex offenders who were divided into groups based on victim age. The researcher found that offenders with child victims were more emotionally expressive, lacking in self-confidence, and more self-effacing than offenders with adult victims, while offenders with adolescent victims were somewhere in the middle. Kalichman suggested that sex offenders' treatment strategies should differ based on the age of victims.

Marshall and Pithers (1994) evaluated several treatment programs for adult and child sex offenders. From the results, the authors suggested that classification of these offenders into subgroups may aid in future treatment methods or development of new models of treatment for particular offenders.

Not only is classification important to treatment agendas but also to management/supervision agendas. Currently, in San Bernardino County, probation supervision is given to child sex offenders based on penal code violations. Standard terms are assigned to all offenders who fall into this category regardless of any consideration of pedophilia or predatory behavior. However, preferential child molesters have a much higher potential for reoffending, and their primary targets will be children. Additionally, these offenders are more likely to collect child pornography or erotica. Therefore, a distinction between preferential child molesters and situational offenders could be made at an early stage in the process and specific management criteria imposed on these offenders on a case-by-case basis. As a result, appropriate terms and conditions regarding computer use and access may be determined.

TERMS AND CONDITIONS OF PROBATION

When determining terms and conditions for probationers, one must look at both the legal and practical aspects of enforcement. According to del Carmen (1985), there are four basic constitutional requirements for terms of probation. First, a condition of probation must serve the legitimate purpose of either (1) protecting society or (2) promoting rehabilitation. The second requirement involves the clarity of the condition. It must be clear and understandable to the probationer, outlining exactly what is expected of the offender. The wording of the term cannot be vague or ambiguous.

The third requirement is that the condition must be reasonable. It cannot be excessive or an unnecessary burden on the probationer. The legal test for reasonableness is that a majority of "neutral" persons would find the term reasonable. Finally, a condition of probation must be constitutional. Usually a term is challenged when it is extreme, excessive, or violates fundamental human rights such as religion, speech, and marriage (del Carmen, 1985).

In California, the authority to place term and conditions of probation on offenders is derived from Section 1203.1 subsection j) of the penal code. This section states that

> the court may impose . . . reasonable conditions, as it may determine are fitting and proper to the end that justice may be done, that amends may be made to society for the breach of the law, for any injury done to any person resulting from that breach, and generally and specifically for reformation and rehabilitation of the probationer.

Section 1203.1 has also been determined to limit the authority in which the court may exercise terms. *People v. Richards* (17 Cal. 3d 614, 619, 1976) states that a valid condition of probation must "serve one of the purposes specified in the code section."

The standard by which most terms and conditions are assigned in California are based on two appellate cases, *Lent* and *Keller. People v. Lent* (15 Cal. 3d 481, 486, 1975) states,

> A condition of probation will not be held invalid unless it (1) has no relationship to the crime of which the offender was convicted, (2) relates to conduct which is not in itself criminal, and (3) requires or forbids conduct which is not reasonably related to future criminality. . . . Conversely, a condition of probation which requires or forbids conduct which is not itself criminal is valid if that conduct is reasonably related to the crime of which the defendant was convicted or to future criminality.

In *People v. Keller* (76 Cal. App. 3d 839, 840, 1978), the court of appeals found that a revocation of probation based on a search of the defendant's premises and discovery of contraband resulting from a waiver of the defendant's fourth amendment rights was invalid. The defendant was originally convicted of a misdemeanor petty theft charge and the court imposed search and narcotics terms. The court of appeals stated that these terms were unreasonable in that they were not reasonably related to the misdemeanor crime for which the defendant was originally convicted.

In *People v. Hopkins* (94 Daily Journal D.A.R. 16574, November 24, 1994), a term of probation was considered unreasonable if it (1) is overly harsh in relation to the crime committed, (2) unnecessarily infringes on a constitutional right, or (3) is completely unrelated to the probationer's circumstances. Several terms of probation have been challenged in court, including drug testing, home searches, polygraph testing, birth control and parenting requirements, prohibition of certain types of music, and electronic monitoring.

Regarding home searches, the Supreme Court ruled that "although a waiver of rights under U.S. Const., 4th Amend., as a condition of probation, does not permit searches undertaken for harassment or searches for arbitrary or capricious reasons, a search condition of probation permitting a search without a warrant also permits a search without cause" (*People v. Bravo*, 43 Cal. 3d 600, 1987).

Controversial conditions, or those difficult to enforce, may be of limited utility. While polygraph testing may be a useful supervision technique for sex offenders (Abrams & Ogard, 1986), it may not stand alone as grounds for revocation. Likewise, attempts to "depunk" and "demetal" juveniles with specific terms of probation that include not listening to or wearing clothing associated with punk rock or heavy metal may not be constitutional or provide sufficient justification for revocation (Rosenbaum & Prinsky, 1991).

LIMITING COMPUTER USE OF PREFERENTIAL CHILD MOLESTERS

Obviously, a blanket term imposed on all child molesters would be neither reasonable nor constitutional. Additionally, a term prohibiting computers or computer material for particular offenders may be excessive when applied to the *Lent-Keller* test.

There is little dispute that many child sex offenders possess some type of pornography, erotica, or other material that focuses on children. A common term of probation for anyone convicted of a sex offense against children involves prohibiting pornography. Standard conditions used by the San Bernardino County Probation Department in California read

> Neither possess nor have under his/her control any "matter" (as defined in PC 311(b)) that is pornographic or that depicts or alludes to sexual activity or depicts minors under eighteen.

and

Not associate with persons/females/males under the age of eighteen, except in the presence of a responsible adult who is aware of the nature of the defendant's background and current offense, and who has been approved by the probation officer.

These terms could arguably also apply to use of the computer either to contact minors or to view and collect pornography or other "matter." However, the terms could also be considered too vague and ambiguous when applied to the computer. An offender could argue that contact through e-mail does not constitute an association or that he or she was unaware that the person contacted by e-mail was under the age of 18. Additionally, a "discussion" with a fellow pedophile on the Internet which included graphic language about fantasies may not be considered by the offender a violation of pornographic "matter."

Another standard term that may apply states,

Not associate with known convicted felons or anyone actively engaged in felony activities.

Obviously, this term would ensure that the probationer did not "associate" either in person or through the Internet with other "felons." However, as outlined previously, a pedophile is not necessarily a felon. Therefore, it becomes necessary to extrapolate on the terms and conditions to make them clearly understandable while attempting to keep them reasonable.

As discussed earlier, a preferential child molester is highly likely to collect some form of child pornography or other matter relating to children. Many of these individuals in a lower socioeconomic status may not have the means to utilize a computer for any reason. The first problem that must be addressed is the target population that does have the means and ability to own or use computers. This could occur either at home, in the scope of employment, or as a student. In order to determine an at-risk population, an appropriate investigation must occur before the court imposes terms prohibiting or limiting computer use.

Proficient classification and investigation, as outlined earlier, are imperative to a consideration of specific terms and conditions limiting or prohibiting computer use for an offender. The offender should first fit the classification of a preferential sex molester and, second, must have established a pattern of computer use that is directly related to his pedophilia and criminal behavior. A set of criteria would then be established that outlines term and conditions that apply to that individual. For example, a collection of adult pornography will not fit the criteria necessary for eligibility of a computer term. However, if a convicted offender was found to possess computer child pornography or other material related to children, special terms could be developed to include

Neither possess nor have under his/her control any "matter" that is pornographic or that depicts or alludes to sexual activity or depicts minors under the age of eighteen. This includes but is not limited to any "matter" obtained through access to any computer or any material linked to computer access or use.

The constitutional question here may be "under his/her control." However, based on the *Lent-Keller* standard for imposing specific terms, this term would be reasonable without being excessive as it is directly related to current or future criminality or rehabilitation of the offender.

Along those same lines, if a convicted offender had demonstrated a knowledge or ability with computers, or if he or she required a computer for employment purposes and also fit the criteria of being a preferential child molester and had a history of computer use for criminal behavior, the preceding term would apply. However, additional specific terms could be added, for example,

1. Maintain a complete, current inventory of his or her computer access including but not limited to any bills pertaining to computer access, telephone bills used for modem access, or other charges accrued in the use of a computer.
2. Submit a monthly record of computer use and bills to the probation officer.

In *United States v. Gallo* the court noted that "a condition of probation that is broad or ambiguous on its face may be illuminated by the Judge's statements, the probation officer's instructions or other events." A standard term imposed on all probationers should also be used to ensure compliance and address the potential for computer misuse:

> Cooperate with the probation officer in a plan of rehabilitation and follow all reasonable directives of the probation officer.

Many sex offenders will be placed on intensive supervision. The probation officer may apply the "cooperate" term by instructing the offender on possession of computer materials or computer use, including prohibiting contact with pedophiles or individuals who supply information regarding children through bulletin boards or other networks. The probation officer should give clear and specific instructions to the probationer regarding computer misuse and possession of "matter" and/or computer "paraphernalia" that may result in revocation and follow an aggressive supervision strategy including, if necessary, the ability to access and confiscate materials that may violate probation. These instructions should be monitored and documented in the case file. In order to apply the "cooperate" term to computer use effectively, the probation officer must have an above average knowledge of current computer technology as well as computer "misuse" by pedophiles in general.

Finally, the standard search term must be imposed on all preferential child molesters who fit the criteria.

It is unlikely that all preferential child molesters with a proclivity toward using the computer for their "collections" will stop their activities solely due to threat of revocation of probation if caught. Therefore, probation searches of homes, businesses, or other locations where the offender may hide materials is imperative. Again, probation officers conducting these searches must be knowledgeable about computer misuse, access to potential areas of misuse, and computer-linked materials that may place the probationer in noncompliance.

CONCLUSION

Pedophiles and child molesters will undoubtedly have access to computer networks that provide erotic materials as well as potential contact with child victims. Careful investigation and classification techniques will help establish valid criteria for limiting computer use without unnecessarily infringing on the client's legitimate technological needs. It is also possible that components such as polygraph testing may enhance supervision, allowing officers to question probationers concerning illegal computer access.

The key to finding and managing child molesters who misuse computers is adequate training and awareness by criminal justice agencies. Through accurate documentation and the ability of law enforcement agencies to recognize the offender who uses a computer to further his criminal activities, appropriate measures can be taken to prevent future abuse.

CASES CITED

People v. Bravo (43 Cal. 3d. 600, 1987).
People v. Hopkins (94 Daily Journal D.A.R. 16574, November 24, 1994).
People v. Keller (76 Cal. App. 3d. 839,840, 1978).
People v. Lent (15 Cal. 3d. 481,486, 1975).
People v. Richards (17 Cal. 3d. 614, 1976).
U.S. v. Gallo (20 F. 3d. 7, 1st dr., 1994).

REFERENCES

Abel, G. G., S. S. Lawry, E. Karlatrom, C. A. Osborn, & C. F. Gillespie, (1994). "Screening tests for pedophilia." *Criminal Justice and Behavior,* 21(1): 115–131.

Abrams, S., & E. Ogard. (1986, September). "Polygraph surveillance of probationers." *Polygraphy,* pp. 174–182.

Becket, J., & M. Kaplan. (1989). "The assessment of adolescent sex offenders." In R. Prinz (Ed.), *Advances in Behavioral Assessment of Children and Families* (pp. 97–118). Greenwich, CT: JAI Press.

del Carmen, R. (1985). "Legal issues and liabilities in community corrections." In L. Travis (Ed.), *Probation, Parole, and Community Corrections: A Reader* (pp. 47–72). Prospect Heights, IL: Waveland Press.

Dietz, R. E. (1983). "Sex offenses: Behavioral aspects." In S. Kadish (Ed.), *Encyclopedia of Crime and Justice* (Vol. 4) (pp. 1485–1493). New York: The Free Press.

Gillam, J. (1995, January 2). "California laws '95." *Los Angeles Times,* pp. A3, A18.

Hanson, R. K., R. A. Steffy, & R. Gauthier. (1993). "Long-term recidivism of child molesters." *Journal of Consulting and Clinical Psychology,* 61(4): 646–652.

Kalichman, S. C. (1991). "Psychopathology and personality characteristics of criminal sexual offenders as a function of victim age." *Archives of Sexual Behavior,* 20(2): 187–197.

Lanning, K. V. (1992). *Child Molesters: A Behavioral Analysis* (3rd ed.). Quantico, VA: Federal Bureau of Investigation.

McCary, S. P., & J. L. McCary. (1984). *Human Sexuality.* Belmont, CA: Wadsworth.

Marshall, W. L., & W. D. Pithers. (1994). "A reconsideration of treatment outcomes with sex offenders." *Criminal Justice and Behavior,* 21(1): 10–27.

Penal Code Handbook of California. (1994). Altamonte Springs, FL: Gould Publications.

Rosenbaum, J. L., & L. Prinsky. (1991). "The presumption of influence: Recent responses to popular music subcultures." *Crime & Delinquency,* 37(4): 528–535.

Sussman, V. (1995, January 23). "Policing cyberspace." *U.S. News and World Reports,* pp. 55–60.

Williams, F. R., & M. McShane. (1995). *Erotica and the Internet.* Paper presented at the annual meeting of the Academy of Criminal Justice Sciences. Boston, MA.

Van Curen, E. (1995, January 24). "Travel information superhighway to visit White House, China." *Daily Press,* p. A1.

SECTION 3

SCHOOL AND WORKPLACE VIOLENCE

Perhaps there is no greater concern for parents across the country than the safety of their children at school. With increased frequency, we are consistently hearing of new cases where a child has brought a gun or other potentially lethal weapon to the confines of our neighborhood school. Parents may well be able to protect their children while they are under their care and supervision; however, once their kids enter our nation's schools, they relinquish that responsibility to the teachers, principals, and other professionals that educate our nation's children.

Just as we expect our schools to be a place where it is safe to learn and grow, the same can be said of our places of employment. No wife, husband, mother, or father expects their significant other to be harmed at work. After all, how dangerous can it be to work in an office building, stock shelves at a local grocery store, or teach at the local community college? Despite our sometimes false sense of security, acts of violence in our nation's schools and places of employment do happen and often more frequently than we like to admit.

To explore this phenomenon we have chosen three chapters that relate to the topics of school and workplace violence. These three provide ample coverage to the major issues in these areas: that is, why kids take guns to school and what type of people engage in violence in the workplace.

To explore these issues, the first chapter, "School Violence: Causes, Consequences, and Intervention," explores the issue of school violence in great detail. The authors start out by making the point that our nation's schools are very safe. They cite several studies to back up their claims and even one study that states that the number of children killed at Columbine are killed in acts of domestic violence every two days. Included in this chapter is a discussion of the social and ecological context of schools that experience more acts of school violence than others. They claim that the research seems to indicate that schools in poverty-stricken urban areas are more likely to experience increased rates of violence than other rural or suburban schools. In essence, they argue that it is the community in which the schools reside that dictates how violent the institution will be. However, there are exceptions to every rule. There are many urban schools housed in socially disorganized neighborhoods that have not had a violent incident in the last ten years. The authors claim that this is more likely caused by the positive adult supervision and the blending of public and private resources in the schools to intervene when a youth potentially represents a problem. The authors conclude by stating that while there appear to be ecological forces that seem to serve as correlates of violent schools, there are no steadfast rules that one can follow. Violence in rural or suburban schools can be just as prevalent and deadly as those in the inner city if not enough resources are expended to supervise the children and provide them with positive influences and role models.

The second chapter, "Understanding the Relationship between Carrying Weapons to School and Fighting," takes a different perspective. Instead of looking at the differences between the neighborhoods and what schools are likely and unlikely to experience school violence, it examines the results of a survey of 934 middle school students concerning weapons in schools. The results of the study indicate that while some students do carry weapons to school for bullying purposes, they only do so sporadically. The authors claim that those most likely to bring a weapon to school are those students who have either been a victim of school violence or those that have witnessed this violence first hand. This finding suggests that if school administrators can curtail the number of fights in and around school property, then it is likely that the number of weapons brought onto school campuses will diminish. Thus, schoolwide violent intervention programs may be more effective than simply installing metal detectors at the entry doors.

The third chapter, "Murder in the Workplace," examines the types of people that engage in workplace violence. In this chapter, the authors examine the characteristics of the disgruntled employee as the perpetrator of workplace violence. Great care is given to denoting the distinct qualities of this type of offender. Discussed are the motivation, anticipated gain, victim selection, and the relationship of the victims to the perpetrator of this vile type of crime. The chapter ends with a case study of Joseph Wesbecker, the individual who killed seven individuals and coworkers at the Standard Gravure Printing Company before fatally dispatching himself.

CHAPTER 8

SCHOOL VIOLENCE: CAUSES, CONSEQUENCES, AND INTERVENTIONS

Gordana Rabrenovic, Carol Goodman Kaufman, and Jack Levin

INTRODUCTION

School shootings in places as diverse as Colorado, Oregon, and Kentucky have made many people fearful for the safety of their children. A Scripps Howard/Ohio University poll, for example, showed that one-third of the nation's adults think that children are safer at a shopping mall or walking the streets than they are at school. Similarly, 81 percent of adults believe that children are safer at home than at school (Myers, 2000).

By sensationalizing dramatic episodes of violence, media pundits have fanned the flames of hysteria, and many communities have reacted in kind. Some previously peaceful schools are turning into fortresses, and school administrators are spending scarce financial resources on law enforcement measures such as metal detectors, police patrols, and surveillance video cameras to the detriment of educational programs and services.

Contrary to these popular beliefs, most schools are relatively safe places. Less than one student in two million suffers a school-associated violent death. According to the U.S. Department of Justice, 90 percent of homicide victims younger than twelve years of age are slain by adults, not other children. Indeed, "the number of kids killed at Columbine are killed in acts of domestic violence in just two days" (Myers, 2000).

In 1997, students ages 12–18 were more likely to be victims of serious violent crime away from than at school—about 24 of every 1000 students were victims of serious violent crimes at home, work, or on the streets. In contrast, only 8 out of every 1000 students were victims of serious violent crimes at school or getting there.

Moreover, most injuries that occur at school are not a result of violence. Among children (ages 5–18) admitted to a pediatric trauma unit or children's hospital for an injury sustained at school, 90 percent were injured unintentionally through falls, sports, and school equipment (*Annual Report on School Safety,* 1999, p. 3).

Not surprisingly, educational settings are generally safer because many schools have developed programs and policies to keep children safe and to address potential threats of violence. Schools provide adult supervision and in some instances use security guards and police to maintain order. Schools are also structured environments characterized by procedures such as how to move students in an orderly fashion from one place to another and how to engage them in organized activities.

At the same time, there are still 253,000 serious violent crimes in schools every year (Bureau of Justice Statistics, 2000). It is precisely because schools are expected to be safe environments in which children can learn that school violence is so disturbing. Most observers agree that decreasing levels of violence and conflict are necessary to ensure a school setting in which teaching and learning effectively occur. In addition, there are many acts of aggression in the classrooms and corridors of schools around the country that have not risen to the level of serious violent crimes but nevertheless impair the effectiveness of the teaching/learning process as well as the ability of students to feel comfortable, respected, and secure (Hernandez, 1999).

The effect of violence on academic performance is, of course, not limited just to the classroom. Pattavina (1999) reports a negative correlation between community crime level and academic performance among middle school students, suggesting that being surrounded by the threat of crime in everyday life affects a student's academic success. Moreover, Marans and Adelman (1997) warn that when their development is undermined by poverty, family dysfunction, and threatened or actual physical danger such as that prevalent in the inner city, children's feelings of competence and safety are also threatened. Psychic trauma can result.

In this chapter we first define school violence, consider why it happens, and discuss who is affected. Then we address school responses to violence and offer some suggestions as to how we can make schools a safer environment for all of our students.

WHAT IS SCHOOL VIOLENCE?

There is no clear definition as to what constitutes school violence. According to Furlong and Morrison (2000), "School violence is a multifaceted construct that involves both criminal acts and aggression in schools, which inhibit development and learning, as well as harm the school's climate." In this view, such violence can consist of anything from antisocial behavior to bullying to criminal behavior, including theft, assault, and even murder—and it can occur in classrooms, the hallway, the lunchroom, or in the school yard and school buses. Though not considered violent behavior, minor acts of aggression in the classroom and on the playground often escalate into major incidents of violence between students at schools. Brener and colleagues (1999) found that while aggressive behaviors may not always lead to physical injuries, they are associated with risk for injury, intimidation and threats, and perceptions of fear and vulnerability.

How prevalent is school violence and is it on the rise? In 1996, the National School Boards Association reported that 82 percent of school districts surveyed showed increasing levels of violence within their schools in the past five years. Sixty percent reported weapons violations (U.S. Dept. of Education, 1996). Similarly, Chandler and colleagues (1998) recorded an increase in reports of victimization during this same time period and correlated these reports with drug availability, street gang presence, and guns in the schools.

Levin and Johnson's (1997) study of violence in urban schools found that high school principals report spending virtually every day dealing with episodes of violence and conflict, often responding to incidents between students that may not be criminal but seriously erode the social climate. For example, bullying—which for too long had been considered a mere rite of passage for school children—is more often now seen as a serious problem, especially among the middle school population, where it can easily escalate into violent crime (Kaufman et al., 1998). Even at the high school level, there are numerous reports of verbal and physical aggression that reduce the quality of student culture and impair the ability of students to learn. Painter (1999) states, for example, that 50 percent of high school students have experienced racist comments, and 22 percent of female students have been sexually harassed.

The most recent data show, however, that school violence is beginning to decline. Between 1995 and 1999, the percentage of students who reported being victims of crime at school decreased from 10 percent to 8 percent. Students also seem to feel more secure at school as compared with previous years. Of course, not all types of school crime have decreased, but even the most intransigent forms—such as the number of students in grades 9 through 12 who are threatened or injured with a weapon on school property (7.5 percent) or who report being in a physical fight on school property (15 percent)—have recently remained constant (Bureau of Justice, 2000).

WHAT CAUSES SCHOOL VIOLENCE?

Some researchers have argued that there is a close connection between school location and school violence. Other researchers have examined school violence within the context of youth violence in general. Finally, there is a growing number of researchers who examine the relationship between school characteristics and school violence. The way in which schools react to the needs of adolescents, they argue, can facilitate or prevent violent student behavior.

The Impact of School Location on School Violence

Many studies of school violence have assumed that violence that erupts in school actually has its origins in communities and families exclusively and that little about school structure or policy has the capacity for having a major impact on the propensity of students to act violently. Advocates of this viewpoint have argued that, if anything, certain school policies and programs (e.g., tracking, labeling, or poor academic performance) might merely facilitate, rather than cause, delinquency among at-risk students. O'Reilly and Verdugo (1999) go so far as to state, "Nothing about schools causes students to behave violently or criminally." Indeed, some researchers have even suggested that those communities most severely impacted by school violence simply lack any viable organizations or resources for improving school safety and order

(Menacker et al., 1990). Hence, we see the National Education Association's equation, Safe Schools = Safe Communities + Safe Families, which leaves schools out of the formula except as a result (Hernandez, 1999; Menacker et al., 1990; Metropolitan Life Insurance, 1994; O'Reilly & Verdugo, 1999; Verdugo & Schneider, 1999).

Although violence affects all schools, those in inner-city neighborhoods are more vulnerable than their suburban counterparts. Data indicate (Binns & Markow, 1999; Conway & Verdugo, 1999; Kaufman et al., 1998) that urban areas are more likely than suburban or rural areas to have incidents of theft, violence, and serious crime. In some cases (Donahue et al., 1999), research shows that more than three times as many city schools report violent crime than suburban/town schools; this is more than twice the rate for schools in rural areas.

Similarly, Schiraldi (1999) reports that juvenile homicide is overwhelmingly an inner-city phenomenon. He explains that this is a result of the historically high levels of both poverty and the availability of guns. The United States has a child poverty rate three times that of 17 industrialized nations, while arrests for gun-related homicide are 12 times that of 25 other industrialized nations combined.

Notwithstanding the vulnerability of urban public schools to criminal behavior, it is simply not true that communities with high levels of poverty, unemployment, and crime inevitably produce unsafe schools. It is too often taken for granted that all schools within any given impoverished community will have essentially similar safety records; that any differences among schools in the same community will be minimal, at best (Hernandez, 1999; Verdugo, 1999; Verdugo & Schneider, 1999). As Menacker and colleagues (1990) declared, "Socially disorganized, crime-ridden neighborhoods produce socially disorganized, crime-ridden schools."

Laub and Lauritsen (1998) lamented, "Conventional wisdom holds that school is a reflection of violence in a broader social context, that is, violence is imported into the school by the students, and by intruders from the neighborhood surrounding the school." However, they go on to say that the relationship between neighborhood crime and school violence is a complex one and that it must be examined from all aspects, including that of the school.

Yet even in the most impoverished inner-city neighborhoods, safe schools do exist. Across this nation, schools whose safety and achievement records are comparable to those of their suburban counterparts (see studies by The Charles A. Dana Center, 1999) thrive, even where principals carry no baseball bats. In Worcester, Massachusetts, for example, the University Park Campus School situated in a severely impoverished inner-city neighborhood has had very few violent episodes. In Oakland, California, the Emiliano Zapata Street Academy is a public high school with virtually no fights, guns, or metal detectors, yet its students come from low-income families. In Dallas, Texas, Lincoln High School's crime rate is low despite its location in an impoverished neighborhood (average income is $14,354) where crime runs rampant. In Chicago, Whitney Young High School is situated in the inner-city but hasn't had a violent incident in the last 10 years.

A possible explanation for the existence of at least some safe schools in dangerous neighborhoods is that these schools have taken advantage of local support and resources. They have done this either by bringing the community into their schools (e.g., through partnerships with public and private sources), by bringing their schools into the community (e.g., through community service learning), or both. Important community resources include parents, teachers, clergy, grandparents, local college students, police, and business leaders. The University Park Campus School, for example, has collaborated with a local institution, Clark University, in a number of important programs and has recruited large numbers of parents to volunteer their services as tutors and mentors.

Moreover, recent incidents of violence in suburban schools draw back the curtain on the troubled lives of suburban teens. They also force schools and their communities to examine their practices more critically. Although urban youth are more likely than their suburban counterparts to be victims of violence, school violence potentially affects all schools, regardless of location.

In inner-city urban schools, violence and conflict typically arise in order to resolve disputes, protect drug markets, punish deviants, and reinforce a position of dominance in student subculture. By contrast, revenge was the primary motive in the string of massacres occurring in suburban and small-town schools around the country beginning in February 1996. Almost every tragic shooting incident in obscure places named Pearl, Springfield, Jonesboro, and Littleton involved youthful killers who had felt rejected and alienated by other people—most notably their peers—and decided to get even.

By far the largest school massacre occurred on April 20, 1999, in Littleton, Colorado. After months of careful planning and preparation, 18-year-old Eric Harris and 17-year-old Dylan Klebold armed themselves with guns and explosives and headed off to Columbine High School to celebrate Adolph Hitler's birthday. By the time their assault ended, a dozen students and one teacher lay dead. The two shooters then took their own lives.

Just as in previous school shootings, revenge was implicated in the motivation of Klebold and Harris. At Columbine High, the two friends were generally regarded as geeks or nerds. Though outcasts from mainstream student culture, they banded together with several of their fellow outcasts in what they came to call the "Trench Coat Mafia." Not coincidentally, they targeted especially the most popular and respected members of the student body of Columbine High. Their first victim was a popular black student athlete (Fox & Levin, 2001).

It is not an incidental fact that the recent shootings including Columbine High occurred at suburban rather than inner-city schools. For the last decade, the residents of small town and suburban America have tended to feel immune from what they regarded as big-city crime. As a result, as major cities were gearing up to fight teenage violence by eliminating guns and increasing supervision, small town residents failed to act. Most suburban teenagers—those who felt a sense of belonging and importance in their local networks—never knew the difference. But a relatively few potentially dangerous youngsters failed to receive the positive forms of attention that they so much craved. In a student culture where diversity is not always appreciated and uniformity may be demanded, those who are different tend to be marginalized and alienated. Some begin to see themselves as victims of injustice. When they open fire on classmates and teachers, they seek revenge against their tormentors and, at the same time, hope to gain a position of power and importance with their peers. In perpetrating the Columbine massacre, for example,

Harris and Klebold sought to get even with the students and teachers who had contributed to their feelings of rejection. Just as important, they attempted to create an image of power and dominance—the "Trench Coat Mafia," the gothic incivility, the forces of darkness, the preoccupation with Hitler, and the celebration of evil, Satanism, and villainy (Fox & Levin, 2001).

School Violence and Youth Violence

Another approach to explain school-based violence is based on examining school violence within the broader context of general youth violence. After all, schools do not exist in a vacuum—youth violence has increased dramatically over the past three decades. Prothrow-Stith (1998) has declared youth violence a major public health problem and has called for a multilevel, multifaceted approach, similar to that used for combating tobacco or drug use. Indeed, the long-term effects of violence are just as devastating to our children as are these other menaces and can include anxiety, poor academic performance, aggression, truancy, neurological impairment, and higher rates of crime (Hellman, 1983; Modzeleski, 1996; Osofsky, 1997; Perry, 1997).

Although official documents report that youth violence figures of the late 1990s are relatively low compared to the 1985–1994 period, they are still three to four times those of the 1970s, depending on age group, and unacceptable to a public clamoring for safe schools. Zimring (1998) and Fox and Zawitz (1999) point out that, although the violence statistics for four serious crimes (homicide, aggravated assault, rape, and robbery) are down from their all-time peaks in 1992–1994, the figures for homicide and aggravated assault—among the most violent offenses—are still far above those for 1980. Homicide arrests are double those of 1980, and aggravated assault arrests are 56 percent higher. Between the years of 1985 and 1994, murders committed by teens increased by a startling 170 percent. In other words, the figures are rosy only when viewed against the worst figures of the century!

The ease with which guns can be obtained is reflected in school violence as well. It has been estimated that 35,000 teenagers carry guns to school every day (Blumstein, 1995). Fear is a powerful emotion and breeds more fear. One student bringing a gun to school can provoke others to bring them, simply as a matter of self-defense. In fact, Sheley and Wright (1998) suggested that although a few juveniles did report that they carry weapons to gain respect from their peers, and a full 50 percent felt they could obtain guns easily, the vast majority of their respondents indicated their primary reason for carrying a firearm was self-protection. The Annual American Teacher Survey (The Metropolitan Life, 1999) found that 12 percent of all students carry a weapon to school.

The research on juvenile violence also shows the correlation between demographic characteristics of students and their involvement in risk behavior. Adolescence is a developmental period characterized by physical and emotional changes, unformed social skills, and high vulnerability to peer pressure. Adolescents enter a new school situation with many new demands on their intellectual skills at the very time they are pursuing new personal goals, including social affiliation, social identity, and autonomy (Fagan & Wilkinson, 1998). Osofsky (1997) describes children this age who, in order to gain a sense of belonging, join gangs as a substitute to family. This can lead to violence.

The onset of adolescence seems to be a point of which intervention can make a profound difference. Kaufman and colleagues (1998), citing the National Crime Victimization Survey, shows that total nonfatal crime at (or getting to and from) school among 12–14-year-olds is almost 40 percent higher than among 15–18-year-olds. Theft is almost 28 percent higher, and violent crime is a startling 49 percent higher in the younger age group. The Department of Justice stated that although adolescents make up 14 percent of the country's population, 30 percent of all violent crime is committed against them. And Brener and colleagues (1999) report that ninth graders (right out of middle school) were significantly more likely to engage in violent behaviors. The most recent Annual Report on School Safety (U.S. Departments of Education and Justice, 1999) demonstrated that teachers are more likely to be victimized by middle school students than by either elementary or high schools students for both theft and violent crime.

Most perpetrators of youth violence, and consequently of school violence, are boys (Hill & Drolet, 1999). In a study reviewed by the National Education Association (2000), violent boys were often rated as "popular" by both girls and other boys, whereas violent girls were only described this way by other violent girls. The authors explain this discrepancy as a result of the different socialization processes that each gender undergoes. Violence is still not acceptable for girls, while it has always been "understood" to be part and parcel of boyhood. Courtney (1999) further explains this phenomenon by describing how boys are socialized to repress their pain. Boys have no outlet to discuss any emotional issues they may have. Between this socialization and the raging hormones they experience during adolescence, and with the added factor of the availability of guns, boys are much more likely than girls to become violent. In fact, most school-aged killers are boys.

Using the Youth Risk Behavior Survey developed by the Centers for Disease Control and Prevention, Hill and Drolet (1999) showed that minority students, particularly Hispanics and blacks, are both victims and perpetrators of violence more than other students. Blacks and Hispanics carry weapons to school significantly more often than whites. Only Asian students carry weapons to school less often than whites.

The recent decrease in school violence may be explained in part by the decrease in juvenile violence generally. Researchers are exploring potential explanations for the decrease in violence-related behavior, such as improvements in economic conditions, stabilization of the crack cocaine market, reduction in the accessibility of guns, changes in legislation and law enforcement practices, changes in school policies and the school environment, and improvements in the quantity and quality of youth violence prevention programs. Declines in fighting and weapon carrying among U.S. adolescents after 1991 are encouraging and consistent with declines in homicide, nonfatal victimization, and school crime rates (Rener et al., 1999).

Fox (1997) has argued that the reasons for the recent decline in certain measures of youth violence may simply be a "market correction," a reprieve due to the healthy economy this country is enjoying. This period may just be the "calm before the storm," with an economic downturn spelling disaster. Other observers have said that the decline in homicide rates may have been a result of turf wars between crack dealers having left many of the leading players dead or incarcerated (Blumstein, 1995).

Cities like Boston and New York, which have had great success in reducing youth crime and violence, have inspired some criminologists (see, for example, Levin, 1999) to argue that there is another explanation for the dramatic decreases in overall crime figures. What have these cities—as opposed to Baltimore, New Orleans, and Detroit—done that others could emulate? Did they establish similar policies and programs, or did they reach similar results by following different paths? The explanation that still needs to be examined in more detail is that there has been a concerted, coordinated effort by certain cities to reduce crime and violence. New York has relied on "Zero Tolerance Policing" whereby the police have been asked to become more aggressive and confrontational. Boston, by contrast, has developed partnerships between law enforcement and local residents.

Adolescents and Schools

Many public health surveys show that the majority of high school students engage in some risk behaviors that pose serious threats to their health and safety. Some of the risks that students face in their adolescent years are smoking, alcohol and illegal drug use, violence-related behavior, sexual activity, suicidal behavior, and eating disorders. According to the 1999 Massachusetts Youth Risk Behavior Survey, for example, most of the common risks that students face are frequent alcohol use, cigarette smoking, marijuana use, and fighting. Also, the survey shows that these risk behaviors tend to cluster together. Therefore, students who drink are more likely to drink and to engage in unprotected sex as well.

What youth risk surveys also show is the connection between students' social and emotional level and their cognitive development. For example, 30 percent of Massachusetts's high school students report that "in the past year there had been a period of two weeks or more when they felt so sad and hopeless that they had stopped doing some usual activities" (Massachusetts Youth Risk Behavior Survey, 1999). Even more troubling is the connection between students' sexual development and their psychological well-being. Homosexual or bisexual teens report higher rates than their peers of considering suicide (49 percent vs. 20 percent), making a suicide plan (39 percent vs. 15 percent), actually attempting suicide (29 percent vs. 7 percent), or requiring medical attention for a suicide attempt (18 percent vs. 3 percent). As high as these numbers are, they are actually lower than comparable results from the early 1990s. In response to the epidemic of suicide by young homosexual and bisexual youths reported in a 1989 federal report on youth suicide, the governor of Massachusetts in 1992 appointed a Governor's Commission of Gay and Lesbian Youth. Although this commission worked hard to create a safe learning environment for teens in schools and universities, it came under attack and criticism from some parent organizations for addressing the issue of homosexuality in a public way. Here, we see the conflicting values that exist in the school environment about the appropriate way to address social development issues of children and adolescents.

Another group of students at risk for suicide are youths who, having been victimized at school, believe there is no teacher or staff member they can go to for help. About one-fifth of high school students (19 percent) indicated that they did not believe there was an adult at school that they could talk to if they had a problem. These teens were far more likely than their peers to have made a suicide attempt. The experiences of dating violence and unwanted sexual contact were also associated with suicides (Massachusetts Youth Risk Behavior Survey, 1999).

A source of conflict in many schools is the perceived or real problem of biased and unfair treatment by teachers and fellow students of students because of their ethnicity, gender, race, social class, religion, disability, nationality, sexual orientation, or physical appearance. The data on the prevalence of "bullying" or harassment among 11-, 13-, and 15-year-olds from the survey of Health Behavior of School Children in the United States shows that 15 percent of these youths had been bullied because of their religion or race. Over 30 percent of them had been bullied by means of sexual jokes or derogatory comments or gestures directed to them. There are more and more examples of sexual misconduct at earlier ages ranging from a nine-year-old boy grabbing his classmate's breast to a group of seven-year-olds being accused of forcing a five-year-old to perform a sex act in a bathroom (*New York Times,* 2000).

Although it has long been considered nothing more serious than a youthful rite of passage, bullying has more recently been recognized as one of the more disturbing and prevalent hidden crimes among young students. The National Association of School Psychologists estimates that 60,000 children miss school each day because they fear being bullied. Kaufman and colleagues (1998) report that bullying peaks in the sixth grade and is four times more likely to occur in the sixth grade than in the twelfth grade.

The bullies, according to a study of middle school student interaction by Dorothy Espelage (Hewit, 2000, p. A24) are not always the bigger, older boys or the short-on-friends misfits who struggle not to drop out. Instead, bullies are usually sixth-grade males who are among the most popular kids in schools; many of them are athletes. And their peer groups back them up with support and encouragement. Thus, bullying is actually considered "cool" in many circles. The bullies themselves, however, struggle with serious emotional issues and lash out at weaker peers in order to bolster their relatively poor self-images.

Bullying not only hurts its initial victims but also increases the risks for those who bully when their victim becomes desperate enough to retaliate in kind. Painter (1999) points out that many bullying victims bring guns to school. Moreover, Fagan and Wilkinson (1998) have argued that "bullying is a precursor to stable antisocial and aggressive behavior that may endure into later adolescence and adulthood." As we have discussed earlier, the students who committed the massacres at Columbine High School in Colorado had endured years of taunting and bullying, with the silent acquiescence of teachers and coaches, prior to their rampage. As a result of the recent string of school shootings by teenagers, there is now much more interest in studying the conditions under which bullies bully and their targets react with violence. Another interesting question is the role of onlookers or bystanders. In many schools across the country, students—mostly males—negotiate their social status in a group by establishing a pecking order consisting of bullies, onlookers or bystanders and victims. Usually in the majority, those onlookers who have respect for human dignity can play an important role in dismantling this pecking order, causing bullying to become devalued in student culture.

School Characteristics and School Violence

How do schools respond to student social and developmental needs? How do our school curricula address issues that are relevant for youth: bullying, racial prejudice, peer-to-peer conflict, gang issues, sexual harassment? We know that in order to create a safe learning environment for children we have to create a climate of tolerance in schools that will allow all students to feel comfortable, respected, and secure. A supportive school environment and policies facilitate the development of a positive identity of all students and allow them to perform to their highest potential. These goals are not easy to achieve because they force us to rethink how we envision schools as social institutions.

Schools are bureaucratic organizations based on hierarchical structure and dominated by rules and regulations that define school activities. Most of the early socialization of children in school is based on absorbing school rules and responding according to school expectations. As Brint (1998, p. 12) argues, "In schools, space and time are organized both to control students and to allow for psychologically useful intervals of separation between staff and students." This bureaucratic model of the public school is seen as the most efficient way to provide schooling to a large number of students and to socialize them to the expectations of a workplace.

However, this bureaucratic structure is also seen as a source of school conflict. Noguera (1995) argues that many of the current problems that schools are having have been created by an overemphasis on the need for maintaining order and control over students, as opposed to the need for producing a humane environment in which learning can occur. Similarly, Hawkins and Gaham (1997) argue that schools are often overly managed and have too many restrictive rules and regulations, which suppress adolescent development toward self-organization. This is why conflicts are most visible in middle and high schools.

What complicates the work of schools is that they frequently have conflicting goals. For example, there is currently a debate going on as to which needs—social or academic—schools should address more. Theoretically, they are expected to address them both. What is clear is that adolescents need to adapt socially before they can excel academically. As the U.S. Departments of Justice and Education stated in their 1999 *Annual Report on School Safety,* "fostering and maintaining an effective learning environment means creating a climate of tolerance among students. Determining how to achieve this goal will have ramifications for the future of youngsters now in school, for future generations, and for the communities in which they live." Based on a recent Educational Testing Service study, Barton and colleagues (1998) find that students in safe schools perform better academically than those in unsafe schools. However, although most educators support a developmentally appropriate, child-centered approach, the current emphasis on measuring school outcomes based on standardized tests is moving schools away from addressing students' developmental needs.

Many schools react to students' violent behavior by suspending them. Unfortunately, however, there is a strong connection between school suspension and dropping out of school. The Centers for Disease Control reports that "out-of-school" teenagers are more likely to have been involved in a fight, carried a weapon, used alcohol and drugs, or engaged in sexual intercourse than students who stay in school.

Another important element of school organization is the size of the school. Today's schools are huge. Since 1990 the number of high school students in institutions with an enrollment over 1000 has risen to 71 percent from 64 percent. Big schools can offer advanced-placement courses and expensive equipment for activities. As many studies show, however, in schools where students are grouped in smaller numbers (ideally from 400 to 800), alienation problems decline and students' sense of security increases. Consequently, many large schools are experimenting with the "schools within schools" concept, seeking to create a sense of community despite their large population of students.

RESPONSES TO SCHOOL VIOLENCE

What can schools do realistically to combat the scourge of violence? Many of them have reacted to real or perceived dangers by installing metal detectors, placing armed officers in the hallways and introducing surveillance cameras, drug-sniffing dogs, and random locker searches. Some schools have established safety lines or hotlines for callers to alert officials to drugs, weapons, and impending violence for both students and parents. Many schools have instituted "no-tolerance for bullying" and a tougher weapons policy. Overall, there have been many more school suspensions and expulsions.

Many school officials have taken a hard line on any sort of violence and are implementing zero-tolerance policies. Although such strict policies emerged as a part of the federal Gun-Free School Act of 1994, which requires states to establish a one-year mandatory expulsion for any public school student bringing a "weapon" to school, many local school districts went beyond that. First they expanded the notion of the "weapon" (defined by the Act of 1994 as a gun, bomb, grenade, rocket, missile, or mine) to include bicycle chains, screwdrivers, slingshots, pea shooters, and penknives. According to the National Center for Education Statistics (1997), 94 percent of schools reported the existence of a zero-tolerance policy for firearms and 91 percent for weapons other than firearms. Second, schools have implemented zero-tolerance policies for other forms of unacceptable behavior such as for alcohol (87 percent), drugs (88 percent), and violence (79 percent).

The important question, however, is who gets punished and for how long. There is growing evidence that minority students are more likely to face sanctions or to be punished more severely than their white counterparts. The longitudinal study of eighth-graders by the National Center for Education Statistics (1997) shows that African Americans were more than twice as likely to be suspended than white students. Although, in general, poorer students were more likely to be suspended than wealthier students, the wealthiest African Americans were still suspended almost as often as the poorest whites. Racial disparities in suspensions and expulsions are also supported by other data. For example, more than 43 percent of students expelled from Illinois schools in 1999 were black, though black students made up only 21 percent of the school enrollment (McDermott, 2000, p. A1). Between 1995 and 1999, the Decatur school district, in which only 46 percent of its students are black, expelled 57 students, 47 of whom (82 percent) were black (*St. Louis Post-Dispatch,* 1999, p. B2).

It should be noted also that schools' discipline codes define punishable behavior in subjective terms, such as "disrespect" or "defiance of authority." Minority students are more likely seen by individual teachers and administrators as being defiant or disrespectful and punished accordingly. Also, they are less likely to have parents who can effectively lobby for them to reverse a punishment. Therefore, school disciplinary policies can have a different impact on students of different racial and ethnic backgrounds.

Even the policies born of the best intentions may have unintended consequences that disproportionately punish a particular group of people. For example, the war on drugs began in the 1980s as a sincere effort to rid the streets of inner-city neighborhoods of crack cocaine dealers and users. In the process, however, hundreds of thousands of young black and Latino men were arrested and incarcerated for long periods of time while their white counterparts in suburban communities either went free or received much lighter sentences for essentially the same offenses (Tonry, 1996). Similarly, suspension and expulsion policies that were adopted to combat school violence in the 1990s resulted in a large number of suspensions of students who were disproportionately members of minority groups.

Racial discrimination thus is often an unintended consequence of seemingly benign public policies. Because black and Latino students are concentrated in impoverished urban neighborhoods with few resources, they are more likely to be affected by low-cost, quick-fix punitive policies. In addition, because their schools tend to be more impersonal and larger than suburban schools, minority students with disciplinary problems are less likely to be treated in an informal manner. They are also less likely to have parents who advocate on their behalf. Therefore, not only are students of color more likely to be suspended or expelled, but they are also more likely to drop out of school permanently because of the lack of viable alternative programs available to them.

Another way of dealing with school violence is to increase the support services for students who are in need of assistance. Social workers, school counselors, and psychologists are increasingly available in schools to help teachers, parents, and children deal with violence. In many schools, there are now conflict resolution programs, cultural awareness classes, group mediation, peer counseling, anger management, and programs to develop respect for and resistance to peer pressure.

Unfortunately, many schools address each risk separately. They might have drug councilors, dating violence specialists, and conflict resolution programs, all of which are rarely connected. Thus, there is a need to take a comprehensive approach to risk behaviors rather than to advocate specific programs for each of them. Another problem with existing programs—especially the ones that target high school students—is that they start too late. For some adolescents, risk behaviors begin well before high school. That suggests the need to start with programs in the earlier grades. The emerging number of programs at the middle school level shows the benefits of such an approach.

A fairly recent development in some city school districts is the alternative school. Presently available in more than half of all states, these programs serve students as young as five years of age, who have been assigned to them as a result of violent behavior in the classroom. They provide an opportunity for students to learn positive and appropriate prosocial behavior while attending academic classes and are seen as one part of the strategy for stemming school violence. According to the American Federation of Teachers (1996), for every $1750 spent on alternative schools, communities can save $18,380 per student. This includes money saved on student learning time, reduced grade repetition costs, reduced welfare costs, and reduced prison costs.

In addition, Levin and Johnson (1997) have pointed out that if programs are begun early on in children's education, they will become part of their be-havioral repertoire and will be more likely to be accepted as they get older. By starting such programs later, there is a greater likelihood of resistance on the part of jaded adolescents, who treat the programs as an object of derision. This is especially true of structured after-school programs that depend on parent and teacher volunteers.

Research also shows that when adult supervision of youngsters increases, violence decreases. By supervision, we mean the entire range of parental, teacher, and community involvement that builds a permeable, yet safe, boundary around the school and its students. Fifty-seven percent of the chil-dren in the United States have no parental supervision after school (Fox & Newman, 1997). In low-income, urban areas, it is much less likely that chil-dren have after-school programs and activities to attend, which would keep them busy, off the streets, and away from temptation (Levin & Johnson, 1997). However, Posner and Vandell (1994) found that those low-income children who do have formal, structured programs do better both academically and so-cially. Fox and Newman (1997) suggest that after-school programs can reduce juvenile crime significantly. Similarly, Painter (1999) argues that as the school reaches out to the community and as the community becomes involved in the school, a culture of mutual support and nonviolence will prevail.

According to Petersen and colleagues (1998), the cost of crime prevention in schools has increased dramatically, from the price of metal detectors and video cameras to the expense of replacing teachers burned out by stress. Yet there are studies that show clearly how the much less costly approach of en-hancing the bond between student and school is effective in protecting stu-dents from risk behaviors.

Research suggests that a school that invests in and supports conflict reso-lution on a consistent basis will reap the benefits of lower rates of violence. Particularly in urban areas with poverty, high unemployment, social immobil-ity, single parenthood, and a culture of gangs and drugs, it is only natural to respond to conflict in a violent way if that is the community standard (DuRant et al., 1996; Jones & Offord, 1989). Forty percent of teens report that gangs are present in their schools (Blumstein, 1995). However, we argue that when the school, parents, and the community together stand behind an integrated cur-riculum of conflict resolution and violence prevention, violence will be re-duced. This belief is supported by the findings of a landmark study (Resnick et al., 1997) that shows that students who have strong parental bonds, school connectedness, and high parental expectations participate in significantly fewer risky behaviors.

CONCLUSION

As we can see, schools are not hostage to their social environments, though they may be constrained by characteristics of their students and the neighborhoods in which they reside. Schools even in impoverished environments may also benefit from unanticipated human and community resources. What schools do makes an important difference in determining school climate.

Programs that work share certain characteristics in common: First, they adopt a comprehensive approach to violence, which includes developing sound prevention programs and procedures for intervening quickly when a student is in distress. Second, they start early and are part of a long-term commitment of the school. Third, they have strong leadership and disciplinary policies. Fourth, they emphasize staff development and consequently have competent and caring teachers. Fifth, they encourage parental involvement, making possible a consistent response between school and home to the issues of violence. Sixth, they create interagency partnerships and community linkages in order to provide more resources for children. And seventh, they use a culturally sensitive and developmentally appropriate approach.

Survey after survey shows how American children have become more aggressive, more impulsive, more disobedient, more lonely, and more depressed (Lantieri et al., 1998). The good news is that people's emotional and social capacities can be strengthened, especially at a young age. We need safe and caring schools and communities that enhance social and emotional learning and teach conflict resolution and value diversity. We need age-appropriate programs and activities that give young people opportunities to contribute to their families, schools, and communities. Also, we need to recognize children and youth for their capabilities and participation.

To achieve an optimal effect, school safety should be a schoolwide and communitywide effort. Our success will depend on our ability to develop trusting relationships among all parties involved. It will also require resources to support children's development by supporting families and communities where these youngsters live. Importantly, those schools with the largest number of at-risk students are also likely to need the highest level of resources for implementing comprehensive violence prevention programs. Unfortunately, these are the very schools that are now most lacking in resources.

REFERENCES

Agron, J. (1999). "Lesson Learned." *American School & University,* 1(11): 10.
Alternative Education Programs for Expelled Students. (1996). U.S. Department of Education. www.ed.gov/offices/OESE/ACTGUID/altersc.html

Annual Report on School Safety. (1999). Washington, D.C.: The U.S. Department of Justice and the U.S. Department of Education.

The Appropriate and Effective Use of Security Technologies in U.S. Schools: A Guide for Schools and Law Enforcement Agencies. (2000). Washington, D.C.: U.S. Dept. of Justice, Office of Justice Programs, & National Institute of Justice.

Barth, P., K. Haycock, H. Jackson, K. Mora, P. Ruiz, S. Robinson, & A. Wilkins, (1999). *Dispelling the Myth: High Poverty Schools Exceeding Expectations.* Washington, DC: The Education Trust.

Barton, P. W., R. J. Coley, & H. Wenglisky, (1998). *Order in the Classroom: Violence, Discipline, and Student Achievement.* Princeton, NJ: Educational Testing Service.

Binns, K., & D. Markow, (1999). *The American Teacher 1999: Violence in America's Public Schools Five Years Later.* New York: Louis Harris and Associates.

Blumstein, A. (1995). "Youth Violence, Guns, and The Illicit Drug Industry." *Journal of Criminal Law and Criminology, 86*(10).

Brener, N. D., T. R. Simon, E. G. Krug, & R. Lowry, (1999). "Recent Trends in Violence-Related Behaviors among High School Students in the United States." *Journal of the American Medical Association, 282*(5).

Chandler, K. A., C. D. Chapman, M. R. Rand, & B. M. Taylor, (1998). *Students' Reports of School Crime: 1989 and 1995.* Washington, DC: U.S. Departments of Education and Justice.

Charles A. Dana Center, University of Texas at Austin. (1999). *Hope for Urban Education: A Study of Nine High-Performing High Poverty, Urban Elementary Schools.* Washington, DC: U.S. Department of Education, Planning, and Evaluation Services.

Conway, D., & R. R. Verdugo, (1999). "Fear-Free Education Zones." *Education and Urban Society,* 31(3): 357–367.

Cook, P. (1998). The Epidemic of Youth Gun Violence. In *Perspectives on Crime and Justice: 1997–1998 Lecture Series* (G. L. Kelling, R. Kennedy, D. F. Musto, J. Petersilia, & P. Cook, eds.) (pp. 109–125). Washington, DC: National Institute of Justice.

Courtnay, W. H. (1999). "Youth Violence? Let's Call it What It Is." *Journal of American College Health,* 48(3): 141.

Crawford, D., & R. Bodine. (1996). *Conflict Resolution Education: A Guide to Implementing Programs in Schools, Youth-Serving Organizations, and Community and Juvenile Justice Settings.* Washington, DC: U.S. Departments of Justice and Education.

Deutsch, M. (1992). *The Effects of Training in Conflict Resolution and Cooperative Learning in an Alternative High School.* New York: International Center for Cooperation and Conflict Resolution, Teachers' College, Columbia University.

Devine, J. (1996). *Maximum Security: The Culture of Violence in Inner-City Schools.* Chicago: The University of Chicago Press.

Donahue, E., V. Schiraldi, & J. Ziedenberg. (1999). *School House Hype: School Shootings and the Real Risks Kids Face in America.* Washington, DC: Justice Policy Institute. www.cjcj.org/jpi/schoolhouse.html.

Dunn, M. J. (1999). "Critical Elements in School Security." *American School & University,* 71(11): 13.

Durant, R. H., F. Treiber, A. Getts, K. McCloud, C. W. Linder, & E. R. Woods. (1996). "Comparison of Two Violence Prevention Curricula for Middle School Adolescents." *Journal of Adolescent Health,* 19: 111–117.

Early Warning, Timely Response: a Guide to Safe Schools. (1999). Center for Effective Collaboration and Practice. http:/cecp.air.org/guide/annotated.htm

Etzioni, A. (1998). *Community Watch. What Can the Federal Government Do to Decrease Crime and Revitalize Communities?* Washington, DC: National Institute of Justice Research Forum, pp. 21–23.

Fagan, J., & D. L. Wilkinson, (1998). Social Contexts and Functions of Adolescent Violence. In *Violence in American Schools* (D. S. Elliott, B. A. Hamburg, & K. R. Williams, eds.) (pp. 55–93). Cambridge, UK: Cambridge University Press.

Fickes, M. (1999). "The ABC's of Security Technology." *American School & University,* 71(11): 2.

Fox, J. (1997). Preventing the Coming Wave of Youth Violence. *Congressional Digest, August/September 1996, 206–212.*

Fox, J. A., & J. Levin. (1997). *State-Level Trends and Variation in Teen Murder.* Unpublished paper, Northeastern University.

Fox, J. A., & J. Levin. (2001). *The Will to Kill: Making Sense of Senseless Murder.* Boston: Allyn and Bacon.

Fox, J. A., & S. A. Newman, (1997). *After-School Crime or After-School Programs: Tuning in to the Prime Time for Violent Juvenile Crime and Implications for National Policy.* Report to the U.S. Attorney General. Washington, DC: Office of Juvenile Justice and Delinquency Prevention.

Fox, J. A., & M. W. Zawitz. (1999). *Homicide Trends in the United States. Bureau of Justice Statistics Crime Data Brief.* Washington, DC: U.S. Department of Justice.

Furlong, Michael, & G. Morrison. (2000). "The School in School Violence: Definitions and Facts." *Journal of Emotional and Behavioral Disorders,* 8(20): 71.

Garbarino, J., N. Dubrow, K. Kostelny, & C. Pardo. (1992). *Children in Danger: Coping with the Consequences of Community Violence.* San Francisco: Jossey-Bass.

Heaviside, S., C. Rowland, C. Williams, S. Farris, S. Burns, & E. McArthur. (1998). *Violence and Discipline Problems in U.S. Public Schools: 1996–97.* Washington, DC: U.S. Department of Education.

Hellman, D. (1983). *Analysis of Violence in the Boston Public Schools: Incident and Suspension Data, A Report Submitted to the Safe Schools Commission.* Boston: Northeastern University.

Hernandez, T. (1999). "Community Building in South Florida to Promote School Safety." *Education and Urban Society,* 31(3): 368–374.

Hewit, Paige. (2000). "Focus: Coping with Conflicts; Slammed in Schools; Experts Pay More Attention to Why Bullies Intimidate and How Victims Respond." *The Houston Chronicle.* November 6, 2000, p. A24.

Hill, S., & J. Drolet. (1999). "School-Related Violence among High School Students in the United States." *Journal of School Health,* 69(7): 264.

Indicators of School Crime and Safety. (2000). National Center for Education Statistics and Bureau of Justice Statistics.

Johnson, D. W., & R. T. Johnson, (1995). *Reducing School Violence through Conflict Resolution.* Alexandria, VA: Association of Supervision and Curriculum Development.

Jones, M. B., & D. R. Offord, (1989). "Reduction of Antisocial Behavior in Poor Children by Nonschool Skill Development." *Journal of Child Psychology and Psychiatry,* 30(5): 737–750.

Kaufman, P., X. Chen, S. Choy, K. A. Chandler, C. D. Chapman, M. R. Rand, & C. Ringel. (1998). *Indicators of School Crime and Safety, 1998.* Washington, DC: U.S. Departments of Education and Justice.

Kennedy, M. (1999). "The Changing Face of School Violence." *American School & University,* 71(11): 6.

Kerr, J. (2000). *Violence Rises in California Schools.* Sacramento, CA: Associated Press, 2000.

Lantieri, Linda, Janet Patti, & Marian Wright Edelman. (1998). *Waging Peace in Our Schools.* Boston: Beacon Press.

Laub, J. H., & J. L. Lauritsen. (1998). The Interdependence of Social Violence with Neighborhood and Family Conditions. In *Violence in American Schools* (D. S. Elliott, B. A. Hamburg, & K. R. Williams, eds.) (pp. 127–155). Cambridge, UK: Cambridge University Press.

Levin, J. (1999). "An Effective Response to Teenage Crime is Possible—And Cities are Showing the Way." *The Chronicle of Higher Education,* 35, May 7.

Levin, J., & J. A. Fox. (2001). *The Will to Kill: Murder and Power in America.* Boston: Allyn & Bacon.

Levin, J., & H. Johnson, (1997). "Youth Violence and the Urban Public School Response." *Journal of Research in Education,* Fall, 3–7.

Marans, S., & A. Adelman. (1997). Experiencing Violence in a Developmental Context. In *Children in a Violent Society* (Osofsky, J., ed.) (pp. 202–222). New York: Guilford Press.

Massachusetts Youth Risk Behavior Study (MYRBS). (1999). Massachusetts Department of Education.

McDermott, Kevin. (2000). "Illinois Schools Expel Black Girls Six Times as Often as Whites; Critics Blame Southern Legacy, Culture Clash. *St. Louis Post-Dispatch.* January 19, 2000, p. A1.

Menacker, J., W. Weldon, & E. Hurwitz. (1990). "Community Influences on School and Violence." *Urban Education,* 25(1): 68–80.

Modzeleski, W. (1996) "Creating Safe Schools: Roles and Challenges, A Federal Perspective." *Education and Urban Society,* 28(4): 412–423.

Myers, George, Jr. (2000). "Echoes of Gunfire a Year After Columbine, What Have We Learned." *The Columbus Dispatch,* April 16, 2000, p. A1.

National Center for Policy Analysis. (1996). *Crime Costs.* www.ncpa.org/hotlines/juvcrm/eocp2.html.

National Education Association. (2000). "Portrait of a Young Tough." *NEA Today,* 18(8): 23.

National School Safety Center. (1999). *School Associated Violent Deaths.* National School Safety Center. www.nscci.org.

New York Times. (2000). "Maine Town Disturbed by Harassment Case," June 5.

Noguera, P. A. (1995). "Preventing and Producing Violence: A Critical Analysis of Responses to School Violence." *Harvard Educational Review, 65(2): 189–212.*

O'Reilly, E. M., & R. R. Verdugo. (1999). "Safe School Indicators: Theory, Data, and Social Policy." *Education and Urban Society,* 31(3): 334–348.

Orpinas, P., G. S. Parcel, A. McAlister, & R. Frankowski. (1995). "Violence Prevention I Middle Schools: A Pilot Evaluation." *Journal of Adolescent Health,* 17: 360–371.

Osofsky, J. (1997). Children and Youth Violence: Overview. In *Children in a Violent Society* (Osofsky, J., ed.) (pp. 3–8). New York: Guilford Press.

Painter, P. (1999). "The Washington Education Association Responds to School Violence: A Two-Pronged Approach." *Education and Urban Society,* 31(3): 349–356.

Pattavina, A. (1999). "The Influence of Community Violence on Child Development in an Urban Setting." *Research in Politics and Society,* 7: 163–182.

Perry, B. (1997) Incubated in Terror: Neurodevelopmental Factors in the "Cycle of Violence." In *Children in a Violent Society* (Osofsky, J., ed.) (pp. 124–149). New York: Guilford Press.

Petersen, G. J., D. Pietrzak, & K. Speaker. (1998). "The Enemy Within: A National Study on School Violence and Prevention." *Urban Education,* 33(3): 331–359.

Posner, J. K., & D. L. Vandell, (1994). "Low-Income Children's After-School Care: Are There Beneficial Effects of After-School Programs?" *Child Development,* 65: 440–456.

Prothrow-Stith, D. (1998). Revitalizing Communities: Public Health Strategies for Violence Prevention. *What Can the Federal Government Do to Decrease Crime and Revitalize Communities?* Washington, DC: National Institute of Justice Research Forum, pp. 59–63.

Resnick, M. D., P. S. Bearman, R. W. Blum, K. E. Bauman, K. H. Harris, J. Jones, J. Tabor, T. Beuhring, R. E. Sievings, M. Shaw, M. Ireland, L. H. Bearinger, & J. R. Udry, (1997). "Protecting Adolescents from Harm: Findings from the National Longitudinal Study on Adolescent Health." *Journal of the American Medical Association,* 278(10): 823–832.

Roehl, J. (1998). What Do We Do Next? Research Questions and Implications for Evaluation Design. *What Can the Federal Government Do to Decrease Crime and Revitalize Communities?* Washington, DC: National Institute of Justice Research Forum, pp. 97–102.

School Associated Violent Deaths. (1999). Westlake Village, CA: National School Safety Center.

The School Shooter: A Threat Assessment Perspective. (2000). Washington, DC: Federal Bureau of Investigation.

Tonry, M. H. (1995). *Malign Neglect—Race, Crime, and Punishment in America.* New York: Oxford University Press.

Tonry, Michael. (1996). *Malign Neglect: Race, Crime, and Punishment in America.* New York: Oxford University Press.

Schiraldi, V. (1999). "Making Sense of Juvenile Homicides in America." *America,* 8(12): 17.

Sheley, J. F. & J. D. Wright. (1998). *High School Youths, Weapons, and Violence: A National Survey. National Institute of Justice Research in Brief.* Washington, DC: National Institute of Justice, October, 1–7.

St. Louis Post-Dispatch. (1999). "Black Students Are Expelled More Often, District Admits; But Officials In Decatur, Ill., Say Punishments Are Fair." December 29, 1999, p. B2.

U.S. General Accounting Office. (1995). *School Safety: Promising Initiatives for Addressing School Violence, Report to the Ranking Minority Member Subcommittee on Children and Families, Committee on Labor and Human Resources, U.S. Senate,* Washington, DC.

U.S. Department of Education. (1993). National Center for Education Statistics, *National Household Education Survey.*

Verdugo, R. R. (1999). "Safe Schools: Theory, Data, and Practices." *Education and Urban Society,* 31(3): 267–274.

Ward, J. R. (2000). "Implementing Juvenile Curfew Programs." *FBI Law Enforcement Bulletin.* Washington, DC: Federal Bureau of Investigation.

Zimring, F. E. (1998). *American Youth Violence.* New York: Oxford University Press.

CHAPTER 9

UNDERSTANDING THE RELATIONSHIP BETWEEN CARRYING WEAPONS TO SCHOOL AND FIGHTING*

Stephen M. Cox, Timothy S. Bynum, and William S. Davidson

Abstract: *The study explored the individual characteristics of students who bring weapons to school (number of previous fights, attitude toward fighting, self-efficacy, amount of observed delinquency, self-reported delinquency, attitude toward school, and perception of school safety). Survey responses were obtained from 944 middle school students from a large Midwestern school district. The study found that students who sporadically bring weapons to school are aggressors (males, believe in using violence, often participate in delinquent acts, and have been victimized) while students who frequently carry weapons to school do so for protection. The conclusions center on the importance on relying less on increased school security (metal detectors, armed security guards, and random locker sweeps) and more on school environment improvement programs.*

INTRODUCTION

In-school violence continues to receive a significant amount of attention in the media and from policymakers. While many trends in school crime and violence have decreased since the early 1990s, the occurrence of serious incidents and the high fear of violence among students and teachers remains a concern (U.S. Department of Education, 1999). Many of the problems associated with school violence center on the prevalence of students carrying weapons to school and fights among students (Kenney & Watson, 1998).

During the 1996–1997 school year, 10 percent of all public schools called for police intervention as a result of a serious violent crime (e.g., murder, rape, suicide, fight with a weapon, robbery) (U.S. Department of Education, 2001). Twelve percent of public middle schools and 13% of public high schools

*Please address correspondence to Stephen M. Cox, Department of Criminology and Criminal Justice, Central Connecticut State University, 615 Stanley Ave., New Britain, CT 06050, e-mail: coxs@ccsu.edu

reported at least one physical attack or a fight with a weapon needing police attention. These percentages were much higher for physical attacks or fights not involving weapons (51% of middle schools and 55% of high schools)(U.S. Department of Education, 2001). Furthermore, 18 percent of middle school principals and 37 percent of high school principals reported that their school had at least one serious discipline issue (U.S. Department of Education, 1997).

The number of school-associated deaths increased in the latter half of the 1990s. From 1992 to 1994, there were 105 school-associated deaths (Kachur et al., 1996). Eighty-one percent of these deaths (85) occurred as a result of an interpersonal dispute and 94 percent involved a gun or a knife. During the 1997–1998 school year, there were 58 school-associated deaths (U.S. Department of Education, 1999). Forty-six were homicides (80 percent) and eleven were suicides (one student was killed by a police officer at school). There were five multiple victim homicides during the 1997–1998 school year, the highest number for one school year in the 1990s.

Although the number of deaths in school and the number of multiple victim homicides are relatively low, violent incidents and fear of violence can have a profound effect on the educational process. Schools with high rates of crime and violence are less effective in educating students. These schools have lower levels of student achievement, higher rates of absenteeism, and more dropouts (Binns & Markow, 1999; Christie & Toomey, 1990; Hazler, 2000; Lawrence, 1998; Lowry et al., 1995). Even in schools having a low percentage of students being victimized, a few violent acts can have far reaching detrimental effects for a large number of students. Fear of victimization has been found to inhibit students' educational and psychological development (Asmussen, 1992; Christie & Toomey, 1990).

School-related violence has been attributed to interpersonal fighting among students and weapons being brought to school. A national survey of elementary and secondary school principals revealed that 21 percent of all principals believed that physical fighting was a serious or moderate problem (U.S. Department of Education, 1998a). The Centers for Disease Control (CDC) (1998) found that 37 percent of all students in the ninth through the twelfth grades had been in at least one physical fight in a twelve-month period. Overall, the CDC estimated that approximately 115 physical fights occurred per 100 students.

While students bringing weapons to school is not a new phenomenon, it happens at an alarming rate (Gaustad, 1991; National Center for School Safety, 1993; U.S. Department of Education, 1998). For instance, 35 percent of sixth- through eighth-grade students and 48 percent of ninth- through twelfth-grade students reported they had seen students bring weapons to school (Office of Juvenile Justice and Delinquency Prevention [OJJDP], 1996). Almost one-half of eighth-grade students surveyed had seen a weapon (44 percent), while 38 percent of the seventh graders and 24 percent of the sixth-grade students had observed a student with a weapon. More recently, the Centers for Disease Control reported that 18 percent of students nationwide had carried a weapon to school at least once in the month prior to their survey, and an estimated 74 incidents of weapon carrying took place per 100 students over the same period (Centers for Disease Control, 1998).

The increase in physical fighting and weapon carrying has commonly been explained by social learning theory. Social learning theorists suggest that violent behavior begins with the perception of a disagreement and is followed by a learned response (Bandura, 1973; Goldstein, 1988; Okey, 1992; Pallone & Hennessy, 1992). That is, youth perceive that they have been wronged in some way by another youth and will seek retribution in order to right the wrong. These youth will resort to violence rather than other alternatives because this has become the learned (and often accepted) response to resolving conflicts.

Based on the social learning perspective, physical fighting is a precursor to bringing a weapon to school. Students learn to deal with conflict by using violent methods of resolution. When the conflicts escalate, students continue to use more violent methods of dealing with them, ultimately leading students to carry weapons to resolve the problems. School-based violence intervention programs have been developed and instituted based on the social learning theory that students who bring weapons to school will be the students who are involved in a lot of fights. Therefore, the best way to decrease the number of students carrying weapons is to stop students from fighting. These programs teach students nonviolent ways to deal with interpersonal conflict, most commonly through conflict resolution skills and peer mediation.

While much attention has been dedicated to the level of school violence and characteristics associated with violent acts (e.g., number of incidents, perpetrator-victim relationships, structural characteristics of the school), little research has looked at individual characteristics of those students who bring weapons to school (e.g., gender, grade in school, attitude toward fighting, self-efficacy, amount of observed delinquency, self-reported delinquency, attitude toward school, and perception of school safety) even though many school violence programs target individual characteristics.

STUDENTS AND WEAPON CARRYING

Research suggests that students bring weapons to school for two reasons: bullying and protection (Arnette & Walsleben, 1998; Hazler, 2000). Bullies are highly aggressive children who seek out conflict situations (Besag, 1989; Furlong & Morrison, 1994). They have a need to exercise or confirm their power over others. Usually, bullies are physically stronger and have more energy and confidence than other students (Besag, 1989). Carrying a weapon is a form of bullying. Bullies who carry weapons do so to assure dominance over their victims.

Cotten and colleagues (1994) studied characteristics associated with bullying. They examined the relationship between aggression, fighting behavior, individuals, and family factors. They found that predictors of aggression were age (older students were more aggressive than younger students), attitude toward violence (a positive attitude toward violence was predictive of aggressiveness), and weapon carrying (students reporting ever carrying a weapon were more aggressive than non-weapon-carrying students).

The other reason students bring weapons to school is for protection (Hazler, 2000; National Center for School Safety, 1993). These students have either been victimized or have a fear of being victimized and feel that the only way they can avoid this is to carry a weapon. In addition, as more schools resort to different types of increased security (e.g., metal detectors, armed security guards, random locker searches, police officers stationed in the school), students' fears of being victimized have been increased to where many students feel that they are unsafe without carrying a weapon (Asmussen, 1992; National Center for School Safety, 1993).

Several studies have explored different types of predictors of weapon carrying. These studies have found that weapon carrying is associated with fighting (Lowry et al., 1998), alcohol and drug use (Kingery et al., 1999; Lowry & Cohen, 1999; McKeganey & Norrie, 2000; Valois & McKewon, 1998), having a friend or relative victimized (Vaughan et al., 1996), sexual intercourse (Valois & McKewon, 1996), being a victim or witness of extreme violence (Kingery et al., 1999), positive attitudes toward aggression (Cornell & Loper, 1998), and poor parental relationships (Orpinas & Murray, 1999).

While fighting is believed to be associated with weapon carrying, few studies have tested this relationship. Lowry and colleagues (1998) reanalyzed 1992 data from the Youth Risk Behavior Survey and found that weapon carrying and fighting were common among the 12- to 21-year-olds in the sample. They also found that youth who carried weapons were more likely to have been in a fight than those who did not carry a weapon. However, they were unable to establish a causal relationship between the two.

One study that investigated weapon carrying among middle school students was interested in whether weapon carrying was more of a defensive or an aggressive behavior. Webster and colleagues (1993) attempted to identify several personal factors associated with weapon carrying in two Washington, D.C., middle schools. Their primary hypothesis was that weapon carrying was a function of seven factors: (1) direct and indirect exposure to violence, (2) delinquency, (3) positive attitude about hitting other people under certain conditions, (4) positive attitude about shooting someone under certain conditions, (5) peer support of violence, (6) patterns of aggressive behavior, and (7) belief that having a weapon can provide protection from physical attacks.

Webster and colleagues (1993) found that students who carried knives and guns were more aggressive than students who did not carry weapons. Students who carried knives were more likely to be males and had been threatened or attacked with a knife. The authors speculated that these students were victims due to their propensity to get into a fight more than through random victimization. Gun-carrying students were more aggressive than knife carrying students. These students had been arrested for drug-related charges, had extreme attitudes regarding the use of violence, had a perception of peer support for violence, and had a tendency to start fights. Overall, their findings were not consistent with the belief that innocent victims carry weapons out of fear of being further victimized. Both gun and knife carrying was more of an aggressive than defensive behavior.

The primary drawback of these studies has been that weapon carrying was measured as a dichotomous variable (Cornell & Loper, 1998; Kingery et al., 1999; Lowry & Cohen, 1999; Lowry et al., 1998; McKeganey & Norrie, 2000; Rountree, 2000; Valois & McKewon, 1998; Vaughan et al., 1996; Webster et al., 1993). That is, these studies focused on whether students had *ever* carried a weapon. While researchers did ask for the frequency of weapon carrying over a specific time frame, they did not test for differences between students who carry weapons on occasion versus students who carry weapons on a daily basis. It is possible that the individual characteristics of students who occasionally carry weapons are different from students who frequently carry weapons. For instance, students may carry a weapon once or twice in order to show it off or prove they have easy access as a way to gain status or enhance their bullying image (Greene, 1993). Students who regularly possess weapons may have other reasons such as protection from a reoccuring threat or constant fear of victimization. Haynie and colleagues (2001) and Cotten and colleagues (1994) found that aggressive students who carried weapons were also victimized. Hence, even aggressive students may carry weapons on a daily basis for protection rather than aggressive purposes.

The following study further investigates the relationship between fighting and carrying a weapon to school. Since a large portion of school violence programs are designed to decrease the use of violence as a way to resolve conflict, we will test the assumption that fighting is associated with carrying weapons while examining other individual characteristics as predictors of weapon carrying. The study also explores potential differences between students who occasionally and frequently carry weapons.

METHODOLOGY

Sample

Data for this study were collected from four middle schools in a large Midwestern city. The schools were in the same urban school district but located in different areas of the city. These four schools were selected by research staff and school officials based on their representativeness of middle schools in the school district. The schools were located in low-income residential areas of the city. The principals of these schools believed the area around their school was home to gangs and drug dealers.

Anonymous and confidential surveys were distributed and collected during homeroom periods in each school. The surveys were given to all sixth-, seventh-, and eighth-grade students in attendance. The sample consisted of 944 middle school students across the four schools. Slightly more than half (55 percent) were female and the mean age was 12.6 with a range of 9 to 15 years old. One-third of the students in the sample were sixth graders, 37 percent were seventh graders, and 30 percent were eighth graders.

Measures

The student survey contained several items related to weapon carrying and physical fighting. The constructs contained in the survey were number of times students carried weapons to school and participated in fights at school, students' self-efficacy, attitude toward school, attitude toward fighting, perception of school safety, self-reported delinquency, the amount of delinquency witnessed at school, and victimization. All of these scales were created by summing the scale items and dividing the sum by the number of items with nonmissing responses. Several items were reverse coded to maintain consistency in the direction of the scale.

Fighting and carrying a weapon. The students were asked to report the number of times in the past two months that they had brought a gun or a knife to school and had been involved in a fist fight at school. The possible responses to these questions were "zero," "one," "two," "three," and "four or more."

Self-efficacy. The scale that assessed students' self-efficacy was comprised of twenty items asking students how difficult it would be to use nonviolent methods to resolve potential conflicts. The responses were coded as "very hard," "hard," "easy," and "very easy." A high scale score indicated that a student felt it would not be difficult to avoid conflicts nonviolently while a low scale score indicated that a student did not feel confident that he or she could avoid a conflict situation by employing nonviolent methods. The scale reliability for self-efficacy was .80.

Attitudes toward school. The construct was based on a six-item scale measuring general attitudes toward school (Gold & Mann, 1984). Students were given statements regarding their feelings about teachers, principals, and the school in general and were asked if they "strongly agreed," "agreed," "neither agreed nor disagreed," "disagreed," or "strongly disagreed" with the statement. The scale measured the extent the students liked or disliked school. A high scale score represented a positive attitude toward school. The scale reliability was .75.

Attitude toward fighting. The attitude toward fighting scale measured students' belief that fighting was an appropriate way to handle problems. Students were given seven statements regarding the appropriateness of fighting and asked if they "strongly agreed," "agreed," "did not know," "disagreed," or "strongly disagreed" with each item. A high scale score signified a positive attitude regarding fighting and a low scale score meant the student did not believe that fighting was an acceptable or appropriate method of handling interpersonal conflicts. The scale reliability of this scale was .75.

Perception of school safety. The perception of school safety scale contained five items measuring how safe students felt while they were at school (Clifford & Davis, 1991). For these items, students read a statement regarding a safety issue in their school and reported the extent to which they "strongly agreed," "agreed," "did not know," "disagreed," or "strongly disagreed" with the statement. A high score represented a perception that the school was a safe place while a low score represented a perception that the school was not safe. The scale reliability for perception of school safety was .59.

Self-reported delinquency. The self-reported delinquency scale consisted of six items that focused on school-related misbehavior and were adapted from Elliott and colleagues (1985). The items included in this scale pertained to school vandalism, being sent to the principal's office for misbehavior, skipping a class, skipping an entire school day, threatening other students, and being suspended. Students were asked to report how many times, "zero" through "four or more," in the past two months they had been involved in these activities. The scale reliability for self-reported delinquency was .82.

Observed delinquency. In measuring the amount of school-related violence students had witnessed in school, students were asked to report the number of times in the past two months they had seen: (1) a fist fight between other students, (2) a student threaten a teacher, (3) a student destroy school property, (4) a weapon that was brought to school by another student, (5) the police remove a student from the school, and (6) students possessing drugs in school. Similar to the questions involving fighting and weapons, the possible responses to these items were "zero," "one," "two," "three," and "four or more." The scale reliability was .73 for observed delinquency.

Victimization. School victimization was measured using four self-report items. Students were asked how many times in the past two months they had been physically assaulted, had something physically taken from them, had something stolen from their school locker, and been threatened by another student. These items were also coded with the responses of "zero" through "four or more" times. The reliability for this scale was .67.

RESULTS

The purpose of this study was to examine the relationship between fighting and weapon carrying in four urban middle schools and explore characteristics associated with students who had brought a weapon to school. The first step in the analysis was to compare students who had brought a gun or a knife to school with the number of fist fights in which they had participated. The second step in the analysis employed three multiple regression techniques to determine what individual characteristics were predictive of students carrying weapons to school.

Past literature and research has suggested that students most likely to bring weapons to school are those that are involved in fighting. Some of these students use weapons to intimidate or bully other students while other students carry weapons for protection. The belief is that both types of students will bring weapons to school only after several instances of fighting. We explored this assumption by examining students who had ever carried a weapon to school and the number of fights that these students had been involved (Table 9.1). The column percentages in Table 9.1 shows that the percentage of students who carried a weapon to school increased as the number of fights they have been in increased. For instance, only 8 percent of the students who had never been in a fight had carried a weapon to school, whereas 40 percent of the students who reported being in four or more fights reported carrying a weapon. This finding is consistent with literature on interpersonal violence that has suggested that fighting leads to carrying weapons.

Unfortunately, much of the literature focusing on youth violence and weapons has not extended analysis beyond this conclusion. Most school violence programs use conflict resolution strategies that are based on the belief that the best way to decrease the rate of weapons being brought to school is to decrease the number of fights between students. While it is not the intention of this study to argue that this conclusion is wrong, it is believed that there may be other characteristics explaining why students bring weapons to school than the number of fights. Referring back to Table 9.1, there were 162 students who reported being involved in four or more fights during the two month

Table 9.1
Crosstabulation of Students Carrying a Weapon at Least Once by Number of Reported Fist Fights

Number of fist fights	Zero	Once	Twice	Three	Four or More	Totals
Ever carried a weapon to school						
Yes	41	26	28	19	64	178
	(8%)	(16%)	(28%)	(37%)	(40%)	(18%)
No	472	142	71	33	98	816
	(92%)	(85%)	(72%)	(64%)	(61%)	(82%)
Totals*	513	168	99	52	162	994
	(52%)	(17%)	(10%)	(5%)	(16%)	

Note: All percentages are column percents except for "Totals,*" which are row percentages.

period prior to the survey. However, 60 percent of these students had never brought a weapon to school. If fighting were the major cause of students carrying weapons, we believe this percentage should have been higher.[1]

The relationship between fighting and weapon carrying was further tested using three different regression analyses. In each regression equation, the dependent variables were the number of times students reported carrying a weapon to school. The first regression equation was a linear multiple regression in which the dependent variable was the number of times in the past two months students carried a weapon to school. The dependent variable was coded 0 through 4, representing the response choices of "zero" through "four or more" times. The second regression equation was a logistic regression with the dependent variable, "how many times in the past two months have you carried a weapon to school," coded as a dichotomous variable (0 = never carried a weapon, 1 = carried a weapon). The equation sought to predict which students had ever carried a weapon to school. The third regression equation attempted to predict the characteristics associated with students who carried weapons to school on multiple occasions without being skewed by students who had never brought a weapon to school. The model was a linear regression using a truncated sample that contained only those students that reported carrying a weapon to school (178). The independent variables for all three of these regression equations were grade in school, gender, number of fights in school, self-efficacy, attitude toward school, attitude toward fighting, perception of school safety, self-reported delinquency, observed delinquency, and victimization.

Table 9.2 presents the *t*-values for the independent variables and the model R^2-values for the three regression equations. Similar results were obtained for the linear and the logistic regression equations. In these equations, the significant predictors were gender, attitude toward fighting, self-reported delinquency, and victimization. These results suggest that males, students who believe fighting is a positive way to resolve interpersonal problems, students who have a higher rate of delinquency, and students who are victimized

Table 9.2

T-Values for the Full Prediction Models of Carrying a Weapon to School

Variable	Linear Regression	Logistic Regression	Selected Sample
Grade	.14	.29	.31
Gender*	−2.13**	−2.07**	−1.13
Number of fights	.16	.09	.31
Self-efficacy	−1.00	−1.60	−.54
School attitude	−1.23	.05	−1.64
Attitude toward fighting	2.68**	2.98**	1.11
Perception of school safety	.54	.46	−.35
Delinquency	11.82**	12.05**	1.71
Observed delinquency	1.85	.77	2.57**
Victimization	4.45**	4.86**	1.43
N	994	994	178
R^2	.32	.31	.19

*Gender was coded as males = 1 and females = 2.

** $p < .05$.

are most likely to carry weapons to school. In these regressions, the number of fights was not a significant predictor of carrying a weapon.

The results were different for the selected sample regression equation. The only significant predictor of students' carrying weapons to school on multiple occasions was the amount of observed delinquency. Students who observed a high amount of delinquency committed by other students were more likely to bring a weapon to school on multiple occasions. This finding was interesting given that none of the significant predictors from the linear or the logistic regression were statistically significant in this equation.

The finding that observed delinquency predicted frequent carrying of weapons led to an additional analysis of the selected sample model. The analysis was conducted using the individual items from the observed delinquency scale as the independent variables (Table 9.3). The significant predictors from this equation were the amount of observed fights, the number of observed threats on other students, and the number of times the students saw other students with drugs.

DISCUSSION

The analyses produced three distinct findings. First, this study compared the relationship between number of fights at school and carrying a weapon to school based on the assumption that the more fights a student is involved in, the more likely he or she will carry a weapon to school. The crosstabulation of

Table 9.3

Selected Sample Model Predicting Carrying a Weapon
to School with the Individual Scale Items from the Observed
Delinquency Scale as Independent Variables

Item	Selected Sample
Observed fights between students	2.35*
Observed threats to other students	2.38*
Observed school vandalism	1.78
Observed students with weapons	1.14
Observed the police at school	1.06
Observed students with drugs	2.10*
N	178
R^2	.24

* $p < .05$.

these variables demonstrated that the likelihood a student will carry a weapon to school increases as the number of fights increases, thus supporting the use of social learning antiviolence programs (conflict resolution, peer mediation, etc.) that assume that decreasing the number of fights will decrease the prevalence of weapons in the schools.

However, the strength of the relationship between fighting and weapon carrying was tested against other variables believed to be associated with fighting and weapon carrying. Using three regression equations, we attempted to predict the number of times students' brought weapons to school (linear equation), those students who had ever brought a weapon to school (logistic equation), and of those students who reported carrying a weapon, which students repeatedly carried weapons (selected sample). The number of fights in which the students were involved was not a significant predictor in any of the regression equations. While a relationship exists between fighting and weapon carrying, it appears to be small and does not significantly predict weapon carrying when compared to other individual characteristics.

The second principal finding was that predictors of weapon carrying was higher among students who were male, had a positive attitude toward fighting, high self-reported delinquency, and high victimization. The similar results produced by the linear and logistic regression was likely attributable to the number of students who reported never carrying a weapon to school (82 percent) compared to students who did (18 percent).

The findings from the linear and logistic regression equations reflect earlier beliefs about school violence (Cotten et al., 1994; Haynie et al., 2001; Webster et al., 1993). The students more likely to carry weapons appear to be bullies. These are students who believe fighting is a positive way to resolve conflicts, are involved in a large amount of other delinquent behaviors, and have been victimized. These students are aggressive but need to have a weapon because they have also been victimized, most likely as a result of their own aggressive behavior.

The third principal finding was the differences between the selected sample model and the other two regression models. These differences suggest that students who bring weapons to school are different from students who repeatedly carry weapons. The selected sample model suggests that students who frequently carry weapons do so for the purpose of protection from random victimization. These students were not involved in more aggressive behaviors, nor have they been victimized significantly more than other students. The analysis using the individual observed delinquency items as independent variables provided a more detailed explanation of this initial finding. The students who often carry weapons were more likely to report witnessing fights between other students, students getting physically threatened, and students with drugs. In other words, students who frequently carry weapons appear to have a high fear of school violence, regardless of whether they have been victimized.

CONCLUSIONS

Although this study does support prior research that has found that students carry weapons to school for bullying and for protection, it also found that fighting is not the best predictor of weapon carrying. Bullies appear to carry weapons occasionally, but students who witness violence-related activities in school carry weapons frequently.

School administrators have adapted two strategies for dealing with the increase in student fighting and the prevalence of weapons being brought into the schools. One strategy has targeted the weapons and the other has focused on the students. The first approach has been to take extreme safety measures by placing metal detectors at school entrances, hiring full-time armed security guards, having on-duty police officers stationed inside of the school during school hours, conducting random locker searches, and enforcing stiffer penalties (Gaustad, 1991; Kenney & Watson, 1998). The purpose behind this strategy is to create deterrents that would disallow and prevent weapons from ever entering the school.

The findings from the selected sample model suggest that these types of measures may not serve as a deterrent but as a reason why some students carry weapons to school on a daily basis. Walking past metal detectors and armed security guards may only serve to frighten students to the point they believe they need a weapon for protection. Researchers have questioned the ability of these types of security measures to create a safe school environment (Collins et al., 1992; Noguera, 1995).

The second strategy attempts to deal with the problem of fights between students in a less formal manner. Antiviolence programs have become popular in many urban, suburban, and rural school districts. These programs are grounded in social learning theory and attempt to teach students nonviolent methods to resolve interpersonal conflicts. Social learning–based programs typically consist of teaching students conflict resolution skills, promoting peer mediation to resolving interpersonal conflicts, and impressing on all students the problems associated with using violence. While this approach may be successful in keeping students from fighting, and perhaps keep some students from ever carrying a weapon to school, it does not address those students who bring weapons to school on a regular basis.

The findings of this study suggest that schoolwide violence intervention programs may be more effective in decreasing weapon carrying than individual-level approaches. Conflict resolution programs often target the individual as the level of intervention (Tolan & Guerra, 1994) while schoolwide programs target multiple facets of violence (Commission on Violence and Youth, 1993). G. Gottfredson (1987) pointed out that implementation of programs in schools with a high number of problems is difficult unless the intervention is also aimed at improving the school as a whole. Research on school environment programs is limited (D. Gottfredson, 1987; Lane & Murakami, 1987), but it has indicated that school improvement programs have been moderately successful in improving the school environment, decreasing the number of suspensions, and decreasing the number of delinquent and drug-related activities in school (G. Gottfredson, 1987). Therefore, a school environmental approach appears to be best suited to decrease the fear of school violence for those students who frequently carry weapons.

It is important that school administrators consider all possible effects as they explore different strategies to stop the increase in weapons being brought into their schools. Placing metal detectors at the entrances, posting armed security guards in the hallways, and conducting locker searches may deter some students from carrying weapons, but it appears that these measures may cause other students to feel they need to have a weapon for protection. In addition, while conflict resolution, peer mediation programs, and antibullying programs are able to decrease the instances of students fighting, schoolwide programs that target the overall school environment appear to have more potential for decreasing weapon-related school violence. This study has extended prior research in demonstrating that individual differences exist between students who sporadically and regularly carry weapons. More in-depth research is needed that further examines why students feel they need to carry weapons to school and what measures school administrators can institute that will alleviate these feelings of dismay.

REFERENCES

Arnette, J. L., and M. C. Walsleben. (1998). *Combating Fear and Restoring Safety in Schools.* Washington, DC: U.S. Department of Justice.

Asmussen. (1992). "Weapon Possession in Public High Schools." *School Safety, Fall,* pp. 28–30.

Bandura, A. (1973). *Aggression: A Social Learning Analysis.* Englewood Cliffs, NJ: Prentice Hall.

Besag, V. E. (1989). *Bullies and Victims in Schools.* Philadelphia: Open University Press.

Binns, K., and D. Markow. (1999). *The Metropolitan Life Survey of the American Teacher: Violence in America's Public Schools—Five Years Later.* New York: The Metropolitan Life Insurance Company.

Centers for Disease Control. (1998). *Youth Risk Behavior Surveillance—United States, 1997.* Atlanta, GA: Centers for Disease Control.

Christie, D. J., & B. G. Toomey. (1990). The Stress of Violence: School, Community, and World. In L.E. Arnold (Ed.), *Childhood Stress* (pp. 297–323). New York: John Wiley & Sons.

Clifford, M. A., & M. Davis. (1991). *Evaluation Tests for Student Assistance Programs.* Boulder, CO: National Organization of Student Assistance Programs and Professionals.

Collins, J. J., P. Messerschmidt, & C. Ringwalt. (1992). *The Relationship between School Disruption and School Social Control Activities*. Research Triangle Park, NC: Center for Social Research and Policy Analysis.

Commission on Violence and Youth. (1993). *Violence & Youth: Psychology's Response. Volume I: Summary Report*. Washington, DC: American Psychological Association.

Cornell, D. G., & A. B. Loper. (1998). "Assessment of Violence and Other High-Risk Behaviors with a School Survey." *School Psychology Review*, 27: 317–330.

Cotten, N. U., J. Resnick, D. C. Browne, S. L. Martin, D. R. McCarraher, & J. Woods. (1994). "Aggression and Fighting Behavior among African-American Adolescents: Individual and Family Factors." *American Journal of Public Health*, 84(4): 618–622.

Furlong, M. J., & G. M. Morrison. (1994). "Introduction to Miniseries: School Violence and Safety in Perspective." *School Psychology Review*, 23: 139–150.

Elliott, D. S., D. Huizinga, & S. S. Ageton. (1985). *Explaining Delinquency and Drug Use*. Beverly Hills, CA: Sage.

Gaustad, J. (1991). "Schools Attack the Roots of Violence." *ERIC Digest*, 63, 1–2.

Gold, M., & D. W. Mann. (1984). *Expelled to a Friendlier Place: A Study of Alternative Schools*. Ann Arbor, MI: University of Michigan Press.

Goldstein, A. P. (1988). "New Directions in Aggression Reduction." *International Journal of Group Tensions*, 18(4): 286–313.

Gottfredson, D. C. (1987). "An Evaluation of an Organizational Development Approach to Reducing School Disorder." *Evaluation Review*, 11(6): 739–763.

Gottfredson, G. D. (1987). *American Education—American Delinquency* (Report No. 23). Baltimore: Center for Research on Elementary and Middle Schools.

Greene, M. B. (1993). "Chronic Exposure to Violence and Poverty: Interventions that Work for Youth." *Crime and Delinquency*, 39(1): 106–124.

Haynie, D. L., T. Nansel, P. Eitel, A. D. Crump, K. Saylor, K. Yu, & B. Simons-Morton. (2001). "Bullies, Victims, and Bully/Victims: Distinct Groups of At-Risk Youth." *Journal of Early Adolescence*, 21: 29–49.

Hazler, R. (2000). "When Victims Turn Aggressors: Factors in the Development of Deadly School Violence." *Professional School Counseling*, 4(2): 105–112.

Kachur, S. P., G. M. Stennies, K. E. Powell, W. Modzeleski, R. Stephens, R. Murphy, M. Kresnow, D. Sleet, & R. Lowry. (1996). *"School-Associated Deaths in the United States, 1992–1994." Journal of the American Medical Association*, 275(22): 1729–1733.

Kenney, D. J., & T. S. Watson. (1998). *Crime in the Schools: Reducing Fear and Disorder with Student Problem solving*. Alexandria, VA: Police Executive Research Forum.

Kingery, P. M., M. B. Coggeshall, and A. A. Alford. (1999). "Weapon Carrying by Youth." *Education and Urban Society*, 31: 309–333.

Lane, T. W., & J. Murakami. (1987). School Programs for Delinquency Prevention and Intervention. In E. K. Morris & C.J. Braukmann (Eds.), *Behavioral Approaches to Crime and Delinquency* (pp. 305–327). New York: Plenum Press.

Lawrence, R. (1998). *School Crime and Juvenile Justice*. New York: Oxford University Press.

Lowry, R., & L. Cohen. (1999). "School Violence, Substance Use, and Availability of Illegal Drugs on School Property among U.S. High School Students." *Journal of School Health*, 69: 347–355.

Lowry, R., K. E. Powell, L. Kann, J. L. Collins, and L. J. Kolbe. (1998). "Weapon-Carrying, Physical Fighting, and Fight-Related Injury among U.S. Adolescents." *American Journal of Preventative Medicine*, 14: 122–129.

Lowry, R., D. Sleet, C. Duncan, K. Powell, & L. Kolbe. (1995). "Adolescents At Risk for Violence." *Educational Psychology Review*, 7(1): 7–39.

McKeganey, N., & J. Norrie. (2000). "Association between Illegal Drugs and Weapons in Young People in Scotland: Schools' Survey." *British Medical Journal*, 320: 982–984.

National Center for School Safety. (1993). *Weapons in Schools*. Malibu, CA: Pepperdine University.

Noguera, P. A. (1995). "Preventing and Producing Violence: A Critical Analysis of Responses to School Violence." *Harvard Educational Review,* 65(2): 189–212.

Office of Juvenile Justice and Delinquency Prevention. (1996). *Juvenile Offenders and Victims: 1996 Update on Violence.* Washington, DC: U.S. Department of Justice.

Okey, J. L. (1992). "Human Aggression: The Etiology of Individual Differences." *Journal of Humanistic Psychology,* 32(1): 51–64.

Orpinas, P., & N. Murray. (1999). "Parental Influences on Students' Aggressive Behaviors and Weapon Carrying." *Health Education and Behavior,* 26: 774–787.

Rountree, P. W. (2000). "Weapons at School: Are the Predictors Generalizable across Context?" *Sociological Spectrum,* 20: 291–324.

Pallone, N. J., & J. J. Hennessy. (1992). *Criminal Behavior: A Process Psychology Analysis.* New Brunswick, NJ: Transaction Publishers.

Tolan, P., & N. Guerra, (1994). *What Works in Reducing Adolescent Violence: An Empirical Review of the Field.* Boulder, CO: Center for the Study and Prevention of Violence.

U.S. Department of Education. (1997). *Principal/School Disciplinarian Survey on School Violence.* Washington, DC: U.S. Department of Education.

U.S. Department of Education. (1998a). *Indicators of School Crime and Safety, 1998.* Washington, DC: U.S. Department of Education.

U.S. Department of Education. (1998b). *Violence and Discipline Problems in the U.S. Public Schools: 1996–1997.* Washington, DC: U.S. Department of Education.

U.S. Department of Education. (1999). *Annual Report on School Safety, 1999.* Washington, DC: U.S. Department of Education.

U.S. Department of Education. (2001). *Annual Report on School Safety, 2000.* Washington, DC: U.S. Department of Education.

Valois, R. F., & R. E. McKewon. (1998). "Frequency and Correlates of Fighting and Carrying Weapons among Public School Adolescents." *American Journal of Health and Behavior,* 22: 8–17.

Vaughan, R. D., J. F. McCarthy, B. Armstrong, H. J. Walter, P. D. Waterman, & L. Tiezzi. (1996). "Carrying and Using Weapons: A Survey of Minority Junior High School Students in New York City." *American Journal of Public Health,* 86: 568–572.

Webster, D. W., P. S. Gainer, & H. R. Champion. (1993). "Weapon Carrying among Inner-City Junior High School Students: Defensive Behavior vs. Aggressive Delinquency." *American Journal of Public Health,* 83(11): 1604–1608.

NOTE

1. In addition to the crosstabs presented in Table 9.1, the correlation between fighting and weapon carrying was .32. While this was a statistically significant correlation, we believe that the relationship should have been higher if fighting is the primary predictor of weapon carrying.

CHAPTER 10

MURDER IN THE WORKPLACE

Ronald M. Holmes and Stephen T. Holmes

INTRODUCTION

More than 2 million violent victimizations occur in the workplace (Bureau of Justice Statistics [BJS], 1998). Thus, workplace violence is an emerging problem that results in great suffering and deaths. The BJS report states that

- Each year between 1992 and 1996, more than 2 million U.S. residents were victims of a violence crime while they were at or on duty.
- The most common type of workplace victimization was simple assault, with an estimated 1.5 million occurring each year. U.S. residents also suffered 51,000 rapes and sexual assaults and about 84,000 robberies while they were at work.
- Annually, more than 230,000 people officers became victims of a nonfatal violent crime while they were working or on duty.
- About 40 percent of victims of nonfatal violence in the workplace reported that they knew their offenders.
- Women were more likely than men to be victimized by someone they knew.
- Approximately 12 percent of the nonfatal violence workplace crimes resulted in an injury to the victim. Of those injured, about half received medical treatment.
- Intimates (current and former spouses, boyfriends, and girlfriends) were identified by the victims as the perpetrators of about 1 percent of all workplace violence crime.

Settings vary as far as workplace violence. David Burke was terminated from the Pacific Southwest Airlines (PSA). Angry, he boarded a PSA plane. As the plane was airborne, Burke killed his boss, causing the airplane to crash. Forty-three people on board, including Burke, were killed. In Mississippi, firefighter Kenneth Tornes returned to his firehouse one evening. He killed four supervisors before he was wounded in a gunfight with the police. In

California, Willie Woods, a Los Angeles electrician, went to his workplace and shot and killed two supervisors and two fellow employees. He was arrested at the crime scene by two police officers who happened to be in the area. On April 3, 1995, James Simpson walked into the oil refinery where he once worked and killed his wife, a former boss, and three other employees. He then walked out the back door and killed himself.

There are other disgruntled employees who kill, such as Joseph Harris, 35. A former postal worker, Harris had a reputation of simply disliking people. His coworkers stated that Harris disliked everyone. Harris was fired for refusing to cooperate in an investigation of charges brought against him by his former supervisor. In the early morning hours, Harris walked into the back door of the post office and killed two employees of the post office. Only hours before, he had been to the home of his former supervisor, Carol Ott, and killed her and her fiancé, Cornelius Kasten, Jr.

More than 30 years ago, Robert Earl Mack was fired from his job at General Dynamics, a defense contractor. Mack, 42 years old, had worked for the company for 25 years. Fellow employees noted a change in Mack's work habits and personality. He began to show up late and miss days of work. He was fired. Nine days after he was fired, Mack was scheduled to appear before an appeals board. During a break in the meeting, Mack opened fire and shot and killed his former coworkers. He surrendered to authorities. These examples are reflective of only a small number of cases. Table 10.1 presents a larger picture of contemporary suspected and alleged disgruntled workplace killers.

TRAITS OF THE DISGRUNTLED EMPLOYEE KILLER

Violence committed in the workplace usually takes one of three forms:

- Committed by people who work in the place where the crime of violence took place
- Committed by a present or former customer with the business that the violence took place
- Committed by persons who have no relationship with the business or company

Many of these workplace homicides are committed by those who have some type of relationship with the company or institution (Seger, 1993). Frederick Davidson killed three members of his thesis committee. On first glance, this may not appear to fit the traits or characteristics of a disgruntled employee killer. However, a case can be made that this killer was a "customer" of the university, and Davidson was to receive a product, a degree. He believed that the university was negligent in not assisting him in his employment endeavors as well as delaying granting him his degree. In California more than a decade ago, a Ph.D. graduate student entered the office of his advisor at Stanford University and beat him to death with a hammer. His motivation? He had been in the graduate program for more than eight years and Stanford did not "graduate" him.

The disgruntled employee killer has traits that are fundamentally different from other types of killers.

Motivation is Intrinsic to the Personality of the Disgruntled Killer

The motivation to kill falls within the mind of the killer (O'Boyle, 1992; Roth, 1994). There are no motivations that arise from outside the personality of the offender. Thus, the motivation is within the psyche of the killer. Witness again the case of Harris. He was often belittled by his coworkers (Losey, 1994). The blame for all of his problems rested outside of his own arena of responsibility. The motivation to kill, however, rested within his personality.

Anticipated Gain: The Gain is Expressive to the Disgruntled Employee

The disgruntled employee expects some reward for his act of murder. This anticipated gain is expressive or psychological. The gain is somewhat difficult to understand for many. How could the killing of innocent persons, many of whom were workplace associates, be a psychological pleasurable thing? But for the disgruntled employee, the answer to this question is easy to address. From the actions of one episodic act of homicide, the attention is not only on the person committing the act but also the occurrences that brought about the killings. Of course, these occurrences are in the mind of the killer (intrinsic motivation), but they add substance to the motivation as well as drawing attention from others to those injustices that brought about the killing. Maybe this is a rationalization for the killings, a denial of injury, denial or victims, and a denial of responsibility (Sykes & Matza, 1957).

Table 10.1
Selected Alleged and Suspected Disgruntled Employee Killers

Name	State	Victims
David Burk	California	Killed 43 people in an airplane
Frederick Davidson	California	Killed 3 members of his thesis committee
Gian Ferri	California	Killed 6 people in his attorney's office
Christopher Green	California	Killed 4 people at a post office
Willie Woods	California	Killed 4 coworkers
Eric Houston	California	Killed 4 people at his former high school
Matthew Beck	Connecticut	Killed 4 coworkers
Richard Herr	Delaware	Killed 3 coworkers
Clifton McCree	Florida	Killed 5 fellow workers
Joseph Wesbecker	Kentucky	Shot 7 people at his workplace
Kenneth Jones	Mississippi	Killed wife and four coworkers
Kenneth Tornes	Mississippi	Killed spouse and 4 coworkers
Joseph Harris	New Jersey	Killed 4 people at a post office
James Davis	North Carolina	Killed 3 coworkers
Gerald Clemons	Ohio	Killed 3 people at his former workplace
James Simpson	Texas	Killed wife, boss, and three coworkers
Michael Barton	Georgia	Killed wife, two children, and 7 people at work

Victim Selectivity: Victims Are Selected Randomly by the Disgruntled Employee

Victims are often coworkers or former coworkers. But when the killer enters the place of employment, the victims are selected usually because they appear within the view of the killer. The disgruntled employee killer may also enter the facility seeking a specific target (e.g., a former supervisor), but others are killed because of their propiquinty to the killer. The perpetration of fatal violence is directed toward those people in the workplace who are working that day (Bensimon, 1994). The killer may be looking for a supervisor, but that does not preclude the murderer from killing others at the scene.

Not all disgruntled employees resort to fatal violence against their coworkers. According to Baron there are three levels of personal violence that employees often engage in. It is only this final one that involves the killing of another human being. These levels are presented in Table 10.2.

Victim Relationship: Victims Are Not Related to the Killer

The victims of the disgruntled employee are typically not sanguinely or by marriage related to the killer. They are strangers to the family of the killer; the only ties (not relationships) are those that they all share by working in the same facility, be it a post office, factory, or any other place of employment. For example, In March 1995, Christopher Green, another former postal worker, killed two fellow employees and two customers. His reason? He was in debt and the small post office owed him some past paychecks.

Joseph Wesbecker had been employed for the same company for over twenty years. Certainly he knew some of the people he worked with during those years. However, all admitted that they had never been to Wesbecker's home, and none knew this killer on a personal level. They all suspected Wesbecker was strange, and his behavior bordered on the weird. None admitted to having personal ties with this man. A loner, on medication for his mental illness, Wesbecker had an inordinate interest in weapons and a grudge against the managers of his former employment because of his involuntary separation from his work. Wesbecker ended his own life and prevented a further investigation into his mind and pathology to seek answers to important questions.

Spatial Mobility: The Disgruntled Employee Tends to be Geographically Stable

The disgruntled employee is typically a geographically stable killer. He has roots in community, his family, his worship center, his recreation, and his employment. This was the case of Joseph Harris, who killed in the post office. This was also true for Joseph Wesbecker. This killer usually has community ties. He works for a long period of time in his place of employment. Over time, he builds up a sense of anomie, hate, and revenge. He acts out of this sense of rage. It is apparent that this person is a long-term employee. It takes some time for the employee to build up to the point where violent fatal behavior is manifested.

Table 10.2
Levels of Personal Violence

Level 1
  Refuses to cooperate with the immediate supervisor
  Spreads rumors and gossip to harm others
  Consistently argues with co-workers
  Belligerent towards customers/clients
  Consistently swears and curses with others
  Makes unwelcome sexual comments

Level 2
  Argues increasingly with customers, vendors, co-workers, and management
  Refuses to obey company policies and procedures
  Sabotages equipment and steals property for revenge
  Verbalizes wishes to hurt co-workers and/or management
  Sends sexual or violent notes to co-workers and/or management
  Sees self as victimized by management (it is a "me" against "them" mentality)

Level 3
  Frequent displays of intense anger resulting in:
  Recurrent suicidal threats
  Recurrent physical fights
  Destruction of property
  Utilization of weapons to harm others
  Commission of murder, rape, and/or arson

Source: Baron, S. 1993. *Violence in the Workplace: A Prevention and Management Guide for Business.* Ventura, CA: Pathfinder Publishing Co.

Victim Traits: Physical Traits Are Not Important to the Disgruntled Employee

The disgruntled employee does not kill for sexual reasons. He kills because the anticipated gain is psychological and the reason or motivation is intrinsic to the personality of the killer. He does not, as the lust serial killer, seek out an ideal victim type who embodies certain physical traits, such as hair style or color, body build, or other physical attributes. The latter killer murders for completely different reasons. This killer murders because of a perceived injustice.

The physical characteristics of the victims are inconsequential. They are only in a place where the killing will occur. A victim is killed because he or she shares the physical space of the killer. There is no personal relationship. There is only a sense of happenstance.

CASE STUDY: JOSEPH WESBECKER

On Thursday, September 14, 1989, at approximately 8:30 A.M., a disturbed and angry man went to his former place of employment. Placed on disability leave seven months previously for severe psychiatric problems, he was armed with an AK-47, clips of ammunition, a SIG-Sauer 9-mm semiautomatic assault pistol, a MAC-11 semiautomatic pistol, a bayonet, a .38-caliber Smith & Wesson revolver, a second MAC-11, and several hundred rounds of ammunition. The MAC-11s had been purchased only four days before. Joseph Wesbecker stepped onto the elevator of the Standard Gravure Printing Co., his former employer of over 20 years. He walked from the elevator on the third floor. Sharon LaFollete Needy, age 49, a receptionist, was standing talking with another employee. She had gotten to work a little early that day to attend to some business that needed extra attention. She was the first one shot as Wesbecker opened fire. Her husband, George, said that he was told by the police that Wesbecker started shooting as soon as he stepped out of the elevator. Sharon happened to be at another workstation, not her own (G. Needy, personal interview, May 10, 1998).

Lt. Jeff Moody, homicide unit of the Louisville Police Department, was one of the first police officers to respond to the scene. He remarked that when they entered the plant they found blood and bodies scattered around the building. Moreover, they were not certain where Wesbecker was. After Wesbecker shot Needy, he shot another receptionist, Angela Bowman. She survived. Walking through the hallways, Wesbecker fired randomly at anyone he saw. A few of the workers gathered together in one office and escaped detection of the killer. One worker, lying on the floor, heard some shots, and then there was silence. She dialed 911. The call went through the telephone system at 8:38 A.M. Within the next minute, more than a dozen more calls went through the 911 system, calls asking for aid and protection from a crazed killer who was stalking the premises of the plant.

Wesbecker continued his killings. He encountered one fellow worker, a casual acquaintence, and told him to get away from him. Why Wesbecker did not shoot this man was unclear. By this time, the word had circulated throughout the plant that Crazy Joe Wesbecker was shooting people (Holmes & Holmes, 1998). Many ran and escaped his uncontrolled rage.

Walking down the hallway into the bindery division, Wesbecker shot and killed James Husband. He walked through a tunnel and down to the ground floor. He shot William Gannet, James Wile, and Lloyd White. In the basement, Wesbecker killed Richard Bragger and Paul Sale. Wesbecker also shot thirteen other workers, but fortunately they survived. Finally, the last shot was fired.

Table 10.3
Murdered Victims of Joseph Wesbecker

Name	Age
Richard O. "Dice" Bragger	54
William S. "Bill" Gannet	46
James G. "Buck" Husband	47
Paul S. Sale	60
Sharon L. Needy	49
James F. Wile, Sr.	56
Lloyd R. White	42

Wesbecker took his own life on the ground floor in the pressroom, only a short distance from Wile, one of his victims. He shot himself in the face with one of his pistols. A complete list of his victims can be found on Table 10.3.

What kind of man would go into his place of employment of two decades and kill people who bore no culpability to his medical disability termination? There is no clear answer. But we do know that this was a carefully planned case of murder. Wesbecker started collecting his weapons about a year earlier. Did he start his planning for his rampage a year before?

"Has this been a plotted, methodically planned situation that he finally brought to culmination, or did something happen to him to set him off? We haven't been able to find that," said Louisville homicide detective Sgt. Gene Waldridge, who has been interviewing Wesbecker's relatives and looking into his background. Police, who said Wesbecker suffered from manic depression, still planed to interview a psychiatrist he had been seeing, as well as at least 40 Standard Gravure workers, including Wesbecker's former bosses. But Waldridge said, "The big question—Why?—more than likely will never, ever be answered. You can't talk to that person. You don't know what motivates them." (*Courier Journal*, 1989).

There were special stressors that compelled Wesbecker to shoot twenty people and finally end his own life. Wesbecker had been seeking psychiatric help for the past year. He was a patient in psychotherapy as well as drug therapy. Years later, relatives of the victims would sue the makers of Prozac, which Wesbecker was taking, and claim that he caused him to become a killer. The suit was judged in the favor of the drug company.

Wesbecker, age 47, was apparently tormented by his dismissal from work. He thought that the company failed to compensate him for the time and the stress he had undergone on their behalf. He was angry at supervisors, and he told one fellow employee that if any supervisor came up to him he would "blow out their brains" (*Courier Journal*, 1989). Wesbecker told other employees that he had thought about hiring someone to kill some of the people at the plant. He also related that he had plans to operate a remote control model airplane with plastic explosives that he would guide through the plant to a determined destination. He also told one fellow worker, "Me and old ack-ack will do a job that's been long overdue" (*Courier Journal*, 1989, p. A16). Some workers acknowledged later that they should have taken his threats more seriously. He had a list of people whom he wanted dead. That list included the executive vice-president of the company as well as the owner of the company. As one employee said, "You just figure he was mad at management. You figure it's just a way to get your frustration and your stress out. . . . You don't take it seriously" (p. A16). Another fellow worker said that another employee told him about Wesbecker's explosive plan. He quickly dismissed that Wesbecker was a real and present danger. He added, "I really didn't think he'd ever do anything . . . I'm sure you've had people you work [talk] with about meeting a guy outside, punching him out or whatever. Well, maybe one out of every two or three hundred it might happen. But most of the time a guy thinks about it five or 10 minutes and wonders why he ever made such a dumb remark" (p. A16).

The threats made by Wesbecker to his fellow workers were never made known to the supervisors at the plant. While the remarks by Wesbecker were common knowledge to the people in the factory, the general manager, the plant manager, the vice-president of operations, and other managerial personnel were unaware of the extent of the problem. This made Wesbecker's eventual action more than a real possibility. There could have been legal proscriptions barring Wesbecker from the premises or other legal orders that could have circumvented an action that resulted in twenty innocent people shot and seven killed. Additionally, an argument can be made against the fellow workers who should have taken his comments more seriously and then made these remarks available to those who could have taken legal actions.

Wesbecker is buried with his parents in a small Catholic cemetery in southern Indiana. His gravestone overlooks a peaceful valley and stands among the graves of many early settlers in Elizabeth, Indiana: the Browns, Finks, Johns, and others. St. Peter's Catholic Church held the burial for this killer. The priest asked for forgiveness of the act of this "troubled" man and a belief in the divine plan of God. But perhaps society needs more of its own plan so others innocent victims do not meet the same end. Early identification of troubled employees, psychological services given to needful employees, and other human services could provide important human services that may prevent the murder of innocent victims.

CONCLUSION

There is no completely effective plan that will protect us from the acts of a disgruntled employee. This killer will randomly select his victims from those who shared his workplace. There is no affinity between the killer and the victim; the victims are either complete strangers or know the killer only as fellow workers. If the killer knows the victim in this scenario, as was the case with Wesbecker, the killer will sometime dismiss this person, sparing the individual's life.

Among all killers, the disgruntled employee is perhaps the most visible. The headlines are alive when such a case occurs. Our research for this chapter shows that other types of killers may kill victims, but most of the time these acts are not reported on the front pages of the newspapers.

A possible proactive strategy is to develop a policy within the company that a troubled employee would be encouraged to follow if the company suspects there is a person who presents a danger or peril. Employee education is an important part of any plan to prevent a murder of its most important asset, its employees.

REFERENCES

Bensimon, H. (1994). "Violence in the Workplace." *Training and Development*, 27–32.
Bureau of Justice Statistics. (1998). *Workplace Violence 1992–1996* (Special Report 168634). Washington, DC: U.S. Department of Justice, Office of Justice Programs.
Courier Journal. (1989, September 16). *Courier Journal*, p. A1.
Holmes, R., & S. Holmes. (1998). *Serial Murder* (2nd ed.). Thousand Oaks, CA: Sage Publications.
Losey, J. (1994). "Managing in an Era of Workplace Violence." *Managing Office Technology*, February, 27–28.

Needy, G. (1998). Personal interview. May 10, 1998.

O'Boyle, T. (1992). "Disgruntled Workers Intent on Revenge Increasingly Harm Colleagues and Bosses." *Wall Street Journal*, pp. B1, B10.

Roth, J. (1994). *Understanding and Preventing Violence* (Research in Brief). Washington, DC: U.S. Department of Justice, National Institute of Justice.

Seger, K. (1993). "Violence in the Workplace: An Assessment of the Problem Bases on Responses from 32 Large Corporations." *Security Journal*, 4 (3): 139–149.

Sykes, G., & D. Matza, (1957). "Techniques of Neutralization: A Theory of Delinquency." *American Sociological Review*, 22.

Section 4

Serial and Mass Murder

Serial murder and mass murder have made an impact on the social consciousness of all Americans. The names of the serial killers are well known, and in some circles these killers have become celebrities. All our students know of the name of Ted Bundy, while many cannot tell you who was the president of the United States before Bill Clinton. Mass murderers commit their crimes usually only once, but they too have secured a place in the social consciousness with their heinous crimes. People such as James Oliver Huberty, Richard Speck, and Colin Ferguson have become items for discussion and research despite their crimes.

Regardless of the manner in which we view serial and mass murderers, attention is reflected in the media to their crimes and others who commit such similar crimes. Other than school violence and recent acts of terrorism, serial murder and mass murder remain at the apex of interest and attention. Perhaps this is one reason, and not the only one, that we have chosen to include chapters on these two topics in this section.

The first chapter, "Serial Killers and Their Victims," is written by Steven Egger. Egger is recognized as one of the country's authorities on serial murder. He interviewed Henry Lucas while a graduate student, and his doctoral dissertation dealt with the Lucas case and the "linkage blindness" developed by law enforcement agencies. In this chapter, written especially for this book, Egger deals with some of the basic assumptions of the serial killer. He identifies some of the basic problems in the study of the serial murderer while presenting some basic information on selected ones. The list contains many names, some that are well known (e.g., Douglas Clark) and others that are probably only known by the serial killer researcher (e.g., Michael Swango). He continues by examining selected typologies of serial killers and offers some constructive statements concerning not only the typologies but victimology as well.

The next chapter, "Darkness in the Bluegrass: Kentucky's Ties to Mass Murderers and Serial Killers," is written by Barry Royalty. This author is a new face in serial and mass murder research. This chapter covers serial murder and mass murder as forms of multicide. He introduces Charles Manson as a young person in Kentucky and details how David Berkowitz had ties to the same rural state. The central purpose of this chapter is to alert readers that serial and mass killers can come from small towns and rural communities, not only from large cities and states.

The next chapter is a unique one. "Letters from Convicted and Alleged Serial Killers: A Content Analysis" is written by two of the authors and Angela West, an assistant professor from the University of Louisville. Analyzing letters and other forms of correspondences from killers presently incarcerated in penal institutions across the country, the authors perform a content analysis in which they attempt to garner clues about the motives and anticipated gains of the killers.

The next chapter, "Profiles in Terror: The Serial Murderer," is a classic in the literature of serial murder. Written by Holmes and Deburger, this was the first attempt to categorize the various types of serial murderers. Later revised in subsequent writings, the two authors offered for the first time a new and different way to look at serial murder and how it may differ from other types of murder. The typology, *visionary, mission, hedonistic*, and *power/control*, is used across the world in serial murder investigation, research, and theory construction.

"Masters of Terror: Types of Mass Killers" addresses the feasibility of constructing a typology of mass murderers in the same fashion as Holmes and Deburger did in 1985. Using the work of Park Deitz and adding to it, the author first defines and differentiates mass from serial murder. The author discusses several types of mass killers: disciple, family annihilator, disgruntled employee, disgruntled citizen, ideological, set-and-run, and the psychotic. Using anticipated gains and motivations as a starting point in the examination of the types, Holmes offers the reader an interesting point of reference in understanding the mind and mentality of the mass killer.

Joseph Davis contributes to understanding the mass killer in his chapter, "Violence Expressed through Mass Murder: An Epidemic of Growing Proportion and Concern." Using the theoretical framework developed by Holmes and Deburger as well as Holmes and Holmes, Davis studies the mass killer and delves into the mind and psyche of this type of offender while offering various practical examples of such killers.

CHAPTER 11

SERIAL KILLERS AND THEIR VICTIMS

Steven A. Egger

INTRODUCTION

In 1999, 15,533 criminal homicides were reported nationally to the FBI for a rate of 5.7 per 100,000 population in the United States (U.S Department of Justice, 2000). A portion of these homicides, referred to as serial homicide/murder, is a very special type of homicide and is estimated by some to be less than 1 percent of all homicides (Fox & Levin, 1999), although an actual count is unavailable.

The definition of serial murder developed by Egger (1998) will be used in this chapter:

> A serial murder occurs when one or more individuals (in many cases males) commit(s) a second murder and/or subsequent murder; there is generally no prior relationship between victim and attacker (if there is a relationship, such a relationship will place the victim in a subjugated role to the killer); subsequent murders are at different times and have no apparent connection to the initial murder; and are usually committed in a different geographic location. Further, the motive is not for material gain and is for the murderer's desire to have power or dominance over his victims. Victims have symbolic value for the murderer and/or are perceived to be prestigeless and in most instances unable to defend themselves or alert others to their plight, or are perceived as powerless given their situation in time, place, or status within their immediate surroundings, examples being vagrants, the homeless, prostitutes, migrant workers, homosexuals, missing children, single women (out by themselves), elderly women, college students, and hospital patients (pp. 5, 6).

There is currently no representative database of serial murderers over a period of time from which to generalize to the entire population of serial murderers in the United States. The same can be said for the rest of world, although the uniqueness of serial murder in a sparsely populated country (e.g., Australia) will generally increase the reliability of accounting for serial murders. However, even here, serial killers may be operating within the industrial centers with their crime scenes and victims not being linked by law enforcement agencies. This inability of law enforcement to link unsolved murders was labeled by the author as "linkage blindness," (Egger, 1984). "'Linkage blindness' is the nearly total lack of sharing or coordinating of investigative information and the lack of adequate networking by law enforcement agencies" (Egger, 1998, p. 180). While linkage blindness is certainly a problem for law enforcement to overcome in a serial murder investigation, it also poses a real methodological problem for the researcher attempting to develop a profile or generalization of the serial killer due to missing data when a single kill is not counted as part of a pattern.

In the United States and several other countries throughout the world, serial murder is not generally recognized or collected as a separate category of murder at the national level. Without such official statistics, researchers are required to rely on counts of numbers generated by other researchers or on anecdotal information, or they must take on the onerous task of developing their own database from which to generalize.

DATABASE DEVELOPMENT

Four researchers have taken on the task of collecting and developing a database from which to work. Hickey (1997), in his work on serial murderers and their victims, developed a database of 399 serial murderers responsible for from 2526 to 3860 victims between 1800 and 1995 as the basis for his analysis. Holmes and Holmes (1998) list 184 alleged and suspected modern serial killers identified from 1900 to the 1990s in the United States. The Federal Bureau of Investigation National Center for the Analysis of Violent Crime provided an official summary report to the CNN television network in 1993, which identified 331 serial murderers and almost 2000 confirmed victims of serial murder between January 1977 and April 1992. The FBI's data were challenged and through an independent examination resulted in a substantially reduced number of serial murderers to 140 and victims to approximately 1000 during this time period (Griffiths, 1993). The only other major database under development is by K. Egger from 1900 to 1999 in which over 700 serial murderers have been identified on an international basis.

FIVE SOURCES OF INFORMATION ABOUT SERIAL KILLERS

The research on serial murder behavior is based on five basic sources of information:

1. Scene of the killing
2. Pattern or series of murders
3. Confessions of the killer
4. Victims
5. Published research (Egger, 1998, pp. 16, 17)

First, the scene of the crime will tell us something about the killer or killers. Where the killings took place, how the victim was killed, how the victim was found, whether the victim was hidden from view or displayed for all to see, and what methods were used to subdue or torture the victim are all characteristics or descriptions of the kill site that will allow researchers to deduce explanations about the killer's motivation.

Second, the pattern or series of murders that have been identified as committed by a specific serial killer may give us insight into the mind of the serial killer. In this case the researcher has a larger view of the killer's acts from which to begin to understand the motivation for such killings. The similarities and differences of these murders and how they were carried out provide a clearer picture of these crimes.

Third, the confessions of the serial killer probably provide most of the information used in developing an explanation for his killings. The killer states first to the police, and frequently to the news media, book writers, and researchers, what he has done. In practically all instances the killer is asked "why?" The killer may not know or realize why he has committed these horrific acts, or he may well understand why he has committed these acts (at least in his own mind). The "why?" is of interest to all, but it is not required for criminal prosecution. In many instances, what the killer says is his motives is questioned. How much is fact and how much is fiction? The killer may honestly be telling us why he thinks he killed or he may be telling the police and others what he thinks they want to hear, based on his perception of what serial killers do, his audience's perception of the serial killer, or both.

The fourth basic source is the victims. What type of person has the killer selected as his victims? Are they simply those who crossed his path and provided the opportunity for a "kill" or abduction? Do these victims have some symbolic significance for the killer? Were they selected, abducted, or killed in similar locations?

The fifth source are theories and explanations of serial murder behavior as detailed in published research in journals and monographs. Even though only a small amount of published research has been developed on serial murder since the mid-1980s, much of this research has not been empirically tested and the data that have been collected have been limited in scope. This is primarily because there is no information on serial murder that is collected by governmental agencies on a systematic basis.

Notwithstanding these problems with workable data, we should not overlook the development of case studies of serial killers that have contributed to the growing body of literature on serial murder. A number of researchers and authors have based their analyses on a small number of case studies, and in some instances analysis and conclusions have been based on singular case studies. When multiple cases are made, comparisons can be made across cases.

In addition to research published in journals or monographs (whether they are based on limited data collection or case studies), there is a great deal of information published in newspapers accounts, electronic media, the World Wide Web, true-crime books, and government publications, which may or may not be reliable or valid. From this group of informational sources, newspapers would appear to be a major source for those conducting serious research into serial murder. However, given the nature of the mass media regarding the accuracy of reporting and the "hype" of violent crime, a great deal of crosschecking and triangulation of sources and methods is required.

OBSERVATIONS BEFORE AND AFTER APPREHENSION

Another way of viewing sources of information about serial murder behavior is to consider oneself an observer of the serial killer's behavior. Since we cannot in any practical way observe the actual killings, we must limit ourselves to what can be observed prior to the apprehension of the killer and after the apprehension of the killer.

Prior to the killer's apprehension we can observe

1. Victims
2. Crime scenes
3. Areas surrounding the crime scenes
4. Scenes of abductions
5. Areas surrounding the abductions

After the apprehension of the killer we can observe

6. Background of the killer
7. Physical characteristics of the killer
8. What the killer says about the killings (Egger, 1998, pp. 18, 19)

We can then aggregate these observations of the killings and the killer with other killings and killers and then attempt to make observations across killers.

WHO ARE THESE SERIAL KILLERS?

Who are these serial killers? A nonstratified sample of some of these killers should provide the reader with an idea of the types of individuals committing serial murder across the world.

Most people with a television or a subscription to *Time, Newsweek,* or *People* know Jeffrey L. Dahmer's deadpan stare. In July of 1991 Dahmer was charged by Milwaukee police with the death of sixteen young men and was charged with the death of one young man in Ohio. He confessed to killing and dismembering his victims and at his trial Dahmer pled guilty but insane. The judge decided Dahmer was sane and he was sentenced to 15 consecutive life sentences in Wisconsin, a state that prohibits the death penalty. He was killed in prison.

Arthur Shawcross pleaded innocent to the murders of ten women. His lawyers argued that he was legally insane. He was found guilty of second-degree murder, however, and was sentenced to a minimum of 250 years in prison in New York. He pleaded guilty to killing an eleventh victim (Olsen, 1993).

Richard Ramirez was dubbed the Night Stalker by the press. He claimed to worship Satan. A California jury convicted him of 13 murders and 30 felonies. He is incarcerated in San Quentin Prison in California (Linedecker, 1991).

Theodore Robert Bundy, one of the most infamous serial killers in the United States, was convicted of killing two college girls and a 12-year-old girl in Florida. In addition, he is believed to have killed at least twenty other females in four states. He was executed on July 24, 1989.

Shortly after his arrest on suspicion of killing an 84-year-old woman, Henry Lee Lucas confessed to killing sixty people. Following this arrest he was convicted of 11 homicides for which he was sentenced to six life sentences, the death penalty, two sentences of 75 years, and one sentence of 60 years. He is still considered a prime suspect of an additional 162 murders in 27 different states. His death sentence was commuted to life in 1998.

Wayne Williams pleaded innocent to the killing of two black youths in Atlanta, Georgia. An Atlanta jury found him guilty of two counts of murder. He was sentenced to two consecutive life terms in Georgia. Police at the time believed that Williams was responsible for the killing of 24 youths in what was referred to as the "Atlanta Child Killings." Prosecutors linked Williams to these other murders and effectively closed the files on 29 youths who had been murdered or were missing (Issacson, 1982).

Police in DesPlaines, Illinois found most of the young men killed by John Wayne Gacy, Jr. in a crawl space under Gacy's house. He was convicted of killing 33 young men. Gacy continually maintained his innocence of these killings and called himself the "34th victim." He was executed on May 10, 1994 by the State of Illinois.

Donald Harvey's coworkers called him the "Angel of Death." It seemed that whenever he was working someone died in the hospital. Harvey was charged with killing hospital patients in Ohio and Kentucky. He was convicted of 37 murders, 7 aggravated murders, and one felonious assault. He pleaded guilty to avoid the death penalty. He claims to have killed 87 people (CNN, 1993) and is believed by others to have killed an additional 23 victims (Hickey, 1997, p. 178).

"Hillside Stranglers" Angelo Buono and Kenneth Bianchi were found to have committed nine murders of young women in the Los Angeles, California area in late 1997. Bianchi was also convicted of two killings in Bellingham, Washington after his claim of a multiple personality was found to be a hoax.

For thirteen months in 1976 and 1977 the "Son of Sam" shot thirteen young men and women in eight different incidents in New York City. Six of these victims died. David Berkowitz, a twenty-four-year-old postal worker, was charged with these crimes. Claiming that a dog told him to kill, he pleaded guilty to killing five women and one man. He was sentenced to 25 years to life (Abrahamsen, 1985).

Juan Corona was found guilty in January 1973 of slaying 25 migrant farm workers in California. The prosecution argued that these were homosexual murders, but a motive for these killings was never firmly established. He was sentenced to 25 consecutive life terms. An appeals court ordered a new trial and he was again convicted for all these murders (see Kidder, 1974, or Lane & Gregg, 1992).

Albert DeSalvo claimed he was the "Boston Strangler," but police lacked evidence to bring him to trial for the thirteen female victims who had been killed between mid-1962 and early 1964. He was tried for unrelated assaults, convicted, and sentenced to life imprisonment. He was stabbed to death in his cell in 1973 (Frank, 1967; Lane & Gregg, 1992; Rae, 1967).

Westley Allan Dodd was the first person in over 30 years in this country to be executed by hanging. He was convicted in 1993 for the kidnapping, rape, and murder of three small boys. Prior to these murders he claims to have molested young boys virtually nonstop for fifteen years (CNN, 1993). Dodd is quoted as saying that if he were ever freed, "I will kill and rape again and enjoy every minute of it" (CNN, 1993).

Lawrence Bittaker and Roy L. Norris began committing a series of rapes, torture, and murder of teenage girls during the summer of 1979 in California. They had met in prison the previous year. They dumped their last victim, naked and mutilated, on the lawn of a suburban house so they could see the reaction of the press. They were found guilty of five murders and twenty-one other felonies, including rape, torture, and kidnapping. Norris received 45 years to life in prison and Bittaker received the death penalty (Markman & Dominick, 1989).

Known by the media as the "Sunset Slayer," Douglas D. Clark, together with his partner Carol Bundy, abducted and murdered six young prostitutes and runaways from Hollywood's Sunset Boulevard during the summer of 1980. Clark was found guilty of all six murders and sentenced to death. Bundy, who testified for the prosecution, received two sentences of 27 years to life and 25 years to life to run consecutively. Clark continues to deny all involvement in the murders (see MacNamara, 1990). Clark claims that Bundy (no relation) did all the killings and was attempting to duplicate Ted Bundy's crimes (personal communication, Michael Reynolds, Feb. 5, 1991).

Jerome Brudos, at 17 years of age, forced a young girl at knifepoint to pose in the nude. As a result he spent nine months in a mental hospital. Nine years later, between 1968 and 1969, he began killing young women in his garage under a special mirror he had installed to feed his fantasies. He was convicted of three murders and is serving three life sentences at the Oregon State Prison (Rule, 1980).

Richard Angelo, referred to the "Angel of Death" by the press, worked as a supervising nurse in the intensive care unit and coronary care unit of Good Samaritan Hospital in Long Island, New York. He had conducted experiments with the drugs Pavulon and Anectine on field mice and in 1987 began using these drugs on patients to put them into cardiac arrest. In some cases he would revive these patients; in other cases the patients would die. When a surviving patient complained, an investigation was initiated and 33 bodies were exhumed. Angelo was convicted of second-degree murder and manslaughter for injecting four patients with a deadly drug and was sentenced to 50 years to life. He is suspected of killing as many as 25 patients (Linedecker & Burt, 1990).

Florida law enforcement officials believe Christine Falling murdered six young children. She was found guilty of murdering three children, all under her care as she worked as their babysitter. When she is released she wants to babysit for young children again. She stated to CNN, "I just love kids to death (CNN, 1993).

Gerald Gallego and his wife Charlene went on a killing spree, abducting young women in search of the perfect sex slave and murdering them. Charlene lured women to the car Gerald was driving and often held a gun on the women while Gerald raped them. This team of killers murdered at least ten young women between 1978 and 1980 (Biondi & Hecox, 1988).

As part of a plea bargain to avoid the death penalty, Robert Berdella confessed to killing six men in Kansas, Missouri in the late 1980s. All his victims were killed by injections of an animal tranquilizer after he had tortured them and used them as his sex slave for a number of days. Berdella then dismembered the bodies. One of his victims escaped, and police found skulls and a number of pictures of the victims in his apartment. He died in prison of a heart attack in October of 1992 following a lengthy series of interviews with British television journalists (Clark & Morley, 1993).

Kenneth Allen McDuff was on death row for the murders of three teenagers in Fort Worth, Texas in 1966. His sentence was commuted to life in 1972, and in 1990 he was paroled. Less than two years later he was suspected of killing at least six women in Texas. The body of one of McDuff's victims was discovered just three days after he got out of prison. He was profiled on "America's Most Wanted" television program in May of 1992, and a caller spotted him in Kansas City, Missouri, where he was arrested. He was convicted in 1993 of killing a pregnant convenience store clerk in Temple, Texas. He is still a suspect in the disappearance of several women in the Temple, Texas area. He was sentenced to death and was executed in November 1998 (Fair, 1994).

Roy and Faye Copeland, a farm couple from rural northern Missouri, celebrated their fiftieth wedding anniversary in separate jail cells shortly after they were arrested for killing five transient farm workers with a 22-caliber rifle and burying them on the farm (Miller, 1993). Roy recently died of natural causes in a Missouri prison.

In 1964, when Edmund Kemper was 15 years old, he killed his grandparents and was committed to a California state hospital for the criminally insane. In 1969 he was released as "cured." He then murdered six young female hitchhikers and murdered his mother, all over an 11-month period. After the murder of his mother he drove to Pueblo, Colorado, where he called the local police and confessed to the murders (Cheney, 1976; Leyton, 1988).

Charles Ng, along with Leonard Lake, tortured and killed at least 11 women in their survivalist bunker near Wilseyville, California, between 1981 and 1983. They are believed to have killed at least 14 additional women during this time. Lake committed suicide shortly after his arrest in June of 1985 for theft. Ng, who was with Lake at the time, escaped and fled to Canada. The car that Ng and Lake were in led police to the killers' hideaway, a torture-murder bunker in Calaveras County. Ng was arrested in Canada in 1985 and finally extradited in September of 1991 to California, where he was arraigned on 11 counts of murder. Police found Lake's diary in the bunker. He wrote, "God meant women for cooking, cleaning house and sex and when they are not in use they should be locked up" (Associated Press, Sept., 29, 1991) (Harrington & Burger, 1993). Ng was found guilty in 1999 of 11 counts of murder of three women, six men, and two infants.

In 1997 Andrew Cunanan went on a killing spree that killed five men in Minnesota, Illinois, New Jersey, and Florida. He was referred to by the press as a gay thrill killer who committed random murders. Following the death of his fifth victim, internationally famous clothes designer Gianni Versace, the police tracked Cunanan to a houseboat in Miami. Before the police could apprehend him, he committed suicide.

Between April and December 1995, Robert Silveria killed someone riding the rails once a month. He killed in Oregon, Kansas, and Florida. In addition to the eight killings in 1995, he is suspected of killing dozens more. Nicknamed "Sidetrack," Silveria was a heroin addict who belonged to the Freight Train Riders of America (FTRA). The FTRA is an organization formed by Vietnam veterans who wear lightning-bolt tattoos, are considered welfare outlaws, and have links to the far-right militia and racist groups such as the Aryan Nations. Past and present members of this group are suspected by police of having committed some 300 murders nationwide. Silveria would wait until his victims were asleep and then beat them to death with a blunt object or a baseball bat. He would then assume the identity of his victim to collect more public welfare. When he was arrested in Oregon he had 28 food stamp accounts around the country and was picking up $119 from each one, per month. (Kershaw, 1999).

The south side of Chicago has spawned at least four serial killers between the years 1992 and 1999. In June of 1995 Hubert Geralds, Jr. was charged with the murder of six women. Some of these victims had children. Most did drugs and some had turned to prostitution to finance their drug habits. Geralds's murders were particularly difficult for the police to solve since there was little indication of foul play. Geralds's method of killing his victims was to smother them by covering their noses while pressing his thumb on their throat, leaving no marks associated with strangling.

Derrick Flewellen is also accused of strangling two women during the same time period that Geralds was killing. Ralph Harris, a third suspected serial killer, was charged with killing five men, all believed to have been robbery victims.

In May 1996 Gregory Clepper was charged with killing eight women, who apparently objected when he refused to pay them for sex. The victims in this case, according to police, were all drug addicts and prostitutes. They had all been sexually assaulted, strangled, and left in trash containers on the south side of Chicago.

Another serial murder was identified as occurring on the south side of Chicago. Chicago Police arrested Andre Crawford in January 2000. He was charged with killing 10 women and raping 11 other women between 1993 and June 1999. He confessed to these crimes on videotape to the police. A DNA sample from Crawford linked him to seven murder victims and one woman who survived a brutal assault. Most of Crawford's victims were strangled or received blunt trauma injuries. Many victims had arrest records for drugs and prostitution.

In November 1998 truck driver Wayne Adam Ford walked into the Humbolt County Sheriff's station in Eureka, California with a severed woman's breast. He then proceeded to confess to four murders of women hitchhikers and prostitutes. His trial is currently pending.

Robert Hansen was considered a family man and a respected member of the community. He owned a bakery in Anchorage, Alaska and was a member of the local Chamber of Commerce. Yet in early 1984 he entered a plea bargaining agreement in which he admitted killing 17 women and raping 30 additional women in the Anchorage area. Hansen tortured his victims in his home when his family was away and then killed his victims with a high-powered rifle after he had released them in rural areas outside of Anchorage. He buried his victims.

Like Hansen, Robert Yates, Jr. was considered to be an upstanding member of the community and a good neighbor in Spokane, Washington. He killed prostitutes in the Pacific Northwest. At least 11 Spokane women lost their lives to his brutal assaults, which began in 1996. However, it was not until two years later, at the end of 1998, that Spokane authorities admitted that they were dealing with a serial killer. Yates, the father of five, was to all, including his wife and father, simply living the American dream. That was before he was identified as a serial killer. Yates was finally arrested in April 2000 because of the long, hard work of Spokane detectives. One of his victims was buried in his back yard. After his arrest, Robert Yates pleaded guilty to two killings in Walla Walla, Washington in 1975 and another killing, that of Stacy Hawn, in 1988. The victims in the first case, a college couple, had remained unsolved for a quarter of a century. The case of Stacy Hawn had also gone unsolved. No one suspected the involvement of Robert Yates, Jr., and his admission to these killings came as a shock to the relatives of the victims, who had never suspected that the man they had read about for many months had been their children's killer. The authorities suspect that the modus operandi of these crimes may have established the future pattern of killings of Spokane prostitutes (*The Seattle Times*, Oct.18, 2000). In October 2000 Yates was taken to Tacoma, where he will face charges of killing two additonal women.

Serial killers can be found in almost every country. In October 1999 Luis Alfredo Garavito astonished Columbian police by admitting that he killed 140 children between 1994 and 1999. Most of these young victims were between 8 and 16 years of age and came from poor families whose parents were street vendors. These victims were often left on their own unattended in parks and at traffic lights as their parents approached motorists to sell their goods. Most of these victims had been found with their throat slit and their bodies mutilated; they showed forensic evidence of having been tied up. Columbian police were first alerted to a possible serial killer operating in the country when they discovered the remains of 36 bodies in the western city of Pereira in 1997.

Garavito apparently used a variety of disguises to lure his victims. He reportedly posed as a monk, a charity representative, or a street vendor like the children's parents. He would persuade his victims to walk with him to remote rural areas, where he would tie them up before torturing and killing them. As of October 1999 police had recovered 114 skeletal remains of the victims. Garavito is also suspected of killings in Ecuador, where he had lived previously (BBC, October 30, 1999).

Garavito might be considered an apprentice killer when compared to Pedro Alonzo Lopez. While Garavito exceeded 100 victims, Lopez exceeded 300 victims. Lopez may well be modern history's worst murderer, a serial killer of 350 children. Lopez became known as the "Monster of the Andes" in 1980 when he led police to the graves of 53 of his victims in Ecuador, all girls between 9 and 12 years old. Three years later he was found guilty of murdering 110 young girls in Ecuador and confessed to a further 240 murders of missing girls in nearby Peru and Colombia.

Lopez killed on a regular basis, murdering two or three girls a week over a three-year period. He said that at age eight he was going to be a killer, explaining, "I was the seventh son of 13 children of a prostitute in Tolima, Colombia. My mother threw me out when I was eight after she caught me touching my sister's breasts, and I was taken in by a man who raped me over and over again. I decided then to do the same to as many girls as possible" (Laytner, 1998, p. 19).

Ironically, given Colombia criminal law, Lopez is now a free man having been released after 18 years of captivity (less than one month for each girl he murdered). He was released in 1998 for his good behavior while in prison.

Andrei Chikatilo, a former university professor, know as "Citizen Ch." or the "Monster of Rostov" by the Russian press, confessed to killing and mutilating 22 boys, 14 girls, and 19 women (a total of 55 victims) between 1978 and 1992 in or near the city of Rostov-on-Don in Ukraine, Russia. Chikatilo's first victim was a nine-year-old girl in December 1978. However, it was not until June 1982 that one of the killer's victims was discovered, a 13-year-old girl who had left her village to buy cigarettes, bread, and sugar. And it was not until October of that year that police saw a similarity between three of Chikatilo's victims and organized a special work group of investigators to solve these three killings. Chikatilo became a suspect in these murders in 1984 and 1987, when he was placed at or near the scene of some of the murders. There were no witnesses to these murders and practically no physical evidence, except for a semen sample. Chikatilo was placed under surveillance in 1990 and arrested on November 20 of that year. Nine days later he began confessing to his horrible crimes. He was described by Russian police as having no remorse for his victims and only pity for himself. He was convicted of killing 52 people in October of 1992 and was executed on February 14, 1994 (Conradi, 1992; Cullen, 1993; Krivich, 1993; Lourie, 1993).

Another Russian serial killer is Anatoly Onoprienko, from the Ukraine, who killed 52 people between 1989 and 1996, many of them in small family groups. Though he has confessed to the 52 murders, Onoprienko claims he was not responsible for his actions, saying he was "programmed by a higher force to kill." But, according to Stepan Bilitski, a court deputy, "He is as sane as you or I. A man who was mentally sick could kill one person but then would get caught. To kill so many takes cunning. There is no doubt that he knew what he was doing" (Wroe, 1999, p. 6).

Onoprienko's confession revealed that he had been a lawless drifter throughout Europe. His first killing had been that of his landlady in 1989, at age 30, shortly after leaving the Army and moving to the southern Ukrainian port of Odessa. He continued killing throughout the summer of 1989, shooting couples in cars and stealing their money and jewelry. He then traveled throughout Europe to Germany, Hungary, Greece, Yugoslavia, and Sweden for the next six years. He refuses to talk about this part of his life. Police suspect he may have killed in all of these countries. When he returned to the Ukraine in 1995, his known killings stood at 13 victims. Within five months this death toll would stand at 52. He shot all of his known victims.

Charles Sobhraj doesn't call what he does murder; he calls it "cleaning." By his own confession, he has cleaned many times. During one year, 1976, and for no obvious motive, he befriended and then sadistically killed at least eight travelers on the drug trails through Thailand, Turkey, and India. After his conviction for one of these killings, he escaped from a Delhi high-security prison and may have orchestrated his own recapture in order to avoid being sent to Thailand, where he would almost certainly receive the death penalty for his murders. He is currently serving life imprisonment in an Indian prison. Thailand and Nepal still have a number of outstanding murder charges against Sobhraj (see Thompson, 1979, for a fascinating account of the crimes and travels of Sobhraj, and Lane and Gregg, 1992).

On August 27, 1994, Norman Afzal Simons, 29, who is suspected of being a serial killer dubbed the "Station Strangler," was charged in Cape Town, South Africa with killing 10 people, bringing to 12 the number of murder charges he faces. This serial killer is believed to have killed 21 boys and a young man over an eight-year period in and around Cape Town. In June 1995 Simons was convicted of murdering a young boy. South African police had assembled a team of three police psychiatrists to help track him. These psychiatrists were helping a team of detectives compile a psychological profile of the killer. Simons is referred to as the "Station Strangler" because several of his victims were attacked near railway stations. Most of the victims were children, who were found buried in shallow graves after being sodomized and strangled near Cape Town. A note found on one of his victims read, "one more, many more in store" (Rueters, August 10, 1995).

John Martin Scripps was serving a 13-year sentence in Hertfordshire, England for heroin trafficking when he escaped during weekend home leave in October 1994. His first murder is believed to be when he allegedly chopped up his victim, South African tourist Gerald Lowe, using butchery skills he learned in prison. His victim's remains, minus the head, were found in several black plastic bags floating in Singapore harbor. At his trial he denied that he had killed anyone. A number of police agencies disagree and believe him to have been an international serial killer. Shortly after this murder, Scripps flew to Thailand, where he is believed to have killed two Canadian tourists—Sheila Damude, a school teacher, 49 years old, and her son Darin, 23. Their passports were found in Scripp's possession when he was arrested in Singapore. He is also suspected of killing two British nationals, one in Mexico and the other in San Francisco. He was found guilty of the Singapore killing and executed on April 19, 1996 (The Herald (Glasgow), October 3, 1995).

Australian police have recently arrested a suspect in the "backpacker murders." In late June of 1994 truck driver Ivan Milat was arrested. He protested his innocence and fired his lawyer during a court appearance at which he was again refused bail. Two women backpackers, the latest of the seven backpackers to be slain in an Australian forest, were the first to be found. The forest had been chosen as the site of the Australian national orienteering championships on September 20, 1992. Without the volunteers assisting the police in looking for the missing women, they would still be two names on the missing persons list. On October 5, 1993, the next body was found close to where the first two victims were found. He had been missing in December 1989, after setting off to hitchhike with his girlfriend to a conservation festival in

Melbourne. The girlfriend's body was later found nearby. For the next two months police coordinated a search of the forest with more than four hundred volunteers. They found the remains of three more young bodies who had been stabbed and shot to death. After the discovery of the last of the seven bodies, the Australian government offered a $500,000 reward and a local paper added another $200,000 to the reward. Milat was ordered to stand trial in early December 1994 after a seven-week pretrial hearing. He was found guilty in 1995 (Millikan, 1994).

England has had its share of serial killer with Yorkshire Ripper Peter Sutcliffe, London's Dennis Nilsen, and, of course, the infamous Jack.

Peter William Sutcliffe was first arrested for carrying a hammer in 1969 and was convicted for possessing burglary tools. During that same year he was accused of attacking a woman in the red light district of Bradford, England with a weighted sock; however, he was not charged with this crime. There is no record of Sutcliffe's criminal activities for the next four years. He was married in 1974, and approximately 11 months later he began a series of 20 attacks on women for which he was eventually charged. He tried to kill two women during that year and killed a third in Leeds in October of that year. He used a hammer with each attack, and police began to suspect a serial killer. The British media dubbed these attacks the work of the "Yorkshire Ripper," after Jack the Ripper, the infamous serial killer who killed during the Victorian era in London. In November 1975 another woman was murdered, and by March 1978 Sutcliffe had killed a total of eight women and had tried to kill five others.

Between 1975 and 1981 Sutcliffe (sometimes referred to as the "harlot killer," as most of his victims were prostitutes), who was working as a truck driver, is believed to have killed 13 women and injured seven others who survived his attacks. Others credit Sutcliffe with four other murders and seven additional assaults (Yallop, 1982). He was arrested in the company of a prostitute on January 2, 1981 for theft of a car license plate; however, at the time of the arrest the arresting officers weren't really sure whom they had in custody (personal communication, David Baker, the arresting officer, May 31, 1994). Following his arrest, Sutcliffe confessed to being the "Yorkshire Ripper."

It was not until after his arrest that Sutcliffe had ever seen a psychiatrist. He was diagnosed as suffering from paranoid schizophrenia. Sutcliffe stated during his trial in London, "They [the police] had all the facts for a long time . . . But then I knew why they didn't catch me; because everything was in God's hands" (N. Davies, "Inside the Mind," *The Guardian*, 1981, May 23, p. 6). He was convicted of 13 homicides and sentenced to life in prison (Burn, 1985; see Doney in Egger, 1990; and Jouve, 1986).

Prior to his arrest, Dennis Nilsen had never been incarcerated or suspected of a crime. He had worked as a police officer for a year for the London Metropolitan Police Force. It was only when Nilsen complained to his landlord of blocked drains in his flat in the north part of London that he became of interest to the police. The police quickly found the drains clogged with body parts of Nilsen's victims. When confronted with this evidence he quickly confessed to his crimes. He had murdered 15 men in his flat between 1978 and early 1983. All of his victims were either drifters, homosexuals, or prostitutes. Only 7 of these 15 victims were ever identified. Nilsen kept his victims in his flat for days and sometimes weeks, posing them and holding one-way "conversations" with them. He was found guilty on six charges of murder and sentenced to 25 years to life in prison (Masters, 1985).

Recently, the neighbors of Frederick and Rosemary West were surprised to learn that they had lived on Cromwell Street in Gloucester with a serial killer in their midst for quite sometime. In late February of 1994 police began a search for human remains that would last 114 days and result in the unearthing of 12 female corpses from two houses in the western English city of Gloucester and a field nearby. Frederick West, 52 years of age, was charged with 11 of the murders, including that of his first wife Catherine and two daughters. His present wife Rosemary was charged with nine murders. Two other adult accomplices were charged with sexual assault on some of the deceased murder victims. The remains of nine women were found buried in the garden, cellar, and under a bath at 25 Cromwell Street, central Gloucester. The search then moved to a second house at 25 Midland Road nearby and a country field outside the city close to where West once lived. Police finished searching 25 Midland Road late in May 1994. The last body found, exhumed from the field, was that of a pregnant woman.

Bad management of health services that were seriously short of funds enabled nurse Beverly Allitt to attack children she was caring for, according to a health workers' union representative. Warning signs were apparently overlooked or ignored. Allitt was known to have incurred self-inflicted injuries and feigned illness while a student at the hospital. Her frequent absences should have been investigated and her family doctor asked if she was suitable for appointment as a nurse.

Information about Allitt was either unavailable to hospital management or lost in the hospital bureaucracy. By several criteria, she was unfit to begin work as a nurse. Hospital authorities made "a serious error of judgment" when they recommended Allitt for employment. Allitt, 25, was sentenced to 13 life sentences for the attacks, including four murders. She is detained at Rampton Special Hospital in Nottinghamshire, England.

Another medical professional in London may have killed as many as 150 of his patients. Dr. Harold Shipman, 54 years of age and a father of four, was convicted on March 31, 2000 of murdering 15 of his elderly and middle-aged female patients. Shipman was convicted of administering lethal doses of the drug diamorphine to these patients. He was also convicted of forging the will of one victim to make himself the beneficiary of a $643,000 estate. Shipman was given 15 concurrent life sentences, as there is no death penalty in England. His number of victims would make him the worst serial killer in modern British history. In at least 15 instances police found that Shipman's victims had died after receiving house visits from him, sometimes only five minutes after he entered their home. Police sources have indicated that they have identified an additional 23 alleged cases of murder connected to Shipman and have investigated 136 deaths altogether. Unfortunately, all of these victims were cremated (Moseley, 2000).

Another medical doctor involved in serial killing was Michael Swango, who recently pleaded guilty to killing four hospital patients at Ohio State University Hospital and a Veterans Affairs hospital in Northport, New York. The FBI believes Swango may have killed as many as 60 people in hospitals across the country and in Zimbabwe (see Chapter 4 for more details).

Robert Black is now referred to as Britain's worst child killer, but in 1982 he was a truck driver and not under suspicion for anything. His birth certificate has a blank space under the column headed "name and surname of father." Black's mother didn't know who the father was. Eighteen months after his birth Black was placed in foster care to a widow who died when he was 13 years old. At age 16 he was convicted of indecent assault on a six-year-old girl, and by the age of 20 he had a large collection of child pornography.

During the summer of 1982 a videotape showing a young schoolgirl reading poetry to her classmates was seen by millions of television viewers across the United Kingdom. The police were trying to jog the public's memory, believing that someone somewhere could hold a vital clue to the whereabouts of the missing child. A few days later the schoolgirl was found brutally murdered and was probably already dead when she was seen and heard on television. The police then made another plea to the British television viewers: "Help us find her killer." This was the beginning of a murder investigation (referred to as an "inquiry" in Britain) that would become the biggest manhunt ever by police in Britain. The investigation lasted nine years, utilizing unparalleled personnel resources and costing an estimated five million British pounds to conduct. ("Long Trail to Find Black," 1994). The investigation involved both Scottish and English police and initially four separate police forces.

In March 1986 after the third young victim was found dead (four weeks after she was reported missing) 70 miles from her home near Leeds, 15 police forces attended a Scotland Yard conference on a series of child murders and abductions across the country. The Nottingham police force then joined what was to become the largest computerized murder investigation ever in the United Kingdom.

In July 1990, a six-year-old girl was abducted by Black and dragged inside his van. A neighbor, who saw the incident, took the van's license number and alerted the police. When police located and stopped the van, they rescued the young girl and arrested Black. The victim's hands had been tied behind her back, two pieces of plaster were stuck over her face, and a bag had been placed over her head. (Staff, 1995, Feb. 21, "Serial Killer Loses Appeal").

Black was convicted of abduction and assault in August 1990. He was subsequently found guilty of kidnapping, murder, and improper burial of three young girls, ages five, ten, and eleven. He was also found guilty of kidnapping a fourth girl. Black committed these crimes between 1982 and 1986. On May 19, 1994, Black, 47, began serving a minimum of 35 years in prison for these murders. Police believe he may be responsible for between 13 and 17 other murders of young children.

Donato Bilancia is suspected by Rome police of having killed six prostitutes and two security guards in 1998. Also at the time of Bilancia's arrest in May 1998 he became a suspect in five other killings. The prostitute victims were found near train stations with bullets to the head or neck (Goodfellow, 1998).

When Christine Malevre first admitted to killing 30 people, she received 5000 letters of support and a book contract. She became a heroine to many people in France. Malevre, a 29-year-old nurse who specializes in dealing with the terminally ill, said she "accompanied" her victims to death, because it would have been "inhuman" to do otherwise. However, following two separate psychiatric reports, officials are charging her with premeditated murder. These reports found her to be "a person with true compassion," a person with a megalomaniac desire to be in a "position of power" over her patients (Lichfield, 1999, p. 17).

WHAT DO WE KNOW ABOUT THESE KILLERS

Holmes and DeBurger (1988) found certain elements that allow us to distinguish serial murder from other forms of multicides and begin to tell us about these killers.

1. The central element is repetitive homicide. The serial murderers kill again and again and will continue to kill if not prevented.
2. Serial murders are typically one-on-one.
3. The relationship between the killer and victim is typically nonexistent. Serial murder seldom occurs between people who are intimates.
4. The serial killer is motivated to kill; these are not typical crimes of passion in the conventional sense, nor do they stem from victim precipitation.
5. Apparent and clear-cut motives may typically be missing in most serial killers (adapted to exclude examples and references, pp. 30, 31)

Holmes and Holmes (1998) found most known serial killers to be between the ages of 25 and 35. Hickey (1997), who differentiated gender, found the average male to be 27.5 years and the average female offender 30 years. Although the race of the serial killer has been found to be predominantly white and killings to be intraracial, with few exceptions, Hickey found 20 percent of his sample to be black serial killers.

Contrary to popular misconceptions, serial killers are not highly educated and in most cases do not hold professional jobs. Hickey (1997) argues that the killer's ability to kill without detection appears to be more a function of cunning and deceit than intellectual abilities or academic attainment. Egger (1998) has argued that it is at best this cunning and deceit (or street sense, which he found in his case study of Henry Lee Lucas) in combination with "linkage blindness," law enforcement's inability to link homicides to a serial pattern, which facilitates the killer's success.

Serial killers do not commonly use firearms as their sole means of killing. Mutilation, suffocation, or strangulation are the predominant methods of killing.

Earlier research on the motivation of the serial killer and the "conventional wisdom" of the press and automatic "experts" seemed to point to sexual gratification as the driving force behind the serial killer. This view has changed or been modified as serial murder research has become more serious and sophisticated. Most serious researchers currently believe that sex is only an instrument used by the serial killer to obtain power and dominance over his victim. Although frequently present in a serial murder, the sexual component is not the central factor for the killer but an instrument used to dominate, control, and destroy the victim.

Serial killers are frequently referred to as psychopaths and have a personality disorder involving a range of affective, behavioral, and interpersonal characteristics. The primary personality characteristics identified by Cleckley (1964) include a lack of empathy, guilt, or remorse for those who suffer from the results of their actions, and a callous disregard for the feelings, rights, and welfare of others.

The term *psychopath* has been replaced with the phrase *antisocial personality disorder* in the *Diagnostic and Statistic Manual of Mental Disorders IV* of 1994 (DSM-IV). As in previous editions, many of the characteristics of the psychopath, now antisocial personality disorder, have been derived from Cleckley's work. The problem is that, whatever the label, the typical characteristics or lack of certain characteristics only allow for the ruling out of individuals and do not allow for the ruling in of individuals. Further, as Meloy (1988) notes, the criteria for this diagnosis are "too descriptive, inclusive, criminally based, and socioeconomically skewed to be of much clinical or research use" (p. 6). Hare (1993) argues that antisocial personality disorder refers primarily to a cluster of criminal and antisocial behaviors, while psychopathy is defined by a cluster of both personality traits and socially deviant behaviors. Rather than referring to serial killers as fitting the antisocial personality disorder, it might be more useful to utilize Hare's psychopathy checklist (1993). However, identifying the key symptoms of psychopathy in an individual does not classify him or her as a serial killer.

Inadequate socialization or childhood trauma are possibly the most frequently cited in theories for serial murder behavior. While there does seem to be a strong correlation for these theories, empirical evidence is lacking. The intense rage of the serial killer may be a reflection of the horror suffered in childhood. A number of researchers have found persistent feelings of powerlessness and helplessness (Storr, 1972); wretched states of social and psychological deprivation (Reinhardt, 1962); violent punishing practices (Willie, 1975); abuse and neglect early in life (Hazelwood & Douglas, 1980); and a lack of kindness by parents and a lack of emotional ties to his or her family members (Ellis & Gullo, 1971). It should be noted here that serial killers are frequently found to have unusual or unnatural relationships with their mothers (Bjere, 1981; Egger, 1998; Lunde, 1976; Starr et al., 1984).

The motivational dynamics of serial murder seem to be consistent with research on the nature of rape (Egger, 1985). Power would appear to be the vital component of either crime. As West (1987) has noted, "it may take only a small increase in the desperation of the assailant or the resisting victim to convert a rape into a murder" (p.180). Canter (1994) has recently noticed this similarity in his research by indicating that the admitted rapists he has spoken to have often admitted that they would have killed future victims if they had not been caught.

A serial killer's biological makeup may contribute to his acts. A killer's characteristics may be abnormalities in the brain caused by trauma, brain damage, or genetic traits from birth. Adriane Raine's research in Denmark, England, and the United States strongly implies that birth complications can lead to mild brain damage that may go unnoticed throughout childhood yet predispose a boy to violent behavior in adulthood. Raine's research suggests that birth complications could have produced a prefrontal dysfunction in the brain that leads to low levels of arousal and underaroused people seek our arousal to bring their levels back to normal. One of the ways to do this is through the commission of violent acts (Connor, 1994).

Jonathon Pincus, a noted neurologist, argues that when brain damage, abuse, and psychiatric impairments are all present, a very violent person can be produced. Richard Restak, neurologist and neuropsychiatrist, disagrees with Pincus. Restak argues that behavior doesn't necessarily imply brain damage (Griffiths, 1993).

Unfortunately, serial killers appear on our streets, in our neighborhoods, and on our highways as the average person. They do not appear as a "mutant from Hell." Once a serial killer is caught, we are quick to comment on the killer's appearance: "He looks like he is evil." "He looks like a serial killer." "I wouldn't want to meet him in a dark alley!" However, without the label of serial killer, in most instances the killer looks very ordinary or like everyone else.

Many serial killers are very quiet and hard to spot. When Joel Rifkin confessed to murdering 17 prostitutes in the New York City area, a high school classmate said that he was a quiet, "shy, not the kind of guy who would do something like this." When David Berkowitz, better know as the "Son of Sam," was convicted of murders in New York City, a former Army friend stated, "He was quiet and reserved and kept pretty much to himself." When Westley Allen Dodd was arrested for kidnapping, rape, and murder of three small boys, one of his neighbors stated, "Wes seemed so harmless, such an all-around, basic good citizen" (Griffiths, 1993).

There are female serial killers as well as male serial killers; however, we don't know as much about them. Hickey (1997) found in his analysis of 62 female serial killers that the average number of victims per killer ranged from 7 to 9, or slightly different from their male counterparts (6 to 11). He found that one-fourth of these killers killed strangers and one-third killed at least one stranger. Overall, one-third of the females in Hickey's sample killed only family members and half killed at least one family member. When the victims of these female serial killers were strangers, young boys and girls were the likely target. Hickey also found that when the killers acted alone, patients in hospitals and nursing homes were the preferred target. When family members were the victims, husbands were almost always the targets.

Hickey found that nearly half of the female killers used poison. Very few of them were sexually involved with their victims, nor did they use particularly violent methods of killing. Although motive is difficult to ascertain without primary empirical evidence, Hickey maintains that the women's motives were financial security, revenge, enjoyment, and sexual stimulation, in that order of priority.

According to Homes and DeBurger (1985), there are four general types of serial killers:

1. Visionary—psychotic, suffering from severe break with reality
2. Mission oriented—task or mission to rid community or world of a particular group to people (two subtypes: either demon mandated or God mandated)
3. Hedonistic (three subtypes: either lust killer who commits necrophilia, thrill killer who keeps victim alive as long as possible and feeds off of terror victim, and comfort killer)
4. Power/control—want total control over victim and to hold fate of victim in their hands

Fox and Levin (1999) have since modified Holmes and DeBurger's framework by reclassifying serial murderers into three categories, each with two subtypes:

1. Thrill
   a. Sexual sadist (the most common)
   b. Dominance
2. Mission
   a. Reformist (to rid the world of filth and evil such as prostitutes)—Many are also motivated by thrill seeking
   b. Visionary—Believe they hear the voice of God or the devil instructing them to kill
3. Expedience
   a. Profit
   b. Protection—To cover up criminal activity (adapted from pp. 90, 91)

Egger (1998), in his development of four case studies of serial killers, found a number of similarities across cases. While only four cases were used in this cross-case analysis, some of the resulting similarities would appear to be consistent with other serial murder research. In order to provide consistency, the same variables or dimensional categories were used in the comparison. The four serial killers studied were John Wayne Gacy, Henry Lee Lucas, Kenneth Bianchi, and Theodore Robert Bundy. All were born into a working class family. Only Bundy and Lucas abused alcohol. Bundy, Gacy, and Bianchi were very neat and orderly in their lifestyle. All these murderers had first experienced sexual intercourse in their early to late teens. Gacy, Bianchi, and Lucas all experienced childhood trauma. Gacy experienced blackouts, which were never diagnosed. Bianchi experienced urination problems and reportedly had severe respiratory infections. Lucas suffered the loss of an eye in an accident as a young child. All four killers had a strong interest in law enforcement.

Bundy, Bianchi, and Lucas were illegitimate children who had domineering mothers. Gacy, Bianchi, and Lucas had mothers with emotional problems. Gacy, Bianchi, and Lucas had all been married and then divorced. All four of these killers, with the possible exception of Lucas, were very manipulative of situations and people. All of these killers were either unable or unwilling to establish lasting relationships with others.

Only Lucas and Bundy were known to have a juvenile delinquency record. However, all men were identified by psychiatrists and psychologists as having antisocial personalities. Clinical diagnosis found them to be strongly resistant to authority, obsessed with controlling or manipulating others, and almost never sharing their true feelings with others.

Bundy, Gacy, and Bianchi posed as law enforcement officers to persuade their victims to accompany them. All killers carried corpses of their victims in their vehicles. Many of the killers' victims were particularly vulnerable to assault or abduction because of their lifestyle or perceived powerlessness, such as young girls out by themselves or homosexuals "cruising" for sexual contacts. Three of these killers used strangulation as their primary means of killing. Lucas used a knife as well as strangulation.

All of these murderers saw themselves in control of others either through their manipulative personalities or physical force. In many cases they failed to recognize any of their own faults and tended to rationalize their behavior by blaming others for their situation. All seemed to be unable or unwilling to delay their gratification.

They all showed a strong disdain for law enforcement authorities. Once caught, all seemed to enjoy the celebrity status of being labeled a serial killer.

WHO ARE THE VICTIMS OF SERIAL KILLERS?

While running the risk of becoming a victim of a serial killer is indeed very small, this should not alter our concern for the victims of serial killers or the dynamic of victimization.

Using three mobility types of serial killers, Hickey (1997) found that 20 to 23 percent of victims were killed in specific places, 36 to 43 percent of victims were killed by offenders identified as local killers, and 36 to 41 percent of victims were killed by traveling killers. Hickey also found that 59 to 63 percent of all victims in this database were killed by men and women who generally stayed close to home. However, the victims of these serial killers were more likely to be killed away from home. Hickey found place-specific serial killers to be responsible for the smallest percentage of victims but to have the highest number of victims per case.

Since 1975 Hickey (1997) found an increase of stranger-to-stranger serial killing over acquaintance and family serial killing. During this period, 76 percent of serial killers murdered at least one stranger. Hickey argues that this trend is due to the killer seeking safety from detection (in other words, elimination of witnesses) and the degree of power and control the killer can exert over his victim.

Most victims from Hickey's database (399) were women and children, a group of victims that could certainly be considered weak, helpless, and without power or control. Hickey found that "in general, serial killers have victimized female adults (65%) consistently more than male adults, but half of all offenders surveyed had killed at least one male adult" (1997, p. 112). Also of note, Hickey found that since 1975 cases of one or more elderly victims had risen significantly.

Egger's (1998) research on the victims of serial killers and the preliminary analysis of K. Egger's (1999) database are generally consistent with Hickey's work. It should be noted, however, that K. Egger's work does show a larger percentage of stranger-to-stranger offender-victim relationships than is indicated by Hickey.

WHAT DO WE KNOW ABOUT THE VICTIMS OF SERIAL MURDER?

One of the most frequent victims of the serial killer is the female prostitute. From the killer's view these women are simply available in an area that provides anonymity, comfort from easy detection, and adequate time in which to make a viable selection. It is highly probable that the serial killer selects prostitutes more frequently because they are easy to lure and control during the initial stages of abduction. Potential witnesses of this abduction see a pickup and transaction of paying for sex. Egger's (1998) search of newspapers from October 5, 1991 to October 5, 1993 found 198 prostitutes who were victims of serial killers involving 21 different and distinct murder patterns for an average of nine prostitute victims per murder. No other group of victims was found that frequently among identified serial murder victims during that period. For the female prostitute, lifestyle certainly plays a part in her being an at-risk prey for the serial killer.

It was not only the brilliant acting of Anthony Hopkins portraying Hannibal Lecter in the movie *Silence of the Lambs* that transformed this fictional serial killer from a cruel and sadistic animal to an antihero in our culture. The public is simply preprogrammed to identify with and even laud the role of the serial killer in our society. The victims of serial killers are viewed as valueless strata of society that become the "less dead" (since for many they were less alive before their death and now they become the "never were") and their demise seems to wash away the "less desirable" elements of our society. Victims become those who "had it coming" or whose fate was preordained. While the public may openly abhor this violence, they are privately excusing the killer's acts as utilitarian or derived from motives best explained by a terrible parentage or childhood trauma on the part of the killer.

Victims become less important, and the multiple nature of the killer's acts and his ability to elude the police for long periods of time become the central focus of this phenomenon, which transcends the very reason he is being hunted. The killer's elusiveness overshadows the trail of grief and horror he leaves behind.

If many serial killers were victimized in childhood, as case studies and research suggest, and vulnerable due to their childhood situation, they may in fact be choosing victims like their earlier selves or from the general lifestyle to victimize. While no hard empirical evidence exists to substantiate this, the literature does suggest that many of these killers have been abused, neglected, and victimized in their childhood. Perhaps a number of serial killers are victimizing earlier versions of their youth.

Interviews and case studies of serial killers appear to indicate that these killers depersonalize or make their victims into less than human beings. For the killer these victims are objects. When serial killer Henry Lee Lucas (eleven homicide convictions) was asked how he selected his victims he stated, "Ya don't know what your go'in to get till ya get there." When asked how he felt after killing a victim, he stated, "I was more or less at peace. I didn't feel anything for the victim. She was just an object I had to get rid of" (author's notes of interview in 1985). Apparently, making objects of victims prevents the killer from identifying them as mothers, fathers, children, people who love, and people whose lives have meaning.

Unfortunately, there is a great deal less pressure on the police when the victims of serial murder come from the marginal elements of society or the community. The public has little concern over a serial murderer operating in their area when they have little or no identification with the victim. In this case, the victims seem far from real and little attention is paid to their demise.

As can be seen from press accounts in newspapers and television news reports, victims and survivors receive little attention in mass media accounts of crime. Unless victims are well-known celebrities or people with wealth or power, the central focus of the media is on the crime and the offender. Victims are of little interest, and survivors are, for the most part, ignored and quickly forgotten.

Most of the victims of serial murder are vulnerable, being perceived as powerless or prestigeless by most of society. A lack of power or prestige defines them as easy prey for the serial killer. A careful selection of vulnerable victims does not mean the serial killer is a coward, only that he has the "street smarts" to select victims who will not resist, will be relatively easy to control, and will not be missed. For the killer such a selection protects him from identification and apprehension. The killer is selecting the "less dead."

Much of the research on serial murder has concentrated on finding similarities among the murderers. One of the greatest similarities among serial murderers is their consistent choice of victims, people who tend to be vulnerable or those who are easy to lure and dominate. Part of these victims' vulnerabilities may be the locations that they frequent, or the fact that they are powerless, or that they are considered throw-aways of our society. Many are frequently not missed or reported missing by others. They are the "less dead." K. Egger's (1999) preliminary analysis of a portion of her database between 1946 and 1987 found that 73 percent of the victims killed 367 killers as fitting the definition of the "less dead."

CONCLUSION

As the title of Egger's (1990) monograph, *Serial Murder: An Elusive Phenomenon,* implies, the behavior of serial killers and their victims is not well understood. Many questions remain to be answered. How does the serial killer select his victim, and how have selected victims escaped death? Can at-risk populations reduce the probability of their victimization from a serial murderer? Will the development of refined typologies of serial murder facilitate a clearer understanding of serial murderers and thus increase meaningful research of serial murder? How can the incidence and prevalence of serial murder be determined more accurately? Is the incidence of serial murder increasing in this country? What are the preadolescent and adolescent characteristics of serial murderers that would distinguish them from their birth cohort? Why does the United States appear to have so many serial murderers compared to the number of other countries?

These are only examples of some of the questions that must be answered. These killers and their victims are still among us today and still very elusive. Research continues and, for the sake of the victims, must continue.

REFERENCES

Abrahamsen, D. (1973). *The murdering mind.* New York: Harper & Row.

BBC World News Service. *World: Americas Columbian Child Killer Confesses.* Bbc.co.uk. October 30, 1999.

Biondi, R., & W. Hecox. (1992). *Dracula Killer: True Story of California's Vampire Killer.* New York: Pocket Books.

Bjere, A. (1981) *The Psychology of Murder: A Study in Criminal Psychology.* (reprint of 1927 ed.) New York: De Capo Press.

Burn, G., (1984). *"Somebody's Husband, Somebody's Son": The Story of Peter Sutcliffe.* London: Heinemann.

Burn, G. (1985). *Somebody's Husband, Somebody's Son: The Story of the Yorkshire Ripper* (1st American ed.). New York, N.Y.: Viking.

Canter, D. (1994). *Criminal Shadows: Inside the Mind of a Serial Killer.* London: Harper-Collins.

Cheney, M. (1976). *The Co-Ed Killer.* New York: Walker.

Clark, S., & M. Morley. (1993). *Murder in Mind: Mindhunting the Serial Killers.* London: Boxtree Limited.

Cleckley, H. (1964). *The Mask of Sanity.* (4th ed). St. Louis, MO: Mosby.

Connor, S. (1994, March 6). "Crimes of Violence: Birth of a Solution." *The Independent,* p. 19.

Conradi, P. (1992). *The Red Ripper.* New York: Walker.

Cullen, R. (1993). *The Killer Department: Detective Viktor Burakov's Eight-Year Hunt for the Most Savage Serial Killer in Russian History.* New York: Pantheon Books.

Egger, K. (1999). *Preliminary Database on Serial Killers from 1900 to 1999.* (draft)

Egger, S. (1984). "A Working Definition of Serial Murder and the Reduction of Linkage Blindness." *Journal of Police Science and Administration,* 12(3): 348–357.

——— (1985). *Serial Murder and the Law Enforcement Response.* Unpublished dissertation. College of Criminal Justice, Sam Houston State University, Huntsville, TX.

——— (1990). *Serial Murder: An Elusive Phenomenon.* New York: Praeger.

——— (1998). *The Killers among Us: An Examination of Serial Murder and Its Investigation.* Upper Saddle River, NJ: Prentice Hall.

Ellis, A., & J. Gullo, (1971). *Murder and Assassination.* New York: Lyle Stuart Inc.

Fair, K. (1994, July). "Kenneth McDuff: Death Row." *Police,* pp. 56–58.

Fox, J. A., & J. Levin. (1999). "Serial Murder: Popular Myths and Empirical Realities." In M.D. Smith & M. Zahn (Eds.), *Homicide: A Sourcebook of Social Research.* Thousand Oaks, CA: Sage.

Goodfellow, M. (1998, May 8). "Italian Serial Killer Case Widens." Rueters News Service.

Griffiths, R. (producer and director). (1993). "Murder by Number" (videotape). Atlanta, GA: CNN.

Hare, R. (1993). *Without Conscience: The Disturbing World of the Psychopaths Among Us.* New York: Pocket Books.

Harrington, J. & R. Burger. (1993). *Eye of Evil.* New York: St. Martin's Press.

Hazelwood, R. R., & J. E. Douglas. (1980). "The Lust Murderer." *FBI Law Enforcement Bulletin,* April, pp. 1–5.

Hickey, E. (1997). *Serial Murderers and Their Victims.* (2nd ed.). Belmont, Ca.: Wadsworth Publications

Holmes, R., & S. Holmes, (1994). *Murder in America.* Thousand Oaks, CA: Sage.

——— (1998). *Serial Murder* (2nd ed.). Thousand Oaks, CA: Sage

Holmes, R., & J. DeBurger. (1988). *Serial Murder.* Thousand Oaks, CA: Sage.

——— (1985). *Profiles in Terror. The Serial Murderers.* Paper presented at annual meeting of Academy of Criminal Justice Sciences, Las Vegas, NV, March 18.

Issacson, W. (1982). "A Web of Fiber and Fact." *Time,* March 28, p. 18.

Jouve, N. W. (1986). *"The Street Cleaner": The Yorkshire Ripper Case on Trial.* London: Marion Boyers.

Kershaw, A. (1999, March 27). "Death on the Rails." *The Guardian,* p 38.

Kidder, T. (1974). *The road to Yuba City.* Garden City, NY. Doubleday.

Krivich, M. (1993). *Comrade Chikatilo: The Psychopathology of Russia's Notorious Serial Killer.* Fort Lee, NJ: Barricade Books.

Lane, B., & W. Gregg. (1992). *The Encyclopedia of Serial Killers.* London: Headline House.

Laytner, R. (1998, December 6). "Murderer of 350 Children Free to Slaughter More." *Scotland on Sunday*, p. 19.

Levin J., & J. A. Fox. (1985). *Mass Murder*. New York: Plenum.

Leyton, E. (1986). *Hunting Humans: The Rise of the Modern Multiple Murderer*. Toronto, Ontario, Canada: McClelland & Stewart.

Lichfield, J. (1999, June 18). "French 'Angel of Mercy' is Charged with Murder." *The Independent (London)*, p. 17.

Linedecker, C. L. (1991). *Night Stalker*. New York: St. Martin's Press.

Linedecker, C. L., & W. A. Burt. (1990). *Nurses Who Kill*. New York: Pinacle.

"Long Trail to Find Black," (1994, May 20). *The Independent*, p. 3.

Lourie, R. (1993). *Hunting the Devil: The Pursuit, Capture and Confession of the Most Savage Killer in History*. New York: HarperCollins.

Lunde, D. T. (1976). *Murder and Madness*. Stanford, CA: Stanford Alumni Association.

Masters, B. (1985). *Killing for Company: The Case of Dennis Nilsen*. London: J. Cape.

Miller, T. (1993, Sept.). "Death Row: Ray and Faye Copeland." *Police*, pp. 62–66.

Millikan, R. (1994, December 13). "Backpacker Murders." *The Independent*, p. 15.

Markman, R., & B. Dominick. (1989). *Alone with the Devil: Famous Cases of a Courtroom Psychiatrist*. New York: Doubleday.

Meloy, J. R. (1988). *The Psychopathic Mind: Origins, Dynamics, and Treatment*. Northvale, NJ: Jason Aronson.

Miller, T. (1993, Sept.). "Death Row: Ray and Faye Copeland." *Police*, pp. 62–66.

Moseley, R. (2000, February 1). "Setting Grisly Record, British Doctor Convicted of Killing 15." *Chicago Tribune*, p. 6.

Olsen, J. (1993). *The Misbegotten Son: A Serial Killer and His Victims: The True Story of Arthur J. Shawcross*. New York: Delacorte Press.

Reinhardt, J. M. (1962). *The Psychology of a Strange Killer*. Springfield, IL: Charles C. Thomas.

Reuters News Service. (1995, August 10). "Station Strangler Is Charged."

Rule, A. (1980). *The Stranger Beside Me*. New York: New American Library.

Staff. (1999, October 3, 1995). "Trial Told of Butchery Skills of Alleged British Serial Killer." *The Hearld (Glasgow)*, p. 8.

Staff. (2000, October 18). "Yates to Plead Guilty." *The Seattle Times*, p.1.

Starr, M. et al. (1984). "The Random Killers." *Newsweek*. November 26, pp. 100–106.

Storr, A. (1972). *Human Destructiveness*. New York: Basic Books.

Thompson, T. (1979). *Serpentine*. New York: Dell.

U.S. Department of Justice. (2000). *Crime Report 1999*. Washington, DC: U.S. Government Printing Office.

West, D. J. (1987). *Sexual Crimes and Confrontations: A Study of Victims and Offenders*. Brookfield, VT: Gower.

Willie, W. S. (1975). *Citizens Who Commit Murder: A Psychiatric Study*. St. Louis, MO: Warren H. Green.

Wroe, G. (1999, April 18). "Touching Evil." *The Sunday Herald*, p. 6.

Yallop, D. A. (1982). *Deliver Us from Evil*. New York: Coward McCann & Geoghegan.

DARKNESS IN THE BLUEGRASS: KENTUCKY'S TIES TO MASS MURDERERS AND SERIAL KILLERS

Barry Royalty

If you have been a resident of or visitor to Kentucky, you may have been in the presence of a killer. He may have been driving next to you on one of the interstates, or even eating at a nearby table in your favorite restaurant. Perhaps he had worked alongside you at one time or another, or patiently waited in the shadows as you took an evening stroll in your neighborhood.

Some of the most notorious mass murderers and serial killers have had connections to Kentucky. A few have lived part of their lives there. Others were just passing through. And then there are those who have left Kentuckians in the wake of their trails of terror.

On November 12, 1934, 16-year-old Kathleen Maddox of Ashland, Kentucky gave birth to an illegitimate son in Cincinnati. Hospital records listed the baby as "no name Maddox." He would be later known as Charles Manson.

Charles Manson, in Nuel Emmons's book *Manson In His Own Words*, described his mother as a "pretty promiscuous little broad" who drank a lot and got into trouble. After living with several men, she married a much older man named William Manson. The marriage soon ended in divorce. His biological father was allegedly from Ashland as well, but Charles never knew him. Manson explained, "The guy who planted the seed was a young drugstore cowboy who called himself Colonel Scott. He was a transient laborer working on a nearby dam project, and he didn't stick around long enough to even watch the belly rise."

Kathleen's frequent disappearances from home (one which led to a five-year prison sentence for armed robbery) left Charles to spend his early childhood being passed off from one relative to another. One of his favorite places was the home of his Uncle Jess in Morehead, Kentucky. He fondly recalled, "Uncle Jess lived in a log cabin elevated several feet off the ground by poles. Jess was hillbilly from his heart, with beard, bare feet, bib overalls, moonshine, hound dogs, and coon hunting." But that living situation came to an abrupt end when, upon pursuit by law enforcement, his uncle blew up his moonshine still—and himself.

Following years would take him through a string of foster homes, juvenile institutions, and eventually prison after developing a talent for theft and burglary.

In 1967, the 32-year-old Manson was released from prison. He moved to San Francisco, where he became the charismatic leader of a cult known as "the Family." Mostly comprised of petty criminals and young women from troubled backgrounds, the group resided at a movie stunt ranch, where Manson controlled them with sex, hallucinogenic drugs, and the preaching of his philosophy. He directed his disciples to prepare for "Helter Skelter," a race war from which only the Family would survive to rule the cities.

In August 1969, Manson launched his attempt to induce the racial holocaust and to exact revenge on the Establishment for his frustrated music career. He sent selected members of the Family to director Roman Polanski's home, where they murdered actress Sharon Tate and four others. Tate was eight months pregnant. On the following night, Manson and six accomplices broke into the house of Leno and Rosemary LaBianca, killing them. The crime scenes were grisly. The victims had been shot, beaten with blunt objects, and repeatedly stabbed. Messages such as "DEATH TO PIGS," "RISE," and the misspelled "HEALTER SKELTER" were found scrawled on walls and a refrigerator door from the blood of one of the victims. Manson and other cultists are serving life sentences for their crimes after what had been the longest murder trial in American history.

As developments in this trial gripped the nation, speculation began to circulate that Manson and the Family may have killed in Kentucky. During the evening of May 27, 1969, Colonel Scott's brother Darwin was hacked to death in his Ashland apartment. His body was found pinned to the floor with a butcher knife. Several local residents had claimed to have made a positive identification of Manson as a mysterious man calling himself "Preacher" who came into town on a motorcycle in the spring of that year. Accompanied by several women, he allegedly distributed LSD to area teenagers. The band of strangers attempted to establish a commune in an abandoned farmhouse until April, when vigilantes burned it down and drove them off the property. Fingerprint analysis of the apartment yielded no link between Manson and his followers to Scott's murder, but the case is still open.

During the summer of 1976, 23-year-old David Berkowitz began a series of killings that terrorized New York City for over 13 months. Armed with a .44-caliber revolver, he stalked dark streets and lovers' lanes, shooting his randomly chosen victims at point-blank range as they sat on stoops or in their cars. He left a note at one of the crime scenes and sent another to newspaper columnist Jimmy Breslin that contained such prose as "Hello from the gutters of NYC . . . I am a monster. I am the Son of Sam . . . I love to hunt." Berkowitz was arrested in August 1977, leaving a casualty list of six dead and seven wounded. He told police that he was ordered to kill by a 6000-year-old demon that spoke to him through a neighbor's dog. Determined to be sane, he was convicted of murder and sentenced to over 300 years in prison. He was eligible for parole in 2002.

The "Son of Sam" moniker is widely known. But few are aware that just two years prior to his first murder, David Berkowitz was stationed at Fort Knox in the 8th Battalion, 4th Brigade. Reassigned to the base in 1973, he worked as a clerk despite his qualifications as a trained sharpshooter with the M-16 rifle. His military psychological tests, in fact, had determined that he was "perfect for infantry service." He remained at Fort Knox until his enlistment was finished in June 1974.

Some of those who knew Berkowitz at Fort Knox gave their recollections of him to John Filiatreau of *The Courier-Journal* shortly after his arrest. Diane Heaberlin was a civilian who worked in the office. She recalled, "He was a bird watcher. Sometimes he'd go and stand at the window and watch the birds playing in the grass. I don't know if it helped him think, or what. There would always be this look in his eye, like he was far off somewhere, and I thought he was trying to think of solutions to problems of some kind . . . with this funny look on his face."

David R. Kisselbaugh of Elizabethtown stated, "He had a very good sense of humor, I thought . . . He'd get out and ride his bike on Sunday . . . He told me he had a job lined up for the outside. He never told me what it was and I didn't pry. He didn't drink. He was a trooper."

Sgt. Gary Flammini added, "He was the type of person who didn't leave a lasting impression. He was quiet and shy, just did his job." Berkowitz reportedly would sometimes chat with him about "various weapons and shells and what they would do to a human body," but the discussions were considered at the time to be idle military talk. Flammini lamented, "It is a little shocking to find out that somebody you knew, somebody you used to have little conversations with, now after two or three years is a . . ."

Berkowitz also attended church in Louisville, where many worshipers remembered him as an exemplary Christian. In a letter he sent to me from Sullivan Correctional Facility, Berkowitz himself shared some thoughts on this period of his life and on his experiences since that time. "I was basically a lonely soldier far from home," he wrote. "I enjoyed those Sundays when I was able to go to Beth Haven Baptist Church. Those people were very kind. I went to this church on and off for about six or seven months, I believe. I did not own a car at the time, but they had a bus service that would pick up men from the base. I did not understand much about Christianity, but I was glad to be able to get off the base on Sunday mornings and meet people from what we soldiers used to call the 'free world.' If I could go back in time and do things differently, I would have stayed in Kentucky. I did not know all that would befall me and what path my life would take when I returned to New York City (the Bronx) where I was born and raised . . . I was just hoping for a normal future . . . I am so sorry about what happened and the loss of innocent lives. God knows my heart and He knows my endless regret. Of course words are cheap unless they are followed by actions. And let God be my witness that with every ounce of my strength I am trying to reach out to others, especially troubled teens and other prisoners, to warn them and hopefully keep them from taking the path that I did and from coming to prison. There is so much despair in these places. In the past 22-plus years in prison, I have seen so many young men coming in here. Many of them are doing long sentences and have virtually thrown away their lives."

The reference Berkowitz makes to troubled teens points to the tragic outbreak of violent crimes over the last several years involving adolescents across the nation. Kentucky has not been immune to such incidents. Two of the most bizarre cases are those of murders that were committed by members of teenage occult groups.

In November 1996, a group of teens from a self-proclaimed "Vampire Clan" in Western Kentucky traveled to Florida, where they bludgeoned to death the parents of one of its members. Often wearing black clothing, dark makeup, and accessories such as dog collars, the cult's constituents immersed themselves in a vampire role-playing game. Murray police detective Sgt. Mike Jump enumerated their other activities. "They apparently like to suck blood," Jump said. "They cut each other's arms and suck the blood. They cut up small animals and suck the blood. They honestly believe they're vampires."

Less than five months later, a couple in Tennessee and their six-year-old daughter were fatally shot in a ditch after being carjacked at a highway rest stop. Their two-year-old son miraculously survived his gunshot wounds. The perpetrators were six teens from three Eastern Kentucky counties whose leader would often threaten to cast evil spells on her enemies. The group was allegedly involved in satanic practices such as mixing their blood in a cup and drinking it, and they were seen performing a ritual in a Pikeville motel room just days before the murders. The mother of one of the teens told the *Lexington Herald-Leader* that she doubted a formal cult existed but hinted that something in that motel may have initiated the killings. "From what I hear, maybe Friday they did something that unleashed a powerful demon spirit on them," she said.

As experts from various fields struggle to identify the causes and solutions to teen violence, David Berkowitz relayed to me his unique perspective on the problem. In doing so, he may have offered a glimpse into his own childhood memories. "I am also saddened by all of the violent incidents that have been happening in public schools and on America's streets involving troubled teenagers," he wrote. "I believe that the answer is a personal relationship with Jesus Christ. Young people need to be shown a lot of parental love. They need to learn about the value of another person, and about the sanctity of life. I know that many may scoff at what I am going to say now, but I do believe that 'Hollywood' and the entertainment industry does play a small part in devaluing life. The movies are constantly portraying violent characters, crimes and murders. How many deaths and violent scenes does the average teenager see in the movies or on TV per year? Life is portrayed as cheap and 'wasting' a person as the solution to ending a problem is made to look simple and easy. Mature adults may not be influenced or affected by all the media violence, but impressionistic teenagers see things differently. In the entertainment industry criminals such as street thugs, Mafia gangsters and serial killers become appealing role models to an angry or lonely kid who feels frustrated and powerless at the way their life is going."

The "sanctity of life" was not valued by Theodore "Ted" Bundy, arguably one of the world's most prolific and infamous human predators. "What's one less person on the Earth anyhow?," he stated in a face-to-face interview with Dr. Ronald Holmes, a professor of criminal justice at the University of Louisville. Bundy came through Kentucky as a fugitive in January 1978 after escaping from a Colorado jail, where he was awaiting trial for the murder of a nurse. Prior to that incarceration, the handsome law student had kidnapped, sexually assaulted, and murdered young women in as many as eight states, mostly in the Northwest. Dr. Holmes estimates that Bundy claimed over 100 victims. "He even killed one of them on his way to visiting his grandmother," Holmes said.

Bundy arrived in Louisville in a stolen Volkswagen bug, his preferred vehicle of transportation, that he had used to entrap some of his victims. He reportedly stopped to eat at a Pancake House downtown on Jefferson Street and then fueled his car at a nearby Standard Oil station. From there, he headed south on the interstate with a destination of Florida, making no further stops in Kentucky.

Had it not been for his urgency to stay ahead of a massive manhunt and a desire for a warmer climate, Bundy may have stayed longer in the Bluegrass. Dr. Holmes recounted, "He told me that he thought Kentucky was a pretty state." Unbeknownst to the women of Kentucky, they had nearly fallen prey to a serial killer.

Florida was not as fortunate. Shortly after his arrival in Tallahassee, Bundy unleashed years of pent-up rage and urges to kill. Upon entering the Chi-Omega sorority house at Florida State University, he sexually assaulted, strangled, and bludgeoned to death two co-eds, leaving deep teeth marks on the left buttock of one of the women. Two weeks later, he abducted a 12-year-old girl from the hallway of her middle school, molesting her and slitting her throat. He was finally arrested in Pensacola after a minor traffic violation and was later convicted of the Florida murders. Ted Bundy was executed in Florida's electric chair in January 1989, at which time some may have asked, "What's one less person on the Earth anyhow?"

While Bundy spared Kentucky during his visit, a shadowy drifter brought death to the state in August 1997. Christopher Maier was a 21-year-old junior at the University of Kentucky when he and his girlfriend were attacked while taking a shortcut along some railroad tracks east of the UK campus. Maier was killed. The woman was raped and beaten but survived.

A period of 21 months passed until authorities even had a suspect in the case. The trail eventually led to Angel Maturino Resendiz, aka "The Railway Killer," a 39-year-old Mexican national who traversed the country in railroad boxcars. Maier's slaying would be linked to at least 10 other vicious murders that occurred in Florida, Texas, and Illinois, all near railroad tracks.

Resendiz was placed on the FBI's Ten Most Wanted List in June 1999. The international manhunt that intensified that summer sent Kentuckians into a panic as the elusive murder suspect and master of disguise made his way back into the state. On June 18, a confirmed sighting was made of Resendiz at a homeless shelter in Louisville. As local television stations relayed this news, authorities received over 200 phone calls from anxious residents claiming to have spotted him at numerous locations across Jefferson County. Resendiz sightings were reported from such spots as a SuperAmerica station near Churchill Downs, a laundromat by the University of Louisville, the Dizzy Whizz Drive-In restaurant on West St. Catherine Street, and even the River Falls Mall in Clarksville, Indiana.

The citizens of Lexington were also on the edge of their seats, and for good reason. In a news conference, Assistant Lexington Police Chief Fran Root said, "I've been in police work nearly 30 years, and I can't recall a previous case of a manhunt where such a dangerous suspect had been identified along with such a likelihood he'd strike again." Police there assigned 30 uniformed officers and six detectives to patrol the areas proximal to railroad tracks, going door to door warning residents of nearby homes to keep their doors locked and their lights on.

Despite the vigilance of law enforcement and civilians alike, Resendiz somehow managed to slip out of Kentucky once again. His life on the run ended in July 1999 when he surrendered in El Paso, Texas. Described at the scene as "calm and very pleasant," he reportedly shook the hand of a Texas Ranger before being handcuffed.

Word of the capture held a special interest for the people of Russell County. It was there in the summers of 1996 and 1998 that Resendiz lived and worked on tobacco farms. Eerily reminiscent of the David Berkowitz case, they could not believe that the man they had known would have committed such acts. Some even thought that he must have had an evil twin. He was remembered in the community as a polite and intelligent man who was entrusted to oversee the other migrant workers. Hollis and Collis Stephens had employed Resendiz to work on their farms. In statements made to *The Courier-Journal*, Hollis Stephens remarked that Resendiz slept in his house and had eaten dinner with his family. He also tutored one of the family members in algebra. Collis Stephens added, "Aw, man, we just thought the world of him."

In May 2000, a jury in Texas found Angel Maturino Resendiz guilty of capital murder in the death of Claudia Benton, a Houston-area physician. Resendiz had broken into Dr. Benton's home in December 1998, sexually assaulting her before eventually beating and stabbing her to death. He was sentenced to death just days after the verdict. There are reports that Fayette County Commonwealth's Attorney Ray Larson still wants Resendiz extradited to Kentucky, where he could be tried for the murder of Christopher Maier and the rape of his girlfriend.

Not every fugitive from justice has gotten out of the state before being apprehended. Anyone in the vicinity of Ky. 52 in Madison County during the afternoon of November 13, 1995 could attest to that fact. A white Ford Festiva barreled down the highway at speeds reaching 100 miles an hour, the hulking body of a 6'3", 200-pound Grizzly Adams lookalike crammed behind the steering wheel. At least six police cruisers were in hot pursuit. The driver, Glen Rogers, finished off a twelve-pack of beer and slung a can at a state police detective who had pulled up beside the vehicle. Plowing through a roadblock of parked cruisers, the Festiva absorbed a trooper's shotgun blast. The wild chase went on for two more miles until police forced the car into a ditch in front of the Blue Grass Army Depot. State troopers converged upon Rogers, prying him out of the wreckage with difficulty because he had observed the state seat belt law. He did not resist arrest.

It was less than an hour earlier when a frantic Rogers appeared at the doorstep of his cousins Edith and Clara Smallwood in Lee County, where he had resided in 1993. Edith later told the *Lexington Herald-Leader*, "He said, 'I was going by and I wanted to stop and I wanted to tell you and Clara that I love you all better than anybody.' I said, 'Glen, why don't you give yourself up?' and he cried and he said, 'I don't know what to do.'" Clara recalled, "When he left, he said, 'Pray for me.'" The Smallwoods reported his visit to state police immediately after his departure. Their thoughts might have turned to the previous year when a decomposed body was found tied to a chair in the family's abandoned cabin. The corpse was that of a 73-year-old Ohio man with whom their cousin Glen had lived.

Once Rogers was arrested, his demeanor radically changed from that of the tearful man the Smallwoods saw leaving their home. He laughed as he told police that he was responsible for 70 homicides. Law enforcement agencies across the nation and in Canada called in an effort to question Rogers regarding several unsolved murders. The man they had in custody was the notorious "Cross-Country Killer" who had been featured on segments of "America's Most Wanted."

Rogers was formally charged in the deaths of women in Florida, California, Louisiana, and Mississippi. Most of the victims had met him in bars, where they were smooth-talked into accompanying him elsewhere. The serial killer would receive the death penalty in Florida for the murder of motel maid Tina Marie Cribbs, the owner of the Ford Festiva. She had been stabbed and left to bleed to death in the bathtub of a Tampa motel where Rogers was staying. In July 1999, a California jury gave him a second death sentence for the slaying of Sandra Gallagher, who was found raped and strangled in her burning pickup truck. Gallagher had given Rogers a ride home from a Van Nuys bar after she celebrated a $1250 lottery win.

Rogers was also implicated in another high-profile California murder case. According to the *New York Post*, the attorneys for O. J. Simpson planned to blame Rogers for the 1994 stabbing deaths of Nicole Brown Simpson and Ron Goldman. Los Angeles detectives had at one time considered him a suspect. Rogers was known to have partied with Nicole and her friend Faye Resnick, and he was placed near her home within an hour of her murder.

Back in Kentucky, those familiar with the murder of Vickie Sue Metzger may have been wondering whether Glen Rogers was her killer, though no evidence has surfaced to link him to her death. In June 1992, her remains were found partially hidden under leaves and sticks near a mountaintop rest stop along Interstate 24 in Monteagle, Tennessee. Her assailant had strangled her with bare hands. A nun who had recently asked to be released from her vows, Vickie Sue had been working as a finance manager at the Whitney Young Job Corps Center in Simpsonville. She was driving alone to a job workshop in Atlanta when she died.

The discovery of Metzger's body would be the latest in a series of mysterious deaths known as the "redhead murders" which began in 1983. During that period, the bodies of 12 women had been found along interstates and highways from Pennsylvania to Arkansas. All of them had red hair.

One month prior to Metzger's death, a trucker stumbled on a body behind a truck stop on Interstate 70 north of Cambridge City, Indiana. An autopsy revealed that the woman had been strangled 12 to 36 hours earlier. Meanwhile, the family of Lisa Maria Atwell in Cadiz, Kentucky filed a missing person report. Atwell had taken a bus to Indianapolis to visit her boyfriend. When she did not call home on her mother's birthday, they became anxious. They made countless phone calls to Indiana hospitals, drug rehabilitation centers, and morgues. Atwell's sister, Sandra Thomas, described her tattoos to an Indiana State Police detective. The family's worst fears were confirmed when, through photographs, Thomas identified the "Jane Doe" found at the truck stop as her sister.

There was no family to mourn the death of a young red-haired woman in Knox County. She was unidentified. On April 1, 1985, two men discovered her body in an old refrigerator as they were searching for appliance parts in a dump off U.S. 25 near Corbin. She was wearing only socks and two gold-colored necklaces. The cause of death was determined to be suffocation, but the Knox County Coroner asserted that she was placed in the refrigerator after she was killed. According to witness reports, the woman was last seen alive at King's Truck Stop on Interstate 75 at Corbin around 2 A.M. on April 1. She was reportedly looking for a ride to North Carolina. State police believed that she likely caught a ride with an individual who would become her murderer.

Though no one knew who she was, the people of Knox County paid her their last respects as if she had been their own. The Hampton Funeral Home in Barbourville donated a casket for the woman. Businesses and private citizens donated flower arrangements. An area department store provided a skirt and blouse for her. Nearly 60 people attended the funeral. Bob Deaton, the manager of Hampton Funeral Home, told the *Lexington Herald-Leader*, "We didn't have to do it, but she is somebody's daughter and we think she is somebody's mother." The "redhead murders" remain unsolved.

Rural highways and secluded stretches of railroad tracks are not the only places where Kentuckians could fall victim to a killer. On a Thursday morning in September 1989, a sequence of 911 calls in Louisville revealed how it could happen in the most familiar of surroundings—even in the workplace.

> **Operator:** "911. Do you need police, fire or EMS?"
> **Caller #1:** "Police! Fire! Standard Gravure at 643 South Sixth."
> **Caller #2:** "Get somebody up here to Standard Gravure. Quick. Third Floor. They're shooting."
> **Dispatcher:** "Sir, what's the problem there?"
> **Caller #2:** "I don't know. I'm locked in my office under my desk. Somebody is shooting. Please, get the police here."
> **Officer #1:** "Be advised that security says there's a man inside the building with a gun, and he's firing it . . . Start EMS down here. I've been advised there's people inside that's supposed to be shot. We don't know where the guy with the gun is."
> **Officer #2:** "Be advised I'm on the third floor. I've got two victims, two victims, start EMS."
> **Officer #3:** "He was last seen up here."
> **Dispatcher:** "Where's he at now? He was last seen on the third floor. Is he out of the building now?"
> **Officer #3:** "I'm not sure if he's out of the building or not."
> **Ambulance Crew #1:** "Apparently the assailant is still on the loose."
> **Caller #3:** "There's a shooting incident ongoing in the basement of the Standard Gravure building . . . I just heard six shots, less than a minute ago."
> **Caller #4:** "Yeah, I've got two people shot in the etching room at Standard Gravure. It's in the old Courier Building."
> **Officer #4:** "2205. We got two more. I've got two men shot in the basement."
> **Officer #5:** "Another one down in the basement."
> **Ambulance Crew #2 to Humana Hospital–University of Louisville:** "We're coming in with the first of multiple gunshot victims. There allegedly is a fully automatic rifle, and we're coming in right now with an approximately 53-year-old male with a gunshot wound through the right buttock. He's conscious and alert . . . vital signs are all stable . . . Be prepared for numerous victims."
> **Officer #6:** "I have two people shot on the third floor of the bindery. Three people, one is shot in the head. I need EMS up here as quickly as possible."

Caller #5: "EMS won't be able to go up without a police officer leading in the front."

Dispatcher: "Car One, 421 advised the man committed suicide down in the basement."

Chief Richard Dotson in Car One: "Are we talking about the assailant?"

Dispatcher: "That's affirmative."

Former employee Joseph Wesbecker had walked into the Standard Gravure printing company at approximately 8:30 A.M. armed with an AK-47 assault rifle, two MAC-11 9-mm assault pistols, a 9-mm Sig-Sauer German-made semiautomatic handgun, a .38-caliber revolver, a bayonet, and a gym bag containing hundreds of rounds of ammunition. In a period of 30 minutes, he methodically shot people throughout the building before killing himself. A total of nine would die, leaving 12 others wounded.

Wesbecker had reportedly become disgruntled over the company's handling of his long-term disability status. Coworkers would later disclose that he threatened to shoot Standard Gravure executives in the past. Psychiatric records chronicled Wesbecker's struggles with a long history of mental illness, particularly depression.

Other Kentucky murders have shown that darkness can dwell within the most trusted members of a community, including those in helping professions. The idea of helping for these individuals, however, is somewhat different than most. In his book *Serial Murder*, Dr. Ronald Holmes refers to them as "mission-oriented" serial killers. He explains that this type of killer "typically displays no signs of psychosis, no indications of being out of touch with reality. But in most such killers there are indications of a fervent, seething desire to 'take charge,' to 'do something' about some aspect of life that is seen as undesirable, immoral, or needing drastic correction. When these traits are combined with a high potential for interpersonal aggression and sociopathic tendencies, the resulting behavior may be violent and even homicidal. In some cases, the mission-type killer identifies a category of persons and sets out to 'teach them a lesson.' In fact, a hallmark of this type of killer is the tendency to target a particular category of persons for extinction."

Such a case involved Beoria Simmons, a 29-year-old social worker in Louisville who counseled ex-convicts in a halfway house. Once considered an upstanding citizen and all-around nice guy, he is currently on death row for the kidnapping, rape, and fatal shooting of three women between May 1981 and March 1983. Their bodies were found in or near Iroquois Park. In June 1983, his efforts to claim a fourth victim in the park led to his arrest when a 16-year-old girl fought him off and identified his car to police. Simmons's capture put to a close an exhaustive homicide investigation in which detectives had taken such measures as X-raying a section of a tree in search of a bullet, visiting 50 restaurants to retrace the steps of a victim who had eaten a hamburger with diced onions shortly before her murder, and consulting a psychic.

During his interrogation, Simmons proudly disclosed the motives behind his crimes. He spoke of his plan to rid the community of women whom he assumed to be prostitutes. Dr. Holmes further describes Simmons's mindset. "The sinfulness and immorality of women who 'sell their bodies' or casually dispense their sexual favors was obvious to Beoria Simmons . . . Such women were an abomination and so harmful to the community that only radical action would remove them from the presence of decent people. It became clear to Simmons that his mission was to cleanse the city of such prostituting, disease-spreading vermin."

Another Kentuckian who possessed a convoluted sense of philanthropy was Donald Harvey. The diminutive Owsley County native worked as a hospital nurse's aide in London, Lexington, Northern Kentucky, and Cincinnati from 1970 to 1987. He quickly developed a reputation as a responsible employee who demonstrated a caring manner toward his patients. "He was very personable and he went out of his way to be friendly," Paddy Duncan told *The Cincinnati Post*. Duncan was a nurse who worked with Harvey at Drake Memorial Hospital in Cincinnati. She remembered how Harvey routinely pulled the curtains or closed the doors when he looked after patients out of respect for their privacy.

Over time, Harvey would also become known for being in the vicinity of patients when they died—so much, in fact, that coworkers began to refer to him as "The Angel of Death." Duncan said, "He'd come out and say, 'Oh, I think somebody just succumbed.'" To their horror, the Drake staff would learn that what they had witnessed was not mere coincidence. In April 1987, Harvey was arrested for poisoning a patient after an assistant coroner detected the almond smell of cyanide while performing an autopsy. Harvey later confessed to murdering 24 patients at Drake during the course of his job, as well as claiming 13 victims at Marymount Hospital in London, where he began his career in healthcare. Harvey has stated that he is actually responsible for as many as 87 deaths.

Harvey explained that he killed most of them out of mercy. He worked on hospital units occupied by elderly and critically ill patients who were at times in tremendous pain. He told the *Lexington Herald-Leader*, "I felt what I was doing was right. I was putting people out of their misery. I hope if I'm ever sick and full of tubes or on a respirator, someone will come and end it. I didn't go in and kill someone and come out clapping my hands."

His killings of compassion were reportedly carried out with great precision and attention to detail. During his rounds, he studied patients' charts to get an idea of their condition. He neatly recorded the murders in journals. Harvey's methods of murder were both varied and elaborate, picking up hints from medical books, Agatha Christie novels, and a friend who embalmed bodies at a funeral home. He stole 30 pounds of cyanide from hospital laboratories and stored it in glass containers in his apartment. Mixing poisons in the comfort of his home, he brought the finished product to work, where he secretly put it in patients' food or into their gastric tubes. He killed others with morphine and an assortment of narcotics. Harvey admitted that most of the patients at Marymount Hospital died after he hooked them to oxygen tanks that were virtually empty. Sometimes, he used less sophisticated but highly effective means, such as pillows and plastic bags. Perhaps the most ghastly death occurred after Harvey rammed a coat hanger through a patient's catheter so far that it pierced his bladder. Days after the incident, the patient died from an infection.

While Harvey preferred to see himself as a dispenser of mercy, pure vengeance proved to underlie some of his acts. One such example revolved around an elderly neighbor who had a sweet tooth for cheesecake. When she once got into a dispute with Harvey's lover, he baked her one—laced with arsenic. The woman became violently ill and cried out for some Pepto-Bismol to relieve her cramps. Harvey gave her some—laced with arsenic. Relief from the abdominal distress finally came to her a few days later when she died. His lover did not escape Harvey's wrath. Harvey slowly poisoned him over a period of three years after learning that he had been unfaithful to him. He dealt with a woman whom he found particularly aggravating by making an unsuccessful attempt to infect her with some tissue from an AIDS patient. Ascribing to the belief that persistence is a virtue, he then spiked her tea with hepatitis serum. She somehow survived drinking the wicked brew after coming perilously close to death.

Donald Harvey was ordered to serve a minimum of 60 years in prison for the Cincinnati killings. In November 1987, he appeared in the Laurel County Courthouse amidst a crowd of outraged and curious onlookers. Circuit Judge Lewis B. Hopper sentenced him to eight life terms for the murders at Marymount Hospital and 20 additional years for a manslaughter charge. As news crews and ordinary citizens strained to catch a glance at "The Angel of Death" on that day, Harvey left them with a message. "There are other Donald Harveys out there," he said. "But I think with my story and what has happened, they will be more careful."

CHAPTER 13

LETTERS FROM CONVICTED AND ALLEGED SERIAL KILLERS: A CONTENT ANALYSIS

Ronald M. Holmes, Angela West, and Stephen T. Holmes

INTRODUCTION

Serial killers are popular cultural icons. Interest across the world has made many serial murderers as well known as world politicians, entertainers, and sports figures. Their names roll off lips as a litany of unholy saints. Ted Bundy, Douglas Clark, Richard Sutcliffe, and many others are galvanized to the consciousness of the world's citizens. The media have done its part to alert the world to the existence of these human predators in all societies in the world.

The serial killer is portrayed as a person without a conscious, unable to understand the repercussions of his or her behavior, a "victim" of violent impulses, thus unable to curb violent impulses. Little is known of the personality of the serial killer if for no other reason than that there are many who are unknown. How many? This is a question with no accurate answer. The Federal Bureau of Investigation estimates that 35 serial murderers are currently active in the United States. How does this translate into a world population of serial killers? Again, an unanswerable question. For one reason, we only know about the traits, characteristics, and number of serial killers from those who are really failures of the system, the ones who have been apprehended by the criminal justice system. So what we have done is to extrapolate the knowledge from the apprehended serial killers. How reliable are their statements? Consider, for example, the case of Henry Lee Lucas in the United States. At one time he and his accomplice, Ottis Toole, confessed to more than 300 killings. Police departments across the country closed many of their unresolved murder cases based solely on the confession of Lucas. He only recently died in his prison cell in Texas of natural causes.

There are countless other serial killers who are known and unknown. The focus of this chapter is to examine the writings of four killers: Ted Bundy, a convicted serial killer; Randy W., in prison for one murder but a suspect in several others (Rule, 1988); Gerard Schafer, a convicted killer of two women but a suspect in the deaths of more than 30 others; and Manny C., a killer of two but a suspect in the deaths of more than 20 others. We must stress at this point that only Bundy was a convicted serial killer. The others are considered by others within the criminal justice system as certain serial killers but because of other problems have not been tried with other homicides, certainly one of the main problems in a serial murder case (Holmes & Holmes, 1996). The writings cover a wide range of topics, but we have selected certain themes, perceptions, style, and other items for analysis. In the initial phases of this study, we did not know what direction we would be taken by their written correspondents, but as the research continued certain commonalities emerged. How common these are to other killers we do not know.

THEORIES OF SERIAL MURDER

There are several theories of serial murder (Egger, 1998; Fisher, 1997; Fox & Levin, 2001; Lester, 1995; Hickey, 1997; Holmes & Holmes, 1999; Holmes et al., 1999; Jenkins, 1994; Norris, 1988). These theories offer ideas for discussion and examination. They also have common elements in their theories.

For brevity's sake, let us examine only a couple of the theories. Holmes and DeBurger (1985) believe that serial killers arise from a unique combination of biology, psychology, and sociology. What separates serial killers from other types of murderers is their anticipated rewards and loci of motivation. The strategic definer of a person who is a serial killer from one who is not lies not only in their biological inheritance but also in the sequence of events for the serial killers. This point of view is also accepted by Egger (1998), Lester (1995), and others.

Hickey (1997) reports that serial killers are developed by the social structure of the society of the murderer. That killer, raised in a developed or underdeveloped country, will experience that structure and adapt to that culture using the experiences as well as the biological inheritance from forebearers. Hickey also considers the experience of unique experiences as molding influences.

Holmes and colleagues (1999) report in their *fractured identity theory* that serial killers undergo a traumatic event sometime in their early lives that causes some psychological "fracture" in their lives. This fracture never really heals. The sole medication for the pain is the predation on helpless victims. The "medication" is only temporary, and it is only a short period of time before another act of fatal violence is needed and committed to aid in the management of pain.

Other theories of serial murder share some commonalities with the ones listed in this section. Suffice it to say that no one knows exactly what causes one to become a serial killer any more than one can say what causes one to become the president of a nation, the pope, or a homeless individual. We are only in the beginning stages of this attempt at understanding the impelling forces that shape and even determine a personality.

What we are trying to do here is to develop an understanding of the mind of three American serial killers from the analysis of their letters written to one author. Perhaps after such an analysis we can begin to understand the mind and mentality of the fatalistic predator.

LITERATURE REVIEW

Prior academic research on psychological profiling is scarce (see Holmes & Holmes, 1996). Evaluation of offender writing styles and characteristics, however, is also sparse. In fact, qualitative analysis of the appearance, structure, and content of written correspondence by criminal offenders is nonexistent.

McLaughlin and Sarkisian (1983) examined the utility of graphoanalysis in the area of criminal justice. They indicate that this form of study can aid investigators in developing an understanding of personalities so that investigations can be more focused on likely suspects. They also argue that this understanding also can apply to assessing the credibility of witnesses. They warn, however, that this type of analysis will not prove or disprove guilt. It should only serve to provide direction and to act as an objective guide for initiating surveillance activities and other traditional investigative techniques.

One study using handwriting specimens from convicted criminals and noncriminal persons attempted to examine the validity and utility of handwriting analysis in criminological arenas. Armistead (1983) found that experts could more accurately distinguish criminal from noncriminal handwriting by using the handwriting to construct a specific criminal personality type. However, when criminal writing samples were replaced with noncriminal samples that exhibited criminal traits, the predictive accuracy of the experts decreased. He concludes that such writing analyses may be helpful in discerning traits, but those same traits may not always be indicative of similar tendencies or behaviors. So, while offender populations may share certain writing traits, the presence of these traits does not always indicate criminality.

Finally, handwriting analysis can be useful as a supplement to more objective investigative methods. Lewis and colleagues (1997) reported significant success in identifying characteristics and traits indicative of dissociative identity disorder and severe abuse during childhood among 12 adult murderers. These authors obtained data on these 12 individuals from existing records (e.g., prison records, social service records, medical and psychiatric records) and supplemented these with interviews and handwriting analyses. They found that symptoms of dissociative identity disorder in childhood and adulthood were corroborated among all the sources in all 12 cases. Evidence of severe abuse was indicated in 11 of the 12 cases. According to the authors, their findings provide conclusive evidence of the link between early severe abuse and dissociative identity disorder among murderers.

Identity disorders also have been linked to varieties of murder, including serial murder. Serial killers have been identified as being in many cases psychopathic and in some cases psychotic; many kill for sexual gratifications that include sexual paraphilias. There are some serial killers, for example, who practiced cannibalism (Bundy, Gein, Dahmer, and others). There are some who receive their gratifications from other forms of sexual aberrations. Regardless, their disorders have been mentioned by Fox and Levin (2001), Hickey, (1997), Holmes & Holmes, (1998), and others. But each author made a distinction between causes and traits or characteristics. While it may be important to list some of the common characteristics of male, young, educated, and so on, we believe it is important to attempt some discovery of the etiology of the serial killer. While this is a noble effort, fortunately for us, this is not the primary focus of this chapter.

STUDY RATIONALE

This research is different from the more common evaluation of handwriting in that it is inductive. Generally, handwriting analysis, or graphology, is used to detect forgery, fraud, or to examine changes over time as the result of psychological or physiological impairments. Commonly, handwriting is analyzed to narrow a possible list of suspects. In this study, the authors (the killers) are known, and their handwriting is being used to inductively assess similarities and differences in relation to the similarities and differences of their killing methods.

As a result, the conclusions drawn here have limited generalizability, as with most qualitative research. The data analyzed will allow possible generalizations to killers who use similar methods as the four evaluated in this project. Although the characteristics of killers and their crimes vary somewhat, study in this area has highlighted many common traits among killers, such as age, gender, race, education, occupation, and mobility.

The evaluation of these writings began with a clear understanding of the authors' killing traits. That is, we know what they did and what methods they used. We are not using their writing to determine their identity. We are using their writing to better understand if traits, habits, and characteristics of their killing spill over into traits, habits, and characteristics in their writing.

If more of these types of inductive studies resulted in the compilation of a database of information about killers and their handwriting styles, perhaps it would aid in future investigations of unsolved killings. That is, any additional information to aid criminal investigators in the construction of killer profiles is useful.

METHODS

Letters from four notorious American killers were collected over a 13-year time span. These letters were analyzed in several ways. First, the appearance of the letters was considered, including such criteria as neatness, consistency, and use of headings and closings. Next, the structure was examined as it concerned letter and word formation, grammar, spelling, punctuation, language, and organization. In addition, the content was examined as it related to tone, theme, purpose, focus, and detail. While this was not a scientific handwriting analysis, per se, conclusions are made as to the personalities and tendencies of the writers as can be determined from the letters. These are, in turn, connected to the characteristics of the murders with which each author is credited.

Four killers corresponded with one of this study's authors over various time frames. Ted Bundy wrote seven letters from January 1985 until March 1986. Manny C. wrote 58 letters from July 1986 until October 1998. Randy W. wrote 18 letters from July 31, 1986 until April 1993. Finally, Gerard Schaefer wrote five letters to his then girlfriend, Sondra London, and various correspondence to his attorney and to one of this study's authors from January 1991 to July 1994. Therefore, this study examined over 90 letters for structure and content. Letters from Schaefer to his girlfriend and attorney were obtained as evidence in a lawsuit launched against one of the authors (R.M.H.) for libel.

This suit was withdrawn by the killer only a few days before it was to appear before the court.

This chapter examines each author's letters, making specific conclusions about appearance, structure, and content. In addition, commonalities and distinguishing traits are discussed, and generalizations are made regarding the writers and their common crime of murder.

APPEARANCE

General Overview

What was striking about the appearance of these letters was the obvious writing patterns and consistency. While the degree of "neatness" varied, with Manny's writing almost obsessively neat and Randy's bordering on sloppy, all were fairly consistent among letters as far as letter formation, unusual characteristics, and arrangement.

Bundy's letters were interesting in that his loose script gave the impression of rambling across the page. He averaged about four and a half pages per letter. He had consistently patterned letter formation, spiky letters instead of more rounded, with fairly large loops on letters such as lowercase g and y. One unique characteristic of Bundy's letters was that he began all lowercase letters (except g, o, p, and sometimes y and a) of each line on the left-hand margin, with a long precursor line leading to the beginning of the letter.

Manny's writing was so consistent that it had the appearance of being typewritten. In addition, the number of words per line in Manny's letters was significantly greater than anyone else's. That is, his style was much more compact, allowing him to write more in less space. So while his page lengths were often low (average of just over two pages), he often said more than another killer did in significantly more pages.

Randy wrote an average of just over one page per correspondence (1.31). As previously mentioned, his was the writing that looked the sloppiest, especially when compared with the others. Objectively, however, it was fairly neat, as well. What made his writing appear more chaotic was his habit of running letters together in a hybrid cursive/print.

Schaefer's letters, while fairly consistent, were not overly neat. His letters make up the smallest proportion of correspondence. He was, however, the most prolific writer, averaging over eight pages per letter.

Differences in length can be explained primarily by differences in target audience and content. While Schaefer most often was writing to a girlfriend, the other three were writing to a less intimate acquaintance. Moreover, Schaefer spent a great deal of time "story-telling," providing long descriptions of events. The others did not do this as often.

Pagination

Different authors had different methods of noting page numbers. Bundy consistently numbered his pages with the number at the top center of each page (except the first), surrounded by dashes. Manny was inconsistent in numbering. When he did number pages, however, he also numbered at the top center.

Instead of dashes, he circled his numbers. Randy also was inconsistent in using page numbers, but placed his numbers in the top left corners without circles or dashes.

Schaefer was the most inconsistent in style and placement of page numbers. While he always numbered his pages, some letters were numbered at the bottom right of the page, surrounded by boxes. In other letters, he used numbers at the bottom center of the page. Finally, one letter contained a mixture of boxed numbers and bottom-centered numbers.

Writing Style and Consistency

This category examined letter and word formation, the degree of control indicated by these formations, and the consistency throughout each authors' series of letters.

Bundy, as previously mentioned, had spiky letters with large loops, with a moderate to severe right slant. His letters gave the impression of being written impulsively, without much forethought. Although the initial appearance is one of impulsivity, a great degree of control is evident in that his lowercase "t" is crossed deliberately and precisely. Moreover, while he often created large loops in his letters, those loops never overpower the letter to seem out of control. The consistent placement of the beginning word on each line also indicates an unusual degree of control. Bundy rarely emphasized any words, but when he did, he used a heavily drawn squiggly underline.

Some inconsistencies with Bundy's letters are noteworthy. Three of the letters in the Bundy series differ significantly from the others. The fourth letter is characterized by less pressure on the pen, resulting in much lighter letters. In addition, his writing appears loopier and the letter formations are not as consistent. In this letter, his writing is not as controlled as in the prior three. In the fifth letter, he regains some consistency, but still is exerting much less pressure on the pen. Letter number six is obviously different from the others. Lack of control is evident in the size of the letters, their formations, and the size of the loops. In this writing, the letters appear to be falling over with huge, uncontrolled loops that infringe upon other letters. The final letter from Bundy is the one in which he ends the relationship with his correspondent. He is, once again, in total control. The letters are more precisely formed, the writing is darker, and the loops are smaller. It is interesting to note that the letters changed in appearance at the time Bundy's execution date was nearing and he had appealed for a stay.

Manny's unusually controlled style was another small cursive/print hybrid with a moderate right slant. While a few letters were all printed, both styles were extremely consistent, characterized by small letters and loops. His writing also is characterized by precise and consistent placement of crosses, dots, and punctuation. Interestingly, the printed letters were straight (no slant) and were characterized by the curious capitalization of all letters "f." For emphasis, he used capitalization and underlining.

Randy, while the least neat of the four, was fairly consistent in that he used the same all capitals, print/cursive hybrid. His letter formations are large and sprawling, and either upright, or slanted slightly left. The combination of all capitals and large, sprawling style makes it appear that his words are demanding attention. They seem to be yelling at the reader. Other characteristics of Randy's letters reinforce this idea, such as his tendency to frequently emphasize words by underlining, capitalizing, and using multiple exclamation points, often in combination.

Schaefer wrote in a compact style with a moderate right slant. His writings are noteworthy in that he completely printed, with the exception of a few places where he used a mixture of cursive and print. In that case, the printed words were used for emphasis. He also emphasized words and phrases by underlining and capitalizing. In fact, letters printed in all capitals are used frequently throughout his writings.

Extraneous Materials

These letters also were examined for any additions to the written words on the pages, such as drawings or "doodlings." Two of the four writers included nothing extra in their correspondence (Bundy and Manny). The other two (Randy and Schaefer) included smiley face icons, ellipses, and parenthetical comments. Randy relied heavily on parenthetical comments, such as "(smile)," "(wink)," and "(Ha!)," while Schaefer peppered his pages with incongruous smiley faces. Randy also included smiley faces at various points, but not nearly as consistently as Schaefer. When either author was upset, as indicated by the tone and content of the letter, use of these lighthearted mechanisms disappeared.

Headings, Greetings, and Closings

The way a writer heads, opens, and closes a letter may also indicate something of his or her personality. Headings generally include the date of the letter and information about a return address. Greetings or openings pertain to the manner in which the writer begins communication with the reader, and closings pertain to how the writer ends communication.

All of the writers except Randy consistently used some heading, although the format of that heading often varied. Bundy was the most consistent, dating every letter with the month, date, and year. He often also included his return address. Manny also was very consistent in including the month, date, and year, although he often mixed formats (written and numerical). Randy was the least consistent, often specifying the month and date, but not always the year. Schaefer also mixed numerical and written formats. Unlike Randy in providing information, he often included the day of the week and the time of day in his letters.

The greetings are especially interesting to trace from start of correspondence to end. All four of the killers began their letters in a more formal manner, as would be expected ("Dear Dr." or "Dear Mr."). These quickly evolved into more personal greetings among all of the writers ("Dear Ron"). Two of the four maintained that level throughout the writings (Bundy and Manny). Even when Bundy ended the corresponding relationship, he still maintained the tone of informality, not indicating in the letter's opening his displeasure with the reader.

Schaefer is somewhat different in that his initial correspondence to the author was to inform of a potential lawsuit, which of course demanded more formality and did not become less formal and more personal over the course of the relationship. Schaefer's letters to London (his girlfriend) began less formally, with his use of a pet name ("Dear Sandi"), then evolved into more formality as the intimate and trusting relationship evaporated in the last letter wherein he threatened harm to her daughter ("Dear Sondra"). It is curious that he seems to have misspelled her name on the second letter ("Dear Sandy").

Randy's letters show a clear progression from formal to informal and back to formal again ("Dear Dr.," "Dear Mr.," "Dear Ron," "Greetings Professor," "Hi Dr. Holmes," "Dear Mr.," "Mr. Holmes"). The tone and content of these letters change accordingly (see following sections). As the relationship begins, Randy is optimistic about the relationship he is forming with his correspondent. As a result, he becomes exceedingly intimate and informal. As it becomes clear that Randy is not getting what he wants out of the relationship, he becomes more distant and formal, finally dropping the "Dear" altogether and addressing the reader as "Mr."

The closings were again fairly predictable for two of the authors (Bundy and Manny). Bundy's letters contained two closings: "peace," and "Best Regards." The word "peace" consistently was written all in lowercase. Most unusual is the fact that Bundy signed his name as "ted," also always in lowercase letters.

Manny took a more traditional approach, using "Sincerely," "Sincerely yours," "Respectfully," "Respectfully yours," and "Your friend." His signatures varied between signing his full first name, middle initial, and last name, to signing "Manny" and "Manuel." Although he was not one to include extraneous doodlings, such as smiley faces and parentheticals, he did often sign "Manny" with a highly stylized "y" at the end.

Again, Randy and Schaefer used varied closings. Randy started out formally ("Sincerely yours," "Sincerely," and "Yours truly"), moved to a more informal closing ("Keep in touch," and "Take care"), then back to very formal ("Very truly yours") before becoming sarcastic in his last correspondence ("Have a nice day [Ha]"). He also varied in how he signed his name, ranging from the more formal ("Randy Woodfield," "Randall Woodfield,") to more informal ("Randy," "Randy W."), to extremely formal ("Randall B. Woodfield") to insulting ("RW").

Schaefer varied each time, from generally optimistic ("Stay well & happy," "Your friend," and "Your reformed warrior") to supportive ("You can lean on me," "Your faithful partner & friend"), to rather maudlin and insincere ("Ever accommodating," and "I wish you happiness and success"). His signature was consistent, however, in its indecipherability. It appears to be a capital cursive G or J with lowercase letters "er" following.

Handling of Errors

Another potentially significant indicator of personality relates to how each killer handles errors in his writing. Generalizations may be made as to how each killer handles mistakes in other areas of his life.

Bundy, for all the outward impressions of care and control he always exhibited, made multiple errors in his writings. These are handled in various ways. Some mistakes are messily scratched out and some are overwritten with dark, heavy print. Commonly, he handled omissions by drawing arrows to text to be inserted. In addition, several margins were full of additions and/or corrections to the main text. This adds to the overall appearance of being hurriedly written without much forethought, although this does indicate some level of proofreading.

Mistakes were more rare for Manny. When it was necessary, corrections were made by precisely placed inserts, or dark, heavy, and carefully made scratch-outs. Careful forethought and planning characterized his writing, so mistakes were few but handled in a neat, precise manner. Evidence of proofreading also was strong for Manny. Given the detail, preciseness, and absence of mistakes, it appears that these letters were painstakingly written, probably proofread along the way.

Randy handled errors by white-out, messy overwrites, and by arrows or lines indicating inserts. It appears that his mistakes were caught right after they were made and altered at that time, rather than being found and altered after careful proofreading.

Schaefer's writing gave no evidence of mistake correction. There were no inserts, marginal additions or corrections, scratch-outs, or overwrites. Schaefer either was a very careful writer or erased mistakes very thoroughly. It appears that he may have just had a natural talent for story-telling in that several times his letters evolve into almost "stream of consciousness" narratives.

Structure

Structure involves the form of the letters, including the organizational schemes and the use of grammar, spelling, and punctuation. These letters were characterized by very little structural variation. Each killer knew how to develop sentences and paragraphs. Each one also had a fairly good grasp of topical organization. One characteristic they all seemed to share was the tendency to write as they might speak. This lent a very conversational air to most of the letters (see the following section on content). Additionally, they each had a tendency to form run-on sentences. Each author was fairly consistent with his use of grammar. That is, word selection and usage varied little among letters.

Manny formed complete sentences that almost were rhythmic. They also were characterized by a near obsessive attention to detail, with particular attention to word choice. Schaefer also seemed to choose his words carefully, picking those with the most descriptive impact on the reader.

Randy did not take as much care with word selection or sentence structure as did the other writers. He tended also to use rhetorical questions more often than anyone else. Schaefer also included rhetorical questions that he often answered himself. Bundy shared this characteristic of asking a question that he would then answer himself.

Schaefer also compulsively used abbreviations and initials. Several persons and phrases would be unidentifiable without the aid of an affidavit from Sondra London in which she defines all the abbreviations. He so consistently used this technique that he identified himself by the initials "GS" or "GJS" instead of referring to himself in the first person (i.e., as "I," or "me").

Of additional note was the writers' use of slang and inappropriate language. Bundy used no slang and only twice cursed ("hell" and "damn"). Similarly, Manny was spare in using such language. He only seemed to do so when trying to be funny or for emphasis. He rarely used slang and never used inappropriate language, even when obviously upset at the reader. Schaefer, on the other hand, frequently used both. With some words he frequently omitted the "g" at the end ("lyin,'" "cheatin,'"), and others he deliberately misspelled for emphasis ("e'nuff," "gonna"). The language was frequently offensive and most often derogatory toward women ("cunt," "whore," "bitch"), to whom he often referred as "Kates," "Sandies" (after women with whom he had prior relationships), or "prosties" (prostitutes).

All the killers seemed to have a natural affinity for the written word, seeming glib and charming in writing. One can imagine these men as friendly, smiling, and personable, with a natural command of the English language.

Misspellings and word misusage was rare. Bundy never misspelled anything, but often left the letter "s" off of plural words or omitted small words such as "a." Manny was similar in that he rarely misspelled anything but frequently omitted letters. Randy was not as good at spelling but still made few mistakes. Schaefer also seemed to be very good with spelling, usually only misspelling the most difficult words. Overall, this group had an excellent grasp on word usage and spelling.

One very interesting similarity was how each writer spoke of himself in his letters. Bundy referred to "Theodore Bundy," although he called himself "ted." Schaefer also had the habit of referring to himself in the third person, as "GS," or "GJS." While Manny occasionally did this, referring to himself by his full name, Randy never did. Randy always spoke of himself in the first person (i.e., "I," "me," or "my").

The level of vocabulary development among these men was exceptional, especially among Bundy, Manny, and Schaefer. Randy seemed to have the weakest vocabulary, although it was still fairly advanced. An advanced vocabulary may be one sign of higher intelligence (indicating that these men were among the more intelligent in our society).

Purpose, Content, and Tone

Content of the letters varied with the purpose of the writing. For Schaefer, this was different because he was writing to someone he considered an intimate personal companion. The others were not, although they displayed a level of trust in the reader. Tone and content are connected in that the content of the letter dictates the tone. Thus, if a killer is writing to voice a concern or complaint, this will obviously impact the letter's tone.

Bundy wrote for a fairly self-serving purpose, even though he gave the appearance of only trying to be helpful. His purpose was self-serving in that he hoped to persuade an "open-minded" researcher that he could explain the myth of the serial killer, that he could provide all the answers if only someone was willing to "expand their minds" and listen. While he often requested information, books, and materials on other serial murderers (e.g., Edmund Kemper), he was disparaging of such research efforts.

Bundy's letters contained content that was meant to be informative, to build on topics discussed in personal meetings. These letters initially were guarded and suspicious. Then, after an initial personal meeting, Bundy seemed almost eager to provide assistance. He was extremely complimentary to the researcher. When the writing style changed around the time of his pending execution date, the tone of the letters indicated depression. Bundy himself complained of feeling "lethargic" and not being able to write. Finally, his tone became self-righteous in his last letter in which he ended the corresponding relationship. It had a quality of justified pessimism because Bundy saw himself as able to provide a unique perspective on the problem and was upset when the reader was not receptive to his ideas. He wrote the following in his last letter:

> I don't believe any worthwhile purpose would be served by me continuing to communicate with you. I regret having to reach this decision, but you have sent me certain material in the last month that indicates I was wrong in my assessment that you were capable of making use of information I would give you.

Manny also wrote for self-serving purposes, to tell his story and somehow atone for his evil deeds. His letters are informational and descriptive, almost confessional. In fact, he initiated contact with one of the authors after Randy received a letter requesting his correspondence (they are incarcerated in the same prison). Manny was not charged with or convicted of the number of murders that would make him a "serial killer" (i.e., three or more, with a "cooling off period in between") (Holmes, & Holmes, 1999)). He still wanted to "cleanse his soul" with regard to his crimes. One must consider, however, that people often take credit for crimes that they did not commit to appear more "evil" in the eyes of others (Holmes, & Holmes, 1997). In fact, he mentions that his stories often are marked by inconsistencies. Therefore, while Manny was only convicted of two homicides, he claimed many more. It is interesting to note that Manny often referred to Bundy and other killers in his letters.

Randy's letters were characterized by need. Each letter contained a request for action on the part of the reader. Randy was using these correspondences to gain as much as he could from the relationship. In each letter, he asked a favor of the reader, either in the form of information or assistance. The tone of the seventeenth letter, which was his "notice of intent to sue" the reader, was formal and threatening. The last letter had an almost jubilant tone, somewhat petulant, but triumphant after he thought the reader was going through a time of suffering. Interestingly, this notice to sue was sent a week before the Christmas holidays.

Schaefer's letters were similar in that they expected something from the reader, some type of assistance. These also were typified by a high degree of description in an attempt to convince the reader (London) that he had been the "#1 SK" (serial killer). In fact, he describes Bundy (with whom he was incarcerated) as "an amateur."

Schaefer used these letters as a way to tell his story. Each line practically oozed with self-aggrandizement, so egocentric that he and his past accomplishments were the focus of each letter. Although he only was convicted of two homicides (in which he insisted there was a "FU," or "frame-up" by the investigating officers), he was eager to describe the full extent of his genius (the "TS," or "true story") to his girlfriend, who was planning on publishing his story for profit.

THE ROLE OF FANTASY

Each killer exhibited a differing degree of fantasy involvement. Bundy, for example, mentioned nothing in terms of his fantasies, although in other media he admitted to active participation in pornographic fantasies (both written and visual) (Holmes & Holmes, 1996). Manny also highlighted the importance of pornographic fantasy. He portrayed his sadistic sexual beginnings as stemming from the discovery of his uncle's violent porn magazine in preadolescence. Randy's letters did not get into this area. Schaefer, however, frequently referred to the fulfilling of violent fantasies, and newspaper articles detail an extensive history with violent pornography.

Other frequently mentioned fantasies involved the spiritual/demonic world. Manny, for example, mentioned satanic influences and fantasies involving this realm. Schaefer also referred to his popularity with satanic cults, hinting that he would use this to inflict harm upon London and her daughter. Overwhelmingly, these fantasies involved the exertion of control over various populations (in these cases, mostly helpless female populations).

Control

Each author demonstrated the need for control in the relationship with the reader. Bundy's letters were characterized by clear manipulation. He insisted on control over the direction of research, the "correctness" of conclusions formed, and how information would be used. Manny also demonstrated this requirement in his relationship with the reader and in his relationship with his girlfriend, Marlene. Randy insisted on clear control of the direction of the research, as did Schaefer.

Schaefer made control a necessary precursor to telling the entire "TS" ("true story") to his girlfriend/publisher, London. Moreover, control was a prominent theme in his illustrations of previous behaviors. Ropes, hand-cuffs, and nylons were recurring restraints in his "fictional" accounts. Additionally, Schaefer insisted on control over the time, place, method, and victim. In fact, Schaefer frequently gloated over the fact that his victims were tracked over a period of at least six months, and followed from one state to another (e.g., from Fort Lauderdale, Florida to Atlanta, Georgia).

Schaefer also attempted to control the ability of the reader (London) to testify against him by offering a marriage proposal to provide marital immunity. In this capacity, there was the hint of an escape attempt (plans "contingent upon my getting out," and "You and I need to have a strategy about that"). With London, manipulation was clear in that Schaefer insisted on final say in publications. Moreover, he asserted control over London and her daughter when he insinuated that he could have London's daughter's life taken at any time, just by saying the word.

Finally, Schaefer admitted that his actions were not dictated by sexual gratification but by control over life and death when he said, "killing is not a sex thing, but a death thing." Manny reinforced Schaefer's assertions by describing his attempt at seizing control over the lives and deaths of young, attractive women.

Rationalizations

Bundy rationalized his behaviors by diverting attention from his actions to the media frenzy and to the failure of law enforcement (i.e., whether catching someone after they had killed 50–100 people really was law enforcement?). Manny, on the other hand, rationalized his behaviors by placing the blame on violent porn, left in his room by a visiting uncle when he was 10 years old. He saw his susceptibility to this as having been enhanced by a relationship with his father in which he was abused, a pervasive belief that he was somehow "different," "superior," and a "freak," or as of somehow being chosen by a spiritual element ("them").

While Randy steadfastly denied any responsibility in any of the murders for which he is credited and/or suspected, Schaefer saw himself as a moral avenger, expressing "moral outrage" against prostitutes. His letters contain religious references to support his contentions, with the firm conviction that he was truly reformed in the eyes of God.

Denial of Responsibility

Randy was the biggest denier of responsibility. In fact, letters from Manny mention the fervor with which Randy denies involvement in acts with which he is credited. Randy repeatedly requested from the reader that an investigation of another person, "Larry," be fully instigated. Repeated requests of the reader were made regarding Moore, his priors, and even his blood type. A conspiracy theory was suggested as the reason more investigation was not being done regarding Larry. In fact, each letter mentions Moore and asks the reader's progress on investigation.

Bundy never denied responsibility in any of his letters. In fact, he almost appeared to relish the role of "expert" given his unique situation. The only time in which he seemed disturbed about being labeled a "serial killer" is when he was credited with a list of victims including both those for which he had been convicted and those for which he had not. He did not protest too strongly, however, and admitted to one of the authors' that his official list of victims was inadequately short (personal interview, Starke, Florida, 1986).

Manny's denials involved his abusive father, his uncle's violent pornography, the spiritual "them," and rejecting judgmental society. Although he seems to accept final responsibility and to seek absolution, he consistently places the blame for his actions on others.

While Schaefer provided vivid descriptions of his heinous acts, he consistently claimed that he was framed (the "FU" or frame-up) by legal authorities. In fact, after a reference was published by one of this study's authors that Schaefer was a "serial killer," Schaefer filed suit, claiming that he was a victim and signing his letters as such ("Gerard Schaefer, victim").

Ending Relationships

Each killer seemed to have a unique way of ending the corresponding relationship. Bundy asserted control over the arrangements, portraying himself as having been deceived and betrayed, then establishing ultimate control by writing to end the working relationship because it was not going the way he wanted it to go.

Randy and Schaefer both seemed to enjoy ending relationships litigiously, by filing suit against their correspondents. With Schaefer, this tendency also was accompanied by threats of harm against one of the readers' daughters. The corresponding relationship between Manny and the author is still ongoing.

Psychological Factors

While the "compulsive factor" of killers has been documented, these killers actually mention these factors in their correspondence. Bundy consistently refers to the focus of media attention on "Theodore Bundy," effectively distinguishing "Theodore" from himself as "ted." Manny describes the vague feeling of being different, of being involved with a spiritual world, where "they" dictate behaviors.

While Randy consistently denies killing, Schaefer refers to his "post-kill depression," which may be analogous to the "cooling-off period" described by researchers (Holmes & Holmes, 1996, 1997). In fact, this malaise led to the quick disposal of bodies for Schaefer. Perhaps this is indicative of trouble dealing with the reality of dead bodies after the fantasies were over. Schaefer also viewed his behaviors in a militaristic fashion. His kills were "executions," "slaughters," and "scores." As most serial killers are apt to identify and to name their compulsive factors, so did Schaefer. He consistently referred to the "evil entity," "murder demons," "the Ghoul," and "the Murder Channel" when describing his fatal compulsions.

SUMMARIES REGARDING EACH WRITER

Bundy

Bundy wrote nice letters that were complimentary toward the reader. He did not rant about the system or his treatment, and he seemed to want nothing from the reader except the opportunity to enlighten him. He expressed disgust with the state of knowledge in the field regarding serial murder. He claimed it was just rehashed psychobabble that perpetuated misperceptions and did nothing to help prevent serial killing.

The language in Bundy's letters was formal and friendly but superficial. The reader is left with the impression that Bundy is providing no introspection but only a surface glimpse. There is no sense of Bundy's personality in these letters. They actually seem devoid of personality. Bundy becomes most animated when he believes that the reader is going to do what he wants (i.e., examine the serial murder phenomenon according to Bundy's advice and perspective). At this point, the writing gets bolder, faster, and more mistake ridden.

Several interesting things typify Bundy's writing. First is his consistent reference to "this person called Theodore Bundy." Similarly, his habit of closing his letters by signing "ted" all in lowercase. It is as if he disassociates himself from the person of Theodore Bundy, preferring to view himself as "ted."

Theodore Bundy is an infamous man, well known and important. "ted," on the other hand, is a nobody whose name isn't even worth capitalizing.

Bundy began each line with a "lead-in" tail to nearly all of his lowercase letters. Exceptions were rare. It appears that he is trying to ground his words, give them a stable foundation, although this does not seem to be intentional. There is no evidence that he ever went back to a letter and added a tail. He never closed the loops on letters such as o, g, a, d, and p. As he seems to write more quickly, he becomes even less consistent with loop closings.

Overall, while it is apparent that he was a man of significant intelligence, he also seemed to be a man in a hurry who did not pay much attention to detail (i.e., leaving out letters, using incorrect tenses). Although he was in a hurry, he was not disorganized. His letters follow a logical order. He also took the time to proofread his work, although not very carefully. His writing gives the impression that his mind was moving faster than his hand could write, and he makes mistakes, leaves out thoughts, and has to insert corrections and additions in the margins.

Manny

Obsessively consistent in form, style, length, and content, Manny's letters appear to have been painstakingly written. A high degree of control is evident given the size of the letters and the spacing between letters and words. Even when obviously upset or emotional about a topic, Manny's writing remains controlled and consistent. Moroever, the only stylization in his writing (besides the artful formation of his letters) is in his signature. The form of his writing is an interesting hybrid of cursive and print.

Like Bundy, Manny was fairly direct in his letters, with very little rambling. Like Schaefer, he was a descriptive story-teller, painting mental images for his readers.

While Manny frequently appears to want a forum within which to "spill his guts," the reader is often left with the impression that Manny was just providing the reader with the standard line of psychological rationalizations about the motivations of serial killers (abusive dad, violent porn, rejection and social isolation). Again, however, a high level of intelligence is clear, given his advanced vocabulary, excellent sense of logic, and highly developed problem-solving skills.

A clear picture of organization and care evolves as one reads Manny's letters. One of the most interesting things in Manny's writing was his habit of capitalizing all letters "f," whether they began or came in the middle of words. Moreover, his was the most strikingly patterned of the letters. Manny actually mentions his obsessive preoccupation with writing in one of his letters and explains that he always wanted his writing to be neat. Unlike Bundy, Manny always closed the loops of his letters (o, a, g, p).

Randy

Randy wrote with the intent of being aided by one of this study's authors. Letters always began on a friendly note, thanking the reader for a previous letter, or inquiring about the reader's health and family. Later in the corresponding relationship, his letters are full of whining complaints about the system, the police state, and being betrayed by those he trusted. He says that his purpose in writing is to "prove to the people I love most that I have been used as a 'scapegoat' and that our system does have faults."

When Randy obtains information about a book in which he is mentioned by one of this study's authors, he sends letter #17, notifying the reader of his intent to sue. Although his tone changes from previous letters, it is not extremely harsh. The worst he does is to call the reader a "hypocrite" and a "liar." The last correspondence (#18, nearly 3 years later) is more taunting, expressing joy over what he perceives to be suffering in the reader's life.

Although Randy's language does not necessarily demand attention, his writing certainly does. He writes in all capitals and uses underlining and exclamation points for emphasis. Of particular note was the repetitive use of parentheticals to illustrate side comments.

As with Manny and Schaefer, Randy often portrays himself as a conspiracy victim that was framed for acts he did not commit. While Randy seems to have less intellectual ability than the others (his vocabulary is weaker and his writing style is not as sophisticated), he still is obviously above average in that department.

Schaefer

Schaefer was the most captivating, yet repulsive, writer, weaving complex stories around his acts that were packed with highly descriptive, highly emotive language. The reader is morbidly drawn into his tales that were unusually descriptive of place, act, and person. Schaefer describes his past in complete detail with associated smells, expressions, and feelings. He chronicles his feelings of hatred, anger, sexual violence, power, control, and gratification. In one particularly graphic story, Schaefer describes the murder of a "whore" with a road flare. He relates how he took the "classy call girl" to a remote area in the swamps of Florida and told her how he was going to kill her. While she tried to save herself by offering sex, Schaefer caught the "smell of terror" mixed with her sour sweat. He dangled her by her wrists from a tree branch, then after a period of torture, shoved a lighted road flare into her vagina, describing the look on her face and the likely damage the flare was doing to her insides. It is obvious that he understood "the dynamics of reducing a confident sex pot call girl to a whimpering lump of ravaged flesh that begs for death."

In other stories he delights in the smells of urine and excrement, and "the coppery smell of blood." He also sprinkled these narratives with dialogue between himself and his victims. Maybe this was necessary for his fantasy fulfillment. Nonetheless, these sections are filled with depictions of sadism and the feelings realized from the fatal predations of helpless and, just as importantly, innocent victims.

Schaefer saw himself as a highly skilled and efficient lover and killer, whose methods and intellect were far superior to other serial killers (e.g., Bundy, Green River Killer, Toole, and Lucas). He bragged, "When I was hanging 'Kates' I did so with EFFICIENCY," and "I am no doubt the most SKILLFUL killer."

He also ridiculed those who tried to develop profiles of serial killers. Although he only was credited with two homicides (but claimed he was framed in these investigations), he boasted about how prolific a killer he was, making reference to over 80 "scores" from 1965 to 1972. This statement was to be used against him when he sued one author for $10 million for libel. He claimed in his suit that he was not a serial killer, but in this letter he claimed 86 murders. Regardless he withdrew the suit the day before it was to go to a federal court.

His true nature is revealed in his last correspondence with London in that he threatens harm to her daughter, writing,

> I'm going to warn you one last time: the very next time you say or do anything that causes me problems, and that includes crying to me about what you threw away so recklessly, I am going to encourage my dope addled Satanist pals in Georgia to go pick up your nigger slut daughter and teach her some sex education.
>
> Yes, there is indeed a satanic underground . . . and they do love young girls. My offer is simple: You don't fuck with me; I won't fuck with your kid. I don't like whores and I don't like half-breed teenaged nigger sluts; I know exactly what to do about them.

CONCLUSION

These four men committed unspeakable acts in their lifetimes. Two of those lives are over. Bundy was executed in a Starke, Florida prison in 1989, and Gerard Schaefer was hacked to death by a fellow inmate in that same facility. Manny and Randy are incarcerated in prison.

We do not know exactly how many lives these killers collectively took. Estimates range from 8 to 50 and may be as many as 504. One killer suggested to one author that he had killed ten score plus 2 (202). Bundy suggested that the "ted killer" could have killed as many as 200 victims. Schafer wrote in one of his letters that he had killed 86 women. Randy is thought to be responsible for at least 16 murders (Rule, 1995).

Although killers with multiple victims comprise a small proportion of murderers, probably less than 2 percent (Holmes & Holmes, 1999), they claim disproportionately more lives, particularly of the weaker and more disadvantaged segments of our society, such as runaways, prostitutes, vagrants, and drug addicts (Egger, 1998; Hickey, 1997, Holmes & Holmes, 1999).

While we have developed some insight into the serial killer, there is much we still do not know. This project attempted to develop insights into these four particular personalities based on the appearance, structure, and content of their writings.

What we have attempted to show is the various means of written communications used by violent personalities. While only one of the letter writers is an adjudicated serial killer (Ted Bundy), we believe the three others have killed at least three predicated on research we have conducted in each case. Thus, each satisfies the parameters we believed to be imperative for inclusion into this study.

Each letter writer has a distinct personality and means and methods to communicate. Each one had a goal and an anticipated gain in continuing the communications. We believe by an analysis of the content of the letters as well as the style, appearance, grammar, punctuation, and so on that we are moving another notch in the understanding of a serial killer, a cultural icon, but a dangerous one nonetheless.

REFERENCES

Armistead, T. (1983). "A Critique and Blind Experiment in the Criminological Utility of Handwriting Analysis." *American Journal of Police*, 2(2): 167–191.

Egger, S. (1998). *The Killers among Us: An Examination of Serial Murder and Its Investigation*. Upper Saddle River, NJ: Prentice Hall.

Fisher, J. (1997). *Killer among Us: Public Reactions to Serial Murder*. New York: Praeger.

Fox, J., & J. Levin. (2001). *The Will to Kill*. Boston: Allyn and Bacon.

Hickey, E. (1997). *Serial Murderers and Their Victims*. Pacific Grove, CA: Wadsworth Publishing Co.

Holmes, R., & J. DeBurger. (1988). *Serial Murder*. Newbury Park: Sage.

Holmes, R., & S. Holmes. (1996). *Profiling Violent Crimes: An Investigative Tool*. Thousand Oaks, CA: Sage Publications.

Holmes, R., & S. Holmes. (1997). *Serial Murder* (2nd ed.). Thousand Oaks, CA: Sage.

Holmes, R., & S. Holmes. (1998). *Serial Murder* (2nd ed.). Thousand Oaks, CA: Sage Publications.

Holmes, R., R. Tewksbury, & S. Holmes. (1999). "Fractured Identity Syndrome: A New Theory of Serial Murder." *Journal of Contemporary Criminal Justice*, 15(3): 262–272.

Jenkins, P. (1994). *Using Murder: The Social Construction of Serial Homicide*. New York: Aldine De Gruyter.

Lester, D. (1995). *Serial Killers: The Insatiable Passion*. Philadelphia: The Charles Press.

Lewis, D. O., C. A. Yeager, & Y. Swica. (1997). "Objective Documentation of Child Abuse and Dissociation in 12 Murderers with Dissociative Identity Disorder." *American Journal of Psychiatry*, 154(12): 1703–1710.

McLaughlin, C. G., & B. A. Sarkisian. (1983). "Graphoanalysis." *Security Management*, 27(10): 40–41.

Norris, J. (1988). *Serial Killers: The Growing Menance*. New York: Doubleday.

Rule, A. (1988), *The I-5 Killer*. New York: Signet Books.

CHAPTER 14

PROFILES IN TERROR: THE SERIAL MURDERER[1]

Ronald M. Holmes and James E. Deburger

Homicide is a crime that has historically galvanized public attention to the work of law enforcement personnel. In past decades, when the situational context of most homicides ensured or at least enhanced the probability of rapid solution, law enforcement personnel were lauded for their investigative skills. In recent years, however, both the public and those in law enforcement have expressed frustration and concern regarding the growing number of un-solved murders in this nation. Since 1960, the solution rate for homicides has declined from over 90 percent to approximately 76 percent in 1983 (*Newsweek*, 1984). This dramatic decline in the solution rate coincides with a period of in-creasingly sophisticated technology and an increase in the number of police officers per capita. Given the increased technology available for scientific in-vestigation of these violent crimes, a fair conclusion is that the decrease in the solution rate can be attributed more reasonably to the character of many con-temporary homicides than to the ability of the investigators. While about 20 percent of all homicides today have no apparent motive, in 1966 only 6 per-cent of all homicides were motiveless. Many of the currently unsolved homi-cides are believed to have been perpetrated by serial murders.

Serial murder, the focus of this chapter, is not a totally new kind of crimi-nal behavior. Generally, however, this crime represents the emergence of a form of homicide that is very different from murders commonly investigated in earlier times. Stranger-perpetrated, this form of murder often reflects nei-ther passion nor premeditation stemming from motives of personal gain. More frequently, it tends to reflect nonrational or irrational motives or goals and its victims stand in a depersonalized relation to the perpetrator. One alarming as-pect of contemporary serial murder is the extent to which its perpetrators be-lieve that violence against human beings is a normal and acceptable means of implementing their goals or motives. While the major purpose here is to de-scribe a systematic typology of serial murders, an initial comment will be

---

[1]This chapter first appeared in *Federal Probation*, Vol 44, No 3 (September 1985), pp. 29–34.

made on the significance of violence in the everyday social context as a possible contributory factor in the emergence of this form of violent crime.

SOCIAL-CULTURAL CONTEXT OF VIOLENCE

There is growing evidence to support the view that social and cultural factors in postindustrial American society tend to enhance the probability of interpersonal causes and perpetration of criminal violence. It also seems likely that serial murder represents an advanced form if not an ultimate extension of violence; for here is a form of homicide that by rational standards is pointless and unaccompanied by remorse or a sense of responsibility on the part of the perpetrator. Studies by Wolfgang and his associates on the subculture of violence (Wolfgang & Ferracuti, 1982; Wolfgang & Weiner, 1982) have clearly demonstrated the ways in which personal and contextual factors may interact to produce violent criminal behavior. It is difficult to establish the specific mechanisms by which a culture of violence may be translated into specific criminal acts such as serial murder. But it seems likely that the basic processes of socialization that affect individual behavior from childhood through adulthood are saturated with a potential for violence in interpersonal relations.

Both in terms of contemporary life in America and in terms of this society's European roots, there is a fertile cultural seedbed of violent examples for behavior. Currently, violence as a "normal" or appropriate response in many situations has explicit or implied approval in many facets of our American cultures. This may stem largely from the recurrent, extensive, and essentially "pointless" violence that is commonly portrayed in mass media. There is a sensitivity-dulling exposure to it that reaches all age groups and pervades the waking hours of both children and adults. Television depicts violence in movies and in videos; rock stars, in their entertainment acts, make use of hammers, swords, clubs, and so on. One study of children's TV programs by a Senate committee found 16 violent incidents per broadcast hour. Such material connotes at least passive acceptance of violence. The news media provide further real-life examples of recourse to violence in politics, racial and ethnic relations, labor relations, and the American family. The role of TV as an influence on personal acceptance of violence and as a precursor of violent behavior is still being researched and debated.

Historical and sociological study of American life has provided many examples of violence throughout our history. From very early days in this society, a passive acceptance of violence has existed. Our frontier was characterized by a poor system of law enforcement, little assurance that a judge would arrive in time for a hearing or trial, and a generally weak and uneven judicial system. In some areas, these conditions paved the way for initiation of a vigilante system. Vigilantism was a unique and often violent response to the conditions of frontier America. Often, vigilante leaders were social conservatives attempting to maintain what they perceived as necessary social order. Their victims, unfortunately, included a wide range of easily identified people—blacks, Catholics, and others whose chief offense lay in their unacceptable or unwelcome status. Even in contemporary America, political ideology of the powerful tends to legitimize the use of violence to protect the interests of the powerful. Our cultural norm that grants some acceptance to this use of violence probably stems largely from the frontier ideology.

Widespread individual acceptance of the perpetration of violence appears to be more predominant in the South and the West; however, it is suggested that there is a general increase in acceptance of violence throughout the nation. Many urban minorities are arming themselves for protection against new urban predators who seek to take their property or take their lives. The person growing up in American society tends to learn subtle lessons about violence that reinforce the positive aspects of interpersonal violence in certain situations.

Many people believe that violence is justifiable under certain circumstances; witness, for example, the growing acceptance of executions during the past decade. While many are repulsed by the idea of taking the life of another person under any circumstances, others would justify this action in case of self-defense or other valid circumstances. In terms of criminal behavior, research clearly indicates that some have no reluctance whatever in resorting to violence in the course of crimes that are essentially property related. Toward the polar end of the continuum of violence acceptance are those who see little or no intrinsic wrong in the murder of another human being. For example, serial killer Gerald Stano remarked that the killing of his victims was no different than stepping on a cockroach.

Aside from the contemporary social context and its possible contribution to violence, there exists a history of violence that includes commentary on an extreme form of violence—serial murder. A speaker recently introduced an address on this topic by saying that "serial murder is a product of the 1970s." But this is not accurate. The notoriety of the contemporary serial murderer has been widely covered by the printed media and also by television. Thus, a general impression exists that this type of homicidal predator has emerged only in the last few years. But this perception is not supported by a careful examination of literature on the topic, despite the fact that the names of contemporary serial murderers roll off the lips of criminal justice students like a litany of unholy saints—Gacy, Williams, Bundy, Lucas, Toole, Berkowitz, and others.

But historical study reveals other criminals who lived in much earlier times and committed atrocities of such magnitude that their names are not likely ever to be forgotten by serious students of homicide. Gilles DeRais, a fifteenth-century nobleman and confidant of Joan of Arc, is known to have tortured, raped, and killed more than 800 children. The gratification he received from his sadistic actions and necrophilia derived more from mutilation of the children than from traditional sexual relations. In the latter part of the nineteenth century, a man known as the "ogre of Hanover"—whose real name was Fritz Hairman—sodomized and murdered scores of young boys. Haarman reportedly obtained sexual pleasure by ripping out the throats of his young unfortunate victims (Holmes, 1983). But probably the most famous serial killer in all history was Jack the Ripper, who lived in late-nineteenth-century England. His predilection for London prostitutes made his name a household word. According to learned estimates, however, his victims numbered not more than seven. The crimes of Jack the Ripper pale in comparison with the serial murders committed by contemporary killers such as Bundy, Lucas, and Toole.

SERIAL KILLERS: GEOGRAPHICALLY STABLE AND TRANSIENT

It should be apparent that there is a difference between mass murderers and serial murderers. Mass murderers kill a number of people in one place at one time. This type of killer usually exhibits a momentary frenzy and kills in his frenzy. He probably will not kill again. The serial killer murders a number of people over a long period of time.

There is a need to first identify serial killers in terms of their degree of spatial mobility. Two major forms can be noted. The geographically stable killer is one who typically lives in a particular area and kills his victims within the general region of his residence. John Wayne Gacy, for example, lived in Chicago. He was a well-known personality, a self-employed businessman, and an entertainer of children. Suspected of killing 33 young men and boys, he not only murdered his victims in or near his home but buried them in such places as his crawl space in his home, in his attic, between his walls, under his patio and driveway, and other such unlikely places. Albert Fish, a resident of New York and self-confessed lust killer and cannibal of more than 200 young boys and girls, also was a geographically stable serial killer. One of the most famous recent serial killers is Wayne Williams. He was convicted of only two killings. However, his probable involvement in more than 30 killings of young black males in Atlanta qualifies him for classification as a geographically stable, serial killer.

This type of homicidal predator is often employed in his own community and is well known and well respected. His killings may occur over several years before his apprehension. The senselessness of his acts is a puzzle to law enforcement personnel since the usual motives for murder—spurned love, money, or revenge—are missing. An additional source of great frustration is the lack of physical evidence usually accompanying homicide in these kinds of cases. The serial murderer kills for more exotic reasons—and these are reasons that are not immediately evident to the investigating officer. Very frequently, the motive is sexual in nature and the predator may slaughter a selected group of victims.

The other type who presents a different set of problems to law enforcement is the geographically transient serial killer. This type of serial murderer travels continually throughout his killing career. Typically he kills in one police jurisdiction and shrewdly moves on to another. Consider Ted Bundy. Ted, a handsome former law student from Washington state, is suspected of killing more than a score of women in Washington, Utah, and Colorado. He eventually was apprehended and sentenced for the kidnapping of Carol DaRonch in Murray, Utah. Later taken to trial for the killing of Caryn Campbell, he escaped. His trail led to Chicago, East Lansing, Louisville, and, finally, to the campus of Florida State University in Tallahassee. Less than 2 weeks after his arrival, Bundy brutally attacked Lisa Levy, Margaret Bowman, Karen Chandler, and Kathy Kleiner at the Chi Omega Sorority House. Two blocks away, he broke into the home of Cheryl Thomas and assaulted her. Lisa and Margaret died as a result of this crime. Two weeks later, Ted killed his last victim, 12-year-old Kimberly Leach. When Don Patchen, supervisor of the Homicide and Assault Unit of Tallahassee Police Department, interviewed Bundy regarding 36 cases of unsolved murder victims, Ted calmly told the veteran police officer that he could add one digit to that number. Patchen believes that

Bundy has murdered more than 300 young women throughout the United States; many of these victims were from the great northwest. When Bundy was queried regarding the number of states in which he has killed, he admitted that his "entity" had killed in six different states (Michaud & Anyesworth, 1983; Patchen, 1984a).

At this time, there is little known about Henry Lee Lucas. But it can safely be said that his victims may number in the hundreds. At least 142 of his crimes have been verified. At times he has claimed responsibility for 365 killings and has led police officers to many grave sites.

TYPOLOGY OF SERIAL MURDERS

As is true of any specific type of human behavior, different people may have the same basic motivation but behave differently. This variation in behavior may stem from many factors. Social and behavior scientists have developed a wide range of models for describing behavioral models. These models will not be reviewed here since our focus is on a specific type of a typical behavior—serial murder. A typology is described next that categorizes the major types of serial murderers. Within each type the motives that seem to predominate will be examined. In each type it will be apparent that the motives function to provide for the serial killer a personal justification for the violence he commits.

Visionary Type

Most serial murderers would not be considered psychotic. They are in touch with reality but have no feelings for others. By contrast the "visionary type" is impelled to murder because he has heard voices or has seen visions that demand that he kill a certain person or a category of persons. For some the voice or vision that is perceived may be that of a demon; for others it may be from God. Consider the case of Harvey Carignan; he was convicted of killing six women. But it is believed he killed many, many more. All of these victims fell prey to Carignan because God told him to do it. He perceived the women as "bad" people and himself as God's instrument to do away with evil in the world. Another illustrative case is one in which a young male decapitated a 76-year-old woman and stabbed her lifeless body over 200 times. Within the next two weeks he assaulted three other elderly women, each time stabbing them in the neck and chest area. Upon apprehension, he related that he was possessed by a red demon who demanded this action and that he could find comfort only through killing.

Both killers heard voices that were only in their heads. Both operated because of a vision. One was god mandated, the other was demon mandated. These two subtypes give different justification for their actions even though the end product is the same, a homicide. The perpetration of violence is legitimized by the vision the serial killer "experienced." There is little doubt about the mental state of this type of serial killer. At times he is clearly out of touch with reality. He hears voices and sees visions. In psychiatric terms, this type of serial killer could be termed psychotic. A shrewd defense attorney could certainly make the case of an insanity plea.

Mission-Oriented Type

The serial killer who has a mission to fulfill is one who consciously has a goal in his life to eliminate a certain identifiable group of people. He does not hear voices or see visions. However, he may decide on his own that it is his role to rid the world of a group of people who are "undesirable" or unworthy to live with other human beings. Recently, there was a case of four young women who were similarly murdered. All four victims frequented local night spots. One was a known prostitute, and the others had alleged reputations for casual sexual encounters. Their dress style appeared to advertise their personal availability and their willingness to participate in sex for money. The murderer of these women had a personal mission, a mission to rid his community of prostitutes. During the interrogation of the killer, not only was he aware of his killings but he verbalized a sense of pride because of rendering the community such a great service.

The mission-oriented serial murderer is not psychotic; he does not hear voices or see visions. He has a self-imposed duty to rid the world of an unworthy group of people. The victim group may be prostitutes, young women, Catholics, or any other group he defines as unworthy to live with decent people. He may be either an organized nonsocial or a disorganized asocial type (Hazelwood & Douglas, 1980, p. 2). He lives in the real world and interacts with it on a daily basis. Typically when this type of killer is arrested, his neighbors cannot believe that he is the person responsible for the deaths of so many people. Take the case of a geographically stable, serial killer from Louisville. Neighbors described him as a nice young man who cared for the people in the neighborhood and was a social worker in a group home for convicted felons. No one had suspected him of murdering young women in his community.

Hedonistic Type

Physical evidence accompanying murders committed by the hedonistic type tend to be most striking and bizarre. Consider these examples.

The nude body of a young woman was discovered in an alley; her body had been mutilated, both breasts had been removed, and her vaginal vault had been crudely excised. In another case, in the summer of 1984, a street wino was found dead in a walkway in an urban area. The cause of death was internal bleeding. He was nude, and a crutch was found inserted seventeen inches into his rectum. As yet, no one has been arrested in either of these cases.

Interview records with the hedonistic type reflect a perverted means of thrill seeking. A young male presently awaiting sentencing in a multiple killing of young boys described, with a gleam in his eyes, the great pleasure he received in killing the young men. He said that he felt a rush of excitation when he put the knife into the ribs of the young boys. Killing for him was a thrill, it was "pure" enjoyment. This is typical of the hedonistic serial murderer.

As difficult as it must be for most people to realize, there are some people who can kill simply for the thrill of it. These people kill not because of a goal in their life to rid the community of undesirables; neither do they kill because they hear voices or see visions. They kill because they enjoy it. They kill because the thrill becomes an end in itself. The lust murderer can be viewed as a subcategory of the hedonistic type because of the sexual enjoyment experienced in the homicidal act (Hazelwood & Douglas, 1980, p. 3). Anthropophagy, dismemberment, necrophilia, or other forms of sexual aberration are prevalent in this form of serial killing. Often this type of serial killer is typically intelligent; less intelligent ones tend to be street smart. Apprehension of the hedonistic type is very difficult especially if he is geographically transient. His method of killing, while sadistic and immeasurably pleasurable to him, makes investigation difficult for the law enforcement professional. He may be able to escape detection for years.

Power/Control-Oriented Type

The power/control-oriented type receives gratification from the complete control of the victim. Ted Bundy obviously experienced some great pleasure from exerting power and control in the killing of his victims. While one description of the killing of Kimberly Leach reports Bundy's sexual pleasure connected with the act, the fundamental source of pleasure is not sexual, it is the killer's ability to control and exert power over his helpless victim (Michaud & Aynesworth, 1983). In another case where there are indications of power-oriented behavior; the Red Demon Killer experienced orgasm while stabbing his victim (picquerism). Holding the power of life or death over a victim is symbolically the ultimate control that one person can exert over another.

By exerting complete control over the life of his victim, the murderer experiences pleasure and excitement, not from the sexual excitation or the rape but from his belief that he does indeed have the power to do whatever he wishes to do to another human being who is completely helpless and within his total control. This type of serial murderer is not psychotic; he does live in the world and is aware of the rules and regulations that he is expected to abide by. He chooses, however, to ignore them. He lives by his own code and typically fits the patterns of a psychopathic or sociopathic type of personality. His behavior indicates a character disorder, not a break from reality. While the power/control-oriented type and the hedonistic type are probably both psychopathic, they differ in that killing for the hedonist is simply pleasurable. The hedonist receives sexual gratification in the process of killing another person and may experience orgasm from knifing the victim (picquerism) or having sex with the corpse (necrophilia). The pleasure derived from the killing by the power/control-oriented type derives from his capture and control of his victim, rendering his victim powerless and helpless while forcing the captive to obey his every command. The power/control-oriented type experiences a selfinflated sense of importance and power.

SERIAL KILLER: GENERAL CHARACTERISTICS

While it may be beneficial to cast serial murderers into various categories depending on their motives, it is just as necessary to indicate some of the general characteristics of the offender. These should be seen as characteristics, not causes of behavior. A fundamental difference exists between the two words; *characteristics* describe only what appear to he common variables whereas *causes* explain why certain behaviors occur. Rule (1984), an expert on serial murder, argues that it is impossible to speak in absolute terms when one is dealing with an aberrant personality. The majority of serial killers appear to share certain characteristics. First, most are white and are in the age group of 25 to 34 years of age. They are intelligent or at least "street smart." They are charming and charismatic; and many of them are psychopathic. Many, such as Edmund Kemper, are "police groupies" and are fascinated by police work. Kemper frequently associated with off-duty police officers and questioned them about the progress that was being made on unsolved murders that he had committed. Serial killers often focus on one type of victim. Bundy selected young women, all with dark long hair, parted in the middle. Williams chose young black males. It appears that the victim group shares two basic features: They are vulnerable and easy to control. Often the serial murderer will use a ruse to gain access to their victims. Bundy, for example, frequently used a cast to simulate a broken arm to solicit sympathy and aid.

It is also interesting to note that serial killers appear to be highly mobile. Many will travel almost constantly (e.g., geographically transient type). They appear to be "night people." They appear to select, to stalk, and to kill their victims when most people are not as alert or aware of their personal vulnerability. They kill with "hands-on" weapons such as knives, hands, fists; they have physical contact with their victims. In the beginning, their killings are elaborately planned. Toward the end of their killing careers, the plans disintegrate. They kill more in a "panic" and some kill more than one person at a time. Witness again the case of Bundy. He savagely attacked five women in the space of less than 2 hours; five were brutally beaten, and two killed. Normally, the serial killer waits, stalks, kills, waits, stalks, kills (Rule, 1980). Toward the end of his murderous career, there is little time between the waits and the kills.

Many of the known serial murderers were born out of wedlock. As children many were physically, sexually, or emotionally abused. These killers tend to abuse alcohol or drugs, and often this abuse exacerbated their sadistic fantasies. For example, their interest in media would lie more in the area of sadistic porn or other depictions of violence. Many are intimately involved with women who have no knowledge of their partner's homicidal activities. Sexual relationships with these women are often characterized by binding and other forms of sadistic behavior.

SERIAL KILLERS: A PROBLEM FOR THE CRIMINAL JUSTICE SYSTEM

The apprehension of serial killers by professionals in criminal justice appears to occur almost by accident. Due largely to the senselessness of their crimes, their mobility, and their intelligence, they may go on for years without being apprehended. Their killings are not of the "smoking gun" variety. One criminologist estimated that the number of serial murderers has tripled over the past two decades and that the overall murder rate has more than doubled. Currently it is estimated that about 5000 people each year are victims of serial killers. Contrary to the FBI's estimate of 30 serial killers roaming throughout the United States, this same criminologist believes that there are over 100. In a personal interview on death row in Florida, Ted Bundy suggested that the number is much higher (Bundy, 1985; Rule, 1984).

Regardless of the number of serial murderers, the number of victims is significant. While other crimes such as robbery clearly affect more people, there should be no confusion when one speaks of the quality of an act versus the quantity of an act. In view of the mission of criminal justice, there can be no standard that uses numbers solely as a yardstick for action. The consideration of violence in the cultural context and comments here on the general characteristics of serial killers are intended solely to shed light on contemporary types of serial killers. But one compelling fact is apparent: There has appeared in contemporary times a class of homicidal predators who pose a clear and present danger to more than 5000 Americans yearly. Certainly this is evidence enough that the criminal justice system must take notice and develop a plan of action.

REFERENCES

Bundy, Theodore. (1985). Personal interview.
Darrach, Brad, & Joel Norris. "An American Tragedy." *Life,* August 1984, p. 58.
Hazelwood, Robert R., & John E. Douglas. (1980, April). "The Lust Murder." *FBI Law Enforcement Bulletin,* p. 1.
————. "The Random Killers." *Newsweek,* November 26, 1984, p. 100.
Holmes, Ronald. (1983). *The Sex Offender and the Criminal Justice System.* Springfield, IL: Charles C. Thomas Publishing Co.
Michaud, Stephen, and Hugh Aynesworth. (1983). *The Only Living Witness.* New York: Linden Press.
Patchen, Donald. (1979, August). "The Mind of the Mass Murderer." *Time;* August.
————. (1983). "Catching a New Breed of Killer." *Time,* November 14, p. 47.
————. (1984a). Personal interview.
————. (1984b). "Profiling Serial Murders." *Science Digest,* October, p. 47.
Rule, Ann. (1980). *The Stranger Beside Me.* New York: W.W. Norton.
Rule, Ann. (1984). Personal interview.
Wolfgang, Marvin E., & Franco Ferracuti. (1982). *The Subculture of Violence.* Beverly Hills, CA: Sage Publications.
Wolfgang, Marvin E., & Neil A. Weiner. (1982). *Criminal Violence.* Beverly Hills, CA: Sage Publications.

MASTERS OF TERROR: TYPES OF MASS KILLERS

Ronald M. Holmes

INTRODUCTION

George "Jo Jo" Hennard drove his pickup truck through a window in a crowded restaurant. He fired into the crowd of innocent people as they were eating their lunches. As some lay upon the floor, he screamed at them, "Is it worth it?" A disgruntled citizen, he then killed himself. James Oliver Huberty walked into a McDonald's restaurant and killed 21 people; then a marksman from the local police department killed him. Another disgruntled citizen. Fourteen-year-old Michael Carneal went to school early one morning in Heath, Kentucky, and he shot eight fellow students. Three young female students died in his onslaught. A school shooter as well as a mass killer. William Baker, age 66, was a former worker for a Navisar plant in Melrose Park, Illinois for 39 years. Fired six years ago in 1995, he returned to the plant and killed four employees and wounded four others before killing himself. This is an example of the disgruntled employee mass killer.

When did this all start? Perhaps our attention to the problem of mass murder commenced with the actions of Charles Whitman. This killer shot 46 innocent victims from atop the tower at the University of Texas and killed 16. He was shot to death by police officers at the scene. Certainly there were other mass killers prior to this crime, but for some reason this crime in 1966 galvanized the attention concerning the crime of the mass killer.

WHAT IS MASS MURDER?

Mass murder is one of three forms of multicide, that is, the killing of a number of people.

- Mass murder—the killing of three or more people at one time and in one place
- Serial murder—the killing of three or more people in more than a thirty-day period with a significant time distance between the killings

- Spree murder—the killing of three of more people within a thirty-day period usually accompanied with the commission of another felony

Mass murder differs from the other two forms of multicide in time and distance. Simply said, mass murder is the killing of a number of people at one time and in one place. The number three is the baseline number in this definition for mass murder. Holmes and DeBurger (1985, 1988) and Hickey (1997) agree that the number three is the appropriate number. To muddle the waters, Dietz (1986) offers a unique definition: "we define mass murder as the willful injuring of five or more persons of whom three or more are killed by a single offender in a single incident" (p. 480).

This last definition is burdensome. No one else adds nonfatal victims to the definition of mass murder. So, regardless of the number of people injured, if less than three are killed, it is still not a case of mass murder. While it is agreed that the injured should not be an integral component of the mass murder definition, a number of fatally injured should remain constant, and for the purposes in this definition, the number should be three.

Time and place are two additional elements to the number of murdered victims. Usually the act of mass murder is carried out at one time and in one place. Joseph Wesbecker, for example, returned to his former place of employment and committed an act of mass murder. On the other hand, Carl Drega killed two people at the parking lot of a local mall and then went into town where he killed two more. Both are acts of mass murder. The "one place" element is missing in the latter case, but it is important to recognize that it was a continuous act. Drega left the parking lot and drove to the center of town to complete his rage. Thus mass murder may be carried out over a longer period of time, sometime minutes or even a few hours, and also at more than one geographical area.

There are other differences between the mass killer and the other two types of multicide. The mass killer, for example, will often commit suicide at the site; other times he will "force" the police to kill him or her, perhaps a form of "suicide by proxy." In rare instances they will turn themselves in to the police. This is not true of serial or spree killers. They continue their acts of fatal predation until something occurs that circumvents their crimes (e.g., they are apprehended, they are incapacitated in some fashion, they die, etc.).

The mass murder scene erupts with a violence that almost paralyzes the community. There is widespread fear and with some a panic that is not present with a serial killer. With the latter, there is a continuing lingering of fear and it continues under the edge of consciousness only to emerge temporarily with a new murder. This is evident in the serial murder case of the Green River Killer in Seattle. This case dates to the 1980s and is still unresolved. Other cities and communities have similar cases, although perhaps not as many victims, but still the attention devoted to a mass killing scene is dramatic and foreboding.

Perhaps it is because it is perceived that there is no real protection from the mass killer that there is such an alarm among the citizens of a community. True, the serial killer attacks strangers as does sometimes the mass killer. But the mass killer may open fire from the dining room of a hotel or from the factory upon his former or current coworkers. Thus the feeling of vulnerability permeates those who witness the mass killing or simply are exposed to it in a second-hand fashion, from a media report or a column in a newspaper.

The mass killer is often viewed as a deranged person, one who is mentally ill, suffered some type of catatrosophic episode, and has some other demented personality alteration. The serial killer is often viewed not unlike one's next-door neighbor, his social face charming, not showing any form of pathology. This was seen in the cases of Ted Bundy, Douglas Clark, Donald Harvey, and a host of other serial killers. But with mass killers, the likes of Huberty, Whitman, and others hold a story of those who "were wronged" by society and the killer is to right that wrong with an act of mass killing.

INCIDENCES OF MASS MURDER

Mass murder is not a new criminal phenomenon. In compiling data for this chapter, it was noted that since 1949 there has been a gross increase in the number of mass murders. In 1949, for example, Howard Unruh killed thirteen neighbors. The next year, William Cook killed five family members. There were few others. In 1966, Charles Whitman, the Charles Manson family, and Richard Speck captured the headlines with their killings. Since that time the incidence of mass murder has grown. There are some who believe that there are at least three cases of mass murder a month in the United States. This may be underestimated. Regardless, there are many people who take the lives of many others in this country with no apparent reason until after the crime occurs; it is only then that the experts talk about the warning signs and what could have been done to prevent such a crime.

The cases of school shootings illustrate the growing number of mass killings that occur within the perceived safety of the classroom. Within a relatively short period of time, eight young males assaulted 114 classmates and teachers and killed 31 people, including one mother, a set of parents, and two teachers. Strangely, this epidemic of school shootings has stopped, at least temporarily and hopefully forever. However, we do not think this latter to be the truth.

TYPES OF MASS KILLERS

In an attempt to understand the social problem of mass murder, it is important to develop some form of typology of mass killers. Using a similar methodology developed to distinguish types of serial killers (Holmes & DeBurger, 1985, 1988; Holmes & Holmes, 1999), an attempt is made to understand the mass killer using certain and selected items for analysis. These traits are provided in Table 5.1 along with their corresponding type of mass killer that is likely to exhibit them.

Behavioral Background

There is no clear understanding concerning the basic formation of the personality of the mass killer. It is at least influenced by the unique experiences that a person undergoes as he or she develops from a child to an adult. It is not solely those experiences but the unique experiences as well as the sequence of those experiences.

Additionally, the biological inheritance of the individual must be considered. The inheritance is unique to that person and, as far as the research found, there are no identical twins found wherein the one was a mass killer and the other not.

The experiences and the biological inheritance form the personality of the mass killer. Certainly there is no one factor that determines the personality of an individual. There are multiple causes, and it is also recognized that some mass killers have mental or physical problems that could have influenced their deeds. For example, Charles Whitman was found to have a brain tumor. Joseph Wesbecker was diagnosed with severe mental problems prior to his killing at his former place of employment. Richard Speck was thought to have an extra Y chromosome. Norris and Birns (1988) claimed that a blow to the head as a youth is responsible for the development of a violent personality. However, it has not been scientifically demonstrated that the possession of any one biological anomaly is the sole responsible agent for the mass killer (Hickey, 1997; Holmes & Holmes, 2001; Sears, 1991). The other popularly held beliefs that poverty, female-headed families, and mass density cause the mass murder mentality also do not hold true for empirical verification (Holmes & Holmes, 2001).

As stated by Holmes and DeBurger (1988), Hickey (1997), and Holmes and Holmes (1998, 2001), bad neighborhoods, economic stress, family instability, and other such social ills do not by themselves produce a killer. It is a myriad of factors interacting in a unique fashion that produces a mass killer.

Motivation

Motivation is another element that is used to categorize the mass killer. The motivation to kill an unknown number of strangers or family members lies either within the personality of the killer or rests outside the personality, in the instance where someone is paid to fatally injure a group of people. The motivation is complex and can be easily misunderstood. A partial answer may rest within the location of the motivation to kill (that is, intrinsic or extrinsic to the personality of the killer).

There may be something deep within the personality of the killer that impels the person to kill. A vision from God, a voice from a spirit has been enough for some mass killers. Priscilla Ford, for example, believed that God had spoken directly to her demanding that she kill innocent people walking down the streets of Reno, Nevada. On the other hand, James Oliver Huberty struck back at innocent persons as responsible representations of a society that had done him wrong. He killed not because of voices or visions; he killed out of rage because of the injustices he perceived he received from society. The victims stood as reminders of those wrongs that he had to right.

Anticipated Gain

What is the reason for an act of mass murder? What does the mass killer hope to realize from the act of mass murder? There are two types of anticipated gain. The first is psychological gain; the second is material. The psychological gain holds a potential that others will now realize who the killer is and what was the wrong he wronged. People will now take notice of the troubling issues that are important to the mass killer. The material gain is represented by money, goods, business interests, insurance claims, or other such items of some value. Regardless, the examination of the anticipated gain is important in distinguishing among the various types of mass killers.

Spatial Mobility

Most mass murderers are geographically stable. That is, they live, work, and kill in one area, and they are not nomadic in their killings. Of course, there are two types that will be discussed that do travel, but they are the exceptions rather than the rule.

Victim Characteristics

The traits of the victims usually play no role in their selection process for the mass killer. Sometimes the victims are members of the killer's family. Sometimes the victims are complete unknowns and strangers. Again, Hennard killed strangers at the restaurant; Whitman murdered strangers walking across the campus at the University of Texas. Conversely, Ronald Gene Simmons killed relatives and family members; John List killed his family. Regardless of the persons victimized, there are no physical traits that are important to the mass murderer. Hairstyle, hair color, occupation, and so on play no role in their selection by the mass killer.

TYPES OF MASS MURDERERS

Dietz (1986) and Holmes and Holmes (2001) list several types of mass killers in their research: the disciple, the family annihilator, the religious/ideological killer, the disgruntled citizen, the disgruntled employee, the set-and-run killer, and the psychotic mass killer. In distinguishing the types of mass killers, behavioral background, the motivation, anticipated gain, and victim characteristics were examined to determine what type of mass killer each case represented.

The Disciple Mass Killer

The disciple mass killer murders because of a connection that is made by the killer and the leader of the group or organization. The reason for the affiliation may be political or simply based on the charismatic personality of the leader. This was true in the case of Charles Manson, who allegedly instructed a group of his followers to murder Sharon Tate, Steven Parent, Abigail Folger, Jay Sebring, and Voyteck Frykowski, and then the next night to kill Leno and Rosemary LaBianca. These killers, including Patricia Krenwinkel, Leslie Van

Houten, Susan Atkins, and Tex Watson, killed in response to the perceived directions of Manson himself.

Using a format to distinguish each type of mass killer, motivation, anticipated gain, victim selectivity, victim relationship, spatial mobility, and victim traits, it is noted that each type of mass killer is different. For example, the disciple mass killer's motivation to kill is extrinsic to the personality of the killer. That is, the leader of the group is the one who commands the death of others, and it is the disciple who will carry out such demands or wishes. There is nothing intrinsic to the personality of the killer himself or herself that wishes to kill a certain group or people. This is the desire of the leader and it is the duty of the disciple to carry out such demands.

The anticipated gain for the disciple is expressive, or psychological. To become a member of the chosen inner circle with the leader is the hope of the disciple killer. This person will kill because it is the commandment of the leader and by doing so will gain some form of acceptance into the group. The disciple will play no role in the determination of the victims to be killed; this is left to the leader. Unless the victims are members of the group itself, which may be the case in rare situations, the victims are strangers. As such, the victims have no physical traits that are apparent in the selection of them as victims.

As far as geographical mobility, this type of mass killer will follow the movements of the leader. So, if the leader decides to move to another location, the disciple will follow. Thus, the disciple may be geographically transient depending on the whims and wishes the group's leader. The decision to move from one locale to another is the responsibility and the choice of the leader. The disciple merely follows the dictates of the leader.

Table 15.1

Traits of Various Types of Mass Killers

Types of Mass Killer	Motivation	Anticipated Gain	Victim Selectivity	Victim Relationship	Spatial Mobility
Disciple	Extrinsic	Psychological	Random	Strangers	Transient
Family annihilator	Intrinsic	Psychological	Nonrandom	Relatives	Stable
Disgruntled employee	Intrinsic	Psychological	Random	Coworkers	Stable
Ideological	Intrinsic	Mixture	Often members of the group, sometimes strangers	Often members of the group, sometimes strangers	Transient
Set-and-run	Intrinsic	Material	Random	Strangers	Transient
Disgruntled	Intrinsic	Psychological	Random	Usually strangers	Stable
Citizen psychotic	Intrinsic	Psychological	Random	Strangers	Stable

Family Annihilator Mass Killer

The family annihilator is bent on taking the lives of his family and relatives. What would impel someone to take the lives of their own family, nuclear or extended? There are many such examples of family annihilators: John List, Ronald Gene Simmons, and many others. For example, Leonardo Morita was plagued by financial setbacks. He set his house afire, killing his wife, his three children, and his housekeeper. James Cooper confessed to the murder of his wife and three children. Only recently a former Army Ranger received the death penalty for the murder of his three children. Jeffrey Hutchinson also confessed to the murder of his wife; he received the death penalty in Florida.

What are the traits or characteristics of the family annihilator? How different is this type of mass killer from the other types treated in this chapter? First, the family annihilator's motivation to kill is intrinsic to the killer's personality; it lies within the psyche of the person who has made a decision to kill. Unlike the male serial killer, who often kills for some type of sexual gratification, this killer kills for a nonsexual purpose. It may be to rid oneself of the burdens and obligations of raising a family (John List is such an example), or it may simply be to obliterate a family because of an involvement with another person outside the marriage. Regardless of the reason, there is something within the personality, the psyche, the mental state of the mass killer to move this individual to take the lives of his family and/or relatives.

The anticipated gain for this killer is psychological or expressive. There is no material gain to be expected unless it is to rid oneself of the financial burden of a family, but this is typically an ancillary gain, not the primary gain. Sometimes this is ascertained quite easily. Take, for example, the cases of John List and Ronald Gene Simmons. However, in the case of another family annihilator, Dr. Jeffrey MacDonald, this is difficult especially because MacDonald has consistently maintained his innocence. Some believe that MacDonald wanted to live a different lifestyle and his family hindered that goal (Holmes & Holmes, 2001). Jeffrey Hutchinson was said to have suffered from the Gulf War syndrome, and he was unaware of what he had done despite calling the 911 operator and saying he had shot his family.

MacDonald was eventually found guilty in his slaying of his family. He was given three consecutive life sentences, granted an appeal, and was eventually returned to prison in 1983. His case is still under appeal.

The victims of the family annihilator are not selected on a random basis. They are members of his family or other relatives. In this case the killer knows his victims, and they all live in close physical proximity. This is not true for many other mass killers. For example, the Manson family members did not personally know the victims; Hennard was not acquainted with the diners at Huby's Restaurant. These victims are chosen by who they are; they are members of the killer's family. Thus they are chosen because of the affinity they share with the mass killer. Again, the victims are related, usually family members, not strangers. In Lowell, Massachusetts, Peter Contos killed his girlfriend, and then he killed their two children and stuffed them into his locker at his workstation at a military base. Interestingly, the wife and girlfriend were apparently unaware of each other (Holmes & Holmes, 2001, p. 56).

Regarding geographical mobility, the family annihilator tends to be a long-time resident of the community. He may have been born in the area, worked in that area, and participated in a wide range of social activities. Too, the victims are long-term residents of the area. Unlike some of the other mass killers, the family annihilator has no need to travel to find victims.

The Disgruntled Employee Mass Killer

The disgruntled employee has a vendetta against his present or former employer. For whatever reason, real or imagined, this mass killer has a mission to rectify a wrong that was committed against him for an action taken by his employer.

Joseph Wesbecker returned to his place of employment armed with handguns, an AK-47, a bayonet, and hundreds of rounds of ammunition. Seven months earlier his employer placed him on mental disability leave. He had warned that he would return someday and kill some people. He did. He killed seven people and then killed himself. The disgruntled employee is not a new phenomenon. Thirty years ago, a defense contractor fired Robert Mack from his job, where he had worked for 25 years. He appealed his firing and at that meeting he opened fire on his former coworkers.

What kind of person is the disgruntled employee? First, the motivation to kill lies within the psyche of the person. There is unrest within the personality that causes a disturbance and impels that person to such an action. Thus the gain is psychological. There is no other person who commands the killer to act; no money, insurance, and so on that will be realized by the act of mass murder. From the action of mass murder, immediate and often national attention is brought to the killer. The victims are selected at the place of work. They are sometimes coworkers known to the killer but sometimes they only happen to work there, unknown to the killer. They are not relatives; they happen to be at the location. Sharon Needy, a victim of Joseph Wesbecker, arrived at work an hour earlier than normal because she had to attend to some personal business on her lunch hour. She was talking to a secretary across the door from an elevator. Wesbecker stepped off the elevator, opened fire, and she was killed. Had she arrived at work at her normal time, had she not been talking to someone apart from her own work station; she may not have been a victim and may still be alive today. The victims are randomly selected; Needy was there. Wesbecker continued down the halls, into the cafeteria, into the basement, where he shot and killed those unfortunate to be in his path.

The disgruntled employee tends to be a long-term resident of his community. Often he has worked for the same employer for a number of years. Neighbors know him; he is not a stranger, although some neighbors may say later that he often acted strange.

Ideological Mass Killer

Marshall Applewhite was ultimately responsible for the deaths of his Heaven's Gate cult. The leader ordered their deaths by suicide because of the cult's belief that there was a space ship behind the Hale-Bopp comet. This space ship would transport them to a better place in the next life. Jim Jones ordered more than 900 of his cult to kill themselves. Some were reluctant to do, so they were "helped" by other members of the cult. Some drank a poisonous drink, some were shot, and others stabbed. Jones told his followers they would all be killed by American agents in retaliation for the killing of Congressman Lee Ryan. The only way to escape and to gain everlasting salvation was to die alongside "Father Jones."

It is apparent that the motivation for the ideological mass killer rests within the personality of the person. There appears to be a search and a need for power and control. There is no greater power than the control over another person's fate. This is apparent in the cases already described in this section. Thus, the motivation is within the personality of the mass killer.

What does this mass killer hope to realize from the killing of a number of people? In many cases, the anticipated gain is a mixture of gains, some psychological and some material. If the killer does not die at the scene, as Jim Jones or Marshall Applewhite, the gain is psychological. It is an expression of his power and control. If the deaths of the followers leave the mass killer with the wealth, possessions, and goods of the victims, then the gain is material. These are now the property of the cult and ultimately the mass killer.

In many instances, the killer knows the victims. They are members of the cult or group. In some instances the victims are members of the group itself. In Heaven's Gate, the 39 victims were members of the group. They, including Applewhite, knew each other because of the relatively small number of persons. In Jonestown, more than 900 were members of the group. Terrorists are ideological killers. We recall the horrific act of terrorism in the killing of the Olympic athletes during the games in Germany. This type of mass killer may be propelled by intrinsic motivations, but the reason may be further fueled by a political overtone. Netter (1982, pp. 228–237) offers the following:

- *No rules.* Terrorists differ from soldiers in war and police action in that terrorists consciously violate all conventions.
- *No innocents.* The "unjust system" includes a fight against all people within that system who do not side with them.
- *Economy.* By a single act of terrorism, the acts serves to frighten tens of thousands, even millions, of people.
- *Publicity.* Terrorists seek publicity, which in turn encourages terrorism. Well-publicized violence advertises the terrorist's cause.
- *Individual therapy.* Fighting may be fun to some fanatics to a cause. Engaging in a battle gives purpose to life, and all the more to lives that are meaningless.
- *Varied objectives.* One goal of a terrorist act is to exercise power and to get more of it. However, members of a group may variously conceive of what power is used for.

Those involved in ideological warfare against another group or within their own group are willing to exercise violence in the most brutal fashion. The ideological mass killer may move from one location to another; thus, the killer is geographically transient or nomadic. Jim Jones's ministry started in Indiana, moved to California, and finally to Guyana. The Heaven's Gate cult started in Oregon and ended in California. And, of course, victim traits are unimportant to the ideological mass killer.

The Set-and-Run Mass Killer

Jack Graham, a petty criminal, was upset with his doting mother. One Christmas season, his mother visited him in Denver, and he presented her with a present as she boarded the plane. The "present" contained 14 pounds of dynamite. After taking off the bomb exploded and 44 people were killed. He was executed in 1957.

In Chicago, in 1982, a killer who tampered with Tylenol killed seven people. The motivation to kill in this case is unknown because the killer has never been caught. Why should this be considered a mass killing rather than a serial killing? The medication was tampered with and placed on the shelves in one continuous activity according to the police.

In Oklahoma City, Timothy McVeigh bombed the Murrah Federal Building. One hundred and sixty-eight innocent men, women, and children were killed. Arrested shortly after the bombing in April 1995, McVeigh refused to answer questions as to why he would kill so many innocent people.

With the set-and-run mass killer, the murderer is not present at the time of the act of mass murder. He has fled. This was true in all three of the cases cited above. Graham was on his way home; McVeigh was trying to drive away from the scene, perhaps on his way back to meeting with other terrorists of the same ilk.

What motivates a set-and-run mass killer? The locus of motivation rests within the personality of the mass killer. Revenge may be one motivation. Anger, political purpose, or some other motivation may be other reasons. Regardless, the motivation lies within the personality of the mass killer.

What is to be gained from the act of mass murder? The anticipated gain is certainly expressive or psychological. This killer does not kill for financial or material gain. With this said, there may be some professional killers who kill a number of people with a firebomb or some other device. And with this type of mass killer, which is highly unusual and probably more accidental than intended, the anticipated gain is material. This type of mass killer is the rare exception. Perhaps a subtype or even a different type could be termed mass murderer for hire.

Victim selectivity is at a random basis. The site, however, is deliberately selected. McVeigh deliberately selected the Murrah Federal Building because the federal building represented the enemy for this set-and-run killer. The innocent victims were only objects that represented the enemy, the American government. He never personally viewed the 168 victims; he was far from the scene when the bomb exploded. Likewise the victims are strangers to the set-and-run killer. They are not selected because of physical traits of the victims, unlike the sexually motivated mass killer. This is also true for the Tylenol killer. Another set-and-run killer, Julio Gonzalez set fire to a social club in New York City. He had a disagreement with his girlfriend and became incensed when he saw her dancing with another man. Eighty-seven innocent people died in this fire. Bystanders identified him as he ran from the social club. The girlfriend escaped unhurt.

The set-and-run mass killer tends to be nomadic or transient. McVeigh was not from Oklahoma City. Gonzalez was originally from Cuba, relocated to Florida and then to New York City (Holmes & Holmes, 2001, p. 91). As with the other mass killers, physical traits are unimportant.

The Disgruntled Citizen Mass Killer

There is a group of people who are so upset with the society that they lash out with fatal violence at citizens of that society. These killers do not return to their workplace; they lash out at people on the street with no care about relationships or any other personal concerns of their victims. Hubert de la Tore was so angry at the world that he set an apartment complex on fire. Twenty-five residents died as a consequence of that fire. In Scotland, Thomas Hamilton was terminated as a scoutmaster after authorities found photographs of bare-chested young boys in his possession. Twenty-five years later he vented that simmering rage. He entered a primary school and killed 16 students and a teacher. In Florida, William Cruse entered a shopping center and killed six innocent shoppers. In California, Alan Winterbourne was upset because he could not find employment. He entered a state unemployment office and killed three state workers. Of course, one of the most infamous was James Oliver Huberty. He had been fired from his job in Ohio, relocated in California, and when he lost his job as a private security guard, he killed 21 customers at McDonald's.

What are some of the traits of the disgruntled citizen mass killer? Using the same format as with the previous mass killers, the following mental image appears:

1. The locus of motivation for the act of mass murder for the disgruntled mass killer is intrinsic to the personality. The killer perceives that society has committed a gross injustice, and the only way to correct that perceived injustice is to kill. The injustice, real or imagined, must be remedied; it is within his mind that the origins for mass murder rest.

2. The anticipated gain is psychological or expressive. The gain is also personal. Although the killer is murdering strangers who have no role in the acts of injustice as judged by the killer, the mass murder episode stands as a sign for the injustice. Now people will not only know who the killer is, but they will also know the injustice perpetrated against the mass murderer. Society can no longer ignore the injustice, and the killer may, at least for a time, bask in the reflected glory of what has been done, the mass killing episode.

3. The victims are selected randomly. The victims are strangers. In the same fashion that Priscilla Ford ran over pedestrians on the streets of Reno, the disgruntled citizen mass killer shares no affinity or relationship with the victims. Colin Ferguson killed on a subway; James Oliver Huberty murdered in a McDonald's; William Cruse committed his act of mass murder in a shopping mall. Thus, the victim selectivity and victim relationship involve randomness and a stranger relationship.

4. The disgruntled citizen mass killer tends to be geographically stable. This person usually does not move around the country, seeking victims for killing. The murderer usually has lived in the area and worked in that same area for an extended period of time. There are exceptions. Huberty is such an exception. True, he moved from Ohio to California. But the reason for his move was to find employment, not to seek victims.

Again, the physical traits of the victims are of no consequence for this mass killer.

The Psychotic Mass Killer

Perhaps the most mysterious mass killer is the psychotic mass murderer. This type of killer has a severe break with reality. With some, this break is long lasting; with others; the breaks with reality are short lived. The killer may hear voices or see visions. One needs to know the difference between one who is psychotic and one who is psychopathic or possesses a character defect. The psychopathic person has the following characteristics:

- Above-average intelligence
- Absence of delusions, hallucinations, or other signs of psychosis
- Chronic lying
- Inability to feel sorrow or remorse
- Inability to learn from experiences
- Ongoing trouble with the legal system
- Charming and personable
- Unreliable (Cleckley, 1982)

This character defect personality appears early in life, and by the teenage years the person may have been involved in numerous brushes with the law. However, with the psychotic individual, the appearances are not so much with the criminal justice system as with the mental health system.

Ellen Church killed her children because of the voices that commanded her to kill. Priscilla Ford heard the voice of Jesus Christ and saw the image of Christ. According to her, she then drove downtown to obey the word of the Lord to drive her car on the sidewalk, where she killed seven people.

What kind of killer is the psychotic mass murderer? What are the traits and the characteristics? First, the motivation to kill lives within the psyche of the psychotic mass killer. True, the person may believe that voices or visions command the act of mass murder. But realistically, the impaired mental condition of the mass killer comes from inside the demented state of being. It is the psyche of the killer that accounts for the decision to kill (Holmes & Holmes, 2001, p. 107).

What does one have to gain from the killing of strangers? The anticipated gain is psychological. This may come from a form of appreciation or notoriety that results from the mass murder incident. The killer's name will be in the media. The killer will have more than 15 minutes of fame.

The victims are strangers and they are randomly selected. There are no physical traits responsible for their selection as victims. In rare occasions does the psychotic killer kill family members. Ronald DeFeo confessed to killing family members. DeFeo at one time stated that one day he came home and found his father, mother, two brothers, and two sisters dead. The next day he confessed to the killings, stating that a face appeared on the TV set and instructed him to kill his family and place them face down in their beds.

Because of the mental condition of this mass murderer, the mass killer tends to be geographically stable. The individual does not have the mental health to relocate, start life over again with a new home, new job, and new friends. In many cases, the psychotic mental condition demands that the person live with his parents, relatives, or in some type of assisted care situation. The voices or visions demand the action within a comfort zone (Holmes & Holmes, 1996).

CONCLUSION

Mass murder in its various forms has become a serious social problem in this country. Mass murderers are as different as serial killers, and this chapter is an attempt to describe the various traits and elements that distinguish one type from the others. This is really the first step in declaring an investigation into the mind and mentality of the mass murderer. The elements chosen to distinguish among the various types of mass killers form a theoretical framework for analysis. This is truly the first step in the attempt at some type of resolution to the serious social problem of mass murder in the United States.

REFERENCES

Cleckley, H. (1982). *The Mask of Sanity.* New York: Plume.

Dietz, P. (1986). "Mass, Serial, and Sensational Homicide." *Bulletin of the New England Journal of Medicine,* 62: 477–491.

Hickey, E. (1997). *Serial Killers and Their Victims.* Belmont, CA: Wadsworth Publishing Co.

Holmes, R. (1990). *Sex Crimes.* Thousand Oaks, CA: Sage Publications.

Holmes, R., & J. DeBurger. (1985). "Profiles in Terror: The Serial Murderer." *Federal Probation,* 56: 53–61.

Holmes, R., & J. DeBurger. (1988). *Serial Murder.* Thousand Oaks, CA: Sage Publications.

Holmes, R., & S. Holmes. (1996). *Profiling Violent Crimes: An Investigative Tool.* Thousand Oaks, CA: Sage Publications.

Holmes, R., & S. Holmes. (1998). *Serial Murder.* (2nd ed.). Thousand Oaks, CA: Sage Publications.

Holmes, R., & S. Holmes. (2001). *Mass Murder in the United States.* Upper Saddle River, NJ: Prentice Hall.

Netter, G. (1982). *Explaining Murder.* Cincinnati: Anderson Publishing.

Norris, J, & W. Birnes. (1988). *Serial Killers: The Growing Menace.* New York: Dolphin Books.

Sears, D. (1991). *To Kill Again.* Wilmington, DE: Scholarly Resources.

CHAPTER 16

VIOLENCE EXPRESSED THROUGH MASS MURDER: AN EPIDEMIC OF GROWING PROPORTION AND CONCERN[1]

Joseph A. Davis

Abstract: Although still quite rare when compared to other violent crimes, mass murder commands the attention of academics, criminal behavior scholars, threat assessment, security and risk management professionals, and public safety personnel. Mass murder will always pose a significant threat to our safety and security because many preincident indicators are often veiled threats dismissed by many and the prediction of future violence from such threats can be quite complex to many who are untrained in the assessment of these indicators. A commonly accepted definition of mass murder is "a homicidal action that involves four or more victims in one location, during one event, with no lapse of any time period in between." Mass murderers themselves can be placed into one of several different categories or typologies: the disciple, the family annihilator, the pseudocommando, the disgruntled employee, the set-and-run killer, and the atypical killer. Mass murderers are placed in one or more of these categories or types depending on the factors surrounding the mass murder event itself. These factors include such aspects as location, behavioral resources, emotional triggers, situational triggers, locus of control, motivation, anticipated gain, killer-victim relationship, and victim selection. This chapter will discuss mass murder, identify the types of individuals who engage in such behavior, and provide some case examples of those who have committed in multicide in our society.

INTRODUCTION

California State University at Fullerton, California; University of Texas at Austin; McDonald's Restaurant, San Ysidro, California; Edmond, Oklahoma; Escondido (Orange Glen), California; Cleveland Elementary School, Stockton, California; Luby's Cafeteria, Killeen, Texas; Murrah Building, Oklahoma City, Oklahoma; and, most recently, Columbine High School, Littleton, Colorado:

---

[1] I acknowledge my former graduate students in forensic psychology and psychology-law, John Yurcak and Terri White, for their valuable assistance and support in researching this topic for the publication of this manuscript.

All have been the unfortunate sites of mass casualties and critical incidents from human-made events called mass murder. Infamous historical names such as Howard Unruh, Ronald Gene Simmons, Richard Speck, Charles Whitman, Edward Charles Allaway, Jim Jones, Patrick Henry Sherill, Sylvia Seegrist, Carl Robert Brown, James Huberty, George Banks, James Pough, George Hennard, Marc Lepine, Patrick Edward Purdy, William Bonner, Thomas McIlvane, Joseph Wesbecker, John Merlin Taylor, and, of more recent times, Gang Lu, Joseph Harris, Colin Ferguson, Albert Petrosky, Alan Winterbourne, Richard Farley, Timothy McVeigh, Mitchell Johnson, Andrew Golden, Kipland Kinkel, Dylan Klebold, Eric Harris, Mark Barton, Larry Ashbrook, and Bryan Uyesugi, to name only a few, are associated with mass murder in modern American society.

With the incidents of mass murder committed by Bryan Uyesugi in November 1999; Larry Ashbrook in Ft. Worth, Texas, in September 1999; and Richard Labatt in Sacramento, California in August 1999 as well as Richard Baumhammers in Pittsburgh, Pennsylvania, who killed five in April, and Robert Wayne Harris in Irving, Texas, who also killed five in March of this year, mass murder or multicide appears to be growing in frequency. This uncomfortable rate of violence and aggression is becoming a problem in our industrialized American nation. However, solutions are not easily found or quickly forthcoming when trying to predict future violence and risk potential to protect society from potential mass murderers.

Mass Murder: A Growing Concern with No Immediate Solution

Mass murder. These infamous words frequently conjure up from the depths of our psyches and vision a nightmare from a horror movie or from a story-book fictional character who is dazed, drugged out, or perhaps out of touch with reality; someone presumed to be psychotic, insane, or at least someone deranged who is frequently armed with a semiautomatic weapon or strapped to an improvised explosive device, ranting and raving incoherently as he threatens to blow up a building or kill his family or who is randomly shooting into a crowd of innocent victims before talking his own life. This vision, partly sensationalized by the media, partly dramatized by story-book fiction, and part byproduct of several high-profile cases that have occurred over the last few decades or so is now becoming our American reality.

As often observed from case histories, mass murderers have varying demographic and ethnic backgrounds: Many come from the obviously psychotic or deranged, to the quiet and apparently harmless but slightly eccentric man who lives next door, to the boyish kid who just didn't fit in.

WHAT DETERMINES MASS MURDER?

Mass murder or multicide involves the killing of a multiple number of persons. Depending on the definition and its context, mass murder usually involves 4 or more victims killed (definitions range from a minimum of 3 to 5 victims) at one time, during one event and at one place without an "cooling-off" period (Holmes, 1992; Levin & Fox, 1985; Ressler et al., 1988). Multicide

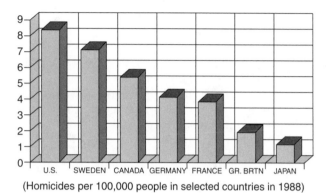

(Homicides per 100,000 people in selected countries in 1988)

Figure 16.1 Homicides Globally *(Excerpted from the Associated Press, 1991)*

is not just a problem within the borders of the United States. Studies on mass murder show that other countries have similar problems with such acts of violence. Unfortunately, the United States is the leader in these specific homicides (Figure 16.1).

Violence researchers and experts such as criminologists, psychologists, and psychiatrists and some sociologists who attempt to offer an rational explanation for the gradual rise in mass murder see this as an exclusive American phenomenon that has grown out of the proliferation of guns in the country, the disintegration of traditional American society, and the decline in the standard of living in recent years as millions of relatively high-paying jobs have been lost. Except for the tragic event of mass murder at Columbine High School in Colorado, in 1999, the mass shooting in Killeen, Texas, has been the worst in recent decades. The death toll in Killeen, Texas, totaled 23 (Holmes and Holmes, 2001).

Although experts may suggest that lenient gun laws and lack of gainful employment, the loss of tradition, and a decline in the standard of living play a role, another expert offers another explanation as to why mass murder is steadily growing. Park Dietz, a forensic psychiatrist who has studied mass murderers, believes that, "mass murderers acquire their fantasies from various media accounts" (Dietz, 1991). Dietz also suggests that if the media didn't give these events so much attention, there would be a possible decline in mass murders because the mass murderer's fantasy of media attention would be nonexistent.

Psychological Profile Considerations of Mass Murderers

The characteristics of a mass murder can be examined to develop a demographic profile. Such demographic findings have implications directing attention to individuals who may be a possible threat now and in the future. The demographic profile can often aid in completing a comprehensive picture of any subject and indirectly answer why a person would or could commit such a crime as mass murder.

The possible demographic profile of a workplace mass murderer is as follows:

- Generally a Caucasian male (rarely are there female mass murderers).
- Approximate age between 35 and 45 years.
- GED or high school level educated.
- Typically not psychotic; knows intent, directed and focused actions and destructive outcome of behavior.
- Often plans to take his own life or will force a police assisted suicide act or suicide by cop action.
- Aggressive or action-oriented personality style.
- Has access to weapons or resources involving firearms or bombs; fantasy with weapons.
- Victim mentality; externalized blame to others.
- Possibly clinically depressed; may use drugs or alcohol.
- Generally plans event long before it takes place; not an impulsive act.
- Generally tells others of plan or action (direct or veiled), which is often dismissed by those who overhear such statements of intended actions.
- Although demographic data exist on mass murderers, psychological profiling the individual is difficult as most mass murderers are known and quickly identified.
- Most mass murderers have histories of previous violence or aggressive behavior that have come to the attention of public safety.
- Most offenders of this nature do not start out as mass murderers as they often vent their frustration on property, animals, or on their children or spouses.
- Some mass murderers use substances to deal with their repressed or suppressed emotions; typically, acting out as self-medication has limited therapeutic value.
- Low self-esteem, self-concept.
- Recent failure or setback often acts as an antecedent trigger that leads to aggression and violent behavior (Davis, 1996; Holmes & Holmes, 1992; Ressler et al., 1988).

The Disciple   This type follows a leader. "The motivation for mass murder for the Disciple Killer rest outside the killer" (Holmes, p. 57). The leader of a group will demand an action. The disciple, attempting to gain acceptance from the leader, will carry out the requested action.

The Family Annihilator   The family annihilator is defined as "one who kills and entire family at one time. This killer may even murder the family pet" (Holmes, p. 57). The demographics of this killer is that he is an older male, depressed, and perhaps has a history of alcohol abuse.

The Pseudocommando   The pseudocommando is described as being "preoccupied with weaponry. This killer's homicide usually occurs after a long period of deliberation and careful planning" (Holmes, p. 58). Examples of such infamous offenders are Patrick Henry Sherill, James Huberty, Patrick Edward Purdy, and Charles Whitman, and Joseph Wesbecker.

Table 16.1
Typologies of Mass Murderers

Types of Mass Murderers

1. Disciple type
2. Family annihilator type
   a. Family type
   b. Classic type
3. Pseudocommando type
4. Disgruntled employee type
5. Set-and-run type
6. Atypical type

Source: Holmes, R. M., & S. T. Holmes. (1992). "Understanding Mass Murder: A Starting Point." *Federal Probation,* 56(1): 53–61.

The Disgruntled Employee   A workplace offender "is often a former employee of a company who has been dismissed or placed on some form of medical leave or disability" (Holmes, p. 59). The person may feel that there is some injustice to his termination of employment and must find a way to seek justice or equality. Furthermore, a person does not necessarily have to be an employee to be determined a workplace violence type offender. In addition to this author, workplace violence prevention experts like Anthony Baron and Steve Albrecht suggest that any person engaging in a violent act in the workplace setting who has a direct or prior relationship (a.k.a., disgruntled employee), indirect relationship, or no relationship with that setting can be considered a workplace violence offender (Albrecht, 1997, Albrecht & Mantell, 1994; Baron, 1993; Baron & Wheeler, 1994; Davis, 1999). A somewhat forgotten case of mass murder in the workplace but no less devastating is the historical example of Edward Charles Allaway. Allaway committed mass murder by killing seven people in 1967 in the campus library of the California State University at Fullerton.

Perhaps a more contemporary example of such extremism in the workplace involved the mass murder of eight individuals in the law firm of Petit & Martin at 101 California Street in San Francisco, California, in 1993 by a disgruntled client, Gian Luigi Ferri.

VIOLENCE LEVELS AND BEHAVIORAL DESCRIPTORS

According to many experts on the causes and prevention of violence and human aggression (Albrecht, 1997; Albrecht & Mantell, 1994; Baron, 1993; Baron & Wheeler, 1994; Davis, 1996, 1999; Holmes & Holmes, 1992; Holmes et al., 1994), workplace aggression can be difficult to assess.

OSHA, the Occupational Health and Safety Administration, U.S. Office of Personnel Management (OPM), Cal-OSHA, and various others (Albrecht, 1997; Albrecht & Mantell, 1994; Baron, 1993; Baron & Wheeler, 1994) report that violence in the workplace can vary based on certain levels of aggression. Some

Table 16.2
Levels of Violence and Aggression

VIOLENCE LEVEL I
Refuses to cooperate with others
Consistently argues with coworkers
Belligerent toward fellow peers and/or customers
Spreads rumors within company to harm others
Excessive profanity (primarily sexual in nature)
Makes unwanted sexual comments toward peers or customers
VIOLENCE LEVEL II
Argues with others (customers, vendors, coworkers, managers, etc.)
Refuses to obey company policies and procedures
Sabotages company equipment
Steals company property
Verbalizes desire to hurt others
Sends provocative sexual or violent notes
Sees oneself as a victim of others
VIOLENCE LEVEL III
Recurrent physical fights
Recurrent suicidal threats
Recurrent homicidal threats
Destruction of company property (i.e., equipment, computers, etc.)
Murder, rape, property or arson incidents
Utilization of weapons for the purposes of harm to self or others

suggest that from an assessment standpoint, violence can be broken down into three levels, such as Level I, Level II, Level III. Examples are contained in Table 16.2.

> Experts agree that the person is likely to be a loner, often angry, paranoid, and depressed, with a fascination for weaponry. An individual may be undergoing a private stressful situation, like a death or divorce in the family, which is compounded by workplace difficulties. For many of them, the workplace may be the source of their identity and sense of well-being. When their job is jeopardized, they strike back (excerpted from Pennings, 1995).

The more workplace violence incidents occur, the more accurate the perpetrator traits and overall profiles will become. There have been a sufficient number, to date, of regularly occurring incidents and homicides that experts have been able to develop a noticeable identification. The following is one example of such profile provided by colleague and workplace consultant, Anthony Baron, from his popular book, *Violence in the Workplace: A Prevention and Management Guide for Business:*

> The data on hand indicates that the likely perpetrator is male, 35 years of age or older, has a previous history of violence toward women, children, or animals,

owns a weapon, and reflects self-esteem externally connected with his job, concurrent with minimal outside interests. He is likely to be withdrawn, or a loner, and is characterized by a tendency to externalize blame for his life disappointments. There is a high probability of military history, and substance abuse and/or mental health concerns may be prominent, although often identified only after the fact (excerpted from Baron, 1993).

From the author's viewpoint, various cases, compiled clinical data, and information based in psychological personality theory, management styles, and organizational behavior suggest a possible correlation with high incidents of violence in the workplace.

Offered here are 16 key points (characteristics) from various case studies of violence in the workplace that are often found regarding troubled or strained employee versus employer relations.

1. Problems are not acknowledged and resolved.
2. Preferential treatment because of title and responsibilities.
3. Employees are viewed as tools; they are expendable and replaceable.
4. Senior management does not do what they say (i.e., "management supervisor walk doesn't match the management supervisor talk").
5. Rules for success in the organization are unclear.
6. Lack of mutual respect in the departments and among employees.
7. Ineffective horizontal and vertical communication. Communication is typically not direct, specific, or behavioral.
8. Employees often feel confused as management appears to attack attributes of character and personality (which cannot be changed) instead of performance (which can be appraised, assessed, evaluated, and changed).
9. Increased work load with less resources and greater expectations. The working atmosphere is repetitive, monotonous, and unfulfilling.
10. Rules and roles are inconsistent in application.
11. Overly aggressive "autocratic" management style showing no compassion for the employee.
12. Ineffective discipline and grievance procedures.
13. Externalized blame, orientation, and position toward "labor-management" issues.
14. Supervisory and management defensive posturing toward employee.
15. Insufficient attention to physical environment and security measures.
16. Ineffective or lack of communicative, dispute resolution and mediation skills that exacerbates employee a loss of dignity, by which "management looses credibility" (Pennings, 1995; Davis, 1996; Albrecht and Mantel, 1994; Baron, 1993; Baron & Wheeler, 1994).

The aforementioned organizational/management list of characteristics and its identified culture frequently contribute to a dysfunctional employer/employee relationship and disgruntled would-be offender. The aforementioned management approaches and styles toward personnel combined with an "aggressive-type personality style" of an employee who has increasingly sensed or perceived a loss of worth, respect, and dignity from his company lend significantly to a future credible threat of violence (Davis, 1996, 1999).

Set-and-Run Offender

The set-and-run killer is another type of mass murderer. "Spurred by motive for revenge, sometimes for anonymous infamy, and sometimes simply for creature comfort is reason this killer is qualitatively different from the others discussed" (Holmes, 2001, p. 69). The tainted Tylenol capsules that involved the poisoning of several victims years ago would be an example of such a case. The perpetrator would set the tainted capsules in place, leave, and some unsuspecting person would become the next victim. The offender committed these crimes without knowledge of the victim.

Atypical Offender

The atypical killer does not fit into any of the other category based on the definition. Although George Hennard, who committed the atrocity at Luby's Cafeteria in Killeen, Texas, in 1991, was unemployed, it appeared based on his actions and his history that he would not fit into any of the aforementioned categories (Davis, 1996). However, he committed an act of mass violence in the workplace like Patrick Purdy, in Stockton, California, at Cleveland Elementary School; both are also considered to be a workplace violence perpetrator. Purdy would also meet the criteria as a pseudocommando-type offender as well, much like that of Charles Joseph Whitman (University of Texas in 1966) and James Oliver Huberty (McDonald's in 1984).

Mass murder is not exclusively an American or even a modern phenomenon. History provides many accounts of mass murder the world over. During the past 50 years or so, mass murder has crept further and further into the limelight, taking on the appearance of a growing epidemic, with America suffering the most casualties.

What triggers a mass murderer? Surely, such a senseless crime as mass murder must be the result of a sick, psychotic, or deranged mind. Is insanity really the root of these horrendous acts? Can mass murderers be identified and thwarted before they can carry out their terrible crimes? These are just some questions that will be addressed herein.

MASS MURDER: A WORKING DEFINITION

The term *mass murder* (a.k.a. multicide) is often used improperly by the media, lay public, and even law enforcement officials and frequently interchanged with serial murder and spree murder (Davis, 1999). Actually, all of these terms involve a type or a subset of homicide called multicide or multiple murder (Holmes & Holmes, 1992, p. 53), and each has its own somewhat specific set of applied criteria.

Mass Murder: A Four-Point Criteria

The criteria for mass murder may be best understood and defined by examining four distinct characteristics: the number of victims; the location of the murders; the time of the killings; and the distance between the murder locations (Holmes & Holmes, 1992, p. 53). However, there is some disagreement over what exactly defines and constitutes a mass murder. Some sources define mass murder as "a homicide involving four or more victims in one location, and within one event" (Ressler et al., 1988, p. 138), while others have set the minimum number of victims at three. Holmes and Holmes (1992, p. 53) suggests that the problem of setting such number limits, citing a hypothetical example in which only two people are killed but many people are seriously injured and are saved by prompt medical attention, could alter the outcome an otherwise attempt at mass murder. The case of Joseph L. Neale in Riverside County in California in 1998 somewhat reflects this impression. In October of that same year, a disgruntled Neale broke into a city council meeting after a long-standing dispute over how he had been treated by the city and county. In total, he shot six individuals, but no one was left fatally wounded. Had it not been for prompt intervention, a possible mass murder would have been imminent (Albrecht, 1999; Davis, 1999). The intent of Neale, with gun in hand, was not to mediate his problems but to do as much harm as possible.

Additional definitional problems arise when discussing the time and location portions of the mass murder criteria. Ressler and colleagues (1988, p. 139) assert that to be considered mass murder, the event must have occurred within one event at a single location, although they are not specific as to what constitutes "a single location." This is done to distinguish mass murder from spree murder, which involves "killing at two or more locations with no emotional cooling off period between murders," and serial murder, which involves "three or more separate events with an emotional cooling off period between homicides" (Ressler et al., 1988, p. 139). Holmes and Holmes (1992, p. 53) propose that an incident may still be classified as mass murder even if the murders occur minutes or hours apart and at locations that may be blocks away, or even across town.

As one can evaluate, there is an obvious gray area differentiating mass murder from spree murder, whereas a particular multicide can either be one or the other, or even both, depending on the definition used. For the purposes of this chapter, we will use the definition of mass murder that sets the minimum number of deaths at four and that allows for flexibility regarding elapsed time and differing locations between murders, so long as the time and location differences between the murders are not substantial.

CLASSIFYING THOSE WHO COMMIT MASS MURDER

Although Ressler and colleagues (1988, p. 138) place mass murderers into two categories, classic and family, this chapter will use the typology promoted by Holmes and Holmes (1992, pp. 57–60). Admittedly, such categorizations are not perfect, as they tend to generalize, and some cases may involve two or more topologies. The use of these topologies allows for easier handling and discussion of the subject matter. Holmes and Holmes (1992, pp. 55–60) examine the following factors in order to classify mass murderers.

Behavioral Background: Basic Sources

These are the elements that combine to produce the foundation for a mass murderer's behavior, an area that is vastly complex and not well understood. Consequently, numerous theories exist. What is known is that the behavior of a mass murderer is the product of a combination of sociological, biological, and psychological factors, with each combination being unique (Davis et al., 1999).

In terms of threats of violence, no one single factor can be positively singled out as possessing the causal link to mass murder (Davis et al., 1999). A problem arises due to the fact that this applies to every other individual. Thus, the question asks, Why do some individuals become mass murders while the vast majority typically do not even though murderers and nonmurderers may share nearly identical backgrounds and may find themselves in nearly identical circumstances? Not surprisingly, this question remains basically unanswered by many psychiatrists, psychologists, and criminologists.

What can be done in the interim is that the factors that suggest an individual's potential for violence can be identified and examined. Psychiatrist John M. MacDonald proposed that a history of three factors—bedwetting, firestarting, and torturing small animals (a behavioral triad)—were indicators of potential homicidal violence (Levin & Fox, 1985, p. 27).

G. S. Evseeff and E. M. Wisneski targeted childhood experiences, such as physical and/or sexual abuse and parental abandonment, as causal factors regarding "homicidal proneness" (Levin & Fox, 1985, p. 29). Others rely on a broader range of factors, such as an individual's demographics, past history of violent behavior, comparison of the individual's violent behavior with those of similar backgrounds and stressors in the individual's present environment (family, peer, and employment) (Ewing, 1985, pp. 16–23) when trying to assess an individual's proclivity toward violence and aggression.

Unfortunately, the problem of false positives and skewed observations based on small case pools make predicting violent behavior, specifically homicidal behavior, an "educated guess" in many instances. Most mass murderers are brought to the attention of evaluators after the fact, followed by an expected flurry of Monday morning quarterback comments such as, "We should have known," "He showed all the signs," or "Nobody ever took his crazy comments seriously." Rather than prediction, the task at hand now becomes one of historical reconstruction and analysis.

As to the question of insanity in mass murder cases, there is dissension among the experts. Donald Lunde, considered a medical expert witness in the field of criminal and forensic psychiatry, contends that mass murderers are almost always insane (Lunde, 1976, p. 48). Others note that mass murderers do not always display psychotic signs, at least not at the time of the actual murders.

What most experts do agree on, however, is that an examination of a mass murderer's behavioral history will often show at least one, if not both, of the following trends. The first trend is the presence of paranoid personality traits, or the actual disorder itself. Indications of a paranoid personality disorder include such symptoms as "hyper-vigilance, chronic anger, explosiveness, perceived malevolence, arrogance, social reclusiveness" ("the mass murderer," 1988, p. 1), "suspicious demeanor, hallucinations" (usually "hearing voices"), and "delusions of grandeur and/or persecution" (Levin & Fox, 1985, p. 33).

The second trend involves the presence of indicators of an antisocial personality disorder. These indications include "the ability to suspend any empathetic regard for potential victims, and the ability to carefully plan and carry out violent acts that involve a certain amount of preparation, deception, and time." The lack of empathy for the victims frees the mass murderer of any guilt, allowing him to kill ("the mass murderer," 1988, p. 2).

One must realize, however, that the presence of one or both of the aforementioned trends does not necessarily mean that an individual will commit mass murder. What is required is a triggering factor, something to set the killer into action. The "triggering factor" is usually something beyond the control of the killer. These triggering factors can range from the semiobvious, such as the loss of a job or family problems ("the mass murderer," 1988, p. 2), to the subliminal and numinous, never to be ascertained.

Motivation to Kill in Mass Numbers

Motivation is the mass murderer's reason for acting and may be either internal or external to the killer. The mass murderer's motivation may remain speculative, especially in cases where the killer dies before authorities can question him.

Anticipatory Gain

Anticipated gain is what the mass murderer is seeking to gain from his actions. These gains can be either expressive (psychological) or instrumental (material). Examination of the anticipated or perceived gain may be of use to the investigator when trying to determine the killer's motivation (Holmes & Holmes, 1992, p. 56).

Victimology

In some cases, a mass murderer will select his or her victims. Therefore, victims of a mass murder event may or may not share common traits, depending on the particular incident. As part of an investigation, this aspect should be carefully analyzed.

Victim-Offender Relationship

This is the relationship between the victim(s) and the killer at the time of the murder. There may or may not have been a relationship prior to the actual murder. Again, this may or may not be a factor. Examination of this item can also assist the investigator in completing a more accurate assessment of the murder scene and the murderer.

MASS MURDERER TYPOLOGIES TAKEN FROM CASE EXAMPLES

The Disciple-type Mass Murderer

Charles Manson, Charles "Tex" Watson, Patricia Krenwinkel, Linda Kasabian, and Susan Atkins were all members of the infamous Manson family, led by the self-proclaimed father/messiah, Charles Manson. On the night of August

8, 1969, Manson ordered the foursome to go to 10050 Cielo Drive in Beverly Hills and kill the residents. The foursome obliged, and before the night was over they shot and brutally stabbed five people, including actress Sharon Tate, who was eight months pregnant at the time. Allegedly, Kasabian did not actually participate in the actual murders (Blashfield, 1990, pp. 150–152).

The following night, Manson ordered the foursome to commit another massacre, but this time they were accompanied by Manson himself, along with two other individuals: Steve "Clem" Grogan and Leslie Van Houten. At random, they selected a house at 3301 Waverly Drive, near Griffith Park in the Los Feliz section of Los Angeles, home of Leno and Rosemary LaBianca. Breaking in, they tied up the LaBiancas. Soon afterward, Manson and some others left, leaving Watson, Krenwinkel, and Van Houten, who then stabbed and mutilated the LaBiancas (Blashfield, 1990, pp. 155–157).

Shortly afterward, the police apprehended everyone involved in the Tate-LaBianca murders. They were brought to trial and found guilty of murder, except for Linda Kasabian (Blashfield, 1990, p. 161).

CASE EXAMPLE: JIM JONES AND JONESTOWN

On November 19, 1978, at the People's Temple in Jonestown, Guyana, self-styled religious leader and cult dictator Jim Jones ordered his followers to line up and receive a fatal dose of cyanide-laced grape "Kool-Aid." Volunteers squirted the deadly mixture into the mouths of the infants. The older children were next, followed by the adults. Armed guards stood by to coerce those who were the slightest bit hesitant or had intentions other than those of their leader. As a grand finale, Jim Jones shot himself in the head. In a single day, the mass murder/suicide claimed the lives 913 members (some accounts say 912) of the People's Temple that included 276 children (Davis, 1999; Levin & Fox, 1985, pp. 80–81).

The disciple mass murderer is one who kills at the command of a charismatic leader (Holmes & Holmes, 1992, p. 57). The motivation of the disciple to commit mass murder appears to stem from the leader's complete control over his followers. Charles Manson is said to have had a unique, mysterious charisma, which he used along with his self-generated religious and moral philosophies to attract vulnerable teenage runaways and castoffs. Desperate for love, attention, and acceptance, these young people found what they sought in Charles Manson. Manson had convinced his followers that he possessed great power, and some Family members even thought he was Jesus Christ (Levin & Fox, 1985, p. 90). Thus, Manson's followers were motivated to kill by a perceived psychological (expressive) gain; specifically, increased acceptance by their leader (Holmes & Holmes, 1992, pp. 56–57).

In the case of the Jonestown massacre, Jim Jones created an atmosphere of complete physical and psychological dependence between himself and his followers. Isolated from friends, family, and the reality of the outside world, Jones provided for all their needs. Seeing his vision of paradise nearing an end, Jones ordered his followers to end not only their own lives, but the lives of others. By and large, his "flock" blindly obeyed (Levin & Fox, 1985, p. 90). Again, the perceived gains were expressive.

The disciple can actually be examined using theories of organizational behavior. Often group dynamics will play a role, causing individuals to commit acts that they never would have committed as an individual. Such theories have been advanced to explain the actions of those individuals involved in carrying out Hitler's "Final Solution" (Levin & Fox, 1985, pp. 84–85).

Additionally, Maslow's hierarchy of needs may no longer apply. The disciple's need to gain the acceptance of the leader and/or the group may rank higher than physiological or even survival needs, as seen in the Jonestown case. However, regarding self-preservation, since the disciple's primary motivator is acceptance by the leader, in cases where the leader requires further action, the disciple may place survival needs at a higher priority. Consequently, suicide or intervention by the police would not be a viable option for the disciple (Holmes & Holmes, 1992, p. 57) such as in the Manson case, where the disciples made conscious efforts to avoid apprehension.

As for the victims, the disciple usually chooses strangers selected at random or kills those that the Disciple's leader has selected, as in the Manson and Jonestown cases (Holmes & Holmes, 1992, p. 57).

The Family Annihilator

The family annihilator is a person who murders numerous members of his own family at once (Holmes & Holmes, 1992, p. 57). Victim selection and the relationship between the killer and the victims are obviously critical factors here. This category comprises almost half of all mass murder cases (Levin & Fox, 1985, p. 100).

CASE EXAMPLE: JAMES RUPPERT

It was Easter Sunday, 1975. The location was Charity Ruppert's house in Hamilton, Ohio. Scattered between the kitchen and the living room were Charity, her son, Leonard, Leonard's wife, Alma, and their eight children. Her other son, James, was upstairs in his bedroom. As the Ruppert clan was preparing to sit down for their Easter dinner, James Ruppert came downstairs and entered the kitchen carrying a .357 revolver, two .22 pistols, and an 18-shot rifle. He told everyone he was going out target shooting, an activity that he frequently enjoyed and at which he was quite proficient. Seconds later, he opened fire. Within minutes, 11 members of the Ruppert family were dead. Three hours later, James Ruppert called the police and reported, "there's been a shooting here" (Levin & Fox, 1985, pp. 107–108).

At his criminal trial, James Ruppert entered a plea of not guilty by reason of insanity. His defense team painted him as a deeply disturbed and frustrated man. Expert witness for the defense, Dr. Howard Sokolov, testified that Ruppert was suffering from "a paranoid psychotic state" in which there was a "departure from reality in terms of thinking and behavior" and went on to say that he had a tendency to be excessively suspicious, jealous, and angry" (Levin & Fox, 1985, p. 112).

Often frail and physically ill as a youth, Ruppert was constantly teased by other children and was a loner for most of his childhood and teen years. His father died when he was 12, leaving him only bitter memories of an unsuccessful, unaffectionate man who had a violent temper and a vocal lack of confidence that his son, James, would ever amount to anything (Levin & Fox, 1985, pp. 115–116).

According to Ruppert, his mother did little to improve the situation. She often told him that he was a mistake; that she had actually wanted a girl instead. She would beat and taunt him, egging his older brother Leonard to join in. His mother made no attempt at concealing her overwhelming affection for her older son. At age 16, James ran away and attempted suicide (Levin & Fox, 1985, p. 116). As James grew older, his own failures and insecurities were exacerbated by Leonard's relatively successful life. Leonard was everything that James had aspired to but failed to be. James soon came to believe that Leonard and his mother were plotting against him.

In 1965, the local police department had traced an obscene phone call back to James Ruppert. He admitted to making the call, but he believed that his mother and Leonard were trying to discredit him by telling everyone what he had done. He also believed they had told the FBI that he was a communist and a homosexual. Consequently, James was convinced that the FBI now had bugged not only his home phone but also the phones at the various bars and restaurants he frequented. By 1975, James included the State Highway Patrol, the local Sheriff's Department, private detectives, and the Hamilton Police Department in the conspiracy against him (Levin & Fox, 1985, p. 117).

The prosecution contended that James Ruppert killed his family for financial gain in that following the murders, he stood to inherit close to $300,000. The prosecution argued that Ruppert was trying to be found not guilty by reason of insanity so that he would be committed to the state mental hospital, be eventually found sane, and then be released to collect the family fortune (Levin & Fox, 1985, p. 113).

In the end, Ruppert was found guilty of murdering his mother and brother but was found not guilty by reason of insanity in the other murders. He is currently serving two consecutive life sentences (Levin & Fox, 1985, p. 121).

Who typifies the family annihilator and what are the base sources for the act? Ironically, the family annihilator is often found to be the senior male in the family (Holmes & Holmes, 1992, p. 57). The family setting itself is often filled with stress. This stress may be the result of "possessiveness or jealousy toward the spouse, parental rigidity, isolation of family members, and in extreme cases, sexual abuse of family members, including children" ("the mass murderer," 1988, p. 1).

CASE EXAMPLE: RONALD DEFEO, JR.

Ronald Defeo, Jr., who in 1974 shot and killed his parents, two brothers, and two sisters, felt he was under constant pressure at home. He failed to live up to the high expectations set by his father, who thought that beating his son would somehow solve the problem. Defeo's father also refused to let Ronald go off and live on his own and would bribe him with money to stay with the family (Blashfield, 1990, pp. 162–180).

CASE EXAMPLE: RONALD GENE SIMMONS

In 1987, Ronald Gene Simmons shot and killed 14 family members, among others. Relatives claimed he abused his wife and may have fathered his daughter's baby, all of whom were among those killed (Johnson & Shapiro, 1988, p. 20).

Other stress factors, such as severe depression, alcohol or drug abuse, presence of a paranoid personality disorder or paranoid traits, loss of/or inability to find employment, and actual or possible estrangement from wife and/or family can all add up to creating a potentially explosive emotional and physically violent situation, just waiting for that one certain factor to set it off. The family now becomes the object that must be retaliated against ("the mass murderer," 1988, p. 1).

Several days prior to that infamous Easter Sunday, James Ruppert lost his job, and his mother told him he could no longer live at her house. When he entered the kitchen with his guns, James's brother, Leonard, asked him about his Volkswagen. James Ruppert was convinced that his brother had been trying to sabotage his car for the past several months and had actually done so. James felt that Leonard was scolding him with the question concerning his car. That is when James flew into his murderous rage. This seemingly innocent question was James Ruppert's triggering factor (Levin & Fox, 1985, p. 101–120).

It is not uncommon for the internal family problems or stresses to be transparent to the outside observer. Both John List and William Bradford Bishop had what appeared to be on the surface, normal, well-adjusted family lives. List was a successful insurance salesman. Bradford was a promising mid-level career diplomat with the State Department. In 1972, List shot and killed his wife, mother, and three children. In 1976, Bishop beat to death his wife, mother, and three children. In both cases, the basic sources and motivations for the killings are still speculative at best. Both men became federal fugitives (Ressler et al., 1988, p. 139).

Psychiatrist Sherver Frazier has suggested two motivations that may explain some of the family annihilator cases. Each motivation is based around two completely opposite emotions: love and hate. The family setting is filled with spousal conflict. The man may be either willingly or unwillingly removed from the family setting. Lacking the emotional support and security of the family structure, and feeling lost, alone, and angry, his thoughts turn to revenge. Even though the family annihilator's main anger is directed at the spouse, he views killing "her" children as a way of gaining complete revenge. Frazier refers to this as "murder by proxy" (Levin & Fox, 1985, p. 100).

On the other end of the emotional spectrum, in cases where the male has lost his job, is unable to find employment, or has committed some act that in his mind will bring unspeakable shame on family, the family annihilator decides to spare his family the imagined suffering by mercifully killing them, confident that they will be brought back together under better circumstances in the hereafter. Frazier calls this "suicide by proxy" and goes on to say that "the parent may identify so strongly with his children that he sees them as an extension of himself. Therefore, to kill his children is, in his mind, to commit suicide" (Levin & Fox, 1985, p. 100).

The motivation behind the killing is often based on conjecture or speculation; the motivation is only really known to the killer, who may take this secret to the grave. It is not uncommon for family annihilators to commit suicide following the act. Without a proper understanding of the motive, it may be difficult to determine whether the family annihilator's perceived gains were expressive (psychological) or instrumental (material) (Holmes & Holmes, 1992, p. 56).

The Pseudocommando-type Offender

CASE EXAMPLE: PATRICK EDWARD PURDY

Recess was in full swing at the Cleveland Elementary School in 1989 in Stockton, California, as Patrick Edward Purdy parked his car nearby. Purdy's thoughts probably drifted back to the time many years ago, when he had attended this very same school. He put on a flak jacket bearing the words "LIBYA" and "DEATH TO THE GREAT SATIN [sic]" before picking up his semiautomatic AK-47 rifle with the word "HEZBOLLAH" carved into the stock and his Taurus 9-mm pistol with the word "VICTORY" painted on its weapon grip. Before he started his car, Purdy lit the fuse to a gasoline bomb that was to act as a diversion/dramatic enhancement to the act which he was about to commit. He then walked into the schoolyard and, devoid of emotion, proceeded to fire 105 rounds into the crowd of over 300 elementary school children. As police sirens began to sound in the distance, the 26-year-old Purdy put the Taurus 9-mm semiautomatic pistol to his head and pulled the trigger. By the time the police had arrived, five children were dead, and 29 others, along with one teacher, were wounded (Caputo, 1989, pp. 137–154; Foreman, 1992, pp. 73–75; "Slaughter in," 1988, p. 29).

The pseudocommando is the image that usually comes to mind when one hears about a mass murder. Mass murderers are often loners; introverts lacking social skills or possessing antisocial personality traits such as incidents of "repeated conflicts with society" and low frustration levels (Toch, 1979, p. 323). As Holmes and Holmes (1992, p. 58) put it, "the Pseudocommando lashes out at society in a most grotesque way." Something in his world is not correct, and he will "teach the world a lesson" by his behavior.

Paranoid tendencies are often the thinking patterns found in pseudocommando mass murders. Howard Unruh, who is considered by many to have been one of the first contemporary mass murderers, walked through his Camden, New Jersey, neighborhood on September 6, 1949, shooting and killing 13 people, some of whom were his neighbors. He later told psychiatrists he believed that some of his neighbors had been slandering him. Psychiatrists at the time diagnosed Unruh as having "dementia praecox, mixed type, with pronounced catatonic and paranoid coloring" (Foreman, 1992, p. 58).

Former librarian William Bryan Cruse, who in 1987 gunned down six people at a Palm Bay, Florida, shopping mall, was convinced that his neighbors gossiped about him and were spreading rumors that he was a homosexual. Several psychiatrists for the defense testified that Cruse was a "paranoid schizophrenic beset by delusions" (Foreman, 1992, p. 68). Pseudocommandos are typically infatuated with weapons, usually firearms, to a degree far beyond that of an enthusiastic collector. The pseudocommando often thinks about his act far in advance and may make elaborate plans and preparations.

CASE EXAMPLE: CHARLES WHITMAN

Charles Whitman, who in 1966 gunned down 44 people, killing 15 (some accounts say 16) from the University of Texas at Austin's campus clock tower, had visited the university psychiatrist four months prior to the massacre and told him of the recurring thought he was having of "going up on the tower with a deer rifle and start shooting people" (Blashfleld, 1990, Davis, 1996; pp. 206–207). The list of items Whitman brought with him to the tower read like a grocery or sporting goods store stock list:

> Cans of meat ravioli, Spam, Vienna sausages, peanuts, sliced pineapple, fruit salad, and liquid diet formula; a jar of honey, boxes of raisins, sandwiches, and a vacuum flask of coffee; vitamins, Dexidrine, Excedrin, earplugs, jugs of water and of gasoline, matches, charcoal lighter fluid, rope, binoculars, canteens, a machete, a hatchet, three knives, a transistor radio, toilet paper, a Gillette razor, and a plastic bottle of Mennen deodorant; a 6mm Remington bolt-action rifle with a four-power Leopold scope, a .35-caliber Remington pump rifle, a .30-caliber carbine, a sawed-off 12-gauge Sears shotgun, a 9mm Luger pistol, a Galesi-Brescia pistol, a .357 magnum Smith & Wesson revolver, and 700 rounds of assorted ammunition (Foreman, 1992, p. 31).

Whitman even rented a mover's dolly earlier that day in order to move everything from his car to the tower; this was a well-planned event. There usually exists no prior relationship between the pseudocommando and his victims. In some instances, such as the Unruh case, the killer kept a "grudge list" of individuals whom he perceived as having wronged him in some way (Foreman, 1992, p. 58). More often than not, the actual victims are not the ones on the list.

Victim selection may or may not be a factor. Sometimes the victims just happened to be at the wrong place at the wrong time, as seen in the Charles Whitman case. Other times the killer seeks out victims that fit into a broad category.

CASE EXAMPLE: MARC LEPINE

In 1989, Marc Lepine entered classroom C-230 at the University of Montreal's *École Polytechnique* armed with a Ruger Mini-14 semiautomatic rifle and 100 rounds of ammunition (Foreman, 1992, pp. 141–159). Telling the students, "I want the women" (Doerner & Graff, 1989, p. 30), he ordered the males out of the room. Just before opening fire on the remaining female students, Lepine shouted, "You're all a bunch of feminists, and I hate feminists" (Came et al., 1989, p. 14). He continued his rampage throughout the building before committing suicide. As a result of Lepine's attack, 14 women died. Lepine was also rejected from entering the military because he was, in their view, antisocial (Foreman, 1992, pp. 141–159).

As for the motivation of the pseudocommando, it is not always clear, and sometimes, as in the cases of Purdy and Whitman, it is a complete mystery. In other cases, such as the Lepine case, Holmes and Holmes (1992, p. 59) surmise that the killer was calling attention to an issue he felt was important. Marc Lepine felt women were overstepping their bounds and were taking away opportunities from men (Foreman, 1992, pp. 141–159). He applied to, but was never accepted into, the *École Polytechnique,* where the killings occurred.

Holmes and Holmes (1992, p. 59) hypothesized that another motivating factor is the anticipated fame that the killer would receive following a mass murder. When Robert Smith, who killed five women in a Mesa, Arizona, beauty salon in 1966, was asked by police officers why he did it, he replied, "I wanted to make a name for myself . . . I wanted people to know who I was" (Foreman, 1992, p. 60).

The Disgruntled Employee Murderer

CASE EXAMPLE: JOSEPH WESBECKER

On September 21, 1989, Joseph Wesbecker walked into his former place of employment armed with an AK-47 and a 9-mm pistol and shot 20 former coworkers, killing seven, before committing suicide. Wesbecker had a well-documented history of mental health problems and previous suicide attempts and had been placed on long-term mental disability leave from work prior to the incident. Doctors said that Wesbecker was a manic-depressive who had been taking medication for his condition. His medication had been changed the day before the shooting took place ("Another AK-47," 1989, p. 27).

The disgruntled employee category encompasses those workers who have been dismissed, placed on medical or disability leave, or disciplined by their employer and then return to their former workplace, seeking revenge. As revenge is the typical motivator, the perceived gains are psychological. Additionally, as in Wesbecker's case, many disgruntled employees possess vast degrees of mental illness and may actually be undergoing treatment or taking medication at the time of the incident.

They also share some of the characteristics of the pseudocommandos—those of paranoid personality traits and deliberate, long-range planning. Coworkers said that Wesbecker had talked about getting revenge a year before he actually carried it out. One coworker said, "He's paranoid, and he thought everyone was after him" ("Another AK-47," 1989, p. 27).

Victim selection is also a factor. The disgruntled employee normally targets those individuals whom the killer perceives as having done him an injustice. However, victims other than the intended targets frequently appear on the list of casualties. This may be due to the killer's sense of frustration in not being able to find particular targets and consequently unleashing that frustration on targets of opportunity instead. The victim-killer relationship is also a factor. Many victims are known to the killer, and the relationships may be employer-employee, supervisor-employee, employee-employee.

The Set-and-Run Mass Murderer

CASE EXAMPLE: JACK GRAHAM

On November 1, 1955, Jack Graham saw his mother off at the airport in Denver, Colorado. Prior to his mother boarding the plane, Graham obtained $86,500.00 worth of insurance policies on her. Eleven minutes after takeoff, United Flight 629 exploded in midair, killing all 44 people aboard, including Jack Graham's mother. Ten days later, taken into the custody by the FBI, Jack Graham confessed to being the one responsible for the bombing. Although the insurance money obviously played a role in Jack Graham's actions, it became known to investigators that Jack wanted to get back at his mother for wanting to leave him, while at the same time he wanted to free himself from the dependence he had on her (Blashfield, 1990, pp. 121–123).

Of all the categories of mass murderers, the set-and-run killers are probably the easiest to understand. Prone to violence, they often display antisocial personality traits. Their motivations run from money or revenge, or both as in the Graham case, to self-preservation. On February 14, 1983, Willie Mack and Benjamin Ng robbed the patrons of the Wah Mee Club, a private gambling club frequented by Chinese, located in Seattle's Chinatown area. In order to ensure there would be no witnesses, all 13 people present were tied up, forced to lie on the floor, and were shot in the head (Levin & Fox, 1985, p. 15). Getting away and staying alive are key components of the set-and-run killer character, setting him apart from most other types of mass murderers.

Anticipated gains, victim selection, and victim-killer relationship are all dependent on the killer's motivation. Since the killer will avoid being apprehended, analysis of these factors will be crucial to the investigation and bringing the killer to justice (Holmes & Holmes, 1992, pp. 59–60).

A Class All His Own

CASE EXAMPLE: GEORGE HENNARD

George Hennard fit the demographic profile at the time of his mass murder. He was 35 years old (falling within the age range of 35–45) and Caucasian. In addition, he graduated from Las Cruces High School in 1974. Although people who knew him would describe him as strange, a loner, or rude, he was aware of what he was doing and of the consequences. Police officers describe the killings in an interview. In regard to Hennard being aware of what was going on they reported, "He told us he was not going to give up." The officers stated that they were so close that they could see him "wide-eyed and visibly frightened." According to this interview, "the incident ended when he shot himself in the right temple." It is the impression of the author that it is typical for mass murderers to include themselves in the killings saving the last live round for themselves (Davis, 1996).

PROVIDING SOME POSSIBLE ANSWERS OR EXPLANATIONS

Front-versus Back-Stage Behaviors

Mass murderers often include themselves as part of the macabre events. Their death ends the tragedy but leaves society without an explanation as to why this had to occur. Analyzing the behavior of the mass murderers may provide some type of answer to the question why. Two specific forms of behavior are noted by colleague Ronald Holmes, a professor of administration of justice and an applied criminologist at the University of Louisville, who has written extensively on this subject. Holmes suggests that "front stage" or "overt aggressive behaviors" and "back stage" or "covert aggressive behaviors" are common among all mass murderers (Holmes & Holmes, 1992).

Front-stage behavior is the behavior that is openly displayed to others. "This is an outward directed behavior that is noted as hatred, anger or rage.

Often, a display which those who bother to notice would see as atypical" (Holmes & Holmes, 1994). An example of front-stage or overt behavior is that of George Hennard. Judy Beach was threatened by Hennard. Beach and her son were searching for a baseball glove near Hennard's home and he was shouting epithets at her and her son. "I'll never forget how he was looking at me in a threatening manner" and screaming "Bitch!" (Woodbury, 1991; p. 33). Yet still another example of front-stage or overt behavior is the letter that Hennard wrote to two sisters. In the letter, he indicated that women were vipers. Hennard's letter to the girls and his threatening behavior resulted in a complaint being filed against him. It was noted by the neighbor who filed the complaint, "If something had been done in June, those 23 people could have been saved" (Woodbury, 1991, p. 33).

Back-stage behavior is defined as "the screened or secretive behavior only the offender sees or witnesses (Holmes & Holmes, 1992). The victims are usually the recipients of the back-stage behavior when the front-stage behavior has been typically glossed over, dismissed, or ignored" (Davis, 1996). Hennard's victims happened to be at the wrong place at the wrong time. Quite simply, Hennard intended on killing. His victims were shown no mercy, with the exception of one woman who had an infant. He told her to leave. Of the 23 victims, 14 were women. The victims in the murder were not of significance to Hennard other than to be victims. Their identity and life were not important to Hennard. The victims that Hennard claimed before taking his own life included an Army Lieutenant Colonel stationed at Fort Hood, who was about to retire in two weeks, and another victim who was a grandmother of two and who happened to be "one of the most prominent black women in Marlin."

Locus of Control

Externalized versus Internalized Triggers of Aggression Emotional triggers as defined by this author are "psychological set points that typically center on levels of arousal or stimuli which can set-off the offender based on inappropriate or maladaptive forms of behavioral release" (Davis, 1996, 1999). Hennard's gain and violent aggressive release was psychological. Hennard had anger built up inside against women. He did not trust women and his opinion of women was negative. Hennard did not have a good relationship with his mother and apparently did not have any significant relationship with other women. This could be due to his anger toward women, and the less contact the more the negativity grew. Hennard perhaps blamed his trouble on women and more specifically he probably blamed his mother for the core of his problems.

Hennard was the second of two children. He was the son of an Army surgeon. This transient life of moving from one duty station to another could have prevented him from having a meaningful relationship with the opposite sex. This inability to form a meaningful relationship with women may be the reason for the antisocial personality, the repressed anger, and violence toward women. Furthermore, he displayed a paranoid personality disorder stemming from distrust and his further hatred of women.

Although the answer to the question why will never be accurately answered, George Hennard's background provides a basis for possible triggers that led him to his hatred toward women. Whatever led him to drive his pick-up truck through the plate glass of Luby's Cafeteria and begin murdering 23 people before taking his own life will possibly never be answered.

CONCLUSION

Many aspects of mass murder and the individuals who actually perpetrate these acts remain a mystery. The exploration and understanding of the human mind are still in their infancy stages, and much remains to be discovered. Perhaps we should follow Truman Capote's suggestion concerning mass murderers: "Such people, whom we do not begin to understand and therefore cannot pretend to 'treat,' should be confined in humane circumstances in a very secure place, and observed every day of their lives" (Levin & Fox, 1985, p. ix).

Mass murders are shocking and leave one anxiously looking for an explanation—any explanation, unfortunately one that is not frequently found or readily available. Father Hartz, who sermonized Marilyn Dreesman, along with five other members of the Dreesman family, were killed by another family member, may have summed up mass murder the best: "this kind of tragedy crashes into our world without warning, a cruel, uninvited guest . . . we can neither anticipate it before the fact, nor understand it after the fact" (Rowan, 1991, p. 12).

Finally, the usefulness of categorizing mass murderers yields a twofold purpose. First, it may be possible to identify individuals who demonstrate a strong potential for violence, specifically mass murder, using the various indicators and characteristics discussed within each of the five categories. In several of the cases outlined in this chapter, warning signs were present prior to the actual murders but were mostly ignored or dismissed. The ability to recognize these preincident indicators, link them to possible acts of violence, and take preventive steps greatly increases the chances of avoiding a tragedy. Second, the characteristics of each type of mass murderer can be of extreme utility to the investigator. The ability to place the perpetrator into a certain category could provide crucial information, insight, and direction in otherwise enigmatic investigations (Davis, 1996, 1999).

It is evident that the media's coverage of mass murders is extremely superficial, lacking in analysis and accuracy. The media are quick to dismiss the mass murderer as a "nut" or "deranged lunatic," delving no further into his motivations than those that are readily apparent. Another trend is to bypass any meaningful analysis and proceed straight to identifying a scapegoat, typically the mental heath care profession. *Time* magazine is also especially fond of blaming mass murders on the availability of various types of firearms and what are in their opinion "lax gun control laws." Almost every one of their articles covering a mass murder incident blames one or both of these as reasons for the occurrence of mass murder. This, in the author's opinion, draws attention from the core aspects and promotes ignorance regarding the issue. However, when psychologically examining mass murder from the demographic data available and by analyzing the mass murderer's behavior patterns, an educated assumption can explain the possible reasons for mass murder and hopefully prevent such acts of heinous violence.

REFERENCES

Albrecht, S. (1997). *Fear and Violence on the Job: Prevention Solutions for a Dangerousness Workplace.* Book Forward by Dr. Joseph Davis. Durham, NC: Carolina Academic Press.

Albrecht, S. (1999). *Violence in the Workplace Setting.* Chapter in-service presentation, American Society for Industrial Security (ASIS), San Diego, CA.

Albrecht, S. F., and M. Mantel. (1994). *Ticking Bombs: Defusing Violence in the Workplace.* Irwin Publishers, Burridge, Illinois.

Annin, P. (1991, October, 28). "You Could See the Hate." *Newsweek,* p. 35.

"Another AK-47 Massacre." (1989, September). *Time,* 134(13): 27.

Baker, J. N., & A. Murr. (1989, September). *Newsweek,* 114(13): 22.

Baron, A., & E. Wheeler. (1994). *Violence in Our Schools: Hospitals and Public Places.* Ventura, CA: Pathfinder Publishers.

Baron, A. (1993). *Violence in the Workplace.* Ventura, CA: Pathfinder Publishers, p. 39.

Blashfleld, J. F. (1990). *Why They Killed.* New York: Warner Books.

Bilski, A. (1991, October). *Tragedy in Texas.* p. 34

Came, B., D. Burke, G. Ferzoco, B. O'Farrell, & B. Wallace. (1989, December). "Montreal Massacre." *Maclean's,* 102(51): 14–17.

Caputo, P. (1989. December). "Death Goes to School." *Esquire,* 112(6): 137–154.

Celis, W. (1991a, October, 21). "Autopsy of Man Who Killed 23 in Texas Finds No Drugs or Tumor." *The New York Times.*

Celis, W. (1991b, October, 19). "Town in Texas Quietly Gathers for a Memorial." *The New York Times,* Section National.

Davis, J. (1996a). *Confidential Excerpted Interview and Defusing with a Disgruntled Employee.* Workplace Violence Case and Threat Analysis in Sacramento, California. Scripps Center for Quality Management, Inc., San Diego, CA.

Davis, J. (1996b). *Criminal Investigative Analysis: Elements of Psychological Personality Behavioral Assessment.* San Diego: Author.

Davis, J. (1997). *Management Styles, Profiling and Aggressive Workplace Behavior.* Unpublished lecture and presentation to San Diego Business Executives. San Diego: Author.

Davis, J. (1999). *The Psychology Behind Crime and Trauma.* San Diego: Montezuma Publishing.

Davis, J., L. Stewart, & R. Siota. (1999). "Future Prediction of Dangerousness and Violent Behavior: Psychological Indicators and Considerations for Conducting an Assessment of Potential Threat." *Canadian Journal of Clinical Medicine,* 6(3): 52–59.

Dietz, P., D. Matthews, D. Martell, T. Stewart, D. Hrounda, & J. Warren. (1991). Threatening and Otherwise Inappropriate Letters to Members of the United States Congress. *Journal of Forensic Sciences,* 36(5), 1445–1468.

Doerner, W. R., & J. L. Graff. (1989, December). The man who hated women. *Time.* 134(25): 30.

Ewing, C. P. (1985). *Psychology, Psychiatry and the Law.* Sarasota, FL: Professional Resource Exchange, Inc.

Foreman, L. (1992). *Mass Murderers.* USA: Time-Life Books.

Hayes, T. (1991, October, 17). "Gunman Kills 22 and Himself in Texas Cafeteria." *The New York Times,* Section A.

Holmes, R. M., & S. T. Holmes. (1994). *Murder in America.* Thousand Oaks: Sage Publications.

Holmes, R., & S. Holmes. (2001). *Mass Murder.* Englewood Cliffs, NJ: Prentice Hall.

Holmes, R., & S. Holmes. (2001). *Murder in America* (2nd ed.). Thousand Oaks, CA: Sage Publications, Inc.

Holmes, R., & S. Holmes. (1996). *Profiling Violent Crimes* (2nd ed.). Thousand Oaks, CA: Sage Publications.

Holmes, R. M., & S. T. Holmes. (1992). "Understanding Mass Murder: A Starting Point." *Federal Probation,* 56(l): 53–61.

Johnson, T. E., & D. Shapiro. (1988, January). "A mass murder in Arkansas," *Newsweek,* 11, p. 20.

Levin, J., & J. A. Fox. (1985). *Mass Murder.* New York: Plenum Press.

Lunde, D. T. (1975). *Murder and Madness.* The Portable Stanford. San Francisco: San Francisco Book Company, Inc.

Lunde, D. (1976). *Murder and Madness.* New York: W.W. Norton.

Meloy, J. R. (1988). "The Mass Murderer: A Clinical Profile." *Newsletter: Academy of San Diego Psychologists,* pp. 1–2.

Pennings, B. W. (1995). *Workplace Violence.* San Diego Marshal's office, Marshal's Association of California. San Diego, CA: Author, pp. 1–28.

Ressler, R. K., A. W. Burgess, & J. E. Douglas. (1988). *Sexual Homicide: Patterns and Motives.* New York: Lexington Press.

Rowan, R. (1991, April). "A Time to Kill, and a Time to Heal." *Time,* 137(14): 11–12.

"Slaughter in a School Yard." (1988, January). *Time,* 133(5): 29.

Terry, D. (1991, October, 18). "Portrait of Texas Killer: Impatient and Troubled." *The New York Times,* Section A, p. 14.

Toch, H. (1979). *Psychology of Crime and Criminal Justice.* New York: Holt, Rinehart, and Winston.

Turque, B., & M. Colin. (1989, December). "Massacre in Montreal." *Newsweek,* 114(5): 39.

Wallace, B., G. Ferzoco, & B. Bergman. (1989, December). "The Making of a Mass Killer: A Youth's Hidden Rage at Women." *Maclean's,* 102(51): 22.

Woodbury, R. (1991, October, 28). "Ten Minutes in Hell." *Time,* pp. 31–34.

SECTION 5

CHILD-PERPETRATED VIOLENCE

Ⅰn this section we have chosen a selection of readings that deal with the impact and ramifications of child violence. Since our nation's children are our most valued and prized commodity, special attention has to be paid to keeping them safe and making sure they are raised in an environment free of violence.

The first chapter, "Breaking the Cycle of Violence," examines how our juvenile justice system deals with youthful offenders. The author begins by noting that while most child offenders are not predatory or violent criminals, the system must make every effort to detect, intervene, and prevent youth that have gone astray from engaging in a life of crime. These efforts, the author claims, must be most pronounced in major urban areas, where the cycle of juvenile violence is more prevalent. The author notes recent ethnographical evidence that for many inner city youth, engaging in crime and going to prison is often considered badge of honor or even a rite of passage. She claims that this simply is not acceptable. She argues that federal, state, and local officials need to be cognizant of their plight and work in meaningful ways to prevent these youth from adapting a deviant and criminal lifestyle. She states that it is critical that society invest more time, effort, and money in both public and private crime prevention programs since increasing prison terms or toughening the penalties associated with juvenile crime simply will not do anything to address this problem.

The second chapter examines the effects of the victimization on our nation's youth. Cathy Spatz-Widom states in her chapter, "Childhood Victimization: Early Adversity, Later Psychopathology," that physical abuse, sexual molestation, and neglect have both immediate and long-term effects on children. To examine these effects, the author began examining and comparing 908 subjects under the age of 11 who had fallen victim to some type of childhood victimization in the Midwest between 1967 to 1971. These subjects were then tracked into adulthood and compared to a similar sample of 667 individuals who did not suffer a similar victimization experience. Overall, the author found evidence that the victimization experience appears to hinder their intellectual performance as measured by their IQ scores. Not only did the abused sample score lower on these standardized exams, but when they recorded their current occupation 20 years after the experience, the experimental group held more menial and semiskilled jobs than did the control group. The differences between the groups did not stop there. Divorce and separation from their partners were more prevalent among these youth when they became adults. And the abused group was 1.9 times as likely to have been arrested as those that had not been abused.

While this study is still underway, the preliminary findings are startling. Youth who are abused suffer greatly from their victimization experience, not only immediately but well into the future. The policy implications of the results of the study are clear: Childhood victimization in contemporary society must be taken seriously. And those that perpetrate these crimes must be held to account not only for the immediate harm that they cause to their victims but that harm that may follow their victims into adulthood.

The third chapter in this section examines the deadly nexus of drugs, guns, youth and violence. Alfred Blumstein notes that while the crime rate has been leveling off across all the major demographic factors, there is one that remains an anomaly. This of course is age. He states that we are increasingly seeing more violence committed by our nation's youth. In this article he explains this nexus and offers broad policy implications that may help curb this growing trend.

CHAPTER 17

BREAKING THE CYCLE OF VIOLENCE: A RATIONAL APPROACH TO AT-RISK YOUTH*

Judy Briscoe

A certain segment of the population of kids today, to whom John J. Dilulio, Jr., a leading criminologist, refers to as superpredators, are born into and reared in abject moral poverty. According to Dilulio,

> Moral poverty is the poverty of being without loving, capable, responsible adults who teach you right from wrong. It is the poverty of being without parents, guardians, relatives, friends, teachers, coaches, clergy and others who habituate you to feel joy at others' joy, pain at others' pain, happiness when you do right, remorse when you do wrong. It is the poverty of growing up in the virtual absence of people who teach these lessons by their own everyday example, and who insist that you follow suit and behave accordingly. In the extreme, it is the poverty of growing up surrounded by deviant, delinquent, and criminal adults in chaotic, dysfunctional, fatherless, Godless, and jobless settings where drug abuse and child abuse are twins, and self-respecting young men literally aspire to get away with murder.

Maximum security prisoners agree. When Dilulio asked what was triggering the explosion of violence among today's young street criminals, a group of long- and life-term New Jersey prisoners did not voice the conventional explanations such as economic poverty or joblessness. Instead, these hardened men cited the absence of people—family, adults, teachers, preachers, coaches—who would care enough about young males to nurture and discipline them. In the vacuum, drug dealers and "gangsta rappers" serve as role models. "I was a bad-ass street gladiator," one convicted murderer said, "but these kids are stone-cold predators."[1]

Over the next 15 years the number of juveniles under 17 will grow to about 74 million. Most experts agree that the number of juveniles arrested for

---

*This chapter originally appeared in *Federal Probation*, 67(3): 3–13.

murder, rape, robbery, and aggravated assault will more than double by 2010.[2] Dilulio notes,

> As James Q. Wilson, a professor of public policy at the University of California at Los Angeles has written, Americans rightly believe that "something fundamental has changed in our patterns of crime," namely the threat of serious crimes committed by "youngsters who afterwards show us the blank, unremorseful stare of a feral, pre-social being."
>
> Some have denied this "superpredator" reality by noting that "only" one-half of 1 percent of all juveniles are arrested for a violent crime each year. But that translates into more than 150,000 juveniles arrested for violent crimes, including utterly senseless drive-by shootings, gang assaults and "joy killings."

For the last several years crime has been consistently rated as the public's number one concern, but, more particularly, juvenile crime has had staggering increases. However, the latest Federal Bureau of Investigation Uniform Crime Report (UCR) noted that juvenile arrests for violent crime declined in 1995 for the first time in nearly a decade. Most encouraging is that this decline was greatest among young juveniles.

During 1995, law enforcement agencies in the United States reported the following:

- There were an estimated 2.7 million arrests of persons under the age of 18, or 18 percent of all arrests.
- Juvenile arrests for Violent Crime Index offenses (murder, forcible rape, robbery, and aggravated assault) declined 3 percent.
- The number of juvenile crime arrests was 12 percent greater than in 1991.
- The number of juvenile crime arrests was 67 percent above the 1986 level.

Other recent findings from the UCR are as follows:

- Juveniles were involved in 32 percent of all robbery arrests, 23 percent of weapon arrests, and 15 percent of murder and aggravated assault arrests in 1995.
- Juveniles under age 15 were responsible for 30 percent of juvenile violent crime arrests in 1995, but they accounted for more than one-half (55 percent) of the decline in these arrests between 1994 and 1995.
- Juvenile murder arrests declined 14 percent between 1994 and 1995.
- Juvenile Property Crime Index arrests showed no change between 1991 and 1995.
- Juveniles were involved in 13 percent of all drug arrests in 1995, a 138 percent increase since 1991.
- Arrests of juveniles accounted for 14 percent of all violent crimes cleared by arrest in 1995—9 percent of murders, 15 percent of forcible rapes, 20 percent of robberies, and 13 percent of aggravated assaults cleared by arrest.
- Decline in violent crime arrests was greater for younger juveniles.

- One in four juvenile arrests in 1995 were arrests of females.
- Juvenile violent crime arrest rates declined for the first time since 1987.[3]

Although a 1-year decline cannot be considered a trend, the newest Federal Bureau of Investigation arrest statistics give hope for the future.

Even with those daunting statistics, it is important to keep in mind several things about the potential juvenile crime challenge. First, the vast majority of juvenile offenders are not violent predators. They are neither violent nor incorrigible, and the juvenile justice system needs to be able to address the entire range of at-risk, delinquent, and criminal youth. Solutions must span the entire spectrum—from prevention to early intervention to swift and sure punishment for chronic/violent offenders.

Because the majority of crimes are concentrated in the major metropolitan areas of a half-dozen or more states, youth of these communities are disproportionately vulnerable to violent crime, either as a victim or as a victimizer. Society must focus efforts at revitalizing communities where violence is bred. Children must be allowed to be children without the fear of themselves, their families, or their neighbors being harmed.

Professor Marvin Wolfgang, in *Delinquency in a Birth Cohort* and *From Boy to Man, From Delinquency to Crime,* coined the 6 Percent Rule that about 6 to 7 percent of all boys in a given birth cohort will go on to become chronic offenders. *Chronic* was defined as having five or more arrests before reaching one's eighteenth birthday. He also found that these chronic offenders were responsible for about half of all crimes, and two-thirds of all violent crimes, committed by the entire cohort by age 18.[4] Wolfgang's studies have been well replicated. The sheer increases in numbers of adolescent males in the next decade bode disastrously for society unless parents, government, businesses, churches, schools, and individuals become collaboratively responsible for the outcome of these youth. Children cannot rear themselves.

A growing body of statistical and ethnographic research suggests that many of today's persistent young offenders cannot be deterred from committing crimes simply by toughening the criminal penalties. As Professor Neal Shover argues, some of today's "young offenders know little and care less about the schedule of penalties."[5] In fact, for many youth, going to prison is a badge of honor or a rite of passage.

Not only must a graduated network of juveniles-only secure facilities be built, but juvenile probation officers, juvenile corrections officers, and juvenile parole officers must be recognized, rewarded, and retrained for the increasingly difficult job of monitoring and mentoring the growing numbers of severely troubled and potentially dangerous juveniles for whom they have responsibility.

Public concern about crime has been influenced by several factors: first, by the ever-increasing politics of crime by national, state, and local leaders; second, by the reporting, exaggerating, and sensationalizing of crime by the media; and third, by the failure of academicians, criminal justice experts, and policy makers to agree on how best to manage crime. Whether that concern is perception or reality is not important. What is important is that policy makers not be infatuated by sound bites and expedient get-tough approaches but work toward a rational, comprehensive approach to delinquency prevention.

There are some fundamental principles on which society must begin to act. There is growing evidence that certain types of social programs can succeed in keeping at-risk youth out of trouble. A RAND Corporation study entitled *Diverting Children from a Life of Crime*[6] identified several modes of early intervention to prevent crime:

- Early-childhood interventions for children at risk of later antisocial behavior
- Interventions for families with children who are "acting out"
- School-based interventions (e.g., incentives to graduate)
- Interventions for troublesome youths early in delinquency

The RAND team concluded that such demonstrations would be an investment worth the cost.

It is critical that society invest more time, money, and effort in both public and private crime prevention efforts that encourage responsible, caring, prosocial adult role models to become involved in the lives of at-risk youth. Society must place a priority on educating its children and instilling those values that make them responsible citizens. Communities must identify those factors that place children at risk and then mobilize forces to eradicate bad influences and build or strengthen those factors that provide protection and hope. Economically depressed, crime-ridden neighborhoods must be revitalized so that youth can experience hope and dreams for a better way of life.

Juvenile justice professionals must argue vigorously to maintain separate juvenile and criminal justice systems. Legitimate public concerns justify imprisoning dangerous, repeat offenders; however, research shows that housing juvenile offenders with adult felons is not the answer to decrease the rate of violent crime. Youth who get into trouble with the law need adult guidance, and suitable role models won't be found in prison. People must understand that the development of children and youth is a process that allows for learning, growing, changing, and maturing. Just as youth are vulnerable to negative influences, they are just as likely to be amenable to positive influences if adults can figure out how to reach them or recognize that they must be reached. Citizens must maintain hope for rehabilitation; for without that, society will surely self-destruct.

In the last 20 years, social order has changed dramatically. An increasing number of children are living with only one parent, and that parent often depends on government assistance or works two jobs to keep food on the table. People have become more transient, which precludes establishing roots and having access to extended families and long-term friendships. Neighborhoods are no longer stable, and many are violent and poverty ridden. For people with economic means, burglar alarms, fences, and private security systems keep them safe; for people without means, violence is a fact of life. More children are born into poverty to unwed, uneducated, young mothers who don't understand the basics of nurturing their child, much less being a teacher or role model. Poverty can create a sense of hopelessness that becomes a self-fulfilling prophecy. The church is no longer a focal point, and children grow up without a spiritual connection and with no sense of right and wrong. Reverend Eugene Rivers, III, who established a youth ministry in inner city Boston, developed a 10-point plan "to save children" and "mobilize churches to combat youth violence and despair," based in part on his conversation with one of the neighborhood's most notorious drug merchants. At the end of a long and complicated discussion of why so many of the community's children had fallen prey to drugs and crime and violence, the drug dealer cast a cold eye on Rivers and his fellow ministers and declared plainly, "I'm there, you're not."[7]

Drugs and alcohol have become a way of coping. More substance abuse by juveniles leads in many cases to more trouble with the law and violence. Numerous studies have found that juveniles who drink alcohol to the point of drunkenness are far more likely than juveniles who do not drink to get into fights, get arrested, commit violent crimes, and recidivate later in life.[8] If one thinks about television commercials, some of the most clever and popular ones glamorize drinking beer. Many parents mistakenly think that if their children drink beer, they're at least not taking drugs. How wrong they are.

When crack cocaine emerged in the mid-1980s in the United States, the face of crime changed dramatically. Along with crack cocaine and its devastating addiction came the opportunity for young people to make money as never before and the need to defend themselves and their territory with guns. The combination of drugs and weapons has had a lethal impact on society. Gangs, which have always existed but remained in the background, became pervasive and much more violent.

Every year guns end the lives of thousands of young people in the United States. Their families and friends are left to cope with the loss of a life barely lived and to face a future overshadowed by violence. The National Crime Prevention Council[9] reported the following:

- Every day 15 children under the age of 19 are killed by gunfire and many more are injured.
- Homicide is the second leading cause of death for youths ages 10 to 19. Most of these offenses are committed with firearms—especially handguns.
- Youths between 10 and 19 years old commit suicide using handguns every 6 hours.
- Firearms kill more people between the ages of 15 and 24 than all natural causes combined.
- An estimated 1.2 million elementary-aged children who return to an empty house after school have access to guns.

Although many communities believe they are immune to these kinds of statistics, it is important to be aware of potential problems and develop preventive measures. Many states in the United States ignored the problems of gangs, assuming they were a problem for the major cities, only to be inundated later with gang violence. Problems such as guns, drugs, and gangs cannot be ignored. They will manifest without constant vigilance to keep communities safe from negative influences and without constant efforts toward building and enhancing resources to keep youth out of trouble.

Many professionals and practitioners have known intuitively for some time that violence begets violence, but until recently there have been few scientific studies that have shown the correlation empirically. One exceptional longitudinal study completed by Cathy Spatz-Widom, professor of criminal justice and psychology and director of the Hindelang Criminal Justice Research Center at the State University of New York at Albany, was entitled *The Cycle of Violence.*[10]

Widom's study tracked 1575 cases from childhood through young adulthood, comparing the arrest records of two groups: a study group of 908 substantiated cases of childhood abuse or neglect and a comparison group of 667 children not officially recorded as abused or neglected and matched to the study group according to age, race, sex, and approximate family socioeconomic status. The design also featured clear operational definitions of abuse and neglect, which permitted the separate examination of physical abuse, sexual abuse, and neglect. The findings were as follows: Those who had been abused or neglected were

- 53 percent more likely to be arrested as juveniles
- 38 percent more likely to be arrested as adults
- 38 percent more likely to be arrested for a violent crime
- 77 percent more likely to be arrested if they were females

The study further showed that abuse and neglect cases were more likely to average nearly 1 year younger at first arrest, commit twice as many offenses, and were arrested 89 percent more frequently. A more troubling conclusion was that a child who is neglected is just as likely as a child who is abused to be arrested for a violent crime. And unless there is neurological damage from the abuse, neglect has a longer term, more damaging impact to the development of a child.

Preliminary Phase Two findings of Widom's study, based on follow-up interviews with 500 study and comparison group subjects, indicated other negative outcomes to be as common as delinquency and violent criminal behavior. Widom's subsequent findings included mental health concerns (depression and suicide); educational problems (inadequate cognition, extremely low IQ, poor reading ability); health and safety issues (alcohol and drug problems); and occupational difficulties (lack of work, employment in low-level service jobs).

Not only do abuse and neglect have a psychological and emotionally devastating impact on the individual, but they are also having a tremendously negative economic impact on the nation. The cost of child abuse and neglect is overwhelming.

Violent crime has imprisoned the economy. Ted R. Miller, director of the safety and health policy program at the National Public Services Research Institute, published an article entitled "Victim Costs of Violent Crime and Resulting Injuries" in *Health Affairs,* Winter 1993. He cites Mark Cohen's Vanderbilt/Urban Institute Cost of Crime Study of 1993, which estimates that each year adds another $178 billion in lifetime costs to victims of violent crime. Michael Mandel's article "The Economics of Crime," appearing in the December 13, 1993 issue of *Business Week,* estimates that if property loss, urban decay, private protection, and criminal justice costs are included, the annual financial loss to the nation is a staggering $425 billion.[11] In an unpublished study partially funded by the National Institute of Justice and employing similar analytical techniques to his earlier Urban Institute Cost of Crime study, Cohen estimated that the monetary value of diverting a high-risk youth from a criminal career through successful intervention is between $1.5 and $2 million per juvenile.[12] Thus, delinquency prevention should not be just an altruistic phenomenon but should be considered an economic imperative. It defies logic that lawmakers are reluctant to embrace proven programs to keep youth out of trouble and yet willingly fund bricks and mortar to house youth who have gotten into trouble.

What do children need? They need, first, to be born healthy. So prenatal care is extremely important. This is a public health issue and needs to be treated as such. Children need to be nurtured so they are well loved, well fed, immunized against childhood diseases, read to, touched, taught right from wrong, encouraged creatively, and allowed to bond. The Carnegie Corporation of New York studied the importance of the first 3 years of a baby's life in terms of brain development. We now know the following:

- The brain development that takes place before age one is more rapid and extensive than previously realized.
- Brain development is much more vulnerable to environmental influence than ever suspected.
- The influence of early environment on brain development is long lasting.
- The environment affects not only the number of brain cells and the number of connections among them but also the way these connections are "wired".
- There is new scientific evidence for the negative impact of early stress on brain function.

The Carnegie study identified many risk factors in a child's life (e.g., personality, physical health, family, social/peer influence, neighborhood, community, school, and individual interaction with the environment). Risk factors are often multiplicative, not additive, in their effects. "When children showed only one risk factor, their outcomes were no worse than those of children showing none of the identified risk factors. But when children had two or more risk factors, they were four times as likely to develop social and academic problems."[13] Community networks that meet the basic emotional, medical, educational, and spiritual needs of children must be built.

The road to *violence* begins in childhood. It is imperative that society understand what puts children at risk:

Research identifies many risk factors that contribute to youths' propensity for violence and delinquency. Crime-prone youth are more likely to come from families where parents are abusive or neglectful, provide harsh or erratic discipline, or exhibit marital discord. They tend to live in communities rife with drugs, crime, guns, and poverty, where positive role models and safe, constructive recreational opportunities are scarce. They are likely to associate with peers who are delinquent or drug-abusing or to participate in youth gangs. In many cases they are tracked at school into classes dominated by low-achieving and trouble-making students.

Several individual characteristics—such as hyperactivity, attention deficit disorder, low intelligence—have been linked to delinquency. The presence or lack of self-control, problem-solving skills, and beliefs condemning violence have been identified as key determinants of criminality. Other personal factors—a strong and sustained relationship with at least one adult, an even temperament, and an ability to evoke positive responses in others—have been identified as "protective factors" that can help insulate even high-risk youth from the danger of falling into delinquency. Prevention can address the risks facing many children while boosting protective factors, making them less likely to become delinquent.[14]

To help ensure that children are properly nurtured, communities can replicate a program that began in Hawaii, called Hawaii Healthy Start. This program has social workers go into the hospital and interview mothers shortly after they have given birth. If the mother agrees, a risk assessment is administered to determine whether the mother might be at risk for abusing or neglecting her child. If the risk assessment indicates the possibility of abuse or neglect and the mother agrees to participate in the program, a home visitor schedules a time to meet with her once she leaves the hospital. The home visitor teaches her parenting skills, helps her access government services for which she is eligible, and establishes a relationship with a primary care physician for the baby. That family is monitored for the first 5 years of the baby's life. Among those mothers who agreed to participate, child abuse and neglect was averted in 99.7 percent of the cases.

To ensure that children are prepared to learn, preschool programs should be implemented. As stated in *Significant Benefits: The High/Scope Perry Preschool Study Through Age 27* by Lawrence J. Schweinhart and David P. Weikart, "High-quality, active learning preschool programs can help young children in poverty make a better transition from home to community and thus start them on paths to becoming economically self-sufficient, socially responsible adults."[15] The High/Scope Perry Preschool Project was a study that assessed whether high-quality preschool programs could provide both short- and long-term benefits to children living in poverty and at high risk of failing in school. The study followed into adulthood the lives of 123 such children from African American families who lived in the neighborhood of the Perry Elementary School in Ypsilanti, Michigan, in the 1960s.

Findings at age 27 indicated that in comparison with the no-program group, the program group had

- Significantly higher monthly earnings at age 27 (with 29 percent vs. 7 percent earning $2000 or more per month)
- Significantly higher percentages of home ownership (36 percent vs. 13 percent)
- A significantly higher level of schooling completed (with 71 percent vs. 54 percent completing 12th grade or higher)
- A significantly lower percentage receiving social services at some time in the previous 10 years (59 percent vs. 80 percent)

- Significantly fewer arrests by age 27 (7 percent vs. 35 percent) with 5 or more arrests for crimes of drug making or dealing (7 percent vs. 25 percent).[16]

There are many programs with successful outcomes from which expertise and experience can be drawn. Most of these are not expensive and are easily replicable. If society can reweave its fabric so that ethical behavior and moral decisions are fundamental, delinquency can be manageable. Skills such as anger management, *violence* prevention, and school-yard mediation can be taught. Programs such as Fight-Free Schools, developed by the principal of an elementary school in St. Louis, Missouri, have changed the culture of many schools around the country. Youth need recreation centers and community centers so that they can congregate in prosocial activities. Mentors can make a significant difference in a child's life by teaching prosocial conduct and permissible ways of problem solving and by acting as a role model and a resource in developing problem-solving skills. Further,

- A caring adult parenting figure is often associated with a good outcome for the child.
- A caring adult is the most significant and consistent prevention influence during or after a major disaster, trauma, deprivation, or abuse.
- A caring adult causes the child to see himself or herself as likable and important.
- Abused children who have a good association with a caregiving adult are less likely to carry on the abuse when they become parents.[17]

Intergenerational programs have had amazing success for both youngsters and the elderly. Two such programs are Telefriends, a program that connects children who are home alone with older volunteers, by telephone; and Grandfriends, where retired senior volunteers share their time, their love, and a lifetime of wisdom with children in child care centers and preschools. The ever more fast-paced society has forgotten what tremendous wisdom and life experiences an elderly person can provide.

A growing body of empirical research supports the efficacy of church-centered approaches to battling crime, delinquency, and other economic and social problems. "Just as the density of liquor outlets in a neighborhood correlates with negative phenomena, the density of churches correlates with positive ones."[18] "Several recent econometric studies find that controlling for all relevant individual characteristics (race, gender, education, family structure, etc.), urban youth whose neighbors attend church are more likely to have a job, less likely to use drugs, and less likely to be involved in criminal activity. In other words, church-going has what economists term 'positive externalities.' In this case, church-going affects the behavior of life prospects of disadvantaged youths whether or not they themselves attend church."[19]

The Texas Youth Commission created the Office of Delinquency Prevention specifically to provide information about programs such as those mentioned previously, as well as the latest research on issues relating to early childhood development, adolescence, family problems, juvenile justice, and delinquency prevention. There is a tremendous need for this information, as evidenced by the requests received from all over the world. The address for the Prevention Web site is www://tyc.state.tx.us/prevention/.

There is no one program to fit every community or every situation. An array of programs along the developmental continuum where there is citizen investment has the most promise for success. But while citizens are trying to figure out what to do, the following must be kept in mind: A child who is not nurtured is a child who doesn't learn to trust, doesn't develop empathy, doesn't accept responsibility for his or her behavior, and will hurt others with impunity. Children must have a safe and secure environment in which to grow and mature. Even impoverished youth living in crime-ridden neighborhoods tend to make it if they have an adult parent, teacher, coach, or clergy to protect and guide them. Youth who commit the worst crimes have almost always been raised without adult care and supervision. The presence or absence of a positive adult mentor is a principal element in whether or not a teen is able to oppose criminal conduct. One study discovered that 85 percent of the mentees from a high-risk area in Washington, D.C. had no court involvement. That same study found 53 percent of the mentees believed theft mentors helped them resist illegal drugs.[20]

For those youth who have already broken the law, a responsive juvenile justice system is imperative. To establish a frame of reference, the juvenile justice system can exercise control over an adjudicated offender for only a limited time. Texas will be an example of such a responsive juvenile justice system. The age of accountability varies among states and countries. Juvenile court jurisdiction in Texas begins at age 10, so if a child commits a crime before that age, he is legally not accountable and must be served through whatever human services are available. For youth who do meet juvenile court age, if placed on probation at the community level, the youth must be discharged from the system no later than his or her eighteenth birthday; if committed to the state Texas Youth Commission, his or her twenty-first birthday. In some instances, juveniles can be transferred from juvenile to criminal court. If the offense was committed while the youth was 15 or 16 and was a felony, or for a capital or first degree felony committed by a 14-year-old, then after a hearing the juvenile court may transfer the case to criminal court for prosecution under adult law. In 1995, 535 youth were certified to stand trial as adults in Texas.

In 1995, the Texas legislature passed into law a continuum of progressive sanctions guidelines designed to balance public protection, offender accountability, and rehabilitation. From prevention and early intervention programs to secure incarceration, the services are designed to hold youth accountable at each sanction level. Decision makers are given flexibility and are encouraged to determine a sanction level based not only on the seriousness of the offense but also on the child's prior delinquent history, special needs and circumstances, and the effectiveness of prior intervention efforts. Progressive sanctions guidelines describe seven levels with each one being more restrictive and demanding than the previous one. The premise of the law was that consequences of delinquent conduct should be reasonably predictable so youth know what to expect from the juvenile justice system but flexible enough to fashion sanctions and services uniquely suited to the needs of the youth.

Progressive sanctions establish a system of accountable early interventions and progressively predictable sanctions that give youth the message that a criminal career will not be tolerated. The purposes of progressive sanctions guidelines are as follows:

- Ensure that juvenile offenders face uniform and consistent consequences and punishments that correspond to the seriousness of each offender's current offense, prior delinquent history, special treatment or training needs, and effectiveness of prior interventions.
- Balance public protection and rehabilitation while holding juvenile offenders accountable.
- Permit flexibility in the decisions made in relation to the juvenile offender to the extent allowed by law.
- Consider the juvenile offender's circumstances.
- Improve juvenile justice planning and resource allocation by ensuring uniform and consistent reporting of disposition decisions at all levels (Texas Family Code Section 59.001).

Table 17.1 illustrates the types of offenses and the recommended sanctions.

The first five sanctions levels are under the auspices of the local juvenile probation departments, with sanctions ranging from counseling, to informal

Table 17.1
At-Risk Youth Progressive Sanctions Guidelines

Offense		Recommended Sanctions
Conduct indicating a need for supervision, other than a Class A or Class B misdemeanor	1	**Require counseling.** Inform child of progressive sanctions for future offenses; Inform parent(s) of responsibility to impose restrictions on child; Provide information to child & family on needed social services; Require child or parent(s) to participate in services from STAR (Services To At Risk Youth); Refer child to citizen intervention program; release child to parent(s) or guardian(s).
Class A or B misdemeanor, other than a misdemeanor involving the use or possession of a firearm;	2	**Deferred prosecution or court-ordered or informal probation for 3–6 months.** Inform child of progressive sanctions for future offenses; Inform parent(s) of responsibility to impose restrictions on child; Require restitution to victim or community service restitution (CSR); Require parent(s) or guardian(s) to identify restrictions to be imposed on child;
Delinquent conduct under Section 51.03(a)(2) or (3)		Provide information to child & family on needed social services; Require child or parent(s) to participate in services from STAR; Refer child to citizen intervention program; Additional conditions of probation as appropriate.

(continued)

Table 17.1

At-Risk Youth Progressive Sanctions Guidelines (*Continued*)

Offense		*Recommended Sanctions*
Misdemeanor involving use or possession of a firearm, state jail felony; third-degree felony	3	**Court-ordered probation for less than 6 months.** Require restitution to victim or CSR; Impose specific restrictions and requirements for child's behavior; Require probation officer to closely monitor child's activities and behavior; Require child or parent(s) to participate in programs or services as appropriate; Additional conditions of probation as appropriate.
Second-degree felony	4	**Not less than 3 months intensive and regimented program PLUS court-ordered probation for 6–12 months.** Require restitution to victim or CSR; Impose highly structured restrictions and requirements on child's behavior; Require probation officer to closely monitor child; Require child or parent(s) to participate in programs or services as appropriate; Additional sanctions if appropriate.
First-degree felony, other than a felony involving the use of a deadly weapon or causing serious bodily injury	5	**6–9 months court-ordered structured residential placement PLUS court-ordered probation for 6–12 months.** Require restitution to victim or CSR; Impose highly structured restrictions and requirements on child's behavior; Require probation officer to closely monitor child; Require child or parent(s) to participate in programs or services as appropriate; Additional sanctions if appropriate.
First-degree felony involving the use of a deadly weapon or causing serious bodily injury, or aggravated controlled substance felony	6	**Commitment to Texas Youth Commission, where Commission may impose the following:** 9–12 months highly structured residential program; Require restitution to victim or CSR; Require child or parent(s) to participate in programs or services as appropriate; Additional sanctions if appropriate; Parole with highly structured restrictions and requirements on child; Parole supervision for not less than 6 months; Other parole supervision conditions as appropriate.

(*continued*)

Table 17.1

At-Risk Youth Progressive Sanctions Guidelines (*Continued*)

Offense		*Recommended Sanctions*
Determinate sentence for first-degree felony involving the use of a deadly weapon or causing serious bodily injury; determinate program; sentence for an aggravated controlled substance felony; capital felony	7	**Determinate sentence to the Texas Youth Commission, where Commission may impose the following:** 12 months to 10 years highly structured residential program; Require restitution to victim or CSR; Require child or parent(s) to participate in programs or services as appropriate; Additional sanctions if appropriate; Parole with highly structured restrictions and requirements on child; Parole supervision for not less than 12 months; Other parole supervision conditions as appropriate.

Source: Texas Juvenile Probation Commission Progressive Sanctions Handbook, December 1995.

probation, to intensive probation, to placement outside the home. In Texas, juvenile boards, comprised of district judges, the county judge, and any designated juvenile court judge in the county, are responsible for the administration of local juvenile probation services. Texas has 254 counties, with 172 juvenile boards administering services in all the counties and providing approximately 70 percent of the funding. The state of Texas, through the Texas Juvenile Probation Commission, establishes state standards, provides training and technical assistance, compiles transactional data on incidence of crime from the local level for statewide purposes, and provides 30 percent of the funds.

Levels six and seven refer to commitment to the Texas Youth Commission (TYC), the state agency responsible for the most seriously delinquent and disturbed youth. Juvenile courts can commit youth to the TYC in two ways: Level six provides for an indeterminate commitment to the agency where the TYC determines minimum length of stay by internal policy, the least of which is 9 months, and level seven provides for a determinate sentence of up to 40 years for youth who commit certain violent offenses. For a determinate sentence, third-degree felony has a minimum length of stay of I year; second-degree, 2 years; first-degree, 3 years; and capital felony, 10 years, without juvenile court approval for release.

In the mid-1980s, there was an increasing number of violent offenses being committed by youth under age 15, which led to the belief that the juvenile justice system was incapable of adequately dealing with these youth. As a result, the determinate sentencing statute was created and has been amended to deal more appropriately with the violent offender as young as 10 years of age and as old as age 16.

The major significance of the determinate sentencing act was that it did not transfer the youth to criminal court for prosecution but kept the youth in juvenile court and yet provided all the procedural protections that an adult being prosecuted in criminal court would possess. It provided an extended term of control—up to 40 years—with confinement beginning in a juvenile facility; then at age 18, after a hearing by the juvenile court, the youth could be released on juvenile parole, recommitted to the TYC for an indeterminate sentence until age 21, or transferred to the adult institutional facility to complete the rest of the sentence.[21] The original law included five of the most violent offenses for which a youth could get a determinate sentence. The 1995 legislative session made two major changes: It expanded the list for which youth could get a determinate sentence to virtually all aggravated offenses against a person, or chronic and serious offenses; and it lowered to 16 the age at which the TYC could return to court for possible transfer of those youth who continue to be a danger to themselves or others and who refuse to participate in the treatment program.

The courts have upheld the constitutionality of the determinate sentence scheme, but, equally important, the scheme gives prosecutors, judges, and juries another viable option to transfer to criminal court and extends the time over which the TYC has control.

Although the rhetoric of the "get-tough" approach to juvenile crime usually calls for transfer, research is almost unanimous in concluding that transferring juvenile offenders to adult court will ultimately do more harm than good. In reality, there are many unintended consequences, not the least of which is that transfer usually results in a less severe sanction than would have been received in the juvenile justice system. Determinate sentencing, on the other hand, gives juvenile justice professionals the opportunity to work with these youth to better determine whether or not they are amenable to treatment and if they continue to pose a risk to society.

The TYC, which operates institutions, halfway houses, boot camps, and aftercare services, is the ultimate sanction in the juvenile justice system and the last hope for many of these youth. Traditionally, the TYC handles the most seriously disturbed and delinquent 2 to 3 percent of the youth who are arrested. In 1995, 133,866 youth were referred to juvenile court and 2387 youth were committed to TYC. Last year, 1996, 36 percent of the youth were committed to the TYC for violent offenses, a 356 percent increase since 1988. The following characteristics provide a profile of the types of youth for whom the agency is responsible[22]:

- 41 percent known gang members
- 23 percent diagnosed as having severe mental illness
- 77 percent known drug or alcohol users
- 35 percent classified as special education, with median reading and math levels at fifth grade
- 77 percent minority youth
- 43 percent considered dangerous to others
- 16 percent considered dangerous to self
- 7 percent history of setting fires
- 64 percent history of cocaine/crack abuse
- 73 percent history of marijuana abuse

- Vast majority have history of abuse and neglect
- Vast majority have family members with history of substance abuse, criminal behavior, and/or mental impairments
- 58 percent come from poverty
- 71 percent come from chaotic environments
- 80 percent of families lack discipline skills

In 1995, the TYC began implementing a therapeutic approach that utilized the best elements of various treatment modalities including those cited in research for having the most successful outcomes. This treatment program, called Resocialization, is based on the premise that youth have been "socialized" to a delinquent/crime-prone subculture, must be held accountable for their behavior, and must be helped to understand and to develop the skills necessary to become positive, prosocial individuals. Resocialization uses a variety of interventions with emphasis on therapeutic community concepts and cognitive-behavioral interventions in a continuum of care context.

The Resocialization philosophy is as follows:

- Children are not born delinquent.
- Delinquency is learned behavior that is influenced by
    - Early family relationships that shape thoughts and feelings about the world
    - Social environment
    - Biological factors that impact skills and abilities
    - Subcultural norms and values that justify criminal behavior

The Resocialization goal is to involve youth in a positive social contract. For example,

- Members of society agree to uphold certain rules of behavior for the good of all society's members.
- Individuals must be accountable for their own actions.
- Reparations should be made when harm has been caused intentionally.

Resocialization requires

- Accurate assessment of causative and contributing factors to delinquency
- Provision of a safe, positive environment
- Intervention to stop negative behavior patterns
- Rehabilitation to promote prosocial behavior
- Supportive community reintegration[23]

The Resocialization program is built around the agency's four cornerstones: education, work, disciplinary training, and the core group curriculum.

To maintain a safe environment, behavior groups deal with such issues as positive peer norms, conflict resolution, and problem solving. To intervene with delinquent behavior, treatment groups include the following:

- Layout describes who the student is, what he or she has done, and what he or she needs to change.
- Thinking errors are excuses for criminal behavior.
- Life story identifies the motivation for delinquent behavior.
- Offense cycle identifies patterns of thoughts and feelings that prompt delinquent acting out and devises strategies to interrupt that behavior.
- Values development promotes social obligation and individual accountability for behavior.
- Victim empathy inhibits aggression and exploitation of others.
- Success plans identify goals and objectives for productive community reintegration and prevention of recidivism.

The *Rehabilitation Element* includes skills groups that help youth learn such things as anger management, life skills, independent living skills, education, and vocational training.

The five phases of Resocialization were designed to take approximately 12 months to complete. Phase I, the Orientation/Control Phase, takes about a month and relies primarily on external controls. Youth adjust to program norms, learn the rules, are introduced to the core program concepts, and experience a safe environment.

Phase II, Discomfort/Motivation Phase, takes about 2 months. Youth recognize how thinking errors are used to justify hurting others, confront their delinquent need gratification, recognize critical life events that have led to delinquent lifestyles, and identify unmet needs.

Phase III, Hope/Positive Expectations Phase, takes about 3 months. Youth recognize that choices change lives, experience the effects of positive reinforcement for prosocial attitudes and choices, accept responsibility for their own choices, and understand the impact those choices had on their victims, and recognize the connection between values and behavior.

Phase IV, Personalization/Experimentations Phase, takes about 3 months. During this phase, youth practice new ways of getting needs met in prosocial ways, assume greater leadership responsibility, increase their use of coping skills, and begin efforts at restitution.

Phase V is the Integration/Maintenance Phase, during which time the youth are on parole. At this point, youth recognize high-risk situations, practice realistic relapse prevention strategies, consistently self-interrupt their delinquent offense cycles and thinking errors, develop and implement realistic success plans, and understand and experience family support.

Each phase has objective criteria, and youth must demonstrate mastery of the skills required in each phase. Workbooks are available, homework is assigned, staff are trained, curriculum-driven groups are consistently held, and controls are in place for verification and documentation. Education, discipline training, and work—the other three cornerstones—are complementary to the Resocialization program.

In addition to the Resocialization program, to which all youth have access, the TYC operates four specialized treatment programs: the capital offender program for youth who commit murder, sex offender treatment, chemical dependency treatment, and programs for youth with emotional disturbance. Of all the youth who are committed to the agency, approximately 80 percent have a need for one or more of the specialized treatment programs. Unfortunately, the TYC only has resources to provide the specialized treatment to approximately 30 percent of the youth with special needs.

The Texas legislature required the TYC to report on the outcome effectiveness of the four specialized treatment programs. The review examined the following five outcome measures:

- 1-year rearrest rate
- 1-year rearrest severity rate
- 1-year reincarceration rate
- 1-year rearrest rate for a violent offense
- 3-year reincarceration rate

The highlights of the review are as follows:

- Youth receiving specialized treatment matching their needs were initially found on 13 of 16 measures to recidivate either significantly less or marginally less than youth with these needs who did not receive this treatment.
- Even after statistically removing initial differences in recidivism propensities between groups, three of the four specialized treatment programs (chemical dependency, capital offender, and treatment for emotional disturbance) had at least one outcome measure demonstrating treatment effectiveness of youth receiving the specific treatments compared to youth with the same needs who did not.
- The other specialized treatment category, sex offender treatment, had evidence of effectiveness at one facility, which suggests that there may be better implementation of the sex offender treatment program at that facility. Steps have been taken to bring the other sex offender treatment program in line with the program that showed effectiveness.
- The chemical dependency treatment program showed the greatest evidence of treatment effectiveness, with youth receiving specialized chemical dependency treatment being less likely to recidivate on three of the four outcome measures (rearrest within 1 year, reincarceration within 1 year, and reincarceration within 3 years).
- The capital offender program was found to reduce by 53 percent the likelihood of capital offenders being arrested for a violent offense within a year of release.
- There was evidence that recidivism could be reduced in some manner by youth in all four of the specialized needs categories if they received at least one of the four specialized treatments.[24]

While the programs were not able to eliminate subsequent crime or significantly reduce the likelihood of future crime on all measures, as the TYC continues to improve its programs based on evolving benchmarks and from additional monitoring and evaluations, these programs should only get better.

All of the TYC treatment programs are designed to hold youth accountable for their own delinquent behavior. Their willingness to hold themselves accountable depends on their acquisition of sufficient internal control and prosocial skills for need gratification. Through accurate assessment, provision of a therapeutic environment, appropriate intervention, effective skills training, and meaningful community support, the TYC attempts to remove youth's justification for continued delinquency and provide the tools necessary for lasting behavior change.[25]

Several states have expressed an interest and obtained copies of the law that created the Progressive Sanctions guidelines and may introduce similar legislation. The TYC's Resocialization program and its capital offender program have received national and international recognition and have been visited by corrections professionals from several states and foreign countries.

Although the TYC programs show statistically significant reductions in recidivism, people should not have to be hurt or killed before these youth get help. Institutional programs are not only expensive, but they are also too late for many youth and their victims. Policy makers, funding bodies, and citizens need to focus on the front end—prevention—where the return on the dollar is the greatest and the chance to succeed is best.

ENDNOTES

1. John J. Dilulio, Jr., "Fill Churches, Not Jails: Youth Crime and 'Superpredators," statement before the United States Senate Subcommittee on Youth Violence, February 28, 1996. [Online] Available: John Dilulio Testimony <http://www.brook.edu/pa/hot/dilulio.htm>
2. John J. Dilulio, Jr., "Stop Crime Where It Starts," *The New York Times,* July 13, 1996. [Online] Available: John J. Dilulio, Jr. Oped. <http://www.brook.edu/pa/hot/arttoppics/diiulio.htm>
3. Juvenile Arrests 1995 (Office of Juvenile Justice and Delinquency Prevention, February 1997). [Online] <http:www.ncjrs.org/txtfiles/163813.txt>
4. Marvin E. Wolfgang, R. Figlio,& T. Sellin. *Delinquency in a Birth Cohort* (University of Chicago Press, 1972), and *From Boy to Man, From Delinquency to Crime* (University of Chicago Press, 1987).
5. Neal Shover, *Great Pretenders: Pursuits and Careers of Persistent Thieves* (Westview, 1996), pp. 178–179.
6. Peter Greenwood, K. Model, C. Hydell, & J. Chiesa. *Diverting Children from a Life of Crime: Measuring Costs and Benefits* (RAND Research Brief, May 1996).
7. *Preventing Crime, Saving Children: Monitoring, Mentoring, & Ministering* (Council on Crime in America, February 1997), p. 20.
8. Helene Raskin White, S. Hansell, & J. Brick, "Alcohol Use and Aggression Among Youth," *Alcohol Health and Research World,* 1993, pp. 144–150.
9. National Crime Prevention Council report (Gene O'Neal, editor), Washington, DC.
10. Cathy Spatz-Widom, "The Cycle of Violence," *National Institute of Justice Research in Brief,* October 1992.
11. Michael J. Mandel, P. Magnusson, J. E. Ellis, G. Degeorge, & K. L. Alexander, "The Economics of Crime." *Business Week,* December 13, 1993, pp. 72–85.
12. Mark A. Cohen, *The Monetary Value of Saving a High Risk Youth,* unpublished paper, Vanderbilt University, November 1995, p. 52.
13. Starting Points: Meeting the Needs of Our Youngest Children, The Report of the Carnegie Task Force on Meeting the Needs of Young Children, 1991.
14. Richard A. Mendel, "Prevention or Pork? A Hard-Headed Look at Youth-Oriented Anti-Crime Programs" (Article on the Internet) [Online] Headline: Prevention or Pork? <http://www.handsnet.org/ handsnet2/Articles/art.822520502.html>
15. *The High/Scope Perry Preschool Study through Age 27,* edited by L. J. Schweinhart and D. P. Weikart (Ypsilanti, MI: High/Scope Press, 1993).

16. Ibid.
17. Michelle Lea Cherne Anderson, "The High Juvenile Crime Rate: A Look at Mentoring as a Preventive Strategy." *Criminal Law Bulletin,* Vol. 30, No. 1 (1994), pp. 54–75.
18. *Preventing Crime, Saving Children: Monitoring, Mentoring, & Ministering,* p. 21.
19. John J. DiIulio, Jr. "Fill Churches, Not Jails: Youth Crime and 'Superpredators,'" Prepared statement submitted to the Senate Judiciary Committee February 28, 1996.
20. Anderson, "The High Juvenile Crime Rate."
21. Robert O. Dawson, *Texas Juvenile Law* (4th ed.), May 1996, p. 335.
22. Information courtesy of Research and Planning Department, Texas Youth Commission.
23. Linda Reyes, *Core Curriculum in Resocialization,* Texas Youth Commission, 1995.
24. Charles Jeffords and Scott McNitt, *Review of Treatment Programs* (Texas Youth Commission report, December 1996).
25. Linda Reyes, *Resocialization Approach* (Texas Youth Commission report, 1996).

CHAPTER 18

CHILDHOOD VICTIMIZATION: EARLY ADVERSITY, LATER PSYCHOPATHOLOGY*

Cathy Spatz-Widom

Childhood physical abuse, sexual abuse, and neglect have both immediate and long-term effects. Different types of abuse have a range of consequences for a child's later physical and psychological well-being, cognitive development, and behavior. But there is another side to the issue: Because these crimes often occur against a background of more chronic adversity, in families with multiple problems, it may not be reasonable to assume that before being victimized the child enjoyed "well-being." Parental alcoholism, drug problems, and other inadequate social and family functioning are among the factors affecting the child's response to victimization. Gender differences add to the complexity. Disentangling all these factors is difficult, as researchers have found.

Clearly, more needs to be learned about the long-term consequences of childhood victimization and the processes linking it to outcomes later in life. This chapter discusses what is known from earlier studies and also presents the findings of more recent research.[1]

CONSEQUENCES AND WHAT GIVES RISE TO THEM

Child maltreatment has physical, psychological, cognitive, and behavioral consequences. Physical consequences range from minor injuries to brain damage and even death. Psychological consequences range from chronic low self-

---

*This chapter first appeared in the *National Institute of Justice* Journal, January 2000, pp. 3–9. NCJ 180077.

The research described in this chapter was supported by grants from the U.S. Department of Justice, National Institute of Justice (86-IJ-CX-0033, 89-IJ-CX-0007, and 94-IJ-CX-0031), and the U.S. Department of Health and Human Services, National Institute on Alcohol Abuse and Alcoholism (AA09238) and National Institute of Mental Health (MH49467).

The author wishes to thank Patricia J. Glynn and Suzanne Luu for their help in the preparation of this chapter.

esteem, anxiety, and depression to substance abuse and other self-destructive behavior and suicide attempts. Cognitive effects include attention problems, learning disorders, and poor school performance. Behavioral consequences range from poor peer relations to physical aggression and antisocial behavior to violent behavior. These consequences are influenced by such factors as gender differences and the context in which victimization occurs.

Gender Differences

Differences between men and women in manifesting the effects of childhood victimization have received only limited attention from scholars. Some researchers, exploring how men and women differ in showing distress, have suggested there is some conformity to traditional notions of male and female behavior.[2] Some have noted that differences between men and women in manifesting the consequences of abuse may parallel gender differences in the way psychopathology is expressed. Thus, aggression (in males) and depression (in females) may express the same underlying distress, perhaps reflecting gender-specific strategies for maintaining self-esteem in the face of perceived rejection.[3]

Differences in the way boys and girls react to abuse have been reported in a few studies. In one, boys were found to have more externalizing and girls to have more internalizing symptoms.[4] An examination of depression and conduct disorders in sexually abused children revealed that girls were more likely than boys to develop depressive disorders and less likely to develop conduct disorders.[5]

Family and Community—The Context

The long-term impact of childhood trauma may depend on the larger family or community context.[6] In a study of children kidnapped and held underground, preexisting family pathology was identified as a factor in the victims' long-term adjustment. Four years after the incident, the children from troubled families were more maladjusted than those from healthier families.[7] The findings of other research were not as clear; rather, subsequent maladjustment was linked more to whether victimized children received appropriate play materials and maternal involvement than to whether they were abused.[8] Parental alcoholism is another contextual factor linked to child abuse[9] and to alcoholism later in life in the offspring.[10]

In the same way, practices of the community and the justice and social service systems may have long-term effects. Researchers have called attention to the ways in which children who are members of racial and ethnic minorities encounter discrimination, which diminishes their self-esteem and exacerbates the effects of victimization.[11] Elsewhere, researchers have suggested that victimized children are more likely to develop problem behavior in adolescence partly because of juvenile justice system practices that disproportionately label them as juvenile offenders and adjudicate them as such.[12]

Studying the Long-Term Effects in Depth

In a systematic study of the long-term consequences of early childhood abuse and neglect, the author is examining the experiences of more than 900 people

---

How the Study Is Being Conducted

The study is based on a "prospective cohorts design," so called because it follows a group of people (a cohort) for an extended period, enabling researchers to examine sequences of development over time. In the case of this study, the design helps sort out the effects of childhood victimization from other, potentially confounding effects traceable to different causes. The subjects were told they were part of a study of the characteristics of people who had grown up in the area in the late 1960s and early 1970s.

The cases of children who were abused and/or neglected were drawn from county juvenile and adult criminal court records in a metropolitan area of the Midwest between 1967 and 1971. The children were young—age 11 or younger—at the time of the incident.

The comparison group. To create a control group against which to compare the abused and neglected children, a group of children who had not been reported as victimized but who were similar in other respects to the study subjects were identified. To match children younger than school age at the time of the incident, county birth records were used. To match school-age children, records of more than 100 elementary schools were used.

Sample size and characteristics. The original sample consisted of 1575 people, of whom 908 were study subjects and 667 were controls. Of these, 1196 were interviewed for the study. Just under half the interviewees were female, about two-thirds were white, and the mean age at the time of the interview was 28.7. There were no differences between the abused/neglected group and the controls in gender, race/ethnicity, or age.

Some caveats. Because the study findings were based on court cases, they most likely represent the most extreme incidents of childhood abuse and neglect. What is more, they were processed before enactment of child abuse laws, when many cases went unreported and thus never came to the attention of the authorities. The findings are therefore not generalizable to unreported or unsubstantiated cases of abuse and neglect.

Because cases brought before the courts disproportionately represent people at the lower end of the socioeconomic spectrum, the study's subjects and controls were drawn from that stratum. For this reason, it would be inappropriate to generalize to cases involving people from other socioeconomic strata.

---

who were victimized in childhood. Begun in 1986, the study first focused on the extent to which, as the victims grew into adulthood, they became involved in delinquency and crime, including violent crime.[13] The current focus is on how their intellectual, behavioral, social, and psychological development was affected. This second phase began in 1989, more than 20 years after the victimization. (See "How the Study Is Being Conducted.")

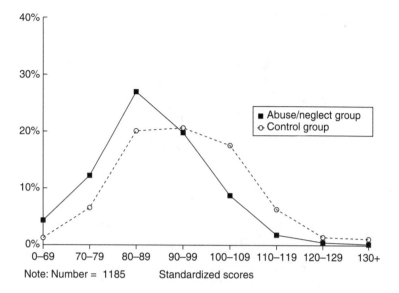

Figure 18.1 IQ scores—abused/neglected group and control group.

IQ scores are based on the Quick Test. See Ammons, R. B., and Ammons, C. H., "The Quick Test (QT): Provisional Manual," Psychological Reports 11 (1962): 11-162 (monograph supplement 7-VII).

Intellectual Performance

When tested at about age 29, the study subjects and the comparison group both scored at the lower levels of the IQ scale, with the majority in both groups below the standard mean of 100 (see Figure 18.1). Those who were abused or neglected, however, scored significantly lower than the comparison group, and these lower levels persisted irrespective of age, sex, race, and criminal history.

Overall, both groups averaged 11.5 years of schooling, but the abused and neglected group completed significantly fewer years. Thus, the childhood victims were less likely to have completed high school: Fewer than half, in contrast to two-thirds of the people in the control group.

Behavioral and Social Development

The occupations of both groups ranged from laborer through professional. In the sample overall, the median job level was that of semiskilled worker, with fewer than 7 percent in the two groups holding managerial or professional jobs (see Figure 18.2). The abused and neglected individuals had not done as well as the control group: Significantly more of them held menial and semiskilled

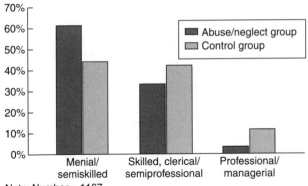

Figure 18.2 Occupational status—abused/neglected group and control group.
Occupational status was coded according to the Hollingshead Occupational Coding Index. See Hollingshead, A. B., "Four Factor Index of Social Class," New Haven, CT: Yale University Working Paper, 1975.

jobs. Conversely, a larger proportion of people in the control group held higher level jobs, ranging from skilled worker through professional.

Unemployment and underemployment disproportionately affected the abused and neglected group (see Figure 18.3). In both groups, more than one-fifth had been unemployed in the 5-year period before they were interviewed for the study. Not surprisingly, people in the control group were more likely than the victims to be employed. For underemployment, the story is similar: Significantly more victims of childhood abuse and neglect were underemployed in the 5 years before the interview than were controls.

The quality of interpersonal relations also is affected by childhood victimization, and here again there are no surprises (see Figure 18.4). Using marital stability as the measure of success, child abuse and neglect victims did not do as well as control group members. Almost 20 percent of the controls reported a stable marriage, compared to only 13 percent of the abuse and neglect group. Frequent divorce and separation were also more common among abused and neglected people.

As reported in previous research, childhood victimization also increases the risk of criminal behavior later in life-as measured by arrests for delinquency and adult criminality, including violent crime.[14] The current study confirms these findings. The odds of arrest for a juvenile offense were 1.9 times higher among abused and neglected individuals than among controls; for crimes committed as an adult, the odds were 1.6 times higher (see Table 18.1). Childhood abuse or neglect increases the risk of being arrested for violent crime, whether in the juvenile or adult years, as well as for crime in general. It is perhaps most important to note, however, that a substantial proportion of the abused and neglected children did not become delinquents or criminals.

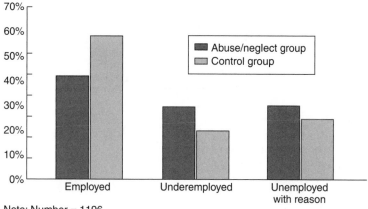

Note: Number = 1196

Figure 18.3 Employment history—abused/neglected group and control group
Employment history findings are based on a measure used in Robins, L. N., and D. A. Regier, eds., Psychiatric Disorders in America: The Epidemiological Catchment Area Surveys, New York: Free Press, 1991: 103.

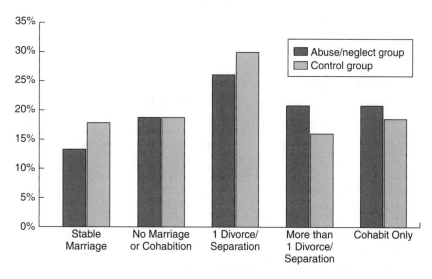

Figure 18.4 Marital history—abused/neglected group and control group

Table 18.1
Childhood Victimization and Later Criminality

	Abuse/Neglect Group (676)	Control Group (520)
	%	%
Arrest as juvenile	31.2**	19.0
Arrest as adult	48.4**	36.2
Arrest as juvenile or adult for any crime	56.5**	42.5
Arrest as juvenile or adult for any violent crime	21.0*	15.6

*$p \le .05$.

**$p \le .001$.

Psychological and Emotional Fallout

Suicide attempts, diagnosis of antisocial personality disorder, and alcohol abuse and/or dependence were some of the measures of psychopathology. The abused and neglected individuals were significantly more likely than the controls to have attempted suicide and to have met the criteria for antisocial personality disorder (see Table 18.2), findings irrespective of age, sex, race, and criminal history. High rates of alcohol abuse were found in both groups (more than 50 percent in each), although the abuse/neglect victims were not at greater risk than the controls, a finding that departs from other research but that methodological differences might explain.[15]

Table 18.2
Childhood Victimization and Later Psychopathology

	Abuse/Neglect Group (676)	Control Group (520)
	%	%
Suicide attempt	18.8**	7.7
Antisocial personality disorder	18.4**	11.2
Alcohol abuse/dependence	54.5**	51.0

*$p \le .05$.

**$p \le .001$.

Note: Numbers in parentheses are numbers of cases.

Diagnosis of antisocial personality disorder and alcohol abuse/dependence was determined by using the National Institute of Mental Health DID-III-R diagnostic interview.

Table 18.3

Childhood Victimization and Later Psychopathology, by Gender

	Abuse/Neglect Group (676)	Control Group (520)
	%	%
Females	(338)	(224)
Suicide attempt	24.3***	8.6
Antisocial personality disorder	9.8*	4.9
Alcohol abuse/dependence	43.8**	32.8
Males	(338)	(276)
Suicide attempt	13.4**	6.9
Antisocial personality disorder	27.0**	16.7
Alcohol abuse/dependence	64.4	67.0

*$p \leq .05$.

**$p \leq .01$.

***$p \leq .001$.

Note: Numbers in parentheses are numbers of cases.

Diagnosis of antisocial personality disorder and alcohol abuse/dependence was determined by using the National Institute of Mental Health DID-III-R diagnostic interview.

As other research has shown, gender can affect the development of psychopathology in abused and neglected children later in life. The current study revealed some of these gender-based differences. Females abused and neglected in childhood were more likely than controls to attempt suicide, to abuse alcohol or be dependent on it, or to suffer from an antisocial personality disorder. Like females, male victims were found at greater risk than controls of attempting suicide and developing an antisocial personality disorder, but they were not at greater risk of developing alcohol problems (see Table 18.3).

The findings of males' higher risk for antisocial personality disorder and females' higher risk for alcohol problems parallel previous research revealing conformity to gender roles. However, the finding that females are, like males, at risk for antisocial personality disorder (as well as criminal behavior)[16] may call for reconsidering the assumptions of externalizing and internalizing as the respective pathways of male and female response.

The Context of Victimization

The findings confirmed earlier research identifying context as a factor influencing the long-term outcome for victims. This became evident in analyzing the relationships among childhood victimization, having a parent who had been arrested, and the likelihood of the offspring's developing antisocial

Table 18.4

Antisocial Personality Disorder in Offspring—Relation to Parental Criminality

	Abuse/Neglect Group	Control Group	Row Significance
	%	%	
Either parent arrested	21.9 (365)	18.8 (170)	n.s.
Neither parent arrested	14.2 (365)	7.4 (350)	**
Column significance	*	**	

*$p \leq .05$.

**$p \leq .001$.

n.s. = not statistically significant.

Note: Numbers in parentheses are numbers of cases.

Diagnosis of antisocial personality disorder and alcohol abuse/dependence were determined by using the National Institute of Mental Health DID-III-R diagnostic interview.

personality disorder. The analysis revealed that among people who had a parent with a history of arrest, abuse or neglect in childhood did not increase the likelihood of their developing an antisocial personality disorder (see Table 18.4).

However, where there was no parental criminality, being abused and/or neglected did increase the risk for this disorder. This complicates attempts to understand the consequences of childhood victimization and also suggests multiple factors in the development of antisocial personality disorder.

A different picture and set of relationships were found for alcohol abuse. When parental alcohol/drug abuse, childhood victimization, and subsequent alcohol problems in offspring were analyzed, the parents' substance abuse problem emerged as the critical factor in the development of the same problem in the children, and this held true whether or not the child had been victimized (see Table 18.5). The study also showed that, as a group, the children who were abused or neglected were no more likely than controls to develop alcohol problems, whether or not the parent had the same problem.

The strong influence of parental characteristics on the offspring, regardless of victimization, warrants more careful consideration but is consistent with earlier literature on the genetic transmission of alcoholism.

Multiple Mechanisms

The study generated more and more systematic evidence that the consequences of childhood victimization extend well beyond childhood and adolescence, persisting into young adulthood. Such victimization affects many functions later in life, and what was revealed in this study most likely represents only the tip of the iceberg, which further research could bring to light. On the other hand, some expected outcomes (such as increased risk for alcohol

Table 18.5

Antisocial Personality Disorder in Offspring—Relation to Parental Alcohol/Drug Problems

	Abuse/Neglect Group	*Control Group*	*Row Significance*
	%	%	
Either parent alcohol/drug problem	63.2 (389)	56.6 (196)	n.s.
Neither parent alcohol/drug problem	42.6 (284)	47.5 (324)	
Column significance	*	**	n.s.

*$^*p \leq .05.$

*$^{**}p \leq .001.$

n.s. = not statistically significant.

Note: Numbers in parenthesis are numbers of cases.

Diagnosis of antisocial personality disorder and alcohol abuse/dependence were determined by using the National Institute of Mental Health DID-III-R diagnostic interview.

problems in abused and neglected children) did not materialize, raising questions for further study.

Disentangling the Pathways

One of the difficulties in assessing risk of negative consequences is sorting out the children's multiple problems and those of their parents. As previous research has shown, adverse effects interact, so that the combined effects of two types of problems may be greater than their sum.[17] Whether this interaction effect applies to childhood victimization is not known, although it is likely.

This study has not yet tried to distinguish among the many mechanisms by which childhood victimization affects development and psychopathology. When it comes to the influence of contextual factors, children may simply be modeling their parents' behavior. But it also is possible that abuse or neglect may produce immediate effects that then irremediably affect subsequent development, which in turn may affect still later outcomes.

Direct and Indirect Pathways

Some pathways may be direct, persisting into adulthood. Abused and neglected children may show aggressiveness and behavior problems in childhood, delinquency in adolescence, and antisocial and criminal behavior in adulthood. It also is likely that this path leads to abusive behavior in the home, manifested in spouse or child abuse. In other instances there may be a delayed reaction, occurring years later.

Abuse or neglect may encourage certain dysfunctional ways of coping. An example is impulsive behavior that in turn gives rise to deficiencies in problem solving or in school performance, less than adequate functioning on the job, or antisocial personality disorder. Adaptations that might serve well at one stage of development may no longer do so at a later stage, placing the person at risk for further unfavorable situations or subsequent victimization that may trigger psychopathology.

Some early, adverse experiences may be indirect, creating byproducts. They may change the environment or the family situation, which in turn may predispose a person to problem behavior. They also may expose the child to further harmful experiences. In this way, the consequences may be due not so much to the abuse or neglect but to the chain of events it triggers.

No doubt there are many other mechanisms by which abuse and neglect affect a child. Hopefully, future models that explain long-term consequences will examine some of them, because finding a single mechanism that explains all cases of abuse and neglect is highly unlikely.

ENDNOTES

1. This chapter summarizes the author's "Childhood Victimization: Early Adversity and Subsequent Psychopathology;" in *Adversity, Stress, and Psychopathology,* ed. B. P. Dohrenwend, New York: Oxford University Press, 1998: 81–95.

2. Downey, G., et al., "Maltreatment and Childhood Depression" in *Handbook of Depression in Children,* ed. W. M. Reynolds and H. F. Johnson, New York: Plenum, 1994; Dohrenwend, B. P., and B. S. Dohrenwend, "Sex Differences in Psychiatric Disorders," *American Journal of Sociology* 81 (1976): 1447–1454; Horwitz, A.V., and H. R. White, "Gender Role Orientations and Styles of Pathology among Adolescents" *Journal of Health and Social Behavior* 28 (1987): 158–170; and Widom, C. S., "Sex Roles, Criminality, and Psychopathology" in *Sex Roles and Psychopathology,* ed. C. S. Widom, New York: Plenum, 1984: 87–213.

3. Downey et al., "Maltreatment and Childhood Depression."

4. Friedrich, W. H., A. J. Urquiza, and R. L. Beilke, "Behavior Problems in Sexually Abused Young Children," *Journal of Pediatric Psychology* 11 (1986): 47–57.

5. Livingston, R., "Sexually and Physically Abused Children," *Journal of the American Academy of Child and Adolescent Psychiatry* 26 (1987): 413–415.

6. Briere, J., and M. Runtz, "Symptomatology Associated with Childhood Sexual Victimization in a Nonclinical Adult Sample," *Child Abuse and Neglect* 12 (1988): 51–60; Harris, T., G. W. Brown, and A. Bifulco, "Loss of Parent in Childhood and Adult Psychiatric Disorder: A Tentative Overall Model," *Development and Psychopathology* (1990): 311–328; Terr, L. A., "Chowchilla Revisited: The Effects of Psychiatric Trauma Four Years after a School-Bus Kidnaping," *American Journal of Psychiatry* 140 (1983): 1543–1550.

7. Terr, "Chowchilla Revisited."

8. Gibbin, P. T., R. H. Starr, and S. W. Agronow, "Affective Behavior of Abused and Controlled Children: Comparison of Parent-Child Interactions and the Influence of Home Environment Variables," *Journal of Genetic Psychology* 144 (1984): 69–82.

9. Famularo, R., et al., "Alcoholism and Severe Child Maltreatment," *American Journal of Orthopsychiatry* 56 (1986): 481–485; Reider, E. E., et al., "Alcohol Involvement and Violence toward Children Among High-Risk Families," Paper presented at the annual meeting of the American Psychological Association, New Orleans, Louisiana, August 11–15, 1989.

10. Goodwin, D.W., et al., "Alcohol Problems in Adoptees Raised Apart from Alcoholic Biological Parents," *Archives of General Psychiatry* 28 (1973): 238–243; Goodwin, D.W., et al., "Alcoholism and Depression in Adopted-Out Daughters of Alcoholics," *Archives of General Psychiatry* 34 (1977): 751–755; Cloninger, C. R., et al., "Psychopathology in Adopted-Out Children of Alcoholics: The Stockholm Adoption Study" in *Recent Developments in Alcoholism*, Vol. 3, M. Galanter, ed., New York: Plenum, 1985.

11. Wyatt, G. E., "Sexual Abuse of Ethnic Minority Children: Identifying Dimensions of Victimization," *Professional Psychology: Research and Practice* 21 (1990): 338–343.

12. Smith, C. P., D. J. Berkman, and W. M. Fraser, *A Preliminary National Assessment of Child Abuse and Neglect and the Juvenile Justice System: The Shadows of Distress*, Washington, D.C.: U.S. Department of Justice: Office of Juvenile Justice and Delinquency Prevention, 1980.

13. Widom, C. S., "The Cycle of Violence," *Science* 244 (1989): 160–166.

14. These findings, based on the study of 1196 of the original 1575 subjects (the 908 abuse/neglect victims plus the 667 in the control group) should not be confused with findings from studies published previously (Widom, "Cycle of Violence," and Maxfield, M. G., and C. S. Widom, "The Cycle of Violence: Revisited Six Years Later," *Archives of Pediatrics and Adolescent Medicine* 150 (1996): 390–395, which report on the entire original sample of 1575.

15. See Widom, C. S., T. Ireland, and P. J. Glynn, "Alcohol Abuse in Abused and Neglected Children Followed-Up: Are They at Increased Risk?" *Journal of Studies on Alcohol* 56 (1995): 207–217.

16. These findings are not shown here. See Maxfield and Widom, "The Cycle of Violence: Revisited."

17. Rutter, M., "Protective Factors in Children's Response to Stress and Disadvantage," in *Primary Prevention of Psychopathology: Social Competence in Children*, Vol. 3, ed. M. V. Kent and J. E. Rolf, Hanover, NH: New England Press, 1979: 49–74.

VIOLENCE BY YOUNG PEOPLE: WHY THE DEADLY NEXUS?*

Alfred Blumstein

INTRODUCTION

Despite evidence that aggregate rates of crime have been leveling off or even declining in the past two decades,[1] there continues to be widespread concern about the issue on the part of policymakers and the public. Indeed, among all issues, crime may be the one perceived by Americans as most pressing.[2] When aggregate crime data are broken down by certain demographic and other variables, however, the otherwise flat trend shows major distinctions, indicating that the concern is understandable. Although gender and race account for much of the differences in crime rates, age is the variable whose effect has been changing significantly in recent years. And while many of the national trends have remained strikingly flat, there has been some dramatic change in violent crime committed by young people.

THE RISE IN JUVENILE CRIME

Data gathered from a variety of sources indicate that after a period of relative stability in the rates of juvenile crime, there was a major turning point in about 1985. Then, within the next seven years, the rate of homicides committed by young people, the number of homicides they committed with guns, and the arrest rate of nonwhite juveniles for drug offenses all doubled. The sudden upward surge in all three of these indicators, beginning with the increased drug trafficking of the mid-1980s, is the topic of this chapter.

Particularly relevant to future crime, and to consideration of prevention and intervention strategies, is the size of the current teenage population. The age cohort responsible for much of the recent youth violence is the smallest it

---

*This chapter originally appeared in *National Institute of Justice Journal*, August 1995, Issue 229, pp. 2–9.

has been in recent years. By contrast, the cohort of children ages 5 to 15, who will be moving into the crime-prone ages in the near future, is larger.

This suggests that if current age-specific rates do not decline, planning needs to begin now to address the increase in crime likely to occur as this group grows older.

THE AGE FACTOR

That young people commit crime at a high rate is no revelation. Age is so fundamental to crime rates that its relationship to offending is usually designated as the "age-crime curve." This curve, which for individuals typically peaks in the late teen years, highlights the tendency for crime to be committed during an offender's younger years and to decline as age advances.

For example, figures on rates of robbery and burglary, broken down by age, indicate that for both these crimes, the peak age of offending has been about 17, after which there is a rapid decline as the offender gets older. For burglary, the rate falls to half the peak by age 21, whereas the falloff for robbery is somewhat slower, reaching half the peak rate by age 25. The age-specific patterns are about the same for the most recent year data are available (1992) as they were in 1985.

Young People and Murder

The age-specific patterns for murder present quite a different pattern; the trends for this crime have changed appreciably in the past decade. First, the peak is much flatter. For a fairly long period—1965 to 1985—the age at which the murder rate was highest remained fairly stable, with a flat peak covering ages 18 to 24. In other words, during this 20-year period, people in this age group were the most likely to commit murder, and it was in the age group of the mid-30s that the rate dropped to half the peak. Then, in 1985, an abrupt change began to take place, with the murder rate moving to a sharp peak at age 18 instead of the more traditional flat peak covering the entire 18-to-24 age group (see Figure 19.1).

The change over time in the age-specific murder rate is striking, especially for the peak ages 18 to 24 (see Figure 19.2). Following an initial increase from 1965 to 1970, the rate remained stable (and about the same for all ages in this group) for about 15 years—from 1970 through 1985. Among people at the older end of this age spectrum—the 24-year-olds—there has been no strong trend since 1970. But beginning shortly around 1985, murder by people under 24 increased, with the rate of increase inversely related to age. For people age 18, the increase was dramatic—it more than doubled.

For people at all ages under age 18, the increase was equally dramatic—it too more than doubled. For 16-year-olds, for example, whose murder rate before 1985 was consistently about half that of the 18-to-24 peak rate, the increase between 1985 and 1992 was 138 percent. By contrast, for ages older than 24, there has been no growth, and even a decline for ages 30 and above.

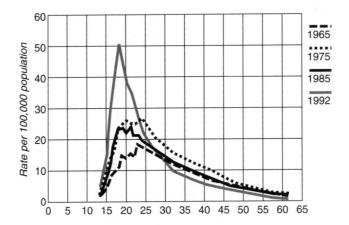

Figure 19.1 Age-specific murder rate: 1965–1992.
Source: Age-Specific Arrest Rates and Race-Specific Arrest Rates for Selected Offenses, 1965–1992. Uniform Crime Reporting Program, Federal Bureau of Investigation, Washington, DC: December 1993.

"Excess" Murders Committed by Young People

The increase in murder by very young people after 1985 has not at all been matched by increases among the older groups (ages 24 and over). Among them murder rates have even declined. Thus, much of the general increase in

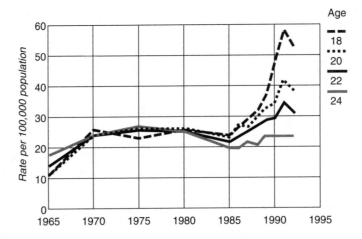

Figure 19.2 Trends in age-specific murder rate: Trends for individual peak ages
Source: Age-Specific Arrest Rates and Race-Specific Arrest Rates for Selected Offenses, 1965–1992. Uniform Crime Reporting Program, Federal Bureau of Investigation, Washington, DC: December 1993.

the aggregate homicide rate (accounting for all ages) in the late 1980s is attributable to the spurt in the murder rate by young people that began in 1985.

One can calculate the "excess" murders attributable to the rise in murder by young people over and above the average rate that prevailed for each of the young ages in the period 1970–1985—in other words, the number of murders that would not have been committed had the youth murder rate remained at its earlier, flat average. For the eight ages, 15 through 22, in the 7 years of 1986 through 1992, the number of "excess" murders is estimated to be 18,600. The number is a significant component of the overall number for that period; it accounts for 12.1 percent of the annual average of about 22,000 murders in those years.

RACE

There are important race differences in involvement in murder, both in the rate itself and the change since 1985. Among African American males ages 14 to 17, murder rates have been about four to five times higher than among white males of the same age group, although for both groups the rates had remained fairly stable from the mid-1970s until the mid-1980s (see Figure 19.3). Then, beginning about 1985, the rates rose for both groups, though the growth rate was much faster among blacks. For white males in this age group, their annual rate for murder was 8.1 per 100,000 in the period 1976 to 1987, after which it almost doubled in the next four years (from 7.6 in 1987 to 13.6 in 1991). In

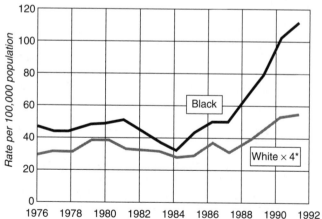

*This rate is scaled up by a factor of 4 to put it on a scale comparable to that of blacks.

Figure 19.3 Homicide arrest rate of 14–17-year-old males.

Source: The data were generated by Glenn Pierce and James Fox from the FBI's Supplementary Homicide Reports, which are based on reports of individual homicides submitted by the nation's police departments.

those four years, the arrest rate for murder by black males in this age group rose even faster, more than doubling (from 50.4 to 111.8 per 100,000).

FACTORS GENERATING FEAR

Strangers

Persistent fear of crime is not caused by reviewing the aggregate rate of homicide and noting the absence of a trend. Rather, distinctive incidents or changing patterns of crime stimulate the anxiety levels. In particular, because young people are generally perceived to be more reckless than their elders, the growth in youth homicide conveys a sense that their killing is random. This is confirmed by the greater extent to which homicide by the young is committed against strangers. When victims seem to be selected at random, vulnerability is heightened: Anyone can be a target. For example, the FBI's Supplementary Homicide Report for 1991 noted that 28 percent of the homicides committed by people under 25 were against strangers, whereas only 18 percent of those committed by offenders age 25 and above were against strangers.

Guns

Also intensifying the fear of crime is the increasing involvement of guns in homicides committed by young people. This factor generates fear because of the recognition that young people are less likely to exercise the restraint necessary to handle dangerous weapons, particularly rapid-fire assault weapons. Data on the use of weapons in homicide reflect the same patterns described above: After a period of stability came an abrupt increase in the mid-1980s. Thus, from 1976 to 1985, a very steady average (59 percent) of homicides committed by juveniles involved a gun. Beginning in 1985, there was steady growth in the use of guns by juveniles in committing murder, leading to a doubling in the number of juvenile murders committed with guns, with no shift in the number of nongun homicides (see Figure 19.4).

JUVENILE VIOLENCE AND THE DRUG–CRIME CONNECTION

The public also has a vague sense of a link between the growth in juvenile violence and drugs. In part, this derives from recognition that, especially in the past decade, a major factor affecting many aspects of criminal behavior has been the illicit drug industry and its consequences. Beyond the offenses of drug sale or drug possession, the drug-crime link has been described as taking several forms:

- Pharmacologically/psychologically driven crime, induced by the properties of the drug. (The most widely recognized connection is between alcohol and the violence it induces.)
- Economic/compulsive crimes, committed by drug users to support their habit.

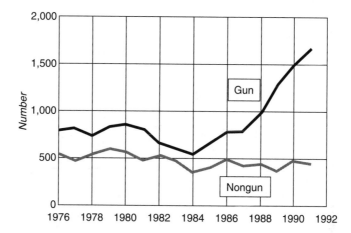

Figure 19.4   Number of gun and nongun homicides:
Juvenile offenders (ages 10–17).

*Source: The data were generated by Glenn Pierce and James Fox from
the FBI's Supplementary Homicide Reports, which are based on reports
of individual homicides submitted by the nation's police departments.*

- Systemic crime, which includes the crimes committed as part of the
  regular means of doing business in the illicit drug industry. (An example is the violence used to resolve disputes between competing
  traffickers.)[3]

There is a fourth, still broader connection of drugs to crime: the community disorganization effect of the illicit drug industry and its operations in the
larger community. This effect includes the manner by which the norms and
behaviors of the industry, which can become a significant activity in some
communities, influence the behavior of people who themselves have no direct
connection to drug trafficking. The effect could, for example, include the influence on others of the widespread possession of guns by drug sellers. When
guns are so prevalent, people in the community might arm themselves, perhaps for self-defense, perhaps to settle disputes that have nothing to do with
drugs, or perhaps just to gain respect. In other words, once guns are used
within the illicit drug market, they become more prevalent in the larger community and used for purposes unrelated to buying and selling drugs. Hence,
they add to community disorganization well beyond what happens as a direct
result of the drug industry.

Juveniles and Illicit Drug Marketing

Drug arrest rates, especially for nonwhites, began to move upward in the early
1980s and then accelerated appreciably after 1985 as the distribution of crack
cocaine became widespread, particularly in inner city areas. Among nonwhite

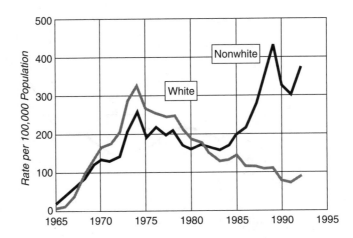

Figure 19.5 Drug arrest rate—juveniles.

Source: Age-Specific Arrest Rates and Race-Specific Arrest Rates for Selected Offenses, 1965–1992. Uniform Crime Reporting Program, Federal Bureau of Investigation, Washington, DC: December 1993.

juveniles, drug arrest rates were lower than those of whites in the 1970s and were also fairly constant, until they began a very rapid acceleration until about 1985, doubling by 1989. This pattern contrasted with that of the 1960s and 1970s, when the rate at which young whites were arrested for drug-related offenses followed the pattern of whites, but stayed somewhat low. The arrest rate of whites then peaked in 1974 and then began a steady decline (see Figure 19.5.)

The acceleration in drug arrests of young nonwhites (primarily blacks) reflected a major recruitment of sellers to market crack, which required many more street transactions. The racial differences in arrest rates indicate the extent to which drug enforcement has focused on blacks more than on whites. The black–white difference is magnified also because black drug sellers tend much more often to operate in the street, where they are vulnerable to arrest, whereas white sellers are much more likely to operate indoors. The amenability of inner city nonwhite juveniles to recruitment into the illicit drug industry was undoubtedly enhanced by their pessimism—or perhaps even hopelessness—as they weighed the diminishing opportunities available to them in the legitimate economy.

A PROPOSED HYPOTHESIS

This striking array of changes in juvenile crime since 1985—a doubling of the homicide rate, a doubling of the number of homicides committed with guns, and a doubling of the arrest rate of nonwhites for drug offenses, all after a period of relative stability in these rates—cries out for an explanation that will link them all together. The explanation that seems most reasonable can be traced to the rapid growth of the crack markets in the mid-1980s. To service that growth, juveniles were recruited, they were armed with the guns that are standard tools of the drug trade, and these guns then were diffused into the larger community of juveniles.

Recruitment

The process starts with the illicit drug industry, which recruits juveniles partly because they work more cheaply than adults, partly because the sanctions they face are less severe than those imposed by the adult criminal justice system and partly because they tend to be daring and willing to take risks that more mature adults would eschew. The plight of many urban black juveniles, many of whom see no other comparably satisfactory route to economic sustenance, makes them particularly vulnerable to the lure of the profits of the drug industry. The growth in the drug arrest rate of nonwhite juveniles is evidence of this recruitment.

Guns as a Means of Self-Protection

These juvenile recruits, like all participants in the illicit drug industry, are very likely to carry guns for self-protection, largely because in that industry guns are a major instrument for dispute resolution as well as self-defense. People involved in the drug industry are likely to be carrying a considerable amount of valuable product—money or drugs—and are not likely to be able to call on the police if they are robbed.

The Diffusion of Guns

Since a considerable number of juveniles can be involved in the drug industry in communities where the drug market is active, and since juveniles are tightly "networked," at school or on the street, other juveniles are also likely to arm themselves. Again, the reason is a mixture of self-protection and status seeking. Thus begins an escalation: As more guns appear in the community, the incentive for any single individual to arm himself increases, and so a local "arms race" develops.

The Violent Outcome

The recklessness and bravado that often characterize teenage behavior, combined with their lack of skill in settling disputes other than through physical force, transform what once would have been fist fights with outcomes no more serious than a bloody nose into shootings with much more lethal consequences because guns are present.

This sequence can be exacerbated by the socialization problems associated with extreme poverty, the high proportion of single-parent households, educational failures, and the pervasive sense of hopelessness about one's economic situation.

It does appear, however, that by the time these young people move beyond their early twenties, they develop a measure of prudence. It may be that the diffusion process is far slower because adults are less tightly networked and less prone to emulate each other's behavior. Even within the drug industry, they appear to act more cautiously when they are armed, and to otherwise display greater restraint. However, there is some concern that the restraint that normally comes with age may not materialize in this particular age group. It is possible that a cohort effect may be occurring, with the possibility that the 18-year-olds currently responsible for the higher homicide rates may continue their recklessness as they get older. This possibility needs to be monitored and explored.

Evidence of the Diffusion

The possibility that guns are diffused from drug markets to the larger community through juvenile recruits is further confirmed by the pattern of white and nonwhite arrests for murder. Since 1980, the murder arrest rates for adults, both white and nonwhite, have followed the same downward trend, and have shown no growth since 1985 (see Figure 19.6). By contrast, among juveniles the murder arrest rates for whites and nonwhites have grown markedly between 1985 and 1992. The increase among nonwhite juveniles was 123 percent (from 7.1 to 15.8 per 100,000). Among white juveniles the murder arrest rate also increased markedly, although by a lesser amount—80 percent (from 1.5 to 2.7 per 100,000) (see Figure 19.7).

What is notable in these figures is that the murder rate rose among white as well as nonwhite juveniles since 1985, at a time when the drug arrest rate for nonwhites alone began to climb. Thus, the apparent absence of significant involvement of white juveniles in the drug markets during this time has not

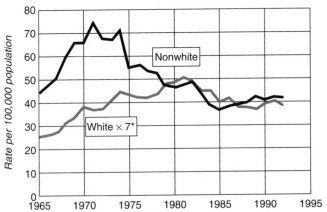

*This rate is scaled up by a factor of 7 to put it on a scale comparable to that of blacks.

Figure 19.6   Murder arrest rate—adults.
Source: Age-Specific Arrest Rates and Race-Specific Arrest Rates for Selected Offenses, 1965-1992. Uniform Crime Reporting Program, Federal Bureau of Investigation, Washington, DC: December 1993.

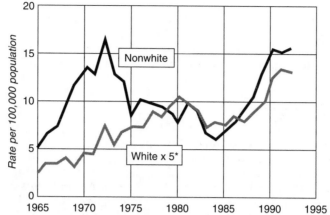

Figure 19.7 Murder arrest rate—Juveniles.
Source: Age-Specific Arrest Rates and Race-Specific Arrest Rates for Selected Offenses, 1965–1992. Uniform Crime Reporting Program, Federal Bureau of Investigation, Washington, DC: December 1993.

insulated them from the growth of their involvement in homicide, possibly through the suggested process of the diffusion of guns from drug sellers into the larger community.

When the arrest trends of young nonwhites for homicide and drug offenses are compared (Figure 19.8), it is evident that both rates climbed

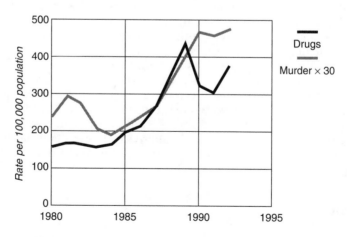

Figure 19.8 Nonwhite juvenile murder/drug arrest rates.
Source: Age-Specific Arrest Rates and Race-Specific Arrest Rates for Selected Offenses, 1965–1992. Uniform Crime Reporting Program, Federal Bureau of Investigation, Washington, DC: December 1993.

together from 1985 through 1989, suggesting the relationship between the two. The drug arrest rate declined somewhat after 1989. There was a flattening out, but no corresponding decline in the murder arrest rate. In other words, the continued high rate of murder arrests seems to demonstrate that once guns are diffused into the community, they are much more difficult to purge.

REVERSING THE TRENDS

If the explanation outlined above is at all valid, it implies the need for solutions, some immediate and others longer range. One immediate approach would involve aggressive steps to confiscate guns from juveniles carrying them on the street. Laws permitting confiscation of guns from juveniles are almost universal, but they require more active and skillful enforcement. The need is particularly urgent in communities where homicide rates have risen dramatically, probably coincident with the appearance of drug markets. James Q. Wilson has made some concrete proposals for pursuing such efforts, including better devices for detecting guns from a distance.[4]

Also, in contrast to the intense pursuit of drug markets by law enforcement over the past 15 years, very little attention has been paid to the illegal gun markets through which guns are distributed to juveniles. This issue clearly needs much greater attention. More complex in its implications for policy are the links among the magnitude of the criminal drug market, the use of guns in drug markets, and the juvenile homicide rate—the subject of this discussion. The presence of guns in drug markets results from the fact that these markets are criminalized. This does not, of course, warrant an immediate call for legalization of drugs. Any policy in the broad spectrum between full prohibition and full legalization involves carefully weighing the costs of criminalization (of which homicide is but one) against the probable consequences of greater use of dangerous drugs. The complexity of this issue prohibits its discussion here. However, if the diffusion hypothesis is correct, the impact on juvenile homicide represents one component of the cost of the current policy.

To the extent that efforts to diminish the size of the illegal drug market could be pursued (through greater investment in treatment, more effective prevention, or other health care initiatives responsive to addicts' needs), then although illegal markets would continue, the demand for drugs and the volume of drugs sold in the markets would diminish. A cost-benefit comparison of current policies and possible alternatives is needed but has yet to be made. Perhaps concern about the recent rise in the juvenile homicide rate might lend urgency to the issue.[5]

THE AUTHOR

Alfred Blumstein, Ph.D., is J. Erik Jonsson University Professor of Urban Systems and Operations Research at Carnegie Mellon University's H. John Heinz III School of Public Policy and Management.

The research reported in this chapter is being extended with the aid of an NIJ grant on juvenile violence and its relationship to drug markets. Recently,

Dr. Blumstein led a seminar about this research at NIJ; a 60-minute videotape of his presentation and responses to audience questions is available for $19.00 ($24.00 outside the United States) from the National Criminal Justice Reference Service, PO Box 6000, Rockville, MD 20849-6000; telephone 800-851-3420 or e-mail askncjrs@aspensys.com. Ask for NCJ 152235.

ENDNOTES

1. *Criminal Victimization in the United States: 1973–92 Trends—A National Crime Victimization Survey Report*, Washington, DC: U.S. Department of Justice, Bureau of Justice Statistics, July 1994: 1. In the period 1973–1992, the highest rate of violent victimization was 35.3 per 1000 persons, reported in 1981. That number fell until 1986, then started to climb, reaching 32.1 in 1992 (pp. 1, 9). National Crime Victim Survey data do reveal a 5.6 percent increase between 1992 and 1993 in victimization for violent crime, principally because of a rise in attempted (as opposed to completed) assaults. "Crime Rate Essentially Unchanged Last Year," press release, U.S. Department of Justice, Bureau of Justice Statistics, October 30, 1994. Homicide rates show a flat trend similar to that for violent victimization (homicide figures are not included in the victimization survey). The homicide rate per 100,000 people was 9.5 in 1993, but the historical high occurred in 1980, when the rate was 10.2. *Crime in the United States, 1993: Uniform Crime Reports*, Washington, DC: U.S. Department of Justice, Federal Bureau of Investigation, December 4, 1994: 13, 283.
2. *A New York Times*/CBS nationwide poll reported early in 1994 indicated crime or violence as the leading issue (cited by 19 percent of respondents), followed by health care—the subject of considerable public discussion at the time—with 15 percent. See Richard L. Berke, "Crime Joins Economic Issues as Leading Worry, Poll Says," *New York Times*, January 23, 1994.
3. This taxonomy of the drug-crime connection was developed by Paul Goldstein in "The Drug/Violence Nexus: A Tripartite Conceptual Framework," *Journal of Drug Issues* 15 (1985): 493–506.
4. James Q. Wilson, "Just Take the Guns Away," *New York Times*, March 20, 1994. National Institute of Justice is now sponsoring research to aid in detecting concealed weapons.
5. In my presidential address to the American Society of Criminology in November 1992, I suggested proposing establishment of a Presidential Commission to examine the costs and benefits of our current zero-tolerance policy and to contrast that with various possible alternatives. Such an assessment would require major research support from the National Academy of Sciences. (See Alfred Blumstein, "Making Rationality Relevant," *Criminology* 30: 1–16.)

SECTION 6

TERRORISM, HATE GROUPS, AND INSTITUTIONAL VIOLENCE

The tragic acts of September 11, 2001 awoke in the American public an awareness of the appalling consequences of terrorism. There was an initial inclination to include in this section chapters that dealt solely with domestic and international terrorism. This was especially strong when the authors visited the site of the Twin Towers. The site was a strong reminder of the evil that lurks in terrorism. The attempt to understand the mind and mentality of the domestic terrorist is no easy task regardless of the race or nationality of the offender. But on further reflection, we decided that we must examine terrorism in all its manifestations, including hate groups and institutional violence.

We have included in this section five chapters. Each examines a different type of personal violence, each with a varied focus, and each with conclusions and recommendations that are important and relevant.

The first chapter, "Individual and Institutional Determinants of Police Force: An Examination of Threat Presentation," examines the use of violent force by the police in the performance of their duties. Utilizing a multifaceted approach in analyzing factors that may contribute to the use of physical force, and in some cases violence, in carrying out of law enforcement duties, the authors identify some of these factors and offer recommendations for police and interested others in dealing with this issue.

The next chapter, "Criminalizing Hate: An Empirical Assessment," is a classic in the analysis of hate. It examines hate crimes in Florida and then draws conclusions about the extent of hate, the many examples of hate, indicators of hate and their motivations, and finally a profile of what is a hate crime. While the typical hate crime may vary with time and location, the author draws on his experience and tells the reader what a typical hate crime is. The author calls for refining the manner in which hate crimes are reported and warns that we should be cognizant of new groups that will emerge as potential victims of those who commit such acts of violence.

The third chapter deals with the alleged fact that hate crimes are not new in the United States. Petrosino offers evidence that hate crimes have extended throughout America's young history. Examining hate crimes in terms of race, the manner in which hate crimes are viewed by society and those in authority, and other societal variances, "Connecting the Past to the Future: Hate Crimes in America" suggests that those who commit hate crimes may not be as variant as once thought and may even be seen as a form of domestic terrorism.

John Lewis's chapter, "Fighting Terrorism in the Twenty-First Century," is timely in light of the numerable acts of terrorism occurring throughout the world today. Identifying terrorist groups worldwide, and with a recitation of various acts of terrorism, the author identifies manners in which certain groups, including our own government, have gone about planning to combat terrorism successfully. The author believes that the Federal Bureau of Investigation (FBI) must take a lead in a prevention program to combat this serious and deadly problem.

The last chapter, "Religious Movements and Violence: Incidents, Causes, and Policy Implications," offers an idea that is strangely ignored by many: There is often a relationship between religion and violence. This is apparent in the current state of affairs. Recognizing this relationship, social scientists are becoming more cognizant of the relationships and are studying ways and means to combat this social concern. Bromley and Dawson discuss some of the popular misconceptions about religious movements and violence (For example, cults are remarkably similar and can be identified by a set of common characteristics). Discussing the David Koresh case, as well as the Solar Temple and Heaven's Gate scenarios, the authors call for a plan of action in which law enforcement readies for gross acts of terrorism that will surely follow, maybe not today, but in the future.

CHAPTER 20

INDIVIDUAL AND SITUATIONAL DETERMINANTS OF POLICE FORCE: AN EXAMINATION OF THREAT PRESENTATION*

Stephen T. Holmes, K. Michael Reynolds,
Ronald M. Holmes, and Samuel Faulkner

Abstract: This chapter is based on previous research denoting the primary factors that influence officer decisions regarding the use of differing levels of force in police–citizen encounters. Using a totality of the circumstance approach, primary emphasis is directed toward explaining those factors that contribute to officers' estimation of the perceived level of threat inherent in police–citizen encounters. Officers' perceived level of threat presented by a suspect or the situational context of an encounter is important because in 1989, the Supreme Court in the Graham v. Connor *decision mandated that the appropriate amount of force that can be utilized depends on the following four primary factors: the threat, offense severity, actual resistance offered and whether the suspect is trying to escape custody. These criteria were tested and placed into a predictive model along with other indicators the literature has found to be correlated with situations in which police force is used more often. The findings suggest that while the threat presented to officers is important and related to the level of force that is deemed appropriate by the police profession, many additional elements must be taken into consideration when interpreting if an officer used force correctly.*

INTRODUCTION

Whenever police officers use force, officers, supervisors, the department, and the political body they represent are placed in jeopardy for claims of excessive use of force. While attention in the past has been primarily given to cases in which officers have used deadly force, the use of less than lethal force can present just as much of a problem to officers and their departments.

The consequences of police officers using force historically have plagued the public perception of the police. Some have noted that public perceptions concerning the misuse of force were some of the precipitating causes of the Chicago riot of 1919, the Harlem disturbance of 1935, the Watts riot of 1965, the Miami riot of 1980, and the Los Angeles riots immediately following the

*This chapter first appeared in the *American Journal of Criminal Justice,* Vol. 23, No. 1, 1998.

Rodney King decision (Lasley, 1994; Montgomery, 1980; Pate & Fridell, 1995; Smith, 1994). Given the significance of the problem and possible community ramifications, it is not surprising that police force has received considerable attention lately. Citizens, academics, practitioners, and legislators have begun to ask such questions as, What circumstances precipitate the use of force? Which officers are more likely to use it? How does organizational culture relate to the level of force used by officers? And, most important, how do officers, administrators, judges, and other agents of the criminal justice system define and differentiate between appropriate and inappropriate force?

Recent attempts to answer these and other questions have been met with limited success. More than two million federal research dollars has been spent over the past three years to better understand how police use and implement force. This expenditure has produced little substantive information useful for explaining the dynamics of police–citizen encounters in which force is used. There are two principal reasons for this failure. First, the use of police force at any level is a rare occurrence. Force is thought to occur in fewer than 3 percent of all police–citizen encounters (Friedrich, 1977; Fyfe, 1995; Garner et al., 1995; Klockars, 1995; Reiss, 1967; Worden, 1995). Second, because police force is rare, a large amount of actual field research time is required to observe and record the factors related to the modal (appropriate) level of force that the profession uses in police–citizen encounters. Moreover, the expense of conducting field observations has forced researchers to look only at a given municipal police agency over a short time period. Pate and Fridell (1993, p. 21) claim that, as such, our current knowledge base on police force has come from researcher intuition, personal experiences, and limited ride-alongs with the police.

Measuring the amount of force or the frequency with which police use either reasonable or excessive force is not the focus of this chapter. Nor is it the purpose of this chapter to examine when officers should use deadly force. Instead, by focusing on the various kinds of situations that officers face every day, this chapter seeks to develop insight into two major components that influence use of force outcomes. The first component concerns officers' perception of the threat level or risk inherent in a police–citizen encounter to either the respondent or others in the immediate area. The second component is to understand more fully how officers respond given the totality of the situation. The chapter also seeks to explain factors that contribute to variations in officers' collective responses concerning when and how much force are appropriate. Thus, this chapter seeks to explain the factors that officers believe contribute to their estimation of the dangers inherent in police–citizen encounters. In doing so, this chapter presents empirical evidence to suggest that while threat and perceptions of the appropriate amount of force that should be utilized in a given situation are related, the indicators of these two concepts are not the same. Moreover, these data indicate that the predictors of these two related concepts fail to share some common, expected elements.

REVIEW OF LITERATURE

The extant literature states that the application of police force depends on various individual, situational, and organizational factors that are present when officers intervene and interact with citizens. Friedrich (1980) divided the predictors of police force into individual, situational, and organizational categories. He stated that the individual approach explains the use of police force in terms of the characteristics of officers or citizens involved in police–citizen encounters. He tested to see if officers' individual characteristics—such as race, age, sex, experience, and years on the job—would help predict when and how often officers used physical force to resolve police–citizen encounters. What he found was that very few individual-level characteristics of police officers influence officers' behavior. However, other studies have indicated otherwise. For instance, Croft and Austin (1987) found that the amount of time officers spend on the job and the number of arrests they make are related to the number of times force is used each year.

Friedrich (1980) also tested the individual-level characteristics of suspects and again found little support. Other studies, however, have suggested that suspect characteristics play a significant role in the application of police force (Black, 1971; Bogomolny, 1976; Friedrich, 1977; Lundman et al., 1978). Race is reported to be highly correlated with the frequency of arrest. Several investigators have found that African Americans are more likely to be stopped, interrogated, and arrested than whites. Binder and Scharf (1980) claim that youth and minority group membership stand out as important predictors of police force since these elements may point to the actual or perceived amount of danger or threat inherent in an encounter. Even though it is reported that race is a factor, some also report that minorities tend to exhibit more disrespectful behavior and outward hostility toward police officers (Mulvihill & Tummin, 1969). Thus, this type of behavior may be an aggravating factor and lead to more arrests and, potentially, police use of force. However, others have found that when the seriousness of the offense is held constant, the effect of race disappears (Black, 1971; Black & Reiss, 1970; Bogomolny, 1976; Friedrich, 1977; Lundman et al., 1978).

Gender differences also impact arrest rates. Women have been found to be less likely to be questioned, detained, or arrested than men (Visher, 1983). One possible explanation is that women are less threatening and not perceived to be as dangerous as men are. Also, the typical police encounter with women is usually for minor offenses that would not necessitate an arrest. When victim reports are compared with official arrest reports, female offenders appear to be overrepresented in arrest statistics for serious offenses (Friedrich, 1977; Hindelang, 1979; Pastor, 1978; Rubinstein, 1973).

One of the most important, and highly debated, characteristics is suspect demeanor. Antagonistic or hostile behavior by suspects has been found to increase the chance of arrest (Black 1971; Black & Reiss, 1970; Lundman et al., 1978; Pilivin & Briar, 1964; Reiss, 1967; Bittner, 1970; Sykes & Clark, 1975). Conversely, suspects who submit to police authority are not arrested as often. It is claimed that "hostility directly increases the odds of arrest" and is "part of the criminological canon" (Klinger, 1994, p. 477). Concerning the demeanor of suspects, Klinger found the relationship between force and demeanor to be overstated because it is often operationalized to include attacks on the police. On the other hand, Worden and Shepard (1996) found support for the demeanor hypothesis even when additional variables are examined to control for the potential bias in the operationalization of demeanor.

The incident location is another important aspect of the officer–citizen interaction. Previous studies have examined public versus private places and found that more arrests are made for incidents that occur in public spaces (Lundman, 1994). Another factor that relates to public space is the presence of others who are not directly involved (Westley, 1970). There is evidence that when bystanders are present, police officers may perceive a need to exercise a higher level of visible formal control. This exercise of formal authority often leads to more arrests than would occur in a nonpublic location. There is also evidence that when more than 10 individuals are present, the likelihood of arrest increases (Friedrich, 1977). It is clear that location has an effect on police officer response and that when the interaction occurs in a public space, the likelihood for some formal police action is greater than in a nonpublic environment (Friedrich, 1980; Westly, 1970).

Another critical aspect of police citizen encounters involves how the police are called to a situation. In general, the extant literature maintains that the majority of police–citizen encounters are reactive, rather than proactive (Black, 1971). What makes this important is the finding that police-initiated offenses generally involve less serious offenses and appear to differ substantially from reactive encounters. Thus, officers in proactive mobilizations may be granted less legitimacy and react more aggressively to establish a position of authority (Friedrich, 1977). However, the police may have a greater range of options when they react proactively because the call is not necessarily part of departmental records. Therefore, we may find that the type of mobilization may impact the level of force chosen, depending on the type and level of the perceived seriousness of the offense.

While each of the aforementioned factors is important in determining the frequency and amount of force that may be used in police–citizen encounters, what we are interested in determining here is how these factors affect the perceived level of threat inherent in police–citizen encounters. We assume that these same factors will also contribute to the threat or risk inherent in these encounters. Thus, we must measure the attitudes and perceptions of police officers concerning the amount of threat they perceive and the amount of force that they would consider appropriate in a police–citizen encounter in a context that includes the aforementioned independent variables.

THE IMPORTANCE OF MEASURING THE PERCEPTIONS OF THE POLICE

Measuring the attitudes of the law enforcement profession with regard to the factors that contribute to estimating when force is most often and appropriately applied is important because the Supreme Court in *Graham v. Conner* (1989) mandated that the correct standard for judging the efficacy of police officers' nonlethal coercive behavior is best determined by police professionals. Hence, the reasonableness of an officer's behavior is not subject to interpretation from others outside the policing profession. The Supreme Court created the "objective reasonableness" standard, stating that actions of officers involving questions about the appropriate use of force should be judged without regard to the intent or motivation of the responding officer. Further, such decisions should be made "from the perspective of a reasonable officer coping with a tense, fast evolving scene, rather than with 20/20 hindsight" (Graham, 1989, p. 1872).

The *Graham* decision provides a basis that can be used to examine the role and factors that are important to the legal determination and evaluation of the "reasonableness" of officers' actions. However, the decision clearly states that "reasonableness . . . is not capable of precise definition or mechanical application" (Graham, 1989, p. 1981). It is evident that no policy or other organizational procedure is capable of providing a precise statement as to the appropriateness of any officers' conduct concerning how much force could or should be used. Thus, the only approach that can approximate this standard is one that roughly estimates the situational context in which the event occurs. Kappeler (1997, p. 72) states that these factors include

1. Whether the suspect poses an immediate threat to the officer or others,
2. The severity of the crime,
3. Whether the suspect is actively resisting arrest, and
4. Whether the suspect is attempting to escape custody.

The importance of the factors illuminated by Kappeler (1997) and the *Graham* decision cannot be overstated. What these factors represent is the apparent danger or element of risk both inherent and perceived by officers as they arrive at a scene and interact with citizens and suspects. These factors go beyond Skolnick's (1966) "symbolic assailant" in that the elements of the encounter are not only possessed by the suspect but are a combination of individual, situational, and ecological elements. Thus, in looking again the list provided by Kappeler, all the elements point to the inherent perceived risk to either the officer or others in the immediate area.

There appear to be at least three elements that need to be included in any examination of the efficacy of police response. The first is threat. Threat is a multidimensional phenomenon and includes situational clues emanating from the suspect as well as in the environment. The second element is the severity of the offense to which the officer is responding. Depending on the experience of the officer, the severity of the offense may put the officer on guard as to what type of person or situation to expect. While the severity of the offense may be considered part of the overall threat perceived by the officer, we have chosen to include offense severity as a predetermining factor of the overall threat. We do this because we assume that officers generally have some knowledge of the type of offense they are responding to, either through radio contact or from the events they witness. Thus, it would follow that officers generally view and classify the suspects they are or will be dealing with by the type of call. This call type classification is primarily determined by the reported offense.

The final element that is essential is the level at which the suspect is resisting or attempting to get away. In an ideal world (barring extralegal factors from consideration), this is and should be the only element that determines if an officer acted correctly in the implementation of physical force. However, given the nature of society and the unpredictability of the human element in police–citizen calls, other situational factors must be considered. While Kappeler lists "escape" as a fourth element, we assume that an actively resisting individual is indeed attempting to escape the custodial attempts of the officer.

DATA AND RESEARCH METHODS

A factorial approach will be used to investigate what individual, situational, and community-level factors officers believe contribute to the perceived threat inherent in police–citizen encounters. The factorial method is a proven, robust analytic strategy designed to enunciate critical points in complex decision making that influence outcomes or decisions. The factorial method in its most general form uses a series of vignettes comprised of randomly drawn elements placed in standardized prose. The result is a series of unique scenarios, each randomly drawn, to which the respondent is asked to respond and state an opinion.

The use of this method allows researchers to overcome prior methodological limitations by providing the respondent with a context in which an opinion may be shaped or formed. This context is critical to police officers since they are often asked to intervene in situations where there is an inherent danger or risk.

The survey used in this study was administered to 662 officers attending either routine or in-service training on the use of force, defensive tactics, or weapons retention courses at the Ohio Peace Officers Training Academy (OPOTA) in London, Ohio. The reason for choosing OPOTA and officers from Ohio is based primarily on two criteria. The first is a matter of convenience, and the second lies in the similarity of the population of the state of Ohio to the United States as a whole (Tuchfarber, 1988, p. 15). This view was bolstered and applied to Ohio's law enforcement community by Faulkner (1991), who found little difference in the opinions of citizens and the law enforcement community of Ohio from those in any other state concerning issues about the efficacy of police force.

Included in each survey was a list of demographic information about themselves and their department and a randomly constructed vignette depicting an encounter with a resisting suspect. Within each vignette, the values of 15 independent variables that the literature on police force has found to affect the likelihood that the police will use force are rotated in to comprise a situation that officers can easily comprehend and relate to. The use of the factorial method in this context allows a fictitious police–citizen encounter to be modified in several dimensions. Since this method does not depend on actual use of force events, it allows the researchers to simulate field conditions and avoid its time and expense. Furthermore, by controlling for all of the included variables, this approach allows researchers to determine which factors or dimensions of an encounter influence the police officer's response. This methodology is appropriate to study police force because it closely approximates and is even superior to the current practice of asking court-appointed expert witnesses to render opinions about the appropriate use of police force. Its superiority is demonstrated by the fact that the opinions presented are not those of one person, but of the 662 officers contained within this sample.

THE DEPENDENT VARIABLES

Measuring the level of threat that an officer perceives or attempting to quantify when officers perceive an actual threat is a tenuous and challenging methodological exercise. In order to acquire the data, it is important that the researcher define what the concept of "threat" is supposed to be measuring. *Merriam-Webster's Collegiate Dictionary* (1996, p. 1228) defines *threat* as "an expression of intention to inflict evil, injury or damage." According to this definition, threat must involve some type of intention on the part of a suspect to injure the officer or those around him or her. The question remains, however, What factors influence an officer's perception of the suspect's intention? And how broad of a concept is threat?

If threat is intended to measure the totality of the circumstances that piques the suspicions of officers, then it may be prudent to ask such a question as, What is the likelihood that this situation will result in injury to you, another officer, or an innocent bystander? This probe, while technically correct, is problematic for officers because of the inherent supposition that the respondents (police officers) may not be able to handle a situation or will allow it to get out of control. Responses to questions worded this way are likely to be answered with limited variation. This question was pretested and our suspicions were confirmed.

An alternative to phrasing the question this way was to ask the officers how many warnings they would issue prior to using physical force. The variable representing this concept was coded as a limited range ordinal measure ranging from 1 to 5, with higher values denoting that officers are likely to issue fewer warnings. Preliminary analysis of pretest data confirmed significant variation in responses and a direct relationship between the number of warnings an officer would issue and the level of force that they perceived as appropriate. This question was kept and a similar one was added to test for construct validity.

The second dependent variable asked officers directly to rate how serious the situation was, thus avoiding the negative connotation that the officer may not be able to handle a situation. The question representing the direct presentation of threat was worded as follows: "As the responding officer, how much of a threat does the situation or suspect described in the scenario present to you?" Responses to this question were also coded and treated as a limited range dependent variable (range of 1–5), with higher scores denoting higher levels of threat. While direct and to the point, wording of the question in this manner allows officers to interpret on their own how they define threat.

Because threat is such a critical concept, a decision was made to keep both measures of threat to see if they not only measured the same concept, but to see if the predictors were the same. Regression models were run comparing the results predicting the concept of threat using both the straightforward probe versus that attained by asking the respondents how many warnings they would issue prior to using physical force.

The third dependent variable used in these analyses measures the amount of force that officers believe should be applied in this situation. Remember it is anticipated that the threat contained in a situation should predict rather well the amount of force that officers believe is appropriate in a given police–citizen encounter. This measure was operationalized using Faulkner's (1991) Action Response Use of Force Continuum. Faulkner's continuum consists of eight differing force alternatives that may be applied to a resisting suspect. The use of this particular continuum is important because it is the one adopted and used by the Ohio Attorney General's Peace Officers Training Academy, and it is the basis on which many of the respondents' prior training on the use of force has been built.

THE INDEPENDENT VARIABLES

The independent variables included in this study are comprised of the key elements that Kappeler (1997) denotes as essential in determining the efficacy of an officer's forceful behavior (the threat that the elements of the situation present to the officer, the level of suspect resistance, and offense seriousness) as well as others that the literature has found to be related to situations in which force is most frequently used. In these data, the severity of the original offense to which the officer is called is measured as a 10-item variable consisting of the offenses of shoplifting, disorderly conduct, burglary, domestic violence, aggravated assault, robbery, rape, drive-by shooting, arson, and homicide. The selection of these offenses represents a cross section of the types of calls to which officers respond.

The level of resistance offered by the suspect (or, in Kappeler's terms, if the suspect is attempting to escape custody or if he or she is actively resisting) is measured using nine categories. The first level represents situations in which the suspect is using only the weight of his/her body to resist. The second represents those situations in which the suspect pulls away to resist the officer's prodding. The third category stands for those situations in which the suspect pushes the officer away each time the officer attempts to take control of the suspect. The fourth presents situations in which there is a push-pull match after the officer has touched the suspect. The fifth represents a situation in which the suspect squares up, clenches his or her fists, and makes verbal threats to the officer. The sixth entails an encounter in which the suspect starts resisting by punching and kicking. At the seventh level, the suspect viciously attacks the officer and attempts to choke or gouge the eyes of the officer. The eighth is comprised of situations in which the suspect attempts to take the officer's weapon away. The final resistance level is reached when the suspect produces a weapon and is intent on using it.

Other independent variables utilized were coded into three different categories. These categories involve individual attributes of officers, suspects, and situational elements.

In the categories of individual-level attributes of officers, the following variables were entered into the full model: age, gender, race, years of service, education, years of residence, weight, height, hours of defensive tactics training, number of physical confrontations, and number of times the officer had been injured in physical confrontations in the past year. Similarly, the individual-level characteristics of suspects that were entered were suspect's age, race, gender, size, appearance, and emotional stability and whether the officer suspected the suspect was under the influence of alcohol or drugs. The third level of indicator variables are the situational elements. These elements are not individual to the officer or the suspect, but rather emanate from or are present on the social stage in which the encounter occurs. These variables include the time of the encounter, whether the encounter occurs in a public or private place, the call frequency of an area, the socioeconomic status of an area, the number of officers present, and the number of citizens present. Codes and frequency distributions of these variables are contained in Table 20.1.

Table 20.2 presents the characteristics of the sample. A glance at this table reveals that the officers surveyed were predominately from small to medium-sized departments that serve mixed urban/rural communities. Further, over 90 percent of the respondents were white males. Also important is the notation

Table 20.1
Frequency Distributions and Codes of Independent Variables

		N	*Percent*
Level of Resistance			
1	Dead weight	76	11.5
2	Pulls away	76	11.5
3	Pushes away	84	12.7
4	Push-pull match	62	9.4
5	Squares off	74	11.2
6	Punching and kicking	59	8.9
7	Viciously attacks	81	12.2
8	Grabs firearm	75	11.3
9	Produces weapon	75	11.3
		662	100.0
Suspect Gender			
0	Female	347	52.4
1	Male	315	47.6
		662	100.0
Offense Severity			
1	Shoplifting	58	8.8
2	Disorderly conduct	71	10.7
3	Burglary	64	9.7
4	Domestic violence	68	10.3
5	Aggravated assault	75	11.3
6	Robbery	62	9.4
7	Rape	52	7.9
8	Drive-by shooting	64	9.7
9	Arson	78	11.8
10	Homicide	70	10.6
		662	100.0
Demeanor			
1	Calm and collected	129	19.5
2	Non-responsive	130	19.6
3	Nervous and agitated	132	19.9
4	Belligerent and threatening	130	19.6
5	Abusive and violent	141	21.3
		662	100.0
Suspect Size			
1	Small	230	34.7
2	Medium	220	33.2
3	Large	212	32.0
		662	100.0

(continued)

Table 20.1
Frequency Distributions and Codes of Independent Variables (*Continued*)

		N	Percent
Mobilization Type			
0	Proactive	322	48.6
1	Reactive	340	51.4
		662	100.0
Officer Carry OC Spray			
0	No	39	7.0
1	Yes	518	93.0
		557	100.0
Number of Other Officers Present			
1	None	148	22.4
2	One	182	27.5
3	Two-three	161	24.3
4	Four or more	171	25.8
		662	100.0
Officer Black			
0	No	616	93.9
1	Yes	40	6.1
		656	100.0
Emotionally Disturbed			
0	No	469	70.8
1	Yes	193	29.2
		662	100.0
Alcohol or Drug Use			
1	None	135	20.4
2	Alcohol	131	19.8
3	Marijuana	128	19.3
4	Cocaine	136	20.5
5	Mixed	132	19.9
		662	100.0
Time of Day			
1	6:00 A.M.	93	14.0
2	9:00 A.M.	80	12.1
3	12:00 P.M.	81	12.2
4	3:00 P.M.	89	13.4
5	6:00 P.M.	72	10.9

(*continued*)

Table 20.1
Frequency Distributions and Codes of Independent Variables (*Continued*)

		N	*Percent*	
Time of Day (*continued*)				
6	9:00 P.M.	89	13.4	
7	12:00 A.M.	71	10.7	
8	3:00 A.M.	87	13.1	
		662	100.0	
Years Lived in Community*				
	Less than 5 years	92	14.2	
	6 to 10 years	70	10.8	
	11 to 15 years	54	8.3	
	16 to 20 years	22	3.4	
	21 to 25 years	60	9.2	Mean = 24.3
	26 to 30 years	121	18.6	
	31 to 35 years	87	13.4	
	36 to 40 years	59	9.1	
	40 Years or more	85	13.1	
		650	100.0	
Call Frequency of Area				
1	Rare	219	33.1	
2	Infrequent	243	36.7	
3	Frequent	200	30.2	
		662	100.0	
Number of Citizens Present				
1	None	131	19.8	
2	1 person	129	19.5	
3	2–3 persons	133	20.1	
4	4–5 persons	142	21.5	
5	More than 6 persons	127	19.2	
		662	100.0	
SES of Encounter Area				
1	Lower class	137	20.7	
2	Lower to middle class	144	21.8	
3	Middle class	138	20.8	
4	Middle to upper class	111	16.8	
5	Upper class	132	19.9	
		662	100.0	

* Data in Models were run at actual values. Data are collapsed here for presentation only.

Table 20.2
Characteristics of Officers and Departments Included in Sample

	N	*Percent*	
Officer Age			
20–25	58	8.8	
26–30	184	27.9	
31–35	158	23.9	Mean = 34.5
36–40	105	15.9	
41 and over	155	23.5	
	660	100.0	
Department Location			
Urban	179	27.2	
Mixed	359	54.6	
Rural	120	18.2	
	658	100.0	
Officer Gender			
Female	44	6.6	
Male	618	93.4	
	662	100.0	
Department Size*			
25 and under	222	33.6	
26–50	226	34.2	
51–75	34	5.2	
76–100	40	6.1	Mean = 223.6
101–125	16	2.4	
126–150	10	1.5	
Over 150	114	17.3	
	660	100.3	
Years of Service*			
5 and Under	238	36.1	
6–10	185	28.0	
11–15	95	14.4	Mean = 9.7
16–20	85	12.9	
21 and over	57	8.6	
	660	100.0	
Officer Race			
White	596	90.9	
Black	40	6.1	
Hispanic	12	1.8	
Asian	8	1.2	
	656	100.0	

(continued)

Table 20.2
Characteristics of Officers and Departments Included in Sample (*Continued*)

	N	*Percent*
Rank in Department		
Patrol officer	450	68.0
Sergeant	132	19.9
Trainer	10	1.5
Detective	26	3.9
Lieutenant	26	3.9
Captain	12	1.8
Chief	6	0.9
	662	100.0
Department Sued		
No	333	50.3
Yes	329	49.7
	662	100.0

Sample size may not equal 662 due to missing data.

Percentages may not total to 100 due to missing data.

*Data in models were run at actual values. Data are categorized here for presentation purposes only.

that two-thirds (67.6 percent) of the officers surveyed were from departments with 50 or fewer officers. While this overrepresentation of officers from small to medium-sized departments appears on the surface to be problematic, it must be remembered that over 75 percent of all police agencies employ fewer than 25 sworn personnel (Langworthy & Travis, 1994).

Further examination reveals that those respondents included in the sample were not rookies or law enforcement agents fresh out of law enforcement training academies. The typical respondent was 34 years old and had been a police officer for a little less than 10 years.

The majority of respondents were patrol officers (68 percent) or first-line supervisors (19.9 percent). While there were a number of officers participating that held a higher rank, this group comprised only 10 percent of the total sample. Finally, half of the officers had knowledge of a suit that had been filed in the past against their department for the use of excessive force.

FINDINGS

The results of the two models predicting the level of threat that officers perceive are presented in Table 20.3. These models list all the independent variables that were placed into the full model using threat presentation directly and as a proxy measure. Both models predict rather well the variation in

Table 20.3

Comparison of the Models Predicting Situational Threat

	Model 1: Predicting Level of Threat Situation Presents			Model 2: Depicting the Number of Appropriate Verbal Warnings		
	Beta	*t*	*Sig.*	*Beta*	*t*	*Sig.*
Resistance	.697	20.698	.000 ***	.525	13.204	.000 ***
Suspect Gender	−.116	−3.389	.001 ***	−.043	−1.072	.284
Carry OC	−.005	−.152	.879	.005	.122	.903
Years of Service	−.064	−.900	.368	−.160	−1.932	.054 *
Years of Education	−.007	−.207	.836	−.052	−1.285	.199
Years in Community	.001	.025	.980	−.039	−.742	.458
Offense Severity	.061	1.806	.072 *	.004	.093	.926
Suspect Demeanor	.065	1.927	.055 *	−.002	−.044	.965
Officer Black	.063	1.826	.069 *	.024	.589	.556
Officer Weight	−.046	−1.024	.307	.036	.679	.498
Mobilization	.029	.863	.389	.107	2.714	.007 ***
Suspect Size	.058	1.733	.084 *	−.039	−.974	.331
Emotionally Disturbed	.046	1.370	.172	−.040	−.996	.320
Age of Officer	.051	.794	.428	.094	1.235	.218
Alcohol or Drug Use	.042	1.235	.217	−.010	−.240	.811
Building Type	.004	.133	.894	−.048	−1.180	.239
Call Frequency of Area	−.007	−.210	.834	−.051	1.297	.195
Appearance/Dress	−.043	−1.270	.205	−.021	−.513	.608
Defensive Tactics Year	−.010	−.300	.764	.021	.508	.612
Injured in Physical Year	.009	.254	.799	−.048	−1.161	.246
Time of Day	−.002	−.059	.953	.040	1.027	.305
Gender of Officer	.027	.735	.463	−.055	1.247	.213
Height of Officer	.023	.535	.593	.017	.344	.731
Number of Citizens Present	−.020	−.597	.551	−.042	−1.043	.297
Officers Present	−.059	−1.732	.084 *	−.025	−.621	.535
Physical Confrontation Year	−.047	−1.336	.182	−.021	−.506	.613
SES	.014	.401	.689	.047	1.180	.239
Suspect Age	−.018	−.516	.606	.043	1.076	.283
Officer Asian	−.033	−.928	.354	.008	.201	.841
Officer Hispanic	.004	.116	.908	−.031	−.627	.531
Suspect Asian	−.052	−1.254	.211	−.021	−.422	.673
Suspect Black	.033	.791	.429	.055	1.119	.264
Suspect Hispanic	−.016	−.383	.702	−.031	−.627	.531
	$R^2 = .531$			$R^2 = .345$		

* $p < .10$

** $p < .05$

*** $p < .01$

officers' perception of the inherent risk involved in each vignette. The strength of the two models is indicated by the high R^2 statistic ranging between .53 and .34.

Looking at the model predicting threat directly, seven independent variables distinguish their unique influences over all the other variables. These seven indicators are level of resistance, gender and size of the suspect, severity of the offense, suspect demeanor, whether the officer was black, and the number of officers at the scene. This model notes that large, abusive, and violent males suspected of committing more serious offenses and who more actively resist are more likely to be perceived by officers as a more serious threat than passive females suspected of committing less serious offenses. Further, non-black officers who respond to situations alone are more likely to rate a situation as less threatening than black officers responding with backup.

It is important to note that some of the traditional measures that the literature has found to be associated with situations in which police arrest or use other coercive techniques did not attain statistical significance. Thus, it is apparent that such factors as the race of the suspects, if they were mentally or emotionally disturbed, their physical appearance, and the suspected use of alcohol or drugs did not trigger the predicted response.

The second model, presented in Table 20.3, contains the same predictor variables as the first. This model uses the proxy variable to represent the risk or threat inherent to the officer in each vignette. In this model, the context in which the question is answered changes and so do the perceptions of the responding officers. This change of context affects the variables that trigger the perceptual cues to which officers respond. When officers were asked how many warnings they would issue prior to using force, the officers based their responses on three criteria. These criteria are the level of resistance offered by the suspect, the number of years (or experience) they have been police officers, and whether the situation is police or citizen initiated. Thus, less experienced officers who are called to a situation by a citizen reporting an offense and who encounter actively resisting suspects through a citizen report are likely to perceive a suspect as more of a threat and as less deserving of a second chance before they resort to using physical force.

The differences in the models predicting the level of threat or risk inherent in each encounter were unexpected. Intuitively, it makes sense that the same predictors that put officers on "alert" would also prompt them to give or not give suspects one or more warnings before resorting to physical force. These data, however, do not support this contention. Instead, the data reveal that these concepts are in fact two distinct concepts. Thus, officers' perception of the level of threat that a police–citizen encounter entails seems to be comprised of many individual elements that emanate from the demographics of the participants. In this instance, belligerent and threatening males who are suspected of more serious offenses are more likely to be perceived as a greater threat to both the officer and the maintenance of their authority. Further, black officers who encounter large suspects perceive threat at higher levels even when controlling for the socioeconomic status, call frequency, and size of the suspect.

In order to clarify these findings further, a condensed model was run using the variables that predicted overall either threat, the number of warnings, or the appropriate level of force that officers in this sample considered appropriate. The rationale for including all of the significant predictors of these variables in this model was to see if each had a direct influence on the level of force that officers believe is appropriate in each scenario. If both of the primary indicators of threat significantly affect the perceived level of force considered appropriate, we can state that each predictor of the composite indices of threat will have an indirect effect on the level of force considered appropriate. Thus, this model seeks to determine if there is a direct influence.

Table 20.4 contains the coefficients and results of this test. When all of the significant predictor variables that affect either of the three dependent variables are included in each model, there is no change in either the significance level or direction of the variables predicting the level of threat that officers perceive once they arrive at a scene. Thus, it is clear that this model and its predictors are stable. The model predicting threat by the proxy variable fluctuates. While the levels of resistance and mobilization type retain theft effects in the predicted direction, the importance of the number of years an officer has been on the force diminishes.

The third model in Table 20.4 notes the indicators of the level of force that officers consider appropriate for each of the fictitious police–citizen encounters. In this model, of the 14 independent variables entered, only two were not associated with either the direct or proxy measure of threat. These two include the number of years an officer has lived in the community he/she polices and if the officer carries oleoresin capsicum (OC) spray. According to traditional wisdom, older officers who are well entrenched within their community should be less likely to use force, but these data indicate the opposite to be true. Officers in this sample who are longtime community residents are more likely to rate police–citizen encounters as deserving of higher levels of force than those who had lived in a community for fewer years.

Furthermore, these data indicate that officers who carry OC spray are more likely to state that a situation calls for higher levels of force than those who do not use or carry chemical agents. While OC and other chemical agents were designed to reduce the number of incidents in which officers become physically involved in encounters with suspects, this finding may be easily discounted since the continuum used as the dependent variable in this analysis counts OC and other chemical agents as level 5 (out of 8) force alternative. Thus, if officers have come to count on using chemical agents as alternatives to physical force, it is likely that their answer will be higher than those who either do not approve of it, are not permitted to use it, or simply are not issued it as standard equipment.

Other factors that contribute to predicting the perceived level of force for the encounter include the level of threat, the number of warnings issued, the level of suspect resistance, suspect gender, offense severity, and the number of years the respondent has been a police officer.

Of these factors, two of the strongest indicators of the appropriate amount of force that officers believe to be reasonable are the level of threat they perceive and the number of warnings they would issue prior to using force. These two variables produce a strong direct linear effect on the amount of force considered appropriate. Thus, if the officers perceive a situation as more threatening or they believe they should issue fewer warnings before using force, they are more likely to rate higher levels of force as more acceptable. Along the same line, if there is a direct effect between these two measures and force, then it follows that the indicators of the two original dimensions of threat are

Table 20.4

The Condensed Model Comparing Suspects' Presentation of Threat and the Officers' Perceptions of the Appropriate Amount of Force

	Model 1: Predicting Level of Threat Situation Presents			Model 2: Depicting the Number of Appropriate Verbal Warnings			Model 3: Predicting the Appropriate Level of Force		
	Beta	t	Sig.	Beta	t	Sig.	Beta	t	Sig.
Number of Warnings	***	***	***	***	***	***	.175	5.494	.000***
Threat Level	***	***	***	***	***	***	.451	11.744	.000***
Resistance	.700	22.892	.000***	.235	4.784	.000***	.287	7.844	.000***
Suspect Gender	−.139	−4.540	.000***	−.013	−.360	.719	−.109	−4.231	.000***
Offense Severity	.075	2.442	.015**	.007	.200	.842	.046	1.815	.070*
Suspect Demeanor	.054	1.759	.079*	−.022	−.623	.534	.014	.553	.580
Suspect Size	.058	1.885	.060*	−.094	−2.700	.007***	.002	.070	.944
Mobilization	.018	.605	.545	.092	2.641	.009***	−.035	−1.381	.168
Carry OC	−.007	−.216	.829	−.008	−.221	.825	.055	2.189	.029**
Officers Present	−.055	−1.786	.075*	.022	.624	.533	−.016	−.635	.526
Officer Black	.059	1.899	.058*	.016	.446	.656	.017	.646	.519
Years of Service	.000	.007	.994	−.064	−1.400	.162	−.071	−2.146	.032**
Years in Community	−.015	−.369	.712	−.044	−.967	.334	.067	2.039	.042**
	$R^2 = .519$			$R^2 = .381$			$R^2 = .675$		

* p < .10

** p < .05

*** p < .01

322 Terrorism, Hate Groups and Institutional Violence

likely to produce both a direct and indirect effect on the level of appropriate force. Out of the seven composite indicators of threat measured directly, only four variables (level of resistance, gender of suspect, offense severity, and number of officers present) also produce a direct effect on the amount of force that officers consider reasonable. The three indicators that do not produce a direct effect on the amount of force considered appropriate are the size of the suspect, his/her demeanor, and whether the officer is black.

Similarly, of the three variables in both the full and condensed models that significantly predict the proxy measure of threat, only the level of suspect resistance retains its significance and has a direct effect on the level of force considered appropriate. Thus, in the opinions of these officers, the size of the suspect, whether the situation is reactive or proactive, and the years a respondent has been a police officer may put him/her on "alert," but this does not mean that his/her actual physical response would be influenced by these factors.

DISCUSSION AND CONCLUSION

This effort set out to determine which factors determine the level of threat an officer perceives as he/she arrives and interacts with citizens during a police–citizen encounter. To do this, we measured the concept of threat in two ways. First, we operationalized threat using a direct approach, asking the officers in this sample how much of a threat the situation or suspect described in the scenario presented. We also operationalized threat using a proxy measure by asking officers how many warnings they would issue to suspects before resorting to physical force. It was hypothesized that both measures would yield the same predictors since each measure was designed to tap the seriousness of or how much risk was inherent in each encounter. The results obtained by comparing the predictors of these two variables indicated otherwise.

With the exception of the level of resistance offered by the suspect, none of the indicators of the direct indicator of threat corresponded with the significant indicators of the number of warnings officers would issue prior to using force. This finding lends credence to the notion that when officers interact with citizens in their official capacity, there may be at least three different and distinct dimensions or stages that need be analyzed. We call the first stage the introduction. In this stage, the officers arrive at a scene and gather some preliminary intelligence based on their experience and cues from the external environment. They may or may not have firsthand knowledge of the offense to which they have been called or the suspect involved, but they are able to ascertain from the situational cues who the main suspect is and if their own demographic attributes affect how they will be perceived. Officers may issue an order to which the suspect is expected to comply, but the two parties will not fully engage each other. By the end of this stage, the officers are able to tell with some degree of certainty how the suspect will respond to their imposed authority.

The second stage we call reflection. In this stage, the officers are ready to or have already fully engaged the suspect. The officers have some baseline information on the type of suspect with whom they are dealing, are aware of their options, and have a good idea of how best to proceed. The initial plan of action at this stage is not set. The final determination of the officers' response is based on the suspect's response to their formal intervention. During the reflection stage, officers fully engage the suspect and if the suspect resists or fails to pay heed to the officer's authority, force may be used to gain compliance.

The third stage is the stage of last resort. Officers in this stage have exhausted all means within reason to subdue the suspect in a peaceful manner. Based on the cues already collected and on the physical prowess of the suspect, officers will move to subdue the suspect in the quickest, most effective manner without injuring either themselves or the suspect. In this stage, more experienced officers may be better fit and more adept at defensive tactics techniques so that they do not feel the need to escalate force to levels at which either permanent or visible physical injury to the suspect is likely.

In respect to the main goal of this research, we were able to measure the amount of threat that officers experience when dealing with citizens in situations where force may be required. As indicated in both Tables 20.3 and 20.4, we are able to account for over half of the variation in responses by asking officers directly how much of a threat this situation or suspect presents to them. We are thus confident that the level of suspect resistance, severity of the offense, demeanor of the suspect, mobilization type, number of officers present, and the race of the officer each play a role in determining the level of perceived threat.

However, knowing the determinants of an officer's perception of threat is not enough. We can take into account all the factors noted by Kappeler and the "objective reasonableness" standard as handed down by the *Graham* decision. However, these elements do not reconcile with the findings of these data that threat, the number of warnings an officer would issue, and preferred levels of physical force have different predictive elements. It is also necessary to consider other individual and situational elements that account for the officer's reactions to the suspect when the officer officially intervenes. These include the following: (1) the suspects' ability to cause potential injury to the officer or others, (2) the officers' experience or tools they have on hand designed to de-escalate potentially volatile situations, (3) the officers' experience with such encounters, and (4) any inherent biases toward others acquired either through experience or socialization.

While we do have multiple measures designed to tap the experience of officers, they are very crude at best. It is important to know how long officers have been on the force, as well as the amount of training and number of physical confrontations in which they have been involved in the past year, but the interplay between these variables has not been explored. Not all officers experience the same type and number of physical confrontations. Hence, it is likely that the measures employed in the sample to denote the experience of officers do not fully address the interplay between experience, training, and other situational or individual attributes.

While the basic findings of this endeavor support the factors mandated by the Supreme Court in the *Graham* decision, and later clarified by Kappeler (1997), there is still much more to learn. Subsequent studies should be more creative in exploring new ways to measure and learn about the intangibles of police–citizen interactions. Further, subsequent research must focus on or at least pay more attention to the operationalization of the concepts utilized in examining police force. Often, published studies on police force use data sets collected for some alternative purpose. Little attention is paid toward construct validity. For instance, Lundman (1994) operationalized demeanor using a series of binary coded variables looking only at arrests for public drunkenness and juvenile encounters with the police. These types of measures, while empirically correct, do not portray the feelings and beliefs of officers in the variety of situations that officers face. Instead, we are left with a fractured view of when and how the demeanor and resistance of suspects affect law enforcement officers.

In this study, we have violated some of the basic assumptions of ordinary least squares regression by presenting models with a limited range of dependent variables and discussing their results. This violation is easily justified since the focus here is to provide officers with a real-world "totality of the circumstances" approach in order to determine which factors contribute to the escalation of threat and appropriate levels of police force. While we could have easily collapsed categories and run logistic regression, this approach would curtail the focus that certain key indicators act in a linear fashion affecting how officers rate differing levels of force based on individual and situational elements. In this case, we feel the ends justify the means.

REFERENCES

Binder, A., & P. Scharf. (1980. November). "The Violent Police–Citizen Encounter." *Annals of the American Academy of Political and Social Science,* 452: 111–121.

Bittner, E. (1970). *The Functions of Police in Modern Society.* Washington, DC: Government Printing Office.

Black, D. (1971, June). "The Social Organization of Arrest." *Stanford Law Review,* 23: 1087–1110.

Black, D., & A. Reiss. (1970). "Police Control of Juveniles." *American Sociological Review,* 35: 63–70.

Blumberg, M. (1986). Issues and Controversies with Respect to Use of Deadly Force by the Police. In T. Barker & D. Carter (Eds.), *Police Deviance.* Cincinnati: Pilgrimage.

Blumberg, M. (1989). Controlling Police Use of Deadly Force: Assessing Two Decades of Progress. In G. Alpert & R. Dunham (Eds.), *Critical Issues in Policing.* Prospect Heights, IL: Waveland.

Blumberg, M. (1991). Police Use of Deadly Force: Exploring Some Key Issues. In T. Barker & D. Carter (Eds.), *Police Deviance.* Cincinnati: Anderson.

Bogomolny, R. (1976). "Street Patrol: The Decision to Stop a Citizen." *Criminal Law Bulletin,* 12(5): 544–581.

Croft, E., & B. A. Austin. (1987). *Police Use of Force in Rochester and Syracuse, New York, 1984 and 1985.* Albany: New York State Commission on Criminal Justice and the Use of Force.

Demaris, A. (1992). *Logit Modeling: Practical Application.* Newbury Park, CA: Sage.

Faulkner, 5. (1991). *The Action Response Use of Force Continuum.* London, OH: Ohio Peace Officers Training Academy.

Friedrich, R. (1977). *The Impact of Organizational, Individual and Situational Factors on Police Behavior.* Unpublished doctoral dissertation, University of Michigan, Ann Arbor.

Friedrich, R. (1980, November). "Police Use of Force: Individuals, Situations and Organizations." *Annals of the American Academy of Political and Social Science,* 452: 82–87.

Fyfe, J. (1995). Training to Reduce Police–Citizen Violence. In W. Geller & H. Toch (Eds.), *And Justice for All* (pp. 151–175). Washington, DC: Police Executive Research Forum.

Garner, J., T. Schade, J. Hepburn, & J. Fagan. (1995). *Understanding the Use of Force by and against the Police.* Washington, DC: National Institute of Justice.

Hindenlang, M. (1979, Spring). "Sex Differences in Criminal Activity." *Social Problems,* 21: 580–593.

Kaminski, R. (1997). *Opening Remarks.* Paper presented at the National Institute of Justice's Cluster Conference on Police Use of Force, Washington, DC.

Kappeler, V. (1997). *Critical Issues in Police Civil Liability.* Prospect Heights, IL: Waveland.

Kennedy, P. (1992). *A Guide to Econometrics.* Cambridge, MA: MIT Press.

Klingler, D. (1994). "Demeanor of Crime? Why Hostile Citizens Are More Likely to Be Arrested." *Criminology,* 32: 475–493.

Klingler, D. (1995). "Policing Spousal Abuse." *Journal of Research in Crime and Delinquency,* 32: 308–324.

Klingler, D. (1996). "More on Demeanor and Arrest in Dade County." *Criminology,* 34: 301–323.

Klockars. C. (1995). A Theory of Excessive Force and Its Control. In W. Geller & H. Toch (Eds.), *And Justice for All.* Washington, DC: Police Executive Research Forum.

Kroes, W. (1985). *Societies' Victims: The Police.* (2nd ed). Springfield, IL: Charles C. Thomas.

Langworthy, R., & L. Travis. (1994). *Policing in America: A Balancing of Forces.* New York: Macmillan.

Lasley, J. (1994). "The Impact of the Rodney King Incident on Citizens' Attitudes toward Police." *Police and Society,* 3: 245–255.

Lundman, R. (1994). "Demeanor or Crime? The Midwest City Police–Citizens Encounter Study." *Criminology,* 32(4): 631–656.

Lundman, R., K. Sykes, & J. Clark. (1978). "Police Control of Juveniles." *Journal of Research in Crime and Delinquency,* 15(1): 74–91.

Menard, S. (1995). *Applied Logistic Regression Analysis.* Thousand Oaks, CA: Sage.

Merriam-Webster's Collegiate Dictionary (10th ed.). (1996). Springfield, MA: Merriam-Webster, Inc.

Montgomery, P. (1980, May 19). "Anger Long is Rising among Miami Blacks." *The New York Times,* p. Al.

Mulvihill, D., & M. Tummin. (1969). *Crimes of Violence* (Vol. 12). Washington, DC.: Government Printing Office.

Office of Criminal Justice Services. (1983). *The Use of Force in Patrol Work.* Columbus, OH: Author.

Pastor, P. (1978, Spring). "Mobilization in Public Drunkenness Control: A Comparison of Legal and Medical Approaches." *Social Problems,* 25: 373–384.

Pate, T., & L. Fridell. (1993). *Police Use of Force: Official Reports, Citizen Complaints, and Legal Consequences.* Washington, DC: The Police Foundation.

Pilivin, I., & S. Briar. (1964). "Police encounters with Juveniles." *American Journal of Sociology,* 70: 210–212.

Reiss, A. (1967). *Studies on Crime and Law Enforcement in Major Metropolitan Areas* (field surveys no. 3). Washington, DC: President's Commission on Law Enforcement and the Administration of Justice.

Rubinstein, J. (1973). *City Police.* New York: Farrar, Strauss and Giroux.

Skolnick, J. (1966). *Justice without Trial: Law Enforcement in a Democratic Society.* New York: John Wiley and Sons.

Smith, M. R. (1994). "Integrating Community Policing and the Use of Force: Public Education Involvement and Accountability." *American Journal of the Police,* 13(4): 1–21.

Sykes, R., & J. Clark. (1975). "A Theory of Deference Exchange in Police–Civilian Encounters." *American Journal of Sociology,* 81(3): 584–600.

Tuchfarber, A. (1997). Personal Communication with Director of the *Ohio Poll* on the National Generalizability of Opinions of the Citizen's of Ohio. June 12th.

Visher, C. (1983). "Gender, Police Arrest Decisions, and Notions of Chivalry." *Criminology,* 21(1): 5–28.

Westley, W. (1970). *Violence and the Police: A Sociological Study of Law, Custom and Morality.* Cambridge, MA: MIT Press.

Worden, It. (1995). The Causes of Police Brutality: Theory and Evidence on Police Use of Force. In W. Geller & H. Tech (Eds.), *And Justice for All.* Washington, DC: Police Executive Research Forum.

Worden, R., & R. Shepard. (1996). "Demeanor, Crime and Police Behavior: A Reexamination of the Police Services Study Data," *Criminology,* 34(1).

CASES CITED

Graham v. Connor, 409 U.S. 386, 109 5. Ct. 1865. (1989).

Johnson v. Glide, 481 F 2nd 1028, 1033 (2nd Cir.), cert denied, 414 U.S. 1033 (1973).

CHAPTER 21

CRIMINALIZING HATE:
AN EMPIRICAL ASSESSMENT[1]

Eugene H. Czajkoski

INTRODUCTION

Inexorably, the general movement in this country toward protecting both individual and group rights and sensitivities has spawned a number of innovative ideas and control mechanisms. These range from what might be subsumed under political correctness to particular penalty devices in criminal justice. This chapter examines one specific outgrowth of the movement (i.e., hate crime). Moreover, this hate crime examination is mainly descriptive in nature and is limited to the experience of one state, Florida.

Although not concerned with the rather complex social and political forces that have led the country through turbulent rights adjustments culminating in the criminalization of hate, it is important to have some understanding of the background. Fortunately, that understanding is widespread, thanks to the advanced state of public communications media, and requires little explication here. It is, perhaps, sufficient to note that the very concept of hate crime is of relatively recent origin and can best be understood in the context of what has been happening in this country in regard to changing and expanding notions of individual, group, and minority rights. The concept of hate crime does not encompass hatreds in general. One will not find hatred of either Republicans or Democrats, of either Bostonians or New Yorkers, or even of either criminals or noncriminals, in any way proscribed by the criminal law. Usually, it is only when hatred focuses on race, religion, ethnicity, gender, or sexual preference that the criminal law comes into play. Furthermore, hatred in one of those areas, by itself, is not criminal. It is only when some traditionally established crime (e.g., assault, vandalism, theft, etc.) can be legally shown to have been motivated by hate against restrictively specified groups that the punitive hate crime mechanism becomes active.

It is difficult to precisely trace the origins of an evolutionary process, but certainly the activities of the Anti-Defamation League of B'nai B'rith must be

---

[1]This chapter first appeared in *Federal Probation*, Vol. LVI, No. 3. Sept 1992 (pp. 36–40).

328 Terrorism, Hate Groups, and Institutional Violence

regarded as seminal in regard to notions of hate crime. The League has been tracking one kind of hate crime, anti-Semitic vandalism, since 1960. In 1979, it first began to publish an annual "Audit of Anti-Semitic Incidents." These audits, from the beginning, revealed an alarming trend of increasing anti-Semitic vandalism and violence. The League responded by making greater efforts in terms of education, public exposure, and demands for law enforcement support. In 1981, the League's legal affairs department drafted a model hate crimes legislative bill, and the League continues to hold a leadership position in promoting hate crime statutes.

Other organizations, notably Afro-American groups, have also played a leadership role in pursuing hate crimes legislation. In 1985, the National Organization of Black Law Enforcement Executives published a law enforcement guidebook on racial and religious violence. In 1983, the U.S. Commission on Civil Rights published an influential report entitled *Intimidation and Violence: Racial and Religious Bigotry in America*. In 1984, with a seed grant from the State of Maryland, the National Institute against Prejudice and Violence was established. The Institute, whose advisory board represents an impressive cross section of prominent people from several different racial, religious, and ethnic groups, seeks to suppress violence and intimidation motivated by unwarranted prejudice. The Institute's program includes operating a clearinghouse, conducting research, and helping to analyze and draft model legislation.

In reviewing materials published by organizations promoting the hate crime concept, one can discern a thrust aimed at mobilizing the special interests of the law enforcement community. Violence motivated by specified hatreds is presented as a threat to law and order in society. Police agencies are logically hooked into the hate crime business not on the basis of moral arguments but on the straightforward basis of public safety and order maintenance. Economic costs of hate crime and the related costs to police efficiency are part of the argumentation supporting hate crime legislation. As of this writing, there are at least 48 states that, along with the federal government, have some form of statute addressing hate crime. The Federal Bureau of Investigation (FBI) has held training conferences for state and local law enforcement agencies charged with enforcing hate crime statutes. On July 18, 1990, the FBI developed a draft of hate crime data collection guidelines, and there is clearly federal leadership in this area. The International Association of Chiefs of Police has promulgated a model racial, religious, and ethnic violence policy statement as a guide for police executives, and there are numerous relevant handbooks, executive orders, and guidelines developed by law enforcement agencies throughout the country. In light of a recent event involving Los Angeles police officers, it is interesting to note one example of such hate crime policy among police.

Policy: It is the policy of the Los Angeles Police Department to ensure that the rights of all people guaranteed by the constitutions of the United States and the State of California are protected. When such rights are infringed upon by violence, threats or other harassment, the Department will use every necessary resource to rapidly and decisively identify the suspects, arrest them and bring them to justice.

Acts or threats of violence motivated by hatred or prejudice are serious. Such acts generate fear and concern among victims and the public and have the potential of recurring, escalating, and possibly causing counter-violence (Special Order No. ii, dated August 10,1987, Office of the Chief of Police, Los Angeles, California).

After stating the policy, the order proceeds to delineate responsibilities and tasks for implementation.

HATE CRIME IN FLORIDA

In 1989, the Florida Legislature passed a statute known as the Hate Crimes Reporting Act (Section 877.19, Florida Statutes). The Act states that

> The Governor, through the Florida Department of Law Enforcement, shall collect and disseminate data on incidents of criminal acts that evidence prejudice based on religion, ethnicity, color, ancestry, or national origin. All law enforcement agencies shall report monthly to the Florida Department of Law Enforcement concerning such offenses in such form and in such manner as prescribed by rules adopted by the department.

A companion statute (Section 775.085, Florida Statutes) specifies enhanced penalties as follows:

1. The penalty for any felony or misdemeanor shall be reclassified as provided in this subsection if the commission of such felony or misdemeanor evidences prejudice based on race, color, ancestry, ethnicity, religion or national origin of the victim.
   a. A misdemeanor of the second degree shall be punishable as if it were a misdemeanor of the first degree.
   b. A misdemeanor of the first degree shall be punishable as if it were a felony of the third degree.
   c. A felony of the third degree shall be punishable as if it were a felony of the second degree.
   d. A felony of the second degree shall be punishable as if it were a felony of the first degree.

The Act also provides for treble damages in civil actions arising out of hate crime incidents.

The first report on hate crimes in Florida was an interim one covering the period October through December 1989. The interim report consisted of data from 32 law enforcement agencies showing 76 offenses derived from 60 hate crime incidents. The first full year of reporting hate crimes was 1990. During that year, 80 law enforcement agencies reported 259 hate crime incidents involving 306 criminal offenses. What follows is an analytical description of the 1990 data.

COLLECTION OF DATA

In order to facilitate the statewide data collection required by law, the Florida Department of Law Enforcement promulgated, to all law enforcement agencies in the state, a lengthy manual known as the *Hate Crime Report Manual*. The manual provides certain codes for uniform reporting and attempts to deal with the most difficult aspect of hate crime, which is its definition. The manual declares that motivation is the "key element in determining whether an incident is hate-related." According to the manual, motivation can stem from hatred based on race, color, religion, or ethnicity/national origin. Only one motivation can be listed so that the conceivable circumstance of an incident motivated by hatred of both a religion and a race would have to be reported as one or the other motivation, not both.

The manual goes into considerable detail as to the possible indicators of motivation. Some of the indicators are fairly concrete like gestures, words, and symbols. Other indicators offered by the manual are somewhat harder to grasp. For example, the manual lists a holiday/date indicator where an incident may coincide with a specific holiday like Martin Luther King, Jr. Day or Rosh Hashanah.

The manual lists several possible hate-related activities, such as cross burning, threatening placement of animal parts, spitting, defecating, urinating, graffiti placement, wearing of intimidating clothing, and tattooing. Among the possible symbols listed are swastikas, colors, gang signs, and ritualistic markings.

Recognizing the difficulty of determining when a crime is motivated by a statutorily proscribed hatred, the manual stresses the importance of law enforcement officers relying on their "investigative judgment."

An important thing to keep in mind when pursuing the concept of hate crime is that expressions of proscribed hatreds, which occur during the course of an otherwise motivated crime, do not amount to hate crimes. A hypothetical example might help to clarify this point. If during the course of a barroom fight, which started from an argument about some sporting event, the combatants call each other names like nigger, spic, or honky, the event does not rise to the level of a hate crime because it was not a proscribed hatred that precipitated the assaults.

It should be noted that in 1990, offenses motivated by gender hatred or hatred of homosexuals were not covered by the Florida Hate Crimes Act, and such incidents were not reportable then. However, they are expected to be reported in the future.

The data on which this research is based were drawn from the raw reports of law enforcement officers as submitted to the Florida Department of Law Enforcement on a prescribed form titled, "Florida Hate Crime Statistical Report Form." These reports were sometimes scribbled and were frequently incomplete, but never in essential categories relating to victim and hate characteristics. Only a few had narrative explanations of incidents scrawled on the backs of the forms.

DATA PRESENTATION

Race of Victim

As shown in Table 21.1, whites represent the highest number of victims followed by blacks, who are 12 percent fewer.

Table 21.1
Race of Victim

Race	Number	Percent
Black	97	38
White	129	50
Asian	3	1
Unknown	30	11
Total	259	100

Age and Sex of Victim

Male victims outnumber female victims by more than 2 to 1. Twenty percent of victims are under 21 years of age; 54 percent are between 21 and 55; and 7 percent are over 55. In 19 percent of the incidents, age of victim is unknown or not applicable.

Race of Offender

There is a high percentage of unknowns in this category perhaps because race of offender is not essential to the official definition of a hate crime. Black and white were the only specific races recorded among the 259 reports submitted by law enforcement agencies. The number of white offenders exceeded the number of blacks by 6 percent. (See Table 21.2.)

Table 21.2
Race of Offender

Race	Number	Percent
Black	69	27
White	85	33
Unknown	105	40
Total	259	100

Sex and Age of Offender

Because sex and age of offender are also not essential to the official definition of hate crime, there is a high percentage of unknowns in these categories. Fifty-three percent of offenders are male and only 4 percent are female. Offender sex is unknown in 43 percent of the incidents recorded. Twenty percent of offenders are under 21 years of age; 22 percent are between 21 and 55; and 1 percent are older than 55. Age of offender is unknown in 57 percent of the incidents.

Hate Crime Target and Offense

The hate crime reporting scheme calls for information regarding whether offender action is taken against a person or against some inanimate object separated from a person. The vast majority (82 percent) of hate crimes are directed against the person with other targets being property, religious facility, and organization. Assault is the dominant (43 percent) offense category followed by damage to property (31 percent). Intimidation is the offense in 18 percent of the incidents with other offenses covering 8 percent of the incidents.

Indicator of Hate Motivation

Objective indicators of criminal actions motivated by hate are pivotal to determining a hate crime. "Investigative judgment" is obviously indispensable in identifying such indicators. Words are clearly the most frequently found indicator (Table 21.3).

Table 21.3
Indicator of Hate Motivation

Indicator	Number	Percent
Words	141	54
Gestures	15	6
Words and gestures	26	10
Symbols	38	15
Other	37	14
Unknown	2	1
Total	259	100

Racial hatred is the principal motivation for hate crime incidents (Table 21.4).

Table 21.4
Motivation

Motivation	Number	Percent
Race	177	68
Religion	54	21
Ethnicity	28	11
Total	259	100

Offender Race versus Victim Race

A comparison of the race of offenders to the race of their specific victims is shown in Table 21.5. By a slight margin, there are more incidents of blacks committing hate crimes against whites than incidents of whites committing hate crimes against blacks. Overall, there are more white offenders than black offenders. Because the law enforcement agency reports frequently omit offender race, the following covers only the 148 incidents where race of both the victim and the offender is indicated.

Table 21.5
Offender Race versus Victim Race

Offender vs. Victim	Number	Percent
Black vs. white	63	43
White vs. black	58	39
Black vs. black	5	3
White vs. white	22	15
Total	259	100

Offender Age versus Victim Age

There are 105 reported incidents where the age of both the offender and victim are known. Most hate crimes are committed by adults against other adults. The percentages in Table 21.6 are rounded.

Table 21.6
Offender Age versus Victim Age

Offender vs. Victim	Number	Percent
Youth vs. youth	26	25
Youth vs. adult	23	22
Youth vs. elderly	1	1
Adult vs. youth	11	10
Adult vs. adult	39	38
Adult vs. elderly	2	2
Elderly vs. youth	1	1
Elderly vs. adult	1	1
Elderly vs. elderly	1	1
Total	105	100

INCIDENT NARRATIVES

A few of the official hate crime report forms, submitted by law enforcement agencies, contain very brief narrative descriptions of the recorded incidents. Most are intended to clarify motivation indicators. The following is a condensed sampling of these narratives:

- Painted cross and "Nigger go Home."
- Satanic symbols—triangles burned.
- Shot at passing motorists—wanted to shoot a "cracker."
- Left note with these words—"The eyes of the Klan are upon you, you can't sleep with niggers and stay in this neighborhood. Move!"
- "That's what you get for being white."
- Swastikas on sidewalk.
- Trashed house and left "You were hit by the Jack Crew. You will die tonight. Hitler lives."
- Potato stuck in the tailpipe of a Jew's car with the word Jew scratched on side of car.
- KKK sprayed on a predominantly black elementary school.
- Suspect claims to have committed rape because his grandmother was raped by white men.
- "White whore" written on car because of dating a black male.
- Windows shot out of a synagogue.
- Offender defecated in chair and wrote "No Niggers."
- "Go back to China."
- "I'm going to shoot you white cracker."

SUMMARY AND DISCUSSION

An examination of the 259 incidents officially reported during the first full calendar year of the operation of the Florida Hate Crimes Reporting Act provides a rough picture of the newly defined concept of hate crime. Critical to the concept is the distinction made between hate indicators incidentally manifested during a crime and indications of hate actually motivating a crime. It hardly merits saying, but not all hatreds are condemned by the criminal statutes. In 1990, only hate based on race, ethnicity, national origin, or religion incurred criminal penalty and only if such hate triggered one of the ordinarily established crimes. Waiting in the wings are plans to include crimes motivated by hatred of gender and homosexuality.

Based on the data herein described, it is possible to set a profile of a hate crime in Florida. The typical hate crime is racially motivated, is committed by an adult male against another adult male, and is directed against the person. Words are the most frequent indicator of the hate motivation, and assault is most often the underlying offense. Most victims are white, and most offenders are white. When race of victim is matched to race of offender, there are slightly more blacks victimizing whites (43 percent) than whites victimizing blacks

(39 percent). Given the proportion of whites to blacks in the population and further given the generally known pattern of racism against blacks, the unexpected finding that blacks victimize whites slightly more often than whites victimize blacks warrants some further investigation. Although there is no firm indication of it among the data at hand, it is possible that there is a racial differential in the way victims take advantage of the new hate crime statutes. The finding might also be a function of the way the hate crime law is enforced.

Florida is a state with a rich mix of minority groups. There are precarious balances involving Haitians, blacks, Jews, Cubans, and Indians. There are also many migrant farm workers from Mexico. An enormous annual horde of tourists further complicates the task of maintaining harmonious interpersonal and intergroup relations. Seen in the context of Florida's diverse people, the number of hate crime incidents is less than appalling. This is far from saying that a significant problem does not exist or that efforts at reducing hate crime should not be increased.

As reporting mechanisms become refined, and as additional groups are placed under the protection of hate crime laws, it is reasonable to expect that the incidence of reported hate crime will rise. The question of whether such increase will be due to worsening intergroup relations or to bureaucratic effects is worthy of further study. The present research provides a minimal baseline for future studies.

SELECTED BIBLIOGRAPHY

Anti-Defamation League of B'nai B'rith. (1988a). *Hate Crime Statutes: A Response to Anti-Semitism, Vandalism and Violent Bigotry.*

Anti-Defamation League of B'nai B'rith. (1988b). *Hate Groups in America: A Report of Bigotry and Racism.*

National Institute Against Prejudice and Violence. (1986). *Striking Back at Bigotry: Remedies Under Federal and State Law for Violence Motivated by Racial, Religious, and Ethnic Prejudice.*

National Organization of Black Law Enforcement Executives (NOBLE). (1985). *Racial and Religious Violence: A Model Law Enforcement Response.*

National Organization of Black Law Enforcement Executives (NOBLE). (1986). *Racial and Religious Violence: A Law Enforcement Guidebook.*

State of California, Office of the Attorney General. (1986). *Racial, Ethnic and Religious Crimes Project: Preliminary Steps to Establish Statewide Collection of Data.*

State of Florida, Office of the Attorney General. (1991). *Hate Crimes in Florida, January 1, 1990–December 31, 1990.*

State of Florida, Florida Department of Law Enforcement. (1989). *Hate Crimes Report Manual.*

United States Commission on Civil Rights. (1983). *Intimidation and Violence: Racial and Religious Bigotry in America.*

United States Department of Justice, Federal Bureau of Investigation. (1990). *Hate Crime Data Collection Guidelines* (revised draft July 18, 1990).

CONNECTING THE PAST TO THE FUTURE: HATE CRIME IN AMERICA

*Carolyn Petrosino**

Abstract: This chapter argues that hate crimes are not a modern-day phenomenon but extend throughout the history of the United States. Using a definition based on intrinsic justice rather than codified law, selected events in the seventeenth through early nineteenth centuries are examined. Comparative analysis indicated similarities and differences between historical and modem events. The distillation of conditions surrounding hate crime dynamics both past and present, along with the examination of current trends suggest the following summary factors: (1) Racism is a primary predictor of hate crime through time; (2) the efficiency and degree of harm potential in hate crime is a function of opportunity and technology; (3) hate crimes will occur more frequently and be more difficult to prevent; (4) notwithstanding the repugnant nature of hate crime, many Americans are becoming more sympathetic to the hate crime perpetrator's cause; and (5) hate crime, on some levels, is becoming indistinguishable from domestic terrorism.

On June 7, 1998, James Byrd, Jr., a black man, was hitchhiking home following a relative's bridal shower when a truck pulled up. However, instead of receiving a lift home, Byrd was kidnapped, taken to a wooded area, beaten to unconsciousness, chained to the back of the truck, and then dragged for several miles. His head and right arm were torn from his body during the dragging and were later found in a ditch along the road. His assailants were three white men with links to racist groups (Hohler, 1998). It is believed that the genesis for this gruesome murder was racial hatred.

Hate crimes are despicable acts. Their toll only begins with the victim. Harm expands to the victim's family, group, and society itself. Its greatest cost

*The author wishes to thank Mark Hamm, Ann Mulvey, Joe Lipchitz, Gerald Hotaling, Mike Israel, and the anonymous reviewers for their helpful comments on an earlier draft of this chapter. Special thanks to Anthony Petrosino for his encouragement and editorial comments, along with an unnamed supporter who never falls me. This chapter first appeared in the *Journal of Contemporary Criminal Justice,* Vol. 15, No. I, February 1999, pp. 22–47.

is not only measured in property damages, medical expenses, or the loss of wages, but also in the depreciation of the human spirit in dignity, liberty, and security. Furthermore, lethal hate crimes like the Byrd murder take on a quality of frenzied killing; they attest to a revelry in the destruction of a human being. Hamm (1998a) refers to this as "the carnival of violence" (p. 250). The costs of such acts upon society are immeasurable.

The savagery that ended Byrd's life is not an isolated incident; it has occurred over and over in U.S. history (Bureau of Justice Assistance, 1997; J. Levin & McDevitt, 1993). This examination reviews a sample of historical events in light of recent hate crime legislation. The primary objective here is to answer the question that some scholars have posed: Is American hate crime a distinctively modern phenomenon? (Czajkoski, 1992). As this chapter will show, substantial evidence exists to suggest that hate crime as a behavior has existed in America for more than 300 years; however, only recently—relatively speaking—has it become recognized as a violation of law.

Searching for examples of historical hate crimes means moving away from legal definitions. Instead, a definition based on intrinsic justice is needed because many hate crimes discussed here were not considered illegal at the time (Jordan, 1968; Miller, 1979; Stampp, 1956; Steinfield, 1973; Takaki, 1994a, 1994b; Wells-Barnett, 1969). Intrinsic justice is an inherent balance scale of justice. Natural law is written on the conscious of humankind by our Creator, allowing us to discern good versus evil (Devlin, 1986). It is an internal compass causing consciousness of moral and immoral behavior (for more information on this topic, refer to St. Thomas Aquinas [Feinberg & Gross, 1986], or the Holy Bible, Book of Romans 2:14–15). Intrinsic justice has great value because it overrides self-serving special interests that sometimes lead to codified law. It possesses a universal quality causing most community members to collectively consider a behavior right or wrong (e.g., incest [Pallone, 1990]). Harms perpetrated on individuals because of their race, gender, culture, or social status may meet this universal standard. Such behaviors are malum in se or wrong in themselves; they are naturally evil.

In addition to responding to the initial question posed, this chapter accomplishes four objectives: to (1) redefine hate crime, permitting a definition that covers legal but immoral acts in history; (2) identify historical events that meet the new definition; (3) provide a comparative analysis of past and present hate crimes; and (4) predict the scope of future hate crimes and system response.

DEFINING HATE CRIME ACTS

Contemporary hate crime legal concepts are often varied and complex. What identifies a hate crime in one jurisdiction may not be useful in another (Martin, 1996). Similar to this, statutory definitions of hate crimes vary across jurisdictions (Hamm, 1994). For instance, some statutes will list race, color, religion, or national origin as specific categories protected by hate crime legislation. Other states may also include gender, sexual orientation, and the physically disabled in their laws. Hate crime scholarship argues that victim categories extend from the traditional—race, ethnicity, religion, and sexual orientation—to gender, disabilities, age, class, and even political persuasion

(Bureau of Justice Assistance, 1997; Gerstenfeld, 1992). Historically, such perspectives of crime victims were nonexistent.

To begin constructing a more adequate definition, characteristics of modern American hate crime victims were identified. These include the following: (1) Most victims are members of distinct racial or ethnic (cultural) minority groups (Bureau of Justice Assistance, 1997; Hamm, 1994); (2) most victim groups are decidedly less powerful politically and economically than the majority group (Hamm, 1993); and (3) victims represent to the perpetrator a threat to their quality of life (i.e., economic stability and/or physical safety) (J. Levin & McDevitt, 1993). These common factors suggest the following base definition of hate crime: the victimization of minorities due to their racial or ethnic identity by members of the majority. This definition focuses on the imbalance of power between the perpetrator (majority) and the victim (minority), emphasizing harm potential in hate crimes. Although hate crimes certainly occur across racial and socioeconomic categories (i.e., perpetrators can be minorities and victims from the majority group), the most typical incidents are covered by the base definition (Bureau of Justice Assistance, 1997).

Although hate crimes are more easily identified today, this is not true historically. Among the reasons for this include the lack of criminalization; the absence of constitutional, statutory, or other legal rights of victims; the normative values of past eras that denied personhood to victims; and the cornplicitous or direct role of governments and other authorities in hate acts.

Recorded history reveals that although acts such as assault, theft, murder, and rape were considered crimes under the common law, the same acts when motivated by racism or ethnocentrism were not (Hoffer, 1992; Jordan, 1968). The reasons lie in the foundation of law itself. Laws and the criminal justice system often express the intent of powerful interest groups (Mann, 1993; Walker et al., 1996). Few would argue that the protective authority of the law in America did not routinely extend to the poor or nonwhites. In fact, many states disallowed nonwhites full legal redress particularly in matters that accused whites (Perlmutter, 1992; Steinfield, 1973; Takaki, 1994a, 1994b).

The Value of Intrinsic Justice and Moral Theory

Although the law emphasizes some aspects of morality, it does not pronounce all moral behavior. It has biased qualities that at times reflects the interests of only some segments of society while ignoring others (Messner & Rosenfeld, 1997) and is inherently flawed (Hoffer, 1992; Mackie, 1977; Pollock-Byrne, 1989). Moreover, some laws could be viewed as immoral (e.g., Three Strikes Law, the death penalty, abortion, the federal sentencing guidelines for powder cocaine vs. crack cocaine offenders). To some, such laws legitimize immoral acts. Although laws fall short of embodying morality, intrinsic justice transcends the moral shortcomings of codified law (Haskins, 1969; Pound, 1938).

In some ways, intrinsic justice is reflected in morality. The dominant moral theories in American—as well as in most Western cultures—are teleological and deontological in nature. To define briefly, teleological moral theory states that the rightness or wrongness of an action depends on its consequences, whereas deontological moral theory states that the rightness or wrongness of an action is intrinsic to the act itself. More familiar than the term *teleological* is utilitarianism that defines moral behavior as that which brings the greatest good to the greatest number. Kantian ethics[1] best illustrates deontological theory, and it advocates that one has a duty to act according to universal principles of morality. These theories appeal to a rational logic that determines moral behavior. However, deontological theory more closely resembles intrinsic justice because of its appeal to universal standards. Under the lens of deontological theory, hate crimes are clearly immoral due to their inherent nature.

A Definition of Hate Crime and Selection Criteria for Historical Events

In this chapter, the following definition of hate crime is used: the victimization of minorities due to their racial or ethnic identity by members of the majority. However, an additional measure was applied to further underscore the imbalance of power between the victim and perpetrator. The consideration of whether the legal authorities of that time would have responded to the acts in a similar fashion if victims were white Anglo-Saxon[2] Protestants.

Selection of historical events was based on the following criteria: (1) moral offensiveness; (2) the presence, at least in part, of a racial or ethnic bias motive; (3) intentional harming; (4) existence of the likelihood that the justice system would have responded differently if the victim(s) had been white; and (5) an event that occurred before the first wave of hate crime legislation in the 1980s.[3]

Most events selected occurred during the seventeenth, eighteenth, and nineteenth centuries. In addition, the incidents were drawn from the historical experiences of racial minority populations in America. Although historical hate crimes were not an experience solely of racial or ethnic minorities, longevity of victimization uniquely applied to them (Perlmutter, 1992). This pattern is also reflected in contemporary hate crime statistics (Bureau of Justice Assistance, 1997). It is recognized that other ethnic and racial groups have sustained prolonged periods of persecution (i.e., Jewish and Mexican Americans). However, the documented evidence of harms in the form of murder and other destructive acts perpetrated against Native Americans, blacks, and Asians is very compelling. It is further noted that although there are countless historical events that could have been selected, it is not the purpose of this chapter to document each episode; rather, the purpose is to highlight those events that demonstrate the nature of historical hate crime. Historical records as reported in secondary and tertiary sources are relied on in the examination of selected events due to their high recognition and frequent representation in archival and other sources.

MANIFEST DESTINY: THE AMERICAN CULTURE OF HATE

Before reviewing specific historical incidents, it is important to describe an essential feature in American culture that helped to foster racial hatred. Several scholars have noted that hate crime acts are rationalized through an established ideology (Arendt, 1963; Gibbs, 1989; Hamm, 1994; J. Levin &

McDevitt, 1993). The hate crime perpetrator is often ethnocentric and devalues his or her victims. Such beliefs are not created in a vacuum. American culture, both past and present, includes similar beliefs and values. Systematic bigotry and discrimination, or the "culture of hate" (J. Levin & McDevitt, 1993), continuously reaffirms the identity of unworthy members of society, thus instigating and ensuring their victimization. In this chapter, manifest destiny is examined as a contributor to ethnocentrism, intolerance, and hate crime in America.

Manifest destiny was the belief that America was to be governed by white Anglo-Saxon Protestants, as ordained by "God Almighty." Although not a formal policy until 1845, its tenets were evident from the earliest moments of white colonization (Horsman, 1981; Perlmutter, 1992). The idea of a divine mission was present in the seventeenth century (Horsman, 1981; Perlmutter, 1992). Colonial America linked Christianity to racial purity or whiteness and heathenism with racial impurity or nonwhiteness. Therefore, destiny, Christianity, and racial identity were culturally conjoined early in American history (Jordan, 1968). In fact, racial superiority permeated American culture to the point where being American was synonymous with being white. Other races were viewed as foreigners. Prophylactic measures were applied to maintain the distinctions. Thus, practices such as systematic exclusion and discrimination further legitimized bigotry and hatred. Manifest destiny, in the minds of many, justified American expansionism by any means necessary (Merk, 1963). Therefore, if discrimination, racism, fraud, theft, rape, kidnapping, and even murder achieved destiny objectives, such acts were considered to be acceptable consequences.

The following sections examine a selected sample of historical events. After a brief description of the racial attitudes comprising the social climate of that era, a review of the incident and a discussion of its legitimacy as a hate crime are presented.

NATIVE AMERICANS AS VICTIMS OF HATE CRIME

The Social Climate

Many historians have described early contacts between Europeans and Native Americans as nonviolent. However, the nature of their relationship changed with the self-serving acts of the Europeans[4] (Sanders, 1978; Spindler, 1972; Steinfield, 1973; Tebbel & Jennison, 1960). The term *noble savage* came to represent the European image of the Native American (Farb, 1968; Harjo, 1998), a phrase that indicated both disdain and regard. Eventually, this image became more malevolent. As Native Americans increasingly resisted European encroachment and deceptive practices, they were depicted as barbaric (Harjo, 1998; Riding In, 1998). Frequently infantilized stereotyped groups are perceived as dangerous when docile behavior is replaced with assertiveness (J. Levin & Levin, 1982; J. Levin & McDevitt, 1993). Records maintained by the Department of Indian Affairs illustrate attitudes once held toward the Native American.[5]

Historical Events: The Near Genocide of the Yuki and Cheyenne Indians

The Yuki of northern California numbered approximately 5000[6] when first encountered by white settlers in 1848. By this time, many atrocities had been routinely committed against Native Americans in the form of kidnapping, theft, fraud, forced indentured servitude, sexual assault, intentional spread of disease, depletion of food supplies, starvation,[7] and murder (Riding In, 1998). Targeting the Yuki for similar treatment, therefore, was not an aberrant act. Military records indicated interest in exterminating them for the sake of white settlements (Miller, 1979). Private efforts were substituted by state sponsored kill parties to affect the goal (Chalk & Jonassohn, 1990; Perlmutter, 1992). The following is an excerpt of the 1851 annual state message given by California Governor Burnett (Perlmutter, 1992, p. 136):

> A war of extermination will continue to be waged between the two races until the Indian race becomes extinct . . . while we cannot anticipate this result with but painful regret, the inevitable destiny of the race is beyond the power and wisdom of man to avert.

As a result of Burnett's pogroms, the Yukis lost 90 percent of their population in a 32-year period (Chalk & Jonassohn, 1990).

The Cheyenne were victims of similar acts as described in the 39th U.S. Congressional record, 2nd session, Senate Report 156. The following is an account of a mass murder on November 28, 1864, as told by eyewitness Robert Bent (Brown, 1970, p. 73):

> When the troops fired, the Indians ran . . . . I think there were six-hundred Indians in all . . . about sixty [men] in all . . . I saw five squaws under a bank for shelter . . . but the soldiers shot them all . . . There seemed to be indiscriminate slaughter of men, women, and children. There were some thirty or forty squaws collected in a hole for protection; they sent out a little girl about six years old with a white flag on a stick; she had not proceeded but a few steps when she was shot and killed. Everyone I saw dead was scalped. I saw one squaw cut open with an unborn child. . . . I saw the body of a leader, with the privates cut off, and I heard a soldier say he was going to make a tobacco pouch out of them. I saw quite a number of infants in arms killed with their mothers.[8]

Argument for the Classification of These Events as Hate Crime

Few would disagree that these acts were anything less than barbaric, but are they hate crimes? The acts committed against the Yuki and Cheyenne clearly intended to cause significant harm. The nature of the acts also indicates a potent disregard of the victims' humanity. Evidence of racial animus toward Native Americans, which permeated white American culture then, is prolific (Berthrong, 1963). For instance, it was not until 1891,[9] that a U.S. Supreme Court decision declared that Indians were human beings. Note the writing of an Oregon settler (Kennedy, 1959, p. 10):

It was customary [for the Whites] to speak of the Indian man as a buck; of the woman as a squaw; until at length in the general acceptance of the terms, they ceased to recognize the tights of humanity in those to whom they were applied. By a very natural and easy transition, from being spoken of as brutes they came to be thought of as game to be shot, or as vermin to be destroyed.[10]

It could be concluded that racial bias was a primary motive in the events described. The case for moral offensiveness is apparent. Kant's morality test includes whether it would be desirable and appropriate if such acts were universalized, thus permitting any person to commit them. The genocidal actions described would not have been embraced by nineteenth-century America if the aggressor and victim groups were reversed. It is unlikely that the government would have financed genocidal acts of Native Americans against whites, nor would the justice system have remained passive to such acts (Riding In, 1998).

AFRICANS AND AFRICAN DESCENDANTS AS VICTIMS OF HATE CRIME

The Social Climate

It is well documented that perceptions of Africa and African people have been articulated through a Eurocentric perspective (Fredrickson, 1991; Jordan, 1968; Pieterse, 1992). Although the early images of Africans were dynamic,[11] once Europe focused economic interest on the New World, the utility of a particular image was needed. Some have argued that early African enslavement by Europeans was based on culture rather than race, yet some evidence suggests otherwise. The racial characterizations attributed to African people by Europeans were inextricably linked to the devaluation of African cultures. For example, Jordan (1968) and others contend that the British associated blackness with negativity, evil,[12] and foulness. The Africans' skin color and non-Christian religious practices made it less complicated for the British to view them as uncivilized heathens. Subsequently, it became rational for them to associate heathenism—with its inferences to inferiority—with blackness.

By 1625, Africans were enslaved internationally (Jordan, 1968). In fact, being African became synonymous with being enslavable (Morris, 1996; Rome, 1998). The perception of the African as inferior did not change in the colonies. From their earliest experiences in colonial America, Africans were treated in a debased manner. This discriminatory treatment[13] predated the institution of slavery (Horsman, 1981; Morris, 1996). When the legalization of African slavery occurred in the colonies, the scientific community offered evidence of the African's racial inferiority. Moreover, the Black or Slave Codes beginning in 1640 further distinguished blacks from all other groups in America. These initiatives reinforced the racial animus and prejudice whites held toward them.

Historical Event: Black Slavery

Before the actual tenure of slavery began, the transoceanic voyage from the west coast of Africa to the Caribbean and then to the colonies proved to be an extraordinarily brutal event. The following account is an observer's description of the nature of the Middle passage voyage (Perlmutter, 1992, p. 18):

> The sense of misery and suffocation was so terrible that in the 'tweendecks— where the height was sometimes only eighteen inches, so that the unfortunate slaves could not turn around, were wedged immovably in fact, and chained to the deck by the neck and legs—that the slaves not infrequently would go mad before dying or suffocating. In their frenzy some killed others in the hope of procuring more room to breathe. Men strangled those next to them and women drove nails into each other's brains.

Conservative estimates place the death toll during the voyages at approximately 100,000 (Higginbotham, 1978). Shortly after slavery was established, it received the legal status of perpetual (Jordan, 1968), making the loss of freedom lifelong and complete. The status of children born to slaves was clarified when slavery was defined by law as an inherited condition. Servitude dismissed the humanity of blacks in white society. As chattel, a black's value was simply contingent on age, health, strength, and other factors related to work ability. The value of African women was determined by their ability to bear future slaves and work the fields; they were viewed as beasts of burden. As a result, they were often made to give birth in plantation fields (Jordan, 1968).

Despite an enormous effort from religious, political, and scientific quarters to justify slavery, there existed a flaw in the proslavery thesis. Blacks were forced to accept their natural status. Slaveholders often employed various techniques to coerce blacks to accept their conditions (Stampp, 1956). Military protocols for breaking the will of Africans and creating manageable slaves were implemented (Jordan, 1968; Stampp, 1956). The system of slavery necessitated crimes of fraud, kidnapping, assault, torture, inhumane treatment,[14] forced labor, rape, and psychological abuse propelled by economic interests, and racial bias.

Historical Event: Lynching

The history of American lynching has not been widely studied, despite the significance of its occurrence. Named for Charles Lynch, who popularized the act during the eighteenth century, lynching or lynch law involved the execution of an accused individual without due process of law. Although whites were also lynched, blacks were disproportionately victimized (Cutler, 1969). For example, the victimization rate of blacks in southern states was 350 percent greater than that of whites (Cutler, 1969; Dennis, 1984; Wells-Barnett, 1969).

Black lynching in southern states escalated following emancipation. It was a response to the federal government's effort to remove legal constraints on black participation in America's political, social, and economic systems. Little provocation was required for blacks to be victimized. Social activist Ida

B. Wells provided commentary on two 1892 lynchings, epitomizing the vulnerability of blacks at that time (Wells-Barnett, 1969, p. 17): "John Hughes of Moberly (Missouri) and Isaac Lincoln of Fort Madison (S. Carolina) and Will Lewis in Tullahoma, Tenn. suffered death for no more serious charge than that they were 'saucy' to white people."

According to some records, "lynching was so common it was impossible to keep accurate accounts" (Perlmutter, 1992, p. 151).[15] The *Chicago Tribune* reported that between 1882 and 1903, a total of 3337 blacks were known to have been lynched by white mobs (Cutler, 1969). The following is an account of a July 15, 1921, lynching in Moultrie, Georgia. An eyewitness described the incident for a local newspaper (Steinfield, 1973, pp. 40–42):

> Williams was brought from Moultrie on Friday night by sheriffs. . . . Saturday court was called . . . The trial took half an hour. Then Williams, surrounded by fifty sheriffs armed with machine guns, started out of the courthouse door toward the jail . . . 500 poor pecks rushed the sheriffs, who made no resistance. . . . They tore the negro's [sic] clothing off. . . . The negro [sic] was unsexed, as usual, and made to eat a portion of his anatomy. . . . The negro [sic] was chained to [a] stump. . . . The pyre was lit and a hundred men. . . . women, old and young, grandmothers among them, joined hands and danced around the negro [sic] while he burned.

Argument for the Classification of These Events as Hate Crime

Both slavery and lynching were uniquely applied to blacks,[16] indicating a bias motive. Particularly in the case of slavery, only Africans were selected for perpetual bondage (Higginbotham, 1978; Stampp, 1956). The intentional harm incorporated in both acts are obvious—including the theft of another's liberty for economic gain and the theft of another's life without due process. Moreover, slavery and lynching are morally reprehensible,[17] inasmuch as neither fit Kant's criteria for moral behavior. It is unlikely that either would have been embraced as appropriate universal behavior. If whites had been routinely the victims of activities necessary to enslave or lynch, governmental and law enforcement bodies would have responded differently (Morris, 1996).

ASIAN IMMIGRANTS AS VICTIMS OF HATE CRIME

The Social Climate

Asian laborers were invited to the United States to assist the transcontinental railroad construction and to work Hawaiian sugar plantations (Healey, 1995). Although initially viewed as industrious, images of Asians were influenced by several factors. During the latter nineteenth century, the scientific community focused on racial classifications. Not unlike Africans and Native Americans, Asians did not fair well in these schemes. For instance, some contended that the adult Mongoloid was equivalent to an adolescent Caucasian (Gould, 1981). Many stereotypes used to depict Native Americans and Africans were used against Asians as well (Takaki, 1994b, p. 66).

White workers called the Chinese "nagurs," [sic] and a magazine cartoon depicted a Chinese man as a bloodsucking vampire with slanted eyes, a pig tail, dark skin, and thick lips. Like blacks, the Chinese were described as heathen, morally inferior, savage, childlike, and lustful. Chinese women were condemned as a "depraved class" and said to resemble Africans.

Several states enacted laws during the 1800s to constrain Asian liberties. These statutes segregated them and culminated in an effort to banish them from the United States. The pervasiveness of anti-Asian sentiments from that era is illustrated by a statement attributed to Theodore Roosevelt. He never approved of Japanese immigration, and regarding the Hawaiian islands, he said that they should have "a white population representing American civilization" (Takaki, 1994b, p. 76). Roosevelt also believed America should be preserved as a heritage for "Whites, and that because Asians were entirely different, they should not live in the country" (Takaki, 1994b).

Other political organizations echoed similar sentiments. The Native Sons of the Golden West is credited with the following statement (Chronister, 1992, pp. 40–41): "that the state of California should remain what it had always been and God himself intended it shall always be the White Man's Paradise . . . the 31st star shall ever become dim or yellow?"

Historical Event: Kearneyism

Asian unemployment surged at the completion of the railway, but it was short lived. Most took jobs that whites declined, or they started their own businesses. Asians found steady work in menial labor, and white unemployment became an increasing problem.[18] Labor leader Denis Kearney and others inflamed anti-Asian sentiments (Steinfield, 1973). He sent a very clear message that the presence of Chinese people was among the chief causes of economic woes for the region. Moreover, with their removal, the economic problems of whites would eventually dissipate. This message, along with preexisting norms of prejudice and racism, created an atmosphere that prompted spontaneous acts of violence against Asians. During this period of Kearneyism, Asian-owned businesses were frequently vandalized and burned down. Asians were also robbed, assaulted, and murdered. However, because they lacked basic civil liberties, little was done by the legal system in response to their victimization. The murder of Asians became so casual that the print media frequently chose not to report its occurrence (Steinfleld, 1973; Takaki, 1994b).

Historical Event: The Japanese Internment

Following Pearl Harbor, Roosevelt issued Executive Order 9066 (Steinfield, 1973). Pursuant to the order, the land borders of the United States were closed to all enemy aliens and all persons of Japanese ancestry, even American citizens. This caused the mass arrest and incarceration of more than 100,000 persons of Japanese ancestry—of which two-thirds were American citizens. Based on race, this action occurred as a result of long-standing suspicions and prejudice. Evidence of this attitude is demonstrated in a statement attributed to Commanding General John DeWitt (Chronister, 1992, p. 43):

In the war in which we are now engaged racial affinities are not severed by migration. The Japanese race is an enemy race and while many second and third generation Japanese born on US [sic] soil, possessed of US [sic] citizenship have become "Americanized," the racial strains are undiluted.

Those destined for the internment camps required only one eighth of Japanese blood to lose their liberty (Chronister, 1992). This determination of guilt was based on racial heritage—an abnormal evidentiary standard. Besides mass incarceration, the urgency of the evacuation and relocation caused many Japanese to lose accumulated wealth and possessions (Daniels, 1993; Takaki, 1994a).

Argument for the Classification of These Events as Hate Crime

Both Kearneyism and the internment camp experience caused significant psychological, physical, and economic harm. Total disruption of family and community life, compounded with the sudden loss of financial security, brought irreparable damages. Also, these incidents were morally offensive. Based on Kantian principles, the victims were treated merely as ends rather than as means (i.e., ridding white males of job competitors and the incapacitation of an imagined threat to national security that was easy to identify). Evidence of racial bias is easily perceived.

Once again, such attitudes were prevalent in American culture. For example, during the early 1900s, the *San Francisco Chronicle* printed a series of articles that depicted Asians in a contemptuous manner: "Brown Men Are Made Citizens Illegally"; "Japanese a Menace to American Women"; "Brown Men an Evil in the Public Schools"; and "The Yellow Peril-How Japanese Crowd Out the White Race" (Steinfield, 1973; Takaki, 1994a). In addition, in 1981 the Commission of Wartime Relocation formally acknowledged that the internment of Japanese Americans was based on racism (Daniels, 1993). The United States was also at war with Germany and Italy, yet German and Italian Americans were not subjected to the same collective suspicion and persecution at the hands of the federal government. The government's position reflected the mindset that white Americans would not be scrutinized due to their ethnicity or race as were Asian Americans. Likewise, the consequences of Kearneyism would have been brought under control quickly had the attackers been Asian and the victims white Americans.

DISCUSSION

Similarities Between the Past and Present

America's current hate crime problem is not a distinctly modern phenomenon; rather, it has deep historical roots. Harmful acts motivated by racist attitudes and ethnocentrism have frequently occurred throughout American history.

There are many parallels between historical and present-day hate crimes. The most apparent similarity is the presence of white racism in American culture. Racially motivated acts are born out of racist attitudes, making those attitudes powerful predictors of subsequent hate crime (Hamm, 1993). Racism was as prevalent in the past as it is today. Evidence of it was found in institutional and cultural practices. Governmental policies encouraged institutional racism with Indian relocation programs, black codes, and anti-Asian legislation. Social sentiment supported and was reinvigorated by such policies. Evidence of modern racist attitudes, unfortunately, is also well documented (Barkan & Cohn, 1994; Brown, 1995; Hacker, 1995; Mann, 1993).

Other similarities between past and present hate crimes include characteristics of the crimes, perpetrators, and victims. Table 22.1 summarizes these factors. In addition, Table 22.1 compares historical and modern hate crime acts. Historical events are those that occurred before the first wave of hate crime legislation beginning in the 1980s. The two categories are compared using common characteristics gleaned from a review of the historical events.

Factors A to D are concerned with the prevailing attitudes of the times and indicate a social and political environment that facilitated division and acts of intolerance. Modern and historical social climates are viewed similarly across these elements. Factors F and 0 describe the identities of the typical perpetrator and victim of hate crime. Similarities are found once again. With regard to Factor H, historical hate crimes frequently involved significant bodily harm and death, whereas most modern hate crimes do not. Some research indicates

Table 22.1

Comparisons between Historical and Modern Hate Crime Factors

Common Items From Historical Events	*Historical Events*[a]	*Modern Events*
Factor A: Perpetrators group reflected ideas similar to the mainstream	X	X
Factor B: Perpetrator group believed the target group to be inadequate, inferior, and undeserving (culture of hate in place)	X	X
Factor C: Diversity not well tolerated	X	X
Factor D: Targets were identified as anti-American, blamed for the ill of the country, inflation, unemployment, crime, loss of morality	X	X
Factor E: Perpetrator rarely punished	X	—[b]
Factor F: Perpetrators were primarily white males	X	X
Factor G: Targets were primarily people of color	X	X
Factor H: Hate crime was characteristically violent	X	—[c]
Factor I: Targeted groups have constitutional protections by federal and state law	—	X
Factor J: Hate groups were affiliated with legitimate political parties (or sought affiliation)	X	X[d]

[a]An event is considered historical if it is pre–hate crime legislation.

[b]Punishment is relatively lenient.

[c]Much of it is crime against properties, yet incidents of violence are increasing.

[d]For example, extremists infiltrated the Buchanan and Dole organizations and the David Duke and Tom Metzger early runs on Democratic and Republican tickets.

that a higher percentage of bias crimes result in physical harm than nonbias offenses; however, the clear majority of hate crimes are property related (B. Levin, 1992–1993).

Factor J denotes the presence of affiliation of organized hate groups like the Ku Klux Klan with legitimate political parties. In historical events, government officials were often active participants in the crimes, implying representation in mainstream political organizations (Jordan, 1968; Steinfield, 1973). Likewise, modern events indicate infiltration of extremists in traditional political parties (Hamm, 1993).

Factor E compares the level of punishment received by hate crime perpetrators. Analysis of historical events suggests that perpetrators acted with impunity—punishment was a rare occurrence. Modern hate crime perpetrators often receive lenient punishment due to their age and absence of prior record (J. Levin & McDevitt, 1993). However, these offenders are recognized across all jurisdictions as criminals. Factor I compares the level of constitutional or other statutory protections afforded hate crime victim groups. Historical evidence indicates the general absence of such protections, whereas modern victims have received the benefit of various legal mechanisms for protection.

The Future of American Hate Crime

Recent changes in hate crime suggest their prevention and control will become more difficult. They include the following: (1) a greater ability to cause mass destruction, (2) a growing acceptance of extremist ideology in the marketplace of political ideas, (3) the legal protection of extremists in the court system, (4) an increase in religious zealotry among hate crime perpetrators, and (5) an increase adoption of extremist agenda into the concerns of middle America.

Mass Destruction

Whereas the examined historical events caused the victimization of countless persons, they also required the participation of many. Conversely, modern hate crime perpetrators have the capacity to cause large-scale destruction singlehandedly. In 1989, Patrick Purdy, described as a dysfunctional transient with a criminal record, acquired a semiautomatic assault rifle and shot Asian children during recess in their Stockton, California elementary school. Purdy wounded 30 children and killed 5 (J. Levin & McDevitt, 1993). Likewise, Colin Ferguson, the Long Island shooter, wounded 19 and killed 6 (Van Biema, 1995); and Terry Nichols and Tim McVeigh wounded more than 400 people and caused the death of 168 persons (Federal Emergency Management Agency, 1995).

In addition, hate crime perpetrators have learned the value of forming alliances and coalitions (Christensen, 1994; Hamm, 1994; J.Levin & McDevitt, 1993). Information is shared regarding bomb manufacturing, as well as other techniques to disrupt vital infrastructure such as energy sources, water systems, and telecommunications and transportation systems (Southern Poverty Law Center Report, 1997a). With computer technology, such coalitions transverse states as well as continents. The Federal Bureau of Investigation has long reported links between American hate groups and middle-eastern state-sponsored terrorist organizations (J. Levin & McDevitt, 1993; Sloan, 1997). These developments have enabled modern perpetrators to compile arsenals that give pause to many law enforcement agents. Raids have uncovered a panoply of sophisticated weaponry (Valentine, 1995), in addition to plans to secure missiles, biochemical agents, and nuclear weaponry (Southern Poverty Law Center Report, 1997a). Thus, modern advancements allow hate crime perpetrators to become major threats to society. As we approach the new millennium, several watch groups report that extremists are planning acts with the potential for massive loss of life (Hamm, 1998b).

Growing Acceptance of Extremist Ideology

Even more disturbing is the quiet acquiescence and adoption of extremist views in mainstream political platforms and ideologies (Hagan, 1997; Horowitz, 1996; J. Levin & McDevitt, 1993; McLemee, 1997). Although Tom Metzger is considered by some to be the leading force behind the revitalization of the racist skinhead movement in the United States (Hamm, 1994), he consistently sought to enter into the foray of mainstream politics early in his career. He supported Republican Presidential Candidate Barry Goldwater in 1964 and George Wallace in 1968, and he found agreement in much of the Reagan platform. Metzger ran for a congressional seat in 1980. His extreme views were present in his political vision; he may have been one of the original critics of affirmative action policies (Hamm, 1993). Today, affirmative action is moot in California, and it is currently under challenge in several other states. Also, Metzger advocated legislation to end immigration with particular emphasis on sealing U.S. borders from Mexican illegals. Similar to this, Patrick Buchanan, in his Republican primary bid, announced a platform that harmonized strongly with many of Metzger's views (Project Vote Smart, 1992–1998).

Gain of Legal Protection

The courts may be ineffectual in stemming actions that facilitate intolerance. Court decisions reveal increasing hesitancy to interfere with hate speech. First Amendment purists argue for the constitutional right of extremists to espouse their vitriol in public (Heumann & Church, 1997)—even cross burning has been construed as protected speech (see Lawrence [1996] discussion of *R.A.V. v. City of St. Paul, Minnesota*). Using the same First Amendment argument, extremist organizations are using the Internet to provide provocative information. They are able to proselytize, to announce rallies and White Power rock concerts and to provide additional disturbing information (Hamm, 1993; Southern Poverty Law Center Report, 1997b). Hate advocates have discovered a market in how-to-books, such as *Bacteriological Warfare: A Major Threat to North America—A Guide for the Development, Preservation and Deployment of Biological Agents,* authored by Larry Wayne Harris; and William Powell's *Anarchist Cookbook.* Chapters include the following: "How to Make Tear Gas in Your Basement," "How to Build a Silencer for a Submachine Gun," or "How to Make Nitroglycerin." These works have been protected by the U.S. Constitution and the courts.

Increase in Religious Zealotry

Although America has denounced religion-based terrorism in Ireland, Bosnia, India, Pakistan, and the Middle East, some contend that the United States is witnessing the start of the same turmoil on its own soil (Southern Poverty Law Center Report, 1997a). American hate crime perpetrators, organized groups, and other extremist affiliations are often connected by a mutual belief in Christian Identity theology. A pseudoreligion, Christian Identity promotes a doctrine that the white race will be involved in a cataclysmic war against other races and political enemies (Barkun, 1994). This religion has been repeatedly claimed by many organized extremists such as the Aryan Nation and the White Aryan Resistance (Barkun, 1994; Christensen, 1994). Timothy McVeigh reportedly was influenced by the Identity movement. These individuals are devoted to their theology.

Middle America is Becoming More Sympathetic

Since the popularity of political conservatism in the 1980s, Americans have continued to embrace conservative beliefs and values. Although the Clinton administration and many economists describe America's economic health as robust, some Americans are skeptical. As corporations, businesses, and banking institutions merge and local economic conditions are affected, Americans become increasingly concerned and increasingly conservative (Bryjak & Soroka, 1997). In fact, working-class Americans are a growing populace of alienated, hostile, frustrated individuals who are expressing views not unlike some extremists (Horatio Alger Association, 1996; "Pool Points," 1996). Scapegoating is at an all-time high. Not unlike the viewpoints of the patriot, separatist, survivalist, supremacist, militia, or other anarchist movements, anxiety-filled working-class Americans have pointed the finger of blame at everything from working women, the nation of Israel, and non-English-speaking Hispanics to liberalism, the New World Order, and the Bureau of Alcohol, Tobacco and Firearms. Add to this mix Americans who are seduced by extremist rhetoric, and the potential is there for an escalation of hate crimes or domestic terrorism in this country that is fueled by racial hatred (Goldhagen, 1996).

CONCLUSION

Historical hate crimes were shaped by the forces of their day. Prevailing societal attitudes that legitimized ethnocentrism provided conditions that facilitated attacks on the devalued, disfranchised, and isolated subpopulations in America. With the involvement of the government in several instances, historical hate crime had a subsuming and fatalistic quality. Historical victims had little to no legal rights, let alone the capability of mounting adequate defense strategies. In addition, because they were frequently isolated and/or segregated physically and psychologically from the dominant populace, their victimization was largely unnoticed.

Although modern hate crime perpetrators are far more dangerous (i.e., greater access to weapons of mass destruction [Wooden, 1994]), today's hate crime targets do not have the disadvantages of historical victims. Minority populations are generally more integrated and far less isolated, making targeting more difficult. They also have a greater ability to engage political and economic platforms that would prevent or frustrate attacks. Nevertheless, it is clear that the potential of modern hate crime exponentially surpasses harms that were committed in the past.

Scholars such as Sloan (1997) recognize a blurring of the line between foreign and domestic terrorism. Likewise, in several ways hate crime and domestic terrorism have converged (Gibbs, 1989; Hamm, 1994). Due to the growing political sophistication of hate organizations (J. Levin & McDevitt, 1993), American hate crime has clearly evolved into domestic terrorism. The National Advisory Committee's Task Force on Disorders and Terrorism's Report included the definitions of various forms of terrorism. The objective of political terrorism corresponds with the goal of most hate organizations: (Hagan, 1997, p. 134): "violent criminal behavior [is] designed primarily to generate fear in the community for political purposes."

Some would say that much of hate crime targets property and, therefore, does not approach any degree of terrorism. This author disagrees. Even the anonymous spray painting of a swastika on a tombstone evokes fear, intimidation, and sends a political message even if that was not the intention. Hate crime perpetrators range from naive impulsive teenagers to trained members of well-structured and financed organizations bent on procuring destruction. Both terrorists and hate crime perpetrators use fear to achieve purposes that often extend beyond immediate objectives.

Lessons from the past, the present, and the evolving nature of hate crimes suggest further examination of the problem as a form of domestic terrorism. This would be an important change in law enforcement and prosecutorial attitude toward hate crimes. Hate crime viewed as a form of domestic terrorism increases its priority. Law enforcement training, resource allocation, and intelligence gathering would likely receive greater emphasis and fiscal support. However, law enforcement and prosecutors may be hesitant to embrace this new perspective due to the general undercurrent of systemic devaluation of minority, poor, homosexual, and female crime victims (Hernandez, 1990). To upgrade legislatively the classification of hate crime as a form of domestic terrorism is to impute additional importance on the hate crime victim. Perhaps only then will society have sent a cogent message—not sent historically, nor well sent today—that the victimization of the James Byrd, Jr.s of the world will receive a higher standard of justice than what has occurred through the last 300 years.

REFERENCES

Arendt, H. (1963). *Eichmann in Jerusalem: A Report on the Banality of Evil.* New York: Viking Press.

Barkan, S. E., & S. F. Cohn. (1994). "Racial Prejudice and Support for the Death Penalty by Whites." *Journal of Research in Crime and Delinquency,* 31: 202–209.

Barkun, M. (1994). *Religion and the Racist Right: The Origins of the Christian Identity Movement.* Chapel Hill: University of North Carolina Press.

Berthrong, D. J. (1963). *The Southern Cheyennes.* Norman: University of Oklahoma Press.

Brown, D. (1970). *Bury my Heart at Wounded Knee. An Indian History of the American West.* New York: Holt, Rinehart & Winston.

Brown, T. (1995). *Black Lies, White Lies.* New York: William Morrow.

Brown v. Board of Education, 347 U.S. 483 (1954).

Bryjak, G. I., & M. P. Soroka. (1997). *Sociology: Cultural Diversity in a Changing World* (3rd ed.). Boston: Allyn & Bacon.

Bureau of Justice Assistance. (1997). *A Policymaker's Guide to Hate Crimes* (BJA Monograph #NCJ 162304). U.S. Department of Justice: Office of Justice Programs.

Bust, R. A. (1994). Foreword. In M. S. Hamm (Ed.), *Hate Crime: International Perspectives on Causes and Control* (pp. v–x). Cincinnati, OH: Anderson Publishing and Academy of Criminal Justice Sciences.

Chalk, F., & K. Jonassohn. (1990). *The History and Sociology of Genocide: Analyses and Case Studies.* New Haven: Yale University Press.

Christensen, L. (1994). *Skinhead Street Gangs.* Boulder, CO: Paladin Press.

Chronister, A. (1992). *Japan-Bashing: How Propaganda Shapes Americans' Perception of the Japanese.* Unpublished master's thesis, Lehigh University, Bethlehem, PA.

Cutler, J. E. (1969). *Lynch-Law. An Investigation into the History of Lynching in the United States.* Chicago: Negro Universities Press.

Czajkoski, E. H. (1992). "Criminalizing Hate: An Empirical Assessment." *Federal Probation,* 56(8): 36–40.

Daniels, R. (1993). *Prisoners without Trial. Japanese Americans in World War II.* New York: Hill & Wang.

Dennis, D. (1984). *Black History.* New York: Writers and Readers Publishing.

Devlin, P. (1986). Morals and Criminal Law. In Feinberg & H. Gross (Eds.), *Philosophy of Law* (3rd ed.). Belmont, CA: Wadsworth.

Farb, P. (1968). *Man's Rise to Civilization as Shown by the Indians of North America from Primeval Times to the Coming of the Industrial State.* Chicago: E. P. Dutton.

Federal Emergency Management Agency. (1998, January 19). Oklahoma City bombing disaster [Online]. Available: Internet http:llwww.fema.gov/okc95/okcudt8.htm

Feinberg, J., & H. Gross. (1986). *Philosophy of Law* (3rd ed., pp. 11–23). Belmont, CA: Wadsworth.

Fredrickson, O. M. (1991). *White Supremacy. A Comparative Study in American and South African History.* New York: Oxford University Press.

Freeman, S. M. (1992–1993). "Hate Crime Laws: Punishment which Fits the Crime." *Annual Survey of American Law,* 4.

Gerstenfeld, P. B. (1992). "Smile when You Call Me That! The Problems with Punishing Hate Motivated Behavior." *Behavioral Sciences and the Law,* 10: 259–285.

Gibbs, J. P. (1989). "Conceptualization of Terrorism." *American Sociological Review,* 54: 329–340.

Goldhagen, D. J. (1996). *Hitler's Willing Executioners. Ordinary Germans and the Holocaust.* New York: Vintage.

Gould, S. 1. (1981). *The Mismeasurement of Man.* New York: Norton.

Hacker, A. (1995). *Two Nations Black and White, Separate, Hostile, and Unequal.* New York: Ballantine.

Hagan, F. B. (1997). *Political Crime: Ideology and Criminality.* Needham Heights, MA: Allyn & Bacon.

Hamm, M. S. (1993). *American Skinheads: The Criminology and Control of Hate Crime.* Westport, CT: Praeger.

Hamm, M. S. (1994). Conceptualizing Hate Crime in a Global Context. In M. S. Hamm (Ed.), *Hate Crime: International Perspectives on Causes and Control* (pp. 173–189). Cincinnati, OH: Anderson Publishing and Academy of Criminal Justice Sciences.

Hamm, M. S. (1998a). The Laundering of White Crime. In C. R. Mann and M. S. Zatz (Eds.), *Images of Color Images of Crime* (pp. 244–256). Los Angeles, CA: Roxbury.

Hamm, M. S. (1998b). Terrorism, Hate Crime, and Antigovernment Violence: A Review of the Research. In H. W. Kushrier (Ed.), *The Future of Terrorism: Violence in the New Millennium.* Thousand Oaks, CA: Sage.

Harjo, S. S. (1998). Redskins, Savages, and Other Indian Enemies: An Historical Overview of American Media Coverage of Native Peoples. In C. R. Mann and M. S. Zatz (Eds.), *Images of Color Images of Crime* (pp. 30–46). Los Angeles, CA: Roxbury.

Haskins, G. L. (1969). The Beginnings of Partible Inheritance in the American Colonies. In D. H. Flaherty (Ed.), *Essays in the History of Early American Law* (pp. 204–244). Chapel Hill: University of North Carolina Press.

Healey, J. F. (1995). *Race, Ethnicity, Gender and Class. The Sociology of Group Conflict and Change.* Thousand Oaks, CA: Sage.

Hernandez, T. K. (1990). "Bias Crimes: Unconscious Racism in the Prosecution of 'racially motivated violence.' " *Yale Law Journal,* 99: 845–864.

Heumann, M., & T. W. Church. (1997). General Introduction. In M. Heumann & T. W. Church (Eds.), *Hate Speech on Campus. Cases, Case Studies and Commentary* (pp. 3–13). Boston: Northeastern University Press.

Higginbotham, A. L., Jr. (1978). *In the Matter of Cob: Race and the American Legal Process: The Colonial Period.* New York: Oxford University Press.

Hoffer, P. C. (1992). *Law and People in Colonial America.* Baltimore: Johns Hopkins University.

Hohler, B. (1998, June 28). "Klan Rally Bares Hatred, But Jasper Thwarts Violence." *The Boston Globe,* pp. Al, A16.

Horatio Alger Association. (1996). Immigration polls: Why doesn't Congress listen to the American people [Online]. Available: Internet http://www/horatioalger .cornlpubmatJpubmat.htm

Horowitz, C. (1996). Anti-Semitic Violence Is Increasing. In P. A. Winters (Ed.), *Current Controversies Series: Hate Crimes* (pp. 18–24). San Diego, CA: Greenhaven.

Horsman, R. (1981). *Race and Manifest Destiny. The Origins of American Racial Anglo-Saxonism.* Cambridge, MA: Harvard University Press.

Jordan, W. (1968). *White over Black American Attitudes Toward the Negro, 1550–1812.* Chapel Hill: University of North Carolina Press.

Jost, K. (1993). "Hate Crimes." *CQ Researcher,* January, pp. 3–19.

Kennedy, S. (1959). *Jim Crow Guide to the U.S.A. The Laws, Customs and Etiquette Governing the Conduct of Nonwhites and Other Minorities as Second-Class Citizens.* Westport, CT: Greenwood.

Lawrence, F. C. R. (1996). Hate Crimes Violate the Free Speech Rights of Victims. In P. A. Winters (Ed.), *Current Controversies: Hate Crimes* (pp. 60–67). San Diego, CA: Greenhaven.

Levin, B. (1992–1993). "Bias Crimes: A Theoretical and Practical Overview." *Stanford Law and Policy Review,* Winter, pp. 165–180.

Levin, J., & W. C. Levin. (1982). *The Functions of Discrimination and Prejudice.* New York: Harper & Row.

Levin, J., & J. McDevitt. (1993). *Hate Crimes. The Rising Tide of Bigotry and Bloodshed.* New York: Plenum Press.

Mackie, J. L. (1977). *Ethics: Inventing Right and Wrong.* New York: Penguin.

McLemee, S. (1997). The Militia Movement Is Dangerous. In C. P. Cozic (Ed.), *The Militia Movement. At Issue. An Opposing Viewpoints Series* (pp. 50–58). San Diego, CA: Greenhaven Press.

Mann, C. R. (1993). *Unequal Justice: A Question of Color.* Bloomington: University of Indiana Press.

Martin, S. (1996). "Investigating Hate Crimes: Case Characteristics and Law Enforcement Responses." *Justice Quarterly,* 13(3): 455–480.

Merk, F. (1963). *Manifest Destiny and Mission in American History. A Reinterpretation.* New York: Knopf.

Messner, S. F., & R. Rosenfeld. (1997). *Crime and the American Dream* (2nd ed.). New York: Wadsworth.

Miller, V. P. (1979). *Ukomno'm: The Yuki Indians of Northern California.* Socorro, NM: Ballena Press.

Morris, T. D. (1996). *Southern Slavery and the Law, 1619–1860.* Chapel Hill: University of North Carolina Press.

Pallone, N. J. (1990). *Rehabilitating Criminal Sexual Psychopaths.* New Brunswick, NJ: Transaction.

Perlmutter, P. (1992). *Divided We Fall. A History of Ethnic, Religious, and Racial Prejudice in America.* Ames: Iowa State University Press.

Pieterse, J. N. (1992). *White on Black Images of Africa and Blacks in Western Popular Culture.* New Haven, CT: Yale University Press.

Pollock-Byrne, J. M. (1989). *Ethics in Crime and Justice. Dilemmas and Decisions.* Pacific Grove, CA: Brooks/Cole.

"Pool Points to Conservative Electorate." (1996). *USA Today* [Online].

Pound, R. (1938). *The Formative Era of American Law.* Gloucester, MA: Little, Brown.

Project Vote Smart. (1992–1998). Candidate for President of the United States. Patrick Joseph Buchanan [Online].

Riding In, J. (1998). American Indians in Popular Culture: A Pawnee's Experiences and Views. In C. R. Mann & M. S. Zatz (Eds.), *Images of Color Images of Crime* (pp. 15–29). Los Angeles, CA: Roxbury.

Rome, D. M. (1998). Murderers, Rapists, and Drug Addicts. In C. R. Mann & M. S. Zatz (Eds.), *Images of Color Images of Crime* (pp. 85–95). Los Angeles, CA: Roxbury.

Sanders, R. (1978). *Lost Tribes and Promised Lands. The Origins of American Racism.* Boston: Little, Brown.

Sloan, S. (1997). "An Unholy Alliance. The Internationalization of Domestic Terrorism. *Intelligence Report.*" Winter 1997 (Vol. 85, pp. 10–11). Atlanta, GA: Klanwatch.

Southern Poverty Law Center Report. (1997a). *Intelligence Briefs. Intelligence Report.* Winter 1997 (Vol. 85, p. 2). Montgomery, AL: Klanwatch Publishers. A Project of the Southern Poverty Law Center.

Southern Poverty Law Center Report. (1997b). *New Kianwatch Project Monitors Internet Hate* (Vol. 27, p. 3). Atlanta, GA: Southern Poverty Law Center.

Spindler, W. H. (1972). *Tragedy Strikes at Wounded Knee and Other Essays on Indian Life in South Dakota and Nebraska.* Verinillion: University of South Dakota Press.

Stampp, K. M. (1956). *The Peculiar Institution. Slavery in the Ante-Helium South.* New York: Vintage.

Steinfield, M. (1973). *Cracks in the Melting Pot. Racism and Discrimination in American History* (2nd ed.) New York: Glencoe.

Takaki, R. (1994a). *Issei and Nisei. The Settling of Japanese America.* New York: Chelsea House.

Takaki, R. (1994b). *Journey to Gold Mountain. The Chinese in 19th-Century America.* New York: Chelsea House.

Tebbel, J., & K. Jennison. (1960). *The American Indian Wars.* New York: Harper & Row.

U.S. Congress. 39th. 2nd session. Senate Report 156.

Valentine, B. (1995). *Gang Intelligence Manual. Identifying and Understanding Modern Day Violent Gangs in the United States.* Boulder, CO: Paladin.

Van Biema, D. (1995). "Justice. A Fool for a Client." *Time Domestic,* 145(6).

Walker, S., C. Spohn, & M. DeLone. (1996). *The Color of Justice.* New York: Wadsworth.

Wells-Barnett, I. B. (1969). *Wells-Barnett: On Lynchings Southern Horrors a Red Record Mob Rule in New Orleans.* New York: Arno Press.

Wooden, W. S. (1994). *Renegade Kids, Suburban Outlaws.* New York: Wadsworth.

ENDNOTES

1. See J. M. Pollock (1994, p. 18) for a substantive discussion of Kantian ethics. The following are some principles of Kant's ethical formalism:

    1. Act only on that maxim which you can at the same time will that it should become a universal law. In other words, for any decision of behavior to be made, examine whether that behavior would be acceptable if it were a universal law to be followed by everyone.

2. Act in such a way that you always treat humanity, whether in your own person or that of any other, never simply as a means but always at the same time as an end. In other words, one should not use people for one's own purposes.
3. Act as if you were, through your maxims, a lawmaking member of a kingdom of ends. This principle directs that the individual's actions should contribute to and be consistent with universal law. Also, because we freely choose to abide by moral law and these laws are self-imposed rather than imposed from the outside, they are a selection of the higher nature of humans.

2. See Horsman (1981, p. 4) for more information on Anglo-Saxon. The term *Anglo-Saxon race* is truly a misnomer. In reality, the term represents a combination of different European ethnicities, including Germanic and Celtic tribes, and Nordics and Normans who conquered and eventually settled among the indigenous people of England. However, the term began to represent the distinction between English-speaking Caucasians in general and Native Americans, Africans, descendants of Africans, Mexicans, and Asians.

3. One could argue that the antecedents for modem hate crime legislation lie in the Thirteenth and Fourteenth Amendments or in the seminal U.S. Supreme Court decision of *Brown v. Board of Education* (1954). However, in 1981 the Anti-Defamation League drafted the model legislation for hate crimes that stood to facilitate state legislatures (for additional information see Freeman [1992–1993] or Jost [1993]). Based on Freeman (1992–1993) and Jost (1993), the writer uses 1980 as indicative of the hate crime legislation era.

4. See Steinfield (1973, p. 56), regarding the early treatment of Indians.

5. The following is a statement made by Commissioner W. A. Jones in the Annual Report of the Commissioner of Indian Affairs in 1903 (Steinfield, 1973, p. 52):

> It is probably true that the majority of our wild Indians have no inherited tendencies whatever toward morality or chastity, according to an enlightened standard. Chastity and morality among them must come from education and contact with the better elements of the whites.

6. Some have set their approximate numbers closer to 20,000.

7. "They were practically starving on government rations, and the government had told them that they could no longer supplement their diets by hunting game" (Carnes, 1995, p. 62; cited in Spindler, 1972).

8. See Brown (1970, p. 90), "Robert Bent's description of the atrocities was corroborated by Lieutenant James Connor:"

> In going over the battleground the next day I did not see a body of man, woman, or child but was scalped . . . Bodies were mutilated in the most horrible manner; I heard another say he had cut the fingers off an Indian to get the rings. . . . I also heard of numerous instances in which men had cut out the private parts of females and stretched them over the saddle-bows and wore them over their hats while riding in the ranks.

9. Native Americans did not legally receive some form of citizenship until 1924, as a result of their significant participation in World War I.

10. Regarding the manifestation of the dehumanization of the American Indian, as noted in Kennedy (1959, p. 10), "In the opening up of Oregon to white settlement, even Methodist clergymen expressed no regret at seeing Indian women being clubbed to death and Indian babies dashed against trees by white settlers." Found in Brown (1970, p. 90), and in Berthrong (1963, p. 1850), in a public speech made in Denver, Colonel Chivington advocated the killing and scalping of all Indians, even infants: "Nits make lice" he declared.

11. See Pieterse (1992) for further clarification on the change in Africa's image. A summarizing paragraph is found on page 29:

From antiquity to the early Middle Ages the dominant image changed from positive to negative, while the early to late Middle Ages saw the transformation of the black from an infernal demon to the highly honoured representative of a remote Christendom-Europe's redeemer and help in distress.

The developments described are significant against the background of later developments, when gradually a negative image of Africans comes again to predominate.

12. See Jordan (1968, p. 24), on the symbolism of color and spiritual values:

In the Christian period a significant break occurred with the views of antiquity. In the writings of several of the church fathers of western Christendom . . . the color black began to acquire negative connotations, as the color of sin and darkness. Origen, head of the catechetical school in Alexandria in the third century, introduced the allegorical theme of Egyptian darkness as against spiritual light. The symbolism of light and darkness was probably derived from astrology, alchemy . . . in itself it had nothing to do with skin color, but in the course of time it did acquire that connotation.

13. See Horsman (1981, p. 100):

The process of debasing blacks had been carried out in the daily life of America, and whatever the theory, blacks in practice were not regarded merely as men and women of a different complexion. Blacks were not simply regarded as debased because they were slaves: they were also enslaved because of what was regarded as their different and debased nature. Whites, by the very laws they passed and the attitudes they assumed, placed blacks on a different human level.

Also, in Pieterse (1992, p. 41),

In his study of British attitudes vis-à-vis blacks at the time of the slave trade, Anthony Barker argues that before 1770 blacks were regarded as inferior more on grounds of cultural traits, and the traditional association in Christian culture of blackness with evil, than on those of any theory of in-bred racial inferiority.

See Horsman, (1981, p. 123). Thomas R. Dew's review of the debate (regarding Virginia debates on emancipation and equality):

Dew's main contention was that to end slavery would be a disaster. . . . Dew thought that the presence of large numbers of free blacks would be disastrous to both races. Slaves, were "utterly unfit for a state of freedom among the whites," Blackness, not slavery, was the essential cause of the Negro condition, for "the emancipated black carries a mark that no time can erase; he forever wears the indelible symbol of his inferior condition."

14. See Stampp (1956), regarding the systematic effects of slavery on black mortality rates.

15. Wells-Barnett (1969, p. 54) on the casualness of lynch incidents:

Perhaps the most characteristic feature of this record of lynch law for the year 1893, is the remarkable fact that five human beings were lynched and that the matter was considered of so little importance that the powerful press bureaus of the country did not consider the matter of enough importance to ascertain the causes for which they were hanged. . . . Lynch Law had become so common in the United States that the finding of the dead body of a Negro, suspended between heaven and earth to the limb of a tree, is of so slight importance that neither the civil authorities nor press agencies consider the matter worth investigating.

16. See Jordan (1968) regarding the significance of color and the political status of slavery.

17. See Perlmutter (1992, p. 144) regarding the Dred Scott decision. "Unlike European immigrants who could become citizens after 5 years, Blacks born abroad or in America could not. They were simply property. This was the ruling in the 1857 Supreme Court case of Dred Scott v. Sanford."
18. Cited in Steinfield, (1973, p. 132) from Elmer Clarence Sandmeyer in The Anti-Chinese Movement in California (1939). Sandmeyer quoted Senator Morton:

> There would have been a depression in 1870s if the entire population had been made up of lineal descendants of George Washington . . . If the Chinese in California were white people, being in all other respects what they are, I do not believe that the complaints and warfare against them would have existed to any considerable extent.

CHAPTER 23

FIGHTING TERRORISIM
IN THE TWENTY-FIRST CENTURY

John Lewis

Although not new to the United States, the threat of terrorism is changing and becoming more deadly. Over the last several years, the FBI has noted a new trend in terrorism within the United States that involves a transition from more numerous low-level incidents to less frequent but more destructive attacks, with a goal to produce mass casualties and attract intense media coverage. While the number of terrorist attacks in the United States has declined in the past decade, the number of those killed and injured in distinct acts has increased.[1] A single attack in 1993 killed 6 people and injured nearly 1000 when terrorists bombed the World Trade Center in New York City. Less than 2 years later, an attack in Oklahoma City resulted in the worst act of domestic terrorism in the United States and the deaths of 168 people. The number of attempted terrorist acts in the United States remains equally alarming to the law enforcement community.

> *"While the number of terrorist attacks in the United States has declined in the past decade, the number of those killed and injured in distinct acts has increased."*

The FBI, working in conjunction with its state and local counterparts, prevented 5 acts of terrorism in 1996 and 20 acts in 1997 (U.S. Department of Justice, 1998, 1999). How can law enforcement agencies best work together to fight terrorism today and into the twenty-first century? Investigators must consider the sources of today's international and domestic terrorism threats.

CURRENT TERRORIST THREATS

International Terrorism

International terrorism against the United States is foreign based or directed by countries or groups outside the United States. In past decades, international terrorists have attacked the United States primarily by targeting U.S.

citizens and interests overseas. The most memorable attacks include the abduction of hostages in Lebanon in the mid-1980s; the December 1988 bombing of Pan American Flight 103 over Lockerbie, Scotland, which killed 189 Americans; the June 25, 1996 detonation of an explosive device outside Al-Khobar Towers in Dhahran, Saudi Arabia, in which 19 U.S. military personnel were killed; and the August 7, 1998, bombings of the U.S. embassies in Nairobi, Kenya, and Dares Salaam, Tanzania, which resulted in the deaths of 12 Americans. With one exception, no attacks by international terrorists were recorded in the United States between 1984 and 1992 (U.S. Department of Justice, 1992, p. 14). All of this changed, however, on February 26, 1993, when foreign terrorists bombed the World Trade Center in New York City. The suspects intended to destroy the tower and murder over 35,000 people.

The FBI divides the current international terrorist threat to the United States into three categories. The first threat to Americans comes from the activities of foreign sponsors of international terrorism. The U.S. Department of State has designated seven countries as state sponsors of terrorism: Iran, Iraq, Syria, Sudan, Libya, Cuba, and North Korea. These sponsors view terrorism as a tool of foreign policy. However, their activities have changed over time. Past activities included direct terrorist support and operations by official state agents. Now, state sponsors generally seek to conceal their support of terrorism by relying on surrogates to conduct operations. State sponsors remain involved in terrorist activities by funding, organizing, networking, and providing other support and instruction to formal terrorist groups and loosely affiliated extremists.

Formalized terrorist groups, such as Lebanese Hizballah, Egyptian Al-Gama'a Al-Islamiyya, and Palestinian HAMAS, pose the second threat to the United States. These autonomous organizations have their own infrastructures, personnel, financial arrangements, and training facilities. They can plan and mount terrorist campaigns overseas, as well as support terrorist operations within the United States. Some groups use supporters inside the United States to plan and coordinate acts of terrorism. In the past, these formalized terrorist groups engaged in criminal activities in the United States, such as illegally acquiring weapons, violating U.S. immigration laws, and providing safe havens to fugitives.

The third category of terrorist threats stems from loosely affiliated international radical extremists, such as those who bombed the World Trade Center. These extremists do not represent a particular nation. Loosely affiliated extremists may pose the most urgent threat to the United States at this time because they remain relatively unknown to law enforcement. They can travel freely, obtain a variety of identities, and recruit like-minded sympathizers from various countries.

Domestic Terrorism

The devastating bombing of the Alfred P. Murrah Federal Building in Oklahoma City on April 19, 1995 and the pipe bomb explosion in Centennial Olympic Park during the 1996 Summer Olympic Games underscore the ever-present threat that exists from individuals determined to use violence to advance their agendas. From 1982 to 1992, a total of 165 terrorist incidents occurred domestically (U.S. Department of Justice, 1992, p. 8). The majority of these attacks were conducted by domestic terrorist groups, particularly Puerto Rican groups, left-wing extremist groups, and special interest groups.

Domestic terrorism involves groups or individuals who operate without foreign direction entirely within the United States and target elements of the U.S. government or citizens. Domestic terrorist groups represent extreme right wing, extreme left wing, and special interest beliefs. The major themes espoused today by extremist right-wing groups include conspiracies regarding the New World Order, gun control laws, the approach of the millennium, and white supremacy. Many of these extremist groups also advocate antigovernment, antitaxation, or antiabortion sentiments and engage in survivalist training to ensure the perpetuation of the United States as a white, Christian nation.

One current troubling branch of right-wing extremism is the militia or patriot movement. Militia members want to remove federal involvement from various issues. They generally are law-abiding citizens who have become intolerant of what they perceive as violations of their constitutional rights. Membership in a militia organization is not entirely illegal in the United States, but certain states have legislated limits on militias, including limits on the types of training (e.g., paramilitary training) that militias can offer legally. The FBI bases its interest in the militia movement on the rise of violence or the potential for violence and criminal activity stemming from the movement.

Experts have traced the growth of the militia movement in part to the effective use of modern communication mediums. Videotapes and computer bulletin boards and networks, such as the Internet, have been used with great effectiveness by militia sympathizers. Exploiting yet another medium, promilitia facsimile networks disseminate material from well-known hate group figures and conspiracy theorists. Organizers can promote their ideologies at militia meetings, patriot rallies, and gatherings of various other groups espousing antigovernment sentiments. Left-wing extremist groups generally profess a revolutionary socialist doctrine and view themselves as protectors of the American people against capitalism and imperialism. They aim to change the United States though revolutionary means rather than participating in the established political process.

During the last 3 decades, leftist-oriented extremist groups had posed the predominant domestic terrorist threat in the United States. Beginning in the 1980s, however, the FBI dismantled many of these groups by arresting key members for their criminal activities. The transformation of the former Soviet Union also deprived many leftist groups of a coherent ideology or spiritual patron. As a result, membership and support for these groups has declined.

Special-interest terrorist groups differ from extreme left- and right-wing terrorist groups because members of these groups seek to resolve specific interests rather than pursue widespread political changes. Members of such groups include animal rights advocates, supporters of environmental issues, and antiabortion advocates.

> *"the FBI anticipates a greater number of terrorist attacks aimed at U.S. citizens and interests abroad."*

Terrorist Threat Warning System

Warning remains critical to the terrorism prevention effort. In 1989, the FBI developed its Terrorist Threat Warning System to transmit information and intelligence to other members of the law enforcement community. Acting as the lead federal law enforcement agency in combating terrorism in the United States, the FBI manages this system to ensure that vital information regarding terrorism reaches those in the U.S. law enforcement and counterterrorism communities. The warning system ensures the accurate, timely, and orderly dissemination of new information to those responsible for countering terrorist threats against individuals, property, and facilities within the United States. All federal government agencies and departments are reached through the warning system. If the threat information requires nationwide unclassified dissemination to all federal, state, and local law enforcement agencies, the FBI can transmit such messages via the National Law Enforcement Telecommunications System, or NLETS.

The Awareness of National Security Issues and Response (ANSIR) Program is designed to provide unclassified national security threat and warning information to as many as 40,000 U.S. corporate security directors and executives, law enforcement personnel, and other government agencies. ANSIR represents the first initiative by the U.S. government to provide this type of information to individual U.S. corporations with critical technologies or sensitive economic information that foreign governments or organizations may target. Each FBI ANSIR coordinator meets regularly with industry leaders and security directors for updates on current national security issues.

While some consider the causes that special-interest groups represent understandable or even noteworthy in nature, they remain separated from traditional law-abiding special-interest groups because of their criminal activity. Through their violent, criminal actions, these terrorist groups attempt to force various segments of society, including the general public, to change their attitudes about issues they consider important. Therefore, special-interest groups will continue to present a threat.

Unconventional Weapons

Along with the risk posed by groups and individuals, both foreign and domestic, a threat stemming from the choice of weapon used also exists. Although terrorists continue to rely on such conventional weapons as bombs and small arms, several cases suggest that terrorists and other criminals may consider using unconventional chemical or biological weapons in an attack in the United States at some point in the future.

The Cyberterrorism Threat

The FBI defines cyberterrorism as terrorism that initiates, or threatens to initiate, the exploitation of or attack on information systems. The U.S. government, state and local governments, and the private sector have become increasingly dependent on computer hardware, software, networking, and communications technologies for accomplishing operational and administrative goals. However, greater infrastructure sophistication presents new vulnerabilities and cyberterrorism threat scenarios. Compromise or damage to critical computer systems can jeopardize public safety and U.S. national security. In February, March, and June of 1998, the FBI's Terrorist Threat Warning System disseminated four separate warnings related to threats received against computer systems in the United States.

As the twenty-first century approaches, the FBI has prepared to address this new and growing threat in a variety of ways. The FBI's National Infrastructure Protection Center (NIPC) has developed the capability to identify, analyze, and characterize specific cyber threats and incidents. The NIPC uses the FBI 's criminal investigative and counterterrorism resources and expertise in carrying out its mission. The center works proactively to monitor all physical and cyber threats, to maintain relations with the greatest number of federal government agency watch centers, and to disseminate infrastructure threat information to government agencies, state and local law enforcement, and corporate security directors and executives.

Criminal and national security issues have converged in the cyberterrorism threat. Law enforcement can achieve success against this and other terrorism threats by forging strong links among law enforcement at the federal, state, and local levels, and through broad federal government agency and public sector participation.

FIGHTING TERRORISM TODAY AND TOMORROW

Just as the threat from terrorism has changed over the last several years, so has the FBI response to this serious national security threat. In preparation for the next century, the FBI continues to bolster its ability to prevent acts of terrorism before they occur and to respond effectively to such acts once they have taken place.

An example of the FBI's readiness for the next century is the Strategic Information and Operations Center (SIOC) at FBI Headquarters. This 24-hour operations center was recently enlarged and modernized with state-of the-art technology. SIOC is available for use by FBI employees and representatives from other federal, state, or local agencies during times of national crisis, such as following the commission of an act of terrorism.

The linchpin of FBI efforts remains promoting its counterterrorism capabilities and strengthening its ties with other agencies on the federal, state, and local law enforcement levels.

FBI Counterterrorism Mission

The FBI counterterrorism mission is to prevent acts of terrorism before they occur or to react to them after they happen by bringing the perpetrators to justice. To enhance this mission, the FBI established a Counterterrorism Center in 1996 to combat terrorism on three fronts: international terrorism operations, domestic terrorism operations, and countermeasures pertaining to both international and domestic terrorism. The center helps law enforcement and intelligence communities to counter threats of terrorism within the United States more effectively by combining the experience and special skills of each represented agency in a coordinated effort directed at the threat of terrorism or in response to a terrorist act.

Twenty other federal agencies participate in the FBI center, and their representatives are fully integrated into its operation. These representatives serve as specific points of contact for their agencies, thereby enhancing the flow of intelligence and allowing for a collaborative exchange of information. The FBI believes that this interaction has increased the ability of the U.S. government to counter domestic and international terrorism, both at home and abroad.

Objectives of the FBI Terrorism Program

Major objectives within FBI domestic and international terrorism programs include identifying and preventing the activities of terrorists prior to the commission of terrorist acts and pursuing the arrest and prosecution of responsible individuals. As part of this prevention effort, the FBI collects foreign intelligence information relating to those international terrorist groups and individuals whose activities threaten the security of the United States. Pursuant to attorney general guidelines, the FBI analyzes the information collected and works with other members of U.S. intelligence agencies and law enforcement and counterterrorism communities to exploit such information.

In the fight against terrorism, the FBI Counterterrorism Center uses various resources, which include multiagency task forces; ongoing liaison with all federal, state, and local law enforcement agencies; its Legal Attache program; the Terrorist Threat Warning System; and the introduction of new federal legislation.

JOINT TERRORISM TASK FORCES

The FBI combats terrorism through its participation in 16 formalized Joint Terrorism Task Forces (JTTFs) around the country. The JTTFs, composed of federal, state, and local law enforcement personnel, strive to increase the effectiveness and productivity of limited personnel and logistical resources. They avoid duplication of investigative effort and expand cooperation and liaison among federal, state, and local law enforcement.

JTTFs have been highly successful in several critical operations around the country. The FBI–New York City Police Department Joint Terrorism Task Force, for example, has worked on many critical cases, including the massive World Trade Center bombing investigation, the plot to bomb major New York City landmarks, and the crash of TWA Flight 800.

Legal Attache Program

The FBI currently counters global terrorism threats through meaningful cooperation with allied governments around the world. In coming years, the FBI anticipates a greater number of terrorist attacks aimed at U.S. citizens and interests abroad. Cooperation with other governments remains indispensable in countering this heightened threat of global terrorism. The FBI presently has 36 Legal Attaches overseas, and the program's success has resulted in the recent establishment of new offices in Israel, Saudi Arabia, Pakistan, and Egypt. The trust and good faith developed through this cooperation are hallmarks of FBI relationships overseas. Among the many benefits of establishing Legal Attaches is the close working relationships FBI personnel form with the local law enforcement agencies, which have practical and operational familiarity with terrorist organizations that may pose a threat to Americans. These relationships further enhance the ability of the FBI to maintain a proactive, rather than reactive, posture in addressing terrorist threats. If a terrorist attack targeting U.S. citizens or interests does occur, Legal Attaches can provide the FBI with an immediate on-scene presence in the first critical hours of a postincident investigation.

The Antiterrorism and Effective Death Penalty Act

Federal law enforcement efforts received a significant boost in the fight against terrorism with the passage of The Antiterrorism and Effective Death Penalty Act of 1996 (Public Law). This law, enacted and signed by President Clinton on April 24, 1996, includes several new measures aimed at countering terrorism. Highlights of the law include measures that enhance the powers of the federal government to deny visas to individuals belonging to groups designated as terrorist and that simplify the process for deporting aliens convicted of crimes. The new law also bans all U.S. aid to countries that provide assistance or military equipment to terrorist states, allows U.S. citizens to sue foreign nations in federal court for terrorist acts committed against U.S. nationals abroad, and authorizes approximately $1 billion over 4 years to strengthen federal law enforcement in the fight against terrorism. Additionally, the omnibus law broadened federal jurisdiction over crimes linked to terrorism and included new federal criminal statutes for participating in international terrorist activities in America.

A key provision of the law authorizes the secretary of state, in conjunction with the attorney general and the secretary of the treasury, to designate an organization as a foreign terrorist organization (FTO). By designating an FTO under the law, the United States seeks to hinder the fund-raising ability of terrorist organizations. The law allows law enforcement to seize the funds of designated terrorist organizations. Because FTO branches within the United States function primarily as fund-raising arms for the overseas parent organization, the law could have a significant impact on their terrorist activities within the United States.

Additionally, the presence of Legal Attaches abroad has proven crucial in facilitating U.S. criminal extraterritorial jurisdiction. The U.S. government has successfully returned terrorists from other countries to stand trial for acts or planned acts of terrorism against U.S. citizens. There have been over 350 extraterritorial jurisdiction cases since legislation was enacted in 1984 and 1986.

One recent case involved the rendition of a subject from Pakistan wanted for the shooting deaths of two CIA employees in Langley, Virginia. The Legal Attache in Islamabad, Pakistan, coordinated extensive liaison with various foreign entities and U.S. intelligence agencies. Ultimately, the Legal Attache coordinated the delivery of the subject to an FBI arrest team in Pakistan. The Legal Attache's on-scene role was critical to the successful rendition of the subject to the United States, where he stood trial.

The Domestic Preparedness Program

The Domestic Preparedness Program represents a major part of FBI liaison with state and local law enforcement agencies. The FBI coordinates efforts with other U.S. government agencies to train federal, state, and local emergency response personnel to deal with terrorist events involving weapons of mass destruction. Over the next 5 years, this initiative will support the training of emergency responders in approximately 120 cities, selected according to population density, upcoming large-scale security events, critical infrastructure, and geographic orientation. Workshops and seminars include 1 week of training curriculum that addresses various levels of instruction.

To further facilitate this major outreach effort, the FBI has established a National Domestic Preparedness Office (NDPO). The NDPO will serve as a clearinghouse for information on weapons of mass destruction training programs and will work to spur development of other national preparedness assistance initiatives.

CONCLUSION

Terrorism has become a worldwide problem and a major threat to U.S. national security. FBI Director Louis J. Freeh has stated that law enforcement agencies must do everything within their power to prevent terrorist incidents ("What Can Be Done about Terrorism," 1996).

The FBI remains committed to its leadership in counterterrorism—a vital part in maintaining the security of the United States. The steps federal, state, and local law enforcement take today will strengthen the fight against terrorism in the twenty-first century. Effective means of identifying and preventing terrorist acts before they occur, enhanced communication and liaison with various levels of law enforcement, close cooperation with agencies of the federal government, timely dissemination of threat information, and effective analysis of trends and developments have better prepared the law enforcement community in addressing terrorist threats. With the continued cooperation of law enforcement at all levels, the FBI will continue to enhance its ability to protect the American people from the threat of international and domestic terrorism.

REFERENCES

Public Law 104-132.
U.S. Department of Justice. (1992). *Terrorism in the United States, 1982–1992.* Washington, DC: FBI.

U.S. Department of Justice. (1998). *Terrorism in the United States: 1996*. Washington, DC: FBI.

U.S. Department of Justice. (1999). *Terrorism in the United States, 1997*. Washington, DC: FBI.

"What Can Be Done about Terrorism." (1996, January). *USA Today Magazine*.

NOTE

1. Officially classified acts of terrorism include four attacks in 1993, no attacks in 1995, three attacks in 1996, and two attacks in 1997.

CHAPTER 24

RELIGIOUS MOVEMENTS AND VIOLENCE: INCIDENTS, CAUSES, AND POLICY IMPLICATIONS

David G. Bromley and Lorne L. Dawson

Religion and violence are hardly strangers. Millions have died from religious wars and persecutions throughout history, and in contemporary times religion continues to prompt outbreaks of collective violence around the globe. At this moment there are violent clashes between Protestants and Catholics in Northern Ireland, Israelis and Palestinians in the Middle East, Muslims and Hindus in India, Hindus and Christians in India, Muslims and Christians in the Sudan, Christians and Muslims in Indonesia, Sunni and Shiite Muslims in Pakistan and in Iraq, and Christians and Muslims in Nigeria. While elsewhere throughout the world people are dying, as victims or martyrs, to preserve their religions in the face of secular forms of persecution (e.g., the members of Falun Gong in China, Muslim fundamentalists in Egypt and Algeria, Buddhists in Chinese controlled Tibet). There have been significant incidents in American history as well. In the nineteenth century, for example, the Mormons, fearing persecution, dressed as Indians to attack settlers in the Mountain Meadows massacre, and federal troops crushed the resistance of the Native American spirit dancers at Wounded Knee. More recently, Ervil LeBaron's Church of the Lamb of God, a polygamy-practicing group that had emerged from the Church of Jesus Christ of Latter-Day Saints, killed members and former members of the church, as well as members of competitor churches, in an attempt to consolidate control over a group of polygamy practicing churches (Bradlee & Van Atta, 1981; LeBaron, 1981). Or, to provide another example, there were the murders of members of rival Muslim organizations carried out by the original Nation of Islam, under the leadership of Eiljah Muhammad (as distinct from the reorganized Nation of Islam now led by Louis Farrakhan). Many other cases could be cited.

The relationship between religion and violence has been a subject of growing concern to social scientists studying a broad range of religious groups and traditions. Law enforcement officials have also developed an interest, as they find themselves confronted with a number of dangerous and complex situations involving religious groups. In this chapter the focus is on a particular kind of violence that has been attracting a great deal of media attention, *collective violence* involving *new religious movements* (NRMs), or what are more popularly and pejoratively called "cults." By collective violence we have in mind the acts committed by individuals in the name of some religious movement, or the acts committed against religious individuals or movements by agents of social control and legitimated by some organizational purpose. The religious movements under consideration are part of the large cohort of groups that appeared in western societies, or experienced rapid growth in these societies, since the mid-1960s. These movements attracted a primary membership base of higher status and relatively well-educated young adults. Like most religious movements throughout the ages, including those involved in the founding the great religions of the world, these new groups proclaim themselves to be simply in search of spiritual enlightenment, personal development, or contact with immanent/transcendent forces, entities, or knowledge. But they often exhibit anomalous belief and organizational attributes when compared to the traditional, mainstream churches of today.

The impetus to understand the involvement of NRMs in violence, on the part of both scholars and law enforcement officials, stems from a series of episodes of collective violence involving NRMs during the last half of the twentieth century. Benchmark cases would include the Manson Family murders in 1969; the murder-suicide of 914 members of The Peoples Temple at Jonestown in 1978; the death of 80 people during the standoff at the Branch Davidian compound outside of Waco in 1993; the murder-suicide of 74 members of the Solar Temple in Switzerland and Quebec in 1994, 1996, and 1997; the Aum Shinrikyô murders of about 23 members and opponents as well as 12 other innocent subway passengers in Tokyo in 1995; the collective suicide of 39 members of Heaven's Gate in California in 1997; and the murder-suicide of about 780 members of The Movement for the Restoration of the Ten Commandments of God in Uganda in 2000. In addition, there have been a number of instances in which violent confrontations were narrowly averted or a peaceful resolution was achieved (e.g., the Montana Freemen episode; see Rosenfeld, 1997; Wessinger, 2000).

Here we will briefly examine three of these incidents: the Branch Davidian debacle at Waco, the Solar Temple deaths, and the mass suicide of Heaven's Gate. As these cases will illustrate, the eruption of violence stems from the interaction of a diverse array of external circumstances and internal processes, and as Robbins and Anthony (1995) have argued, "the relative weight or significance of the contributions of exogenous and endogenous factors [varies] from one . . . event to another" (pp. 237–238). For the Branch Davidians external factors loom large, for Heaven's Gate the violent end was born largely of internal processes. In the case of the Solar Temple the tragic deaths were precipitated by a more difficult to differentiate play of internal and external factors.

With the brief case studies in hand we will then delineate the challenge posed by violent religious movements to law enforcement agencies. But first we must pause to consider some common misconceptions about the violent propensities of new religious movements before sketching the dynamics of violence in the three episodes selected.

POPULAR MISCONCEPTIONS

There are a number of popular misconceptions about NRMs and violence that have led people to simplistic and formulaic interpretations of the violent incidents we are considering. These misconceptions suggest that cults are inherently unstable and prone to initiating violence either in the form of attacks on outsiders, including law enforcement officials, or in the form of mass suicides. Anticult activists have a vested interest in perpetuating these misconceptions, playing on the public's fear of violent behavior to invoke state sanctions against new religious movements. Three such misconceptions will be briefly considered here, beginning with a more general problem from which two more specifically relevant issues arise.

The first and more general misconception is that *cults are remarkably similar and can be identified by a set of common characteristics.* Most specifically it is assumed that cults "brainwash" their members, allowing authoritarian leaders to maintain almost total control over their followers. In fact, however, NRMs are extraordinarily diverse. New movements have emerged out of the Christian, Buddhist, Hindu, New Age, Human Potential, Neopagan, and UFO traditions. They display very different types of organization, means of social control, and leadership styles (Lofland & Richardson, 1984; Stark & Bainbridge, 1985). Nonetheless some scholars have lumped all cults together under a more manipulative and coercive model of how members are recruited to NRMs (e.g., Singer & Lalich, 1995). Most social scientists involved in the study of NRMs, however, reject these efforts (e.g., Barker, 1984; Bromley & Richardson, 1983; Dawson, 1998). Some controversy, however, persists (e.g., Zablocki & Robbins, 2001).

The second misconception is the assumption that *one of the common features of NRMs is their violent tendencies.* Both the number of religious groups that currently exist and the proportion of those that have formed in recent decades are extraordinary. As Melton's compilation of religious groups reveals (Melton, 1998), there are more than 2000 religious organizations now functioning in the United States, and more than half have been established since 1960. In Africa, Asia, and elsewhere, of course, there are thousands more. Melton's survey, moreover, does not take into account the many quasireligious communal, New Age, and other groups, which possess some religious characteristics but do not define themselves as religious organizations. In the face of these numbers, it should be apparent that incidents of violence are actually quite rare. But the false impression exists that violence occurs frequently because the few high-profile incidents mentioned previously have received extensive media coverage, and these media reports tend to imply that there is a significant probability that other cults will engage in violence. Incidents of violence in NRMs are immediately linked by the media to previous episodes, and all are equally attributed to certain "cultic" qualities of these groups. In fact, instances of personal murder or suicide are likely to attract a disproportionate amount of media attention if the individual has an affiliation with a NRMs. By contrast, violent or criminal acts committed by members of mainstream religions usually are not attributed to their religious affiliation, as the current revelations concerning pedophilia in the Catholic Church amply illustrate. The reality is that since the murders committed by the Manson Family some thirty years ago, only twenty groups can be implicated in violent incidents involving multiple homicides or suicides. There is then an important phenomenon to be understood, but most of the events in question do not bear much resemblance to the stereotypical notions of cult violence.

The third misconception, characteristic of the stereotype of violent cults, is that *movements with millennial/apocalyptic beliefs and charismatic leadership are particularly prone to violence.* Millennialism is in fact a common feature of life in NRMs. But it is shared as well by many millions of Americans in mainstream Christian churches. Numerous movements throughout American history have entertained expectations of an impending apocalyptic moment when godly and satanic forces would be locked in mortal combat and the messiah would return to lead the world to a divinely ordained order (see, e.g., Jenkins, 2000). One illustration is found in the nineteenth-century Millerite movement. William Miller prophetically declared that Christ would return in 1843, and when this date was not fulfilled and he made successive further predictions that also failed. Yet thousands of people kept their faith in his message and over the next several decades more than a hundred different churches arose from the Millerite movement, including two major international organizations, the Seventh-Day Adventists and the Jehovah's Witnesses. More recently, there were dire predictions of violence by millennial groups with the approach of Y2K. Despite great fanfare, however, there were no cases of religiously inspired violence by millennial groups (Canadian Security Intelligence Service, 1999; FBI, 1999; Vise & Adams, 1999). The presence of millennial beliefs, it has been argued, may be a necessary precursor to much religious violence, but it is by no means sufficient as a predictor of such violence (Dawson, 1998; Robbins & Anthony, 1995).

The situation is the same with respect to the charismatic character of so many leaders of NRMs. The media preoccupation with the exceptional personal magnetism and power of such figures as Reverend Jim Jones of The Peoples Temple and David Koresh of the Branch Davidians has created the impression that charismatic authority is intrinsically unstable and prone to violence. But one has to look no further than a number of religious leaders associated with established religious groups have been regarded as extremely charismatic—Billy Graham (Southern Baptist), Oral Roberts (United Methodist), Fulton Sheen (Roman Catholic), and Jimmy Swaggart (Assemblies of God)—to recognize that matters are more complicated (see Dawson, 2002). Some of these well-known figures are respected and others reproved, but none are not suspected of harboring violent tendencies.

THREE CONTEMPORARY CASES OF COLLECTIVE VIOLENCE

While violence involving NRMs is rare and there is no evidence to support widely publicized stereotypes about violence prone cults, there have been several recent cases of collective violence. In this chapter we select three episodes of violence that have occurred in the 1990s—the Branch Davidians (Bromley & Silver, 1995;), the Solar Temple (Mayer, 1999), and Heaven's Gate (Hall et al., 2000) incidents—to examine the relationship between NRMs and collective violence. If violence cannot just be automatically attributed to millennial, charismatic, and possibly unstable cults, as popular stereotypes suggest, then it becomes imperative to develop a more sophisticated understanding of the eruption of violence in some NRMs. In presenting the three cases, we will demonstrate how *both* internal factors related to movement organization *and* external factors related to control agency organization and action can contribute to violent outcomes, but in varying degrees. As indicated previously, external factors are most prominent in the first case, least significant in the last case, and complexly intertwined with internal processes in the second case.

Branch Davidians

The group that ultimately became the Branch Davidians existed for 50 years before the arrival of David Koresh as a small, secluded community at Mt. Carmel outside of Waco, Texas. The group was founded as a schismatic offshoot of Seventh-Day Adventism in 1919. In the half century before Koresh's arrival, the Davidians lived extended periods of religiously committed life punctuated by moments of instability during the transition between leaders. The group remained largely independent of the surrounding community and experienced conflict only with the Seventh-Day Adventist church from which the Davidians actively recruited members.

When David Koresh assumed leadership of the Davidians, the community was in disarray. He refurbished the Mt. Carmel buildings, increased membership with an aggressive recruitment campaign, and established businesses that stabilized community finances. Koresh also sought to expand his spiritual authority; he pronounced himself to be the spiritual descendant of the biblical King David, a messianic figure carrying out a divinely commissioned errand. He taught his followers that his messianic role was crucial to human salvation because Christ had died only for those who lived prior to his crucifixion; Koresh's mission was necessary to permit the salvation of all subsequent generations. His special duty was to open the Seven Seals, contained in the New Testament Book of Revelation, which reveal the end-time events. Under his leadership, the Davidians gradually assumed a more radical posture. One key development was Koresh's prophesy that the battle of Armageddon, the final struggle between the forces of God and Satan, would commence with an attack on the Davidian faithful. He also created a more tight-knit, hierarchical organization; the lifestyle was communal, males and females were segregated, and members' standing within the movement was determined by their personal relationship to Koresh.

The single development that most dramatically heightened tensions with control agencies was Koresh's pronouncement of his "New Light" doctrine that established the "House of David." According to this doctrine, Koresh would father with women in the community a new lineage of God's children; the children created through these unions would erect the House of David and ultimately rule the world. Koresh selected wives and daughters of Davidian members to participate in the House of David, and some of the daughters were legally minors. The House of David triggered both internal opposition and the basis for external intervention. Although most families involved appear to have agreed or acceded to participation of female members in the House of David, it is not surprising that sexual jealousies were aroused and parents rebelled at the involvement of their young daughters. When reports of the participation of underage girls reached the state's bureau of Child Protective Services (CPS), the basis for external intervention was established.

A coalition of Koresh's opponents formed beginning in 1989 and gathered strength over the next several years. Family members disturbed about reports of young girls being inducted into the House of David, sexual partners who rebuffed Koresh or were rebuffed by him, and couples involved in child custody disputes banded into an apostate group under the leadership of Marc Breault, a Davidian who had now become the chief opponent of the group. Breault was repulsed by Koresh's relationships with young girls and fearful that his new bride would soon become a candidate for the House of David. This group was successful in cultivating allies, eliciting interest from a television station, which produced an exposé, as well as the state CPS, which opened an investigation. Initial contacts also were established with local and state law enforcement organizations and several federal agencies: the Internal Revenue Service, the Immigration and Naturalization Service, and the FBI. The Bureau of Alcohol, Tobacco, and Firearms (BATF) also took an interest when a parcel service reported delivering hand grenades to Mt. Carmel (which actually were empty grenade casings that the Davidians adapted as lighters and sold at gun shows).

None of the initial investigations resulted in any sanctions, but they did establish a network from which continued pressure and, ultimately, official actions emanated. The situation was one of mounting tension. David Koresh's sexual relationships with females under the age of legal consent constituted a direct challenge to child welfare agencies mandated to detect and prevent abuse. Correspondingly, welfare agency investigations of those sexual practices constituted an explicit challenge to the House of David, a central Davidian mission to establish a divinely authorized lineage through its messianic leader. In addition, both sides undertook additional actions that elevated the other's suspicions. For example, the Davidians were forced to falsify birth records to protect the House of David, and the BATF subsequently gained secret access to the Davidians through an undercover agent, whose identity was subsequently discovered by Koresh. Just as important, the failure of these investigations created frustration, particularly within CPS, over an inability to confirm the illicit activity officials were convinced was taking place. The sequence of events also increased the sense of threat within the Davidian community. It was at this juncture that Koresh began arming his followers and calling members abroad back to Mt. Carmel.

The impetus for the initial raid on the Davidians came primarily from the actions of the BATF. The agency finally assumed responsibility for direct action against the Davidians, apparently for several reasons—its mandate to control weapons violations, a concern that weapons might be used against the surrounding community, and a need to defend its organizational budget and even survival amid governmental reorganization proposals—but it also received significant information and support from CPS and the apostate group. It was from these nonbureau sources that the BATF obtained considerable misinformation, including reports that Koresh rarely left the compound and hence could not be apprehended individually, rumors that the Davidians might be contemplating mass suicide, allegations of widespread child abuse, and false claims of drug manufacturing operations. The rumors of a contemplated mass suicide were critical because they were instrumental in gaining Department of Justice approval for the initial raid in February 1993. These rumors also influenced the choice of a "dynamic entry" that would rely on surprise and rapid suppression of resistance, as opposed to other less violent alternatives that the BATF feared might permit a suicide attempt.

The BATF's initial raid was based on misinformation and a misassessment of the situation, and Attorney General Janet Reno's decision to approve the action was significantly influenced by BATF input. Most directly, the BATF contravened orders to abort the raid if the element of surprise was lost, which it was when the Davidians were informed of the BATF's pre-raid assembly. The initial raid, and in particular the death of federal law enforcement officers, profoundly altered the conflict calculus for the FBI, which assumed control of the situation in the wake of BATF debacle. The conflict now moved to a qualitatively different level and severely constricted the range of solutions available. In each side's scenario the other played a demonic role, and each calculated its position in terms of its ultimate group mandate. For government officials, although a peaceful conclusion was preferable, no goal could supercede bringing those responsible for the homicides to justice and ending what had become an armed insurrection. They awaited battle or Davidian capitulation. For their part, the Davidians were now confronted by the prospect that the end-time events had indeed been set in motion and that the police at their gates were the forces Koresh had prophesied. Still, the die was not cast on either side, and there was a prolonged standoff. The FBI employed a contradictory combination of increased pressure and isolation interspersed with sometimes conciliatory negotiation to dislodge the Davidians. A split developed between negotiating and tactical units, with the latter exercising the greatest influence. As an FBI lead negotiator (Noesner, 1999) subsequently commented, "during the Waco standoff, on-scene managers received sound advice from the negotiation team but often did not follow that advice" (p. 6). During the standoff tactical units gained control and increased pressure through psychological warfare (cutting off electric power, encircling the compound with snipers and armored vehicles, helicopter overflights, broadcasting random sounds at high decibel levels, and flooding the compound with light around the clock), ridicule (referring to Koresh's beliefs as "bible babble" and Koresh as a "con-man," "child molester," "liar," and "coward"), and destruction of possessions (killing of animals, destruction of automobiles) (Wright, 1999). In assessing government strategy, the House of Representatives Committee report later labeled the raid "premature" and concluded that the Attorney General should have known that the Davidians posed little risk and a peaceful settlement remained possible (Committee on Government Reform and Oversight, 1996). During the standoff, Koresh led the Davidians in continuing to unlock the Seven Seals and await divine instruction on the proper course to follow. It appears that the Davidians may have hoped to avoid a stark battle or capitulation choice by producing a revelatory message for the world before surrendering, thus salvaging some semblance of victory. For a variety of reasons, federal agents perceived, perhaps incorrectly, that neither conciliation nor duress would succeed and that continued flouting of legitimate authority could not be tolerated. A CS gas assault on the compound was launched; 74 residents died in the fire, by their own hand, and at the hand of their compatriots.

The Solar Temple

A mystery began to unfurl on the evening of October 4, 1994 that would eventually take law enforcement officials in three nations several years to solve, but never really to anyone's satisfaction. It all began with a fire and apparent suicide reported at a farm outside the hamlet of Cheiry in Switzerland. Soon, however, police discovered secret chambers in which 22 more bodies were found, draped in long robes and ritually arranged. Within hours, these deaths were tied to further fires and bodies found in homes in Granges-sur-Salvan, Switzerland, and Morin Heights, Canada. In the end 53 people, members of an esoteric spiritual group called Order of the Solar Temple (*Ordre du Temple Solaire*) were found either stabbed, shot, poisoned, or suffocated to death. From the evidence at hand the authorities knew they were in the presence of some bizarre combination of murders and suicides, all ritualistically orchestrated to serve a religious purpose. Soon manifestos explaining the deaths as a "transit" from this world to another on higher metaphysical plane began to appear, methodologically prepared and mailed to television stations and newspapers, other members, ex-members, officials, and scholars. Given the rather lavish lifestyle enjoyed by the leaders of the group, the police first suspected the leaders of foul play, and arrest warrants were issued. But within days it was clear that they too had died in the "transit."

Over a year later, in the face of months of intense media and police scrutiny, 16 more members surprisingly took their own lives during a ritual performed in the French countryside, and five more did the same in Quebec in March of 1997. Many other members of the Solar Temple survived, but clearly the authorities were faced with a situation that could not be reduced to a simple criminal investigation. Those who had died were in the grips of a religious motivation, no matter how possibly misguided it may have seemed. But why had they thought that such a transit was necessary? No definitive answer is possible. It is clear, however, that the tragic end was both internally motivated and externally prompted (see Hall & Schuyler, 2000; Mayer, 1999).

The founder of the Order of the Solar Temple, Joseph Di Mambro (1924–1994), was a wealthy Swiss jeweler. He had been involved with these kind of esoteric groups for years, and he had created several such organizations (e.g., the Golden Way Foundation) before finally forming the Order of the Solar Temple. In 1981 he joined forces with a charismatic and charming young doctor named Luc Jouret. Jouret added an amalgam of homeopathic medical and New Age spiritual ideas to Di Mambro's mix of esoteric teachings, and he became the popular front man of the organization. Through his large public lectures the group began to recruit a following of rather well-educated and prosperous followers in Europe, the Caribbean, and Canada. In line with Jouret's teachings, which involved elements of environmental apocalypticism, in 1984 the group began the transfer of its base of operations to the province of Quebec. The granite of the Canadian shield, it was believed, would provide protection against the natural catastrophes that would usher in the dawning of the age of Aquarius.

The focal point of activity for the Solar Temple was a series of secret initiations, rituals, lectures, and encounters with the spiritual manifestations of various great esoteric and religious figures of the past. For years the group went about its business in relative obscurity. Then in the early 1990s a series of defections began to threaten the group with embarrassing revelations about its operations. One discontent ex-member—in particular, Rose-Marie Klaus—sought and received considerable media attention in Quebec and elsewhere, drawing the interest of the anticult movement. There also appears to have been a fairly significant falling-out between Di Mambro and Jouret at this time, leading Jouret to found another distinct yet affiliated organization, *l'Academie de Recherche et Connaissance des Hautes Sciences,* to which he drew many Temple members. Other internal tensions seem to have arisen as well, as evidenced by the elevation of new people to positions of authority and the demotion of others. Most crucially, Tony and Nicky Dutoit defected and fled to Canada. Tony had masterminded the electronic special effects used to create various illusions during the group's secret ceremonies. Details, however, about all that was really happening in the group at this time remain murky.

Doctrinally, a shift was occurring in the early 1990s as well. Jouret's public talks were becoming increasingly bleak and apocalyptic, while Di Mambro and others began to discuss the prospect of a transit. Initially, though, the transit was discussed in terms of some mystical passing over to another existence, like Alice through the looking glass. At times there was talk of UFOs coming to transport those faithfully prepared to another planet. Suicide or other acts of violence were never mentioned. The theme was one of a spiritual elite surviving a coming crisis—common fare in numerous NRMs. But things seem to have changed rapidly in the fall of 1993 and early 1994, resulting in the violent and messy transit that the leaders themselves declared to be "premature" in the letters they posted posthumously. What happened? In truth it is difficult to say. Di Mambro was getting old and he was ill. The group was experiencing a decline in its fortunes. But neither he nor the other leaders, like Jouret, had ever been violent before (unlike the leaders of The Peoples Temple or Aum Shinrikyô).

By all accounts it seems that a simple twist of fate played an inordinately large role in the course of events. For reasons never adequately clarified, in the fall of 1992, a Quebec member of the group, Herman Delorme, was asked by Jouret and another leader to procure a pistol with a silencer. Delorme eventually purchased three illegal handguns, but from a police informant, and he was arrested in March of 1993. His arrest led to a search of various Temple premises, exposing the operations of the group to the police. Still nothing significant was likely to have come from this turn of events if it had not coincided with a series of anonymous threats made to the life of the Quebec Minister of Public Security and several parliamentary deputies. The police chose to link the two completely independent events and launched an extensive investigation of the activities of the Solar Temple and many of its Quebec members. This in turn set off a chain reaction of police investigations elsewhere, in Europe and in Australia, where the group had been engaged in various financial dealings involving millions of dollars. Soon rumors of illegal gun trafficking and money laundering were being circulated in the media and amongst anticult organizations. In the end, even though none of the rumors proved to be true, the reputation of the Solar Temple that its leaders prized was severely tarnished.

In October, many current and past members of the group were invited to a meeting in Switzerland. Some went clearly believing they were going to participate in a glorious and assumably nonviolent transit; others came to seek redress for their grievances and perhaps to retrieve some of the funds they had invested in the group. At the same time two loyal members of the group were dispatched to Morin Heights, in Quebec, to ritualistically stab Tony and Nicky Dutoit and their three-month-old baby to death. The Dutoits had dared to give their son a version of the name the group had reserved for the messiah. This done, it is unclear just what was planned for the others. In one of the letters sent after the event, Di Mambro complains that Jouret ruined everything by violently bungling the transit at Granges-sur-Salvan, forcing his hand, it is implied, to do the same at Cheiry. In each case, though, some care had been taken to prepare and plant incendiary devices in the homes, so it is difficult to distinguish between what was suppose to happen and what, perhaps unintentionally, did happen. In the end, all we know for sure is that some people, presumably defectors and ex-members, appear to have been murdered, while others, including the leaders, seem to have chosen to take their own lives.

There is considerable evidence that the Solar Temple was experiencing internal conflicts and dissension. Some scholars believe that the sad end of the group is best accounted for in terms of the growing desperation of the leaders to check the mounting disintegration of their dream and legacy. Internal social disorganization coupled with deepening personal depression, on the part of Jouret and Di Mambro, led to the violence. The transit was a ritual of "purification" (e.g., Mayer, 1999; Palmer, 1996) designed to expunge all dissonant voices and symbolically assure the mystical superiority of the group and its leaders. In perpetrating so complicated a crime, however, the leaders had to have the assistance of many others, and therefore events cannot be attributed solely to their own spiritual hubris and dementia.

Other analysts of the event have placed more stress on the role of precipitating external events (e.g., Hall & Schuyler, 2000). It is clear that the group was moving toward an internal crisis, but the violence itself may have stemmed largely from an irrational panic that gripped the group when the government investigations began. The authorities proceeded with little genuine concern for the presumptive religious purposes of the Solar Temple, and the objective of official investigations was unclear. Still, it must be realized that numerous other groups have found themselves in similar circumstances—contemplating delegitimation and decline in the face of opposition and embarrassing exposures—without becoming violent (see, e.g., Dawson, 1999). In most cases their common fate is either to just wither away or be reborn in a new guise. The combination of external pressures and internal demoralization apparently made either prospect unappealing to Solar Temple leaders. As Jean-Francois Mayer (1999) concludes, "Di Mambro acted at times like a common swindler, but he very likely remained convinced of his message and

mission until the end. . . . the transit . . . allowed the group to escape from perceived threats and offered a way to assert dramatically its claims before the entire world" (p. 193).

Heaven's Gate

The forerunner to the group that became Heaven's Gate was founded in 1973
by Marshall Herf Applewhite, a teacher, and Bonnie Lu Nettles, a nurse.
Guided by spiritual visions they had prior to meeting, the two felt their part-
nership was ordained and they began a spiritual quest that evolved over two
years into a loosely organized movement. At first they identified themselves
with the Two Witnesses in the Book of Revelation who are martyred and then
rise to Heaven in a cloud. But their cloud was actually a space ship. In their
view, Earth was a garden that members of what they termed the Next Level
had created. Jesus' earthly mission had been to gather the faithful on Earth to
complete the experiment, but humans were not yet ready for the Next Level.
Applewhite and Nettles taught that their followers would be taken to the
Kingdom of Heaven by spacecraft where they would live eternally as androg-
ynous beings. When the two first began telling others about their visions, they
encountered both disinterest and ridicule. In the face of this rejection their
message became more hostile and apocalyptic. With the passage of time they
came to believe that many humans were under satanic influence and that the
garden that was Earth would be destroyed, "spaded under," as they put it.

In 1974 Applewhite and Nettles achieved their first major success. They
first converted two dozen members of another group that had been anticipat-
ing a spiritual ascension. Seeing themselves as shepherds of this new flock,
they playfully took on the names of Bo and Peep. They then launched a recruitment campaign that yielded over two hundred additional converts. Bo
and Peep taught their new followers that preparation for the Next Level required severing themselves from all their earthly ways and former relationships. To this end they adopted a migratory style, often camping in remote
areas of the American west. The communal lifestyle they developed was oriented to cultivating the personal attributes required of life on the Next Level
and replicating the social forms of the Next Level, as closely as possible, in an
earthly setting. Not surprisingly, the movement's success and separatist
lifestyle triggered opposition. Complaints from family members led at one
point to a state police investigation, although it produced no official action. In
another instance, acquaintances attempted to physically "rescue" a new recruit
from the group. More significantly, when members of the group tried to present their views at public gatherings they were regularly mocked, and there
was a spate of caustic media reports belittling the group. This limited opposition constituted the only real hostility that the movement encountered during
its history. But Bo and Peep seem to have been extremely sensitive to opposition. They concluded that the endtime was near and that they were in danger
of being assassinated. So they went into hiding for several months, and the
group lost about half its membership.

Upon rejoining the group, Applewhite and Nettles changed their names
again, this time to the musical notes Ti and Do. From this point on the group
moved in a more radical direction by isolating itself, creating a more totalistic

environment, and concluding that outsiders were a threat to movement goals. Ti and Do organized the group as a "classroom" in which members were meticulously trained for life on the Next Level. The various places in which they lived were organized as the spacecraft they anticipated boarding, and daily life was controlled down to the most minute details. The members developed a new vision of themselves, not as earthlings but members of the Next Level who had been placed on earth for training. They increasingly began to conceive of themselves as an "Away Team" from the Next Level. Then Ti's (i.e., Nettle's) unexpected death from cancer in 1985 led the group to conclude travel to the Next Level would not be in their physical bodies. Their transit would involve shedding their mortal "containers." The movement's ideology also began to shift in a decidedly more apocalyptic direction. In particular, a race of evil space aliens was posited who kept humans in bondage through their connections to religion and sexuality. The group increasingly came to regard conventional society as fundamentally subversive to the movement's goal of reaching the Next Level.

The period beginning in the late 1980s was one in which Heaven's Gate came out of isolation. Members reached out, attempting to disseminate the new discoveries they had made during their years of seclusion. Over the next several years, the group spread its message through videos, advertisements in newspapers and magazines, and public lectures delivered across the country. As a result, the movement, which had dwindled to a few dozen members, doubled in size; but most of the conversions were short lived. The response to the group's published messages was a combination of silence and sarcasm. And so the movement's last major project to save earth had failed. At the same time, there also were internal forces distancing Heaven's Gate from conventional society. The remaining members were continuing to struggle with their own humanness. Efforts to expunge any vestiges of sexual desire, for example, led some male members to arrange their own castration. Members spent much of their time attempting to connect with the Next Level and to ascertain the timing and conditions of the anticipated interstellar transit. The conflagration at Waco in 1993 raised apprehensions within the movement about its own fate, and members briefly considered, but quickly rejected, the idea of provoking a fatal confrontation with government authorities as a means of leaving earth. Instead some members traveled the globe seeking a location that might be more hospitable, but none was found.

The members of Heaven's Gate found less and less reason to continue their mission on earth. The small group of longtime members was aging; Do's health was in decline; their warnings of the end time were unheeded; and their efforts to find a more congenial location to live were unsuccessful. The group began to turn inward and pursue its vision of salvation. Members openly discussed suicide as a means of orchestrating a collective transit. The appearance of the Hale-Bopp comet in 1995 was interpreted as a sign that the time for departure had arrived. Rumors were circulating in the media that a spacecraft had been sighted trailing in the wake of the comet. In an orderly and deliberate fashion they began to prepare for the transit. Members said their goodbyes to outsiders, paid their debts, and completed any remaining obligations. They took one last trip into the world and returned convinced there was nothing left for them here. Heaven's Gate had fulfilled its moral responsibility by offering salvation to those who would receive it; the group could do no more. It was time to leave a planet that soon would be "spaded under" and to demonstrate the truth of the group's message by transcending its earthly existence. In recorded messages, members communicated their eager anticipation of the voyage ahead and sought to refute the imputations of "suicide" that knew were likely to follow. Then on March 27, 1997, outside of San Diego, California, the 39 remaining members of Heaven's Gate systematically drugged and suffocated themselves in three shifts. Dressed in Away Team uniforms, with purple shrouds covering their earthly containers, they headed home.

THE CHALLENGE OF RELIGIOUS MOVEMENT VIOLENCE FOR LAW ENFORCEMENT AGENCIES

The three cases of collective violence involving NRMs presented here demonstrate that each epidosde is unique and complex. None of the movements exhibited any dramatic signs of a tendency toward violence early in their histories; the nature of their beliefs and organization are very diverse; and their reactions to external pressure and intervention varied. These episodes of collective violence therefore pose a singular challenge to law enforcement agencies. While most movements do not become involved in violence, there is a very real prospect that additional episodes of collective violence will occur simply given the number of NRMs. How law enforcement agencies respond may be crucial to the outcomes of future incidents. Three issues stand out as critical: (1) the lack of visibility of many NRMs, (2) the balancing of restraint and intervention, and (3) identifying valid and reliable indices of dangerousness.

One significant problem facing law enforcement agencies is the relative invisibility of NRMs. Most NRMs tend to be small, and many have limited relationships with the surrounding community. As a result, initial awareness of the movement may coincide with a violent episode. This was particularly evident in the case of Heaven's Gate. The movement had existed for two decades in a highly secluded fashion and offered few obvious clues that its collective transit was about to occur. The group displayed no alarming signs to the few outsiders with whom the movement was in contact. The visibility problem is compounded by the international organization of many NRMs. Movements may be conspicuous in one nation but inconspicuous elsewhere. For example, Aum Shinrikyô was the object of considerable media coverage in Japan but maintained only a small coterie of members in the United States. In addition to physical invisibility, many groups are not visible legally since they may not incorporate legally or own property that would inform state agencies of their existence. The probability of any reasonable surveillance or control measures being effective under such circumstances is remote. While there may be no real solution to this problem, two practices are important for law enforcement agencies. It is imperative to have access to organizations that maintain objective information about NRMs. Examples would include INFORM (Information Network Focus on Religious Movements) in London, England and ISAR (Institute for the Study of American Religion) in Santa Barbara, California. It is also prudent to develop response procedures as a violent episode may involve a series of events and not a single event. The Solar Temple is a case in point. There were three separate incidents in the murder-suicides in Switzerland in 1994, France in 1995, and Canada in 1997. The possibility of serial incidents means that procedures for dealing with violent episodes must be in place before incidents occur.

A second problem, which is related to the first, is finding a balance between restraint and intervention. On the one hand, the separation of church and state and constitutional provisions protecting religious expression limit the degree of control government agencies can legitimately exercise over religious groups. On the other hand, the stereotypical cult model would legitimate increased monitoring and surveillance. The problem is that control measures may be either insufficient or excessive. If law enforcement agencies fail to respond to reasonable, plausible evidence of threats to public safety, then movements may engage in destructive action prior to intervention. In the wake of the Aum sarin gas attack on the Tokyo subway, Japanese law enforcement officials were criticized precisely for failing to respond to available evidence of Aum's intentions. However, if law enforcement agencies respond on the basis of misinformation and stereotypes, as federal agents did in the Davidian case, the result can be an unwarranted provocation and a self-fulfilling prophecy. Again, there is no simple solution, but there have been promising instances of alternatives to radical action and inaction. Federal law enforcement agencies increasingly advocate reducing the level of fear and distrust experienced by radical groups, by employing ongoing "low-key negotiations" (Jensen & Hsieh, 1999). In one specific case, the local police department in Garland, Texas was confronted by a millennial group, Chen Tao, that prophesied an impending apocalypse. The department responded by seeking accurate information from scholars studying the movement while avoiding misinformation that was being circulated, initiating a "meaningful dialogue" with the group and preparing contingency plans (Szubin et al., 2000; Wessinger, 2000). Where movement–law enforcement confrontations do develop, agencies are placing emphasis on negotiated rather than forcible settlements. This strategy gives priority to peaceful resolution and the safety of all parties to the conflict (Noesner, 1999).

A final problem is developing valid, reliable indices of dangerousness. Law enforcement agencies and scholars studying religion both have been actively involved in trying to identify the conditions under which violent outcomes occur (Bromley & Melton, 2002; Canadian Security Intelligence Service, 1999; FBI, 1999; Hall et al., 2000; Jensen & Hsieh, 1999; Szubin et al., 2000; Wright, 1995). A variety of NRM characteristics have been proposed, such as a history of clashes with law enforcement, the personal instability of leaders, the stockpiling of weapons and food, dramatic changes in belief and organization, disposing of property and possessions, predictions (with specific dates) of a final struggle between good and evil, and withdrawal and mobilization for the end times.

In the discussion and debate over such factors, several preliminary conclusions seem clear. Dangerousness is not simply a matter of intense controversy. Some of the movements that grew most rapidly during their early histories, unequivocally denounced American society, and were the targets of control initiatives—the Unification Church, Children of God, and Hare Krishna—never evidenced any violent tendencies. Indeed, these movements abandoned many of their most controversial practices and adopted more settled lifestyles within two decades. Likewise, there is no simple list or profile that can be constructed to identify dangerous movements. Lists typically include, for example, characteristics referring to millennial beliefs and totalistic organization. However, as we have already observed, nonviolent millennial and totalistic groups are commonplace presently and historically. Rather, current thinking on this issue emphasizes both the context of specific factors and the relationship between movement and control agencies. Individual factors are likely to be misleading unless placed in the context of the movement's history and current self understanding. This necessitates tapping the views of current members, former members, scholars studying the movements, and other organizations that attempt to collect objective information.

Perhaps the most important lesson from these episodes is that movements and control agencies alike may contribute to escalating violence. In the Branch Davidian episode, law enforcement played a key role in predicating the violence; the Heaven's Gate episode was largely the product of internal dynamics; and the Solar Temple incident revealed a greater mixture of internal and external influences. Accurate analysis therefore must incorporate patterns of organization and action on both sides of any conflict. The common element linking the actions of movements and control agents is polarization of the situation, which serves to create distance between parties and dramatically increase the likelihood of a violent confrontation. Therefore, the preeminent goal of law enforcement should be to always operate to diminish polarization and maintain open lines of communication, even under the most difficult circumstances.

REFERENCES

Balch, R., & D. Taylor. (2002, forthcoming). "Making Sense of the Heaven's Gate Suicides." In D. Bromley and J.G. Melton (Eds.), *Cults, Religion and Violence*. New York: Cambridge University Press.

Barker, E. (1984). *The Making of a "Moonie": Choice or Brainwashing?* Oxford: Blackwell.

Bradlee, B., Jr., & D. Van Atta. (1981). *Prophet of Blood*. New York: G. P. Putnam's Sons.

Bromley, D. G., & J. T. Richardson. (Eds.). (1983). *The Brainwashing/Deprogramming Controversy*. New York: Edwin Mellen.

Bromley, D. G., & E, Silver. (1995). "The Davidian Tradition: From Patronal Clan to Prophetic Movement." In S. Wright (Ed.), *Armageddon in Waco: Critical Perspectives on the Branch Davidian Conflict* (p. 43–74). Chicago: University of Chicago Press.

Canadian Security Intelligence Service. (1999). "Doomsday Religious Movements." *Perspectives: A Canadian Security Intelligence Service Publication*. December: Report # 2000/03.

Committee of Government Reform and Oversight. (1996). *Investigation into the Activities of Federal Law Enforcement Agencies toward the Branch Davidians*. Thirteenth Report by the Committee of Government Reform and Oversight. Prepared in Conjunction with the Committee of the Judiciary. Washington DC: U.S. Government Printing Office.

Dawson, L. L. (1998). *Comprehending Cults: The Sociology of New Religious Movements*. Toronto: Oxford University Press.

Dawson, L. L. (2002, forthcoming). "Crises of Charismatic Legitimacy and Violent Behavior in New Religious Movements." In D. G. Bromley and J. G. Melton (Eds.), *Cults, Religion and Violence*. New York: Cambridge University Press.

Federal Bureau of Investigation. (1999). *Project Megiddo*. Washington DC: Federal Bureau of Investigation.

Hall, J. R. & P. D. Schuyler. (2000). "The Mystical Apocalypse of the Solar Temple." In J. R. Hall, with P. Schuyler & S. Trin, *Apocalypse observed* (pp. 111–148). New York: Routledge.

Hall, J. R., with P. Schuyler and S. Trin. (2000). *Apocalypse Observed: Religious Movements, the Social Order, and Violence in North America, Europe and Japan.* New York: Routledge.

Jenkins, P. (2000). *Mystics and Messiahs: Cults and New Religions in American History.* New York: Oxford University Press.

Jensen, C., & Y. Hsieh. (1999). "Law Enforcement and the Millennialist Vision: A Behavioral Approach." *The FBI Law Enforcement Bulletin,* 68: 1–8.

LeBaron, R. W. (1981). *The LeBaron Family.* Lubbock, TX: The Author.

Lofland, J., & J. T. Richardson. (1984). "Religious Movement Organizations: Elemental Forms and Dynamics." In L. Kriesberg (Ed.), *Research in Social Movements, Conflict and Change* (pp. 29–51). Greenwich, CT: JAI Press.

Mayer, J. F. (1999). "Our Terrestrial Journey Is Coming to an End: The Last Voyage of the Solar Temple." *Nova Religio: The Journal of Alternative and Emergent Religions,* 2: 172–196.

Melton, J. G. (1998). *Encyclopedia of American Religions* (6th ed.). Detroit: Gale Research.

Noesner, G. (1999). "Negotiation Concepts for Commanders." *The FBI Law Enforcement Bulletin,* 68: 6–18.

Palmer, S. J. (1996). "Purity and Danger in the Solar Temple." *Journal of Contemporary Religion,* 11: 303–318.

Robbins, T, & D. Anthony. (1995). "Sects and Violence: Factors Enhancing the Volatility of Marginal Religious Movements." In S. Wright (Ed.), *Armageddon in Waco* (pp. 236–259). Chicago: University Of Chicago Press.

Rosenfeld, J. E. (1997). "The Importance of the Analysis of Religion in Avoiding Violent Outcomes: The Justus Freemen Crisis." *Novo Religio,* 1: 72–95.

Singer, M., & J. Lalich. (1995). *Cults in Our Midst: The Hidden Menace in Our Everyday Lives.* San Francisco: Jossey-Bass.

Stark, R., & W. Bainbridge. (1985). *The Future of Religion: Secularization, Revival, and Cult Formation.* Berkeley: University of California Press.

Szubin, A., C. J., Jensen, III, & R. Gregg. (2000). "Interacting with 'Cults': A Policing Model." *The FBI Law Enforcement Bulletin,* 69: 16–25.

Vise, D. A., & L. Adams. (1999). "FBI Warns '2000' May Spark Violence." *Washington Post,* 31 October, p. A1.

Wessinger, C. (2000). *How the Millennium Comes Violently.* Chappaqua, NY: Seven Bridges Press.

Wright, S. A. (1995). *Armageddon in Waco: Critical Perspectives on the Branch Davidian Conflict.* Chicago: University of Chicago Press.

Wright, S. A. (1999). "Anatomy of a Government Massacre: Abuses of Hostage-Barricade Protocols during the Waco Standoff." *Journal of Terrorism and Political Violence,* 11: 39–68.

Zablocki, B., & T. Robbins. (Eds.). (2001). *Misunderstanding Cults.* Toronto: University of Toronto Press.

VIOLENCE AND POLICY IMPLICATIONS

CHAPTER 25

VIOLENCE AND THE FUTURE

Ronald M. Holmes and Stephen T. Holmes

INTRODUCTION

There is no doubt that the United States is a society deeply entrenched in violence. Whatever the reason, be it the frontier mentality, the insistence on gun ownership, or a variety of other reasons offered by those experts in the field of violence, we know that this country is deeply entrenched in personal violence that is directed in many directions.

There are many forms of violence, some of which have been prevalent for many years, such as violence directed toward children, women, and other minorities by those who hold the power in our society. This manifestation of power has been seen by some as their birthright and to be used without compunction or fear of societal reprisals. It became part of their "normal" routine of interaction with those whom they predated on.

It may be, however, that there are unique forms of violence that are different in focus and content from those we have become familiar and even in some cases accepting. For example, domestic violence has long been a form of personal attack that has been ignored. It has been wrongly seen that it has been the husband's "right" to administer physical punishment, including rape, to the wife without fear of legal reprisals. Fortunately this has changed. But it was slow in coming. For example, in a few states, Kentucky for one, the husband, as long as the wife was living with him, even though they may have been legally separated, could not legally be charged with rape. He could be charged with assault, but not rape. This law has been changed only recently in the commonwealth of Kentucky.

Other forms of personal violence have been with us. Child abuse, both physical and sexual, has long been prevalent. Parents, caretakers, and other adults without regard to the welfare of the child routinely physically disciplined children, once viewed as chattel. Even child labor laws were only recently passed to prevent the exploitation of children in the workplace. It was judged as the right of the adult to have sex with the child for the pleasure or gratification of the adult, as a means of sex education for the child, or just as the "way things should be."

But there are new forms of violence that are emerging onto the American landscape. The form and character of violence is in some fashion connected with society itself and the manner in which society has changed over the last few years. Technology has also played an important role in the direction violence has taken. For example, the computer has opened up an avenue for violence that did not exist in years past. Document fraud, as a form of impersonal violence, can only exist in a developed economic country and by those who understand the complexities of finance and governmental intricacies.

Let us now examine some of the newer forms of personal violence and how society can meet the challenges of these acts.

SCHOOL VIOLENCE

With the shooting at the Columbine High School, America was alerted to a form of violence that was almost unheard of. After Columbine, shootings became almost commonplace. Other shootings occurred at Health High School (Kentucky), Conyers, Georgia, Richmond, Virginia, Springfield, Oregon, Pearl, Mississippi, and many others. After this series of fatal assaults at suburban and rural schools, students were voicing concerns about attending school because of perceived threats against them. After Michael Carneal, Luke Wortham, Mitchell Johnson and Andrew Golden, Eric Harris and Dylan Klebold, and others committed their fatal actions, America launched a campaign for combating school violence (Holmes & Holmes, 2001). Schools put into place policies and plans of action to place themselves into positions of identifying potential violent students and subsequent acts of fatal violence. Other activists called for community action. In San Diego, California, a congressman, Bob Etheridge, joined with the local YMCA and other area YMCA directors to announce a national initiative to combat youth crime and violence, including school violence, to doubling their efforts to serve the youth within their service area ("One Day after Tragic School Shooting Spree in San Diego, Etheridge and YMCA Announce National Initiative to Combat Youth Crime, 3-6-01, FDCH Press Releases, announcement number 32X20019200002708). Spurred on by the series of crimes by children against children and students against students, this effort encouraged not only organized agencies, such as the YMCA, but also other social agencies and community groups to join the battle against this senseless form of violence.

DOMESTIC VIOLENCE

Domestic violence is nothing new. The consequences of such abuse varied from one time to another, from one place to another. In some cases, the abuse was simply ignored. In a few cases, however, the consequences were grave. Martin (2000) reports the case of Peter Lung. Lung and his wife had a history of intoxication and domestic violence. One night, however, the violence went too far and he killed her. He was sentenced to death. His death was unusual in this small community in colonial Connecticut. But Martin reports that the death sentence may have been influenced more by the intemperance temperament in the country at the time rather than the fatal domestic violent act itself. But fatal domestic violence has not faded. It continues into the twenty-first century.

Statistics tell us that the rates of domestic violence that result in homicide have decreased 74 percent in the last two decades. Additionally, there appears to be a racial divide that is becoming more pronounced as we examine those statistics. For example, the number of black men who kill their same race partners has decreased; however, the number of white males who killed their white partners has increased slight. There is no clear reason for this increase or decrease ("Racial Divide in Domestic Violence" *Society*, Jan./Feb. 2001, 38/22-4). It may be that the criminal justice system has been more involved in prevention programs that are directed toward particularly black couples; but it also important to examine the domestic racial rate. For example, James Fox, Northeastern University, stated that black women were victims of domestic violence killings at a rate of 4.5 per 100,000 compared with white women's rate of 1.75 per 100,000.

Regardless of the numbers and the rates, a single assault or a sole homicide resulting at the hands of an intimate partner is too many. Society must look at this form of personal violence as an affront to all. Various social institutions share responsibility to screen cases of potential fatal domestic violence. The medical field, for example, could be a forerunner in the identification of a domestic abuse situation. Tips should be made available to help those in the medical community identify such cases, tips such as interviewing techniques, medical examinations, and the use of posters, all of which will alert the medical members as well as aiding the identification of such victims of are not as yet fatal victims (Kramer, 2001).

Other members of the medical community can play a role. For example, Erickson, Hill, and Siegel (2001) report that in their study of domestic violence, as many as 40 percent of mothers report domestic violence to their pediatricians. They further added that it was their experience that pediatricians had little training, expertise, and time to identify those who are victims of domestic abuse at the time of the medical visit. This was despite the American Academy of Pediatrics recommendation that all pediatricians incorporate a screening for domestic violence as a part of their routine practice with parents.

Employers, too, have a responsibility to their employees who are abused in their home. It is too easy to make a statement that whatever happens in one's home is one's business, but it has an effect on the productivity of the employee besides the humanness of the abuse that becomes evident once becomes aware of the signs of abuse. As Hofman (2001) stated in his article dealing with domestic violence and the role and responsibility of employers, abuse in the home should not have to be a concern for the employer but it is since it affects the victim's work life and the general work life of the employee. So, in effect, the abuse has a detriment effect on the business as well.

Same-sex domestic violence is an often-neglected topic. Perhaps due to homophobic attitudes among social service delivery personnel or prejudiced feelings among others, same-sex violence research has been lacking. The research that does exist seems to be the result of work done by those who are survivors themselves of same-sex violence of other minorities who seem to share some affinity with homosexuals and lesbians (Levanthal & Lundy, 1999). Regardless of prejudicial attitudes, there needs to be a concentrated effort to review the perpetration of fatal domestic violence directed toward those who live a lifestyle different from many others in our society.

MURDER IN THE WORKPLACE

Perhaps one of the more prevalent emerging forms of violence is murder in the workplace. A decade ago, Joseph Wesbecker entered his former place of employment and killed seven former coworkers and then killed himself. In Chicago, William Baker held a gun to a security officer at the plant where he worked before being retired for medical reasons. He opened fire inside the plant and killed four employees; four more were injured, and then he killed himself. Michael McDermott killed seven coworkers and waited for the police to arrive where he surrendered peacefully. There are scores of other fatal incidences like this.

Society is becoming more aware of the social problem of violence in the workplace. Researchers are concerned that the more this type of crime occurs, the more others will try to imitate the fatal actions. For example, Savoye and Belsie (2001) report that workplace violent crime is becoming quickly a copycat crime. They relate that imitation crimes have become a byproduct of a media-saturated age, and the media is one contributing factor in crimes such as workplace violence as well as school violence. To illustrate their point, they stated that Wesbecker left in the bedroom at the house a *Newsweek* article about a mass murder case. George Hennard went into a restaurant in Texas and killed noontime diners. At his home was a video concerning James Oliver Huberty, who killed 21 people at McDonald's in California.

Research indicates a general profile of this type of personality: a life filled with failure, frustration, and isolation. The more employers are aware of the type of person who will or may resort to fatal violence, the less the risk to those in its employ. Additional research and training needs to be done to arrange programs and policies to combat this social concern. James Merchant, the dean of the School of Public Health of the University of Iowa, has urged the federal government to provide funds for research and policy implementation. Pointing out that homicide in the workplace has not been viewed as an occupational safety and health issue until only recently, it is now time for a joint effort by those in the private sector as well as those in the public sector to combine their efforts and expertise to resolve this grave social issue (Merchant, 2001). There may be a situation in which many employers do not train their people to identify potentially violent behavior. Solomon (2001) reports that her research shows that 35 percent of human resource professionals train their managers and supervisors to identify violent behavior. What is so unsettling about this statistic is that the remainder, 65 percent, does not? This must change.

SERIAL MURDER

In the 1970s, we started to see a change in the character of stranger-to-stranger homicides. Names emerged that have become a part of the pop culture of America: Ted Bundy, Edmund Kemper, John Wayne Gacy, and many more. In the 1980s, 1990s, and into the twenty-first century, their names have emerged as an unholy litany of perverse sadists and human predators.

Police were ill equipped to handle such cases. As Egger (1998) mentions in his work there existed at the time of the infamous Henry Lucas case the concept of linkage blindness. This meant that police departments did not share information about their cases, some of which were in common. The information would stay with one department and the progress and evidence would stay with that one department. Fortunately, this has dramatically changed in the last several years. Not only have the departments realized the need to exchange and share information, the federal government has taken the lead to establish a national database for unsolved murders. The media have also taken the lead to alert the public about celebrated cases, some serial murder cases, some not. *America's Most Wanted* television program has emerged as a leading media presentation that has led to the apprehension of killers who have been highlighted in one of their shows.

Law enforcement agencies have educated themselves concerning not only the hard science forensics but now they are becoming more aware of the mind and mentality of the serial killer.

Regardless, it appears that the serial killer will be with us for the foreseeable future. We cannot hope that this menace will crease to exist; we can only hope that when a case does become evident, a quick apprehension can be realized before more lives are lost.

MASS MURDER

As I have said in my classes on a university campus on many occasions, there is no real protection against the mass killer. It is often unfortunately just a matter of being in the wrong place at the wrong time. No one can adequately predict when someone will climb a tower on a university campus and open fire. This happened at the University of Texas when Charles Whitman killed and was then killed. No one can predict when a pickup truck will smash through a window of a restaurant and the driver emerge and start shooting. This happened in Killeen, Texas at a Luby's Restaurant. Those unfortunate people had no relationship with the killer. This lack of a personal relationship is even further removed when we examine mass murder and mass murder in the workplace, where this type of mass murderer often knows his victims because he had once been employed there and may still be at the time of the killing.

In mass murder, there is no need to search for the killer most of the time. The killer either kills himself or "forces" the police to kill him, a suicide by proxy scenario. So the investigation is confined to a smaller area of concern (e.g., crime scene reconstruction, identification of victims, etc). There must be an early identification of the personality of such a person. Research cited in this book will give the investigator insight into the perpetrator. However, there needs to be an earlier identification. Social service agencies, the educational institution, the juvenile justice system, and the mental health profession all need to work together to render an informed decision concerning the potential risk of some who exhibits early behavioral warning signs of a potential mass killer.

IMPERSONAL VIOLENCE

The computer has emerged as a vital element in our technological society. Imagine if you can what the day would be like if there were no computers. Airline schedules, traffic flow, even starting your automobile in the morning would be impossible if not for the computer.

For all the advances in computer in the last several years, computer hackers have kept pace. But this is only one element in this type of violence. On the one end are those who have the expertise to transfer huge amounts of money from one source to another. Others who have such expertise have been able to tap into governmental agencies and have endangered the safety of the country. On the other end of the scale are those who are able to trade, change, or identify PIN numbers and take money from an individual's bank account. In between these two extremes are a variety of crimes that can have terrible personal consequences.

Identity theft is a new form of impersonal violence. Those who rummage through your personal effects, in garbage cans, trash containers at work, and other such resources, can steal your identity. In another case, a thief can set up a telephone account in your name, set a scanner to obtain your cell phone number, or find someone's address and telephone number by logging onto certain Web sites (e.g., www.anyone.com). As one computer thief said, "I can get on the computer and have all of your information in three clicks" (Herron, 2001, p. 9). What are the various and common types of identity thefts? The Federal Commission's Identity Theft hotline (www.ftc.gov/opa/2000/08/caidttest.htm) lists the following:

- *Credit card fraud:* A credit card is opened in a person's name or unauthorized charges are placed on an existing account.
- *Unauthorized telephone or utility service:* The thief opens new telephone service, cellular phone service, or other utility service in the victim's name.
- *Bank fraud:* A new bank account is opened in the victim's name and fraudulent checks are written and unauthorized checks are written on this account.
- *Fraudulent loans:* The thief obtains a loan in the victim's name.
- *Government documents or benefits:* In this instance, the thief obtains or forges a government document (e.g., driver's license, tax return, etc).

What can be done to lessen the potential damages that could result from these types of violent acts? Truly, the victim is not damaged in the same fashion as in domestic violence, serial murder, school shootings, or the other types of violent crimes we have already discussed. There must be an educational effort to instruct those in the field of computers of the real dangers represented and the various methods to lessen or eradicate the problem. As the world becomes more complex, there will be those who will wish to use the system for their own personal gain. That gain too often comes at the expense of innocent persons. We know that from statements made by those who have had their homes broken into, it was like they were personally violated. People who have been violated by those who use the computer to erase savings and other documents may experience this same sense. This form of personal violence does not involve a personal confrontation. But it can be just as devastating.

VIOLENCE AND THE FUTURE

So what does the future hold for violence? This is a difficult question. Certainly there is no reason to believe that crimes of violence will be obsolete. There will be crimes of violence and there will be innocent victims who will fall victim to these types of crime. There will have to be a concentrated effort by those both within and outside the criminal justice system. This effort must include not only the general understanding of the personality but also new scientific advances to help in the investigation and apprehension. The combination of varied factors may be one step toward a further reduction in violent crime in the United States.

REFERENCES

Egger, S. (1998). *Serial Murder: An Elusive Phenomenon.* New York: Praeger.

Herron, M. (2001). "Identity Theft." *Snitch,* 1(8): 9.

Hofman, M. (2001). "The Shadow of Domestic Violence." *Inc.,* 23(3): 85.

Holmes, R, & S. Holmes. (2001). *Mass Murder in the United States.* Upper Saddle River, NJ: Prentice Hall.

Kramer, E. (2001). "Practical Tips for Domestic Violence Screening." *RN* 64(3): 24.

Levanthal, B, & S. Lundy. (1999). *Same-Sex Domestic Violence.* Thousand Oaks, CA: Sage Publications.

Merchant, J. (2001). "Researchers Seek Federal Funds to Study Workplace Violence." *Professional Safety,* 46(7): 10.

Solomon, M. (2001). "Rage in the Workplace." *Computerworld,* 35(31): 32.

Savoye, C., & L. Belsie. (2001). "When Does Imitation Lead to Tragedy?" *Christian Science Monitor,* 93(51): 2.